EVOLUTION OF AWADHI

(A BRANCH OF HINDI)

BABURAM SAKSENA, M.A., D.Litt.,

MOTILAL BANARSIDASS
DELHI :: PATNA :: VARANASI

Head Office : BUNGALOW ROAD, JAWAHAR NAGAR, DELHI-7
Branch Offices : (i) CHOWK, VARANASI (U.P.)
(ii) ASHOK RAJ PATH, PATNA (BIHAR)

2nd Edition
1971

PRINTED IN INDIA BY SHANTI LAL JAIN, SHRI JAINENDRA PRESS BUNGALOW ROAD, JAWAHARNAGAR, DELHI-7 AND PUBLISHED BY SUNDERLAL JAIN, MOTILAL BANARSIDASS, BUNGALOW ROAD, JAWAHARNAGAR, DELHI 7.

PREFACE

This work is based upon a Thesis submitted for the degree of Doctor of Letters of the University of Allahabad in 1931 and approved by a Board of Examiners comprising of Sir George A. Grierson, Professors R. L. Turner, Jules Bloch, S. K. Chatterji and Dr. A. C. Woolner. It was hoped that the University of Allahabad would publish it but owing to financial stringency the then Vice-Chancellor, in spite of his wishes, could not find funds for it. In the circumstances it was kind of The Indian Press, Ltd., to agree to print and publish it.

The main additions to the thesis are (*a*) the origin of sounds in Part I, (*b*) the appendices giving unpublished texts of Early and Modern Awadhi, (*c*) the index of words, and (*d*) the map. I hope these will prove useful.

The transliteration alphabet of the International Phonetic Association has been adopted for transcribing such modern languages as I know intimately and that of the Royal Asiatic Society for the rest. The current abbreviations found in works of Linguistics have been used in this book also.

It remains for me now to acknowledge my gratitude to those who helped me in the preparation of this work. My revered *guru* Professor R. L. Turner planned this work for me in 1921 at Benares and supervised its completion. I received my first and last lessons in Linguistics at his feet and all that I know of the subject is entirely due to him. I am also deeply beholden to the Professor for his kind permission to dedicate this work to him. Professor S. K. Chatterji did me the favour of looking through the manuscript before it went to the press ;

and he made many useful suggestions. Professor Jules Bloch wrote the encouraging Foreword. Mahamahopadhyaya Dr. Ganganatha Jha and Professor P.K. Acharya gave all facilities and encouragement. Dr. Dhirendra Varma kindly saw most of the proofs with me and several improvements in the arrangement of matter are due to his suggestions. Professor Amaranatha Jha looked into the proof of the Foreword and Mr. Bhagwat Dayal corrected the first proof of the Introduction. Mr. Lalta Prasad Sukul collected three specimens of Modern Awadhi and Mr. Siddhanath Choube helped me in the preparation of the statistics of the frequency of pronouns. Mr. Mata Prasad Gupta translated two texts and Mr. Udai Narain Tewari prepared the index. Mr. Shiva Prasad Singh prepared the sketch of the map. To all these kind friends my best thanks are due.

While in London in 1929-30, I received instruction and advice from Professors Daniel Jones and E. W. Scripture and from Mr. A. Lloyd James, Mr. Stephen Jones, Mr. N. B. Jopson and Dr. H. W. Bailey. I am grateful to all these teachers.

This work has been my companion for the last seventeen years ; I am not unaware of its deficiencies. However, I dare submit it to the world of linguists only in the hope that it will receive their kindness and indulgence.

śivās te panthānaḥ santu

December 1st, 1937. B. R. Saksena

FOREWORD

It is gratifying to see Linguistic science settle down and prosper once more in India, its birth-place. It is a well-known fact that grammar, which had been cultivated in Europe with a view to fixing the best usage in each language, did not become a science, capable of universal acceptance and application, until India revealed Sanskrit to the world. Not that Sanskrit was in itself a sufficient revelation: Bopp, it is true, traced all the consequences of the relationship, more than once recognised by others before him, between Sanskrit and the Indo-European languages of Europe, and thus constituted the new science of Comparative Grammar. Earlier Rask had already established the relationship between the Germanic languages and Greek, Latin, Lettic and Slavonic.

All the same, it was the revelation of Sanskrit that permitted the immense and rapid progress of historical Linguistics. But in spite of the numerous instructive archaisms of Sanskrit and clear gradation of sounds and the mechanism of forms in that language, how much less benefit should we have derived from this discovery had we not had the wonderful analysis of these facts by the Sanskrit Grammarians themselves, an analysis a knowledge of which was to lay the foundation not only of comparative and historical grammar, but of a science of general and universal validity? See a powerful mind like Volney's when in 1795 it tackles the problem of the "Simplification of Oriental languages" in a treatise (in recognition of which he was elected an honorary member of the Asiatic Society of Bengal). He took up the subject again in his book on 'the European alphabet applied to Asiatic languages.' There we witness his painful efforts to lay the foundation of Phonetics. He discovers that a vowel, as distinguished from a mere glottal sound, is articulated "in and by means of the cavities of the mouth and nose" and that a consonant is "the contact of two or several parts of the mouth, made perceptible to the ear by the muffled sound of its breaking away." What would he have said, if he had been told that two thousand years before his time these problems had already been solved and thoroughly investigated, that for instance, consonants were actually called contacts—*sparśa?* Without calling to mind all the subtleties of the Prātiśākhyas, all we need remember is the order of the Sanskrit alphabet, where the sounds are placed according to the degree of aperture and the place and mode of articulation, in order to realize that Indian science supplied the one necessary basis for the constitution of that phonetic science that Volney dreamed of, though with still purely practical purposes. In any case it already provided us with the model of a precise classification, enabling European linguists to understand much better the evolution of languages, which was the object of their first researches.

This is not the place for a survey of this research work, but we can sketch the way in which Europe, after having received Sanskrit grammar as a wonderful present from India, gave her back historical Linguistics in exchange. The first application of the method to Indian languages was the "Essay on Pali" by Burnouf and Lassen (1826) in which the latter specified the circumstances of the transition from Sanskrit to Middle Indian. Strangely enough, a roundabout way had to be taken before we arrived at modern Aryan. According to the testimony of Beames himself, it was the initiative of Bishop Caldwell in connection with Dravidian languages (1856) that suggested to his mind the idea of turning to account his perfect fluency in four different languages and his fair knowledge of three others, to draw up a general survey of them. The study of the Indian branch

To

Professor R. L. Turner

with

gratitude, affection and devotio

from

his first pupil

of

Indian Linguistics

of Indo-European languages far-outdistanced as it was, thanks to Grimm, by the researches in the Germanic family, was not then very much behind the study of Keltic, Slavonic and Latin.

Just as with Europe, it was then a general survey that opened the way, the study of particular languages came only afterwards. In this respect Dravidian lost the lead, as Kittel's grammar of Canara was published only in the 20th century. In the Aryan domain, thanks once more to the help of native grammarians, progress was not slow. As early as 1872 Trumpp's Sindhi was published, a descriptive grammar with comparative illustrations; in 1880 Hoernle gave in one book the thorough description of a modern dialect together with its comparative grammar. The method had now taken root in India and was yielding good fruit when applied by Europeans.

Bnt what the Europeans were able to do by adding to their reading knowledge the first-hand practice of native languages, would not the Indians themselves do the same by grafting on their intimate experience of local usage the newly revised method of which the Europeans showed them the use?

The Great Bhandarkar in his fine Wilson Lectures (1877) even before the publication of Beames' volume concerning the Verb, was the first to endeavour to show the development of Indo-Aryan from Vedic down to the present-day languages.

After him perhaps for some time, at any rate, it was not so useful to treat this subject again * as to get a deeper insight into the principal languages. From this point of view the most important Indian contribution is Professor

*Mention should be made here of Professor Bloch's own brilliant work, l'Indo-Aryen (Paris, 1934), a landmark in the field of Indian Linguistics. Obviously the Professor's modesty has prevented him from making a reference to it.

—B. R. Saksena.

Chatterji's "Origin and Development of Bengali Language," a book too well-known for me to characterize it and give it here the praise it deserves.

Here is now Dr. Saksena's contribution. The language he describes is not so illustrious as Bengali or Marathi. Awadhi is but one of the Eastern Hindi dialects; but let not our ignorance blind us to its importance. If we annex Bagheli to it, as Linguistic science bids us to do, Awadhi is the language of a people numbering more than twenty millions and a half. This number is a little less than that of those who use Polish, but definitely more than European Spanish or Dutch; in India it is almost as large as Telugu can boast of, and more than Marathi or Tamil; still all these languages are among the twenty most extensive in the world according to Prof. Tesnière's calculations. Moreover Awadhi glories in a fine literature, though not in the present generation, as Dr. Saksena explains in this treatise. As is well-known the renowned Rāma-charitamānasa of Tulsī Dās was written in an old form of this language. It may be added that this work bears a date, which is extremely important to the philologist; and that some manuscripts are almost contemporary with the work. An earlier record still is the Padmāwat of Muhammad Jāisī, a text which besides its being dated, has the advantage of avoiding Sanskritisms; neither does it excessively Islamise its diction. A language that possesses such masterpieces and that is able to resist victoriously the encroachments of Hindustani in current usage was well worth studying for its own sake.

But it prescribed to the historian a special difficulty which was to prevent him—fortunately to my mind—from following the plan already used by other scholars for Marathi or Bengali.

The documents in Awadhi are not of the same kind in different periods: we have just seen that there is no written Awadhi today. Now, the description of a spoken language entails special problems and imposes duties of its own.

First of all, the scrupulous precise phonetic notation, which is not quite so necessary when the spelling gives useful hints as regards its previous stages, now becomes indispensable if only to avoid an unconscious imitation of neighbouring literary languages. But this phonetic accuracy demands special training; here again Europe gave the clue, the teachings of grammar having been elucidated there by the results of physiology and acoustics. Here the analysis of sounds was carried out with a precision far superior to the powers of hearing, thanks to the artificial palate, which Oakley Coates had borrowed from the dentists (1871) and to the sound-registering instruments borrowed by Rosapelly (1876) from the physiologists who had more or less adopted them from the 18th-century meteorologists.

To master these methods, Dr. Saksena undertook a visit to Europe and devoted himself to a course of tedious laboratory work. The results of this can be seen in the photographs illustrating this book. This is the first time that the historical treatment of an Indian language has been supported by a description carried out according to the graphic method. It is desirable that particularly in this point Dr. Saksena should find followers, and that the Universities in India might offer facilities to their members for a voyage to Europe to enable them to work on these lines.

The description, specially the graphic description, of an unwritten living language, cannot be made in a general way, the whole study must be based on a particular speech, if not on an individual speaker. Dr. Saksena started from his own dialect, which was the right thing to do. His former study of Lakhīmpurī, which he had done under Professor Turner's guidance was already conspicuous by qualities of order and precision and contained important remarks. Later on, thanks to the consent of the Allahabad University, to whom we should all be grateful for this, he was able to explore the other dialects and prepare the still unpublished monographs which served as a basis for the present work. He thus prepared himself for the use of the geographical method, which is one of the most recent achievements of European Linguistics.

The main originality of Dr. Saksena's work lies in the accurate and complete description of both the ancient and modern stages of Awadhi. The historical explanations have been assigned a subordinate position, and rightly so, as the connection of Awadhi with Indo-Aryan in general renders useless the repetition of theories which have already been propounded in the well-known and authoritative works on the subject. In a few places Dr. Saksena has left a few facts unexplained which, in the present stage of our knowledge, are impossible to be tackled. Dr. Saksena has, in such cases, shown the facts and stated the problems connected with them in a clear light. This in itself constitutes great progress.

Dr. Saksena, in the following pages, gives evidence of a close, varied and comprehensive study of his own language and of promise of studies on parallel lines. It is with great pleasure that I underline the merits and novelty of the great work which Dr. Saksena has produced.

JULES BLOCH

CONTENTS

CHAPTER II

VOWEL COMBINATIONS

GRAPHIC ILLUSTRATIONS

Part II

HISTORICAL GRAMMAR OF AWADHI

CHAPTER I

NOUNS

CHAPTER II

ADJECTIVES

CHAPTER III

NUMERALS

Chapter VII

ADVERBS

Chapter VIII

CONJUNCTIONS

Chapter IX

EMPHATIC FORMS

Chapter X

WORD ORDER

APPENDIX I

SPECIMENS OF EARLY AWADHI UNPUBLISHED TEXTS

(With English Translation)

APPENDIX II

MODERN AWADHI TEXTS

(With English Translation)

INDEX

INTRODUCTION

INTRODUCTION

Name of the Language.

§ 1. Awadhī is the main dialect of the Eastern Hindi branch of the Indo-Aryan group of languages spoken in Northern India. The term Awadhī appears to denote the language of Awadh (Oudh), but, as a matter of fact, the language is not confined to the province of Oudh. It is not spoken in parts of the province (Hardoi district and parts of Kheri and Fyzabad), while it extends to the districts of Fatehpur, Allahabad, Jaunpur and Mirzapur of the Agra province. But as it is chiefly spoken in Oudh, the name may be accepted, at least in preference to the other two names, *Pūrbī* (*Linguistic Survey of India*, Vol. V, Part II, p. 43 and Vol. VI, p. 10) and *Kōsalī* (*Linguistic Survey of India*, Vol. VI, p. 9) which have sometimes been employed for it. *Pūrbī* literally means *eastern*, and is sometimes used for Awadhī and at others for Bhōjpurī. It may very well be a suitable name for Eastern Hindi to distinguish it from Western Hindi. Kōsalī may be the name of the language of the Kōsala Kingdom which no longer exists and the boundaries of which cannot be fixed with certainty. Another name employed sometimes to denote this language is Baiswāṛī (*Linguistic Survey of India*, Vol. VI, p. 9), but it is generally and more appropriately used for a restricted area of Awadhī, that of Baiswāṛā—comprising portions of the Unao, Lucknow, Rae Bareli and Fatehpur districts. Baiswāṛā is notorious for its harshness and so is the language of the area. Inquiries made by me from cultured residents of the area bear out this statement. The main difference from other dialects of Awadhī is phonetic—in the pronunciation of **e** as **jʌ**, **o** as **wʌ**, and **eː** as **jaː** and **oː** as **waː**.

The name of Awadh (Oudh) is connected with *Ayōdhyā*, the ancient town, which remained a town of considerable importance during the Mohammedan period as well. Tulsīdās uses the word *Avadha* for *Ayōdhyā* and so does Lāldās Gupta who spells it as *Audha* also.

Linguistic Boundaries of Awadhi.

§ 2. On the West of Awadhī there are two dialects of Western Hindi, *viz.*, Kanaujī and Bundelī, while on its East there is the Bihārī dialect Bhōjpurī. Compared with Awadhī, the distinguishing features of Kanaujī and Bundelī (see *Linguistic Survey of India*, Vol. IX, Part I, pp. 83, 85, 92) are: (1) the agentive postposition **neː** (Awadhī does not have this), and (2) the noun, adjective and past participle (masc. sing.) in **-oː, ʌu,** Awadhī **aː**. The distinguishing features of Bhōjpurī (see *Linguistic Survey of India*, Vol. V, Part II, pp. 43 and 53) are: (1) the present tense with the enclitic **laː** (*e.g.*, **paːiː laː**), (2) the past tense in **-l**, and (3) the dative postposition **laː**. With these distinctive features of its neighbours, we should fix the exact linguistic boundaries of Awadhī chiefly and of Eastern Hindi generally.

On the West, the **-oː** forms appear from Gōlā Gōkaran Nāth (Kheri district). If we draw a straight line from Gōlā to Nērī (Sītāpur district), it will correctly divide Kanaujī from Awadhī. From Nērī, the river Gomati forms the south-western boundary of Awadhī right up to the point where it divides the Hardōī district from Lucknow. From there a line may be drawn to the south-west roughly along the boundary line of the districts of Hardōī and Lucknow, and Unao up to the point where the district of Unao ends. From here, the district of Cawnpore belongs to Western Hindi and the districts of Unao, Fatehpur and Allahabad belong to Awadhī.

Of the Tirhārī specimens given in the *Linguistic Survey of India* (Vol. VI, pp. 152—156), some, we can say, go under Bundelī while others under Awadhī. For instance, the Banda specimen on page 133 combines **neː** (agentive post-position of Bundelī) with an Awadhī verb **dihis (mʌɽʌi neː bãːɽi dihis)**. The Fatehpur specimen of Tirhārī (p. 138) is, however, pure Awadhī. The Hamīrpur specimen (p. 140) has better reason to be with Bundelī than the Banda specimen, because it has both the characteristics of Western Hindi. A few instances of Awadhī verbs are found in this specimen also. The Gahōrā specimen (p. 150) appears as pure Awadhī, while the Juṛār and Banāpharī specimens are the mixtures of Bundelī and Awadhī (Bāghēlī).

Awadhī and Bāghēlī.—Linguistically, Bāghēlī does not differ from Awadhī. In the *Linguistic Survey* 'Its separate existence has only been recognised in deference to popular prejudice' (*Linguistic Survey of India*, Vol. VI, p. 1). The two characteristic points of difference mentioned in the *Survey* (VI, p. 20), *viz.*, 'the enclitic **teː** or **tʌi**' and the **h** form of the 1st person future' are found in other dialects of Awadhī as well. The enclitic **teː** or **tʌi** is nothing but the contracted form of the auxiliary **hʌtɑː, hʌtʌi, hʌtiː** found after the participles. Similar contraction is found not only in other dialects of Awadhī and in Chattīsgaṛhī but in Western Hindi as well. The **-h** form of the 1st person future is similarly found in other dialects of Awadhī, *e.g.*, in Lakhīmpur, Sītāpur, Lucknow and Bārābankī. Other minor characteristics (*Linguistic Survey of India*, Vol. VI, p. 122) similarly are found in other dialects of Awadhī, *e.g.*, the 'tendency to change a **w** to **b** as in **ʌbɑːʤ**' 'a noise' **ʤʌbɑːb** 'an answer'. There are two points, however, (1) adjectives in a strong form in **hɑː**, as in **nikəhɑː** 'good' and (2) the honorific imperative in **-iː**, *e.g.*, **deːiː**, 'be good enough to give,' which are not generally found in other dialects of Awadhī. The strong adjective in **-hɑː** has correspondences sometimes still, *e.g.*, Lmp. **purʌnihɑː** 'old, experienced' and the honorific, imperative form is a borrowing from the neighbouring dialect of Biharī—Bhōjpurī.

From these facts, it appears best to take Bāghēlī only as a dialect of Awadhī and not as a form of Eastern Hindi standing on a par with Awadhī. Gō̃ḍwānī or Maṇḍlāhī (*Linguistic Survey of India*, Vol. VI, p. 158) has more connection with Awadhī than with Bāghēlī, as we do not find the main characteristic of Bāghēlī (**tʌi** enclitic) in it. To the East of Gō̃ḍwānī lies Chhattīsgaṛhī, and to the West Bundēlī. Therefore, as expected, we find in it a fusion of both these dialects.

On the south, Awadhī is bounded by Chattīsgaṛhī, another form of Eastern Hindi. This has several characteristics which differentiate it from Awadhī. The definitive enclitic **-hʌr** is used after nouns and pronouns, the plural is made by adding **-mʌn**, the accusative-dative postposition is **lɑː** (side by side with **kɑː**) and the instrumental postposition is **leː** (which is commoner than **seː**), the genitive postposition **keː** does not change for number or gender, the enclitic for restrictive emphatic form is **-cʌ** (Awadhī **-i**). The pronouns also are different and have something in common with Bhōjpurī. In other points Chattīsgaṛhī agrees closely with Awadhī (for details see '*A Grammar of the Chhattīsgaṛhī Dialect of Hindi* by Hiralal and Grierson published by the C. P. Government—and *Vikāsa*, the official monthly organ of the District Council, Bilāspur, C.P., which occasionally contains articles in the dialect).

On the north, the Awadhī area is bounded by the territory of the Nepal Government. Most of this consists of uninhabited tracts, forests and barren land. Here and there one finds a small village occupied by some aboriginal tribe, *e.g.*, the Ṭhārūs. There are certain market places (*maṇḍīs*) which are occupied by the people from Pilibhit, Kheri, Bahraich and Gonda during the winter season and they carry on a profitable trade with the Nēpālī hillmen who come down to sell their hill-products, woollen blankets, turmeric, etc., and to purchase the products of the plains, tobacco, ornaments, etc. These markets close down by May and from then up to the beginning of December they are deserted. Thus the Awadhī language does not come in close contact with Nepālī.

On the east, Awadhī is bounded by Bhōjpurī. The boundary of the district of Gonda corresponds with the Eastern boundary of the language itself. Then we move towards the East along the river Ghāghrā right up to Tāṇḍā. A straight line from Tāṇḍā to Jaunpur and thence to Mirzapur will correctly represent the south-eastern boundary of Awadhī. Pure Awadhī is spoken right up to a few miles to the west of Mirzapur town. From there the boundary of the Allahabad district on the south-east and the boundary-line of the Rewa territory to the east, form the eastern limits of Awadhī. Only in the south-eastern triangle of Mirzapur district (the Sōn-pār tract, see *Linguistic Survey of India*, pp. 130-31), is Awadhī spoken more or less mixed up with Bhōjpurī. Further south to Sōnpārī one finds Awadhī bounded by the Surgujiā dialect of Chattīsgaṛhī.

Characteristics of Awadhi.

§ 3. Thus Awadhī stands between Western Hindi and Bihārī. Of the three varieties of the forms of the noun-stem—short, long and longer, Western Hindi has generally the short form, Awadhī both the short and the long while Bihārī has the longer and the long generally. Of the observance of the gender of nouns and adjectives, we find Western Hindi rigorous, Awadhī a little loose while Bihārī mostly does not observe the distinction of gender. The direct case (singular) of consonantal bases in Awadhī ends in **-ụ**, in Western Hindi this **-ụ** is absent, particularly in Hindustānī. The direct plural of consonantal bases in some dialects of Awadhī has the termination **-ʌi**. As regards postpositions, Awadhī is clearly distinguished from Western Hindi by the absence of the agentive postposition in the former. In this respect it agrees with Bihārī. The accusative-dative postposition in Awadhī is **kɑː, kə** while in Western Hindi it is **koː, kʌu** and in Bihārī **keː**. The locative postposition in Awadhī is **mɑː** in Western Hindi and Bihārī generally **meː**. The pronouns show considerable distinction. Awadhī personal genitive adjectives are **toːr**, **moːr**, Western Hindi **teːr-, meːr-**; Awadhī oblique of **hʌmɑːr** is **hʌmʌreː** and Western Hindi **hʌmɑːreː**. The nominative singular of the relative and interrogative pronouns has the forms **ɟoː**, **koː** in Awadhī, and **ɟeː**, **keː** in Bihārī. Of the verb, the auxiliary in Western Hindi is **h-** (**hʌi**, etc.) while in Awadhī it is generally **h-** (**hʌi**), **ʌɦ-** (**ʌɦʌi**), **bɑːʈ-** (**bɑːʈʌi**) in the present and **bɑːɽ-** (**bɑːɽeː**) or **ɑːch** (**ɑːcheː**) in Bihārī. The imperfect participle in Awadhī has lost traces of the ancient case termination (except-**i̥** in Western Awadhī) while in Hindustānī **-ɑː** (**ɟɑːtɑː**) or **-u** (**ɟɑːtu**) is generally found. This **-u** may be whispered in actual existence like **-i̥** in Awadhī. The past tense, based on the imperfect participle, adds affixes in Awadhī while it does not do so in Western Hindi. The best Awadhī characteristic is the affix **-isi̥** or **-is**. The future in Awadhī has vestiges of the ancient simple future as well as of the participle in *-tavya*, while in the neighbouring dialects of Western Hindi we find only the former and in Bihārī only the latter.[1]

Origin of Awadhi.

§ 4. To what Prakrit is Awadhī (or Eastern Hindi) connected in origin? To the west of Awadhī are dialects connected with Śaurasēnī and to the east there are Bihārī dialects whose origin is taken back to Māgadhī. It was natural for Grierson, therefore, to connect Eastern Hindi, with

[1] Only Western Bhojpurī retains some forms derived from the ancient simple future.

Ardhamāgadhī—a language said to lie between Śaurasēnī and Māgadhī. But when we come to take up individual characteristics we find difficulties. Śaurasēnī was distinguished by treating the Sanskrit *-t- -th-* as *-d- -dh-* in opposition to the Mahārāṣṭrī (*-y-*) zero- and *-h-* and by the Nominative singular of bases as *-ō* while Māgadhī had *-ē*. The retention of explosion in *d* and *dh* might point to the more archaic character of Śaurasēnī as compared with Mahārāṣṭrī. Śaurasēnī had the dental sibilant (*s*) while Māgadhī had the palatal (*ś*). In Śaurasēnī *r* was retained while in Māgadh it was substituted by *l*. Ardhamāgadhī does not possess the two main characteristics of Māgadhī, *viz.*, *ś* and *l* for Śaurasēnī *s* and *r*. In this it agrees with Śaurasēnī. But it has both *-ē* and *-ō* forms of the Nominative singular. And the texts of Ardhamāgadhī (chiefly Jain canon) amply bear out the double treatment of the base in the Nominative singular *dēvō* or *dēvē*, *sō* or *sē*, *kē*, *jē*)—see *Ardhamāgadhī Reader* by Dr. Banarsi Das Jain.

When we judge Awadhī by the main characteristic of Ardhamāgadhī, we find that the *-ē* treatment of the Nominative singular is traceable only in the imperfect participle in **-i̥** in some dialects and also possibly in **-eː** perfect participle when used in the singular. Neither the nouns nor the postpositions except **keː** (direct singular genitive found in the eastern dialects of Awadhī) have any trace of *-ē*. On the other hand, the **-u̥** of the direct singular clearly points to the Śaurasēnī *-ō*. The **-i̥** and **-eː** in the imperfect and the perfect participles respectively, however, are found in the neighbouring dialects of Western Hindi as well.

Eastern Hindi has more affinity with Pāli than with Jain Ardhamāgadhī. But Pāli represents a much earlier stage of language than Jain Ardhamāgadhī. The texts in the latter language were recast and edited in the fifth century A.D. We can assume that earlier Ardhamāgadhī was different from the later language in character and that this earlier Ardhamāgadhī was the basis of Awadhī.

F. 2

When did the characteristics of the various modern dialects become fixed? The earliest specimens of Braj, Awadhī or Maithilī already bear the characteristics. The Maithila Apabhraṁśa (*avahaṭṭha*), traces of which are found in the language of the *Kīrtilatā* of Vidyāpati, has the characteristics of Maithilī already in several respects. No Apabhraṁśa works corresponding to Eastern Hindi are available [see the article on Apabhraṁśa Literature by Hiralal Jain—*Allahabad University Studies*, Vol. I, pp. 157—185; *Apabhraṁśa kāvyatrayī*—G.O.S. 1927, *Kīrtilatā*—Nāgarī Prachāriṇī Sabhā, Benares, and *Jasaharacariu*, *Nāyakumāracariu*, *Sāvayadhamma-dōhā* (Karanja, Berar) published since Jain's article which mentions the Apabhraṁśa literature available till then—1925].

In the early Muslim period, portions of the Awadhī area were in the kingdom of Jaunpur. In Akbar's period, the territory was under the Sarkārs of Jaunpur, Allahabad and Oudh. It appears that the Hardoi district was more or less always with Kanauj. The armies regularly used to march from Kanauj to Khairabad in the Sitapur district, which indirectly explains the Kanaujī influences in the southern portions of the Sitapur district.

The characteristics probably belong to the pre-Muslim period, a suggestion put forward by Mr. Dhirendra Varma ('Identity of the Present Dialect-areas of Hindustan with the Ancient Janapadas'—*Allahabad University Studies*, Vol. I, pp. 189—201).

The area where the Bāghēlī dialect of Awadhī and Chattīsgaṛhī are spoken is merely an extension of Kōsala towards South—the Dakṣiṇa Kōsala. It was particularly known as Goṇḍwānā in the Muslim period and was inhabited by wild tribes. The colonisation from Oudh extends over a long period, some of the families having migrated from the Rae Bareli and Unao districts only in the latter half of the nineteenth century.

Importance of Awadhi.

§ 5. According to the *Linguistic Survey* (VI, p. 2) Eastern Hindi is spoken by 24,368,099 people of which 3,755,343 are put down under Chhattīsgaṛhī and the rest 20,612,756, under Awadhī (including Bāghēlī).

Awadhī serves an area which has been historically important from ancient times. Here stands Ayōdhyā (also known as Sākēta), the capital of the Kōsala kingdom which was very important up to the Buddhist period. The activities of Buddha were mainly in the Kōsala kingdom and he spent a considerable period of his time in Sāvatthī and the portions round about it. Allahabad is an ancient sacred place and has been politically important during the Gupta, Moghal and British periods. Fyzabad and Lucknow played a very important part during the reign of the later Moghals. The Nawabs of Oudh have been famous for their culture, gaiety and splendour. The Rulers of Rewa have not only been great patrons of learning and art but have themselves been poets and literary men. Tan Sen, the Prince of Indian musicians, was in the court of Mahārāja Ram Chand Singh from where he was taken away by Akbar.

In the literary field Awadhī stands immortalised in the *Rāmacarita-mānasa* of Tulsīdās.

Awadhī today is merely the common language of the people, and is not a literary vehicle. The Hindustānī dialect (whether Hindi or Urdu) is the literary language of the Awadhī area. The uneducated people speak Awadhī amongst themselves and so do the educated people if they are talking amongst Awadhī people. I have found that in the district towns, educated people coming from outside the Awadhī area generally adapt themselves to Awadhī forms and very soon become good Awadhī speakers. In the larger towns, however, such as Lucknow, Allahabad, Fyzabad, where there is a large admixture of educated people from the non-Awadhī area the vehicle of thought amongst educated people is Hindustānī. In the district towns also, as the official work is all in Hindustānī, the educated classes are familiar with both the Hindustānī and Awadhī forms and speak both according to need. At the homes of Awadhī speakers, however, the practice differs with people. In the district towns, girls married to Awadhī people from outside the Awadhī area, adopt Awadhī and discard their dialects within a year or two. But in the larger towns, with the gradual assertion of woman's individuality in the family, a girl normally speaking Hindustānī retains her speech so that her children, when brought up, speak Hindustānī and not Awadhī which is spoken by only a few members of the family. These are the beginnings of the ousting of the unliterary dialect. Individual Awadhī speakers when outside the Awadhī area have adopted the dialect of the place; for instance, girls of Oudh married to the people of the Kanaujī area have discarded Awadhī and adopted Kanaujī. When families shift, however, they retain their dialect longer in their homes, *e.g.*, an Awadhī family settled in the Mēwāṛī area retains Awadhī at home. But the children owing to the close contact of Mēwāṛī speakers very soon adopt Mēwāṛī habits of speech and it is expected that Awadhī will be ousted from the family after a generation or two.

It should be borne in mind that the various dialects of Hindi, Western or Eastern, are mutually intelligible not only with regard to neighbouring dialects but to others also. A speaker of Braj can make himself intelligible in Oudh even to the uneducated people. If he resides in Oudh he will adopt Awadhī but may retain certain characteristics of his original dialect. And this weakness is condoned, though sometimes it does raise a little joke at the expense of the Braj speaker. The strict puritv of the dialect is not ordinarily insisted upon.

Materials for the Study of Awadhi.

§ 6. Awadhī was used as a literary vehicle, side by side with Braj, before they were ousted by Hindustānī in the last century. Braj has still some votaries, but Awadhī has none. It is only occasionally that we find traces of Awadhī in the Hindustānī written by the writers of Oudh. Awadhī forms creep in, particularly in the commentaries written in Hindi (for instance, *Kuṇḍaliyā Rāmāyaṇa Saṭīka* by Baijnāth Kurmī of Mānpur, district Bārābankī and published by the Newal Kishore Press, Lucknow, in 1892, or his *Adhyātma Rāmāyaṇa Saṭīka*).

Quite an important literature, though not as extensive as that of Braj, however, exists in Early Awadhī. The *Rāmacarita-mānasa* (popularly known as the *Rāmāyaṇa*) of Tulsīdās, the most important work in any modern Indo-Aryan language, is in Awadhī. It was written in Saṁvat 1631 (1575 A.D.) and though the plot is mostly a borrowed one, either from Vālmīki's *Rāmāyaṇa* or from the *Adhyātma Rāmāyaṇa* both of which are in Sanskrit, the poetic genius exhibited in the work stands unrivalled in Indian literature. Another important work in Awadhī is the *Padmāvat* of Malik Muhammad Jāyasī written in Hijrī 947 (1540 A.D.). It is a romantic poem of considerable interest and a philosophical allegory runs throughout. The work is linguistically important as Jāyasī was a Mohammedan, and to all appearances ignorant of Sanskrit, and he has used a language which is devoid of Sanskrit or Arabo-Persian diction. His Awadhī is purer than that of Tulsīdās, though strict purity of dialect is absent and should not be expected. The speakers (or the scribes, at any rate) of the various dialects, Braj, Kanaujī, Awadhī, etc., were mutually intelligible in those days as to-day and there was no rigidly fixed literary form par excellence. The writers, therefore, imperceptibly borrowed from the neighbouring dialects.

Tulsīdās has written in Braj quite as successfully as in Awadhī. Several editions of *Padmāvat* and *Rāmacaritamānasa* exist. From the linguistic point of view the *Padmāvat* edited by Grierson and Sudhākar Dwivēdī is excellent and has been referred to in the following pages. The only other known work of the author *Akharāvaṭa* is also in Awadhī Of the editions of the *Rāmacaritamānasa*, the Nāgarī Prachāriṇī Sabhā, Benares edition, is the least objectionable and has been utilised for references here. The text of the *Ayōdhyā-kāṇḍa* based on the Rājāpur manuscript, said to have been written by the poet himself, edited by Lala Sita Ram, has also been consulted. Of Tulsīdās's numerous other works, *Pārvatī Maṅgala* and *Jānakī Maṅgala* are in good Awadhī.

The other published work is *Indrāvatī* written obviously on the model of *Padmāvat*, by Nūr Muhammad in Hijrī 1157 (1757 A.D.), about two hundred years later than *Padmāvat*. The Nāgarī Prachāriṇi Sabhā published about half of the text in 1906. The manuscript was in the Persian character, but only a copy of it in the Kaithī character was available to the Sabhā. The text is, therefore, not very reliable linguistically. The dialect represented is Awadhī of the most eastern area, near about Mirzapur.

Besides the above-mentioned three authors who have been the basis of studies in Early Awadhī and have been extensively drawn upon in the following pages, two important manuscripts described below have been consulted.

(1) *Avadha-bilāsa*—(described under No. 32 in the Report on the search of Hindi manuscripts for the year 1901) in the Library of the Asiatic Society of Bengal, Calcutta (a manuscript of a portion of the book is in Ayōdhyā, see No. 107 of the *Hindi Search Report* for 1914—17). It was begun in Awadha (Ayōdhyā) by Lāldās Gupta in the bright half of the month of Baisākha, in the Saṁvat year 1700 (A.D. 1643), *i.e.*, about a hundred years

after Jāyasī's work. The author gave up the work on the fifth day of the bright half of Phālgun, the same year. The work, even as it is, is extensive, extending over 301 leaves (602 pages) with 20 to 23 lines on each page. It deals with the life of Rāma and is like the *Rāmacarita-mānasa* in the *dōhā* and *caupāī* metres.

It is divided into 18 cantos (*bisrāms*). The first, which ends on leaf 18b, contains a recommendation and an appeal to the readers to study the book, the poet's respect to the deities, his humble attitude and the importance of devotion and good company. The second canto gives a detailed account of Ayōdhyā, the origin of the river Sarayū, an account of the music played in the town and ends (on leaf 55b) with the occupation of Ayōdhyā by Svayambhū Manu with Vasiṣṭha as his priest. The third canto which ends on leaf 77b contains the reasons why Viṣṇu came down to the Earth as Rāma and why the two Gaṇas of Śiva were born as Rāvaṇa and Kumbhakarṇa. The 4th canto (ending on leaf 127b) describes the terrorism of Rāvaṇa and Kumbhakarṇa, Earth's appeal to Viṣṇu and the latter's promise to come down, the story of Rāhu and the quarrel between Śiva and Pārvatī. The 5th describes in detail the charity of Raghu at Sonakhara Tīratha and ends on leaf 139a. The 6th canto named the Entrance of the King (Daśaratha) in Prayāga and his meeting with Lōmapāda ends on leaf 154b. The 7th describes the meeting of the king with Ṛṣyaśṛṅga (ending on leaf 167b) and the 8th brings the youthful sage down to Ayōdhyā (ending on leaf 199a). The 9th is named *Garbhaprakāsa* (ending on leaf 209b) and describes the sacrifice for the sons and the subsequent conception. In the 10th (ending on leaf 226 a) the princes are born and in the 11th (ending on leaf 240a) the festivities and rejoicings in connection with the birth are elaborately described. The 12th canto in the first half describes the childhood of Rāma and in the second it describes the birth of Sītā. It ends on leaf 254b. The 13th ends on leaf 263a and describes the boyhood of Rāma who is represented as having read the various grammars (Śākaṭāyana's, etc.) and Kāvyas (Raghu, Kumāra, Mēghadūta, Naiṣadha, Māgha, Kirāta). This is only one of the many instances of absurd anachronisms. The 14th canto (ending on leaf 265b) describes the all-pervading might of God who has innumerable assistants in the shape of officers, writers and *faujdārs*. Here occurs a mistake in numbering the cantos. The next canto (15th) numbered as 16th ends on leaf 278b and gives a description of Rāma's pilgrimage to holy places and his instructive discussions with the saints. The writer has tried to give a summary of discourses on philosophical topics in this canto. The 16th (numbered 17th) canto ends on leaf 288b and describes the longing of Sītā for Rāma, Viśvāmitra's arrival in Ayōdhyā and his request to the king for Rāma and Lakṣmaṇa, and the story up to the breaking of Śiva's bow in Mithilā. The 17th (numbered 18th) canto (ending on leaf 296b) contains a description of the marriage of Rāma and Sītā and a detailed account of the dowry given by Janaka. The last canto the 18th (wrongly numbered the 19th) describes the happy residence of Daśaratha in Ayōdhyā with his sons and daughters-in-law, a few stories of ideal charity, the giving of boons to Kaikēyī and the departure of Rāma for the forest. After the colophon to the canto in a couplet the writer possibly describes his own departure from Ayōdhyā on the fifth day of the bright half of Phāgun.

From the literary point of view the work is of little value. But it has importance linguistically and as a work which gives details of the every-day life of the poet's time. The character is Dēvanāgarī mixed with Kaithī. The appearance of the manuscript is old, and, as there is no mention of the copyist, the probability is that it is the author's own copy. The orthography is striking. ष represents *j* and ब *b*, and only a dot below them is added to represent *y* and *v*, respectively. ष regularly represents *kh*, च *ch*, श *s*, ढ *ḍh*, ऐ *e* or *y*. The nasalisation has been mostly left unnoted. The mātrā for the long vowel very often represents a short vowel, *grabhahi* represents *garbhahi*, *achara* represents *acchara*. There are many instances of wrong Sanskritisation, *e. g.*, *jakta* for *jagata*. The grammar generally agrees with that of the *Rāmāyaṇa* of Tulsidās.

(2) *Yūsuf-Zulēkhā*.—The manuscript is in the Persian *nastāliq* script, pp. 346 with 13 to 15 lines per page, size 7.5″ × 4.5″. The last leaf and the first three leaves are slightly mutilated, otherwise the manuscript is in good condition. It was in the possession of Hafiz Samiullah Khan Tarin, B.A., LL.B., of Gangyo, district Sultanpur, and has been purchased by the Hindustānī Academy, Allahabad, which is proposing to publish it.[1] The work was written by Shēkh Nisār of Shēkhūpūr, in Hijrī 1200, V.S. 1847, Śaka 1712 or 1790 of the Christian era, as mentioned in the introductory verses. The work gives the well-known story of Yūsuf and Zulēkhā on the model of *Padmāvat* both in subject-matter and in language. It is a fine specimen of the Awadhī language of the last part of the 18th century.

Besides the above, the following manuscripts mentioned in the Reports on the Search for Hindi Manuscripts appear to be in Awadhī :

(*a*) Report for the year 1900.

No. 4. *Mṛgāvatī*—a romantic poem, a precursor of *Padmāvat*, written in Hijri 909 (1512 A.D.) by Quṭban in the reign of Sher Shah's father Husein Shah. This is possibly the earliest available work in Awadhī.

(*b*) Report for the year 1901.

No. 13. *Baitāla Pacīsī* written by one Bhawānī Shankar who lived at Bhadaini in Benares. The date of composition is V. S. 1871 (1814 A.D.).

[1] Since the above was written, a notice of the manuscript has appeared in the "Nāgarī Prachāriṇī Patrikā," Vol. XI, pp. 445—467.

No. 12. *Shrī Rāmāyaṇa* by Jhāma Dāsa written at Vindhācala, Mirzapur, in V. S. 1818 (1761 A.D.).

(*c*) Report for the year 1902.

No. 110. *Bhakta Saktā kā jhagaṛā*, composed in Hijrī 1053 during the reign of Jehangir—Awadhī mixed with Kanaujī.

No. 111. *Haṁsa Jawāhira*, composed in Hijrī 1149, V.S. 1858 (1801 A.D.) by Qāsim Shāh of Dariyabad (Oudh)—pure Awadhī.

No. 112. *Gyāna Dīpa*—by Shēikh Nabī of Jaunpur, composed in 1024 A.H. (1619 A.D.)—pure Awadhī.

(*d*) Report for the year 1904.

No. 7. *Rājā Citramukuṭa kī Kathā*—no information about the author or the date of composition is available from the manuscript—Awadhī mixed with Western Hindi (post-positions *nē* and *kara*).

No. 19. *Kathā cāra Darvēśa* by Bhūpa Narayana composed in V. S. 1841 (1797 A D.)—pure Awadhī. The other two books of the author, No. 29 (*a*) and (*b*) (Report, 1909-11) are not in Awadhī.

No. 32. *Citrāvalī* by Usmān, composed in 1613 A.D. on the model of *Padmāvat*—pure Awadhī.

(*e*) Report for the years 1909-11.

No. 26. *Baitāla Pacīsī* by Bhawānī Sahāya, date of composition not mentioned, date of manuscript 1839 V. S., mixed Awadhī.

No. 49. *Krisṇacaritāmṛta* by Kṣemakaraṇa Miśra of Barabanki district (born in 1771 and died in 1861 V. S.—date of composition not known)—pure Awadhī.

No. 78. *Śabdāvalī* by Dūlanadāsa, about 1760 A.D.

No. 85. *Sumanaghana* (a translation of Gulistān by Gaṅgā Dāsa, written in V.S. 1879).

No. 221. *Upākhyāna Vivēka* by Pahalawāna Dāsa, composed in V.S. 1865. Another manuscript is No. 131 of the Report for 1917-19.

No. 273. *Rasa Ratnāgara* by Saīd Pahāṛa, date not known.

No. 296. *Bhakti Jayamāla* by Siva Rāma, written in V.S. 1787 (1730 A.D.).

No. 318. *Śabdāvalī* by Tõwara Dāsa, written in V.S. 1887 (1830 A.D.).

(*f*) Report for the years 1912-14.

No. 17. *Hari Canda Kathā* by Bēnī Baksa of district Sitapur, written in V.S. 1836 (1779 A D.)—pure Awadhī.

No. 88. *Bacanāvalī* by Yugalānanda Sharaṇa of Ayōdhyā "born about V.S. (1863—1807 A.D.)"—a prose work in Awadhī mixed with Hindustānī (*rākhatē haī*, *mānanā*, *hōyagā*, etc.).

No. 160. *Bhagavata*, by Sabala Siṁha (born about 1645 A.D.).

Nos. 162 and 163. *Prahalāda carita* and *Raghubansu Dīpaka*, by Sahaja Rāma who "flourished about 1732 A.D."

No. 191. *Saguna Vilāsa,* by Udaya Nātha, written in V.S. 1841 (1784 A.D.).

(*g*) Report for the years 1917-19.

No. 13. *Daṅgawa Parva* by Balabīra, composed in V.S. 1608 (1552 A.D.).

No. 36. *Hitōpadēśa* by Canda, composed in V.S. 1563 (1506 A.D.). Another manuscript is No. 28 of the Report for 1920—22.

No. 48. *Mahābhārata Sabhā Parva,* etc., by Dharma Dāsa, written in V.S. 1711 (1656 A.D.). Another manuscript is No. 41 of the Report for 1920—22.

No. 84 (*b*). *Sīya-Rāma-rasa mañjarī*, by Jānakī Caraṇa written in V.S. 1881 (1824 A.D.).

No. 187 (*b*). *Ekādasī Māhātmya*, by Sūraja Dāsa, written in V.S. 1923 (1866 A.D.).

(*h*) Report for the years 1920—22.

No. 118. *Bhāgavata Daśama Skandha Bhāshā* by Navala Dāsa, written in V S. 1823 (1766 A.D.).

No. 185. *Karṇa Parva*, by Śrīpatī of Maūnagara, written in V.S. 1719 (1662 A.D.).

In the catalogue of Hindi manuscripts in the British Museum a book (No. 25 *Līlāvatī*) is mentioned as being in the Baiswāṛī dialect. I had an opportunity of examining the manuscript while I stayed in London and found it to be in Rājasthānī. Of the manuscripts of Hindī in the India Office Library I did not find any in Awadhī (except *Rāma-carita-mānasa* and *Padmāvat*).

It may be pointed out here that the study of Early Awadhī is beset with difficulties. The text of the works has not yet been critically established. It is difficult to find out how far the *tatsama* words found in the texts were correctly pronounced. Or possibly they might represent merely a difference in writing but not in speech. For instance was श pronounced or was it another symbol for स? That ष was normally pronounced ख is clear from the fact that it replaces ख in the manuscripts at many places. The accuracy of the forms also is not authenticated. We sometimes find that the forms of other dialects creep into works in Awadhī, *e.g.*, the *-ga* (Hindustāni) future in the Rāmāyaṇa. These might be due to the carelessness of the scribes or might belong to the authors themselves. As remarked above, the various dialects of Hindi were not mutually unintelligible.

For Awadhi as spoken to-day, the only available material is that contained in the volume on Eastern Hindi of the *Linguistic Survey of India*. On investigation it was found to be fairly correct. This has been amply supplemented by me with folk-tales and songs collected from the Awadhī area. Sometimes in the Hindi dramas of modern days, Awadhī is uttered by the minor illiterate characters, for instance, in the farces written by G. P. Srivastava (Gonda) and in the *Nētrōnmīlan Nātak* by the Misra Brothers (Sitapur and Lucknow). The late Pt. Shridhar Pathak also employed Awadhī occasionally in his poems.

Dialects of Awadhi.

§ 7. Of the main Awadhī area, the dialects can be divided into three divisions—Western, Central and Eastern. The dialects of Kheri (Lakhimpur), Sitapur, Lucknow, Unao and Fatehpur are Western, those of Bahraich, Barabanki and Rae Bareli are Central while those of Gonda, Fyzabad, Sultanpur, Partabgarh, Allahabad, Jaunpur and Mirzapur are Eastern. This division is based on the commonness of certain linguistic traits detailed in the grammar given hereafter.

Formation of Awadhi.

§ 8. In the following pages sounds and grammar of Awadhī, Early and Modern, have been studied in detail. As regards sounds of Modern Awadhī, I have examined my own dialect,[1] Lakhīmpurī, very minutely and have verified the results by experimental phonetics wherever this was practicable. Information about other dialects is based on personal observation of the actual speech of the people. I got tales and songs from the villagers by going to the villages myself and tried to keep them away from the influence of Hindustānī as far as possible. The grammars of the dialects are based on the material thus gathered and have been supplemented by certain data taken from the literate and habitual speakers of Awadhī of the various tracts.

Vocabulary of Awadhi.

§ 9. The vocabulary does not require any special remarks. It is predominantly Aryan, but here and there there

[1] I was born in the Lakhīmpurī area and habitually spoke Lakhīmpurī until I had to leave Lakhīmpur (at the age of 17 years) for University education. I, however spent my vacations at my native place. I have been regularly speaking Hindustānī now, except at my home where even now Awadhī is spoken. The inscriptions and palatograms appended here are all specimens of my speech—taken in London. For want of proper facilities in India, it was not possible to verify the results arrived at by me through experiment, by testing the speech of other speakers of Awadhī.

is a sprinkling of words of the non-Aryan substratum and of foreign origin. It is only in vocabulary that the speech of one class differs from that of another. The Brahmins are fond of Sanskrit words while the Kayasthas, due to their closer association with the Muslim administration, have a larger percentage of words of Persian origin in their speech than other classes of Hindus. The Banias pick up the words of their special trade from the towns and the agricultural classes employ their own words for expressing the concepts of their occupation. The percentage of special words, however, is so small that it is almost negligible and all understand one another without the slightest difficulty.

The speech of women does not differ from that of men in essentials. Women, however, are more emotional in expression. They avoid words expressing reprehensible ideas. Indian women (particularly Hindu women) never utter the names of their husbands and also generally avoid uttering the names of their eldest sons. In quarrels where men would generally come to blows, women satisfy themselves by showering abuse and curses. Their vocabulary of abuse is thus more copious.

Orthography of Awadhi.

§ 10. Awadhī is reduced to-day to writing only for short messages from one village to another. The script is Kaithī in such cases. The Banias write their accounts in Huṇḍīwālī (also known as Muṛiyā). These are merely convenient forms of the Dēvanāgarī script. The educated classes generally use either the Persian or the Dēvanāgarī script.

PART I
AWADHI PHONETICS

CHAPTER I

INDIVIDUAL SOUNDS

Sound-system

A. EARLY AWADHI

§ 11. The texts reveal the following sounds:

(*a*) Consonants

(*i*) mutes

k *kh* *g* *gh*
c *ch* *j* *jh*
ṭ *ṭh* *ḍ* *ḍh*
t *th* *d* *dh*
p *ph* *b* *bh*

(*ii*) nasals

ṅ *ñ* *ṇ* *n* *m* *ṃ*

(*iii*) semi-vowels

y *r* *l* *v* *ṛ* *ṛh*

(*iv*) sibilants

[*ś*] [*ṣ*] *s*

(*v*) aspirate

h [*ḥ*]

(*b*) Vowels

a *ā* *i* *ī* *u* *ū* **e* *ē* **o* *ō* [*ṛ*]

NOTE—The letters given in brackets are found in the texts though rarely. As shown below they are merely orthographic symbols to represent other sounds (*s*, *kh*, *h* and *ri*). The sounds with asterisks are represented in writing by symbols next to them.

B. MODERN AWADHI

§ 12.	BILABIAL.	DENTAL	ALVEOLAR.	PALATAL.	(PALATAL) RETROFLEX.	VELAR.	GLOTTAL.
1. Plosives ...	p b	t d			ʈ ɖ	k g	
,, Aspirates	ph bɦ	th dɦ			ʈh ɖɦ	kh gɦ	
2. Affricates ...				c ɟ			
,, Aspirates				ch ɟɦ			
3. Nasals ...	m		n	(ɲ)	(ɳ)	(ŋ)	
,, Aspirates	mɦ	nɦ					
4. Lateral ...				l			
,, Aspirate				lɦ			
5. Rolled ...			r				
,, Aspirate			rɦ				
6. Flapped ...					ɽ		
,, Aspirate					ɽɦ		
7. Fricative ...			s				h ɦ
8. Semi-vowels ...	w		j				

9. Vowels

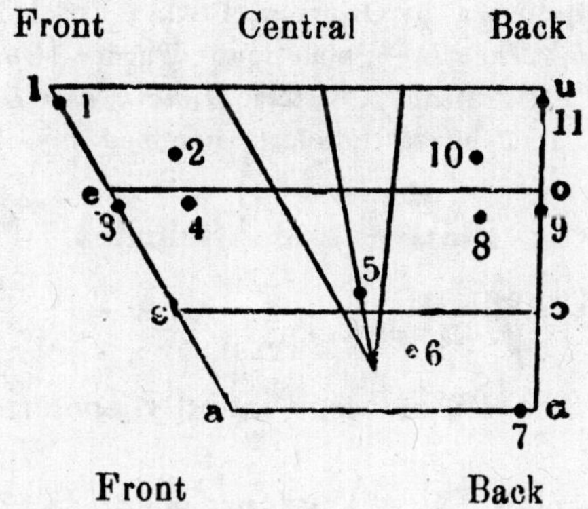

The position of Awadhi vowels is shown by dots in the above chart.

1. **iː, ĩː**
2. **i, ĩ, i̥**
3. **eː, ẽː**
4. **e, ẽ, e̥**
5. **ə**
6. **ʌ, ʌ̃**
7. **ɑː**
8. **o, õ**
9. **oː, õː**
10. **u, ũ, u̥**
11. **uː, ũː**

NOTE.—(1) In the following pages a complete description of sounds of modern Awadhi has been given. This has been verified and attested by experiments wherever it was possible. In the case of Early Awadhi it has not been possible to describe the sounds in detail on account of the absence of evidence. The presumption, however, is that the pronunciation in the early stage also was much the same as in modern Awadhi.

(2) As observed by Dr. Bloch (*Langue Marathe* § 28) 'it is by the grammatical forms chiefly that the Indo-Aryan languages, situated to the east of the Indus, are distinguished from one another. The phonetic system in them is, on the other hand,

perceptibly identical . . . ' Detailed phonology of Indo-Aryan has already been discussed by Grierson (BSOS., Vol. I, Part III. 1920), Bloch (*Langue Marathe*—Phonetique), Turner (*Gujarātī Phonology*, JRAS., 1921-22) and Chatterji (*Origin and Development of Bengali*, Vol. I). I have, therefore, confined myself particularly to Awadhi.

Plosives and Affricates

A. Early Awadhi

Mutes

§ 13. The Mutes occur initially and medially. For instance

k *kēli* 'play' (J. 49), *ākusa* 'goad' (J. 39), *kai* 'of' (T. 164), *ṭikā* 'coronation' (T.159), *kūara* 'prince' (N. 9)., *kanaka* 'gold' (N. 14), *keu* 'some one' (*Lāl*), *dhanuka* 'bow' (*Lāl*), *kamāva* 'earned' (Nisār), *akāratha* 'useless' (Nisār).

kh *khāi* 'having eaten' (J. 121), *likhī* 'written' (J. 121), *khēlata* 'playing' (T. 377), *nirakhata* 'seeing' (T. 374), *khīcahai* 'will drag' (N. 21), *bakhānū* 'description' (N. 21) *khaṇḍa* 'part' (*Lāl.*) *ukhārī* 'uprooted' (Lāl.), *kharī* 'standing' (Nisār), *dēkhi* 'having seen' (Nisār).

NOTE.—In Lāldās the symbol for *ṣ* all through represents *kh*; similarly in Tulsīdās also.

g *gāṭhi* 'knot' (J. 120) *māraga* 'path' (J. 120), *garajai* 'thunders' (T. 375), *māga* 'path' (T. 375), *gosāī* 'master' (N. 21), *jōgī* 'yogin' (N. 21), *gunavārē* 'meritorious' (Lāl.), *jagya* 'sacrifice' (Lāl), *garaba* 'pride' (Nisār), *agyā* 'order' (Nisār).

NOTE.—In Nisār the symbol for *k* represents both *k* and *g*.

gh *ghāli* 'having put' (J. 124), *siṅghala* 'Ceylon' (J. 120), *ghamaṇḍa* 'pride' (T. 375) *nāghehu* 'crossed' (T. 386), *ghaṛī* 'hour' (N. 15), *sugharāhī* 'look pretty' (N. 12), *aghōrahi* 'Aghōra'

(Lāl.), *saṁghārē* 'slaughtered' (Lāl.), *ghāli* 'having put' (Nisār), *paraghaṭ* 'plainly' (Nisār).

c *calĕũ* 'started' (J. 121), *bica* 'middle' (J. 122).

ch *chapāia* 'should not be concealed' (J. 123), *āchai* 'is' (J. 123).

j *jō* 'who' (J. 123), *banija* 'merchant' (J. 127).

jh *jhā̃kā* 'peeped' (J. 61), *samujhi* 'having realised' (T. 383).

ṭ *ṭūṭa* 'broke' (T. 116), *chōṭi* 'small' (J. 140).

ṭh *ṭhakurasohāti* 'pleasing to the master' (T. 163), *jhūṭhi* 'false' (T. 163).

ḍ *ḍagai* 'moves' (T. 108), *bhã̄ḍārī* 'storekeeper' (J. 109).

ḍh *ḍhōla* 'drum' (T. 366), *paḍhī* 'well-read' (J. 83).

NOTE.—Intervocally *ḍ* and *ḍh* are found only after a nasal (*ṇ*) or after nasalisation, otherwise they become *ṛ* and *ṛh* respectively. The manuscripts generally have *ḍ* and *ḍh* (for *ṛ* and *ṛh* also) but the printed books differ. Jayasī's *Padmāvat*, for instance, keeps *ḍ* and *ḍh* throughout in the edition of the Bengal Asiatic Society while the *Rāmacaritamānasa* of Tulsīdās gives *ḍ*, *ḍh* and *ṛ*, *ṛh* distinctly in the Nāgarī Pracāriṇī Sabhā edition. *Indrāvatī* of Nūr Muhammad has promiscuously both the symbols[1].

ṛ, ṛh *baṛa* 'big' (T. 107), *baṛhai* 'increases' (T. 103), *chāṛaū̃* 'I leave' (N. 20), *kāṛhai* 'pulls' (N. 17), but *kā̃ḍhai* in the next line.

t *tumhārē* 'yours' (T. 102), *nakhata* 'stars' (T. 103).

th *thira* 'steady' (J. 70), *mā̃thai* 'on the head' (J. 72).

d *dēkha* 'having seen' (J. 72), *ōdara* 'stomach' (J. 78).

dh *dhani* 'blessed' (J. 80), *gandha* 'smell' (J 79).

p *pūri* 'complete' (J. 79), *dipā* 'shone' (J. 81).

ph *phōrai* 'to be broken' (T. 163), *haripharēuri* 'a variety of fruit' (J. 420).

---

[1] *ṛ* and *ṛh* have been dealt with here, therefore, and not under semi-vowels.

o *bairī* 'enemy' (J. 249), *jāba* 'shall go' (J. 249).

bh *bhūlatī* 'forget' (J. 249), *ūbhi* 'having got bored' (J. 160).

B. Modern Awadhi

p

§ 14. The sound **p** is a breathed bi-labial unaspirated plosive. In a word it can occur initially as in **pʌin**[1] 'sharp', **paːtaː** 'leaf', medially as in **piːpʌr** 'a kind of tree', **upːʌr** 'above' or finally as in **sʌraːp** 'curse', **naːp** 'measure'.

b

§ 15. The sound **b** is a voiced bilabial unaspirated plosive. It is fully voiced, inasmuch as the voice begins earlier than the explosion, and thus slightly differs in shade from English **b** In a word it can occur initially as in **baːp** 'father', **biṭijaː** 'daughter', medially as in **kʌbisaː** 'yellow clay,' and finally as in **ɟaːib** 'shall go'.

Note.—Final **b** is generally unexploded and devoiced (See Ins. I)

t

§ 16. The sound **t** is a breathed dental unaspirated plosive. The passage of breath is closed by making the tip of the tongue touch the points of both the upper and lower teeth (see Pal. 2). In a word it can occur initially as in **tiːni̥** 'three', **turʌt** 'at once', medially as in **pʌturijaː** 'harlot', **kutʌwaː** 'dog', or finally as in **saːt** 'seven', **pʌraːt** 'a big dish'.

d

§ 17. The sound **d** is a voiced unaspirated dental plosive. The closure is made just as to pronounce **t** but the vocal cords vibrate all the time until the explosion. In a word it can occur initially as in **diɦisi̥** 'he gave', **dulʌɦaː**

[1] Unless otherwise stated, the examples given in the following pages have been taken from the Lakhīmpurī dialect.

'bride-groom', medially as in **kuːdʌb** 'to jump', **baːdʌrɱ** 'cloud' or finally as in **tõːd** 'protruding belly,' **gẽːd** 'ball'.

ʈ

§ 18. The sound **ʈ** is a breathed unaspirated retroflex plosive. The closure is made by the touch of the back of the tip of the tongue at the smooth surface of the hard palate right above the rough back of the teeth-ridge (see Pal. 3). In a word, it can occur initially as in **ʈẽːu** 'habit,' **ʈʌʈuaː** 'pony,' medially as in **khʌʈijaː** 'bedstead,' **loʈijaː** 'water-jug' or finally as in **bɦaːʈ** 'bard,' **bɦẽːʈ** 'present'.

ɖ

§ 19. The sound **ɖ** is a voiced unaspirated retroflex plosive. The closure is made just as in **ʈ** but the voice is heard all along until the explosion. It can occur initially in a word as in **ɖeuɽɦeː** 'one and a half time,' **ɖebijaː**, 'casket,' or medially and finally when preceded by its nasal as in **kʌɳɖaː** 'cow-dung cakes,' **mʌɳɖiː** 'grain-market, **lʌɳɖ** 'penis', **ʈhʌɳɖ** 'cold'.

k

§ 20. The sound **k** is a breathed unaspirated velar plosive. The back of the tongue rises up towards the soft palate almost at the point where it meets the hard palate and makes the closure there ordinarily. When a front vowel follows it, however, the closure is made farther forward on the hard palate particularly on the sides (see Pal. 4 and 5). In a word, it can occur initially as in **kʌpəɽaː** 'cloth,' **kinaːriː** 'border,' medially as in **pʌləkaː** 'bed,' **khirkijaː** 'window,' or finally as in **taːk** 'opportunity,' **niːk** 'good'.

g

§ 21. The sound **g** is the voiced unaspirated velar plosive. The closure in the mouth is formed just as for **k**, but here the voice is heard all through until the sound explodes. In a word, it can occur initially as in **goːɦũː** 'wheat,'

gãːṭhi̥ 'knot,' medially as in **leɦẽgaː** 'petticoat,' **bʌgijaː** 'garden' or finally as in **bɦãːg** 'an intoxicating plant,' **ṭãːg** 'leg'.

ph

§ 22. The sound **ph** is the aspirated form of **p.** It resembles the Southern English *p* of stressed syllables with this difference that in the Awadhi sound the aspiration is stronger as with all the aspirated sounds treated below. In a word, it can occur initially, *e.g.*, in **phʌrikaː** 'a gate made of straw,' **phoːrʌb** 'to break,' medially, *e.g.*, in **tʌlphʌti̥** 'writhing,' **sʌphaː** 'clear,' or finally as in **baːph** 'vapour,' **maːph** 'pardon'.

bɦ

§ 23. The sound **bɦ** is the aspirated form of **b.** The voice is heard throughout the aspiration. In a word, it can occur initially as in **bɦaːiː** 'brother,' **bɦiːɟʌb** 'to be wet,' medially, *e.g.*, in **khʌmbɦaː** 'a pillar,' **goːbɦiː** 'cauliflower' or finally, *e.g.*, in **ṭoːbɦ** 'spaces of sewing,' **ɟiːbɦ** 'tongue'.

th

§ 24. The sound **th** is the aspirated form of **t.** In a word, it can occur initially as in **thʌ̃bɦəraː** 'post,' **thuːku̥** 'saliva', medially as in **paːthʌr** 'stone,' **məthʌuriː** 'small tablets made of *urd* and used as meat,' or finally as in **saːth** 'with,' **maːth** 'forehead'.

dɦ

§ 25. The sound **dɦ** is the aspirated form of **d.** The voice is heard throughout the aspiration. In a word, it can occur initially as in **dɦowaːiː** 'washing,' **dɦaːn** 'paddy,' medially in **bãːdɦʌb** 'to tie,' **sẽːdɦi̥** 'an opening in wall made by burglars,' or finally as in **kãːdɦ** 'shoulder,' **bãːdɦ** 'string'.

ṭh

§ 26. The sound **ṭh** is the aspirated form of **ṭ**. In a word, it can occur initially as in **ṭhʌɽɦijaːwʌb** 'to put in standing posture', **ṭhʌur** 'room, space', medially as in **laːṭhiː** 'stick', **mʌɳṭhaː** 'whey' or finally as in **kaːṭh** 'wood', **ḍɦiːṭh** 'obstinate'.

ḍɦ

§ 27. The sound **ḍɦ** is the aspirated form of **ḍ**; the voice is heard throughout the aspiration. It can occur initially in a word as in **ḍɦoːwaː** 'presents', **ḍɦoːlʌk** 'drum' or medially when preceded by its nasal as in **ṭhʌɳḍɦaːiː**' 'cooling beverage'.

kh

§ 28. The sound **kh** is the aspirated form of **k**. In a word, it can occur initially as in **kheːt** 'field', **khoːlʌb** 'to open', medially as in **mukhijaː** 'headman', **ãːkhiː** 'eyes', or finally as in **bɦuːkh** 'hunger', **sʌnduːkh** 'box'.

gɦ

§ 29. The sound **gɦ** is the aspirated form of **g**; the voice is present throughout the aspiration. In a word it can occur initially as in **gɦẽgɦʌrijaː** 'a girl's petticoat', **gɦerʌ̃udaː** 'a baby's toy-house of sand', medially as in **nãːgɦʌb** 'to cross', **sũːgɦẽu** 'I smelt' or finally as in **gɦaːgɦ** 'a person who cleverly hides his motive'.

c

§ 30. The sound **c** is the breathed affricate unaspirated palatal consonant. The closure of the breath is made by the front of the tongue at the rough back of the teeth-ridge and is followed by friction (See Pal. 6). The touch continues a little longer than in the case of other plosives **k, t,** etc., and a slight affrication is perceptible. This affrication is, however, much less than in the corresponding English sound **tʃ**.

c can occur initially as in **cʌnaː** 'gram', **coʈaː** 'thief', medially as in **khãːciː** 'a basket', **pɦ̃icaːni̥** 'cognizance', or finally in a word as in **pãːc** 'five', **naːc** 'dance'.

ɟ

§ 31. The sound **ɟ** is the voiced variety of **c** and may be called a voiced affricate unaspirated palatal consonant. In a word it can occur initially as in **ɟãːgɦ** 'thigh', **ɟʌun** 'which', medially as in **bɦ̃ʌɟʌb** 'to string', **mĩːɟeũ** 'I crumbled (trans.)', or finally as in **raːɟ** 'mason', **mũːɟ** 'a kind of grass'.

ch

§ 32. The sound **ch** is the aspirated variety of **c.** In a word it can occur initially as in **chʌgoriː** 'goat', **chãːʈʌb** 'to wash', medially as in **paːcheː** 'behind', **tirchaː** 'crooked', or finally as in **chũːch** 'empty', **kõːch** 'lap apron'.

ɟɦ

§ 33. The sound **ɟɦ** is the aspirated form of **ɟ.** In a word it can occur initially as in **ɟɦʌloraː** 'mashed vegetable leaves', **ɟɦĩːgaː** 'shrimp', medially as in **mʌ̃ɟɦoːlaː** 'of middling size', **suːɟɦʌb** 'to be visible', or finally as in **sãːɟɦ** 'evening', **ɟɦãːɟɦ** 'an ornament for ankles'.

General Notes on the Plosives.

§ 34. The voiced plosives are generally shorter than the breathed ones. For instance, **t** of **paːtiː** 'leaf' is longer than **d** of **paːdiː** 'broke wind' (See Inscs. 2 and 3). The voiced plosives have strong voice when they are intervocalic. In the initial and final positions the voice is comparatively less strong (Cf. Inscs. 3 and 4).

In an intervocalic breathed plosive, faint voice appears generally in the initial stage of closure (plosion) as well as in the explosion (See **k** of Insc. 1).

The aspirated forms of the plosives are merely plosives with **h** or **ɦ** (see aspirated sounds in Inscs. 1, 4, 7, 10, 15,

19 and 22). The aspiration, however, is united closely with the explosion. It is convenient to treat the aspirates as separate sounds, as they have been so treated all through by Indian grammarians.

A long consonant is about sixty per cent longer than the corresponding short one (See Inscs. 5 and 6, **paːtaː** and **pʌtːaː** 'leaf').

Final plosives preceded by a short vowel are longer than those preceded by a long vowel (See Inscs. 7 and 8 **piʈh** and **piːʈh** 'back').

The general remarks made about plosives are applicable to the affricates also. An affricate is generally a little longer than a plosive, breathed or voiced, (See Inscs. 11 and 12 **cʌʈibaː** 'shall lick' and **sĩcibaː** 'shall irrigate')

C. Origin of Sounds

k

§ 35. Initial Awadhi **k-** is derived from MIA *k-* which came from OIA

(*i*) *k-* *kārya* > **kaːj** 'business'

(*ii*) *kr-* *krośa* > **koːs** 'a distance of two miles'

(*iii*) *sk-* (exceptionally) *skandha* > **kãːdɦ** 'shoulder'.

Medial and final **-k** is derived from MIA

(*i*) *-k-* after *ṅ* *vaṅka* (< Skt. *vakra*) > **bãːkaː** 'crooked'

(*ii*) *-kk-* *cikkaṇa* > **ciːkʌn** 'smooth', OIA *pakva* (MIA *pikka*) > **paːk** 'ripe'.

In words of foreign origin **k** represents foreign *k* and *q*, and sometimes *g*, *e.g.*, **kʌlʌm** < *qalam* 'pen', **dukaːn** < *dukān* 'shop', **bʌkucaː** < *bugcā* 'a load'. **k** is also found in certain words which appear to be *Deśī*. *e.g.*, **boːkaː** 'a bamboo box'.

Besides **k** is found in many modern suffixes, *e.g.*, **bʌɽaː** : **bʌɽkaː** 'big'.

kh

§ 36. Initial **kh-** comes from MIA *kh-* which was derived from OIA

(*i*) *kh- khādya-* > **khaːɟaː** 'a variety of sweetmeat'

(*ii*) *kṣ- kṣetra* > **kheːt** 'field'

(*iii*) *sk- skambha-* > **khʌmbɦaː** 'pillar'.

Medially and finally **kh** comes from MIA

(*i*) *-kkh- pakkhī-* > **pãːkhiː** 'small winged insects', **suːkh** 'dry', **ukhaːrʌb** 'to dig up'

(*ii*) *-ṅkh- *kaṅkha-* > **kãːkhi̥** 'armpit'.

In some words *kh* represents OIA *ṣ* by its pronunciation as *kh*, *e.g.*, **doːkhu̥** < *doṣaḥ* 'defect'.

In foreign loan-words **kh** represents foreign *kh* generally, *e.g.*, **ʌkhʌroːʈ** < *a͟khrōṭ* 'nuts', and in **bʌkhʌt** < *vaqt* 'time' it represents *q*.

g

§ 37. Initially **g-** comes from MIA *g-* which is derived from OIA

(*i*) *g- gata-* > **gaː** 'went'

(*ii*) *gr- grāmaḥ* > **gãːu** 'village'.

g represents *jñ* in *ardhatatsama* words, *e.g.*, ***jñāna*** : **gjaːn** 'knowledge' and *-k-* in **geːraː** < *ekādaśa* and *gh* in **ʌrʌgu̥** < *arghyaḥ* 'offering'.

Medially and finally **-g-** comes from MIA

(*i*) *-gg- aggī* > **aːgi̥** 'fire'

(*ii*) *-g-* after *ṅ*, *aṅga-* > **ãːgaː** 'a sort of coat'.

In foreign loan-words **g** represents foreign *g* and *g*, *e.g.*, **gʌriːb** < *g͟arīb* 'poor', **gumaːn** < *gumān* 'pride'.

gɦ (*gh*)

§ 38. Initial **gɦ-** is derived from MIA *gh-* which itself comes from OIA

gh- ghṛta- > **gɦiu** 'clarified butter'.

In **ghaːn** 'one sweep of material put in pan for baking' **gh** is possibly connected with *g-* (*grahaṇa*).

Intervocal and final **-gɦ** comes from MIA

(*i*) *-ggh-* *vaggha* > **baːgɦ** 'tiger'

(*ii*) *-gh-* after *-ṅ-* *laṅghai* > **nãːgɦʌi** 'crosses'.

In **ʌrəgɦiː** 'a wooden vessel', the possibility of derivation is from 'learned' *arghya-* 'offering' owing to water and flowers, etc., having been offered in such a vessel.

gɦ is also found in many *deśī* words, *e.g.*, **gɦĩːc** or **gɦẽṭuaː** 'neck'.

c

§ 39. Initial **c-** comes from MIA *c-* derived from OIA

(*i*) *c-* *cakra-* > **cʌkiaː** 'stone-mill'

(*ii*) *cy-* *cyavati* > **cuʌi** 'leaks'.

Medially and finally **-c** is derived from MIA

(*i*) *-cc-* *saccaṃ* > **sãːcṇ** 'true'

(*ii*) *-c-* after *-ñ-* *añcala* > **ãːcʌr** 'breast'.

In foreign loan-words *c* represents foreign *c* (**tʃ**) *e.g.*, **ʌckʌn** : *ackan* 'tunic',

ch

§ 40. Initial **ch-** is derived from MIA *ch-* which comes from OIA

(*i*) *ch-* *chedana-* > **cheːniː** 'chisel'

(*ii*) [*ṣ-* in **chaː** < *ṣaṭ* 'six'].

Medial and final **ch** comes from MIA

(*i*) *-cch-* *acchaï-* Early Aw. *āchai* 'is', *maccha-* > **mʌchəriː** 'fish', *macchiā* > **maːchiː** 'fly', cf. **mʌmaːkhiː** 'bee'

(*ii*) *-ch-* after *ñ*, *pauñchai* > **põːchʌi** 'wipes'.

ɟ (j)

§ 41. Initial **ɟ-** is derived from MIA *j-* which comes from OIA

(*i*) *j-* *jihvā* > **ɟiːbɦ** 'tongue'

(ii) *jy-* *jyeṣṭha* > **ɟeːʈh** 'elder'
(iii) *jv-* *jvalati* > **ɟʌrʌi** 'burns'
(iv) *dy-* *dyūta-* > **ɟuãː** 'gambling'
(v) *y-* *yauvana* > **ɟoːbʌn** 'youthfulness'.

Medial and final **-ɟ** is derived from MIA

(i) *-jj-* *ajja* > **aːɟ** 'to-day', **uɟʌr** 'white', **bʌniɟ** 'merchandise'
(ii) *-j-* coming after *ñ* **pãːɟʌr** < *pañjara* 'skeleton'.

In *tatsama* words intervocal **-ɟ-** represents Sanskrit *-j-* *e.g.*, **raːɟaː** 'king'.

In foreign loan-words **ɟ** represents foreign *j* (**ɟʌmaː** < *jamaç* 'collection') and *z* (**mʌɟaː** < *mazaḥ* 'fun'), **ð** (**guɟʌr** < **guðar** 'sustenance'), **đ** (**hʌɟuːr** < **huđur** 'Your Honour'), **ẓ** (**ɟulum** < **ẓulm** 'oppression'), all of which were pronounced as *z* in Persian.

ɟɦ (*jh*)

§ 42. Initial **ɟɦ-** represents MIA *jh-* which is mostly found in onomatopoetic words, and *Deśī* words:

jh- *jhaṭṭa-* > **ɟɦʌʈ** 'soon'.

Medial and final **ɟɦ** comes from MIA

(i) *-jjh-* *bujjhai* > **buːɟɦʌi** 'understands'. *aṇajjhāō* > **ʌɲɟɦaː** 'holiday'
(ii) *-jh-* coming after *ñ-* *sañjhā* > **sãːɟɦ** 'evening'.

ʈ (*ṭ*)

§ 43. Initial **ʈ-** comes from MIA *ṭ-* (OIA *tr-*) and from *deśī* words.

tuṭṭai > **ʈuːʈʌi** 'breaks', **ʈãːg** 'leg'.

Medial and final **-ʈ** is derived from MIA

(i) *-ṭṭ-* *vaṭṭai* > **baːʈeː** 'is'
(ii) *-ṭ-* after *ṇ-* *kaṇṭaa* **kãːʈaː** 'thorn'
(iii) *-ṭṭ-* of *deśī* words, *e.g.*, **peːʈ** < * *peṭṭa* 'stomach'.

In **ɖãːʈʌb** which possibly comes from √*daṇḍa-* **-ʈ-** appears to represent devoiced *-ḍ-*.

In loan-words from English **ṭ** represents English *t*, *e.g.*, **ṭeːm** : English *time*.

ṭh (*ṭh*)

§ 44. Initial **ṭh-** is derived from MIA *ṭh-* and is also found in *deśī* words, *e.g.*, **ṭhaːkur** 'lord', **ṭhʌg** 'robber'.

Medial and final **ṭh** comes from MIA

(*i*) *-ṭṭh- aṅguṭṭha-* > **ãguṭhaː** 'thumb'

(*ii*) *-ṭh-* coming after *ṇ- gaṇṭhī* > **gãːṭhi̥** 'knot'.

NOTE.—In **hũːṭhaː** 'three and a half' < *ardha-caturtha*, OIA *-rth-* which is represented as **-th-** in Awadhī (**cʌuth** <*caturtha*) appears as **ṭh**. The cerebralisation is attested at the Prakrit stage, however (Chatterji: p. 493). Pkt. *-ṭṭh-* in *kaviṭṭha*: Skt. *kapittha* is, however, found as *th* in Aw. **kʌithaː**, cf. Mālvī *kabīṭh*.

Medial and final **ṭh** is found in many *deśī* words also, *e.g.*, **ṭheːṭh** 'entirely'.

N.B.—For *-ṭṭh-* of Pkt. represented as **-ṛh-** in certain cases see below.

ḍ (*ḍ*)

§ 45. Initial **ḍ-** represents MIA *ḍ-* derived from OIA *d daṇḍa-* > **ḍãːṛaː** 'stalk', *daṃśaka* **ḍãːs** 'a biting insect', *dvi-ardha* > **ḍeːṛh** 'one and a half'.

Where Aw. **ḍ-** corresponds with Sanskrit *ḍ-* (*e.g.*, **ḍoːraː** : *ḍora-* 'thread', the latter represents either a late MIA cerebralisation or a loan-word from *deśī*.

ḍ- occurs in many words of *deśī* origin, *e.g.*, **ḍaːr**, 'branch', **ḍõːgiː** 'boat'.

Medially and finally **-ḍ** is found only after **ṇ** and in what appear as modern loan-words from other dialects: **pʌṇḍaː** 'the keeper of a sacred place', **gʌṇḍaː** 'a thread with some mystical influence of some saint, worn on the neck or on the wrist; a group of four', **kʌṇḍaː** 'cow-dung cake.'

NOTE.—In Early Awadhī medial *-ḍ-* possibly represents **ṛ** mostly.

ḍɦ (*ḍh*)

§ 46. Initial **ḍɦ-** is derived from MIA *ḍh-* which comes from OIA

(*i*) *dh* with ṛ, etc., *dhṛṣṭa* > **ḍɦiːʈh** 'naughty'

(*ii*) *ḍh* which is either late cerebralisation or is found in a *deśī* loan-word, *e.g.*, **ḍɦoːwʌː** < *ḍhaukatē-* 'brings, gathers'.

Medial and final **-ḍɦ** is found only after **ɳ** and in few words: **ʈhʌɳḍɦ** cold'.

There are a large number of words where **ḍɦ** occurs initially; these are probably of *deśī* origin, *e.g.*, **ḍɦoːl** 'drum', **ḍɦeːr** 'many', **ḍɦʌkuliː** 'a paddle', **ḍɦũːʈɦʌ** 'searches'.

t

§ 47. Initial **t-** comes from MIA *t-* derived from OIA

(*i*) *t-* *tapta* > **taːt** 'hot'

(*ii*) *tr-* *trīṇi* > **tiːn** 'three'.

Medial and final **-t** represents MIA

(*i*) *-tt-* *putto* > **puːt̪** 'son', *satta* > **saːt** 'seven'

(*ii*) *-t-* after *n-* *danto* > **dãːt** 'tooth'.

In *tatsama* and *ardha-tatsama* words, **-t-** might represent Sanskrit *-t-*, *e.g.*,

ɟʌtʌn ∠ *yatna* 'means'.

In foreign loan-words *t* represents *t*, *e.g.*, **mʌut** 'death'.

th

§ 48. Initial **th-** comes from MIA *th-* derived from OIA

(*i*) *st-* *stana* > **thʌn** 'udder'

(*ii*) *sth-* *sthālī-* > **thʌrijaː** 'dish'

Medially and finally **-th** is derived from MIA

-tth- derived from OIA

(*i*) *tth-* *kapittha-* > **kʌithaː** 'a fruit'

(*ii*) *-kth-* *siktha* > **siːth** 'a grain'

(*iii*) *-rth-* *sārtha-* > **saːthiː** 'companion'

(*iv*) *-st-* *prastara* > **paːthʌr** 'pebble'

th in all positions occurs in *deśī* words also, *e.g.*, **thʌpʌṛaː** 'slap', **thuːthun** 'horse's nostrils'. In *tatsama* and *ardha-tatsama* words Aw. **-th-** might represent Sanskrit *-th-*, *e.g.*, **kʌthaː** 'story'.

d

§ 49. Initial **d-** comes from MIA *d-* derived from OIA

(*i*) *d-* *dadhi-* > **dʌɦiu** 'curds'

(*ii*) *dr-* *droṇa-* > **doːnaː** 'a cup made of leaves'.

Medial and final **-d** goes back to MIA

(*i*) *-dd-* *haliddā-* > **hʌrdiː** 'turmeric', *bhadra-pada-* > **bɦaːdʌũ** 'the Bhādrapada month'

(*ii*) *-d-* after *-n-* *mandu-* > **mãːdaː** 'ill'.

NOTE.— **-d** derived from MIA *-d* after *n* is not found in the Eastern dialects where the nasalisation plus *-d* in such cases is represented by *n*, *e.g.*, Lmp. **cãːdiː**, J. **caːniː** 'silver'.

In Lmp. **dʌurʌb** (Eastern **dɦʌurʌb**), deaspiration of Skt. *dhāv-* 'to run' is possible.[1] *dh-* in this verb is attested by Early Awadhī (Tulsi : *dhāi* 'having run').

dɦ (*dh*)

§ 50. Initial **dɦ-** goes back to MIA *dh-* derived from OIA

(*i*) *dh-* *dhānya* > **dɦaːn** 'corn, paddy'

(*ii*) In Aw. **dɦiː**, **dɦijaː** 'daughter', **dɦ-** goes back to MIA *dh-* (Pāli *dhītā*) representative of *d-* in OIA (*duhitā*).

Medial and final **-dɦ** is derived from MIA

(*i*) *-ddh-* *duddha* > **duːdɦ** 'milk', *giddha* > **giːdɦ** 'vulture'.

[1] (*i*) *dhāvati* > *dhāai*

(*ii*) *dravati* > *davaï* > *dava-ḍa-ï* > *dauṛe*

(*ii*) *-dh* after *n*, *bandhai* > **bãːdɦʌi** 'ties', *randhai* > **rãːdɦʌi** 'cooks'.

NOTE— **-dɦ** derived from MIA *-dh-* after *-n-* is not found in Eastern dialects where the nasalisation plus **-dɦ** in such cases is represented by **-ṇɦ**, *e.g.*, **baːnɦʌi** 'ties', **ʌnɦaːriː** 'darkness'. In Lakhimpurī and other Western dialects **~dɦ** intrudes in other cases also where Eastern dialects have **-nɦ** derived from MIA, *e.g.*, Lmp. **ʝõdɦʌijaː** (Eastern **ʝonɦʌijaː**) < *joṇhā-* 'moonlight'. Lmp. **kʌ̃dɦʌijaː** (Eastern **kʌnɦʌijaː**) < *kaṇha*—'Kr̥ṣṇa'.

dɦ- occurs in certain words which are of obscure origin, *e.g.*, **dɦʌmaːri̥** 'wild sport', **dɦuːm** 'show, pomp'.

p

§ 51. Initial **p-** comes from MIA *p-* derived from OIA

(*i*) *p-* *patrī-* : **paːtiː** 'leaf', *pr̥cch-* : **puːch-** 'to ask'

(*ii*) *pr-* *priya-* : **pijaː** 'beloved', *prasar-* : **pʌsʌr-** 'to lie down'

Medial and final *-p* comes from MIA

(*i*) *-pp-* *uppajjai* : **upoʝʌi** 'is born', *sappa* : **sãːp** 'snake', *appaṇam* : **ʌpʌn** 'one's own'

(*ii*) *-p-* after *-m-* *kampai* : **kãːpʌi** 'trembles'.

p is found in many words of *deśī* origin, *e.g.*, **peːṭ** 'belley', **ṭoːpiː** 'cap'.

p in foreign loan-words represents foreign *p*. In **supeːd** 'white' it stands for Persian *f* (*sufaid*).

ph

§ 52. Initial **ph-** comes from MIA *ph-* derived from OIA

(*i*) *ph-* *phala* : **phʌl** 'fruit', *phālguna* : **phaːgun** 'the month Phālgun'

(*ii*) *sp-* *spand-* : **phãːd-** 'to jump'

(*iii*) *sph-* *sphuṭ-* : **phuːṭ-** 'to break'.

Medial and final *ph* represents MIA

(*i*) *-pph-* *vappha-* : **baːph** 'vapour', *upphaṇāi*: **uphonaːi** 'bursts up as foam'

(*ii*) *-ph-* after *m* *gumpha-* : **goːphaː** 'twining'.

ph occurs in *deśī* words, *e.g.*, **phẽːṭaː** 'a wrapper', **hãːphʌb** 'to breathe deeply when exhausted'.

In foreign loan-words, *ph* represents *f*, *e.g.*, **sʌphaː** clear' : Pers. *sāf*.

b

§ 53. Initial **b-** represents MIA (*a*) *b-* which represents OIA

(*i*) *b-* *budhya-* **buːɟɦ-** 'to understand'

(*ii*) *br-* *brāhmaṇa* : **baːmɦʌn** 'Brahmin'

(*iii*) *dv-* *dvādaśa* : **baːraː** 'twelve' (and so forth in the numerals).

(*b*) *v-* which represents OIA

(*i*) *v-* *vātāvali-* : **bʌjaːr̥i** 'wind', *vismar-* : **bisʌr** 'to forget', *uvaviṭṭha-* : **bʌiṭh-** 'sitting'

(*ii*) *vy-* *vyāghra-* : **baːgɦu̯** 'tiger'.

(*c*) *m-* which represents OIA

m- *mukula* : **bʌur** 'blossom of the mango tree.'

Medial and final **-b** represents MIA

(*i*) *-b-* after *m*, *amba-* (< *āmra*) : **ʌ̃bijaː** 'green mangoes', *tambūla-* : **tʌ̃boːliː** 'seller of betel-leaves'.

(*ii*) *-bb-* *dubbala* : **duːbʌr** 'thin', *kabbura-* : **kʌbraː** 'spotted'.

N.B.—Western Awadhī does not have **-mb-** as **-m** as Hindustānī and Eastern Awadhī have, for instance W. Aw. **kʌ̃bʌriː** (variant **kʌmʌriː**) 'blanket' < *kambala-*, **ɟʌmuniː**

<*jambū-* is a loan-word, the pure Western Awadhī word being **phʌrẽːdaː** <*phalendra-*

In the numerals **-bb-** has been retained, **chʌbbis** 'twenty-six'.

In **bʌɦinị** 'sister' there is evidence of a transference of aspiration from the first to the second syllable.

In *tatsama* or *ardha-tatsama* words *-b-* may represent Sanskrit *-v-*, *e.g.*, **pʌrbiː** < *parvan* 'festival'.

In foreign loan-words and in *deśī* words Aw. **b** represents foreign *b*.

bɦ (*bh*)

§ 54. Initial **bɦ-** represents MIA *bh-* derived from OIA

(*i*) *bh-* *bhikṣā* > **bɦiːkh** 'alms', *bhūmi* : **bɦuĩ** 'ground'

(*ii*) *bhr-* *bhrātṛ-* > **bɦaːiː** 'brother', *bhrāṣṭra-* > **bɦaːṭhaː** 'kiln'

(*iii*) *-bhy-* *abhyantara* > **bɦiːtʌr** 'within'.

In **bɦʌĩsaː** (Skt. *mahiṣa-*) 'buffalo' and **bɦẽːṛiː** (Skt. *mēḍhra-*)- 'sheep'. **bɦ-** is possibly derived from *m* through the transposition of *-h-* (Chatterji, p. 515). Another suggestion is that these words might be *deśī* in origin.

Medial and final **bɦ-** represents MIA

(*i*) *-bbh-* *gabbhiṇī* > **gaːbɦiːnị** 'pregnant', *jibbhā* > **jiːbɦ** 'tongue'

(*ii*) *-bh-* after *m* *kumbhaāra-* > **kũbɦaːr** 'potter'

(*iii*) *-mh* *bāmhaṇa* > **bãːbɦʌn** 'Brahmin' (beside **baːmɦʌn**).

bɦ occurs in several *deśī* words, *e.g.*, **bɦiːr** 'crowd', **bɦʌbːɦʌr** 'agitation'.

Nasals

A. Early Awadhi

§ 55. Out of the five nasals, *ṅ* and *ñ* are found always in the middle of a word before a mute of their own class.

ṇ occurs medially, both intervocally and before a mute of its class, *n* and *m* occur in all positions. For instance :

ṇ *bhūṣaṇa* 'ornaments' (T. 141).

n *nindahi* '(they) blame' (T. 191), *āna* 'another' (T. 190), *kīnha* 'did' (T. 191), *dēotanha* 'gods' (J. 495), *nhāi* 'having taken a bath' (T. 223).

m *māhura* 'poison' (T. 222), *amia* 'nectar' (T. 231), *tumha* 'you' (T. 227).

ṃ always represents one of the five nasals before the mutes of its class, *e.g.*,
maṃgala 'auspiciousness' (T. 198), *puṃja* 'heap' (T. 198), *daṃḍavata* 'obeisance' (T. 199), *suṃdari* 'the Beauty' (J. 488), *saṃmata* 'agreed' (T. 223).

B. Modern Awadhi

m

§ 56. The sound **m** is the voiced bi-labial nasal. It can occur initially as in **mʌɦinaː** 'month', **meɦeruaː** 'woman', medially as in **lʌmbaː** 'long, tall', **seːmiː** French beans', or finally as in **cilʌm** 'a sort of smoking-pipe made of clay', **moːm** 'wax'.

n

§ 57. The sound **n** is the voiced alveolar nasal. It may be noted, however, that the tip of the tongue while touching the gums touches the teeth also (See Pal. 7).

It can occur initially as in **neuraː** 'mongoose', **naːt** 'relative', medially either singly as in **bʌnaːwʌb** 'to make', **miaːnaː** a palanquin', **kʌnːeː** 'the corners of a kite' or before a plosive of its class or before **s** as in **bundaː** 'earrings', **pʌnthiː** 'a posture of sitting with feet on the thighs', **bʌnsiː** 'flute'; before a plosive of another class in compound words as in **kʌnpʌʈiː** 'temples of cheeks', **kʌnʈoːp** 'a head-gear covering the ears also', **kʌnkʌijaː** 'a kite', **kʌnchedonaː** 'the ceremony of piercing the ears', and finally as in **loːn** 'salt', **sʌin** 'beckoning'.

ɳ

§ 58. The sound **ɳ** is the voiced retroflex nasal but is pronounced a little more forward as compared to the plosives **ʈ**, **ɖ** (See Pal. 8). It can occur only medially and there too only before a retroflex plosive, *e.g.*, in **bʌɳʈaːɖɦaːr** 'utter ruin', **mʌɳʈhaː** 'whey', **mʌɳɖiː** 'grain market', **ʈhʌɳɖɦ** 'cool'.

ŋ

§ 59. The sound **ŋ** is the voiced velar nasal (See Pal. 9). It can occur medially and only before a velar plosive, *e.g.*, **sʌŋkʌr** 'Lord Śiva', **sʌŋkh** 'conch-shell', **phʌŋgeː** 'persevering entreaty', **sʌŋgɦʌtiː** 'companion'.

ɲ

§ 60. The sound **ɲ** is the voiced palatal nasal but is pronounced a little more forward as compared to **c**, **ɟ** (See Pal. 10). It can occur only medially and there too immediately before affricate consonants, *e.g.*, in **khoɲcaː** 'a dish of sweets', **tʌmʌɲcaː** 'pistol', **pʌɲchaː** 'features', **pʌɲɟaː** 'paw', **sʌɲɟɦaː** 'evening'.

mɦ

§ 61. The sound **mɦ** is the aspirated form of **m** and occurs only medially, *e.g.* **bʌromɦaː** 'Brahmā'.

nɦ

§ 62. The sound **nɦ** is the aspirated form of **n** and occurs only medially, *e.g.*, **kʌnɦʌijaː** 'Kṛṣṇa'.

General Notes on Nasals

§ 63. Awadhi possesses only two nasals **m** and **n** which are found in various positions in a word and are separate phonemes. The other three **ɳ ŋ ɲ** are found only medially and before the consonants of their class. They come under **n** phoneme. The palatograms show that **ɳ** and **ɲ** are spoken a little forward as compared to **ʈ** and **c** respectively nd that the positions of **ɳ** and **ŋ** are not very different. The aspirated forms of the nasals (*i.e.,* **nɦ**, **mɦ**) are not closely united — they are disintegrated sounds.

A nasal before a plosive is longer than otherwise. For instance, compare the length of **sunti** and **suni** (Inscs. 13 and 14).

A nasal nasalises the previous vowel always, *e.g.*, in **sʌŋkh** (Insc. 15) and also the following vowel, *e.g.*, in **suni** and **mɑɪiː** (Insc. 14 and 46). It nasalises the following voiced consonants, *e.g.*, in **bʌɳɖɑː** (Insc. 16), but does not nasalise a breathed consonant (See **bʌɳʈɑː**, Insc. 17).

NOTE.—A Nasal has become unvoiced in the middle of a sentence expressing the sense of imperative and wonder (*Vide* Charts 3 and 5)

C. ORIGIN

n and nɦ

§ 61. Initial **n**- is derived from OIA

(*i*) *n*- > MIA *ṇ* (except in Paiśācī and Pāli), *e.g.*, *nakṣatra*- > **nʌkhʌt** 'star', *nemi* > **niu** 'foundation'

(*ii*) *jñ*- > *ñ* in Pāli, Māgadhī and Paiśācī but *ṇ* in other Prakrits, *e.g.*, *jñāti*- > **nʌi-ɦʌr** 'a married woman's father's house'.

(*iii*) *sn*- > *ṇh* in MIA and later separated by anaptyxis, *e.g.*, *snā*- > **nʌɦɑː-b** 'to bathe'.

Medially and finally -**n** is derived from OIA

(*i*) -*jñ*- > MIA -*ṇṇ*- (Pāli, Paiś. and Māg. -*ññ*-) *e.g.* *vijñapti*- > **bintiː** 'prayer'

(*ii*) -*ṇ*- √*gaṇ*- > **gʌnʌb** 'to count,' √*śṛṇu*- > **sunʌb** 'to hear'

(*iii*) -*ṇy*- > MIA -*ṇṇ*- *e.g.*, *puṇya* > **punni** 'merit

(*iv*) -*n*- *e.g.*, *navanīta* > **nʌinuː** 'butter', *jānāti* **jɑːnʌi** 'knows' (*v*) *-nn-* *chinna-* > **chinaːri̯** 'a woman of loose character'

(*vi*) *-ny-* *e.g.*, *anya* > **aːn** 'another', *mānya* : **maːni̯** 'honoured relative'

(*vii*) *-rṇ-* MIA *-ṇṇ*, *e.g.*, *karṇa* > **kaːn** 'ear', *varṇa-* > **baːni̯** 'habit'

(*viii*) *-ṣṇ-* > MIA *-ṇh-*, *e.g.*, *kṛṣṇa-* > Eastern Awadhī **kʌnɦʌijaː** 'Kṛṣṇa'

(*ix*) *-sn-* > MIA *-ṇh-*, *e.g.*, *jyotsnā-* > East. Aw. **jonɦʌijaː** 'moonlight'

(*x*) *-hn-* > MIA *-ṇh-*, *e.g.*, *cihna* > **ciːnɦ** 'a token'.

N.B.—In certain modern dialects of Awadhī **-n-** represents ancient **-nd-**, for which see the origin of **-d-** and **-dɦ-** §§ 49-50.

n is also found in words of *deśī* origin and in foreign loan-words.

In a few words **n** represents OIA *l*, *e.g.*, **naːgɦʌb** : *laṅgh-* 'to cross', **noːn** : *lavaṇa* 'salt', **nẽgulaː** : ? *lāṅgūla-* 'the only boy amongst the girls fed on the ninth day of Āśvin in honour of the Devī'; **ʌrgʌniː** : *argalā -* 'a rope hung up for putting clothes on'.

m and mɦ

§ 65. Initial **m** comes from MIA *m-* derived from OIA

(*i*) *m-* *mātā-* : **maːiː** 'mother', *maśaka* : **maːsaː** 'mosquito', *madhu-makṣikā-* : **mʌ-maːkhiː** 'bee'

(*ii*) *mr-* *mrakṣaṇa* : **maːkhʌn** 'butter'

(*iii*) *śm-* *śmaśru* : **moːch** 'whiskers'.

Medially and finally *-m-* comes from MIA *-mm-*, *e.g.*, *sammuha-* : **sʌmʌɦeː** 'in front', *ghamma* : **gɦaːm** 'sun'.

In certain loan-words in the Western dialects, and in the Eastern dialects *-m* represents MIA *-m* + labial mute, *e.g.*, **cuːmʌb** < *cumb-* 'to kiss'.

-mh- comes from *m* + labial plosive or *-mh-* *e.g.*, *m* + *-bh-* **kumɦaːr** < *kumbha -āra* 'potter' *-mh-*, *e.g.*, *bamhaṇa-* : **baːmɦʌn** 'Brahmin'.

m occurs in *deśī* words and in loan-words also.

ɲ ɳ ŋ

§ 66. These three nasals are found in Awadhī before the mutes of their classes only and then also mostly in loan-words either from Sanskrit or foreign languages or in *deśī* words. For examples see §§ 58—60.

Old semi-vowels, Modern semi-vowels and Rolled, Flapped and Lateral consonants.

A. Early Awadhi

§ 67. *y*, *r*, *l* and *v* occur initially as well as medially. For instance :

y *yaha* 'this' (J. 113), *pāyā* 'got' (J. 135).

In the manuscripts the symbol for *y* represents *j* also.

r *rākhā* 'kept' (J. 225), *nīarē* 'near' (J. 225).

l *lēhu* 'take' (J. 273), *hilagi* 'having got entangled' (J. 273).

v *vaha* 'she' (J. 210), *kāvīnī* 'loving woman' (J.)

In the manuscripts the symbols for *v* and *b* are often confused.

Note.—For Early Awadhī *ṛ*, *ṛh* see § 13.

B. Modern Awadhi

j

§ 68. The sound **j** is pronounced like **i**, only the more sonorous character of the following sound gives it a consonantal character (See Pal. 15). The tongue is very much in the position of *i* (short), the air-passage being a little narrower (Compare Pal. 17). It occurs in a few words initially as in **jʌɦu** 'this'. Medially it occurs optionally

F. 7

between two vowels and serves as glide from the less open to the more open vowel, *e.g.*, **piaːs** or **pijaːs** 'thirst', **ḍiʌṭi** or **ḍijʌṭi** 'a lamp-stand'.

w

§ 69. The sound **w** is pronounced like **u**, only the more sonorous character of the following sound gives it a consonantal character. In pronouncing it the lower lip touches the upper lip slightly as also the lower teeth but there is no friction except possibly when it is in the initial position. The lip-rounding required for pronouncing this sound is much less than that for the corresponding English sound **w**.

It occurs initially in a few words, *e.g.*, in **waːr** 'side', **wʌɦu** 'that', medially it occurs between two vowels and serves occasionally as glide from the less open to the more open back vowel, *e.g.*, **puwaː** or **puaː** 'a kind of cake', **soːwaː** 'slept', **sʌwʌṭi** 'co-wife', **gʌ̃waːr** 'villager'.

Note 1.—**w** comes in place of **u** in certain cases of assimilation (See § 152).

Note. 2.—In Bāghēlī, **-w-** is generally pronounced as **-b-**

r

§ 70. The sound **r** is the rolled voiced alveolar consonant (See Pal. 11). In pronouncing it the tip of the tongue taps twice or thrice against the alveolar region above the teeth-ridge. It can occur initially as in **rõːwãː** 'hair on the body', **rĩːdɦʌb** 'to cook', medially as in **beraːm** 'ill', **muraːuː** 'green grocer'. or finally as in **sʌmbaːr** 'Monday', **cʌmaːr** 'cobbler'.

r has an epenthetic vowel before it when it comes initially, *e.g.*, in **raːm se** (Insc. 18) a tiny vowel appears before **r**.

Note —For the elision of intervocalic **-r-** in the Absolutive in the Eastern dialects see below Part II Chapter VI (Verbs).

ɽ

§ 71. The sound **ɽ** is the voiced flapped retroflex consonant (see Pal. 12). The back of the tip of the tongue goes up and taps on the rough back above the gums. It can occur singly, and only medially, as in **ɑ̃ːɽiː** 'bulb', **bɦẽːɽiː** 'sheep', or finally, as in **goːɽ** 'feet', **hɑ̃ːɽ** 'bones'.

The tapping is only once. As the palatogram shows, the contact is perceptibly higher than in the case of **r** but not so high as in the case of **ʈ**.

rɦ

§ 72. The sound **rɦ** is the aspirated form of **r**. It can occur only medially as in **ʌrːɦiː** 'a kind of pulse', or finally as in **riːrɦ** 'spinal cord'.

ɽɦ

§ 73. The sound **ɽɦ** is the aspirated form of **ɽ**. It can occur either medially as in **baːɽɦi̥** 'more', **siːɽɦiː** 'steps', or finally as in **buːɽɦ** 'old'. **koːɽɦ** 'leprosy'

l

§ 74. The sound **l** is the voiced alveolar lateral consonant (see Pal. 13). The tip of the tongue just touches the upper teeth and their root to block the passage and a slight hollow (less than in English **l**) is made, the air passes at the sides. It can occur initially as in **luːʈʌb** 'to rob', **lɔ̃ːdaː** 'a lump', medially as in **kaːli̥** 'tomorrow', **phulʌuriː** 'a variety of scone', or finally as in **caːl** 'trick', **ʌmoːl** 'invaluable'.

NOTE—**l** has a subsidiary phoneme before retroflex sounds.

lɦ

§ 75. The sound **lɦ** is the aspirated form of **l**. It occurs only medially as in **pʌlɦaːwʌb** 'to coax a cow to give milk'.

C. Origin

j (*y*) and w (*v*)

§ 76. These sounds are found very seldom in Awadhī. In the initial position they are found in the pronouns **jʌɦu**, **wʌɦu** which also have alternative forms. In the medial position they serve only as glides between two vowels. They do not occur finally except in some dialects where they stand for **i** and **u** respectively.

Sanskrit *y-* is represented in the initial position by **J** even in the MIA period, and in the medial position it was elided. Sanskrit initial *v-* is represented by **b-** in Awadhī and the medial one by **u** or **b**.

Initial *y-* of foreign words is represented by **i-** or zero in Awadhī (*e.g.*, *yār* Pers.—'friend', Awadhī **iaːr**, *yād-* Pers.—'memory', Aw. **aːdi̥**, **ʌkiːn** 'belief') and *v-*, *va-* generally by **u-** (*e.g.*, Pers. *vakīl* : Aw. **ukiːl**).

In a few words **-w-** medially represents OIA *-p-* (*e.g.*, *sapatnī* : **sʌwʌti̥** 'co-wife'), or with nasalisation it corresponds to OIA *-m-* (*e.g.*, **gʌ̃waːr** : *grāma-* 'villager').

r

§ 77. Initially **r** represents MIA

r- coming from OIA *r-*, *e.g.*, *rātri* : **raːti̥** 'night'.

Medially and finally **r** represents MIA

(*i*) *-r-* coming from OIA *-r-*, *e.g.*, *apara* : **ʌur** 'another', *kēdārikā* : **kejaːriː** 'a bed in a garden', *carma-kāra* : **cʌmaːr** 'cobbler'.

-r- coming from OIA *-t-*, *-d-* in the numerals, *e.g.*, *saptati* : **sʌtːʌri̥** 'seventy', *dvādaśa* : **baːraː** 'twelve', *saptadaśa* : **sʌtːʌraː** 'seventeen'.

(*ii*) *-l-* coming from OIA *-l-*, *e.g.*, *ālasya-* : **aːrʌsu̥** 'lethargy', *prapā -śālā* : **pʌusʌraː** 'a place for supplying water', *phalati* : **phʌreː** 'bears fruit', *phalaka-* : **phʌrɪaɪ** 'plank of wood', *musala-*: **muɪsʌrṳ** 'pestle', *viḍāla*—: **bilaɪriɪ** 'cat'

NOTE.—Braj and Bhōjpuri agree with Awadhī, Hindustānī retains **-l-**.

(*iii*) *ḍ-* coming from OIA *-ṭ-*, *e. g.*, *kaṭu-* : **kʌruɪ** 'bitter', *kīṭa-* : **kirʌwaɪ** 'insect', *viṭapa-* : **birʌwaɪ** 'tree', *puṭa-* : **purijaɪ** 'anything wrapped with paper or leaves'.

NOTE.—Braj and Bhōjpuri agree with Awadhī, Hindustānī represents OIA. *-ṭ-* by **-ɽ-**.

In *ardhatatsama* words, Sanskrit *-r* + consonant is represented in Awadhī by the process of epenthesis, *e.g.*, *dharmu* : **dɦʌrʌm** 'religion', *samartha* : **sʌmʌrʌth** 'powerful'

Evidence of such an epenthesis in earlier stages is found from Skt. *ādarśa-* : Aw. **aɪrʌsiɪ** 'an ornament, containing a mirror, worn on the wrist'.

Intervocal **-r-** is dropped out in certain forms of the verb (see Part II, Chap. VI)

r appears in *deśī* words in all positions, and medially and finally it sometimes corresponds with Hindustānī **-ɽ**, *e. g.*, **raɪrḭ** 'quarrel', **thʌpʌraɪ** (Hin. **thʌpɪʌɽ**) 'slap', **kuɪraɪ** (Hin. **kuɪɽaɪ**) 'rubbish'.

r appears in foreign loan-words also.

rɦ

§ 78. This sound occurs only in what appear to be *dēsī* words (see § 88).

ɽ (*r*)

§ 79. Awadhī **ɽ** which occurs only medially or finally represents MIA

-ḍḍ- *uḍḍēi* > **uɽʌi**, 'flies',

-ḍ after *ṇ-*, in cases where the nasal survives only as nasalisation, *e.g.*, *aṇḍa-* > **ãɪɽiɪ** 'the bulb of a fruit', *ḍaṇḍa* > **ɖãɪɽ** 'oar'.

ɽ occurs in many *deśī* words also, *e.g.*, **goːɽ** 'foot'.

ɽɦ (*ḍh*)

§ 80. Awadhī **ɽɦ** occurs only medially or finally and represents MIA

-ḍḍh- *vaḍḍhai* > **baːɽɦʌi** 'increases', *saḍḍha* + – > **saːɽɦeː** 'and half', *vuḍḍha* – > **buːɽɦ** 'aged'.

Where **-ɽɦ** represents *-ḍh* of the Prakrits, the words are certainly loan-words from other dialects, *e.g.*, **pʌɽɦʌi** < *paḍhai* 'reads', **gaːɽɦ** < *gāḍha* 'thick'.

l

§ 81. Initial **l-** represents MIA

l- coming from OIA, *e.g.*, *lakṣa* : **laːkh** 'a lac', *lajjā* : **laːʒ** 'shame, modesty'. In **laːʈhiː** 'stick' it represents OIA *y-* (*yaṣṭi-*).

Medial and final **-l** represents MIA

(*a*) *-ll-* coming from OIA

(*i*) *-dr-* *bhadra-* : **bɦʌlaː** 'good'.

(*ii*) *-r-* *prerayati* : **peːlʌi** (Pkt. *pellai*) 'enters by force'.

(*iii*) *-ry-* *paryaṅka-* : **pʌlkaː** 'bedstead'.

(*iv*) *-ly-* *kalya-* : **kaːlɦi̥** 'yesterday or tomorrow'.

(*v*) *-ll-* *vallī-* : **baːliː** 'the ear of the maize plant'.

(*vi*) *-lv-* *bilva* : **beːl** 'a particular tree'.

(b) Medial **-l-** in numerals corresponds to MIA, OIA *-r-* in figures 'forty' and in those based on it, *e.g.*, *catvāriṃśat* : **caːlis** 'forty'.

In **lʌʈ-** 'to lose', *l-* would represent *n-* if the word be derived from *naṣṭa-* (Chatterji, p. 545) the loss of aspiration being a difficulty.

Medial **-l-** also corresponds to MIA *ḍ*, *ḷ* derived from OIA *-ḍ-*, *e.g.*, *viḍāla-* : **bilaːriː** 'cat'.

l occurs in *dēśī* and foreign loan-words also.

lɦ

§ 82. This sound occurs only in what appear to be *dēśī* words and from OIA *hl-*, *e.g.*, *prahlādayati* > **pʌlɦaːwʌi** 'coaxes to give milk' (see § 88).

Sibilants and Aspirate

A. Early Awadhi

§ 83. Of the three sibilants, *s* is the normal one. But *ś* also is found particularly in Tulsīdās and in Lāldās. In the latter it sometimes replaces *s* which possibly shows either that *ś* and *s* both represented the sound *s* or there is ultra-Sanskritisation of *s* into *ś*. The symbol for *ṣ* occurs to represent *kh* both in Tulsīdās and Lāldās. It is hardly possible that *ṣ* existed as a sound.

ś *śrutikīrti* 'name of Shatrughna's wife' (T. 139), *śrāpa* 'curse' (T. 93), *dēśa* 'country' (Lāl.), *śō* 'that' (Lāl.).

ṣ *vasiṣṭha* 'Vasiṣṭha' (T. 139), *bhūṣana* 'ornament' (T. 138), *varaṣahī* 'rain' (T. 139), *laṣana* 'Lakṣmaṇa' (T. 192), *bisēṣi* 'particularly' (T. 219); *ṣabari* 'news' (Lāl.), *dēṣi* 'having seen' (Lāl.).

s *suā* 'parrot' (J. 113), *jaisa* 'as' (J. 113), *saguna* 'omen' (T. 295), *bisāla* 'big' (T. 294), *sō* 'that' (T. 295).

Aspirate

h *hai* 'is' (J. 160), *mohī* 'me' (J. 160), *līnhi* 'taken' (J. 160).

ḥ occurs in Tulsīdās and Lāldās in *tatsama* words only, *e.g.*, *jūthaḥ* 'the herd' (T. 295), *niḥkāmī* 'devoid of desires' (Lāl), cf. *niha kalaṃka* 'spotless' (J. 24).

B. Modern Awadhi

§ 84. The sound **s** is the breathed alveolar fricative consonant (see Pal 14). The tip of the tongue touches the upper teeth also. It differs from English **s** in having less friction. It can occur initially as in **soːrʌɦ** 'sixteen', **sẽːtḭ** 'free', medially as in **kʌsʌb** 'to tighten', **pʌsijaː** 'watchman', or finally as in **pʌcaːs** 'fifty', **ṭhoːs** 'solid'.

The sound has no tendency to become voiced in intervocalic position. Final **s** is less pronounced than a plosive.

h

§ 85. The sound **h** is what has been defined as 'Breathed Glottal Fricative'. It 'is the sound of pure breath having a free passage through the mouth.' In a word it can occur initially as in **hʌm** 'we' (see Insc. 47), **huãː** 'there'.

It should be noted that the aspirated forms of breathed plosives and affricate contain this sound as their second element (See Inscs. 7, 8, 15)

ɦ

§ 86. The sound **ɦ** is the voiced variety of **h,** and occurs intervocally as in **kʌɦãː** 'where', **liɦeũ** 'I took', or finally as in **saːɦ** 'banker', **dẽːɦ** 'body'. In the final position, however, the sound finishes with absence of voice, *e. g.*, in **saːɦ**, **ɦ** is **ɦ-h** (see Insc. 20).

It should be noted that the voiced aspirated plosives, affricate, nasals, rolled, flapped and lateral consonants contain this sound as their second element. This second element tends to be voiceless before whispered vowels, *e.g.*, **duːdɦṵ** tends to become **duːdhṵ** (see Insc. 19).

C Origin

s

§ 87. The dental sibilant is the only one in Awadhi as in Braj and Bhōjpurī and represents OIA *s*, *ś* and *ṣ* singly as well as in some combinations, through MIA s or *-ss-*.

s represents MIA. *s*, *-ss-* derived from OIA.

(*i*) *s-* *sapatnī* : **sʌwʌti̥** 'rival, co-wife', *saktu-* : **setuaː** 'barley-flour', *śvāsa* : **sā̃ːs** 'breath', *vas-* : **bʌsʌb** 'to reside'.

(*ii*) *ś-* *śr̥ṅga* : **sĩːg** 'horn', *śuṇḍā-* : **sū̃ːr̥i̥** 'trunk', *āśā* : **aːs** 'hope', *maśaka-* : **maːsaː** 'mosquito'.

(*iii*) *ṣ-* *ṣoḍaśa* : **soːraː** 'sixteen', *mahiṣī* : **bɦʌĩsi̥** 'the buffalo'.

(*iv*) *-sm-* *-vismr̥-* : **bisʌrʌb** 'forget'.

(*v*) *-sy-* *ālasya* : **aːrʌs** 'indolence'.

(*vi*) *-sr-* *srotas-* : **soːt** 'stream'.

(*vii*) *-sv-* *svāmī-* : **saːĩː** 'a saint', *svara* : **sur** 'tune'.

(*viii*) *śm* *raśmi-* : **rʌsʌriː** 'string'.

(*ix*) *śyāmāka* : **sā̃ːwaː** 'a wild rice', *śyāla* : **saːr** 'wife's brother'.

(*x*) *śr-* *śrāvaṇa'*, : **saːwʌn** 'the month of *śravaṇa*', *aśru-* : **ā̃ːsuː** 'tear'.

(*xi*) *śv-* *śvāsa* : **sā̃ːs** 'breath', *śvaśura* : **sʌsur** 'father-in-law'.

(*xii*) *rś-* *parśu-* ; **pʌsuriː** 'rib'.

(*xiii*) *rṣ* *karṣati* : **kʌsʌi** 'pulls'

(*xiv*) *ṣy-* *puṣya* : **puːs** 'the month *pauṣa*' *ruṣyati* : **ruːsʌi** 'gets angry'

NOTE.—In the group *r* and sibilant, epenthesis is witnessed very often, *darśana* : **dʌrosʌn** 'holy sight' *varṣ-* : **bʌrsʌb** 'to rain'.

š and *s* of foreign words are always represented by **s** in Awadhi.

h, ɦ

§ 88. Initial **h**- is derived from MIA *h*- which comes from OIA

(*i*) *h*- *hasta* : **hãːth** 'hand', *haridrā*- : **hʌrdiː** 'turmeric'.

(*ii*) *bh*- in the case of root *bhū*- which is already in the Prakrits found as *ho*-, Aw. **hoːi** 'be' etc.; also in **hãːɽiː** 'a vessel' < *bhāṇḍa*-, Aw. has **bɦãːɽaː** 'treasure', also.

In the pronoun **hʌm** 'we' and its derivations, we find a development of *-sm-* into **h**, through *-mh-* in the Prakrits and in **hʌi**, **aːɦi**, **ʌɦʌi** we find **h** coming from *-st-* through *-tth- th*, possibly.[1]

Medial or final -**ɦ** comes from MIA *-h* which is derived from OIA

(*i*) *-h-* *lauhakāra* : **loɦaːr** 'blacksmith', *phalāhāra* : **phʌroɦʌr** 'fruit-diet'.

(*ii*) *-kh-* *mukha* : **muɦ** 'mouth', *nakha* : **nʌɦ** 'nail', *ākheṭa* : **ʌɦeːr** 'prey', *śikhā-* : **siɦaːb** 'to feel puffed up'.

(*iii*) *-gh-* *māgha* : **maːɦ** 'the month of Māgha', *megha-* : **meɦaːb** 'to get wet', *araghaṭṭa-* : **rʌ̃ɦʌʈaː** 'spindle', *laghu-* : **lʌɦuraː** 'younger', *stāgha* : **thaːɦ** 'bottom', *saghana* : **sʌɦʌn** 'thick'.

(*iv*) *th-* *kath-* : **kʌɦʌb** 'to say'.

(*v*) *-dh-* *avidhavā-tva* : **ʌuɦaːt**, 'non-widowhood', *dadhi-* : **dʌɦiu** 'curds', *putra-vadhū* : **pʌtoːɦ** 'daughter-in-law', *madhūka-* **mʌɦuaː** 'a particular tree'.

(*vi*) *-bh-* *gabhīra* : **gʌɦir** 'deep', *nibhālayati* : **niɦaːrʌi** 'sees closely', *pratyabhijānāti* : **pʌɦicaːnʌi** 'recognises', *sobh-* : **soɦaːb** 'to appear agreeable'

[1] See § 292.

In the numerals *h* represents *ś* (**gezrAß** —' eleven') and *s* (**ekoßAtzArį** —' seventy-one'). This is attested by the Prakrits (see Bloch : *Langue Marathe* § 160). Similarly **ß** of the pronoun **eßu** ' this' goes back to OIA *ṣ*.

In the forms of the **Future** verb **-ß-** represents OIA *-ṣy-* > MIA *-ss* and later *-h-*.

OIA sibilant + nasal which is represented in MIA as *nasal* + *h* is separated by an epenthetic vowel, *e.g.*, *snā-* : *ṇha-* : **nAßaz-** or even **hAnaz-** by metathesis.

mß and **nß** occur in a few *ardhꞇtatsama* words.

Similarly **lß-** comes from OIA *-hl-* in **pAlßazwAb** < *prahlād-* ' to please, to coax '.

Aw. **rß** represents Hindustānī **ṛß** mostly in obscure words, *e.g.*, **rizrß** : Hin. **rizṛß** ' backbone '. the origin of, **Arzßiz** ' kind of pulse ' is obscure.

-ß- appears to mark hiatus in **-Aßi** besides **-Ai**, an affix of Present Tense 3rd pers. sing. < *ati* (compare Bloch : *Langue Marathe* § 161). In **diznß** < MIA *diṇṇa*, the advent of **ß** is obscure.

The treatment of *-st* of loan-words as **ßAtz** - has been noticed below (§132.)

h, -ß is found in *Dēśī* words and in loan-words from foreign languages.

Simple Vowels

A. Early Awadhi

§ 89. The vowels are found in all the positions—initial, medial and final—in a word. For instance .

a *aṃbrita-bēli* 'nectar-creeper' (J. 52), *kadama* ' kadamba ' (J. 53).

ā *āchahī* ' are' (J. 53), *pāsā* ' sides ' (J. 53).

i *ihai* ' this ' (J. 286), *dījia* ' please give ' (J. 286), *tehi* ' *him* ' (J. 286.)

ī *īsa* ' lord ' (T. 86), *tīya* woman ' (T. 106), *bajāī* ' beat (the drum) ' (T. 107) *u* *uṭhai* 'gets up' (T. 107), *suhāī* 'beautiful' (T. 107), *haru* 'remove' (T. 107).

ū *ūpara* 'above' (J. 61), *ṭūṭa* 'broke', (T. 116), *kāū* 'ever' (T. 188).

ṛ occurs only in *tatsama* words and, is mostly represented by *ri*

kṛpā 'favour' (T. 293), *vritti* 'livelihood' (Lāl), *rṛṣi* 'sage' (T. 39), *riṣi* 'sage' (Lāl.)

e The symbol for short *e* is the same in the manuscripts as well as in the printed books as for the long *ē*, only Grierson's edition of the *Padmāvat* has a different symbol. But the existence of *e* is attested by metrical compositions in all the texts—a long *ē* would disturb the metre :

ehi 'this' (T. 160) *jehi* 'whomever' (T. 115), *bhae* 'having become' (J 58).

ē *ēkahi* 'one only' (T. 170), *dēkhu* 'see' (T. 170), *sānē* 'mixed' (T. 207).

o Like *e*, the existence of *o* (as different from *ō*) is inferred from metres; it is found with the symbol in the *Padmāvat* only :

ohī 'the same, (J. 171), *sohāhī* 'appeal' (T. 171)

ō *ōhī* 'to him' (T. 3?2), *dhōla* 'drum' (T. 366).

B Modern Awadhi

iː

§ 90. The sound **iː** is the Close Front Vowel, a little more open than Cardinal No. I (see Pal. 16). The lip-spreading also is less tense than in the Cardinal Vowel.

It can occur initially as in **iːṛhiː** 'stubborn', medially as in **piːseũ** 'I ground', **biːs** 'twenty' or finally in a word as in **pʌthəriː** 'stone', **cʌiliː** 'fuel-sticks'.

i

§ 91. The sound **i** is just like English short *i* (*it*, *pit* etc.) and is pronounced with much less muscular tension than **iː**. The air passage is freer as the tongue does not rise so high. It has been defined as 'Close Front lax unrounded vowel' (see Pal. 17).

It occurs initially, *e.g.*, in **itoraːb** 'to be priggish', **ilːʌti̥** 'botheration' medially as in **pilowaː** 'pup', **mircaː** 'chillies' or finally in a word *e.g.*, in **poːi** 'a variety of vegetable'. **ɟaːi** 'may go'.

e

§ 92. The sound **e** is like the English sound *e* in *get*, *bet*, *pen*, etc. It differs from **i** in being more open and lax. It is very short in quantity as compared to **eː** and is more open also and thus does not give a palatogram.

It occurs initially as in **etːaː** 'so much', **euɟiː** 'officiating', medially as in **dekhibaː** 'shall see', **lifieũ** 'I took', or finally as in **se**, **ke.**

eː

§ 93. The sound **eː** is Half-close Front Vowel pronounced like Cardinal Vowel No. 2 (see Pal. 18). It occurs initially as in **eːkaː** 'unity', **eːraːpheːriː** 'mutual exchange', medially as in **k̨heːlʌb** 'to play', **dfieːlaː** 'half a pice' or finally as in **paːcheː** 'behind', **maːtheː** 'on the forehead'.

aː

§ 94. The sound **aː** is the Back Open vowel. The lips are wide apart and the tongue rests low with a slight rise in the back. It approximates, in quality, to Cardinal Vowel No. 5 and resembles the *a* of *father* in American pronunciation

It occurs initially as in **aːkhʌt** 'grains of rice given to menials on ceremonial occasions', **aːdiː** 'ginger', medially as in **chedaːm** 'one-fourth of a pice', **baːis** 'twenty-two', or finally in a word as in **ghoːɽaː** 'horse' **rʌɦaː** 'remained'.

ʌ

§ 95. The sound **ʌ** is the Half-open Central Vowel. In pronouncing it the tongue rises up, in almost the central position. It can occur initially as in **ʌrsiː** 'linseed', **ʌkaːl** 'famine' or medially as in **ɟʌb** 'when', **dʌs** 'ten'.

This sound is a little longer in open syllables than in closed ones and there tends somewhat towards the back and becomes slightly more open. The ʌ of **ʌkaːl** is such, for instance. In a closed syllable before **r**, it has a slight shade of **ɜ**[1] as in **ʌrsiː**.

ə

§ 96. The sound **ə** is similar in quality to **ʌ** but the tongue in this case is a little more raised and slightly more lax.

It occurs medially or finally and in unstressed syllables. It is at the end of a syllable and never begins a syllable. It is very short in quantity, *e.g.*, in **raːm kə** 'to Ram', **sorəɦĩːː** 'a game with sixteen Cowries'.

This vowel has a tendency to disappear, what remains is merely the explosion of the previous consonant, *e.g.*, **mʌɦətaːriː** is sometimes heard as **mʌhtaːriː** (mother) or **ʌpənaː** is heard as **ʌpnaː**.

oː

§ 97. The sound **oː** is the Half-close Back Vowel, the same as Cardinal Vowel No. 7. It occurs initially in a few words as in **oːs** 'dew', **oːp** 'secret' or medially as in **bʌroːʈh** 'the middle hall', **cʌʈoːr** 'greedy' or rarely finally as in **hoː** 'O'.

---

[1] The vowel which is found before *r* in such words as 'bird' **(bɜd)**

o

§ 98. The sound **o** is similar to **oː** in quality but is slightly more open and removed a little towards the centre. The back of the tongue rises a little less than in the case of **oː**

It occurs initially as in **osoriː** 'turn' **oinaː** 'yarn-hump' or medially as in **bɦorohẽː** in the morning', **dosoraːi ko** 'a second time'.

uː

§ 99. The sound **uː** is the Close Back Vowel just as the Cardinal Vowel No. 8. In pronouncing it, however, the rounding and the protrusion of lips as well as the tension is less than in the ordinary Cardinal.

It occurs initially as in **uːbʌb** 'to be bored' **uːsʌr** 'untilled land', medially as in **duːdɦ** 'milk' **bʌnduːkh** 'gun', or finally in a word as in **naːuː** 'barber', **kʌruː** 'bitter'.

u

§ 100. The sound **u** is similar in quality to **uː** but here the tongue position is a little lower and there is a slight rise towards the centre. It is also less tense than **uː** .

It occurs initially as in **ukilaːb** 'to vomit', **uboɦʌni̥** 'a rope for drawing water from the well', or medially as in **kutijaː** 'bitch', **sukhʌjeũ** 'I dried' or finally as in **aːu** 'come', **kheːu** 'paddle the oars'.

General notes on the vowels

§ 101. The length of a vowel is not fixed but generally speaking, on an average a short vowel has half the length of the corresponding long vowel in the same position (circumstances) in a sentence normally spoken. For instance **-ʌ-** in **bʌɽeː** has a duration of 0·094 sec. as compared to **-aː-** of **raːɟaː** which has 0·187 sec. (Insc. 31).

The length of the same vowel varies very much. The average length of **iː** may be 40 mm. and of **i** 14; **oː** may be 43 mm. and **o** only 14; **aː** may vary in individual words from 50 mm. to 25 mm. while **ʌ** may from 14 to 22 mm. Thus **ʌ** of 22 mm. is short and **aː** of 25 mm. is long only by a convention which has its support from the feeling of the average speaker. For comparative lengths of the vowels, see Inscs. of **sĩːcʌb** and **sĩcibaː** (32 and 12), **deːkhʌb** and **dekhibaː** (4 and 33), **caːʈʌti̥** and **cʌʈibaː** (34 and 11), **sõːcʌti̥** and **sõcibaː** (35 and 36) and **phũːkʌb** and **phũkibaː** (1 and 37)

The nasalised vowel is a little longer than the corresponding unnasalised vowel. For instance, compare **ĩ** of **sĩcibaː** with **i** of **cʌʈibaː** (Inscs. 12 and 11).

The long vowel which begins a word is generally longer than the final long, *e.g.*, compare the length of **eː** in **eːk** with that of **eː** in **bʌɽeː** (Insc. 31).

Two short vowels coming together are generally of th same length as a long vowel, *e.g.*, compare the lengths of the vowels in **deːkhʌu**, **ãːt** and **iu** (Inscs. 38, 39 and 40)

The length of the same vowel in the same position is greater in monsyllabic words than in dissyllabic words.

The length of vowels is maintained except when a vowel occurs in a syllable which is more than two syllables away from the end. In Awadhī length is material for determining metre of verse but is free and immaterial in songs. For instance in

soːwʌu ki ɟaːgʌu moriː aːdɦi bɦʌwaːniː ɟʌgʌt keriː raːniː (Insc. 48) the shorts and longs are not distinguishable.

§ 102. The dialects differ in the pronunciation of **e, eː o, oː**. In a specimen 12 miles south of Gonda town **eː** is pronounced as **jaː** and **oː** as **waː** but not so pronouncedly as in Baiswāṛā. In Sitapur **eː** is **eː** and **oː** is **oː** but when one moves southwards, only six miles south of the town **eː** is found as **jaː** and **oː** as **waː**. Unao district has everywhere this pronunciation. In Fatehpur district on the borders of Cawnpore district **eː** is pronounced as **jaː** and **oː** as **waː**. It appears that in the area where this different pronunciation for **e, eː, o** and **oː** (as **jʌ, jaː, wʌ, waː** respectively) exists, the start was from **e** and **o** but in the latter part of the sound there came about more opening of the mouth which resulted in diphthongs **eʌ, eaː, oʌ, oaː** which later gave **jʌ, jaː, wʌ, waː.** Why these vowels came to be turned into diphthongs is hard to explain. But the area in which this peculiarity of pronunciation exists is considerable.

In Western Awadhī **bolaːwʌb** and Eastern Awadhī **bʌlaːwʌb** 'to call' an alternation of **o : ʌ** is found, in this respect Chhattīsgarhī agrees with Eastern Awadhī. Similar dialectal difference is found in Western **bʌnaːwʌb** and Eastern **bʌnʌub.**

C Origin

ʌ (*a*)

§ 103 Awadhi **ʌ** represents

(*i*) OIA *a*, MIA *a*, *e.g.*, *aṅka* > **ʌniː** 'crisis', *avelā* > **ʌbeːr** 'delay', *aṅguṣṭha-* > **ʌ̃guṭhaː** 'thumb', *antara-* > **ʌ̃tʌraː** 'gap'; *ālasya-* > **aːrʌsu̥** 'sloth', *araghaṭṭa* > **rʌ̃ɦʌṭaː** 'spinning-wheel', *bhaginī* > **bʌɦini̥** 'sister', *nakṣatra* > **nʌkhʌt** 'star'.

(*ii*) OIA *ā*, MIA *ā*, *e.g.*, *ā-loḍ-* **ʌroːrʌb** 'to stir up the grain in the winnowing basket', *ā-cām-* > **ʌ̃cʌwʌb** 'to rinse the mouth', *āṣāḍha* > **ʌsaːṛɦ** 'the month *Āṣāḍha*'; *vātāvali* > **bʌjaːri̥** 'air', *vātākula-* > **bʌuraː** 'dumb'.

Note.—In such instances the old *ā* was either in an unaccented syllable, or if it was otherwise, later it was shortened in Awadhi if it was more than two syllables away from the end (see § 75).

(*iii*) In a few cases -ʌ- is due to anaptyxis, *e.g.*, **rʌkʌt** 'blood', **bɦʌgʌt** 'devotee'.

(*iv*) In the following instances -ʌ- represents MIA *-a-* but OIA *-u-* or *-ṛ-* *mukula* > *maula* >**bʌur** 'blossoms of the mango-tree', *mukuṭa* > *mauḍa* > **mʌur** crown (of the bride-groom)', *guru-* > *garu-* > **gʌruː** 'heavy', *kṛṣṇa-* > **kʌ̃ɖɦʌijaː** 'Krishna' *kṛ-* >**kʌr-** 'to do'.

(*v*) In **nʌriʌr** < *nārikela* 'cocoa-nut' ʌ represents *-e-* (possibly through *-ya-*) and in **bʌɦeːraː** < *bibhītaka* (Chatterji, p. 403) it represents *-i-*.

In foreign loan-words ʌ generally represents *a* and *ā* n the manner of (*i*), (*ii*) and (*iii*), *e.g.*, **ʌrʌgu̥** '—water (*e.g.*, rose-water)' **ʌraːm** 'rest', **ʌɲʤaːd** 'estimate'. In a few cases it represents other vowels as well, *e.g.*, **ʌsturaː** 'razor', **ʌɦisaːnu̥** 'gratefulness for some kind act', **ʌtibaːru̥** 'faith'.

ʌ does not occur finally in Awadhi in modern dialects. It is found in early Awadhi in the documents but the probability is that it was never actually pronounced even then (cf. Bloch : *Langue Marathe* § 38).

aː (*ā*)

§104. Awadhī non-final **aː** represents

(*i*) OIA *ā* > MIA *ā* (before a single consonant) and *a* (before a conjunction of consonants either the same or different), *e.g.*, *āma-* > **ãːu** mucus', *ālaya-* > **aːru̥** 'a niche in the wall to put sundry articles', *ārya-* > **aːʤaː** 'grandfather', *ārdrikā* >**aːdiː** 'ginger', *śṛgāla* > **sijaːr** 'jackal', *nibhāl-* > **niɦaːrʌb** 'to see closely', *santāp-* > **sʌtaːwʌb** 'to oppress', *sārtha-* > **saːthu̥** 'company', *brāhmaṇa* > **baːmɦʌn** 'Brahmin'.

(*ii*) OIA *a*, MIA *a* followed by a conjunction of consonants which was simplified in Awadhī and resulted in a compensatory lengthening of the previous vowel. The long vowel survives only if it is in the final or penultimate syllable of a word, otherwise it becomes **ʌ-**, *e.g.*, *aṅka* > **ãːk** 'number', *anya* > **aːn** 'another', *aṇḍa-* > **ãːɽiː** 'the bulb of a root', *vyāghra-* > **baːgɦɐ** 'tiger' but **bʌgɦʌwaː**, *napita-* > **naːuː** 'barber' but **nʌuwaː**

(*iii*) MIA *aā* or *āa* or *āā*, with or without the glides *y* and *w*, derived from OIA by the loss of intervocalic consonants, *e.g.*, *kumbhakāra* > **kumɦaːr**, *varayātrā* > **bʌraːt** 'bridegroom's party' *rajaputra* > **raːut** 'a particular caste', *dīpāvalī* > **dewaːriː** 'the Diwālī festival'; *koṣṭhāgāra* > **koʈhaːr** 'a zamindar's village-residence.

Awadhī final **-aː** is the result of contraction of vowels :

(*i*) MIA *-au* derived from earlier MIA *-aō* coming from OIA by the elision of the intervocalic consonant or from *-aṃ* or *-as* by levelling out the neuter forms, *e.g.*, *caṇakaḥ* > **cʌnaː** 'gram', *āmalakaḥ* > **ʌũraː** 'myrobalan', *gataḥ* > **gaː** 'went'; Pāli *potthakaṃ* > **poːthaː** 'a book'

(*ii*) MIA *-āo* by the elision of intervocalic *-y-* of OIA or of other consonants, *e.g.*, *anadhyāyaḥ* > **ʌɲɟɦaː** 'a holiday, interruption', *upādhyāyaḥ* > **oːɟɦaː** 'exorcist, snake-charmer', *cakravākaḥ* > **cʌkʌwaː** 'a particular bird'

(*iii*) MIA *-aha* < *-asa* < *-aśa* in numerals, *e.g.*, *dvādaśa* > **baːraː** 'twelve'.

aː is found in foreign loan-words also and generally represents *ā* or *aḥ* of the foreign languages, *e.g.*, **ʌraːm** 'rest', **isʈaːm** 'stamp', **nʌsaː** 'the effect of intoxicants'.

§ 105. Awadhī non-final **i-** represents

(*i*) MIA *i* derived from OIA *i* or *ṛ*, *e.g.*, *indra -as-?* > **ĩdʌrsaː** 'a variety of cake', *itvara-* > **itʌraːb** to be haughty', *bhaginī* > **bʌɦini̥** 'sister' *ghṛtam* > **gɦiu** 'clarified butter', *hṛdayam* > **hijaː** 'heart', *dadhi-* > **dʌɦiu** 'curds', *kapittha-* > **kʌithaː** 'wood-apple', *kādṛśa* > **kʌis** of what sort?'

(*ii*) MIA *ī* derived from OIA *ī*, *e.g.*, *bīja-* > **biaː** 'seed', *dīpa-paṭṭikā* > **ḍiʌṭi̥** 'lamp-stand', *pīḍ-* > **piraːb** 'to pain (passive)', *tīra-* > **tiraːb** 'to come near', *sīv-* > **sĩʌb** 'to sew'.

NOTE.—In all these and in similar cases, the old *ī* is either away from the last two syllables or has become short in Awadhi in roots on the model of other passive verbs (**kaːṭʌb**—'to cut'—active, —**kʌṭʌb** 'to cut'—passive). In **gʌɦir** <*gabhīra* 'deep' and **ʌɦir** <*ābhīra* 'Ahīr', however, the shortening of the vowel remains unexplained

(*iii*) In a few instances **-i-** is due to anaptyxis, *e.g.*, *grahaṇa* > **giroɦʌn** 'eclipse'.

(*iv*) In the following instances **i** represents old *e-* *eṣo-* > **ēhō* > **iu** 'this', *kedārikā* > **kijaːriː** 'a bed of plants', **biṭijaː** 'daughter' < *bēṭā-* son, *nemiḥ* > **niu**, 'foundation'.

(*v*) In **chin** < *kṣaṇa* 'moment', **pĩɟʌraː** < *pañjara-* 'cage', **kinokiː** < *kaṇikā* 'small grain', and **mircaː** < *marica-* 'pepper', Awadhi **i** represents old *a*. Are these loan-words from other dialects? Similarly in the numerals **chijaːlis** 46', **chiɦʌtːʌri̥** '76', **chijaːsiː** '86' old *a-* is represented by Awadhi **i**.

(*vi*) In *ardha-tatsama* words Awadhi **i** represents Sanskrit *-ya-*, *e.g.*, **bithaː** < *vyathā* 'pain', **udːim** < *udyama* 'exertion' and in the beginning, it comes by prothesis, *e.g.*, **istiriː** < *strī* 'wife'.

Awadhi final **-i (i̥)** represents

(*i*) MIA *-ī* derived from OIA *-ī*, *-in*, *e.g.*, *bhaginī* > **bʌɦini̥** 'sister', *śreṣṭhī* > **seːʈhi̥** 'banker', *aggī* > **aːgi̥** 'fire', * *gāvī* > **gaːi** 'cow'

(*ii*) *-ni* of old neut. pl. *-āni* > *āiṃ* > *-āī* > **-ʌi**

(*iii*) **-eː** in pl. masc. perfect participles, *e.g.*, **laːgi̥** besides **laːgeː**, **ʈhaːɽɦi̥** besides **ʈhaːɽɦeː**, and in **kaːlɦi̥** 'tomorrow or yesterday' < *kalye*.

In a few instances final **-i (i̥)** is of modern origin and has been put in as a mark of feminine gender, *e.g.*, **pãːsi̥** 'manure' < *pāṃsu*, Early Aw. *jari* 'root' < *jaṭā*, **baːi** 'gout' < *vāta*.

In foreign loan-words

(*i*) **i** generally represents *i*, *e.g.*, **iɟːʌti̥** 'honour', **inaːm** 'reward'

(*ii*) in a few words **i** represents *ī* or *e*, *e.g.*, **isaːiː** 'Christian', **diɦaːt** 'country-side'

(*iii*) **i** comes by prothesis in words such as **isʈaːm** 'stamp'.

NOTE.—**i** is found initially in very few words of indigenous origin, it is mostly in words of foreign origin.

iː (ī)

§ 106. Awadhi non-final **iː** represents

(*i*) OIA *i*, MIA *ī*, *e.g.*, *mañjīra-* > **mʌ̃ɟiːraː** 'a variety of cymbals', *vīṇā* > **biːn** 'lute'

(*ii*) MIA *i-*, OIA *i-* or *ṛ-* followed by a conjunction of consonants which results in a single consonant in Awadhi and gives a compensatory lengthening to the preceding vowel, *e.g.*, *indhanaṃ* > **ĩːdɦʌnũ** 'fuel', *siktha* > **siːth** 'grain', *piṣṭa-* > **piːṭhaː** 'powdered pulse', *vṛścika-* > **ɓiːchiː** 'scorpion'.

NOTE.—The long vowel survives only in the penultimate syllable, if it is in any anterior syllable, it again becomes short.

(*iii*) MIA ĭ + ĭ, *e.g.*, *sthiti-* > **ṭhiːɦaː** 'reliance', *tṛtīyā* > **tiːɟ** '3rd day'

(*iv*) In **biːtaː** < *vitasti-* 'span', **siːl** < *śītala* 'cold', **bɦiːtʌr** < *abhyantara* 'inside', **iː** represents *i* + *a*, but all these are most probably borrowed words. In **biːtaː** *th* was expected for *t* and in **siːl** *r* for *l* (cf. Aw. **seraːb** 'to get cold'). **bɦiːtʌr** might be from * *bhintara* (*-ya-* > *i*) and not from *abhiantara*.

Final **iː** is the result of contraction of vowels:

(*i*) ĭ + ĭ, *e.g.*, future 3rd pers. sg. termination **-iː** (**kʌriː** 'will do') < *ihi*, *aśīti* > **ʌsiː** 'eighty'; *akṣīṇi* > **ãːkhiː** 'eyes' (the *n* of the termination becoming weakened to *m*, ~ and then being lost) and other plur. dir. and obl. sg. forms of nouns ending in *-i*

(*ii*) *i* + *ā* in the case of fem. nouns in **iː**, *e.g.*, *āryā-* > *ajjiā* > **aːɟiː** 'grandmother', *bhrātṛjāyā-* > **bɦʌuɟaːiː** 'sister-in-law'

(*iii*) *i* + ō in the case of masc. nouns in **iː** derived from *-in* bases of OIA *e.g.*, *prativeśikaḥ* > *padivēsiō* > **pʌroːsiː** 'neighbour', **maːliː** 'gardener'.

NOTE.—As shown below in the case of **gɦiu** 'clarified butter' etc., *i* + ō has survived as **iu**. The double treatment of this group can be explained by the hypothesis that in groups *i* + ō which resulted in **iː**, *i* was pronounced longer than in the other case.

iː occurs in foreign loan-words and there generally represents ī, *e.g.*, **sʌɦnaːiː** 'a kind of musical instrument'.

u

§ 107 Awadhi non-final **u-** represents

(*i*) MIA *u* derived from OIA *u* or *ṛ*, *e.g.*, *udeti* > **uʌi** 'rises', *ud-ghaṭ-* > **ugɦʌrʌb** 'to become uncovered', *ujjvala* > **uɟʌr** 'white', *kumāra* > **kũaːr** 'unmarried', *śuka-*. > **suaː** 'parrot', *nakula* > **neuraː** 'mungoose', *mukha* > **muɦ** 'mouth', *śṛṇoti* > **sunʌi** 'hears', *mātṛ-svasā-* > **mʌusiː** 'mother's sister'

(*ii*) MIA *ū* derived from OIA *ū*, *e.g.*, *bhūmi* > **bɦuĩ** 'ground', *śūkara* > **suʌr** 'pig', *dyūta-* > **ɟũaː** 'gambling', *yūkā-* > **ɟũaː** 'louse', *madhūka-* > **mʌɦuaː** 'a variety of tree', *prāghūrṇa-* > **pʌɦunaː** 'guest'.

N. B.—The shortening of the quantity is due either to accent or to elongation of the final or penultimate vowel in Awadhi.

(*iii*) MIA *va-*, *vа-* derived from OIA *va, pa, ma*, *e.g.*, *svara* > **sur** 'tone', *apara* > **ʌur** 'more', *kaparda-* > **kʌuṛiː** 'cowrie', *kacchapa-* > **kʌchuaː** 'tortoise', *samarpay-* > **sʌũpʌb** 'to entrust', *āmalaka-* > **ʌũraː** 'myrobalan'; particularly in modern loan-words *devatā* > **deutaː** 'deity', *devakī-* > **deukaː** 'a name', *tvarita-* > **turte** (*ardha-tatsama*) 'at once', *dvandva-* > **dundiː** 'naughty'.

Awadhi final **-u (u̥)** represents

Late MIA *u* < early MIA-*o* generally derived from OIA *-aḥ*; but possibly many forms in MIA (particularly in neuter stems) are by analogy, *e.g.*, *grāmaḥ* > **gãːu** 'village', *tāpaḥ* > **taːu** 'heating', **sãːpu̥** 'serpent', *nāma-* > **nãːu** 'name', *dāma-* > **dãːu** 'chance', *suvarṇa-* > **soːnu̥** 'gold', *ghṛta-* > **gɦiu** 'clarified butter'.

The **-u** of the Imperative second person plural and **-u -ụ** of the direct sg. case are thus derived.

u occurs in foreign loan-words and generally represents *u*, *e.g.* **guJʌrʌb** 'to pass away', **umiri̥** 'age'.

NOTE – **u** sometimes dialectically replaces **o**, *e.g.*, *sphoṭa-* > **phurijaː** 'boil', **khaːu** : **khaːo** 'eat'.

uː (*ū*)

§ 108. Awadhi non-final **uː-** is derived from

(*i*) MIA *ū* coming from OIA *ū*, *e.g.*, *sūcikā* > **suːiː** 'needle', *karpūra* > **kʌpuːr** 'camphor'

(*ii*) MIA *u* (derived from OIA *ŭ̄* or *ṛ*) followed by a conjunction of consonants, *e.g.*, *cūrṇa-* > **cuːnaː** 'powdered lime', *truṭy-* > **ṭuːṭ-** 'to break', *pṛcch-* > **puːch-** 'to ask', *vṛddha* > **buːṛɦ** 'old'

(*iii*) **ũːkh** < *ikṣu* 'sugar-cane' and **bũːd** < *bindu* 'drop' are explained by assimilation of *i* to *u* at an earlier stage

(*iv*) **duːn** < *dviguṇa* indicates **uː** < *iu* (possibly first transformed to *uu*)

(*v*) In **chuːraː** < *kṣura-* 'razor' the lengthening of **uː** is unaccounted.

Awadhi final **-uː** is the result of contraction of groups of vowels of MIA

-uː < *-iaō e.g.*, *nāpitakaḥ* : **naːuː** 'barber'

< *-īaō e.g.*, *navanītakaḥ* : **nʌinuː** 'butter'

< *-ūō*, *e.g.*, *godhūmaḥ* : **goːɦũː** 'wheat'

< *-uā e.g.*, *vālukā* : **baːruː** 'sand'.

uː is found in foreign loan-words also.

e

§ 109. Awadhi **e** represents

(*i*) MIA *e*, *ē* (derived form OIA *e* or *ai*), *e.g.*, *kedāra* < **kejaːriː** 'a bed of plants', *nemi-* > **neijaː** 'an earthen support for jars,' *kē-* (Mag form of Pkt. *kō*) > **keɦi̥** 'to whom', *śaivāla* > **sewaːr** 'a kind of green moss-like plant growing in water'.

(*ii*) MIA *ĭ* (derived from OIA *ĭ*, *ya*), *e.g.*, *vipādikā* > **bẽwaːiː** 'a disease of the feet', *tithi-vāra* > **teuɦaːr** 'festival', *dīpāvalī* **dewʌːriː** 'the Diwālī festival', *nīpāvalī* > **newaːri̥** 'a kind of white flower' (Chatterji derives it from *navamallikā*, see Chatterji, p. 409), *vyavahāra* > **beuɦaːr** (possibly through Pkt. *vivahāra*) 'mutual etiquette between families'

(*iii*) MIA *a* (OIA *a*), *e.g.*, *kapāṭa-* > **kẽwaːɽaː** 'shutters,' *kamalā* > **keũlaː** '*Lakshmī*', *nakula-* > **neuraː** 'mongoose'

NOTE.—Both in (ii) and (iii) it will be noticed that *e* is derived from *i*, *ī* or *a* followed by a labial sound.

(*iv*) MIA *īa-* (OIA *ī-* + consonant + *a*) *e.g.*, *śītalāya-* > **seraː-** 'to get cold'. Is the root **seɦolaː-** 'to become moist' connected with this very root?

(*v*) At the end of words **i** corresponds with **e** dialectically, *e.g.*, **khaːi** : **khaːe** '(he) may eat'.

eː (ē)

§ 110. Awadhi non-final **eː-** comes from

(*i*) MIA *e*, *ē* (derived from OIA *e*, *ai* or *ṛ* or *ay*), *e.g.*, *kṣetra* > **kheːt** 'field', *ākheṭa* > **ʌɦeːr** 'shikār', *taila* > **teːl** 'oil', *gairika-* > **geːruː** 'red pigment', *vṛnta* > **bẽːṭ** 'handle', *śayyā* > **seːɟ** 'bed'

(ii) MIA- *ia- e.g. ḍi-aḍḍha* > **ḍeːṛh** 'one and a half', *niara-* (< *nikaṭa-*) > **neːreː** 'near', *viaṇa-* (< *vyajana-*) > **beːnaː** 'fan'

(iii) MIA *-aya- e.g. kadalī-* > *kayalī-* > **keːraː** 'plantain tree', *citrakara-* > *cittayara-* > *citērā* 'painter', *kārya* > * *kayara* > **keːr** 'of'

(iv) In **beːl** < *bilva* 'wood-apple' and **chẽːd** < *chidra* 'hole', **pʌreːwaː** < *pratipadā* '1st day of the Hindu month' **eː** represents OIA *i* possibly through MIA *i* > *e* and in **sẽːdh** < *sandhi* an aperture made in walls by thieves' **eː** corresponds tc *a*, possibly through *saṁdhi*. The words **ɉʌneːu** and **ɉʌneː** < *yajñopavīta* 'the sacred thread' are hard to explain

(v) **eː** occurs in the numerals **geːraː** '11', **teːraː** '13' **teːis** '23', **tẽːtis** '33' and **tẽːtaːlis** '43' where it represents MIA vowel combinations *ēā*, *aya* etc.

eː occurs in many foreign loan-words and represents *ē* or *ai* or *āi*, **ai**, *e.g.*, **teːɉ** 'speedy', **ṭeːm** 'time'.

Final- **eː** in Awadhi represents MIA *-aē, e.g.* * *cittayara-ē* > *citērē* 'painters', OIA *gata-* > MIA *gaaē* > **gʌeː-** plur. of the past participle **gaː** 'went'.

o

§ 111. Awadhi **o** represents

(i) OIA *o, e.g., jyotsnā* : **ɉõdhʌijaː** 'the moon'; Is **sohraːwʌb** 'to rub gently' connected with *śodha-kāra* ? cf. Turner Nep. Dic. p. 624

(ii) OIA *upa-*, *e.g.*, *upaśālā* > **osaːr** 'the ante-room'; Turner derives from *ȧpasāra*

(iii) OIA *au*, *e.g.*, *saubhāgya* > **sohaːg** 'woman's good-luck that her husband is alive';

(*iv*) OIA *ava*, *e.g.*, *ava-ūḍha-* > **oɽɦonaː** 'wrapper', *avasara-* > **osʌriː** 'turn', *ava-tīrṇa-* > **oinaː** 'a spindle on which yarn is put up after spinning'.

NOTE.—In all non-final positions **o** represents ŏ as is clear from the instances, given above. Finally **o** corresponds with **-u** dialectically and stands for late MIA *-u*.

In **okhʌriː** (Skt. *ulūkhala-*) 'a mortar for pounding in' the possibility of Dravidian origin has been suggested (*vide* Turner Nep. Dic. *okhli* p. 61).

oː (ō)

§ 112. Awadhi **oː** represents

(*i*) OIA *o*, MIA *o*, *ō*, *e.g.*, *yoktra* > **ɟoːt** 'yoke', *potikā* > **poːi** 'a vegetable', *oṣṭha* > **õːʈh** 'lip'

(*ii*) OIA *-au-*, MIA ō, *e.g.*, *gaura* > **goːr** 'fair-coloured', *lauha* > **loːɦ** 'iron'

(*iii*) OIA *-ava-*, MIA ō, *e.g.*, *avaśyā* > **oːs** 'dew', *putra-vadhū* > **pʌtoːɦ** 'daughter-in-law', *rasavatī* > **rʌsoːiː** 'kitchen'

(*iv*) OIA *-apa-* MIA *-ava-* > *o*, *e.g.*, √ *kṣapa-* > **khoː-** 'to lose', *liṅga-paṭṭa* > **lɪ̃goːʈ** 'a strip of cloth to cover private parts'

(*v*) OIA *-ama* > **ava̅* in *mama* > *mō* 'mine'

(*vi*) MIA *ua* (derived from OIA *ŭ̄* + consonant + *ă̄*) *e.g.*, *śūkara-* > **soːriː** 'a female pig', *sugandha* > **sõːdɦ** fragrant', *upādhyāya-* > **oːɟɦaː** 'a snake-charmer', *cāṭukara* > **cʌʈoːr** 'one fond of delicious things', *suvarṇa* > **soːn** 'gold'

(*vii*) In *prativeśin-* or *prativāsin* > **pʌroːsiː** 'neighbour', Aw. **oː** represents OIA *-ive-* or *-ivā-*

(*viii*) In words where Aw. **oː** corresponds with OIA *ŭ̄*, the possibility is that *ŭ̄* became *u* in MIA before conjunct consonants and later became *o*. This was lengthened in NIA in order to compensate for the shortening of the consonant, *e.g.*, *mūlya* > *mulla* > *molla* > **moːl** 'price', *pustaka-* > *putthaa* > *potthaa* > **poːthaː** 'a big book'. Similarly we may connect **gophaː** (*gumpha-*) 'twining', **koːkhi̥** (*kukṣi*) 'womb'.[1]

(*ix*) **cõːc** (skt. *cancuḥ*) 'beak' and **mõːch** (skt. *śmaśru*) 'hair on the face' appear to be loan-words from the substratum languages. The *a* > *o* has been sometimes explained, however, to be due to the contamination of *u* in the final syllable, if derived from OIA.

o occurs in loan-words from foreign languages, *e.g.*, *zōr* 'force', **poːt** 'rent' (Pers.), as also from substratum languages, *e.g.*, **ḍɦõːg** 'show'.

Whispered Vowels

A. Early Awadhi

§ 113. There being no special symbols for the whispered vowels, it is not possible to say definitely if Early Awadhi possessed these vowels. The final short vowel makes syllables which fact *a priori* establishes that the final short vowel was pronounced. The fact, however, that the final short could be pronounced long also, however, vitiates the *a priori* conclusion. The possibility is that the final short was pronounced as a vowel but with a very weak quantity.

B. Modern Awadhi

§ 114. Awadhi possesses three whispered vowels **i̥**, **e̥**, **u̥**. These are markedly present in the Western dialects but are absent in the Eastern ones.

A vowel is a sound in which the vocal cords are closely put together and have a certain stretch which results in

[1] The usual explanation of such words is from their *vṛddhi* forms (see Pischel § 125 and Bloch § 80).

musical vibration. In the resonance chamber the tongue does not generally come in contact with the palate, so that a more or less free passage is left for the air. The quality of the vowel is distinguished on account of the position of the tongue. In mere aspiration, the vocal cords are wide apart and the tongue-position leaves a free passage of air. In whisper the vocal cords are closely put together but a small triangular space is left at their base for the passage of air. There is no stretch of the cords and hence there is no vibration and musical note. The resonance chamber assumes the various shapes for pronouncing the full sounds but as there is no vibration of vocal cords (in the case of vowel-sounds and voiced consonants) the full sounds are not heard. Still as the resonance chamber is making the same effort and as the air does come out, though with less force, sounds are heard and distinguished in whisper.

A whispered vowel, thus, is a sound for producing which the tongue in the resonance chamber assumes the position for the regular vowel but there is no vibration of the vocal cords.[1]

The apparatus does not distinguish between a whispered vowel and the explosion of the previous consonant; the acoustic effect is, however, decisive. A complete sentence spoken in whisper gives only breath inscription on the apparatus (See Insc. 25 **tum khaxi axeu**).

§ 115. In Awadhi a whispered vowel occurs only at the end of a word and does not make a syllable.[2] Historically it was a full short vowel **-i**, **-e** or **-u**. It comes after consonants in modern Awadhi—it has a stronger whisper after a voiced consonant than after a breathed one. The whispered vowel gives place to the ordinary vowel (1)

---

[1] See drawings of the Larynx of Mr. S. Jones (Plate 20).

[2] Unlike Japanese where it occurs medially and makes a syllable, *vide* Edwardes: *Phonetique Japanese* § 25.

when it is followed by a voiced consonant of a place of articulation different from that of the consonant which precedes it, *e.g.*, **mʌri̥ gaː** > **mʌri̥ gaː**, **ũːʈu̥ ɟaːti̥** > **ũːʈu ɟaːti̥**; (2) when the elision of a medial vowel makes the consonant preceding the whispered vowel a conjunct one, *e.g.*, **maːrʌti̥** > **maːrti.**

The whispered vowel of the particles is very weak as compared to that of the participial forms The **e** of the particles has the same fate as a whispered vowel, but as its elision cannot be distinguished from the explosion of the consonant which precedes it, it is not possible to say that the whispered **e̥** exists as a separate phoneme.

i̥

§ 116. The sound **i̥** is a whispered vowel in which the resonance chamber is in the position of pronouncing **i** but as the vocal cords are not in vibration the full vowel is not heard (See Inscs. 26 and 27).

It occurs at the end of a word after a single consonant and does not constitute a syllable, *e.g.*, in **ɟaːti̥** 'going', **giːli̥** 'wet', **sãːɟɦi̥** 'evening', **khaːni̥** 'mine'.

u̥

§ 117. The sound **u̥** is a whispered vowel in which the resonance chamber is in the position of pronouncing **u** but as the vocal cords are not in vibration the full vowel is not heard (see Inscs. 28 and 29).

It occurs at the end of a word after a single consonant and does not constitute a syllable, *e.g.*, in **sãːpu̥** 'snake', **haːthu̥** 'hand', **bɦoːru̥** 'morning', **sãːɽu̥** 'bull'.

e̥

§ 118. The sound **e̥** is a whispered vowel in which the resonance chamber is in the position of **-e** but owing to the absence of the vibration of vocal cords, the full vowel is not heard. It occurs at the end of a word and does not constitute a syllable, *e.g.*, **kaɪɦesɐ̥** 'from what?' (see Insc. 30 *sq*).

C. Origin

§ 119. The whispered vowels go back to MIA corresponding short vowels.

Nasalised Vowels

A. Early Awadhi

§ 120. All the vowels shown above have their nasalised forms also. For instance:

ã, ā̃ *bhavãra* 'bee' (J. 35), *kā̃kara* 'gravel' (T. 181)

ĩ *saĩtālisa* 'forty-seven' (J. 35)

ī̃ *parichāhī̃* 'shadow' (J. 37)

ũ *ũjiārā* 'light' (J. 37)

ū̃ *avarāū̃* 'garden' (J. 41)

ẽ *cavẽilī* 'jasmine' (J. 53)

ḗ̃ *piyārḗ̃* 'beloved' (T. 176)

õ *khõcā* 'quiver' (J. 112).

B. Modern Awadhi

§ 121. The dialects possess the nasalised forms of all the vowels (except the neutral and the whispered) described in the foregoing sections and they occur in all such positions as the ordinary vowel can take up. When a nasalised vowel is pronounced, the uvula is slack and thus while the air in its major quantity passes through the mouth a small quantity escapes through the nose also.

The following instances illustrate these vowels :—

(1) **ʌ̃** **ʌ̃dɦʌraɪ** 'blind', **phʌ̃saɪwʌb** 'to ensnare'

(2) **ãɪ** **ãɪkhi̥** 'eye', **gãɪʈhi̥** 'knot', **kʌɦãɪ** 'where'

(3) **ĩ** **ĩdʌrsaɪ** 'a sweet cake of rice', **ɟɦĩgowaɪ** 'shrimp'

(4) **ĩː** **ĩːdɦʌn** 'fuel', **hĩːg** 'Assafætida', **gʌĩː** '(females) went'

(5) **ũ** **ũɽeːlʌb** 'to pour', **ɟũaː** 'gambling', **dɦʌũ** 'whether'

(6) **ũː** **ũːʈ** 'camel', **mũːg** 'a kind of pulse', **goːɦũː** 'wheat'

(7) **ẽ** **ẽʈuaː** 'a seat made of hemp or grass', **gɦẽʈuaː** 'neck'

(8) **ẽː** **ẽːɽiː** 'ankle', **gẽːd** 'ball', **bɦoreɦẽː** 'in the morning'

(9) **õ** **gõʈhibaː** 'shall plait'

(10) **õː** **õːʈh** 'lip', **sõːʈhi̥** 'dry ginger'.

The palatogram of **ĩː** (19) is slightly different from that of the corresponding un-nasalised vowel. In other cases the nasalisation does not show any difference in palatograms.

§ 122. The nasalised vowels are separate phonemes in as much as the absence of nasalisation may entirely change the meaning of a word, *e.g.*, **pãːtiː** 'rows', but **paːtiː** 'leaf', **cãːʈaː** 'slap', but **caːʈaː** 'licked', **laːɽ** 'fondling', but **lãːɽ** 'penis', '**saːiː** an advance to settle an agreement', **sãːiː** 'a tribe of saints', **kʌɦaː** 'said', but **kʌɦãː** 'where'.

A nasalised vowel nasalises the following voiced consonant (but not the breathed one (See Insc. 21) so much so that it would be more accurate to say that a *reduced* nasal comes between the two, *e.g.*, **ĩːdɦʌn**, **ĩːɲgur** and **ĩdʌrsaː** (Inscs. 22, 23 and 24) should be written as **ĩːndɦʌn, ĩːŋgur** and **ĩndʌrsaː**. See also Inscs. 42 and 43 (**bãːɦ** and **hĩːgo**).

When a word ends in a long vowel and there is a nasalised vowel or nasal somewhere in the word, the breath passes through the nose also at the end, see **ĩdʌrsaː** (Inscs. 24). Carefulness in speaking may keep off the influence of nasalisation (cf. **ɟũaː** and **ɟuãː** Inscs. 44 and 45).

§ 123. The pronunciation of intervocalic nasalised **-d-** and **-b-**, aspirated or unaspirated, differs with dialects. In the

Western dialects it is **-d̃**, **-b̃-**, **-d̃ɦ**, **b̃ɦ** although as shown here the nasal consonant appears before the mute. In the Eastern dialects the mute has entirely disappeared so that Western **-d̃-** and **-b̃-** appear as **-n-** and **-m-**, *e.g.*, Lmp. **bʌ̃dɦaː** Sl. **bʌnɦaː**; Lmp. **buːd** Sl. **buːn**; Lmp. **gẽːd** Sl. **genʌwaː**; Lmp. **cʌndʌn** Sl. **cʌnːʌn**; Lmp. **sʌ̃deːs** Sl. **sʌneːs**; U. **sẽːbiː** A. **seːmiː** or **cheːmiː**; Lmp. **kʌ̃bʌriː** Fy. **kʌmʌriː**; Lmp. **kʌdɦʌiː** Fy. **kʌnɦʌijaː**; Lmp. **bɑ̃ːbɦʌn** Fy. **baːmɦʌn**; Lmp. **thʌ̃bɦʌraː** Fy. **thʌmɦʌraː**; Lmp. **pʌĩdɦʌb** Fy. **pʌinɦʌb**.

C. Origin

§ 124. Nasalization in Indo-Aryan has been classed as 'dependent' and 'spontaneous'. The former comes up on account of the influence of a neighbouring nasal or *anusvāra* in OIA or MIA. This variety of nasalization occurs quite frequently in Modern Indo-Aryan including Awadhi; particularly in words where a nasal follows a vowel it has generally left its impress on the preceding vowel, *e.g.*, **dɑ̃ːt** < *danta*. But sometimes a nasal preceding a vowel appears to have nasalized its successor as is clear from the manuscripts where we find *mɑ̃ĩ* for modern **maːiː** 'mother'.

It is also clear that a nasal coming before a voiced consonant leaves nasality longer than one coming before a breathed consonant, *e.g.*, *santāpayati* > **sʌtaːwʌi** 'oppresses', *kaṅkata-* > **kʌkʌwaː** 'comb', *kaṅkaṇa-* > **kʌkʌnaː** 'bracelet' while *andha-* > **ɑ̃ːdɦʌr** 'blind', *kampa-* > **kɑ̃ːp-** 'to tremble; cf. Aw. **pʌseːriː**, Hin. **pʌnseːriː** 'weight of five seers'.

This shows that just as to-day (see 122), nasalization in earlier stages also was less marked before a breathed consonant than before a voiced consonant.

The dependent nasalization is noticed in a few foreign words also, *e.g.*, Pers. *bandar* > Aw. **bɑ̃ːdʌr** 'monkey'.

§ 125. The spontaneous nasalization is very unstable historically and it is not possible to reduce it to general rules.[1] The same word may be found with nasalization at one place and without it at another, *e.g.*, **thuːku** and **thũːku**, **gɦaːs** and **gɦãːs**. But it may be noted that nasalization has been generally noticed where *r*, sibilant or *h* was present somewhere in the word, *e.g.*, *sarpa* > **sãːp**, *akṣi* > **ãːkhi̥** 'eye'.

---

[1] For studies on the subject, see

Grierson: Spontaneous Nasalisation in the Indo-Aryan Languages—J. R. A. S. 1922, p. 381.

Siddheshwar Varma: Nasalisation in Hindi Literary Works—Journal of the Deptt. of Letters, Cal. Univ., Vol. XVIII.

CHAPTER II

Vowel-Combinations

A. Early Awad...

§ 126. All the vowel-combinations given below in the case of Modern Awadhi are generally found in Early Awadhi also. For instance :

īā, e.g., *dīā* 'lamp' (J. 24).
iu, e.g., *nīū* 'lemon' (J. 52).
iē, e.g., *diē* 'gave' (T. 160).
ia, e.g., *piahī* 'drink' (J. 20).
iā, e.g., *duniāī* 'in the world' (J. 20). *tiāgī* 'selfless' (J. 23).
iō, e.g., *biōgī* 'lorn' (J. 45).
iu, e.g., *cāriu* 'all the four' (J. 31).
ēi, e.g., *ṭēi* 'having sharpened' (T. 166).
ēi, e.g., *dēi* 'gives' (J. 22).
ēo, e.g., *mahādēo* 'Śiva' (J. 425).
ēu, e.g., *sēu* 'apple' (J. 52).
ei, e.g., *jei* 'whoever' (J. 23).
eo, e.g., *deotanhi* 'gods' (J. 55).
eu, e.g., *naeu* 'bent' (J. 19).
eū, e.g., *bhaeū* 'became' (J. 23).
aī, e.g., *daī* 'God' (J. 21).
ai, e.g., *caḍhai* 'attacks' (J. 19), *saiuda* 'Syed' (J. 24)
ae, e.g., *mērae* 'unites' (J. 26).
aē, e.g., *gaē* 'went' (210).
au, e.g., *kā̃dau* 'mud' (J. 19.).
aū, e.g., *dūaū* 'both' (J. 273).
āi, e.g., *nāi* 'like' (J. 22).

ai, *e.g.*, *jāi* 'having gone' (J. 19).
āē, *e.g.*, *lakhāē* 'showed' (J. 26).
āe, *e.g.*, *jāesa* 'Jāyas' (J. 33).
āo, *e.g.*, *ghāo* 'wound' (J. 220).
āu, *e.g.*, *niāu* 'justice' (J. 20), *pāu* 'gets' (J. 25).
āū, *e.g.*, *ṭhāū̃* 'place' (J. 45), *jarāū* 'wrought' (J. 57).
oi, *e.g.*, *hoi* 'becoming' (J. 19).
ou, *e.g.*, *dou* 'both' (T. 167).
ōī, *e.g.*, *kōī* 'anyone' (J. 20).
ōi, *e.g.*, *hōi* 'be' (J. 24).
ōa, *e.g.*, *rōahī* 'weep' (J. 254)
ōā, *e.g.*, *rōā* 'wept' (J. 225).
ōu, *e.g.*, *sōu* 'even he' (J. 20).
ōū, *e.g.*, *kōū* 'anyone' (J. 23).
ui, *e.g.*, *dui* 'two' (J. 25).
uē, *e.g.*, *uē* 'rose' (J. 50).
ua, *e.g.*, *chuai* 'touching' (J. 20), *duau* 'both' (J. 25), *cua* 'drips' (J. 41).
uā, *e.g.*, *aguā* 'leader' (J. 26).
uu, *e.g.*, *nauu* 'all the nine' (J. 56).

NOTE.—*ai* and *au* have definite diphthong symbols, but are mostly written as simple vowels.

Nasalised vowels also are frequently found in combination.

B. MODERN AWADHI

§ 127. (*a*) The language has all varieties of combinations of two vowels. The following are the usual ones :

1. **iiː**, *e.g.*, **piiː** 'drunk'.
2. **ieː**, *e.g.*, **ɟieː** 'became alive'.
3. **iaː**, *e.g.*, **ɟiaː** 'elder sister'.
4. **iu**, *e.g.*, **gɦiu** 'clarified butter'.
5. **eːiː**, *e.g.*, **deːiː** 'will give'.
6. **eːi**, *e.g.*, **deːi** 'may give'.
7. **eːeː**, *e.g.*, **kheːeː (cʌlʌu)** '(go on) steering'.
8. **eːu**, *e.g.*, **deːu** 'give'.

9. **eu,** *e.g*, **deukaː** 'a proper name'.
10. **ʌiː,** *e.g.*, **nʌiː** 'new'.
11. **ʌi,** *e.g*, **bɦʌi** 'became'.
12. **ʌeː,** *e.g.*, **gʌeː** 'they went'.
13. **ʌu,** *e.g.*, **tʌu** 'then'.
14. **ʌuː,** *e.g.*, **gʌuː** 'cow'.
15. **aːiː,** *e.g.*, **aːiː** 'came'.
16. **aːi,** *e.g.*, **ɟaːi** 'may go'.
17. **aːeː,** *e.g.*, **khaːeː** 'eaten'.
18. **aːoː,** *e.g.*, **aːoː** 'come'.
19. **aːu,** *e.g.*, **ɟaːu** 'go'.
20. **aːuː,** *e.g.*, **naːuː** 'barber'.
21. **oi,** *e.g.*, **hoi** 'became'.
22. **ou,** *e.g.*, **dɦounaː** 'the wash'.
23. **oːiː,** *e.g.*, **hoːiː** 'will be'.
24. **oːi,** *e.g.*, **hoːi** 'may be'.
25. **oːeː,** *e.g.*, **dɦoːeː** 'washed'.
26. **oːʌ,** *e.g.*, **dɦoːʌn̥** 'the wash'.
27. **oːaː,** *e.g.*, **ɖɦoːaː** 'presents'.
28. **oːoː,** *e.g.*, **dɦoːoː** 'wash'.
29. **oːu,** *e.g.*, **hoːu** 'be'.
30. **uiː,** *e.g.*, **gɦuiː** 'the flower of reeds'.
31. **ui,** *e.g.*, **dui** 'two'.
32. **ueː,** *e.g.*, **ueː** 'rose'.
33. **uʌ,** *e.g.*, **kũʌn** 'the wells' (obl.).
34. **uaː,** *e.g.*, **buaː** 'mother'.
35. **uːiː,** *e.g.*, **ruːiː** 'cotton'.

NOTE.—Of these, the combinations of two short vowels, particularly **ʌi**, **ʌu** have a tendency to become diphthongs.

(*b*) The following are the most common groups of thre vowels:

1. **ieu,** *e.g.*, **pieu** '(you) drank'
2. **iʌu,** *e.g.*, **ɟiʌu** 'live'.
3. **eːeu,** *e.g.*, **kheːeu** '(you) paddled the oars'.

4. **eiaː,** *e.g.*, **neiaː** 'the earthen support of vessels'.
5. **ʌiaː,** *e.g.*, **bɦʌiaː** 'brother'.
6. **ʌuaː,** *e.g.*, **khauaː** 'eater (glutton)'.
7. **aːiu,** *e.g.*, **aːiu** 'you (ladies) came'.
8. **aːeu,** *e.g.*, **kɦaːeu** 'you ate'.
9. **oiaː,** *e.g.*, **loiaː** 'blanket'.
10. **oːeu,** *e.g.*, **dɦoːeu** 'you washed'.
11. **uiaː,** *e.g.*, **gɦũiaː** 'the root of Arum'.

NOTE.—Several dialects show a variation in the combination of vowels. For instance:

Lakhimpuri **eːi, eːu**, **ʌi, ʌu**, **aːi**, **aːu**, **oi, oːi** and **oːu** are represented in the Eastern dialects by **eːe**, **eːo, ʌe, ʌo, aːe, aːo, oe, oːe** and **oːo** respectively.

ʌi is found as **ʌj** in some Central and Eastern dialects. A specimen from Bahraich town records **ʌi** while only twelve miles north of it another specimen records **ʌj.**

ORIGIN

§ 128. The OIA diphthongs had become simple vowels in MIA (*ai* > *o*, *au* > *e*,) which permitted vowels coming side by side without coalescence. The same state continues in Mod IA and particularly in Awadhi. Evidence of diphthongisation is infrequent and in this respect Eastern Hindi stands generally in contrast with Western Hindi where diphthongisation of simple vowels is usually found Awadhi **ʌi** has two simple vowels **ʌ** and **i**, in Braj generally the two have the acoustic effect of a diphthong while in Hindustani of Delhi area this **ʌi** is represented by **æ.** This is found in Rājasthani as **ɛ**

The origin of simple vowels (single) has been discussed in detail above. Vowel-combinations have no separate history.

CHAPTER III

The Syllable

§ 129. A syllable in Awadhī consists of

1. a vowel, *e.g.*, **iː** 'these', **uː** 'that', **i/u** 'this', **bɦʌ-i-aː** 'brother' etc.,

2. a vowel plus a consonant, *e.g.*, **eːk** 'one', **in** 'these' **oːʈ** 'check',

3. a vowel plus the closure of a long consonant (commonly known as a double consonant), *e.g.*, **ot/ːaː** 'that much', **Al/ːaː** 'God (among Mohammedans)';

4. a vowel plus the first of a conjunct consonant, *e.g.*, **ʌr/siː** 'linseed', **ul/ʈaː** 'opposite',

5. a vowel plus a consonant plus a whispered vowel or **ə**, *e.g.*, **ɟaː/iti̥** '(we) going'; **ɟi/ʌti̥** 'living', **ʌpə/naː** 'herself',

6. a consonant plus a vowel, *e.g.*, **raː/ɟaː** 'king', **ki/taːb** 'book',

7. a consonant plus a vowel plus a consonant, *e.g.*, **din** 'day', **bʌs** 'control', **hʌr** 'plough',

8. a consonant plus a vowel plus the closure of a long consonant (commonly known as a double consonant), *e.g.*, **bʌp/ːaː** 'father', **kut/ːaː** 'dog', **bɦuʈ/ːaː** 'an ear of maize',

9. a consonant plus a vowel plus the first of a conjunct, *e.g.*, **khʌŋ/ʈaː** 'sour', **kun/daː** 'log', **bɦiŋ/ɖiː** 'lady's finger', **bʌr/chiː** 'spear',

10. a consonant plus a vowel plus a consonant and a whispered vowel, *e.g.*, **raːmu̥** 'Rāma', **ɟaːti̥** 'going'.

An intervocalic consonant goes with the following vowel to make a syllable and two successive vowels make two different syllables.

§ 130. Most of the syllables in Awadhi are of the variety of a consonant plus a vowel. Out of the eighty-six syllables which make the first three sentences of **gulgulaː waːliː kʌthaː** (Texts No 1), forty-four are of this variety, twenty-two of a single vowel, fifteen of a consonant plus a vowel plus a consonant, two of a vowel plus a consonant, one of a consonant plus a vowel plus a consonant and a whispered vowel and two of a vowel plus a consonant plus a whispered vowel.

§ 131. The syllabic division in Awadhi, as we see from the analysis of syllables, mostly comes after the vowel, the most sonorous element. When there is a long consonant or conjunct consonant, however, the division comes after the closure of the long consonant and after the first consonant respectively.

The general rule in Awadhi is that a long vowel should be followed by a short consonant. A short vowel may be followed by a long, or short or conjunct consonant. A consonant short or long may have a vowel of any quantity after it. In certain verbal formations where **ʌ** has been elided between **r** or **l** and a consonant, we have a long vowel followed by a conjunct consonant, *e.g.*, **baːrʌti̥** > **baːrti** 'burns', **caːlʌti̥** > **caːlti** 'sifts'. We have it in loan-words also, *e.g.*, **baːlṭiː** 'bucket', the dialect-word being **ḍoːlu**.

CHAPTER IV

The Word

§ 132. A word in Awadhi may begin either with a consonant or a vowel. Any vowel may begin a word. As regards consonants, most of them can begin a word—only a few, mentioned in their individual treatment, which occur only medially or finally do not do so. Lakhimpuri avoids the semi-vowels (**y** and **w**) initially.

(*a*) Not more than one consonant (short) may come at the beginning of a word and not more than two vowels together. In the middle of a word we may find one vowel or two or three vowels together. When there are three, the last vowel has a tendency to be separated from the preceding two by a semi-vowel, *e.g.*, **neiaː** 'a support for jars' becomes **neijaː**, **pʌuaː** 'a quarter of a seer' becomes **pʌuwaː**. In the medial position generally there is a short consonant. Sometimes we have it long—mostly in loan-words, *e.g.*, **kutːaː** 'dog', the proper dialect-word being **kuːkur.** Not more than two consonants can come together in the middle of a word and these should be :

1. Nasal and a consonant, *e.g.*, **sʌŋgɦ** 'with', **khoɲcaː** 'a dish of sweets', **piɳɖiː** 'a lump', **bundaː** 'earrings', **bʌmbaː** 'pipe'.

2. **r** plus a consonant, *e.g.*, **bɦurkaː** 'an earthen cup', **bɦurɟiː** 'baker', **bʌrti** 'burning', **bʌrphiː** 'a variety of tofee,' **bʌrsiː** 'anniversary', **bʌrwʌʈ** 'spleen', **ʌrːɦiː** 'a kind of pulse'.

r cannot be combined with a retroflex consonant or with **j** or **l**.

3. **l** plus consonant, *e.g.*, **pʌlkaː** 'bedstead', **kʌlchul** 'spoon, ladle', **baːlṭiː** 'bucket', **bʌldiː** 'exchange', **gʌlphʌr** 'interior of cheeks', **kʌlsiaː** 'a jar', **kʌlːɦi** 'tomorrow'.

The combination of **l** with **r**, **j**, **w** is not found. Group (2) is commoner than group (3).

4. **s** plus plosive. This group is found only in loan-words or in modern compounds, *e.g.*, **bʌstiː** 'habitation', **rʌstaː** 'path', **bʌ̃sphoːr** 'one who makes baskets, mats, etc., from bamboos'.

In the case of loan-words, the group **-st-** is very generally changed into **-ɦʌtː** by all those who are in villages and have little contact with town-life, **bʌstiː** > **bʌɦʌtːiː**, **rʌstaː** > **rʌɦʌtːaː**.

5. a plosive plus a plosive. Both must be either voiced or unvoiced. This combination is very rare and occurs only in compounds, *e.g.*, **khʌṭkirəwaː** 'bug'. In such a case both the plosives are fully exploded.

NOTE.—In one word only, *viz.*, **bʌrmɦaː** 'creator', there appears to be a combination of three consonants together in the medial position. But **-mɦ-** is merely an aspirated form of **m** like **-rɦ-**, **-lɦ-** and should be considered a single consonant for all purposes.

(*b*) A word may end either in a vowel or a consonant. Of the vowels generally long (**iː**, **eː**, **uː**, **aː**), or whispered vowels (**i̥**, **u̥**, **e̥** or **ə**) are found finally. If a short vowel (**i**, **u**) is found it is generally preceded by another vowel.

Only a short single consonant (more generally breathed than voiced) is found in the final position. A conjunct consonant or a long consonant is generally followed by some vowel-sound at the end.

§ 133. A word in Awadhi may contain from one to four syllables but the dis-syllabic word is the most common. Out of the 160 words in the first paragraph of

gulgula:wa:li: kʌtha: (Texts No. 1) 105 are dis-syllabic, 26 tri-syllabic, 25 mono-syllabic and only 4 quadru-syllabic.

The four-syllabic word is unusual for the language, it occurs in some noun-formations and verbal forms or in loan-words.

In a word in Awadhi a long syllable may occur only as the final or penultimate one. Any vowel which is long in a base or root is shortened if it is more than two syllables from the end of a word when declined or conjugated. This occurs only when one of the two syllables is long, or both being short, the word ends in a consonant, *e.g.*, **de:kh + iɦʌũ** > **dekhiɦʌũ, de:kh + ʌten** > **dekhəten** but **de:kh + eu** > **de:kheu.**

NOTE.—When once the shortening has taken place according to this rule it remains in spite of the conditions being disturbed on account of a later elision of a vowel, *e.g.*, **ma:n + otiu** > **mʌnotiu** > **mʌntiu.** Here in spite of the elision of **-o** the first vowel continues to be short.

§ 134. In a four-syallabled word, the medial unstressed syllable with **-ə** tends to lose its vowel, *e.g.*, **mʌɦətija:** 'headman' > **mʌhtija:, ʌdəbʌda:i ko** 'hastily and suddenly' > **ʌdbʌda:i ko, choʈəkʌu:** 'youngest' > **choʈkʌu:, tʌrowa:ri̥** > **tʌrwa:ri̥** 'sword'.

§ 135. A syllable with a long vowel, in the final position, shortens the length before short forms of the post-positions (*vide* Part II Chapter II), *e.g.*, **nʌdi:** 'river' but **nʌdi se̥** 'from the river', **ka:ɦe:** 'why' but **ka:ɦe me** 'in what', **gɦo:ʈa:** 'horse' but **gɦo:ʈʌ se̥** 'from the horse' **go:ɦũ:** 'wheat' but **go:ɦũ se̥** 'with wheat'.

§ 136. The short syllables of the enclitics in the final position, generally in swift speech, disappear, *e.g.*, **ʌu** 'and' > **ʌ, tʌu** 'then' > **tʌ.**[1] This occurs chiefly when the next

[1] An instance of this latter *ta* is available in Tulsīdās, p. 105.

word begins with the same vowel with which the particle ends, *e.g.*, **ʌu** + **unkaː** > **ʌunkaː** 'and to them', **tʌu ui** >**tʌui** 'and they'.

NOTE.—The form and meaning of individual words differ with different districts, *e.g.*, R. **mʌnseːruː**, Sl. **mʌnseːdɦuː**, U. **mʌnsʌwaː** 'husband', Lmp **meɦʌruaː**, Sl. **mẽdɦaːruː**, S. **meɦoraːruː** 'woman', Lmp. **bɦorəɦẽː**, U. **bɦonəɦeː**, B. **bɦinʌɦeː** 'in the morning'; **khisiaːb** in the Western dialects means 'to be ashamed' while in the Eastern its significance is 'to be angry', **dikːə** in Western dialects means 'angry' while in Eastern 'ill'

CHAPTER V

The Accent

§ 137. Awadhi possesses a very weak stress as compared to English or other highly accented languages. That it does possess an accent—and stress accent—becomes quite manifest when Awadhi words are spoken by other Indo-Aryan speakers, say a Gujarati. There the wrong accent can at once be detected. When an Englishman pronounces **khaː/eũ** 'I ate', he puts the stress on the second syllable and has to be corrected. Even when he puts it on the first, he puts it so strong that the word does not sound as Awadhi. A Gujarati person would put the stress on the first syllable in a poly-syllabic word, and it at once becomes non-Awadhi.

§ 138. Mono-syllabic words possess stress only when they come in sentences. In dissyllabic, tri-syllabic or tetra-syllabic words, the stress is put on one of the last two syllables, whichever is long either by nature or posititition. If both are long or short, the accent falls on the penultimate syllable. The following examples illustrate it.

(*a*) Words of Two Syllables

pi-ˈsaːn 'flour', **pʌˈciːs** 'twenty-five', **ˈbaːis** 'twenty-two', **ˈkhaːin̥i** 'they ate', **bɦʌˈwaː** 'became', **ˈsʌnduːkh** 'box', **kʌˈɦis̥i** 'he said', **ˈnʌdiː** 'river', **ˈbɦãːʈaː** 'brinjal', **ˈkutːaː** 'dog', **kuˈdaːr̥i** 'pick-axe', **ˈsaːɟɦaː** 'share', **ˈduleɦin** 'bride', **ˈgãːu** 'village', **ˈbɦaːu** 'rate', **ˈbɦʌrtaː** 'smashed vegetable', **ˈsaːdɦuː** 'saint', **ˈnaːraː** 'pipe, tunnel', **gɦuˈnaː** 'eaten by worms', **bʌˈɦin̥i** 'sister', **ˈbɦaːiː** 'brother'.

(*b*) Words of Three Syllables

lʌriˈkaː 'boy', **ɟɦãːˈpʌi** 'may cover', **ʌˈɽɦaːiː** 'two and a half', **kʌruˈaːtḭ** 'tastes bitter', **kʌˈraːinḭ** 'they caused to do', **soˈwaːisḭ** 'put to sleep', **bɦʌˈwaːniː** 'goddess', **deːˈkheũ** 'I saw', **pʌgʌˈɦaː** 'rope', **sʌˈgaːiː** 'betrothal', **cʌˈmaːrinḭ** 'a Chamar's wife', **bhoreˈhẽː** 'in the morning', **tʌrˈwaːriː** 'swords', **kʌsiˈbaː** 'shall tighten', **bhʌ̃ɽiˈjaː** 'earthen pot', **kʌˈbuːliː** 'admitted', **ʌrˈdaːwʌnḭ** 'the string of the cot', **uˈʈhaːi** 'having taken up'.

(*c*) Words of Four Syllables

kʌriˈɦãːu 'loin', **sirʌɦʌˈneː** 'towards the head of the bed', **kʌceɦeˈriː** 'court', **ɖeɦʌriˈjaː** 'a big earthen granary'.

Note.—Words which have two short vowels together treat them as diphthongs—see Note under § 127 (*a*), *e g.*, **ˈdeutaː** 'god', **lʌgˈwʌibaː** 'shall cause to stick', **bʌɦuˈrʌĩ** 'may come back'.

CHAPTER VI

Assimilation

§ 139. The word has no phonetic definition; it is only a morphological identity. If an illiterate person were asked to divide his sentence into words, he would probably make mistakes astounding to the literate person particularly to the grammarian. However, some idea of a word appears to be present in the sub-conscious mind of the speaker, or else a child would not be able to make up forms from analogy.

The main existence ot a word, thus, is with reference to its use in speech, *i.e.*, in sentences. Here we find that one word considerably affects the form of another. The enclitic is tacked on to the preceding word and loses its strength in certain cases, modifying to some extent its predecessor (*vide* § 135).

Besides, a considerable number of cases of the assimilation of the final sound of a word with the initial of the following have been found. This is particularly noticeable in swift speech. Assimilation in Awadhi is always regressive. It appears that when a speaker reaches the end of a word, his attention comes to rest on the next one, the initial sound of which modifies the final sound of the first word.

Note.—For the purposes of Assimilation, dentals, alvolars, palatals and retroflex palatals fall in one class.

§ 140. A whispered vowel or ə which occurs at the end of a word and stands between two consonants having the same place of articulation. is elided (see Insc. No. 41 **-pə + paː > pːaː)** *e.g.*—

bɦaːgi̥ gʌwaː > bɦaːg gʌwaː 'ran away', **kaːɦeke̥ khaːtir > kaːɦekkhaːtir** 'for what', **khʌʈijʌko kirəwaː > khʌʈijʌkkirəwaː** 'the bug of the cot', **saːgu̥ khaːisi̥ > saːk khaːisi̥** 'ate the vegetable-leaves';

bɦaːɟi̥ cʌlaː > bɦaːccʌlaː 'started running away', **cʌli̥ diɦaː > cʌldiɦaː** 'started', **tiːni̥ dãːi > tiːn dãːi** 'thrice', **kaːɦese̥ saːnini̥ > kaːɦessaːnini̥** 'with what did they mix?' **bɦaːtu daːri̥ > bɦaːd daːri̥** 'rice and pulse'; **pʌɦiri̥ rʌɦaː > pʌɦirrʌɦaː** 'putting on', **tiːni̥ ɟʌneː > tiːnɟʌneː** 'three men', **kʌɦini̥ cʌlʌu > kʌɦin cʌlʌu** '(they) said : let us go', **kʌɦʌti̥ cʌlaː gaː > kʌɦʌccalaː gaː** 'went on saying',

pʌɦiri̥ liɦisi̥ > pʌɦir liɦisi̥ 'he put on.'

kʌɦini̥ cʌlʌu > kʌɦiɲcʌlʌu '(they) said : let (us) go'.

bʌtaːini̥ ɟaːi > bʌtaːin ɟaːi '(they) went and told'.

cʌli̥ diɦaː > cʌldiɦaː 'started'.

dɦʌri̥ diɦisi̥ > dɦʌrdiɦisi̥ '(he) put down'.

pʌɦini̥ liɦisi̥ > paɦinliɦisi̥ '(he) put on'.

§ 141. A voiced plosive at the end of a word becomes breathed before a breathed plosive of the same class in the next word, *e.g.*, **ʌlʌg kʌi deːu > ʌlʌkkʌi deːu** 'turn out', **bɦaːɟi̥ cʌlaː > bɦaːccʌlaː** 'started running', **laːdi̥ tʌu leːiː > laːttʌu leːiː** 'let me first put the burden', **ɟʌb paːniː piː bɦeː > ɟʌppʌːniː piː bɦeː** 'when he finished drinking water', **roːɟu̥ tʌu aːwʌti̥ > roːttʌu aːwʌti̥** 'comes daily'.

§ 142. A breathed plosive occurring at the end of a word (or immediately before a whispered vowel or **ə**) is assimilated with the voiced plosive of the same class in the following word (the whispered vowel or **ə** being elided), *e.g.*,

saːt dãːi > saːddãːi 'seven times',

maːʈiki̥ gɦʌrijaː > maːʈiggɦʌrijaː 'a small pot of clay',

baːp bɦaːiː > **baːbbɦaːiː** 'father and brothers',
saːt ɟʌneː > **saːɟɟʌneː** 'seven persons'.
bɦaːtu̥ d̪aːrisi̥ > **bɦaːd̪d̪aːrisi̥** 'threw the rice'.

§ 143. A breathed plosive coming at the end of a word becomes voiced when followed by a voiced plosive of another class, *e.g.*, **dijʌkḙ dʌrwʌɟɟeː** 'on the door of the lamp (-'s house)', > **diyʌgdʌrwʌɟɟeː, paːku̥ bʌniː hʌi** > **paːgbʌniː hʌi** 'is all right', **koːikḙ ɟuːtaː** > **koːigɟuːtaː** 'somebody's shoes', **khʌʈijʌ po dɦʌriː** > **khʌʈijʌbdɦʌriː** 'placed on the cot', **baːp diɦisi̥** > **baːbdiɦisi̥** 'the father gave'.

§ 144. A nasalisation with the following consonant becomes nasal before a consonant of the same class (place of articulation), *e.g.*, **pʌɦũci̥ ɟaːũ** > **pʌɦuɲɟaːũ** 'I may reach', **pãːc chaː** > **paːɲchaː** 'five or six'. **pãːc saːt paːnsaːt** 'five or seven'.

If the consonant following the nasalisation is aspirated the aspiration is lost, *e.g.*, **bãːdɦi̥ deːu** > **baːndeːu** 'tie (it)'.

§ 145. A plosive occurring at the end of a word (with, or without a whispered vowel or **o** following) is assimilated to the nasal of the same class in the following word, *e.g.*, **dekhaːti̥ naːiː** > **dekhaːnnaːiː** 'is not seen',

baːdi̥ nʌuwʌ kḙ > **baːnnʌuwʌkḙ** 'excepting the barber',

baːp mʌɦotaːriː > **baːmmʌɦotaːriː** 'father and mother',

tʌb mʌɦoraːɟ > **tʌmmʌɦoraːɟ** 'then the Maharaja',

roːɟu̥ naːcʌi > **roːnnaːcʌi** 'may dance everyday'.

But **mʌukepo nʌuwʌu** 'even the barber at the opportunity' remains as it is, because **p** is followed by a nasal of another class.

This assimilation is possible only in the case of labials and dentals as the nasals of other classes do not begin a word.

§ 146. The final consonant is in swift speech united to the initial vowel of the following word, *e.g.*, '**tʌb eːk din raːɟaː** > **ta/beːk din raːɟaː** 'then one day the king'.

This affects only the division of syllables, the most common variety of syllable—consonant plus a vowel--being effected.

§ 147. A plosive or nasal coming at the end of a word loses its explosion if followed by a word beginning with the same plosive or nasal, *e.g.*,

kheːt tiːr > **kheːtːiːr** 'near the field',

maːri̥ kə khisijaːi geː > **maːrikːhisijaːi geː** 'became very much ashamed',

kaːɦemə maːɽeu > **kaːɦemːaːɽeu** 'in what (vessel) did you mix it?'.

§ 148. Final **b** has a tendency to become devoiced before a breathed consonant, *e.g.*,

sʌb+kaː > **sapkaː** 'to all', **ɟʌb seː** > **ɟʌpseː** since'. (See Note to § 15.)

§ 149. Final **-t** or **-th** has a tendency to be assimilated to the following **c-**, **ɟ-**, **r-**, **l-**, and **s-**; the aspiration of **-th** is then lost. The whispered vowel is, of course, elided. For instance:

bɦaːgʌti̥+cʌlaː > **bɦaːgʌccʌlaː** 'went running', **saːth+cʌlʌu** > **saːccʌlʌu** 'come with (me)', **khaːti̥+ɟaːti̥ rʌɦʌi** > **khaːɟɟaːti̥ rʌɦʌi** 'was going eating (on the way)', **ɖɦũːɽʌti̥+rʌɦaː** > **ɖɦũːɽʌrrʌɦaː** 'remained searching', **sʌĩti̥ liɦisi̥** > **sʌĩlliɦisi̥** 'he brushed', **bʌɦut+sãːp** > **bʌɦussãːp** 'many snakes'.

§ 150. Final **-s** has a tendency to be assimilated to the following **c-**, **ɟ-**, **d-**, **ʈ-** and **ɖ-**, *e.g.*,

uː kʌɦisi̥ cʌlʌu > **uːkʌɦiccʌlʌu** 'he said:—come', **dʌs ɟʌneː** > **dʌɟɟʌneː** 'ten persons', **kʌɦisi̥ dʌs birəwaː** > **kʌɦiddʌs birəwaː** 'he said: ten trees', **pʌcaːs ʈhʌĩʈhaː** > **pʌcaːʈʈhʌĩʈhaː** 'fifty points of quarrel', **pʌciːs ɖeraːi geː** > **pʌciːɖɖeraːi geː** 'twenty-five got frightened'.

§ 151. Final **r** is assimilated to the initial **l** or **ɖ** of the following word, *e.g.*,

coːr lʌi gaː > coːllʌigaː 'the thief took away', **caːri lʌrikaː > caːllʌrikaː** 'four sons', **saːr ɖeraːi gaː > saːɖɖeraːi gaː** 'the fool got frightened'. **maːri̥ ɖʌribaː > maːɖɖʌribaː** 'I shall kill'.

§ 152. Final **c, ch, ɟ** are assimilated to initial **ɖ** of the following word, the whispered vowel or **ə** coming between them is elided, *e.g*,

pɑ̃ːc ɖɦeːr > paːɳɖɦeːr 'five heaps', **kuchu̥ ɖaːri̥ deːu > kuɖːaːri̥ deːu** 'do put a little', **bɦaːɟi̥ ʈhaːʈɦ bɦeː > bɦaːʈːhaːʈɦ bɦeː** 'at once ... away'.

§ 153. **h** coming after a plosive or affricate is combined with that plosive or affricate so that an aspirated results. The previous consonant is then pronounced a h longer, *e.g.*,

dʌroːgʌkə + hukum > dʌroːgʌkːhukum 'the order of the police officer', **kaːɦepə hʌ̃seu > kaːɦepːhʌ̃seu** 'what made you laugh ?'.

(*a*) If a whispered vowel or **ə** comes between **h** and the consonant, it is elided if **h** is followed by a similar (back or front) vowel, or becomes **j** or **w** if followed by a dissimilar vowel, *e.g.*,

ɟaːti̥ hʌi > ɟaːtːhjʌi 'goes', but **raːɟʌke̥ hiɑ̃ː > raːjʌkːhiɑ̃ː** 'at the king's', **pɑ̃ːcə + hʌm > pɑ̃ːcːhʌm** 'five to us', but **sɑ̃ːcu̥ hisaːb > sɑ̃ːcːhwisaːb** 'the true account'.

§ 154. If **-i** or **-u** comes between two vowels similar in quality, it becomes **-j** or **-w** respectively, *e.g.*,

lʌi + aːoː > lʌjaːoː 'bring', **gɑ̃ːu + ʌi > gɑ̃ːwʌi** 'to the village'.

§ 155. The forms of the auxiliary 'to be' (present tense only) have a tendency to shorten their syllables when they come after participles. Only their last syllable (with the nasalisation, if one is there) is heard, and there appears to be a slight pause—a silence—in place of the last syllable. For instance :

kʌɦʌti̥ ɦʌi > **kʌɦʌti i** 'he says', **dɦʌreː hʌĩ** > **dɦʌreː ĩ** or even **dɦʌreː ~** 'they are there', **khɑːti̥ hʌu** > **khɑːti u** 'you eat', **deːkhʌti̥ nɑːiː hʌu** > **dːkhʌnnɑːi u** 'aren't you seeing?'.

§ 156. The following cases of doubling (*lit.* lengthening) a consonant and shortening the previous vowel have been noticed:—

kiː tʌnɑː > **kittʌnɑː** 'in which manner', **ɟiː tʌnɑː** > **ɟittʌnɑː** 'in whatever manner'.

Instances of doubling are also noticed in names, *e.g.*, **bʌbːuː**(ordinary **bɑːbuː**), **kʌlːuː** (ordinary **kʌriɑː** 'black') and in appellations of relatives, *e.g.*,

dʌdːuː 'elder brother', **kʌkːuː** 'uncle', **bʌpːɑː** 'father', **kʌkːɑː** 'uncle'.

This doubling seems to be due to emphasis.

CHAPTER VII

THE SENTENCE

§ 157. A sentence in Awadhi is generally small, containing from one to four or five words. In narrative speech these sentences are joined up by conjunctions such as **ʌu** 'and', **tʌu** 'then', **tʌb** 'then', **tʌɦikʌi** 'then' or **ki** 'that' as necessary according to sense. In such conditions, the sentence itself generally forms a breath-group. For instance, the first sentence of **gulgulaːwaːliː kʌthaː** (Texts No. I) will be read as:

eːk raːɟaː rʌɦʌĩ || **ʌu mʌɦətaːriː rʌɦʌi** || **ʌu duləɦin rʌɦʌi** or the last would be read as:

ɟʌiseː unkeː din bʌɦureː || **tʌiseː sʌbkeː bʌɦurʌĩ.**

Long sentences are broken up. In such cases wherever the breath stops it must be the end of a word. A postposition always goes with the preceding word, the two are never separated for breath. The correlative adverb and conjunctions have a stop of breath after them. The subject and the verb when they come one after the other go together and so also the adjective and the substantive. When the adjective, substantive, and the verb come together and a pause is to be made, the breath stops after the adjective. The following are some of the instances:—

eːk | **raːɟaː rʌɦʌĩ** || **ʌu** | **mʌɦətaːriː rʌɦʌi** || **ʌu dulɦin rʌɦʌi. mʌɦətaːriː roːɟu̥** | **chʌpːʌn pʌrkaːlke̥** | **bɦoːɟʌn bʌnaːwʌi** || **ʌu** | **ʌpənaː khaːi** || **ʌu ʌpəneː lʌrikʌk** | **khʌwaːwʌi. dulɦin khaːtir** | **eːk beɟɦʌriki̥** | **roːʈiː sẽːkʌi** || **aːdɦiː roːʈiː** | **ʌu loːnu̥ sʌbeːreː deːi** || **ʌu aːdɦiː** | **sʌɲɟɦʌk. ui** | **maːreː gusːʌke̥** | **roːʈiː ɖeɦʌriʌm** | **ɖaːri̥ deːĩ** || **ʌu loːnu̥** | **gʌgʌrim** | **naːi aːwʌĩ. ʌisʌi** | **kʌrti kʌrti** | **baːraː** | **bʌrsʌi** | **gudʌri̥ gʌĩː.**

§ 158. As noted in § 137, the word-stress in Awadhi is very weak. But in a narrative sentence we have a strong stress on the word which we want to emphasise according to the idea that we want to convey. This falls on the syllable which ordinarily would have the word-stress. For instance, the sentence :

tʌb ui hʌmseː ˈboleː 'then he said to me' would have word-accent only in **ˈboːleː** which is a dissyllabic word, the others being only mono-syllabic But in a sentence even the mono-syllabic words can have stress in order to emphasise a particular word. This sentence may have the following stresses :

ˈtʌb ui hʌmseː ˈboːleː '*then* he said to me',
tʌb ˈui hʌmseː ˈboːlə 'then *he* said to me',
tʌb ui ˈhʌmseː ˈboːleː 'then he said to *me*',
tʌb ui hʌmseː ˈˈboːleː 'then he *said* to me'.

The stressed syllable then becomes a little longer in quantity.

CHAPTER VIII

THE INTONATION

§ 159. Intonation does not play a part in Awadhi to show a difference in meaning of particular words. In normal speech the pitch does not rise or fall considerably. For instance, in the two sentences **eːkə bʌɽeː rɑːɟɑː rʌɦʌti̥ hʌĩ** 'A great king is residing', and **tum khɑːi ɑːeu** 'you have taken your meal', which are mere statements of fact the difference between the frequency of one sound-wave and that of another is not considerable (*vide* Charts 1 and 2). In the former the highest frequency is 160 and the lowest 99, in the latter 133 and 97 respectively.

§ 160. It is in emphatic speech that tone plays a definite part. For the purposes of investigation a sentence was selected which gives four different senses merely by the difference in tone :

1. Statement: **tum khɑːi ɑːeu** 'you came after having eaten (your meal)'.
2. Imperative: **tum khɑːi ɑːeu** 'come after having eaten (your meal)'
3. Question: **tum khɑːi ɑːeu** 'have you come after having eaten (your meal)?'
4. Wonder: **tum khɑːi ɑːeu** 'really! you have come after having eaten (your meal)?'

Charts 2, 3, 4 and 5 depict the rise and fall of tone of these sentences. Chart 2 (statement) shows that the pitch is more or less level. Chart 3 (Imperative) depicts that the sentence begins with a very high pitch (the highest in the sentence), there is an immediate fall, then the tone is more or less level for a considerable length of the sentence. It is only at the end that there is a sudden fall followed by a rise. The highest frequency in this sentence is 181 and the lowest 91.

Chart 4 (question) begins with a high pitch which suddenly falls, then there is a level pitch followed by a gradual rise to the height at which the sentence began; then there is again a fall followed by a level pitch. At the end there is again a gradual rise and a gradual fall. It is thus rise : fall : level : rise : fall : level : rise : fall. The highest frequency in this sentence is 181 and the lowest 87.

Chart 5 (wonder) begins with a very low pitch, there is gradual rise and then a fall almost to the point at which the sentence began. After it, there is a level pitch and then a gradual rise to a very high pitch. The highest frequency in this sentence is 253 and the lowest 85.

§ 161. In individual words, the only scope for the play of tone is when a person is called from far off or when a word expresses acquiescence or prohibition. In the former case the last syllable of the word rises high in pitch besides being elongated, *e.g.*, **bɦʌija** ː ː ː ː 'brother'.

_/

In the latter case, only the interjections like **hãː** are used. Like 'yes' of English, **hãː** is capable of giving different senses by a difference in tone. The following are generally used :

1. **hãː** 'yes' — agreement or acquiescence ¯\
2. **hãː** 'no' — prohibition or disagreement _/

CHAPTER IX

OTHER CHARACTERISTICS

§ 162. As compared with the speech of grown-up people, the speech of children shows the following features:

1. **r** is pronounced as **l**, *e.g.*, **gɦʌr** as **gɦʌl**.

2. **ɽ** is pronounced as **l**, *e.g.*, **gɦʌɽiː** as **gɦʌliː**.

NOTE.—Sometimes a child substitutes **n** for **l**, *e.g.*, **gɦʌr** as **gɦʌn**, **cʌlʌu** as **cʌnʌu**.

3. retroflex mutes are pronounced as dentals, *e.g.*, **kaːʈen** as **kaːten**, **ʈhaːkur** as **thaːkul**, **ɖʌɳɖaː** as **dʌndaː**, **ɖɦoːlʌk** as **dɦoːlʌk**.

4. aspiration in aspirated sounds is very feeble so that they sound as unaspirated, *e.g.*, **gɦʌr** approximates **gʌl**.

5. **s** is pronounced as **ch**, *e.g.*, **sunʌu** as **chunʌu**, **bʌtaːsaː** as **bʌtaːchaː**.

It has been observed that when the child begins to pronounce **s**, he does so in the case of initial **s** first—the medial **s** continues to be pronounced **ch** a little longer.

§ 163. The speech of women does not show any phonetic divergence from that of men. The speech of literate classes sometimes retains foreign sounds in loan-words, *e.g.*, **ʃ**, **f**, **z**. Otherwise there is no phonetic divergence between the speech of one class and that of another. The difference lies only in the adoption of vocabulary (see § 9).

§ 164. Gestures play a part in emotional speech. In ordinary talk men generally do not move their hands. The head rises a little when a question is put and falls when acquiescence is to be indicated. In quarrels, particularly of women, hands play a very expressive part. Challenges and counter-challenges are made by the hand, the persons quarrelling advance towards each other and then retrace the steps. As soon as another telling point is told they again advance and again retrace. The fists are clenched, the teeth are pressed, one set on the other, with spreading of lips and the head moves forward. These gestures, however, are not particular to Awadhi only.

INSCRIPTIONS 1—3

M = Mouth
T = Time
N = Nose

M 1
T

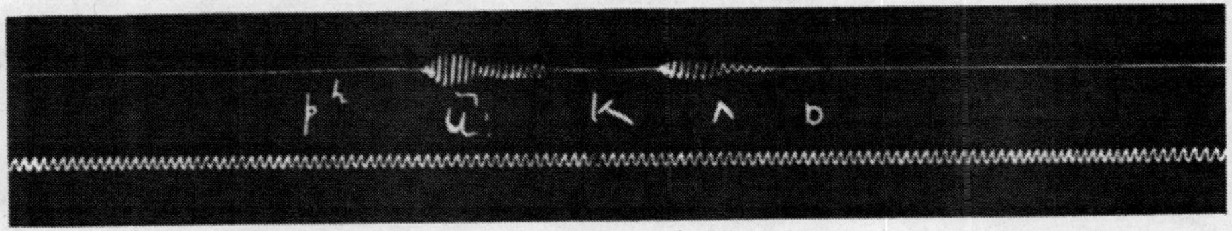

M 2
T

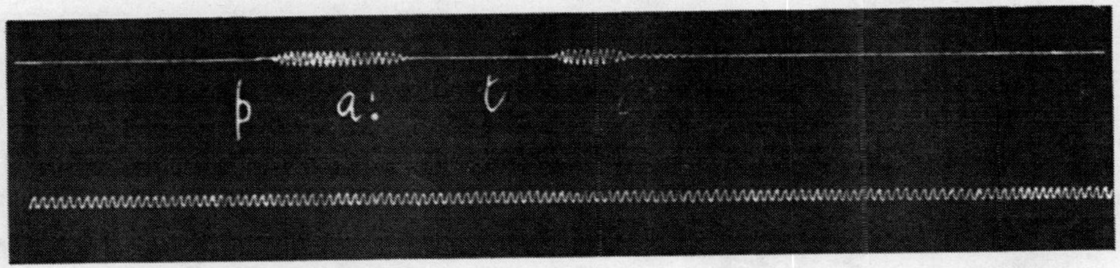

M 3
T

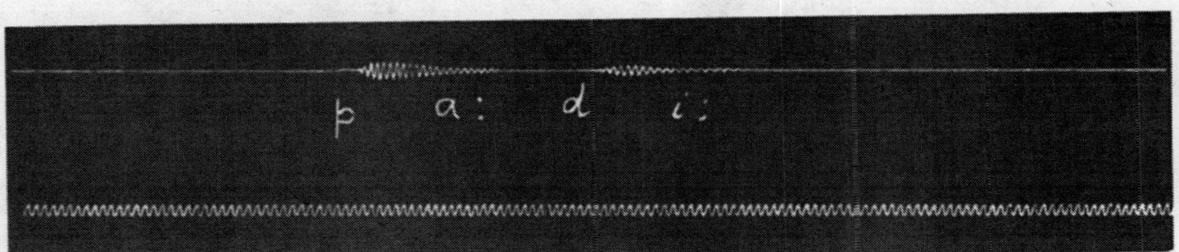

INSCRIPTIONS 4–6

M

4 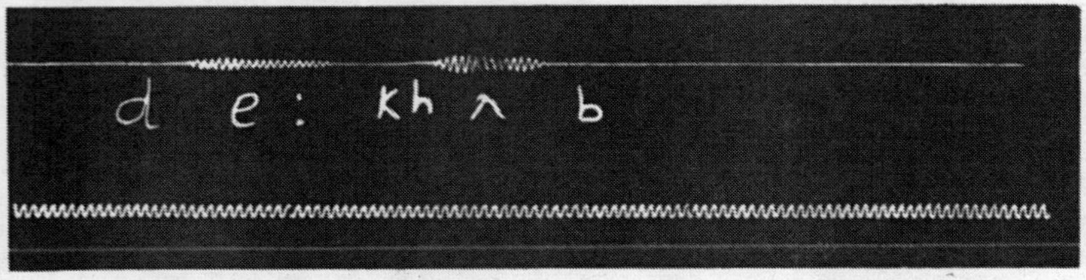

T

M

5 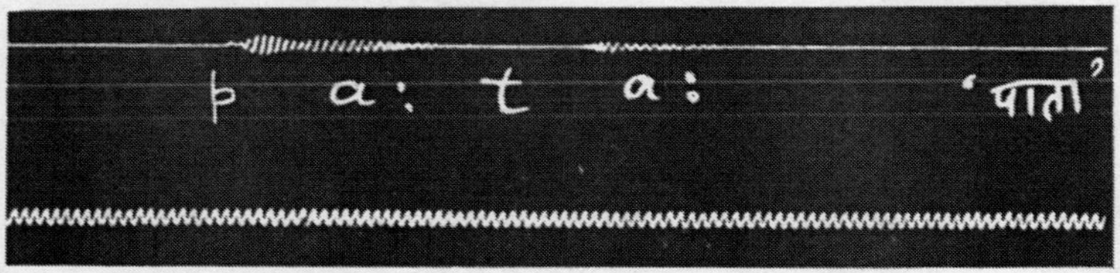

T

M

6 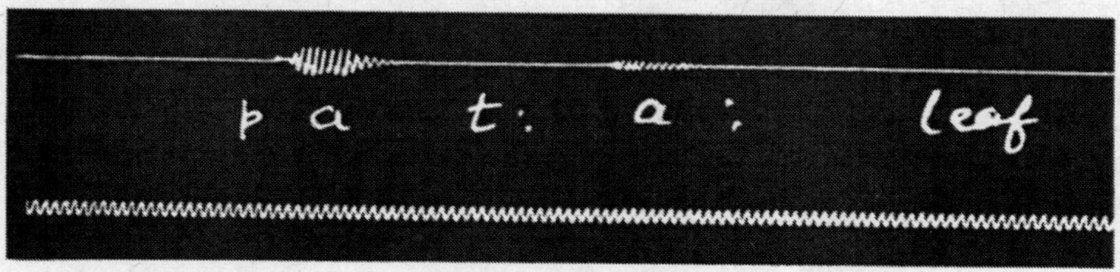

T

INSCRIPTIONS 7–10

M

7

T

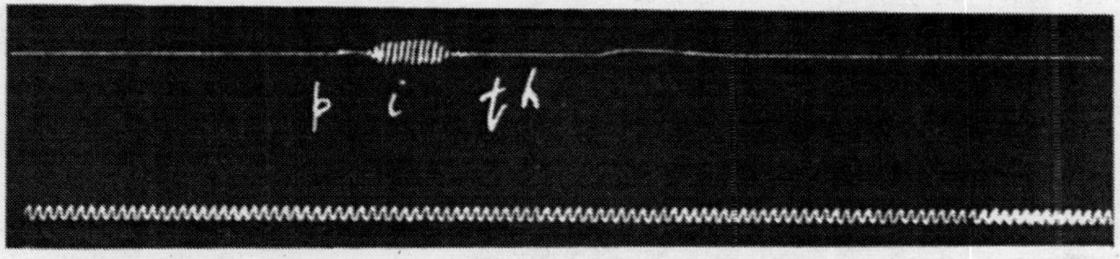

M 8

T

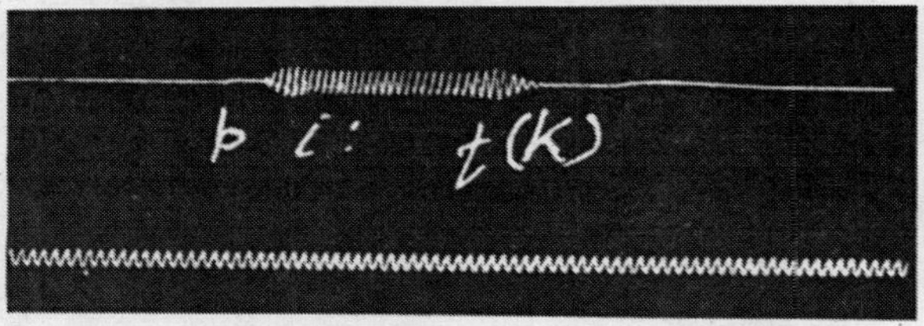

M 9

T

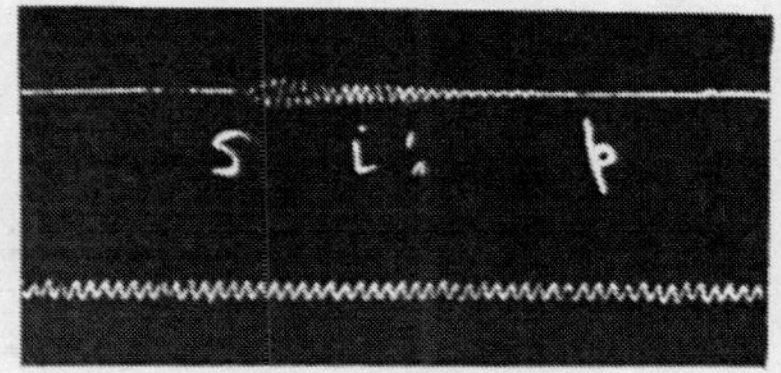

M 10

T

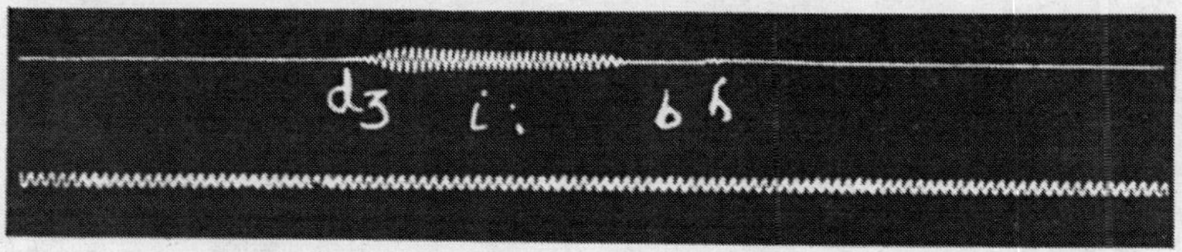

INSCRIPTIONS 11—12

M 11

T

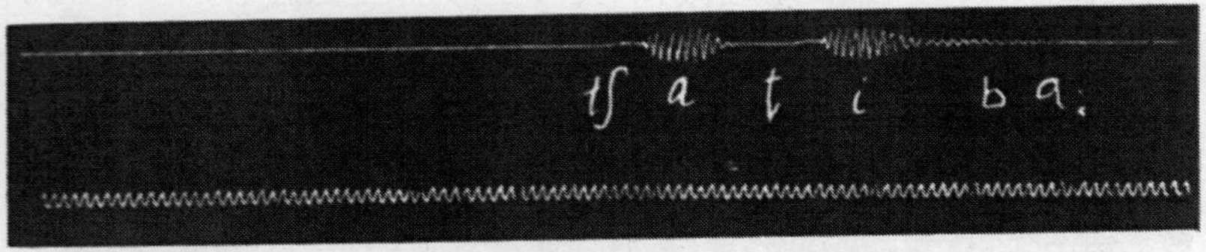

N

M 12

T

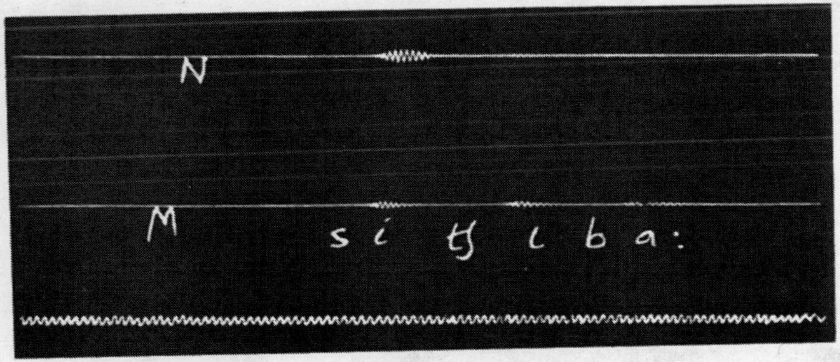

INSCRIPTIONS 13 –14

N

M 13

T

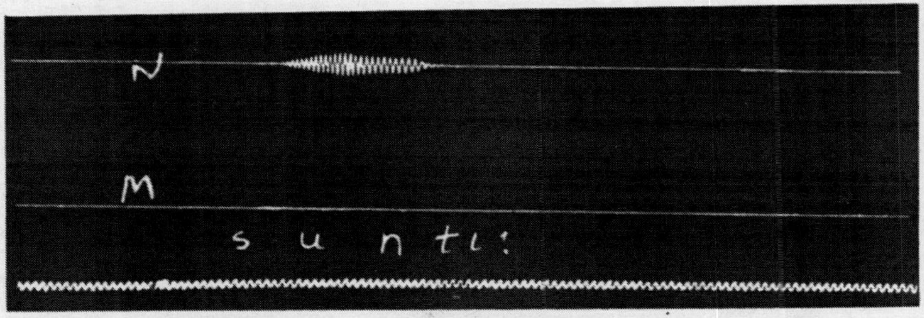

N

14

M

T

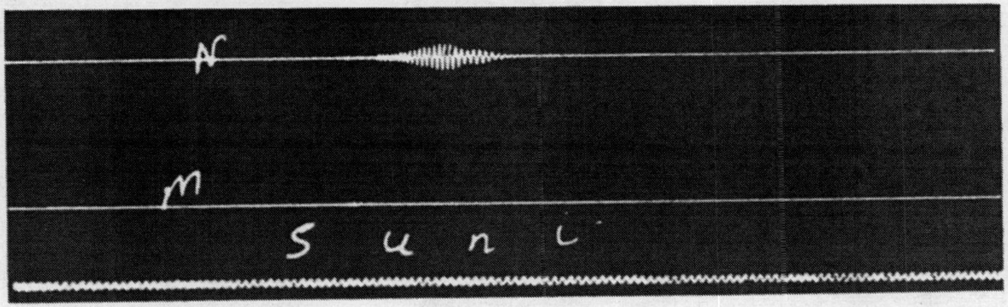

INSCRIPTIONS 15–16

N

M 15

T

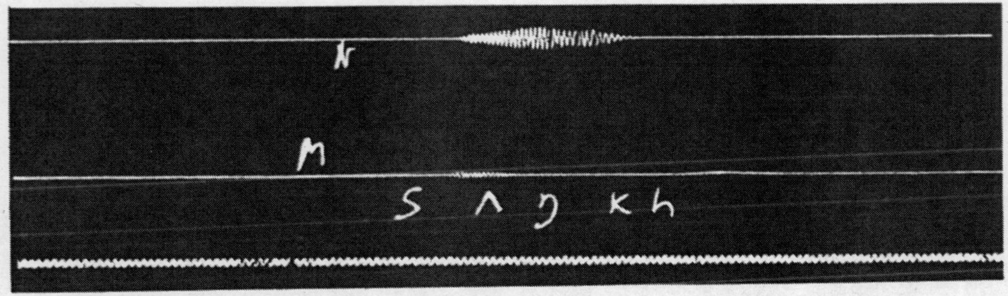

N

M 16

N

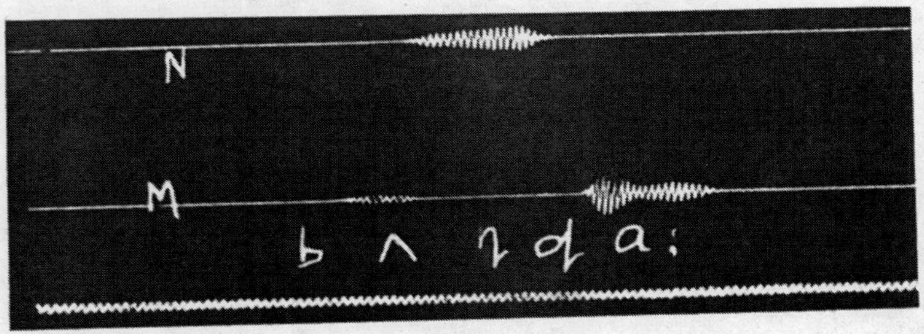

N

17

M

T

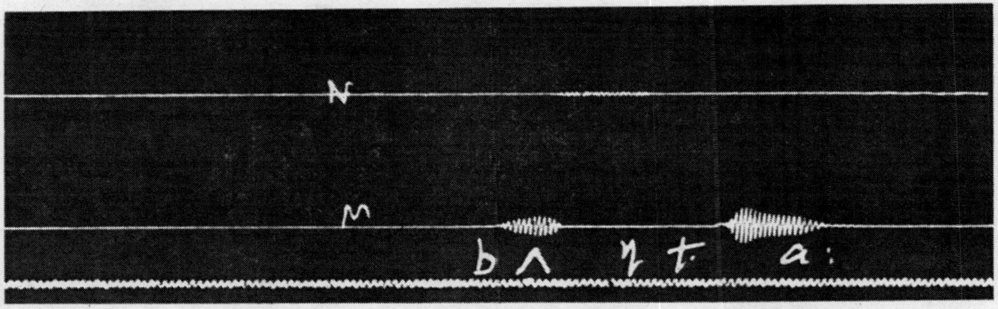

M

T 18

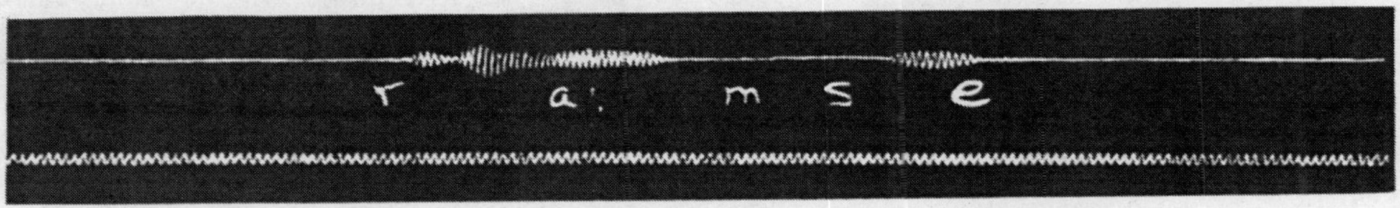

INSCRIPTIONS 19—20

M 19

T

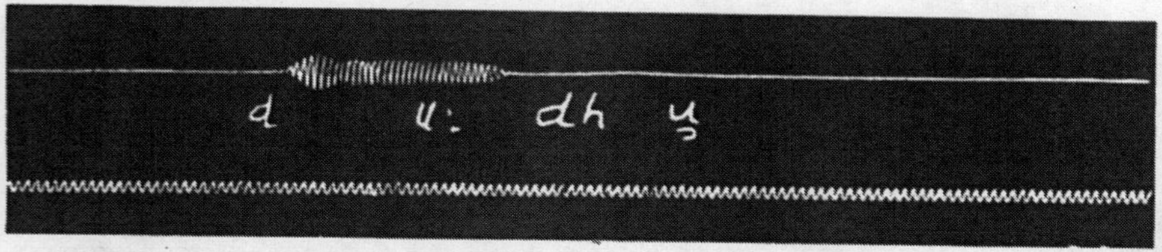

M 20

T

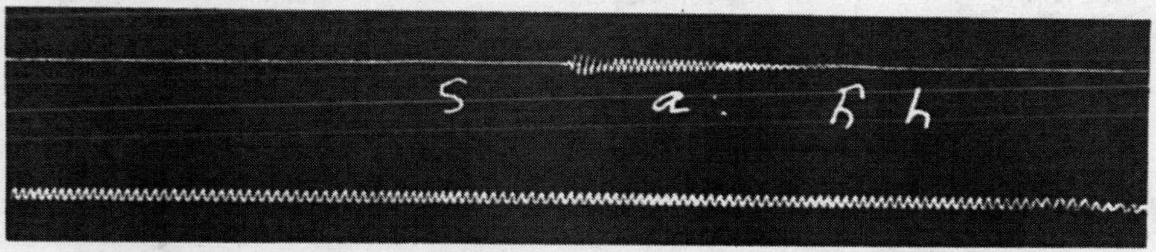

INSCRIPTIONS 21 22

N

M 21

T

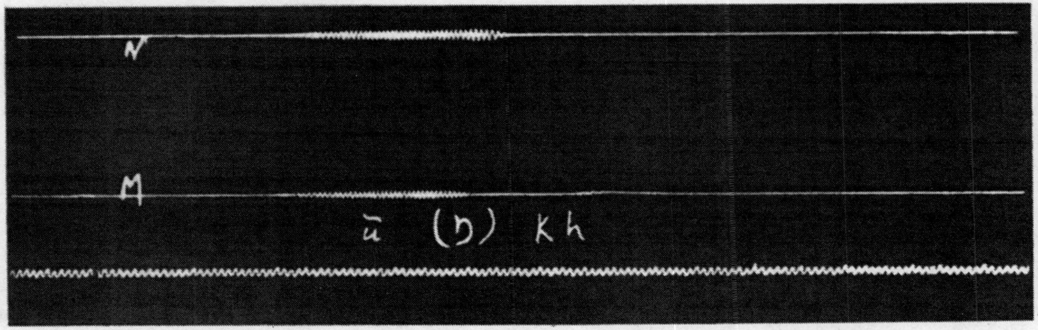

N

M 22

T

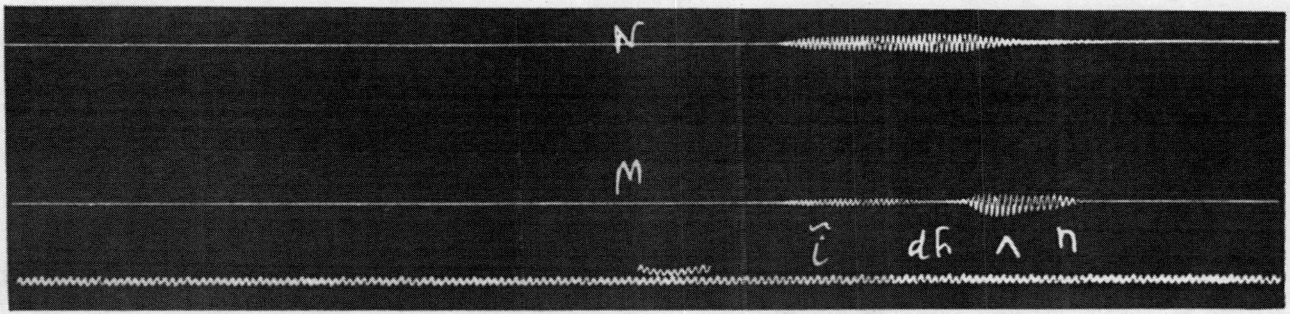

INSCRIPTIONS 23—24

N

M 23

T

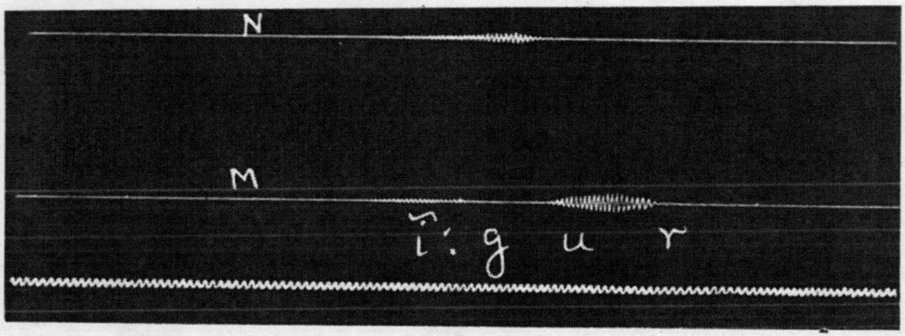

N

24

M

T

M

25 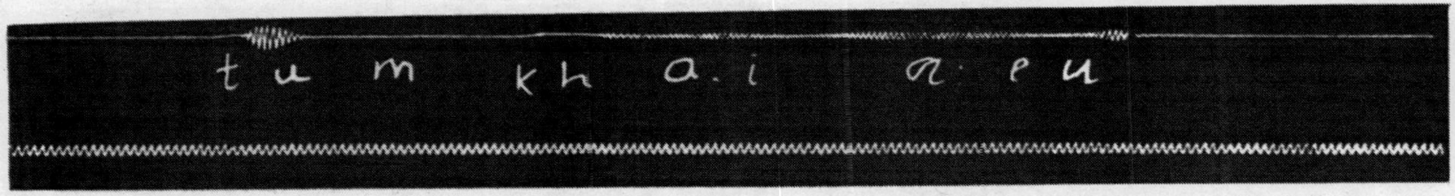

T

M

T 26 

Inscriptions 27—28

N
M 27
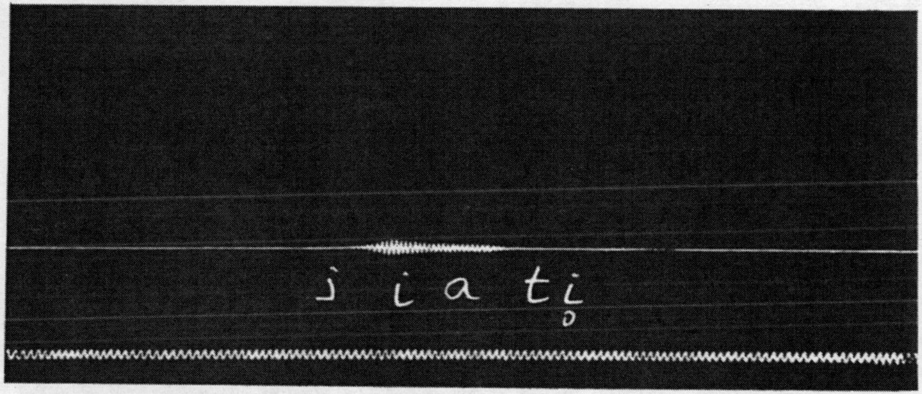

T

N
M 28
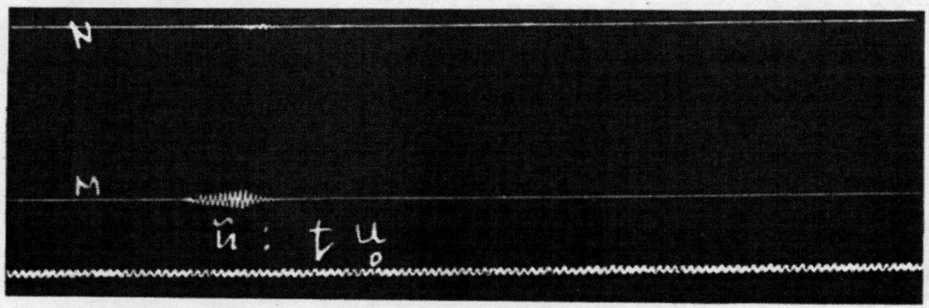

T

N

M 29

T

M 30

T

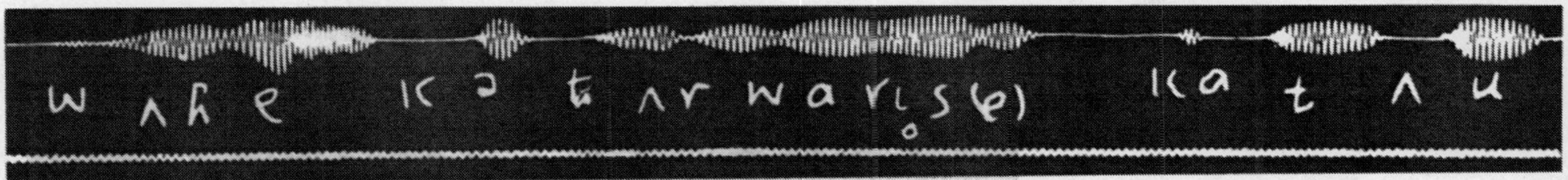

M 31

T

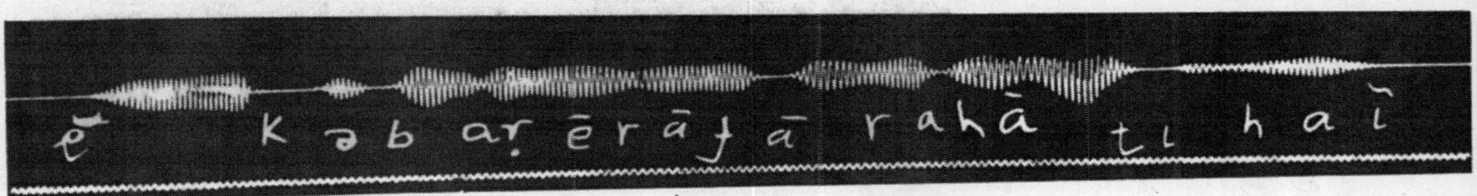

INSCRIPTIONS **32—33**

N

32

M

T

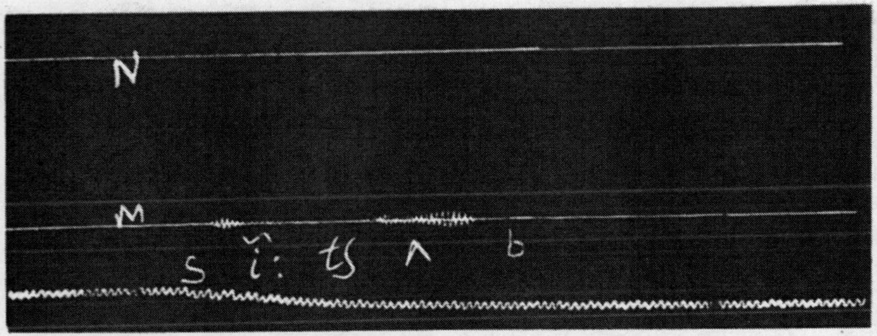

M

T 33

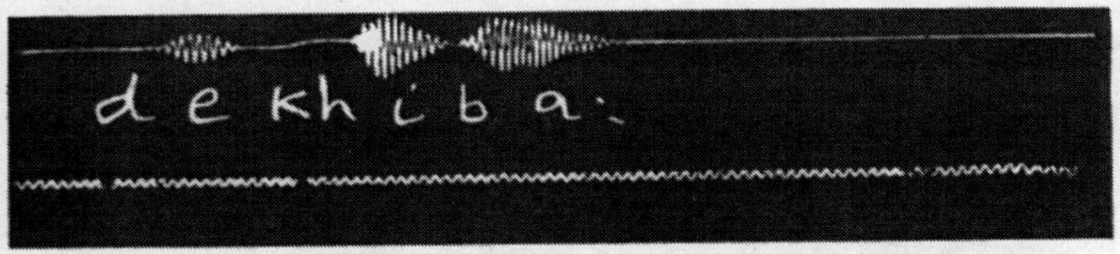

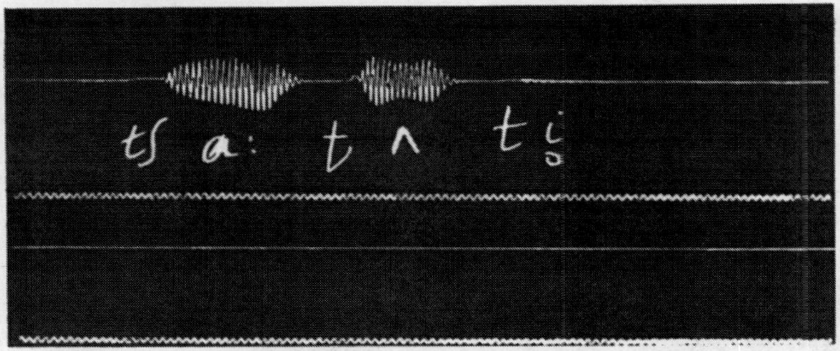

M

T 34

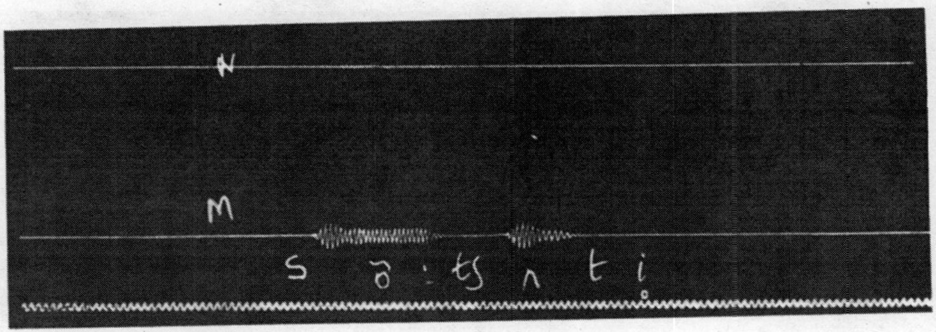

N

M 35

T

Inscriptions 36—37

N

M 36

T

N

M 37

T

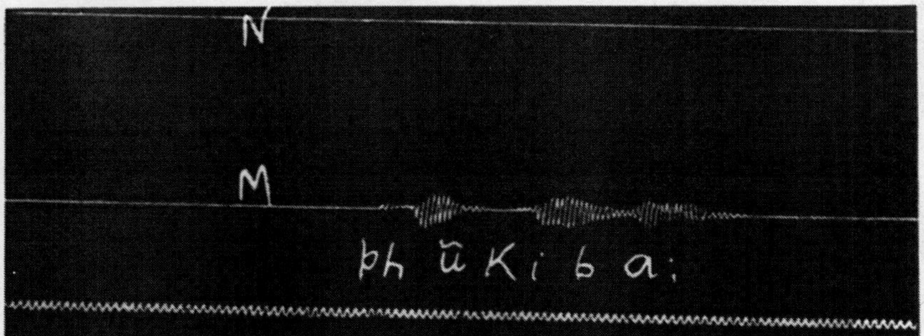

M 38

T

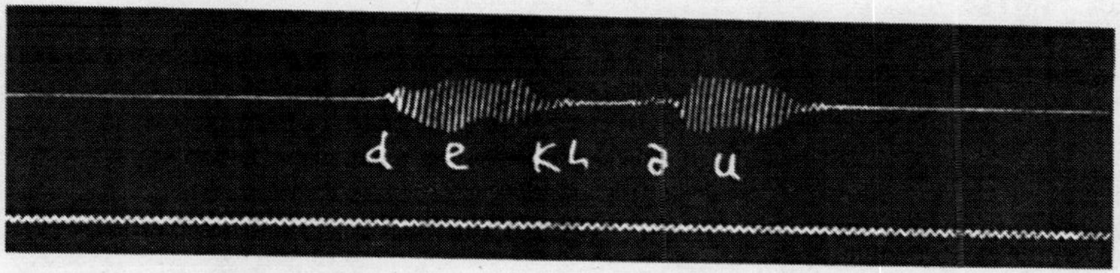

N

M 39

T

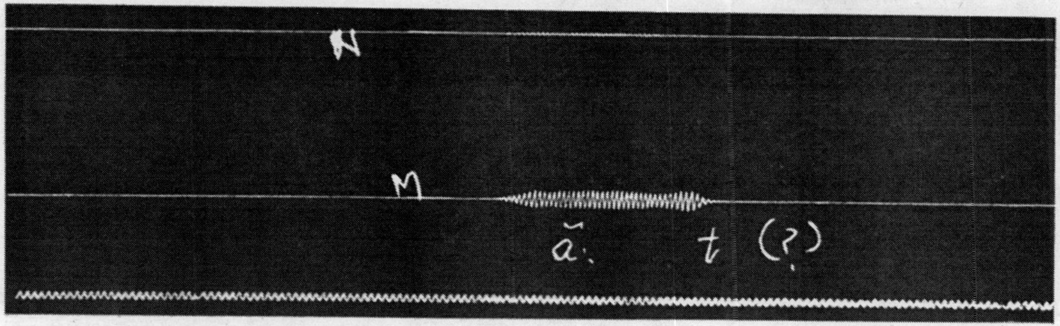

INSCRIPTIONS **40—41**

M 40

T

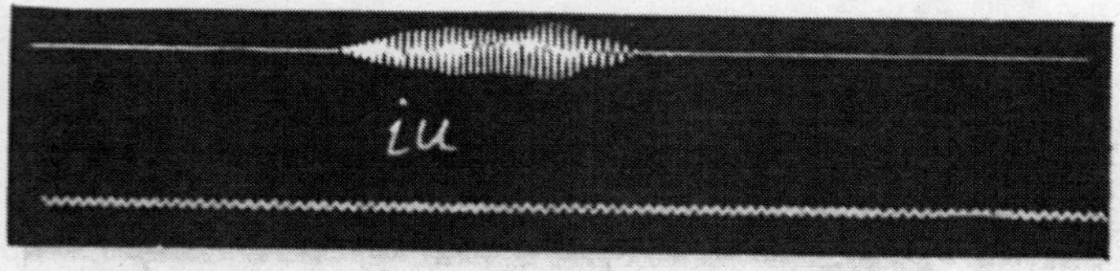

M 41

T

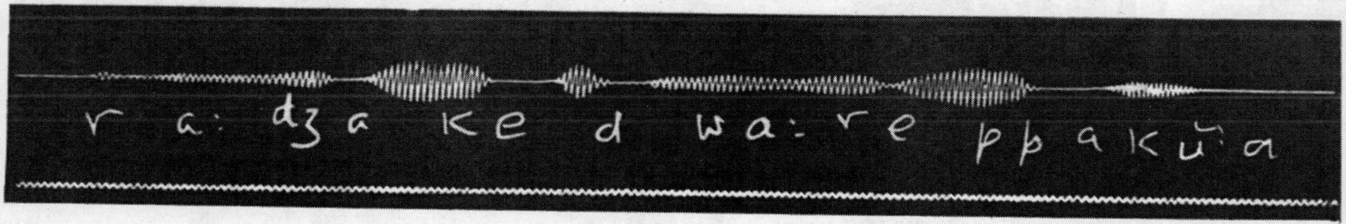

N

M 42

T

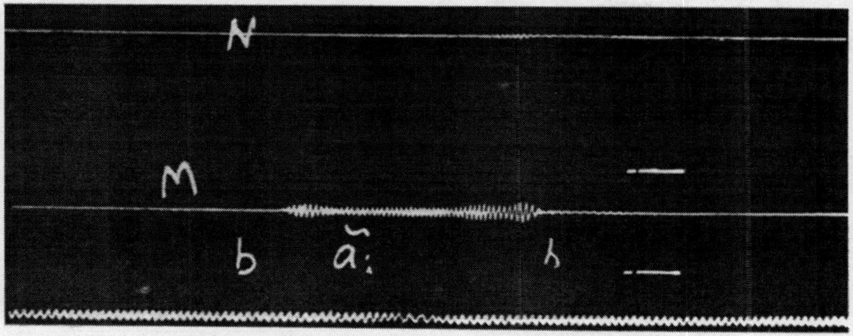

N

M 43

T

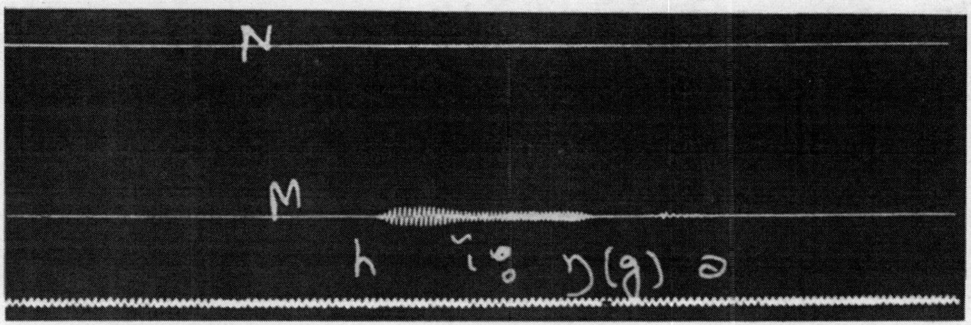

INSCRIPTIONS **44**–**45**

N

M 44

T

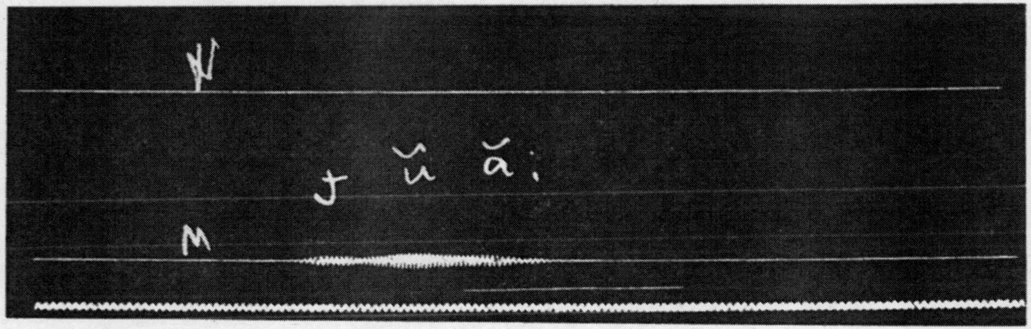

N

M 45

T

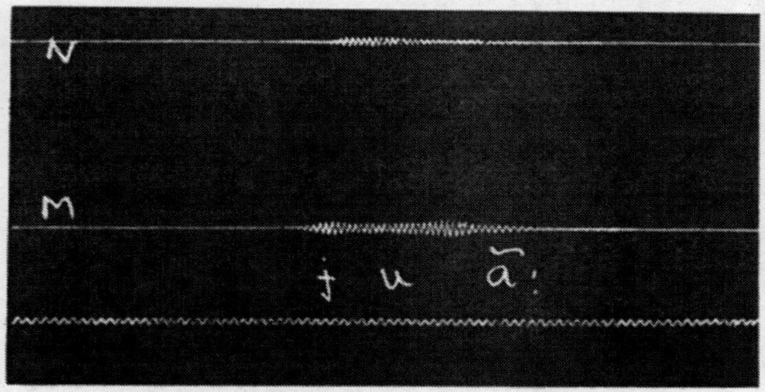

N

M 46

T

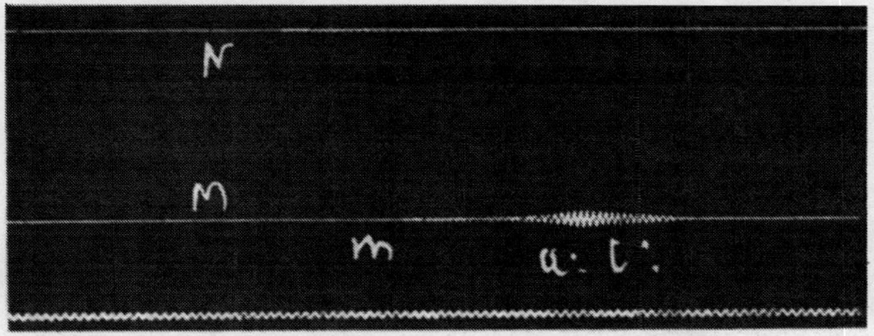

N

M 47

T

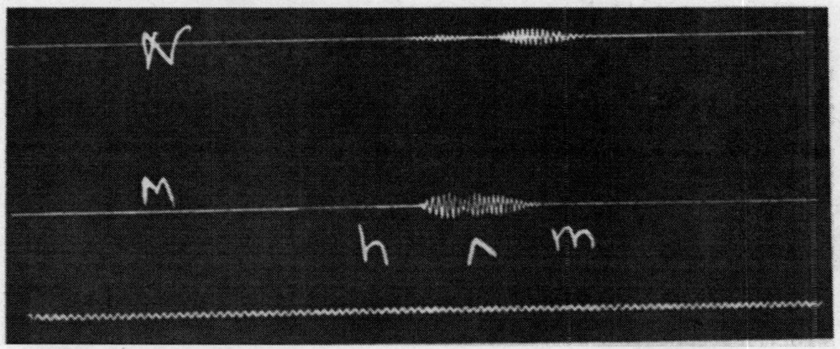

INSCRIPTIONS **48—49**

M

T

M

48

T

M

T

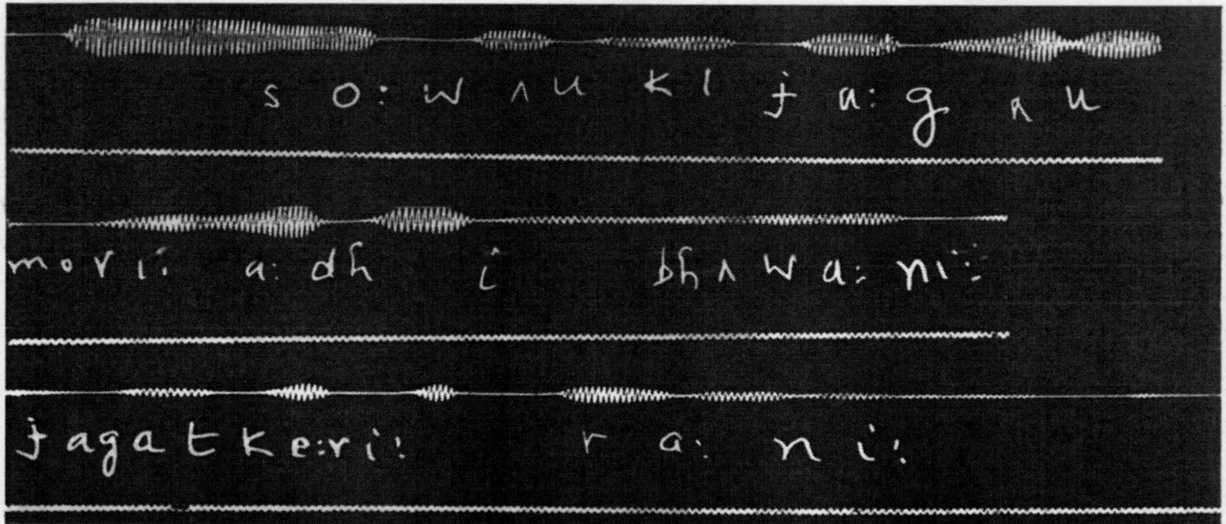

M

T

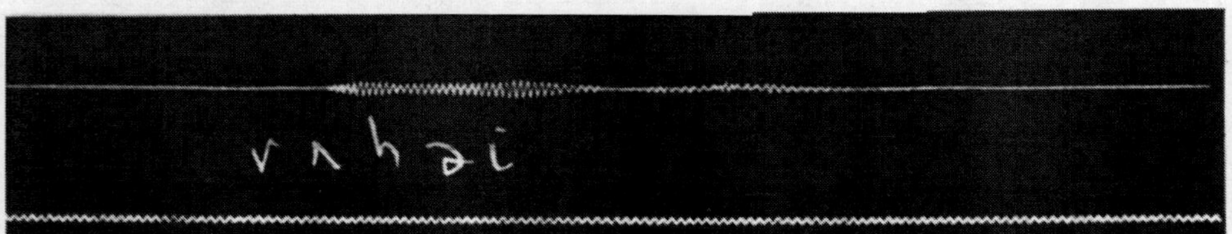

PART II

HISTORICAL GRAMMAR OF AWADHI

PALATOGRAMS

NOTE.—For the convenience of the study, it is proper to divide the palate into parts :—

1. the teeth (dental region)
2. the gums (alveolar region)
3. the rough back above the gums (palate)
4. the smooth back above the rough back (palate where retroflexion is made)
5. the highest portion of the smooth palate (almost where it meets the soft palate—where the so-called velars make a contact).

PALATOGRAMS 1 3

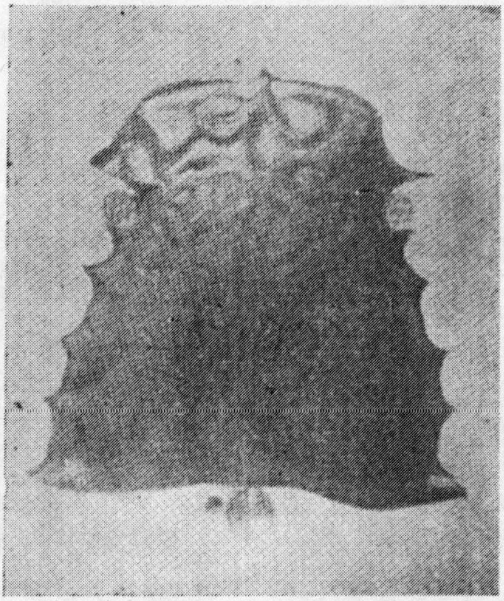

1

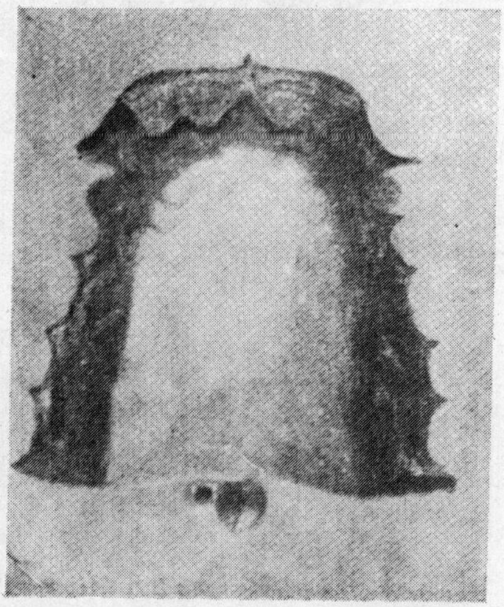

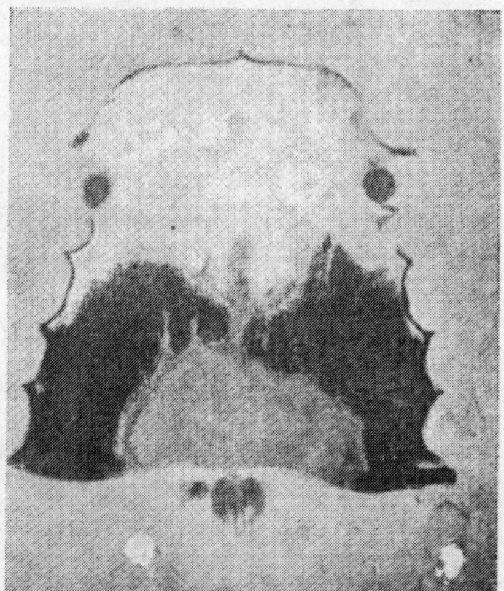

2 t

t 3

PALATOGRAMS 4 7

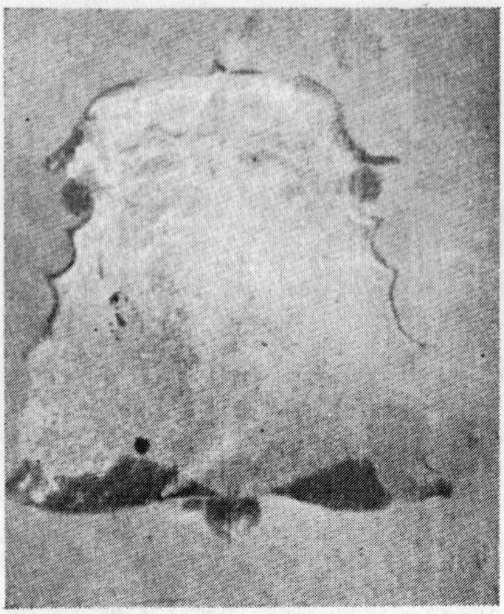

5 ku

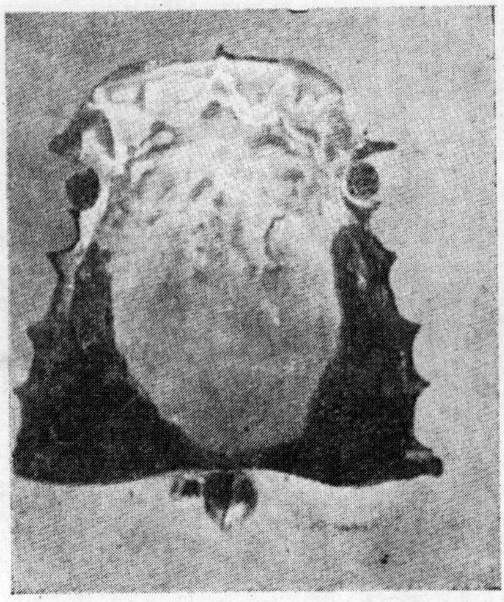

ki 4

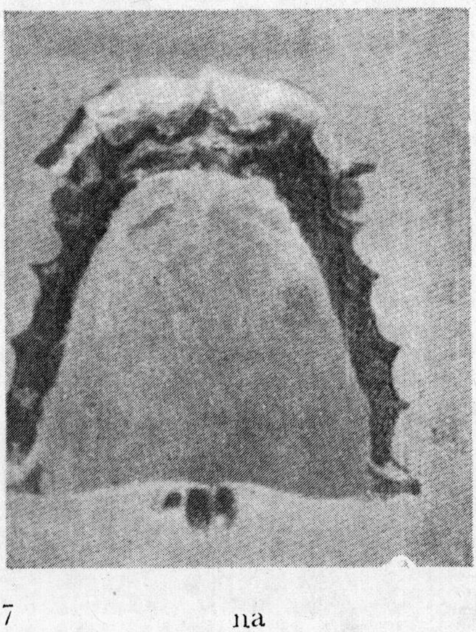

7 na

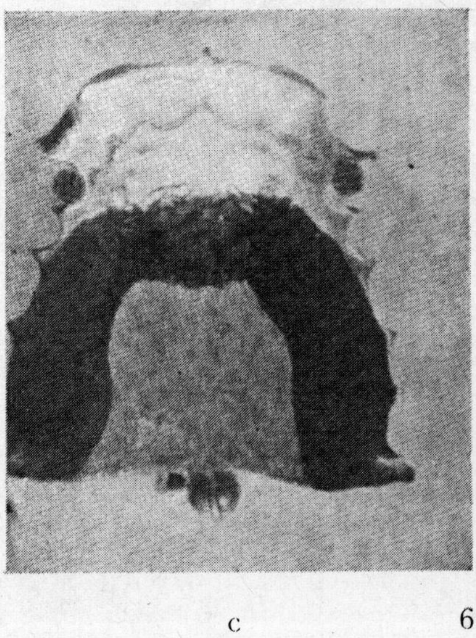

c 6

PALATOGRAMS 8–11

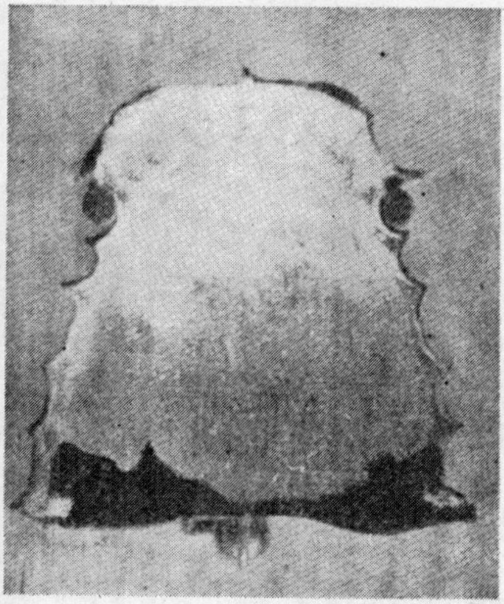

Anga:

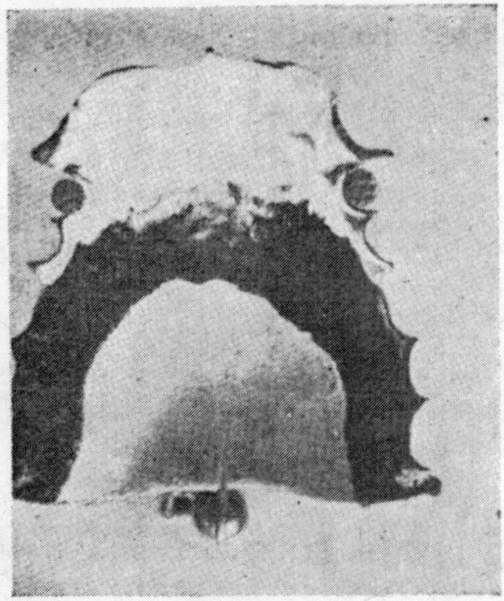

Anga: 8

11 r

Anca: 10

PALATOGRAMS **12—15**

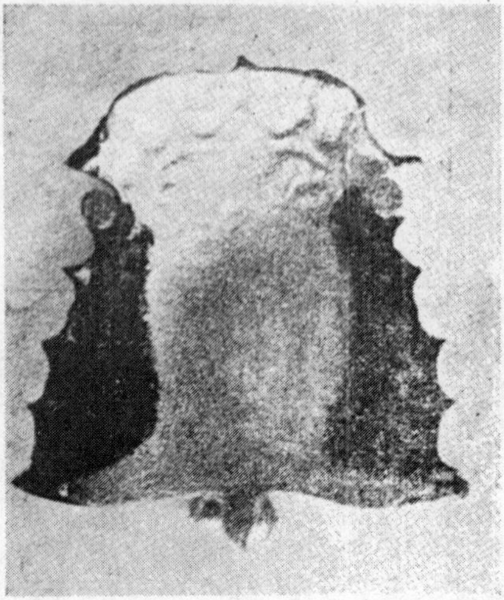

13 l

r 12

15 j

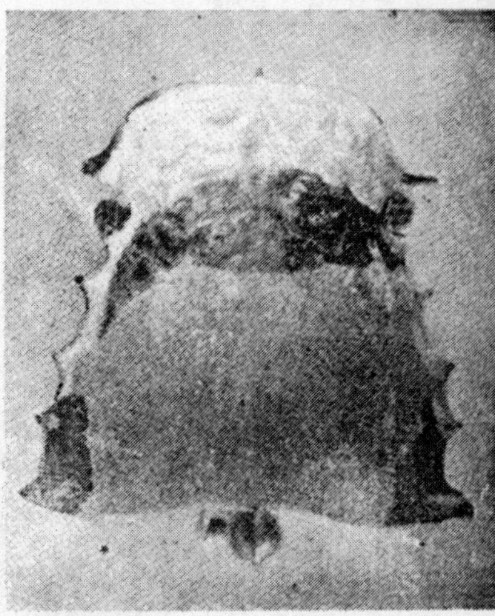

s 14

PALATOGRAMS **16—19**

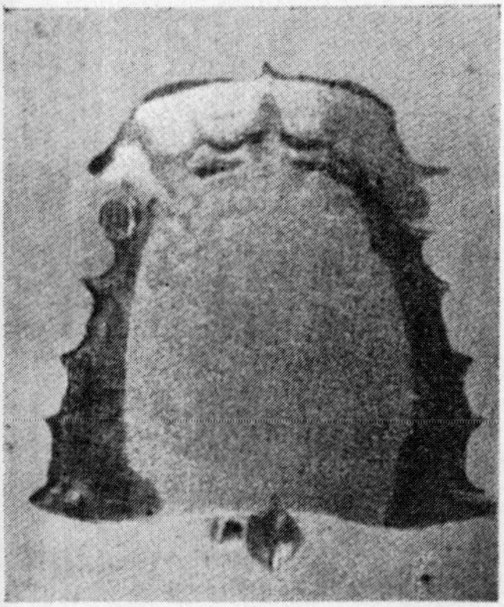

i

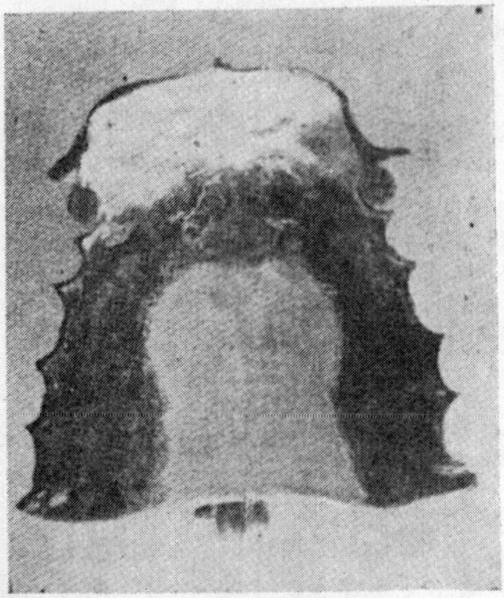

i: 16

19 ī:

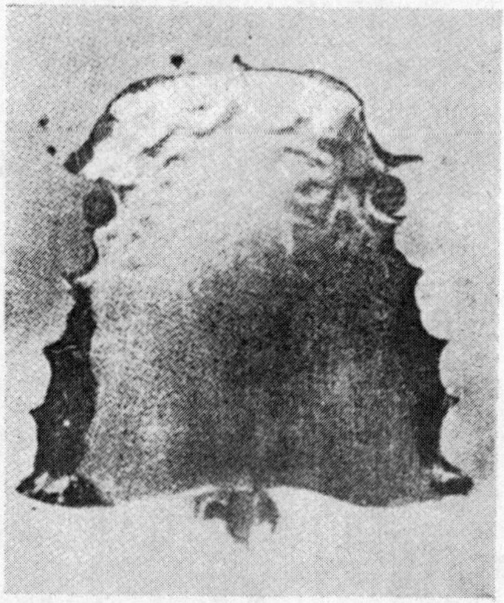

e: 18

Drawing 20

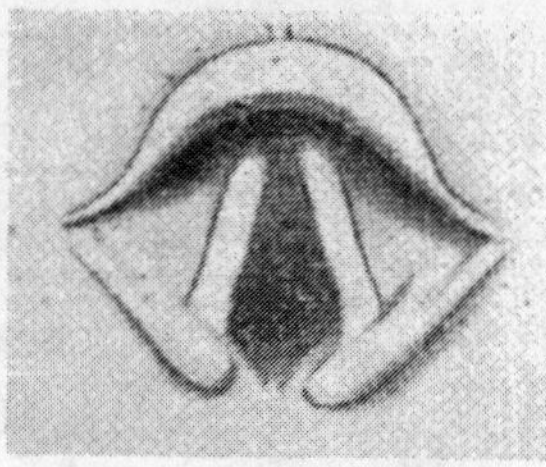

(*a*) breath

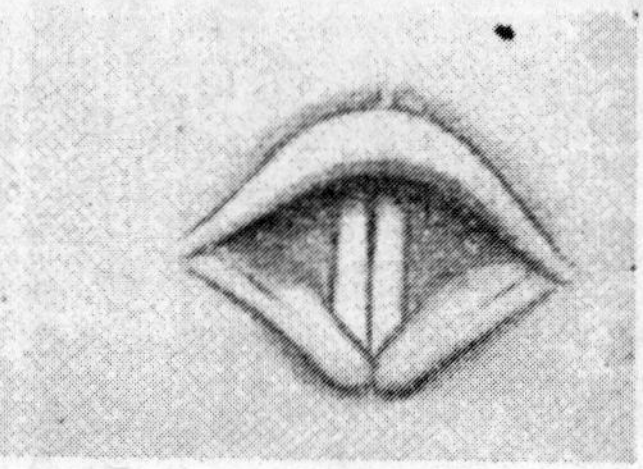

(*b*) voice

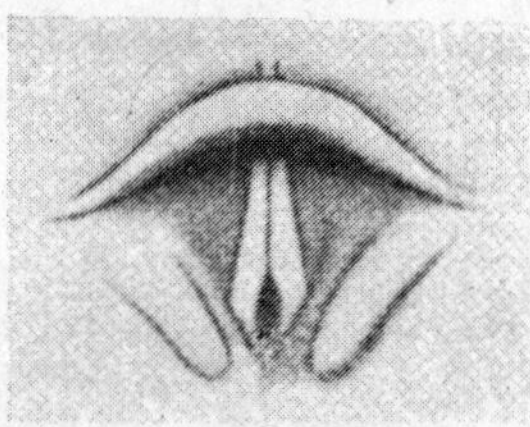

(*c*) whisper

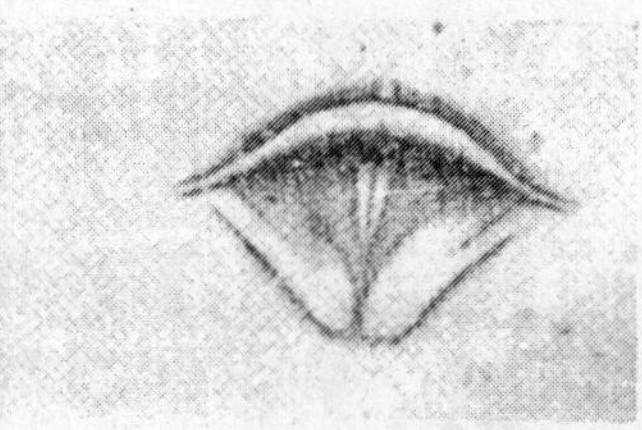

(*d*) closed glottis

CHART 1

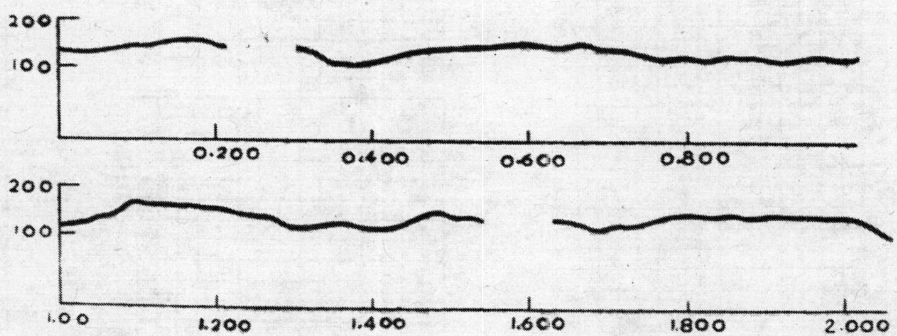

200
100
0.200
0.400
0.600
0.800
200
100
1.00
1.200
1.400
1.600
1.800
2.000

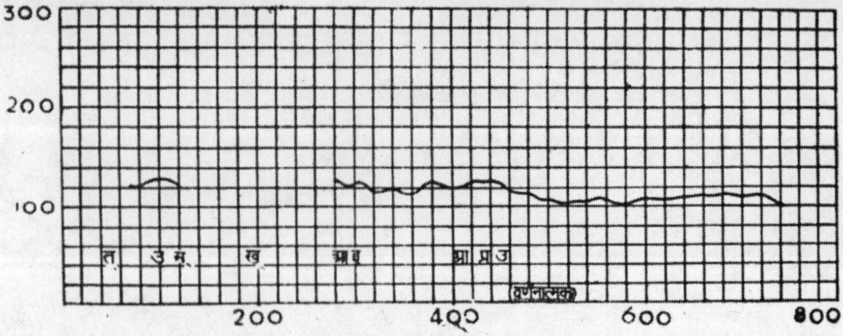
300
200
100
त्
उ म्
ख्
आ
200
400
600
800

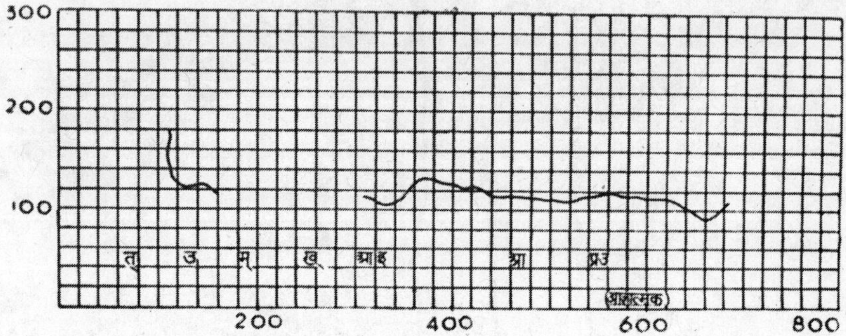
300
200
100
त्
उ
म्
ख्
आ
200
400
600
800

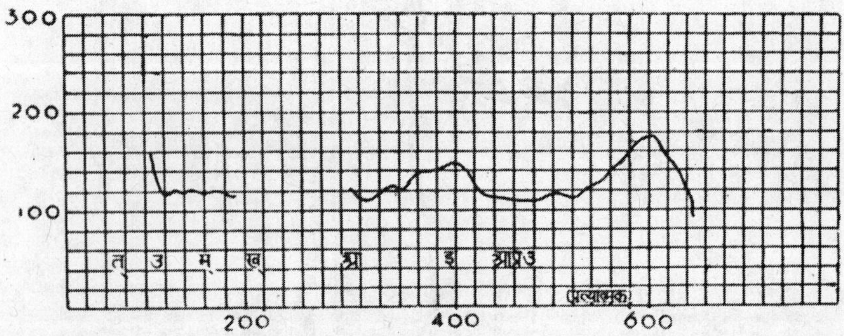
300
200
100
त्
उ
म्
ख्
आ
इ
200
400
600

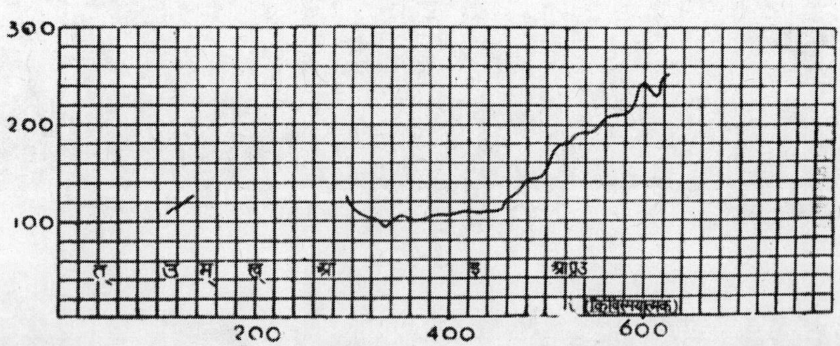
300
200
100
त्
उ
म्
ख्
इ
200
400
600

CHAPTER I

NOUNS

Stem

A. EARLY AWADHI

§ 165. Nouns in Early Awadhi ended in *-a*, *ā*, *i*, *ī*, *u* or *ū*. For instance :

-*a* *ghōra* 'horse', *nakhata* 'star', *maccha* 'fish', *ārana* 'forest', *tāra* 'palm-tree', *sāuja* 'beasts' ; *bhūkha* 'hunger', *ūkha* 'sugar-cane' . . . . Jāyasī.
ghara 'house', *mana* 'mind', *hiya* 'heart' ; *avadha* '*Ayodhyā*', *sikha* 'advice', *bājana* 'musical instruments', *kāja* 'work' . . . . Tulsī.
khambha 'pillar', *bakhāna* 'description', *acarja* 'wonder', *jībha* 'tongue'. *kharihāna* 'granary', *bhaũha* 'eyebrow', *gā̃ṭha* 'knot', *jara* root', *rāta* 'night' . . . . Nūr Muhd.

-*ā* *gilāvā*, 'clay', *lōbā* 'fox', *cā̃ṭā* 'ant', *kũvā* 'well', *dhandhā* 'work', *tarunāpā* 'youth' . . Jāyasī.
badhāvā 'congratulatory concert', *baṭiyā* 'bud', *dōhā* 'couplet' . . . . Tulsī.
cēlā 'disciple', *hiyā* 'heart', *citērā* 'painter', *paṭavā* 'braider' . . . . Nūr Muhd.

-*i* *jari* 'root', *bhuī* 'earth', *sihiṭi* 'Nature', Universe', *raini* 'night', *mahari* 'milk-maid bird' . . . . Jāyasī.
savati 'co-wife', *sudhi* 'recollection', *bhui* 'Earth', *gāi* 'cow' . . . . Tulsī.
gāi (*gāya*), 'cow', *budhi* 'wisdom', *sudhi* 'recollection', *guli* 'ball' . . . . Nūr Muhd.

-*ī* *dharatī* 'Earth', *daī* 'creator', *mākhī* 'fly', *cā̃ṭī* 'ant', *bāvarī* 'big well', *mūṭhī* 'handful', *macharī* 'fish' . . . . Jāyasī.

mahatārī 'mother', *athāī* 'meeting-place', *kahānī* 'tale' . . . . Tulsī.

bārī 'garden', *bovāī* 'sowing', *darabānī* 'stewardship' . . . . Nūr Muhd.

-*u* *sīu* 'coolness', *mīcu* 'death', *bīju* 'lightning', *k*ã*dau* 'mud' . . . . Jāyasī.

rāu 'king', *gālu* 'cheek', *subhāu* 'nature', *pas*ẽ*u* 'sweat' . . . . Tulsī.

gīu 'neck', *ṭhā*ũ 'place', *nā*ũ 'name', *pīu* 'husband' . . . . Nūr Muhd.

-*ū* *nībū* 'lemon', *baṭāū* 'traveller' . . . Jāyasī.

nāū 'barber', *baṭāū* 'traveller'. . . . Tulsī.

pahārū 'watchmen', *ḍiṭhiyārū* 'one who has eyes' . . . . Nūr Muhd.

NOTE—1. A few nouns in Tulsīdās and Nūr Muhammad end -in ō (*e.g. hiyō, cērō* in T.) but they are, to be sure, borrowings from Braj.

NOTE.—2. The quantity of final vowels is very unstable in these texts and it changes for the exigencies of metre. A noun which otherwise ends in a long vowel (*e.g., rānī, cērī*) becomes short (*rāni, cēri*) in the lines of metres and a final short vowel becomes long at the end of a line (*e.g. nā*ũ > *nā*ū̃, *ṭhā*ũ > *ṭhā*ū̃, *karatāru* > *kartārū*).

NOTE—3. Nouns ending in -*ā* are few and those in -*ū* still fewer. Long and longer forms of the stem (§ 167) are not found in Early Awadhi texts except rarely, *e.g., bhāī* : *bhaiyā* (T), *suā-* : *suaṭā* (J 109), *bhikhiyā* (J. 486), *akhiāna* (N. 35), *sejiyā* (N. 38).

NOTE—4. The texts agree with respect to the use of number and gender with modern Awadhi (see below §§ 170—176).

B. Modern Awadhi

§ 166. A noun (stem) may end either in a vowel or in a consonant, *e.g.*, **diaː** 'lamp', **nĩːd** 'sleep'.

(*a*) The final vowels generally are -**aː**, -**i** (**i̥**), -**iː** -**u**, -**uː**. For instance :

-**aː** **kuãː** 'well', **khʌṭijaː** 'bedstead'.

-i(i̥) **seːʈhi̥** 'banker', **gaːi** 'cow', **raːɟi̥** kingdom,' **ãːkhi̥** 'eye', **ɟʌi** 'victory', **bʌjaːri̥** 'wind'.

-iː **thʌbʌiː** 'mason', **dɦoːbiː** 'washerman', **nʌdiː** 'river', **paːniː** 'water'.

-u ũ **gɦiu** 'clarified butter', **ɟiu** 'life', **gʌ̃u** 'chance', **bɦaːu** 'rate', **dʌɦiu** 'curds', **nãːũ** 'name', **gãːũ** 'village', **dãːũ** 'chance', **ãːũ** 'mucus', **naːu** 'boat'.

-uː **naːuː** 'barber', **nʌinuː** 'butter', **baːruː** 'sand', **guː** 'excreta'.

NOTE.—Rarely **-eː, pãːɽeː** 'a class of Brahmins'.

(*b*) The Final consonant may be one of those which can appear finally in a word (see Part I, Chapter I). For instance.

-k **sãːk** 'breath', **noːk** 'point'
-kh **bɦuːkh** 'hunger', **saːkh** 'credit'
-g **sĩːg** 'horn', **mũːg** 'a kind of pulse'
-gɦ **gɦaːgɦ** 'very clever'
-c **kãːc** 'glass', **ãːc** 'flame'
-ch **kõːch** 'the skirt on the lap'.
-ɟ **laːɟ** 'shame' **seːɟ** 'bed'
-ɟɦ **ɟɦãːɟɦ** 'cymbal', **sãːɟɦ** 'evening'
-ʈ **peːʈ** 'belly', **bɦaːʈ** 'bard'
-ʈh **ʈhaːʈh** 'pomp', **hõːʈh** 'lip'
-ɖ **lʌɳɖ** 'penis'
-ɖɦ **thʌɳɖɦ** 'cold'
-ɽ- **hãːɽ** 'bone', **sãːɽ** 'bull'
-ɽɦ **baːɽɦ** 'flood'
-t **kheːt** 'field', **bɦaːt** 'cooked rice'
-th **hãːth** 'hand', **naːth** 'the noose put in the nostrils of bullocks'
-d **nĩːd** 'sleep', **tõːd** 'protruding belly'
-dɦ **kãːdɦ** 'shoulder', **baːdɦ** 'string'
-n **kaːn** 'ear', **soːn** 'gold'

-p	**naːp** 'measurement', **sãːp 'snake'**
-ph	**baːph** 'vapour'
-b	**bʌib** 'a kind of grass', **raːb 'wet molasses'**
-bɦ	**ɟiːbɦ** 'tongue'
-m	**kaːm** 'work', **moːm** 'wax'
-r	**saːr** 'wife's brother', **haːr** 'defeat'
-rɦ	**riːrɦ** 'spinal cord'
-l	**meːl** 'union', **caːl** 'trick'
-lɦ	**maːlɦ** 'a string connecting the spindle with the spinning wheel'
-s	**bãːs** 'bamboo', **sãːs** 'breath'
-ɦ	**bãːɦ** 'arm', **raːɦ** 'way', **nʌɦ** 'nail'

Forms of the Stem

§ 167. In Awadhi, nouns generally have two forms: one short and the other long, *e.g.*, **nʌdːiː : nʌdijaː, gɦoːɽaː : gɦoɽʌwaː, naːuː : nʌuaː, naːuni̥ : nʌunijaː, kʌɦaːr : kʌɦʌrʌwaː.** Some nouns have only what seems to be the long form, *e.g.*, **bilʌijaː** Cf. Hin. **bilːiː, ɖebijaː** Cf. Hin. **ɖibːiː.**

(*a*) Of the dialects, Lmp., S., L., U., F., and Br.[1] generally use the short forms. The long is used only familiarly and sometimes has a tinge of inferiority or contempt. It is never used of superiors but only of inferiors and the younger.

(*b*) Fy. and Sl, the two most eastern dialects, have a third form—longer (also called redundant)—of the stem, *e.g.*,

[1] Lakhimpur (Lmp.), Sitapur (S.), Lucknow (L.), Unao (U.), Fatehpur (F.), Bahraich (B.), Barabanki (Br.), Rae Bareli (R.), Gonda (G.), Fyzabad (Fy.), Sultanpur (Sl.), Partabgarh (P.), Allahabad (A.), Baghēlī (Bgh.)

Of these Lmp., S., L., U., and F. are western dialects, B., Br., and R. are Central dialects and G., Fy., Sl., P. and A. are Eastern dialects (see the map)

kutːaː (short) : **kutʌwaː** (long), **kutʌunaː** (longer). They do not use the short form (except when a noun is used to denote a class, *e.g.*, **gɦoːɾʌkẹ kũːdɦeːpʌi baːr hoːt** Fy. 'the horse has mane on his neck'), but use the long very generally and occasionally employ the longer.

§ 168. To form the corresponding long, **-waː** is added to the masculine short stem if it ends in **-aː** (*e.g*, **kutːaː** : **kutʌwaː**), **-ũ** (*e.g.*, **nĩːũ** : **nʌ̃ũwaː**) or **-uː** (*e.g.*, **naːuː** : **nʌuwaː**) the vowel (together with the preceding consonant) being shortened before the termination and **-ʌwaː** if it ends in **-iː** or a consonant (*e.g.*, **dɦoːbiː** : **dɦobiʌwaː**, **peːʈ**, **peʈʌwaː**). To a feminine short stem **-iaː** is added if it ends in a consonant (*e.g*, **sãːk** : **sʌ̃kiaː**), or **aː** if it ends in **-i** (**i̥**) or **iː** (**gaːi** : **gʌiaː**, **raːɟi̥** : **rʌɟiaː**, **nʌdːiː** : **nʌdiaː**) the whispered vowel becoming full and **-iː** being shortened before the termination. If it ends in **-aː**, **-iaː** is substituted for the final vowel (*e.g.*, **buːɾɦaː** : **buɾɦiaː**).

(*a*) The Eastern dialects add **-naː** after masculine short stem ending in **-aː** or in **-u** (*e.g.*, **kũãː** ; **kũʌnaː**, **suaː** : **suʌnaː**, **sukhdeːu** : **sukhdeunaː**). These do not have the 'longer' form.

(*b*) The longer form is arrived at by adding **-waː** to feminine long forms (*e.g.*, **kutijaː** : **kutijʌwaː**) and substituting **-unaː** for **-waː** of masculine long forms (*e.g.*, **ghoɾʌwaː** : **gɦoɾʌunaː**).

§ 169. Modern Awadhi possesses a respectful long or longer form also, *e.g.*, **serʌwaː** : **serʌuː**, **kutʌunaː** : **kutʌunuː**, **kutiaː** : **kutiʌuː**, **gɦoɾiʌwaː** : **gɦoɾiʌuː**, This is made by substituting **-uː** for the **-aː** and **-waː** of the masculine long and masc. and fem. longer forms and by adding **-uː** to the feminine long forms (shortening **-aː** to **-ʌ** before the terminations).

That this form is respectful is shown by the plural verb

e.g., **serʌwaː aːwaː, serʌuː aːjeː ; gɦoɽiʌwaː gʌi, gɦoɽiʌuː gʌĩː.**

NOTE.—The respectful form of long stems is sometimes found in tales and is particularly applied to powerful and big animals like lions and camels. Otherwise its use is rare.

Gender

§ 170 A noun in Awadhi is either masculine or feminine irrespective of the fact whether it denotes an animate or inanimate object. Bases ending in **-i (i̥)** are generally of feminine gender **(seːʈhi̥** 'banker' m.) while those ending in **-u** and **-eː** are of masculine gender. Those which end in **-aː** are generally masculine **(buːɽɦaː** 'old woman' fem.), but most of such as end in **-iaː** are feminine. Similarly **-uː** bases are generally masculine while those in **-iː** are feminine. But such **-iː** bases as denote an agent are masculine, *e.g.*, **maːliː, dɦoːbiː**. Consonantal bases are found under either gender.

(*a*) The gender of nouns is indicated by the masculine or feminine form of the verb that they take *e.g.*, **gɦʌru̥ ɟʌri̥ gaː** 'the house got burnt', **kitaːb ɟʌri̥ gʌi** 'the book was burnt', the first is masculine while the second feminine. It is also indicated by the agreement of the adjective : *e.g.*, **bʌɽaː ʌdʊmiː** 'a tall man', **bʌɽiː meɦʌruaː** 'a tall woman'.

§ 171. Nouns which denote animate beings take their gender according to the sex that they denote, males being denoted by the masculine gender and the females by the feminine gender. For instance : **mʌnʌiː** 'man', **hʌnːaː** 'deer', **bʌrdɦu** 'bullock', **kʌbutːʌr** 'pigeon', are masculine, while **mʊɦruuː** 'woman', **hʌnːiː** 'deer (she)', **gaːi** 'cow', **kʌbutʌriː** 'pigeon (she)' are feminine.

(*a*) Some nouns, however, are either masculine only or feminine only irrespective of the sex that they denote *e.g.*, **suaː** 'parrot', **sãːp** 'serpent', **neuraː** 'mungoose', are always used in the masculine gender while **mʌinaː** 'magpie', **cirʌijaː** 'bird', **chʌpkijaː** 'lizard' are always feminine. These are cases where the speaker is either unable to observe the sex or does not care to do so.

(*b*) Nouns denoting a collection of living beings may be either feminine or masculine, *e.g.*, **bɦiːr** 'rush of men' (fem.), **ɟʌmaːu** 'collection' (masc.), **sʌwaːriː** 'passenger' (fem.)

(*c*) Where living beings of either sex are to be described together, the masculine noun is used *e.g.*, **lʌrikaː kheːlʌti̥ hʌĩ** 'the boys (for boys and girls) are playing', **hʌnːaː bɦaːgːeː** 'the deer fled away', **meːlʌm bʌɦut ʌdəmiː rʌɦʌĩ** 'there were many men (for men and women) in the fair'.

§ 172. Masculine nouns which denote living beings generally form the corresponding feminine by adding terminations.

(A) Nouns ending in **-aː** substitute:

(*a*) **-iː** for **-aː** *e.g.*, **bʌkoraː** 'he-goat', **bʌkəriː** 'she-goat'

(*b*) **-ini̥** for **-aː**, *e.g.*, **bʌnijaː** 'grocer', **bʌnini̥** 'grocer's wife'

(*c*) **-iniː** for **-aː**, *e.g.*, **lʌrikaː** 'boy', **lʌrikiniː** 'girl'

(*d*) **-ijaː** for **-ʌwaː**, *e.g.*, **bʌchʌwaː** 'cow's male calf', **bʌchijaː** 'female calf', **buɽɦʌwaː** 'old man', **buɽɦijaː** 'old woman', or add (*e*)**-ini̥** *e.g.*, **laːlaː** 'a term of respect for a Kayasth', **lʌlaːini̥** 'his wife'.

(B) Nouns ending in **-iː** substitute **-ini̥** for **-iː** *e.g.*, **maːliː** 'gardener', **maːlini̥** 'gardener's wife', or **-iniː** *e.g.*, **hãːthiː** 'elephant', **hʌthiniː** 'she-elephant'.

Nouns ending in **-uː** either substitute **-uni̥** for **uː**, *e.g.*, **naːuː** 'barber', **naːuni̥** or **-ini̥** 'barber's wife', **saːdɦuː** 'saint', **saːdɦini̥** 'female saint', or add **-aːini̥** *e.g.*, **guruː** 'preceptor', **guruaːini̥** 'preceptor's wife'

The feminine of nouns ending in **-eː** is formed by substituting **-ɑːini̥** for **eː**, **pãːɽeː**, **pʌɽɑːini̥**.[1]

(C) Nouns ending in consonants add:

(*a*) **-i**, *e.g.*, **suʌr** 'hog (male)', **soːriː** < **suʌriː**

(*b*) **-ɑːniː**, *e.g.*, **ɟeːʈh** 'elder to husband', **ɟeʈhɑːniː** 'his wife'

(*c*) **-ɑːini̥**, *e.g.*, **pʌɳɖit** : **pʌɳɖitɑːini̥**

(*d*) **-ini̥**, *e.g.*, **sonɑːr** 'goldsmith', **sonɑːrini̥**

(D) Some feminine nouns form the corresponding masculine by adding terminations, *e.g.*, **mʌusiː** 'mother's sister', **mʌusiɑː** 'mother's sister's husband'.

§ 173. Some nouns which denote inanimate objects form the feminine by adding terminations. The feminine in such cases always indicates a smaller thing, *e.g.*, **rʌsːɑː** 'a big rope' : **rʌsːiː** 'a smaller rope', **guɽʌwʌː** 'a doll' : **guɽijɑː** 'a smaller doll', **gʌgʌrɑː** 'a jar', **gʌgʌriː** 'a small jar'.

§ 174. The dialects of other districts closely agree with Lakhimpuri in forming feminine bases. The terminations are the same. Fy. and R., however, substitute **-i** for **-iː** termination added to consonantal bases, *e.g.*, **suʌr** : **suʌri, kukur** : **kukuri.** The final **-i̥** of feminine forms is sometimes audible and sometimes not. For instance: Fy. records **lʌlɑːin** and **koɦɑːrini̥** both.

(*a*) Sl. gives an example of a new masculine formed from the feminine: **bhʌʈhiiɑːrini̥** 'landlady, innkeeper' thence **bɦʌʈhijɑːren** 'landlady's husband'. The corresponding Hindustani word is **bɦʌʈhijɑːrɑː**.

(*b*) Some nouns are used in one gender in one dialect and in another in the other, *e.g.*, **ɑːluː** is masculine in Lmp. while it is feminine in P., **bʌrs (bʌrʌs)** and **gẽːd** are masculine in Lmp. while feminine in R., **buːtɑː** 'strength' masculine in Fy. while **buːt** 'strength' feminine in Lmp.

---

[1] For shortening of the first syllable see Part I § 133.

Number

§ 175. There are two numbers: Singular and Plural. The singular is employed to denote one and the plural to denote more than one.

The plural is generally used to denote one also when respect is to be shown, *e.g.*, **raːjaː aːjeː** 'the king has come'; the verb shows that the noun is plural, **eːk jʌneː aːeː hʌ̃ĩ** 'one person has arrived' is respectful as compared to **eːku̥ jʌnaː aːwaː hʌi.**

§ 176. Words indicating classes of people add **pʌɲc** (after pronouns generally) and **loːg** (after nouns) to form periphrastic plurals, *e.g.*, **hʌm pʌɲc** 'we people', **wʌkiːl loːg** 'the vakils'.

The terminations to form the various cases are added to **pʌɲc** and **loːg** and not to the preceding substantive, *e.g.*, **kʌħaːr loːgʌn mə, hʌm pʌɲcʌn mə.**

The Eastern dialects which possess a plural form in **-ʌi** do not generally use the periphrastic plurals. The central dialects use them.

NOTE.—The form of **pʌɲc** is **pā̃ːc** in the East.

C. ORIGIN : STEM, GENDER AND NUMBER

§ 177. (*a*) Masc. nouns in **-aː** (Early Aw. *ā*) generally go back to Skt. *-akaḥ* M. I. *-aō* type, *e.g.*, **kūpakaḥ* > **kūao* > **kũaː**. The fem. nouns in **-iaː** are derived from Skt.; *-ikā* > M. I. *-iā* > Mod. I. *-ī*. Thence Awadhi has a further elongation in **-aː**. For instance: **khaṭvikā* > **khaṭṭiā* > *khāṭī*: **khʌṭijaː.**

(*b*) Masc. nouns in **-i** (**i̥**) should be connected with the Nom. sg. of *-in* stems in Skt., *e.g.*, *śreṣṭhī* > *sēṭhi* > **seːṭhi̥**. The fem. nouns

(1) either go back to Skt. stems in *-i*, elongated to **ī** in the Pkts. (*agniḥ* > *aggī*) *e.g.*, *aggī*, > **aːgi̥**, *vātāvaliḥ*, > *vāāvalī* > *vāyāalī* > *bayāli* > **bʌjaːri̥**

(2) or are modern substitutes for **j** stems of Hindustani, *e.g.*, *jayō* > *jayu͂* > **jʌj** > **jɜːi**

(3) or are modern forms, *e.g.*, *jari* (N) < *jaṭā* which became *jar* and then *-i* was added as a distinctive feminine ending. Cf. Ar. *khabar* : Aw. **khʌbʌri̥**, Early Braj. *khabariyā*.

(*c*) Masc. nouns in *-ī* go back to Skt. *-in* stems elongated to *-ika-* Pkt. *-ia-* whence *-ī*, *e.g.*, *mālin* replaced by **mālio* : *mālia* > **maːliː**, **paːniː** < *pānīyam*. Feminine nouns in *-ī* come from elongated *-ikā* stems.

(*d*) Masc. nouns in *-u* in Modern Awadhi go back to Nom. sg. of masc. and neuter bases in *-a* (*grāma*, *dēva*) preceded by a single consonant. The Pkts. would give *-ō*, Ap *-u*. This *-u* has survived (*grāmaḥ* > *gāmō* > **gãːu**), the vocalisation remaining because of the previous vowel. Feminine nouns go back to *-vā* forms **naːu** < *nāvā*.

(*e*) Nouns in **-uː** go back to *-ūkō*, *iaō*, *-īaō* (*nāiaō* < *nāpitakaḥ*, *nayanīaō* < *navanītakō*) types if they are masculine and to *-uā* if feminine (**baːruː** < *vālukā*).

NOTE.—The one stem in **-eː** (only **pãːɽeː**) is possibly from a dialect where *-iaō* > **eː**? Or is it connected with *pāṇḍeya* ?

(*f*) Consonantal bases, if masculine, go back to *-a* bases of Skt. which had a consonant before them in M.I. (*e.g.*, *sarpaḥ* > *sappō*. Early Aw. *sãpu* and *sãpa*). The fem. bases are derived from Skt. *-ā* bases (*lajjā* > Early Aw. *lāja* > **laːj**)

NOTE.—Nouns borrowed from other languages such as Persian, English, etc. all come under this scheme.

§ 178. Modern Awadhi is very fond of elongating its noun-stem. Only traces of it can be found in Early Awadhi. This elongation is practically restricted to the old Ardhamāgadhī area, *i.e.*, to the tracts (Kāsī and Kosala) where Ardhamāgadhī was spoken. It is found in proper names only in Bengali, *e.g.*, Hari—Hariyā > **hore** in standard coll., **ɔoirɛ** in East Bengali ; Rāma—*Rāmuā* > **remo** ; *Rasika—Rasikiyā* > **roʃke** ; *Gopāla—Gopāliyā* > **gopɑle**, E.B. **gopʌilɛ**, etc., contempt is implied. Cf. also Western Hindi **kʌnɦʌijɑː** 'Krishṇa'.

What can be the reason of this elongation? We find that there was a suffix *-ko* in I. E., we find the suffix *-ka* working to an extent in Sanskrit and to a larger extent in Iranian. In Skt. it indicated the idea of the diminutive generally either in affection or in contempt. This diminutive form was more generally used in M.I. as is evident from the declension. It was probably to give a body to the form of the noun. A similar idea seems to be at the root of elongation in Modern Awadhi.

§ 179. The three genders of OIA have been reduced to two in all NIA except in Gujrātī and Marāṭhī. In OIA inanimate objects also had an animate gender (masculine or feminine) when they were conceived of as animate *e.g.*, *apaḥ* 'waters' as opposed to *vāri* 'water'. Also some animate objects were neuter when conceived of as inanimate, *e.g.*, *kalatram* 'women folk'. The tendency to conceive inanimate objects as animate seems to be at the basis of the loss of neuter in Awadhi and in other Mod. I.A. languages. The influence of the substratum also may be responsible. Meillet suggests that the loss of gender in Armenian may be due to Caucasian substratum. In India, we find that the languages which are nearest Tibeto-Burman (where there is no grammatical gender) have practically lost the distinction of gender.[1] Pischel[2] notes that the passage of neuter to masculine is common in Māgadhī but rare in other Prakrits.

§ 180. As has been noted, nouns denoting male beings in Awadhi are masculine and female ones feminine. So, as

---

[1] J. Bloch § 180, Chatterji § 483.

[2] § 357.

far as living beings go, the grammatical gender corresponds to the sexes. It is only in cases where the sex is not noted that the gender depends on the form of the noun. For instance:

suaː 'parrot', and **mʌinaː** 'magpie', are masculine, because most of the nouns ending in **-aː** are masculine, while **chʌpkijaː** 'lizard' is feminine as nouns endings in **-iaː** are generally feminine.

§ 181. The gender of nouns denoting inanimate objects is generally masculine or feminine according as they were masculine or feminine in Sanskrit and M. I. For instance: **baːt** is fem. < *vārtā* fem., **hãːth** is masc. < *hastaḥ* masc. But the gender of the predecessor language is retained only if it fits in with the form of the word, otherwise it changes. For instance: **aːgi̥** (< *agniḥ* masc.) is feminine as it ends in **-i̥** which is a characteristic fem. ending. Similarly **jʌi** 'victory' (< *jayaḥ*) is fem. The word for *jambū* is masc. or fem. according to its form (**jʌmunaː** masc., **jʌmuniː** fem., **phʌrẽːdaː** masc.).

§ 182. Sanskrit neuter nouns were already passing to masculine in Māgadhī Prakrit and we find in Apabhraṃśa forms such as *phalu, ghiu, dahiu*. These are masculine in Awadhi also. Where the form of a noun is in conflict with the inherited gender, we find a difference in dialects. For instance: **moːtiː** 'pearl' < *mauktikam*—**mottiō* is masculine in Lakhīmpurī and feminine in Fyzābādī. The fem. gender of **ãːc** 'flame' shows that it became feminine at a stage when it had *-i* with it.

§ 183. The following words are feminine in spite of their form: **naːu** 'boat', **baːsu** 'smell', **maːru** 'beating', **haːru** 'defeat'. **naːu** retains its gender (Skt. *nauḥ*, Pāli *nāvā*), **baːsu** appears to have its gender owing to contamination with **gʌndɦi** which is feminine. Contamination with **jʌi** 'victory' (fm.), may be responsible for the gender of **haːru** and **maːru**.

It may be noted that Hindi abstract nouns are generally feminine, *e.g.*, **kaːṭ** 'cutting', **jiːt** 'victory'.[1]

§ 184. Loan-words from languages which have a neuter gender for inanimate objects (for instance, English) or have a masculine or feminine gender for them (*e.g.*, Arabic) are generally treated of as masculine or feminine according as the nearest corresponding word in Awadhi is masculine or feminine respectively. For instance: **reːl** (rail) is feminine, the general word for a vehicle in Awadhi being **lʌɽhijaː** or **gaːɽiː**, **kitaːb** 'book' (Arabic *kitāb*—masculine) is feminine because of **poːthiː** fem., the masc. word **poːthaː** < *pustakam* being reserved for a longish book. Where Awadhi does not possess a corresponding word, the borrowed noun takes its gender according to its form, *e.g.*, **kumeːṭiː** (Eng. Committee) is feminine as nouns in *-ī* are mostly feminine. If Awadhi does not possess a corresponding word, the borrowed word from a language distinguishing neuters as masculine or feminine retains its gender, *e.g.*, **mʌut** 'death' (Ar. *maut* fem.).

§ 185. The formation of feminine nouns from masculine ones retains traces of Sanskrit feminine affixes. Fem. **-iː** or **-ijaː** for masc. **-aː** represents *-ikā* : *akaḥ* type in such pairs as **bʌkoraː : bʌkoriː**, **bʌchʌwaː : bʌchijaː** and *-ikā* : *-aḥ* type in such pairs as **suʌr : soːriː.** For the rest **-ni̥** or **-niː** forms the distinctive feminine suffix. For instance: **maːliː : maːlini̥** represent *mālikaḥ* : *mālinikā* type. In some feminine forms the final **-iː** has been preserved (which shows that they are probably later formations) while in others it has survived as **-i̥**. This **-i̥** already is losing ground in some dialects (See § 174).

§ 186. The device of indicating the plural by periphrastic use of the words '**loːg**' and '**pʌɲc**' is modern and has been brought about by necessity. The noun in the direct generally has no distinction in form for number, but a

[1] I owe this suggestion to Prof. Bloch.

distinction becomes necessary, particularly when a class of beings is to be denoted. Thus we find that the periphrastic plural noun is most used in Western dialects of Awadhi where the noun does not keep any distinction of number. All the dialects use the periphrastic plural for pronouns of the 1st person and 2nd person where **hʌm** and **tum** (or **tũː**) are used for both numbers.

loːg (Skt. *lōka*) 'people', **pʌɲc paːc** (Skt. *pañca*) 'people' is generally used for a number of people. It is not used to denote objects. This is an instance of the distinction between animate and inanimate and of the influence of sub-stratum languages.

Case

A. Early Awadhi

§ 187. Like Modern Awadhi, Early Awadhi has two cases of the noun—direct and oblique.

The direct is used generally as

(*a*) the subject, *e.g.*,

rānī utara māna saũ dīnhā 'the queen answered proudly' (J. 140).

cāri mīta kabi Muhamada pāyẽ 'the poet Muhammad found four friends' (J. 31).

kāha na pāvaku jāri saku 'what cannot fire burn' (T. 176).

lasanu ki rahihahī dhāma 'will Lakshmana stay at home?' (T. 176).

sōvai kũara lihaī dhanakōrā 'the prince slept with the beloved' (N. 9).

sugãdha surañga puhupa tahã phūlaī 'flowers of good smell and colour were blooming there' (N. 9).

(*b*) the inanimate direct object, *e.g.*,

katahũ pakhanḍī kāṭha nacāvā 'at some places the hypocrite (juggler) was putting some wood in circular motion' (J. 59).

pahilai tehi kara nāũ lei 'at first having remembered His name' (J. 2).

jaũ na rāmu bana jāhī 'If Rāma does not go to the forest' (T. 170).

lāgi dēna sikha 'began to offer advice' (T. 176). *baranaũ rājakuũra kī bānī* 'I describe the nature of the Prince' (N. 9).

rūpa kanaka kahũ gaṛhaī sonārā 'in some places the goldsmiths were making ornaments of gold and silver' (N. 14).

(*c*) the vocative, *e.g.*,

ē rānī' 'o queen!' (J.)

taba jāyehu bhaiyā! 'O son! then you may go' (T. 178).

mātu 'mother', *hō bhāī* 'O brother!' (N.)

NOTE.—Sometimes the direct is used to indicate the animate object *e.g.*, *savāraũ karatārū* 'I bear in mind the Creator' (J. 2), and it comes also as the first member of genitive compounds *e.g.*, *āgamanu-sūcaka ahahī̃* 'are the indicators of the arrival' (T. 160), *nagaru-banāvũ* 'the decoration of the city' (T. 162), or as genitive (*e.g.*, *sarisa kapāsu* 'like the cotton-plant' (T. 3.) or dative, *e.g.*, *nṛpa jubarāju rāma kahũ dēhū* 'O king give the viceroyalty to Rāma (T. 158).

§ 188. The oblique is used with or without post-positions. For instance:

(*a*) with post-positions:

Singular—

jaga kahã 'to the world' (J. 17), *uparōhita kahũ hari* 'having kidnapped the priest' (T. 74), *sūraja kahã* 'to the sun' (N. 3); *kēli saũ* 'with play' (J. 49) *ratana tē̃* 'with jewel' (T. 15), *hiē tē̃* 'with heart' (T. 24), *gāya sõ* 'with the cow' (N. 9); *gosāī̃ kēra* 'of the lord' (J. 27), *gāḍhē kai sāthī* 'friend in difficulty' (J. 24), *daī kara nāũ* 'the name of the Creator' (J. 41.), *bharata kara sammata* 'the approval of Bharata' (T. 176), *savati kai kathā* 'the tales of co-wives' (T. 164), *cērī kaikei kēri* 'the maid of Kaikēī' (T. 162), *tapī kara ajñā* 'the order of the hermit' (N. 5), *bārī kī nāī* 'in the manner of a garden' (N. 6); *purāna mahā* 'in the Purāṇa' (J. 11), *bhōga mahū* 'in the enjoyment' (T. 12), *phulavārī mahū* 'in the garden' (N. 6).

Plural—

paṅkhinha kahā 'to the birds' (J. 126), *pāḍitanha (kabitanha) saū bhajā* 'spoke to the Pandits' (J. 33), *pakhurinha kai chātē* 'bands of petals' (J. 48), *purukhanha kai ḍīṭhī* 'glance of men' (J. 254), *lōganha pahī* 'in the nearness of the people' (T.), *sakhina sō̃* 'from the friends' (N. 93), *raghubaṁsinha maha* 'among those of the family of Raghu' (T. 108), *kandaranhi mahu* 'in the caves' (T. 40), *biprānha para* 'on the Brahmins' (T. 92), *adharana para* 'on the lower lips' (N. 49).

(*b*) without postpositions:

Singular—

ākusa gaja nāvai 'he tames the elephant with the goad' (J. 39), *bhāya nāma japata* 'utters the name with feeling' (T. 16), *hērahī cakhu nārī* 'the women look with the eye' (J. 49), *ārana rahaī* '(they) live in the forest' (J. 4), *baiṭha ahaū baṭachāhī* 'I am sitting in the shade of the banyan tree' (T. 27), *pūniū karā* 'digit of the full moon night' (J. 25), *cāṭahī karai* '(He) makes the ant' (J. 9), *uparohitahī dēkha jaba rājā* 'when the king saw the priest' (T. 75), *piyahī rijhāi* 'having pleased the beloved' (N. 9), *maī carita sañchēpahi kahā* 'I described the deeds briefly' (T. 49), *sōnai sājā* 'decked with gold' (J. 67), *purukhahi cāhia ūca hiāū* 'lofty heart (courage) is necessary for man' (J. 363), *cōrahī rāti na bhāvā* 'the night is not in the liking of the thief' (T. 162), *samudahī pārā* 'across the ocean' (J. 23), *mōtihi jō malīna hō karā* 'if the glow of the pearl becomes dim' (J. 90), *rāmahī ṭīkā* 'the coronation of Rāma' (T. 159), *ā̃bahi ḍābha na kōi* '(if) there is no blossom in mango' (J. 29), *kuā̃hi khā̃ḍa bahu mēli* 'having put a great deal of sugar in the well' (J. 52), *mā̃thai mōrē* 'on my forehead' (J. 89), *gunahi manu rātā* 'the mind was absorbed in merit' (T. 6), *babūrahī phala lāgahī* 'the fruits come on the *babūl* tree' (N.).

Plural—

saṭhanhi rāma-sammukha kō karata 'who would have turned the wicked towards Rāma' (T. 284), *nayanahī ḍharahī mōti* 'pearls fall from the eyes' (J. 127), *mukhani kahī nija hōnī* 'narrated their birth with mouths' (T. 4), *adharana hā̃sī* 'smiled with lips' (N.), *muni bhāinha asīsa dīnhī* 'the sage gave blessing to the brothers' (T. 102), *paṭavana gharabārā* 'in the houses of the braiders' (J. 56), *sacētanha karanī* 'the deeds of the sensible' (T. 40), *sakhinha lāja* 'modesty of friends' (J. 510), *na nayananha ā̃sū* 'nor a tear in eyes' (J. 242), *jūhī bakucanha lāvā* 'the jasmine flower was planted in plenties' (J. 53), *jhalakā pāyanha jhalakata* 'the blisters shine on the feet' (T. 237), *janaka pīḍhana baiṭhārē* 'Janaka seated them on wooden seats' (T. 142), *mērē hāthana* 'in my hands' (N.).

§ 189. The oblique is also used as the agent of past participle verbs in all the texts. For instance:

rājai sunā 'the king heard' (J. 84)
rājaī putra biāhā 'the king married the son' (N. 7)
pāvā sakhinha 'the friends obtained' (J. 104)
sakhinha kahā 'the friends said' (J. 103)
rājanha sunī 'the kings heard' (J. 83)
siddhanha baḍa mānā 'the great considered (him) to be big' (J. 31)
surana astuti kīnhā 'the gods prayed' (T. 39)
muninha kīrati gāī 'the sages sang the fame' (T. 10)
lōgana jānā 'the people thought' (N.)
sakhina pūchā 'the friends asked' (N.)

sakhiyana pahicānā ' the friends recognised ' (N.).

NOTE.—The oblique singular in *-hi, -i* is used to indicate the inanimate direct object also in a few instances.

bāsuki jāi patārahī cāpā ' Vāsukī went and got hold of the nether-world ' (J. 19), *bajarahi māri uḍāī* ' he turns to pieces the thunderbolt ' (J. 9), *banahī sidhāē* ' went to forest ' (T. 222).

§ 190. Terminations of Cases

(*a*) *Direct Singular*—The bases ending in *-a* form their direct singular either by substituting *-u* for *-a* or like bases ending in other vowels use the base itself as this case.

(*b*) *Direct Plural*—Bases ending in *-a* have a direct plural case in *-ē* (*e.g.*, *tārā* : *tārē*, *chātā* : *chātē* *sapanā* : *sapanē*) and the feminine bases ending in *-a* have a plural in *-ī* (*asīsa* : *asīsaī*, *bhaũha* : *bhaũhaī* (J. 86), *bāṭa* : *bāṭaī* (J. 110), *mūrata* : *mūrataī* (N.). Otherwise the base itself is used as this case.

Traces of *-i* ending for *-a* bases [corresponding to Eastern Awadhi -ʌi ' see § 197 (*b*)] are found in J. *saba rupavantai mukha jō̃hahī* ' all those who have forms look up to the face ', (p. 29), *sapata dīpa kē barai onāhī* ' the birdegrooms of all the seven Dvīpas come up ' (J. 83), *āgai saguna saguniai tākā* ' those who knew the omens saw the omens in front ' (J. 265).

(*c*) *Oblique singular*—the most common form of this is the base. There are two other forms :

1. ending in *-hi*, *-hī*, *-i* *-ī* (shortening the preceding vowel if it is long) for all bases,
2. ending in *-ē* for bases in *-a* and *-ā*.

(*d*) *Oblique plural*—this ends in *-nha*, *-nhã*, *-na*, *-nhi*, *-nhī*, *-ni*. The termination *-nha*, *-nhã* is common in Jāyasī and Tulsī, while *-na* in Nūr Muhammad.

Those in *-nhi*, *-nhī*, *-ni* are rare and are found in Tulsī only.

§ 191. I have taken statistics of the forms of the oblique case in the first five hundred lines of each of the three texts. The results are shown below.

(*a*) Jāyasī

Obl. sg.—there are 30 cases of obl. sg. (excepting the base form used as such) of which 22 end in *-hi*, 4 in *-hī*, 3 in *-i* and 1 in *-hā̃*. The last case (*ēkai nayanāhā̃* 'by one eye only' p 29) has *-ā̃* for *-i* or *ī* (which is expected) probably for the sake of rhyme in the second half of the line (*māhā̃*).

obl. pl.—there are 18 cases of obl. pl. of which 13 end in *-nha*, 4 in *-na* and 1 in *-nhi*. The last case is :

janaũ sabhā deotanhi kai jūrī, p. 55 'as if an assembly of the gods had assembled'. Here it appears that the feminine gender of the word *sabhā* has affected the form of *deotanhi* (expected *deotanha*).

(*b*) Tulsī

Obl. sg.—there are 20 cases of obl. sg. (excepting the base form used as such) of which 9 end in *-hi* and 11 in *-hī*.

Obl. pl.—of the 6 cases 4 end in *-nha* and 2 in *-ni*. The latter are the cases where the connected feminine words appear to have influenced the form of the oblique, *e.g.*, *nija nija mukhani kahī nija hōnī*, p. 4 'have described their birth by their own mouths'—here *hōnī* is feminine ; *sabarī gīdha susēvakani sugati dīnhi raghunātha*, p. 15 'the Lord of the Raghus gave bliss to his good servants the S'abara woman and the vulture'—here *sugati* is feminine.

But in one case *muninha prathama harikīrati gāī*, p. 10 'the hermits first sang the fame of Hari' the feminine gender of *kīrati* has not affected the form of the oblique.

Also in the following cases of *-i* forms no contamination of any feminine noun is present :

karakamalani 'lotus-hands' p. 202, *sīsani* 'on the heads' p. 202, *nija āsramani* 'in their hermitages' p. 210, *sabanhi* 'all', p. 210, *sēvakani* 'to the servants' p. 230, *nayanani* 'with eyes', p. 239, *kōlanhi* 'the *kōls*', p. 245, *-sīkani* 'with drops', p. 247 and *saṭhanhi* 'the rogues', p. 284.

(*c*) Nūr Muhammad—

obl. sg.—There are 30 cases of obl. sg. (excepting the base form used as such) of which 5 end in *-hi*, 4 in ***-hĭ***, 1 in *-i*, 7 in *-ĭ*, 1 in *-ē* and 12 in *-ĕ*.

obl. pl.—There are 12 cases all of which end in *-na*. We thus see that Nūr Muhammad comes very near the practice of Modern Awadhi in dispensing with the *-h-* of the termination.

B. Modern Awadhi

§ 192. There are two cases : direct and oblique.

The direct is used to denote (*a*) the subject (*b*) the inanimate direct object and (*c*) the vocative. For instance:

(*a*) **kutʌwɑː mʌri̥ gɑː** 'the dog died', **kutʌwɑː mʌri geː** 'the dogs died', **gɑːi ɟɑːti̥ hʌi** 'the cow is going', **gɑːiː ɟɑːtiː hʌĩ** 'the cows are going'

(*b*) **gɦʌru̥ no bɑːrʌu** 'do not burn the house', **gɦʌr no ɟɑːrʌu** 'do not burn the houses'; **ɑ̃ːkhi̥ dɦoːi ɖɑːrɑu** 'wash the eye', **ɑ̃ːkhiː dɦoːi ɖɑːrʌu** 'wash the eyes'

(*c*) **lʌrikʌwɑː reː** 'O boy'.

§ 193. The direct is used to denote an animate object in the case of the following verbs:

1. 'to milk'—*e.g.*, **gɑːi** (or) **gɑːiː duɦʌu** 'milk the cow (or) cows'.
2. 'to beg for'—*e.g.*, **rɑːɟʌ sẹ bɦʌĩsi̥** (or) **bɦʌĩsiː mɑ̃ːgeu** 'did you beg for the buffalo (or) buffaloes from the king?'
3. 'to take'—*e.g.*, **tum gʌiɑː leːu mʌĩ bɦʌĩsiː** 'you take the cow, and I the buffaloes'.
4. 'to bring'—*e.g.*, **mʌɟuːr lɑːeu?** 'did you bring the labourers?'
5. 'to give'—*e.g.*, **hʌm kɑː cɑːri̥ ʌdəmiː deːu** 'give me four men'.

6. 'to steal'—*e.g.*, **uː chʌgoriː coraːwʌtḁ rʌɦʌi** 'he was stealing some goats'.
7. 'to stake, to win or to lose a wager'—*e.g.*, **uː ʌpʌnḁ meɦʌruaː dãːupo dɦʌrti hʌi** 'he stakes his wife' **ɟo hʌm bɦʌĩsiː haːriː** 'if I lose the buffaloes', **tʌu tum gaːiː ɟiːtʌu** 'then you win the cows'.
8. 'to capture'—*e.g.*, **gɦoːɽaː pʌkʌrti hʌi** 'he catches the horses', **uː ghoɽʌwaː dɦʌe liɦesḁ** 'he caught hold of the horse'.
9. 'to kill as game'—*e.g.*, **uː mʌchoriː maːrti hʌi** 'he catches the fish'.
10. 'to eat as meat'—*e.g.*, **uː bʌkoraː khaːtḁ hʌi** 'he eats goat.'

§ 194. The oblique is used with the various postpositions. For instance:

(*a*) the singular
with **ko** (accusative)
tum ʌponeːlʌrikaːko maːreu 'you beat your son',
with **se** (instrumental)
mʌĩ ɖʌɳɖʌ sḙ maːreũ 'I beat *with* the stick',
with **ko** (dative)
uː mʌ̃gʌtʌ ko khaːi ko diɦisḁ 'he gave *to* the beggar something to eat',
with **se** (ablative)
birʌwʌ sḙ paːtaː gireː 'the leaves fell *from* the tree',
with **ki** (genitive)
raːm ki lʌũɽiaː marḁ gʌi 'Rām's daughter died'.
with **mo** (locative)
ʌmkhorʌwʌ mo duːdɦṳ naːiː hʌi 'there is no milk *in* the cup'.

(*b*) the plural
with **ko** (accusative)

ʌponeː lʌrikʌn kə kheːdi̥ diɦini̥ ɦʌi 'he has turned out his sons'.

with **se** (instrumental)

phuːlʌn se̥ bʌgiaː mʌɦʌkʌti̥ ɦʌi 'the garden is fragrant *with* the flowers',

with **se** (ablative)

birʌwʌn se̥ paːtaː ɟɦʌreː 'the leaves fell *off* the trees'.

with **ko** (genitive)

kutʌwʌn ke nʌɦ pʌin hoːti̥ hʌĩ 'the nails *of* dogs are very sharp'.

with **pʌr** (locative)

cirʌijʌn pʌr chʌrːaː no cʌlaːoː 'do not fire shot *at* the birds'.

§ 195. The oblique is used without a post-position in the following instances.

1. When a word meaning 'for the sake of' or 'near, with' follows, *e.g.*, **tʌnikʌi baːt khaːtir** 'for the sake of a little thing', **lʌrikʌn khaːtir** 'for the sake of boys', **meɦʌruaː tiːr** 'near a woman', **aːgiː tiːr** 'near the fire.'

2. When a word meaning 'through (the way of)' follows, *e.g.*, **dɦũaːraː ɖʌgʌr** 'through the ventilator', **pʌnaːrʌn ɖʌgʌr** 'through the pipes'.

3 When the noun is repeated and gives a locative sense, *e.g.*, **gɦʌr gɦʌr lʌɽaːiː bɦʌi** 'there was a quarrel in every home', **gãːwʌn gãːwʌn gɦuːmen** 'we roamed in all villages'.

4. When the noun means 'force' and gives an instrumental sense, *e.g.*, **ɟʌbʌrɟʌstiː uʈhaːi laːwaː** 'he brought away by force', **mʌi kaː ɟuːtʌn piːʈisi̥** 'he beat me with shoes'.

(*a*) The oblique plural is optionally employed as the subject of such transitive verbs as are based on the participle, *e.g.*, **bʌmɦʌnʌn** (or **baːmɦʌn**)

sʌb kaːmṳ bigaːri̥ dihini̥ 'the Brahmins spoiled the whole business'.

§ 196. The dialects of other districts agree with Lakhimpuri in the use of the direct and oblique cases.

In the Eastern dialects the obl. pl. case is regularly employed as the subject, *e.g.*, **gʌijʌn khaihʌĩ** 'the cows will eat', **bhʌuɟʌijʌn kʌhaː** 'the sisters-in-law said'.

Terminations of Cases

§ 197. (*a*) *Direct singular*—The simple noun-stem, without any terminations, forms this case, excepting masculine stems ending in consonants to which **-ṳ** is added, *e.g.*, **sãːp : sãːpṳ.**

(*b*) *Direct plural*—All the dialects use the simple noun-stem for this case, except that the feminine stems ending in **-i (i̥)** substitute **-iː** for **-i (i̥)** and the feminine stems ending in consonants add **-ʌi.** For instance **gaːri : gaːriː, ãːkhi̥ : ãːkhiː ; bʌɟaːr : bʌɟaːrʌi; bʌrʌs : bʌrosʌi; kitaːb : kitaːbʌi.**

The dialects of Bahraich (B.), Gonda (G.), Fyzabad (Fy.), Sultanpur (Sl.) and Partabgarh (P.) have a general direct plural case ending in **-ʌi** which is more often used than the simple noun-stem. For instance : **ʈhʌkurowaː : ʈhʌkurwʌi; corowaː : corowʌi; lʌrikʌi niːko ʌhʌĩ** 'the boys are good' (Sl.), **lʌrikiʌi niːko ʌhʌĩ** 'the girls are good' **kutʌunʌi mʌri̥ geː** 'the dogs died'.

§ 198. (*a*) *Oblique singular*—All the dialects use the simple noun-stem as this case except that the final **-i̥** is pronounced as **i.** The bases in **u,** however, substitute **-i** for **-u,** *e.g.*, **pãːu** dir. sg., **pãːi** obl. sg., except **gãːu** which remains so in both the cases.

NOTE.—The obl. sg. of consonantal bases ends in the consonant but in slack pronunciation a final **-o** is audible. It is impossible to know if like dir. sg. **-ṳ**, this **-o** is whispered (see § 115).

(*b*) *Oblique plural*—In all the dialects this is formed by adding (1) **-ʌn** to stems ending in a consonant (*e.g.*, **sɑ̃ːp : sɑ̃ːpʌn; sĩːg : sĩːgʌn**) or in **-u** (the **-u-** then changes to **-w̃**[1]) (*e.g.* **gɑ̃ːũ : gɑ̃ːw̃ʌn; naːũ : nɑ̃ːw̃ʌn**) and (2) **-n** to stems ending in other vowels; the whispered vowel becomes full and the long becomes short (*e.g.*, **kũɑ̃ː : kũʌ̃n; ɑ̃ːkhi̥ : ɑ̃ːkhin; nʌdːiː : nʌdːin; naːuː : naːun; pɑ̃ːɽeː : pɑ̃ːɽen**).

NOTE.—The dialects Fy., Sl. and P. appear to add **-ʌn** (instead of **-n**) to **-uː** stems also (*e.g.*, **ɖaːkuː : ɖʌkuʌn**). This, however, is a case of changing the stem to its lengthened form in **-aː** and not of any difference in formation (**ɖaːkuː > ɖʌkuaː** and then the termination **-n** is added).

Other Cases

§ 199. The dialects possess a vocative plural case which is used to call more than one person. It is formed by adding **-ʌu** to a stem ending in a consonant or **-u**, and **-u** to a noun ending in any other vowel. Before the termination, the vowel undergoes the modification as mentioned above § 198 (*b*). For instance :

kʌɦaːr : kʌɦaːrʌn. The enclitics **reː** (masc.) and **riː** (fem.) are often added after this case, or **oreː** (masc.) **oriː** (fem.) before it (*e.g.*, **oreː kʌɦaːrʌu paːlkiː uʈhaːoː** 'O! *kahars* lift up the palanquin' **oriː məɦʌruʌu gʌunʌiː gaːoː** 'O! women sing the songs'.

(*a*) All the dialects possess this case but such of them as have a direct plural case in **-ʌi** § 197 (*b*) use it oftener as the vocative plural. For instance : **kʌɦaːrʌu** or **kʌɦʌrəwʌi pʌlkijaː uʈhaːoː meɦərʌruʌi gʌunʌiː gaːoː.** These dialects differ also in the use of the vocative enclitic inasmuch as they use **reː** or **oreː** irrespective of the gender of the noun being masculine or feminine. G. and B. avoid using the enclitic altogether.

---

[1] Part I § 154.

§ 200. The nouns **jʌnaː** 'person' and **lʌrikaː baːraː** 'issue' have the direct plural case as **jʌneː** and **lʌrikaː baːreː** in all the dialects. Similarly the nouns **sʌu** 'hundred', **paːu** 'a quarter', **nãːũ** 'name' **dãːũ** 'chance' have **sʌi, paːi, nãːi, dãːi** respectively as their direct plural case. The simple stem does not serve as this case for **jʌnaː** and **lʌrikaːbaːra**, but it does optionally in case of **sʌu, paːu, nãːũ, dãːũ.**

§ 201. An instrumental case ending in **-en** is found in such adverbial expressions as **pijaːsen** 'out of thirst', **bɦuːkhen** 'out of hunger', **ɖʌren** 'out of fear', used with or without the enclitic **maːreː** 'on account of' after them, *e.g.*, **hʌm pijaːsen mʌri̥ gen** or **hʌm pijaːsen maːreː mʌri̥ gen** 'I died out of thirst'.

The Eastern dialects do not possess this case and use the oblique plural for it (Lmp. **pijaːsen** Fy. **pijaːsʌn,** Lmp. **bɦuːkhen,** P. **bɦuːkhʌn.)**

§ 202. A case expressing motion towards a thing is found ending in **-ʌi** (after nouns ending in a consonant or **u**) or **-i** (after those ending in any other vowel) in such usages as **ui gɦʌrʌi geː** 'he went home', **lʌrikaː mʌdʌrsʌi aːeː** 'the boys came to the school', **tum iː gãːwʌi aːjeu** 'you came to this village'. This is used without the postposition.

The Eastern dialects do not possess this case and use the locative in -eː (mentioned below) instead. For instance: Sl. records **gɦʌreː gaː,** while a specimen of 17 miles West of it records **gɦʌrʌi**. G. has **jʌun kuchu̥ mũɦeː aːwaː** 'whatever came *to* the mouth'.

(*a*) The consonantal bases indicating inanimate objects have a locative case (by adding **-e**) in all the dialects. This form is mostly used for the locative (generally without postpositions) but sometimes to indicate other case-relations also. For instance: **ui duaːreː bʌiʈh hʌĩ** 'he is sitting outside (*on* the door)' **ɖãːʈu̥ hʌmoreː maːtheː pʌraː** 'the fine fell to my lot (*on* my forehead)' **waː hʌməreː sʌmʌɦeː nikʌri̥ aːiː** 'she came out *in* my presence', **gɦaːmem na nikʌrʌu** 'do not come out *in* the sun', **hʌm tum kaː sʌpənem deːkhen** 'I saw you *in* a dream', **raːjʌke̥ kaːnem baːt kʌɦi deːu** 'Speak the word *in* the king's ear', **ui kʌuneː kaːme kə geː** '*for* what business has he gone?' **duaːre kə geː,** 'he has gone outside', **bʌraːt jʌnwaːsek aːiː** 'the bridegroom's party came *to* the reception-house', **bijaːɦek sʌrʌnjaːmu̥ kʌrʌu** 'make the arrangements *for* the marriage'.

C. Origin

§ 203. The direct case is the result of the old Nominative-accusative, the direct singular of the singular and the plural of the plural. Thus :

sãːpu̥ represents Skt. *sarpaḥ* : *sarpam*, Pkt. *sappō* : *sappam*, Ap. and E. Aw. *sãpu*, while

sãːp represents Skt. *sarpāh* ; *sarpān*, Pkt. *sappā* : *sappē*, Ap. *sãpā*, E. Aw. *sãpa*.

ãːkhi̥ represents Skt. *akṣi*, Pkt. *akkhī*, Ap. *ãkhi*, E. Aw. *ãkhi*.

ãːkhiː represents Skt. *akṣiṇi*, Pkt, *akkhīiṃ*, Ap. *akkhīï*, E. Aw. *ãkhī*.

§ 204. The direct plural of feminine consonantal bases in Western Awadhi and of all bases in Eastern Awadhi should be derived from the ancient neuter plural ending in *-āni*. The adoption of this neuter ending for nouns of animate gender is attested by some Skt. texts and by Bhāsa's Prakrit[1]. Western Awadhi stands between Eastern Awadhi and Western Hindi in this respect. Eastern Awadhi has it for all nouns, Western Awadhi for consonantal feminine bases only while Western Hindi for all feminine bases, *e.g.*, Hindustānī **lʌɽkiː : lʌɽkijãː; ɔːrʌt : ɔːrətʌĩ**.

[1] Printz : Bhāsa's Prakrit, pp. 26-27.

§ 205. The direct plural of *-ā* bases (*citērā* : *citērē*) in *ē* goes back to the Pkt. accusative ending in *-ē*[1], and pronominal Nominative ending *-ē*. It represents the type *citrakarakaḥ* : *citrakarakāḥ* : *citrakarakān, cittayarаō* : *cittayaraē*. Such forms, however, are very rare in Awadhi and might be loan words from Western dialects. Chatterji derives these from the ancient instrumental plural forms.

§ 206. In Modern Awadhi the traces of distinction between the direct sg. and dir. pl. are found in the case of fem. bases ending in -i̥ (i), *e.g.* **ã:khi̥** 'eye' **ã:khi:** 'eyes' and masc. consonantal bases (**sã:pu̥** 'snake' : **sã:p** 'snakes'). This is explained by the difference in the origin of the two forms : **ã:khi̥** < M.I. *akkhī* and **ã:khi:** < M.I. *akkhīiṃ* or in the case of ancient masculine and fem. forms < *-īō*, *e.g.*, *aggīō*—modern **a:gi:** 'fires', **sã:pu̥** < M.I. *sappō* and **sã:p** < M.I. *sappā*.

Distinction between the direct sg. and the obl. sg. is found only in the case of masc. consonantal bases (*e.g.*, **sã:pu̥** : **sã:p**) and the fem. bases in -i̥ (i). This is also explained by a difference in their origin, the direct being the original nom.-acc.-voc. and the oblique the ancient genitive or dative.

Though other nouns have lost the distinctions to-day, the traces which we find above clearly point to distinctions in the origin.

§ 207. What is the origin of Early Awadhi obl. sg. *-hi* ? Chatterji (§499) explains the *-hi* by a supposed I.E. **-dhi* (> Greek *-θi*), Pāli *-dhi*, a suggestion put forward originally by Hoernle and accepted by Grierson. But this case is not operative in Pāli (the only available form is *sabbadhi* quoted by Wackernagel). It is, therefore, unlikely that such a common case as *-hi* which we find in abundance in Early Awadhi should come from *-dhi*. I have, therefore,

---

[1] Pischel Gram. Prakrit, sec. 367a.

preferred to derive it from the pronominal locative in -*smin* > *mhi* > *hī̃*, *hi*.

I suggested elsewhere[1] that the Early Awadhi -*hī̃*, -*hi* might have come from the ancient plural instrumental ending -*bhis*. That, however, does not explain the nasalisation. Besides the transfer of a plural termination to singular remains unexplained[2].

§ 208. The derivation of the Modern Aw. obl. sg. may be had from the ancient genitive or the dative. The distinction between these two cases is not found in nouns other than -*a* bases in MIA. It would, however, be preferable to derive it from the genitive which was in more common use, *gharassa* > *gharasa* > *gharaha* > Early Aw. *ghara* > Modern Awadhi **gɦʌr**.

The passage of M.I. -*ss*- to late M.I. -*h*- and then its disappearance has a parallel in the forms of the Simple Future : *karissai* > *karihai* > Early Aw. *karihi* and Mod. Aw. **kʌriː**.

As Turner has shown[3], a sound in terminations is likely to have a more rapid (and possibly different) change than the corresponding sound in the body of words.

NOTE.—The nouns in -*u* (**gãːũ** etc.) are all in the dir. case, and the dir. is used with postpositions also. But the use of the dir. thus in place of the obl. appears to be quite a recent development. Even to-day we find some traces of the obl. sg. here: **hʌmaːr ɟiu** dir. but **hʌmʌreː jiː maː, naːũ : naːĩ, daːũ : daːĩ**.

§ 209. The oblique plural in Modern Awadhi in -**n**, Early Awadhī -*nha*, -*nhã*, -*nhi*, -*nhī̃*, -*ni* is based on the ancient genitive plural, Skt. -*nām* : Pkt. -*ṇaṃ*. The -*i* is possibly due to contamination with feminine forms (see §191).

---

[1] Noun-declension in the Rāmāyan of Tulsīdās (Ind. Ant. LII, 1923, p. 5.).

[2] Prof. Bloch sees the possibility of a secondary affix in—*hī̃*.

[3] R. L. Turner : J. R. A. S., 1927, p. 227 and ff., also see J. Bloch : B. S. L. 1928, p. 4.

An objection to this derivation of the oblique plural is that the *-n* of terminations survives in most modern languages only as a simple nasalisation (Marāṭhī *dēvāṃ*, Hindustānī **ghoṛõ**, Rājasthānī **ghoṛã**). But we find the full *n* surviving in the oblique of some Indo-Aryan languages, *viz.*, in Kāshmīrī (L.S.I., VIII, part II, page 271), Sindhī (L.S.I., VIII, part I, p. 25), Singhalese and Gypsy and to some extent in Bengali (Chatterji, sec. 486).

The *n* of neuter plural ending in *-āni*, *-īni* has been lost, but there is a difference between the treatment of *-āni*, *-īni* on the one hand and of *-ānām*, etc., on the other, noticeable in the Pkts. The former became *-āiṃ*, *-īiṃ*, etc., while the latter are found as *āṇaṃ*, *īṇaṃ*, etc. This differentiation has been kept up by Modern Awadhi **-ʌi** < *-āni* and **-n** < *-nām*.

The Early Awadhi *-h* and *-hi* can be explained only as addition to *-na*, owing to the influence of the general oblique singular in *-hi*. Aw. *-nh* could come from *-nn-* also (cf. Marāṭhī *dinkala* : Pkt. *diṇṇa,* Braj **diːnñ**) but no ancient case form in *-nn-* is available.

§ 210. The vocative plural case of Modern Awadhi in **-ʌu** (corresponding with Western Hindi **-oː**) is derived from ancient Nominative-vocative plus the enclitic *-hō*. This enclitic was used in the Prakrit and Apabhraṃśa and by constant use came to form a part of the substantive. The loss of *-h-* and the reduction of *-ō* to **-u** are normal features.

§ 211. The plurals **jʌneː** (sg. **jʌnaː**) < *janaē* and **baːreː** (sg. **baːraː**) < *bālaē* are loan-words from a dialect where *-ā* bases form the plural in *-ē* (Cf. §200). A larger use of these plurals is found in Tulsīdās.

§ 212. The plurals **sʌi** (< *śatāni*), **naːĩ** (< *nāmāni*), **daːĩ** (< *dāmāni*), **paːĩ** (< *pādāni*) are survivals of ancient neuter plurals.

§ 213. The instrumental in *-en* goes back to *-ēna* with elongated forms **ḍaraēṇa* > **ḍʌren** 'out of fear.' The survival of nasal after a front vowel *-ē-* has a parallel in Kāshmīrī also[1].

§ 214. The Modern Awadhi case in **-ʌi** expressing motion towards a thing, represented by Early Awadhi *-hĩ*, *-hi*, *-i* goes back to Skt. ending *-smin* which is found in Prakrits variously as *-mmi* and *-mhĩ* added to nouns alternately with *-ē* (*puttē* or *puttamhi*, *puttammi*). Nouns with this termination indicate other senses, besides locative, in Early Awadhi—chiefly Objective-dative. Modern Western Awadhi has retained this case for expressing motion only. Eastern Awadhi uses the locative in **-eː** to denote this sense.

This case is represented by the dative of Sanskrit (*gṛhāya gataḥ*); but *-āya* would phonetically become *-ā*, and not *-ahi* or *-ai*.

§ 215. The locative case in **-eː** of Modern Awadhi, a few cases of which are found in early Awadhi as well, goes back to the ancient locative singular in *-ē* of elongated forms (*dvārakē*: **duaːreː**). The final *-ē* of *dvārē*, *gṛhē*, etc., would phonetically become *-i*[2] in modern IA, but *-aē* of middle-Indian would survive as *-ē*. The predominantly locative use of this case in Modern Awadhi warrants the derivation from an ancient Locative.

[1] J. Bloch : B. S. L. 1928 p. 5.

[2] as attested by old Rājasthānī texts.

CHAPTER II

ADJECTIVES

§ 216. In Awadhi, the adjectives are very seldom employed and so we find a very small vocabulary of qualitative adjectives. The pronominal adjectives of possession and of quantity are generally in use; they will be treated of under Pronouns. The numerals also have been dealt with separately.

In *Gulgulāwālī kathā* (Texts No. I) in the first paragraph we find 36 nouns but only three adjectives—all pronominal, and eight numerals. Similarly whenever specimens of Awadhi have been searched through it is very seldom that the adjectives have been found.

Gender and Number

A. EARLY AWADHI.

§ 217. (*a*) J. has two genders of the adjective and generally the feminine adjective is used with the feminine noun, *e.g.*, *ghani ībilī* 'dense *Imlī*', *ghana tāra* 'dense palm' (p. 42), *hariara akāsa* 'green sky' (p. 40), *bipati bahu ghanī* 'very dense (great) calamity' (p. 5), *karui bēli* 'bitter creeper' (p. 6), *āgari karā* 'best digit' (p. 22), *khiranī mīṭhī* 'sweet *khirnī*' (p. 41); but *navaũ pauri para* 'on the 9th gatepost' (p. 64), *kinhesi ũkha mīṭha rasa-bharī* 'he created sugarcane, sweet and juicy' (p. 6), where a masculine adjective has been used with a feminine noun.

The *-ā* adjective changes to *-ē* in plural direct and obl. and sg. obl., *e.g.*, *jei pāḍhata sikhē* 'those who are well-read and learned' (p. 15), *dui dīpaka ũjiārē* 'two bright lamps' (p. 25), *apanē apanē ghara* 'in one's own house' (p. 67); *kaunau harē dhūma au kārē* 'some of them were green, dusky and black' (p. 69), *dēkhi tinha ṭhāḍhē* 'seeing them standing' (p. 63).

(*b*) T. has two genders and the distinction is rigorously maintained. For instance:

āgila kāju 'coming business' (p. 162), *āgili bāta* 'coming thing' (p. 164), *dukhu baṛa* 'heavy misery' (p. 165), *sapatha baṛi* 'a heavy curse' (p. 168), *bidhi ati dāhina* 'the Creator is very favourable' (p. 163), *dāhini ā̃khi* 'right eye' (p. 165), *manabhāvati bātā* 'a pleasant thing' (p. 167), *manabhāvata (jī kā)* 'a pleasant (boon)' (p. 168), *avadha ujāri* 'desolate Ayodhyā' (p. 169).

The *-ā* adjective changes to *-ē* for plural direct and obl. and for singular obl. For instance: *rāma-abhiṣēka suhāvā* 'beautiful coronation of Rāma' (p. 160), *bacana suhāē* 'beautiful words' (p. 159), *pachilē pahara* in the last watch (of night)' (p 172).

The adjective has the case-ending like Mod. Awadhi (vide § 221) when the noun is understood, *e.g.*, *baṛehī abhiṣēkū* 'coronation to the elder' (p. 161).

The plural noun when indicating a single individual or thing (vide § 175) has a plural adjective, *e.g.*, *bharata bhōrē* 'the simple Bharata' (p. 171).

(*c*) N. observes the distinction of gender only in *-ā* and *-ī* adjectives. For instance: *piyārā* : *piyārī*, *gāḍhī gā̃ṭha* 'a difficult knot' (p. 4), *bhalī kīrata* 'good fame' (p. 8). In other cases the masculine form is used for the fem. noun also, *e.g.*, *cintā āna* 'other anxiety' (p. 11), *nā ati lā̃ba* 'not very tall (princess)' (p. 19), *mīṭha kōi likhanī* 'the pen (fem.) may become sweet' (p. 13).

The *-ā* adjective changes to *-ē* for the plural, *e.g.*, (*tārē*) *ū̃jiārē* 'bright stars'.

B. Modern Awadhi

§ 218. In Lakhīmpurī, adjectives as a rule have two genders: masculine and feminine, *e.g.*, **nīk** : **nīkị** 'good',

niːk lʌrikaː 'good boy', **niːki̥ lʌũɽijaː** 'good girl'.

The feminine is formed by

(*a*) adding **-i̥** to the masculine ending in a consonant, *e.g.*, **giːl** : **giːli̥** 'wet', **buːɽɦ** : **buːɽɦi̥** 'old', **paːtʌr** : **paːtʌri̥** 'thin'.

(*b*) changing **-aː** to **-iː** in case of a masculine ending in **-aː**, *e.g.*, **thoːraː** : **thoːriː** 'little', **bʌɽaː** : **bʌɽiː** 'big', **lʌmbaː** : **lʌmbiː** 'tall'.

Other adjectives (in **-i̥ baːdi̥** 'useless', in **-iː bɦaːriː** 'heavy', in **-uː kʌruː** 'bitter') do not change for gender.

NOTE.—The change for gender in adjectives in **-uː** (**kʌruː** : **kʌruiː**) sometimes noticed in the speech of the literate, is due to the influence of the literary speech Hindustānī (Hin. **kʌɽuaː** : **kʌɽuiː**).

Adjectives of Persian origin, *e.g.*, **khʌraːb** < *kharāb* **laːjʌk** < *lāyaq*, **laːl** < *lāl*, **sʌpeːt** < *safaid* do not change for gender. The following also do not change for gender:

uɟaːr 'desolate', **kʌriaː** 'black'.

§ 219. The distinction of gender is lost progressively as we proceed to the East. The Western dialects (Lmp. S., L., U. and F.) observe it as detailed above. For instance:

L. has **choːʈ bɦaːiː** 'younger brother' (masc.), **choːʈi̥ raːɟi̥** 'small kingdom' (fem.); **thoːriː bʌɦut ciːɟ bʌsto** 'a few things' (fem.), **thoːraː khaːi leːiː** 'I should eat a little' (masc.). U. has **tʌb sʌroɦʌɟʌirisʌɦiːhoːi laːgĩː** 'then the sisters-in-law began to be angry' (fem.), **buːɽɦ kʌɦʌi laːg** 'the old people began to say' (masc.), **uː ʈhaːɽɦ bɦaː** 'he stood (lit. became standing)' (Masc.).

F. has **buːɽɦ aːdmiː rʌɦʌĩ** 'there were old people' (masc.), **buːɽɦiː meɦoraːruː rʌɦʌĩ** 'there were old women' (fem.).

The Central dialects (B., Br. and R.) are less particular about gender than the Western dialects. For instance:

B. a specimen of 12 miles West to Bahraich records a change for feminine in **hʌm miṭhaːiː ʌb sʌigʌri̥ choːṛi̥ diːn kʌrʌb** 'I shall now leave more (a larger quantity of) sweetmeats' and no change in **pʌɦil meɦaːruː** 'the first wife'. While a specimen of 20 miles East to Bahraich records change for feminine in **-aː** adjectives (*e.g.*, **bɦʌtoraː kaːṭiː, kʌljugʌɦiː** 'the killer of the husband, belonging to *Kaliyuga* (feminine)', it does not record any change in consonantal adjectives (*e.g.*, **hʌmaːr ʌurʌt** 'my wife', **hʌmaːr jindʌgiː** 'my life' (both feminine).

Br. and R. have no change in the singular of consonantal adjectives (*e.g.*, **paːtʌr swãːṭaː** 'a thin stick' (masculine), **paːtʌr chʌṛiː** 'a thin stick' (feminine), **ciːkʌn loːṭaː** 'a smooth jug' (masculine), **ciːkʌn bʌṭuiː** 'a smooth pot' (feminine), but do have it in the plural (*e.g.*, **gʌgoriː juːṛ hʌi** 'the jar is cool' (sg. feminine), **gʌgoriː juːṛiː hʌĩ** 'the jars are cool' (pl. feminine). The distinction of gender is, however, observed in the case of **-aː** adjectives, *e.g.*, **lʌmbaː** (masculine) **lʌmbiː** (feminine) 'tall'.

The Eastern dialects (G., Fy., Sl., P. and A.) do not observe clearly any distinction of gender in adjective. For instance :

G. a specimen of Balrampur records **rʌṇḍiː cʌlaː gʌi**, 'the prostitute went away', where **cʌlaː** (masculine) qualifies (feminine) **rʌṇḍiː** without any change.

Fy. **niːk lʌrikaː** 'good boy' (masculine), **niːk lʌrikiniː** 'good girl' (feminine), **giːl maːṭiː** 'wet clay' (feminine).

Sl. **iː paːniː ṭhʌṇḍɦ ʌɦʌi** 'this water is cold' (feminine), **iː pisaːn giːl ʌɦʌi** 'this flour is wet' (masculine), **iː saːniː giːl ʌɦʌi** 'this fodder is wet' (feminine).

P. **hʌmaːr sʌmʌi rʌɦiː** 'my time was' (feminine).

The Eastern dialects avoid the use of **-aː** (masculine), **-iː** (feminine) (**baṛaː : bʌṛiː**) adjectives by substituting consonantal adjectives for them, *e.g.*, **niːk** for **ʌcːhiː**; **lãːb** for **lʌmbaː, lʌmbiː** and **jeːṭh** for **bʌṛaː, bʌṛiː**).

NOTE—1. In none of the dialects, is the distinction of gender based on the animate or inanimate nature of the object qualified. For instance the adjective **paːtʌr** 'thin' is applied to masculine nouns (animate or inanimate) in Lakhīmpurī and **paːtʌri̥** 'thin' to feminine nouns——**paːtʌr mʌnʌiː** 'a thin man', **paːtʌr bãːs** 'a thin bamboo', **paːtʌri̥ meɦʌruaː** 'a thin woman', **paːtʌri̥ laːṭhiː** 'a thin stick'.

NOTE—2. When a plural noun is used to show respect for an individual, the adjective qualifying it is plural (*e.g.*, **iː thaːneːdaːr bʌṛeː hʌĩ ui choːṭ** 'this police-officer is high, that is low'; here the adjectives qualifying the police-officer are in the plural).

§ 220. The dialectal differences regarding the case and number are generally similar to those of gender—as we proceed towards the East the distinction no longer exists. B., for instance, does not modify the adjective: **raːm ʌcːhaː** (expected **ʌcːheː**) **raːjaː rʌɦeː, khʌṭːaː** (expected **khʌṭːeː**) **aːme kə bʌɦaːi deːu, kũaːri̥** (expected **kũaːriː**) **biṭijʌn kə no maːrʌu.** Of the Central dialects R. and Br. modify the adjective: Br. **juːṛ** : **juːṛeː, goːr** : **goːreː**, R. **suːkh** : **suːkheː** : **suːkhiː**). The modification of **-aː** adjectives (to **-eː**) is noticed in P. and Fy. here and there, otherwise it is absent in all Eastern dialects.

§ 221. The adjective may be used as a noun when the noun used previously is understood in subsequent uses, *e.g.*, **kʌun lʌrikaː aːwaː** 'which son has come?', **bʌṛaː aːwaː hʌi** 'the big (one) has come'.

In such cases the adjective has the necessary case modifications like nouns, *e.g.*, **ʌcːheː lʌrikaː aːi gʌjeː, khʌraːb aːwʌti̥ hoiɦʌĩ** 'good boys have arrived, the bad (ones) must be coming'. **ʌcːhen kə aːwʌi diɦeu khʌraː-**

bʌn ko durijaɪi diheu 'let the good (ones) come in, turn the bad (ones) out'.

NOTE.—Here the plural obl. terminations **-n** and **-ʌn** have been added to the adjectives. It should be noticed that the plural termination is added to the modified form where it exists, *e.g.*, **ʌcɪheɪ** : **ʌcɪhen** in Lakhīmpurī but **ʌcɪhaɪ** : **ʌcɪhʌn** in Fy.

Stem

A. EARLY AWADHI

§ 222. In all the texts the short forms of *-ā* and *-ī* adjectives (*-a* and *-i*) are frequently found, particularly in Tulsīdās in whom the long (*-ā* and *-ī*) are comparatively rare. For instance :

(*a*) J. *ū̃cī pavãrī ū̃ca abāsū* 'high was the gate and high the residence' (p. 55), *koi bhikhāri* 'some beggar' (p. 5), *rājā bhaē bhikhārī* 'the king became a beggar' (p. 60), *saba ṭhāḍha pahārā* 'all the hills standing' (p. 69).

(*b*) T. *sayāni* 'clever', *ujāri* 'desolate', *lagana bhali* 'auspicious time' (p. 161), *phuri bānī* 'true speech' (p. 164), *lāgi madhu* 'the honey which was present' (p. 162), *candini rāti* 'moon-lit night' (p. 162), *nīci karatūtī* 'lowly action' (p. 162), *anamani hasi* 'thou art dejected (p. 162), *kāri janu sā̃pini*, 'as if a black serpent' (p. 162), *jhūṭhi phuri bātā* 'false and true words' (p. 163), *karui mai māī* 'I am bitter, O mother!' (p. 163), *baṛi cūka* 'great mistake' (p. 164), *rāni risāni* 'the angry queen' (p. 167), *sūdha subhāvā* 'a straightforward nature' (p. 165), *bhōra subhāū* 'a simple nature' (p. 168), *baṛa chōṭa* 'big and small' (p. 170), *ṭhāṛhī ṭhāṛhi* 'standing'.

(*c*) N. *ahai ṭhāṛha* 'is standing' (p. 4), *kou ṭhāṛhā hai* 'somebody is standing' (p. 16), *prēma gāṛhā* and *gāṛha* 'great (lit. thick) affection' (p. 13), *rāja rahā mīṭhā* 'sweet was the kingship' (p. 20) and *mīṭha hōi likhanī* 'the pen may become sweet' (p. 20).

When the feminine adjective in *-ī* is shortened in N. it takes the same form as the masculine, *e.g.*, *pahilī rāta* 'first night' (p. 10) and *pakila rāta* 'first night' (p. 12).

B. MODERN AWADHI.

§ 223. The **-aː** (feminine **-iː**) adjectives have sometimes long forms and longer forms, like the noun, *e.g.*, **bʌɽaː : bʌɽʌkaː, bʌɽakʌwaː, bʌɽiː : bʌɽʌkiː : bʌɽʌkijaː.** The Eastern dialects use these long and longer forms oftener than the Western dialects. The **-k-** of these long forms is pronounced long whenever particular emphasis is to be put on the attribute, *e.g.*, **bʌɽʌkaː** or **bʌɽʌkːaː, bʌɽʌkiː : bʌɽʌkːiː.**

NOTE.—Sometimes, particularly in Bgh., an elongation in **-ɦaː** is found, *e.g.* **purʌniɦaː, rogiɦaː.**

§ 224. In Lakhīmpurī, masculine adjectives ending in a consonant (*e.g.*, **kũaːr** 'unmarried') and in **-aː** (*e.g.*, **bʌɽaː** 'big') and feminine adjectives in **-i̥** (*e.g.*, **kũaːri̥** 'unmarried') have modified forms to express the direct plural and oblique singular and plural cases.

The modified forms are obtained by adding **-eː** to consonantal adjectives (**kũaːreː**) and by substituting **-eː** for **-aː** in the case of **-aː** adjectives (**bʌɽeː**) and **-iː** for **-i̥** in the case of **-i̥** adjectives (**kũaːriː**).

The following instances illustrate the use of the modified forms attributively:

Direct singular—

kũaːreː lʌrikaː aːjeː 'the unmarried boys came', **bʌɽeː birowaː giri̥ geː** 'the big trees have fallen down', **kũaːriː lʌũɽijaː aːĩː** 'the unmarried girls came.'

Oblique singular—

kũaːreː lʌrikʌ ko bolaːoː 'call the unmarried boy',
bʌɽeː lʌrikʌ ko bolaːoː 'call the older boy',
kũaːriː lʌũɽijʌ ko bolaːoː 'call the unmarried girl'.

Oblique plural—

kũaːreː lʌrikʌn ke bolaːoː 'call the unmarried boys',

bʌɽeː lʌrikʌn ke bolaːoː 'call the older boys',

kũaːriː lʌũɽijʌn ke bolaːoː 'call the unmarried girls'.

NOTE.—The unmodified form of masculine consonantal adjectives **(kũaːr)** is also used to qualify a direct plural case of the noun, *e.g.*, **kũaːr lʌrikaː aːeː** 'the unmarried boys came'.

The modified form is less in use predicatively; it comes with feminine always **(ui lʌũɽijaː kũaːriː hʌĩ** 'those girls are unmarried', **ui lʌũɽijʌn ke kũaːriː bʌtaːwʌti̥ hʌĩ** 'they say those girls are unmarried') and with the masculine Nom. plural when the adjective is an **-aː** base **(ui lʌrikaː ʌcːheː hʌĩ** 'those boys are good'). Everywhere else the unmodified adjective is used.

Degrees of Comparison

§ 225. Awadhi has no separate forms for the degrees of comparison in adjective.

The sense of the comparative is expressed by (*a*) putting the compared (standard) thing in the ablative (obl. plur. **se)** (*e.g.*, **iu lʌrikaː ui seː goːr hʌi** 'this boy is fairer than that', **uː lʌrikạː iː seː kʌriaː hʌi** 'that boy is darker than this') or by (*b*) using some such word as **ɟaːdaː, bʌɦut, sʌigʌr** meaning 'more' and **kʌm** meaning 'less' (*e.g.*, **iu lʌrikaː ui seː ɟaːdaː goːr hʌi** 'this boy is fairer than that', **uː lʌrika iː seː kʌm goːr hʌi** 'that boy is less fair than this').

The comparison may be made with the rest of the class, *e.g.*, **iu lʌrikaː sʌb seː goːr hʌi** 'this boy is fairer than all the rest.

The sense of the superlative is expressed by the simple adjective preceded by such expressions as **sʌb maː** 'amongst all', **sʌb ʌdmin mo** 'amongst all men', **sʌb lʌrikʌn mo** 'amongst all boys', *e.g.*, **iu lʌrikaː sʌb maː niːk hʌi** 'this boy is the best of all boys', Fy. **iː lʌrikaː sʌbʌn maː goːr hʌi** 'this boy is fairest of all', B. and G. **iː lʌrikaː sʌb maː goroɦʌr hʌi** 'this boy is the fairest of all'—**goroɦʌr** means 'fair'.

C. Origin.

§ 226. The origin of Awadhi adjectives is closely allied to that of the nouns. In OIA and MIA the adjective, unless compounded with the substantive, had the modifications of gender, number and case of the noun qualified. In Modern Awadhi we have traces only of that. It is only the *-ā* adjective which keeps up the modifications to some extent in all Awadhi dialects, in others the base form is generally used.

The masculine oblique singular in **-eː** goes back to *-akē* ending like the noun (vide § 215) and the masculine plural in **-eː** to the Nom. Acc. plural in *-ē* (Cf. **jʌneː** and pronominal forms). The obl. singular feminine *-ī* and feminine plural in **iː** have the same explanation as the corresponding forms of the noun (vide § 203).

The retention of distinction of gender in *-ā*, *-ī* forms in Eastern Awadhi is intelligible from the fact that a large number of these are ancient participles (past passive) in *-aka* elongated forms. We shall find that the distinction of gender in the Verb is maintained only in Participial forms.

We should note that the direct singular and direct plural of consonantal adjectives have different origins, like the noun, **kũaːr** < *kumāraḥ*, **kũaːr** < *kumārāḥ*.

The practice of elongating the adjective-stem accords with the general practice of elongating the noun (vide § 177). The long consonant in these forms is used for emphasis.

CHAPTER III

Numerals

Cardinals

§ 227. The following are the cardinal numbers :—

Number.	Hindustānī.	Lakhīmpurī.	Other dialects.	Early Awadhi.
1	**eːk**	**eːk**	U. **jaːk**	J., T., N. *ēka*.
2	**doː**	**dui**		J., T., N. *dui*.
3	**tiːn**	**tiːni̥**		T. tīni, N. *tīna*.
4	**caːr**	**caːri̥**	Br. **caːr**	J., T. *cāri*, N. *cāra* (but *cāriu*).
5	**pãːc**	**pãːc**	Br. **paːn**	J., T., N. *pãca*.
6	**cheɦ, cheː**	**chaː**	...	T. *cha*.
7	**saːt**	**saːt**	...	J. *sāta*, N. *sāta*.
8	**aːṭh**	**aːṭh**	...	N. *āṭha*.
9	**nɔ**	**nʌu**	...	J., N. *nau*.
10	**dʌs**	**dʌs**	...	J., T., N. *dasa*.
11	**gjaːrʌɦ**	**geːraː**	Fy. **gjaːraː** Br. **egjaːraː** P **egːjaːraː**	N. *egayāraha*.

12	**baːrʌɦ**	**baːraː**	...	J., N. *bāraha.*
13	**teːrʌɦ**	**teːraː**	R. **tjaːraː**	N. *tēraha.*
14	**cɔdʌɦ**	**cʌudaː**	...	J., T. *caudaha*, T. *cāridasa.*
15	**pʌndrʌɦ**	**pʌndʌraː**	...	
16	**soːlʌɦ**	**soːraː**	R. **swaːraː**; Fy. **soːrʌs** ...	J., T. *sōraha*
17	**sʌtːrʌɦ**	**sʌtːʌraː**	R. **sʌtʌraː**	N. *satraha.*
18	**ʌṭhaːrʌɦ**	**ʌṭhaːraː**	...	J., N. *aṭhāraha.*
19	**unːiːs**	**onʌis** ...	B., P. **onːʌis**	
20	**biːs**	**biːs**	...	J. *bīsa.*
21	**ikːiːs**	**ekʌis** ..	B. **ekːʌis.**; G. **ʌkːʌis.**	
22	**baːiːs**	**baːis**	...	N. *bāisa.*
23	**teːiːs**	**teːis**		
24	**cɔbiːs**	**cʌubis**	R. **cʌuːbis**	J. *caubisa.*
25	**pʌcːiːs**	**pʌciːs**	...	T. *pacīsa* (-ā).
26	**chʌbːiːs**	**chʌbːis**		
27	**sʌtːaːiːs**	**sʌtːaːis**		
28	**ʌṭːhaːiːs**	**ʌṭːhaːis**		
29	**untiːs**	**ontis**	Fy. **onʌtːis**; G. **wʌntis** ...	N. *vontisa.*

Number.	Hindustānī.	Lakhīmpurī.	Other dialects of Modern Awadhi.	Early Awadhi.
30	**tiːɛ**	**tiːs**	...	N. *tīsa.*
31	**ikʌtːiːs**	**ekətis**	...	T. *ikatīsa* (-*ā*).
32	**bʌtːiːs**	**bʌtːis**	...	J. *batīsa.*
33	**tẽːtiːs**	**tẽːtis**	...	J. *tītisa.*
34	**cɔ̃tiːs**	**cʌ̃ũtis**		
35	**pæ̃tiːs**	**pʌ̃ĩtis**		
36	**chʌtːiːs**	**chʌtːis**	...	N. *chatīsa.*
37	**sæ̃tiːs**	**sʌĩtis**		
38	**ʌɽtiːs**	**ʌɽtis**		
39	**untaːliːs**	**ontaːlis**		
40	**caːliːs**	**caːlis**	...	N. *cālisa.*
41	**iktaːliːs**	**ekətaːlis**		
42	**bʌjaːliːs**	**bʌjaːlis**		
43	**tẽːtaːliːs**	**tẽtaːlis**	R. **tirtaːlis**	
44	**cɔwaːliːs**	**cʌuaːlis**		
45	**pæ̃taːliːs**	**pʌ̃itaːlis**		
46	**chijaːliːs**	**chijaːlis**	B". **chijãːlis**	
47	**sæ̃taːliːs**	**sʌ̃ĩtaːlis**	...	J. *sartālisa.*
48	**ʌɽtaːliːs**	**ʌɽtaːlis**	...	N. *aṛhatālisa*
49	**uncaːs**	**oncaːs**	R. **ekːʌmpʌcaːs**	

50	pʌcaːs	pʌcaːs	...	T. *pacāsa.*
51	ikːjaːwʌn	ekːjaːwʌn	R. ekːaːwʌn	
52	baːwʌn	baːwʌn		
53	tireːpʌn	tirpʌn		
54	cowʌn	cʌuʌn		
55	pʌchpʌn	pʌchpʌn	G. pʌŋcaːwʌn	
56	chʌpːʌn	chʌpːʌn	...	J. *chappana, chapana.*
57	sʌtːaːwʌn	sʌtːaːwʌn	...	N. *sattāvana.*
58	ʌʈːhaːwʌn	ʌʈːhaːwʌn		
59	unsʌʈh	onsʌʈhi̥	P. onsʌʈh	
60	saːʈh	saːʈhi̥	...	N. *sāṭha.*
61	iksʌʈh	ekəsʌʈhi̥		
62	baːsʌʈh	baːsʌʈhi̥		
63	tireːsʌʈh	tirsʌʈhi̥	...	N. *trīsaṭha*
64	cɔ̃sʌʈh	cʌ̃ũsʌʈhi̥		
65	pæ̃sʌʈh	pʌ̃ĩsʌʈhi̥		
66	chijaːsʌʈh	chãːchʌʈhi̥	B. chaːsʌʈhi̥	
67	sʌrsʌʈh	sʌrsʌʈhi̥		
68	ʌɽsʌʈh	ʌrsʌʈhi̥		
69	unɦʌtːʌr	onɦʌtːʌri̥		
70	sʌtːʌr	sʌtːʌri̥	...	N. *sattara.*
71	ikhʌtːʌr	ekhʌtːʌri̥		
72	bʌɦʌtːʌr	bʌɦʌtːʌri̥		
73	tiɦʌtːʌr	tiɦʌtːʌri̥		
74	cɔɦʌtːʌr	cʌuɦʌtːʌɽi̥		

Number.	Hindustānī.	Lakhīmpurī.	Other dialects of Mod. Awadhi.	Early Awadhī.
75	pichʌtːʌr	pʌchʌtːʌri̥		
76	chiɦʌtːʌr	chiʌtːʌri̥	Br. cheɦʌtːʌri̥. P. cheɦʌtːʌr.	
77	sʌtəɦʌtːʌr	sʌthʌtːʌri̥		
78	ʌṭhʌtːʌr	ʌṭhʌtːʌri̥		
79	unːaːsiː	onːaːsiː	Fy. onaːsiː	
80	ʌsːiː	ʌsːiː		
81	ikːjaːsiː	ekːjaːsiː...	Br. ekːaːsiː Fy. ekaːsiː	
82	bʌjaːsiː	bʌjaːsiː		
83	tiraːsiː	tiraːsiː		
84	cɔraːsiː	cʌuraːsiː	...	J. *caurāsī*.
85	picːjaːsiː	pʌcaːsiː		
86	chijaːsiː	chiaːsiː		
87	sʌtːaːsiː	sʌtːaːsi	Fy. sʌtaːsi	
88	ʌṭhaːsiː	ʌṭːhaːsiː	Fy. ʌṭhaːsiː	
89	nʌwaːsiː	nʌwaːsiː		
90	nʌvːeː	nʌbːeː		

91	**ikːjaːnveː**	**ekːjaːnbeː** ...	Fy. **ekaːnbeː** Br. **ekːaːnbeː** G. **ekːʌnːʌjeː**	
92	**baːnveː**	**baːnbeː** ...	Br. **baːnːʌbeː** Fy. **baːnʌbeː** G. **baːnːʌjeː**	
93	**tiraːnveː**	**tiraːnbeː** ...		
94	**cɔraːnveː**	**cʌuraːnbeː**		
95	**picːjaːnveː**	**pʌɲcaːnbeː**	Fy. **pʌcaːnʌbeː**	
96	**chijaːnveː**	**chaːnbeː**		J. *chā̃nabai.*
97	**sʌtːaːnveː**	**sʌtːaːnbeː**	P. **sʌntaːnbeː**	
98	**ʌʈːhaːnveː**	**ʌʈːhaːnbeː**		
99	**ninːjaːnveː**	**ninːaːnbeː**	G. **ninːaːnʌjeː**	
100	**sɔ** ...	sg. **sʌu** pl. **sʌi**	...	T. *saya*, N. *sau*, *sai*,
1000	**hʌzaːr**	**hʌɟaːr**	...	J. *sahasa.*
100000	**laːkh**	**laːkh**	...	J., T. *lākha.*
10000000	**kʌroːɽ**	**kʌroːri̥**	...	J. *krōḍa*, J. *karōri*, T. *karōrī.*

NOTE.—(1) The Eastern dialects have lost final **-i̥** of the numerals.
(2) From 91 to 99 G. has numerals ending in **-ʌjeː**.

§ 228. As the cardinal numbers as taught at the schools have a tendency to influence and even replace the dialectal forms, I have given the standard (Hindustānī) forms side by side with Awadhi forms.

The people generally count only upto 20, onwards they count by twenties, *e.g.*, **dui biːsiː ʌu caːri̥** '44 *i.e.*, two twenties and four', Fy., **caːr biːsiː rupʌijaː rʌɦiː hʌi** 'there were eighty rupees'. Even within twenty, numbers near twenty are expressed by the help of twenty, *e.g.*, R. **eːk kʌm biːs** 'nineteen'

There is generally the practice of adding **ʈhʌĩ, ʈhʌur** or **ʈhiː** as help-words after numbers, *e.g.*, R. **caːr ʈhʌĩː lʌrikaː** 'four boys', **paːɳʈhʌur rupʌijaː** 'fives rupees', P. **eːk ʈhiː dʌrkhaːs** 'one petition'. A parallel usage in Bengali and Bihari may be noted.

Ordinals

A. Early Awadhi

§ 229. The following cases of the use of ordinal numbers are found in the early Awadhi texts:

(*a*) Jāyasī—

pahila 'first', *dōsara* 'second' (p. 1), with which compare *akasara* 'alone' (p. 401), *dōsari disa* 'on the second side' (p. 561), *tisarai āi cadhāī pūjā* 'the third came and offered the worship' (p. 427), *tēsari hatiā* 'third murder' (p. 470), *chaṭhi rāti* 'sixth night' (p. 80), *navaū̃ pauri* 'the ninth threshold', *dasaū̃ duārā* 'the tenth gate' (p. 64), *dūija* '2nd date' (p. 21), *caudasi* '14th date' (p. 21)

(*b*) Tulsī—

ihai saguna phala dūsara nāhī̃ 'this is just the result of the omen, none else' (p. 160), *dūsara bara* 'the second boon' (p. 168), *dharamu nahī̃ dūjā* 'not a second Dharma' (p. 181), *tiya dūjī* 'second (another) woman' (p. 244), *anubhaeu na dūjē* 'no one else has experienced' (p. 158), *tisarē pahara* 'in the third watch' p. (237). *cauthē pana* 'in the fourth period of age' (p. 174); similarly Greaves[1] cites *dūsari*, *tīsara*, *tīsari*, *tījai*, *cauthi*, *chaṭha*, *chaṭhē̃*, *sātava*, *āṭhava*.

(*c*) Nūr Muhammad

pahila khaṇḍa 'first part' (p. 15), *pahilī rāta ki mūrata* 'the image of the first night' (p. 10), *dūsara rāta* 'second night' (p. 10), *dūsara sakhī* 'another friend' (p. 116), *dūsara*, *tīsara*, *cauthā* 'second, third, fourth' (p. 71), *dusarē tisarē cauthē bana* 'in the second, third, fourth forest' (p. 27), *cauthē khaṇḍa* 'in the fourth part' (p. 15), *pācaē̃*, *chaṭaē̃*, *sataē̃ bana* 'in the fifth, sixth, seventh forest' (p. 28), *dasaī̃ dvāra na khōlata kōī* 'no one opens the tenth door' (p. 46), *akasara* 'alone' (p. 51), *dūjē̃* 'a second time' (p. 59), *duija kai candū* 'the moon of the second date' (p. 38).

B. Modern Awadhi

§ 230. The ordinal numbers in Lakhīmpurī, have two genders, masculine and feminine, like the adjective. Cardinal numbers five and onwards from seven form their ordinals by adding **-ʌwãː** (masculine) or **-ʌĩː** (-**wãː** and **-ĩː** if the number ends in **-aː**), *e.g.*, **pãːc** : **pʌ̃cʌwãː** : **pʌ̃cʌĩː, baːis** : **bʌisʌwãː** : **bʌisʌĩː**.

Note.—11th to 18th, however, insert a short **-ɦ-** in the termination, *e.g.*, **geːraː** : **gerʌɦwãː** : **gerʌɦĩː**

All the other dialects form the ordinals like Lakhīmpurī. Fy., however, does not add **-ɦ-** in 11th and 12th, and B. and G. add **-ɦʌ** before **-wãː (gerʌɦʌwãː)**.

(*a*) Lakhīmpurī forms other ordinals as below :

1st **pʌɦil,** 2nd **doːsʌr,** 3rd **tiːsʌr**, 4th **cʌuth**, 6th **chʌṭːhaː** and their feminines like ordinary adjectives (§ 218).

Fy. has an ordinary form for the 1st **(ekʌwaː** : **ekʌiː)** and the 6th also **(chʌṭhʌwãː** : **chʌṭhʌĩː)**. For 2nd

[1] E. Greaves : Grammar of the Ramayan, p. 17

and 3rd it has **dusarkaː** and **tisarkaː** (**dusarkiː** and **tisarkiː**). Similarly R., Br., P. and Sl.

(*b*) The dates of the Saṃvat era have the semi-tatsama forms (**duiȷ, tiːȷ, cauthī, pañcimīː chaṭhi, satːimiː, aṭːimiː, naumiː, dasmiː** etc.) as contrasted with those of the Muslim and Christian eras where the ordinary forms are used, *e.g.*, **sataĩː** '7th day of Muharram'.

(*c*) The order of sons and daughters (1st son, 2nd son etc.) is generally expressed by the following words:

eldest	**baṛaː**	:	**baṛiː**
2nd	**mãːjɦil**	:	**mãjɦilakiː**
3rd	**sañjɦil**	:	**sãjɦilakiː**
youngest	**choːṭ**	:	**choṭokiː**

Multiplicatives Etc.

§ 231. Awadhi does not possess special numerals of the type of twice or thrice etc. The sense is, however, given by some word expressive of time usually, for instance, **daːĩ** or **daːũ** in Lakhīmpurī and R., **pheːraː, baːr, baːjiː, daːĩ, daːũ, berijaː** in Fy., **beːr, dãːũ** in B. and **baːjiː, dawar, daphe̤ː** in G. Twice is thus resolved to 'two times' **dui daːĩ**; thrice to 'three times' **tiːni̥ daːĩ**. For example:

ham sab janeː din bɦare me eːkai dui daːĩ khaːiti̥ hai, saːɦeb loːg tau pãːc pãːc chaːhaː daːũ ṭipan uṛaːwati̥ haĩ 'we eat our food only once or twice a day while the Sahebs eat tiffin five or six times'.

(*a*) The following words are used for the multiplication tables, in Lakhīmpurī:—

eːkan 'once', **duːniː** 'twice', **tijãː** 'thrice', **cakːuː** 'four times', **pañceː** 'five times', **chakaː** 'six times', **sateː** 'seven times', **aṭhe** 'eight times', **nawãː** 'nine times', **dasaːwan** 'ten times'.

Other dialects use similar words. For instance, Fy. has: **duːniː, tijaːĩː** or **tirakːaː, cauk, pañjeː paceː, chaːk, nawãːĩː, daɦaːĩː**.

(*b*) For expressing the idea of 'double', 'treble', etc., the word **-gunaː** is added to two, three etc., *e.g.*, **dugunaː** 'double', **tigunaː** 'treble', **cʌugunaː** 'four times'. R. adds **-gun,** *e.g.*, **dugun.**

Tulsī—*cauguna cāu* 'four-fold enthusiasm' (p. 177).

(*c*) The following are the most common fractional numerals:—

$\frac{1}{4}$	**pʌuwaː** or **paːu**	$\frac{3}{4}$	**pʌun**		
$\frac{1}{2}$	**ʌdːɦaː** or **aːdɦaː**	$1\frac{1}{4}$	**sʌwaːu** or **sʌwʌijaː**		
$1\frac{1}{2}$	**ɖeːɽɦ** or **ɖeuɽɦ**	$2\frac{1}{2}$	**ʌɽɦaːiː** or **ʌɽɦʌijaː**		

Tulsī—*pahara arhāī* 'for $2\frac{1}{2}$ watches of the day' (p. 266).

C Origin

§ 232. The history of IA numerals has been fully discussed by Bloch (Langue Marathe §§ 211-226) and Chatterji (§§ 511-536). Awadhi numerals do not present any special peculiarities. The following points, however, may be noted:—

(*a*) Cardinals—11 (Br. **egjaːrəː,** P. **egːjaːraː**) in some dialects preserves the original initial *e* while in others it has been lost (Lmp. **geːraː**) leaving only an influence on the vowel of the second syllable (*ekā*—).

16 (Fy **soːrʌs**) is queer on account of the final **-s** which appears to be a recent influence of Sanskrit.

19 (Lmp. **onʌis**) while **-k-** is preserved in 21, 31 etc., it has been softened to **-g-** in 11, but entirely lost in 19, 29, 39 etc. It appears in some Rājasthānī dialects (*e.g.*, Mālvī) where the forms are **gunːiːs guntiːs** and **gupcaːliːs**. 43 R. **tirtaːlis** is curious and is recent.

91—99 **-ʌjeː** forms are recent.

The help-words **ʈhʌĩ, ʈhʌur** and **ʈhi** (< *sthā*—?) are modern devices to give additional force to the number expressed. I have noticed no form in Early Awadhi.

(*e*) Ordinals—the terminations **-wãː** and **-ĩː** are corresponding to *-ma*, *-mī* of Sanskrit in the ordinary ordinals.

pʌɦil < *paḍhilla prath-illa*, **cʌuth** < *caturtha*, **chʌṭːhaː** < *ṣaṣṭhaka*, while **doːsʌr** and **tiːsʌr** have an affix *-sar* (Chatterji, p. 700)—Cf. **ekəsʌr** 'all alone'.

mãːɟɦil < M I *majjha* plus *-illa* and **sʌɲɟɦil**[1] appears to be on its analogy.

[1] This has had the contamination with Persian *seh* 'three' also, most probably. Professor S.K. Chatterji communicates a derivation (suggested by Mr. B. C. Mazumdar) on the analogy of Oriya which is said to have a form *sāna mājha* 'third' —Bengali *sājhuā* > *sejo* where *sāna* < *saṇha* < *ślakṣṇa* 'small' + *mājha* < *madhya* 'middle'. **sʌŋɟɦil** would then be a contracted form from *sāna*+*mājh*—.

CHAPTER IV

PRONOUNS

Introductory

§ 233. As shown below (§ 269) the postpositions are employed oftener with pronouns than with nouns, because the pronouns being used very often and, generally speaking, occupying a comparatively unimportant and meaningless part in speech, become weak both phonetically and semantically. There is thus a quicker disintegration of pronouns than that of nouns and there is consequently a rebuilding and a great variety of forms. Even at the Prakrit stage we find a large number of forms of the various pronouns (see Pischel § 415 for instances of the pronoun of the first person, Bloch § 207). Some of these, doubtless, existed from OIA times.

In the case of all the pronouns we find that the initial sound has subsisted in spite of disintegration and remodelling. Similarly pronouns which have only one syllable (*kō* etc.) have subsisted. This is quite in accordance with the principle of frequent use, *viz.*, that the important element of words of frequent occurrence survives because it is fixed up in the mind.

First Person Pronoun

A. Early Awadhi

§ 234. The texts have the following forms :–

	sg.	pl.
direct		
	maĩ (also *haũ*)	*hama*

	sg.	pl
oblique		
	mō, mohī (mohi)	*ham, hamahī (hamaī)*
genitive adjective		
	mōra	*hamāra*

(*a*) The direct case is employed as the subject. In Jāyasī *haū* is as frequently found in use as *maī*, *e.g.*, *haū jāū* 'I go' (p. 90), *haū mānusa* 'I am a man' (p. 92), *haū lōni* 'I am charming' (p. 134), *haū āwā* 'I came'. *maī* is generally used as the subject of past-participle or future-participle verbs, *e.g.*, *maī pai* 'I got' (p 26), *maī sukha dēkhā* 'I experienced happiness' (p. 90), *maī paiṭhaba* 'I shall enter', *maī jāba* 'I shall go'. But there are a few cases where it stands as the subject of other verbs also, *e.g.*, *maī ravaū* 'I live in enjoyment' (p. 131), *jaū lagi maī phiri āū* 'until I come back' (p. 88). In Tulsī *maī* is the usual form and is used as the subject, *e.g.*, *maī kari prīti parīchā dēkhī* 'I have tested his affection' (p. 163), *karui maī māī* 'O mother! bitter am I' (p. 163), *maī ḍerāū* 'I am afraid' (p. 164), *maī lēbā* 'I shall take' (p. 197). In two instances (*hō-hū kahāwata* 'I also allow to be said' (p. 17), *nātha haū tyāgī* 'my lord has abandoned me' (p. 354), however, *haū* has been used. In an emphatic form (*mahī sakala anaratha kara mūlā* 'I alone am the root-cause of all evil', p. 259) the form *maī* has become *ma-*. In Nūr Muhammad *maī* is used always, *e.g.*, *likhanī maī līnhā* 'I have taken up the pen' (p. 4), *haū maī* 'I am' (p. 4), *maī hōū* 'I become' (p. 21), *maī bōlaū* 'I speak' (p. 110).

In all the three texts *hama* is used as the subject of the verb in plural number, *e.g.*, Jāyasī: *hama tau buddhi gavāū* 'we lost our power of thinking' (p. 113), *hama nicinta* 'I was care-free' (p. 116), *hama gavānaba kālī* 'we shall go to-morrow' (p. 96), *kitu hama* 'where shall we be' (p. 96); Tulsī: *sēvaka hama* 'we the servants' (p. 167), *nātha sanātha bhaē hama āju* 'Lord! we have to-day been endowed with a protector' (p. 209); Nūr Muhammad: *hama nā rahē karabalā ṭhāī* 'I was not in Karbalā' (p. 3), ***hama kehi kārana karaba sīgārā*** 'why shall we decorate ourselves?' (p. 25), ***ōṣada milana kahā̃ hama jāhī*** 'I go to seek for the remedy' (p. 72).

(*b*) The oblique stands for all case-relations except the Nominative. In Jāyasī *mō* is used with postpositions (*e.g.*, *mō kahā̃* 'to me', p. 137, *kō sari mō saũ pāvaī* 'who can gain an equality with me', p. 83) and *mohī* without postpositions (*e.g.*, *tei mohī pantha dīnha ũjiārā*, 'He gave to me a well-lighted path', p. 24, *dēsa dēsa kē bara mohi āvahī* 'suitors of every country come for me', p. 87, *hīrāmani mohī nāũ* 'Hīrāmani is my name', p. 131, *taba guna mōhī ahā* 'then there was merit in me', p. 124).

In Tulsī *mō* is used with postpositions (*e.g.*, *mō para* 'on me', p. 163, *mō kahā̃* 'to me', p. 183) and *mohī* with or without postpositions (*e.g.*, *mohi sana* 'from me', p. 164, *mohi pāhī̃* 'to me', p. 166, *jehi bidhi mōhī* 'as to me', p. 158, *pramudita mōhi kaheu guru* 'the preceptor gladly told me', p. 158, *mōhi achata* 'while I live', p. 159). In one instance *mohi* appears as *muhi*.

In Nūr Muhammad *mō* is generally used with postpositions (*e.g.*, *mō̃ kā̃* 'to me', *mō-mahā̃* 'in me', p. 11, *mō kahā̃* 'to me', p. 21, *mō sẽ* 'from me', p. 107, *mō kaī* 'of me', p. 57) but in two cases without postpositions (*mō manī basā* 'has resided in my mind,' p. 24, *bhãvara na mō tana ḍamka lagāvai* 'the bee does not sting my body' p. 56); *mohi* is used without postpositions (*e.g.*, *mohi bibēka kachu nāhī* 'no discrimination is in me', p. 4, *būjhi mohī parā* 'was realised by me' p 5, *sūjhi parā mohī* 'was visible to me', p. 3, *mohi pāra utārō* 'take me across', p. 2, *mohi karanī kō* 'with me the sailor', p. 2, *dayā dristi mohi ūpara ḍārō* 'cast the glance of mercy on me', p. 2) In one instance (*mahi ghāyala kahā̃* 'to me the wounded person', p. 108) the form of *mohī* appears as *mahi*.

hama as an oblique case is used in Jāyasī both with or without postpositions, *e.g*, ***hama kā*** 'to us' (p. 261), ***hama***

taĩ kōi na āgari rūpā 'no one is superior to me in beauty' (p. 254); *dēha dēha hama lāgu anaṅgā* 'Cupid is sticking to every limb of mine' (p. 87), *gaī hama āū* 'our life has been spent' (p. 112). It is used with postpositions in Tulsī, *e.g.*, *hama para rōṣū* 'anger on me' (p. 120). Only one example is found without postposition: *taji rāma hama* 'Rāma has abandoned us' (p. 191). Nūr Muhammad employs it with postpositions, *e.g.*, *hama kahā̃* 'to me' (p. 2), *hama tẽ* 'from me' (p. 38), *hama sõ* 'with me' (p. 64).

hamahĩ (*hamaĩ* in N.) is used without postpositions in all the texts, *e.g.*, Jāyasī: *hamahĩ lōbha* 'owing to our greed' (p. 116), *hamahĩ garaba* 'owing to our pride' (p. 116), *aba kō hamahĩ karī bhōginī* 'who will make me an enjoyer (of objects), (p. 254); Tulsī: *hamahi kā hānī* 'what harm to me' (p. 163), *dēihi hamahĩ sajāī* 'will give me punishment' (p. 165), *dēu yaha hamahĩ* 'give this to us' (p. 166); Nūr Muhammad: *deihai bahuta hamaĩ asa cērī* 'will give many maids like us' (p. 57), *hamaĩ tumạ cīnhā* 'you recognised (took) me' (p. 83).

(*c*) The genitive adjectives *mōra* 'my' and *hamāra* 'our' are used in all the three texts and modify their forms for case and gender. For instance:

mōra Jāyasī: *jōbana mōra* 'my youth' (p. 87), *hĩchā bhai mōrī* 'I had a wish' (p. 396), *hĩchā pūjai mōri* 'my wish may be fulfilled' (p. 370), *puravahu mōri darasa kai āsā* 'you satisfy my hope for sight' (p. 370), *pitā ki āyasu māthaĩ mōrē* 'father's order is on my forehead' (p. 89), *sēvā mōra* 'my service' (p. 614).

Tulsī: *mōra mana chōbhā* 'my mind became dejected' (p. 163), *mōrē biraha* 'owing to my separation' (p. 189), *mōrē jāna* 'in my knowledge' (p. 258); *āyasu mōri* 'my order' (p. 181), *dahini ā̃khi nita pharakai mōrī* 'my right eye always throbs' (p. 165).

Nūr Muhammad: *prabhu āhai mōrā* 'is my master (p. 24), *kanaka sohāga mōra hari līnhā* 'has robbed me of my golden prosperity' (p. 25), *paṅkha pāya saba mōrē* 'I have wings and feet' (p. 85), *mōrī bairina (gāvahī)* 'my enemies sing' (p. 35).

NOTE 1. In Tulsī and Nūr Muhammad we come across stray forms of the *mērā* adjective which are surely borrowings from another dialect, *e.g.*, Tulsī: ***pūrahu sakala manōratha mērē*** 'satisfy all my wishes' (p. 10); Nūr Muhammad: ***sāthī mērē*** 'my companions' (p. 96), ***hai thōrī budhi pūjiya mērī*** 'I possess very little capital in the shape of wisdom' (p. 4) ***icchā mērō*** 'my wish' (p. 79).

hamāra Jāyasī: *jiana hamāra* 'life is ours' (p. 50), *pitā hamāra na ā̃khi lagāvahī* 'my father does not see (p. 87), *kā pū̃chahu aba jāti hamārī* 'why do you ask (me) about my caste now' (p. 575), *hamarē kahata rahai nahī mānū* 'if you do not believe by my word' (p. 610).

Tulsī: *bacanu hamāra māni* 'having complied with my words' (p. 181), *jē hamāra ari mitra udāsī* 'who are my enemies, friends or are indifferent towards me' (p. 158), *jānati hau basa nāhu hamārē* 'you think the husband is under my control' (p. 163), *bipati hamāri bilōki baṛi* 'having seen our great distress' (p. 162), *baṛi cūka hamārī* 'great is my mistake' (p. 164), *hamārē bayara* 'owing to my enmity' (p. 31), *hamārē bhāyē* 'according to my thinking' (p. 31).

Nūr Muhammad: *jō hamāra dou hātha banawā* 'who made both my hands' (p. 56), *jānata paragaṭa guputa hamārā* 'he knows our open and secret acts' (p. 1), *hōtai mukuta hamāra* 'I would have my liberation' (p. 16), *tohi dāyā sō̃ mukuta hamārī* 'I shall have my liberation by your favour' (p. 2), *thākī nāva hamāra* 'my boat is done up' (p. 35), *bhīkha hamāra* 'my alms' (p. 79), *baṛī hamārī bhāga* 'great is my luck' (p. 156).

NOTE 2. Like ***mōra***, ***hamāra*** also, in Nūr Muhammad, does not generally change for gender.

B. MODERN AWADHI

§ 235. Lakhīmpurī has the following forms :

	sg.	pl.
	mʌi (mʌɦi)	**hʌm**
Genitive Adj.	**moːr**	**hʌmaːr**

(*a*) There are no separate forms for the dir. and obl. —the same form serves for both, only **mʌɦi** is not used as a subject. For instance: **mʌi gʌjeũ** 'I went', **mʌi kaː deːu** or **mʌɦi kaː deːu** 'give to me', **hʌm gʌjen** 'we went', **hʌm kaː deːu** 'give to us'.

(*b*) The genitive adjective changes for gender and case like the ordinary adjective, *e.g.*, **moːr kuːkur mʌri̥ gaː** 'my dog has died', **moːreː kuːkur ko maːrin** '(they) beat my dog', **moːri̥ kutijaː mʌri̥ gʌi** 'my bitch has died', **moːriː kutijʌ ko maːrin** 'they beat my bitch'. Similarly we have **hʌmaːr : hʌmʌreː, hʌmaːri̥ : hʌmʌriː**

(*c*) The forms in other dialects of Modern Awadhi are the same as in Lakhīmpurī. B. and G. specimens give an additional form **hʌmʌi** (emphatic **hʌmːʌi**) which is used as accusative-dative, *e.g.*, **uː hʌmʌi maːrisi̥** 'he beat me', **uː hʌmʌi diɦisi̥** 'he gave to me'. Bgh. has **mʌ̃j** and **hʌmɦ** and **hʌmɦaːr.**

(*d*) The singular form of this pronoun is used less frequently than the plural. The latter replaces the former. The Eastern dialects have entirely lost the singular of this pronoun, the plural '**hʌm** is invariably used as such, *e.g.*, Fy. **hʌm deːkhʌb** may mean 'I shall see' or 'we shall see' according to the context. When a particularisation is to be made, the plural is indicated by adding **sʌb** or **sʌb keuː**, *e.g.*, **hʌm sʌb deːkhʌb** 'we shall see'.

(*e*) The dialectal difference about the change of gender of adjectives exists in the case of the genitive adjective (see § 219).

(*f*) The pronunciation of **mʌɦi** and **moːr** is generally **moɦi (mwʌɦi)** and **mwaːr** in R., Br., U., part of S. and F. and in Bgh.

C. Origin

§ 236 (*a*) *haũ* is not found in Modern Awadhi but was used in Early Awadhi as is attested by its frequent use in Jāyasī and by sporadic instances in Tulsī. It goes back to the extended form *ahakaṃ* (Chatterji § 538). This pronoun fell in disuse in Awadhi almost as early as Tulsī but is of frequent occurrence in Western Hindi.

(*b*) Modern Awadhi **mʌi**, E. Aw. *maĩ* goes back to Pkt. *maẽ* (Skt. *mayā*). This form is used in Jāyasī mostly in participial constructions which shows its origin from an oblique case. The nasalisation in the Early Awadhi form has been explained by Chatterji (§ 539) by an influence of the regular instrumental affix *-ēna*.

(*c*) Early Aw. *mō* goes back to *mama* (Chatterji § 541) and serves as a general oblique. *mohĩ* is super-imposed oblique form by the addition of *-hĩ*, oblique sg termination of nouns. Modern Awadhi **mʌɦi** should be connected with *mohĩ*, and **moːr** with *mō* and the genitive postposition *kara*. The *mērā* form would go back to *mō kēra*.

(*d*) Modern Aw. **hʌm,** E. Aw. *hama* is connected with OIA *asmē* through Pkt. *amhē*, *amha* with the transfer of aspiration to the initial position. Modern **hʌmʌi,** E. Aw. *hamahĩ* is the general oblique form by the addition of *-hĩ*.

hʌmaːr, E. Aw. *hamāra* is *hama* plus the postposition *kara*, *kāra*.

Second Person Pronoun

A. Early Awadhi

§ 237.	sg.	pl.
direct		
	J. *tũ*, *tuĩ*	*tumha*
	T. *tū* (*tũ*) *taĩ*	*tumha* (*tuma*)
	N. *taĩ* (*tui*)	*tuma*

oblique	sg.	pl.
	J. *tō*, *tohi*	*tumha*
	T. *tō*, *tohi*	*tumha* (*tuma*)
		tumhahī, *tumahī*
	N. *tō*, *tohī* (*tohi*)	*tumhai*, *tumahi*
genitive adjective		
	J. *tōra* (*tohāra*)	*tumhāra*
	T. *tōra*	*tumhāra*
	N. *tohāra* (*tōra*)	*tumhāra*

(*a*) The direct case comes as the subject. In Jāyasī both *tū* and *tuī* are used but the latter is generally the subject of past-participle verbs, *e.g.*, *hīrāmani tū parāna parēvā* 'O Hīrāmani bird thou art my life-breath' (p. 91), *tū paṅkhi piārā* 'thou art a dear bird' (p. 92), *ai gosāī tū aisa bidhātā* 'O Master, Thou art such a creator' (p. 107), *dēhi tū cārā* 'thou givest meal' (p. 107), *tū suaṭā paṇḍita hutā* 'O parrot, thou wert wise' (p. 113), *tū bidhi dēhi adhāra* 'O Creator, give (me) support' (p. 122); *tuī suraṅga mūrati vaha kahī* 'thou hast spoken of her, a picture of good colours' (p. 155), *jasa anūpa tuī dēkhī* 'as unique as you have seen (her)' (p. 160), *tuī rājā kā pahirasi kanthā* 'O king why do you put on rags' (p. 232). *tuī dayāla saba kē uparāhī* 'thou art compassionate over all' (p. 370). In one case Jāyasī has *taī*: *taī hari laṅka harāī kēhari* 'by stealing the middle part of your body—as is shown by its being very thin—thou hast defeated the lion' (p. 551). In Tulsī both *tū* and *taī* have been frequently used as the subject, *e.g.*, *jananī tū jananī bhaī* 'mother!, you have been my mother' (p. 220), *kō tū ahasi* 'who art thou?' (p. 220), *tū chala binaya karasi kara jōrē* 'you are practising false supplication with folded hands', (p. 120); *bhagata taī mōrā* 'thou art my devotee' (p. 74), *taī palava sīcā* 'thou hast watered the twig' (p. 220). In Nūr Muhammad the most common form is *taī*, *e.g.*, *mitra taī mērō* 'thou art my friend' (p. 84), *taī jina rahu* 'thou shouldst not remain' (p. 104), *taī na dukhī mana hō* 'do not be distressed at heart' (p. 128), *taĩ dhana kalī samā paṭa māhĩ* 'good woman! thou art like a bud (covered) in cloth' (p. 49), *jā sõ magu taĩ hērā* 'from whom thou hast sought the way' (p. 58), *taĩ marama na pāvā* 'thou hast not reached the secret' (p. 75). In one case (*lābha ki bāta kahī tui gyānī* 'wise man! thou hast uttered words for my benefit' p. 153) we find *tui*.

tumha is used with the plural verb, *e.g.*, Jāyasī: *pātisāha tumha jagata kē* 'you are the king of the world' (p. 17), *tumha rājā cāhahu sukha pāvā* 'you are a king and want to obtain happiness' (p. 229), *tumha abahĩ jẽia ghara pōī* 'you eat finished (food) at home' (p. 229); Tulsī: *tumha kahahu* 'you should say' (p. 25), *tumha pūchahu* 'you are asking' (p. 164), *rāmapriya tāta tumha* 'dear child, you are dear to Rāma' (p. 223), *milehu rāma tumha* 'Rāma! you have met me' (p. 327), *jā para nātha karahu tumha dāyā* 'on whom, my lord, you are compassionate' (p. 354). In Nūr Muhammad the form of this pronoun is *tuma*, *e.g.*, *sumirehu tuma mōhī* 'you should think of me' (p. 4), *tuma gurū* 'you are the teacher' (p. 20), *tuma kāmini mati-hīnī* 'you are a loving woman, bereft of wisdom' (p. 21).

NOTE.—In Tulsī stray cases of *tuma* are found, *e.g.*, *dēkhahu tuma* 'you see' (p. 351).

(*b*) The oblique stands for all case-relations except the Nominative. In all the texts *tō* is used with post-positions and *tohi* (*tohī*) without them. For instance:

Jāyasī : *aihai bhavãra jo tō kahã jōrā* 'the bee who is the mate for thee will come' (p. 383), *au bidhi rūpa dīnha hai tō kā* 'and the Creator has given you beauty' (p. 466), *tō saũ mana lāī* 'having attached his mind with you' (p. 522); *tohi lāyaka bara* 'a bridegroom befitting thee' (p. 87). *karata tohi sēvā* 'while rendering service to thee' (p. 91), *na tohi ḍaru āvā* 'fear did not come to thee' (p. 126).

Tulsī : *sapanehu tō para kōpu na mōhī* 'I have no anger on thee even in dream' (p. 163), *tō sana larata jo sōha* 'who would like to fight with thee' (p. 380); *sikha dīnhiũ tōhī* 'I have given you advice' (p. 163), *bharata sapatha tohi* 'Bharata's swearing by thee' (p. 163), *kahaũ na tōhi* 'I do not tell thee' (p. 165), *jaũ kachu kahaũ kapaṭa kari tōhī* 'if I tell thee anything deceitfully' (p. 167), *tohi sama hitu na mōra saṃsārā* 'nobody is such a well-wisher of mine in this world as thee' (p. 166), *pūchaũ tōhī* 'I ask thee' (p. 25). Nūr Muhammad : *tō sē kō patiyāra* 'what confidence with thee?' (p. 142), *gāṛhī gāṭha parai jahā tōhī* 'wherever you have a difficult point' (p. 4), *tohi dayā sō* 'by thy favour' (p. 2), *sunāvaũ tōhī* 'I tell thee' (p. 14), *sūjha būjha nahī tōhi* 'you do not possess insight or wisdom' (p. 21).

oblique *tumha* in Jāyasī is used with or without postpositions, *e.g.*, *ghaṭai tumha āū* 'your span of life becomes smaller' (p. 64), *mai tumha rāja bahuta sukha dēkhā* 'I have experienced great happiness in your rule' (p. 90); *tumha saũ kōi na jītā* 'nobody has won you' (p. 90), *tumha taī* 'from you' (p. 286).

In Tulsī *tumha* (obl.) is used with postpositions, *e.g.*, *dharma sujasa prabhu tuma kaũ* 'lord, virtue and good glory will accrue to you' (p. 90), *tumha kahā bipati bīja bidhi bayeū* 'the Creator would sow the seed of calamity for you' (p. 165), *tumha sana tāta bahuta kā kahaũ* 'why should I speak to (with) you more, dear sir' (p. 194), *rājahī tumha para prēma bisēkhī* 'the king has a great love for (on) you' (p. 164). In one instance (*tuma samāna tumha tāta* 'dear, you are like yourself', p. 276) *tuma* has been used without a postposition

The accusative-dative form (*tumhahī*, *tumahī*) is used without postpositions, *e.g.*, *tumhahī bidita raghupati-prabhutāī* 'to you the greatness of the Lord of Raghus is well-known' (p. 25), *aba jau tumhahi sutā para nēhū* 'now, if you have affection for your daughter' (p. 35), *cāhata dēna tumhahī yuvarājū* 'wants to give you the title of the crown prince' (p. 161), *tumhahī lei sāthā* 'taking you with me'

(p. 185), *tumahī bolāī* 'having called thee' (p. 238), *tumahī avadhi bhari bāṛi kaṭhināī* 'you have great difficulty throughout the period' (p. 276).

In Nūr Muhammad the oblique *tumhai, tumahi* is used without postpositions, *e.g.*, *tumhai...jōga na chājā* 'Yōga is not suitable for you' (p. 21), *jhūṭha kahānī tumahi sunāeu* 'told you a false story' (p. 23), *tumhaī merāihi pīya piyārā* 'will make thy dear beloved meet with thee' (p. 41), *tumhai sapana mō̃ dēkhaū̃ tahā̃* 'I see you there in a dream' (p. 72), *pitā tumhai kārana dukha sahā* 'your father bore unhappiness on your account' (p. 144); with postposition in *tumhai nita* 'for your sake' (p. 72).

(*c*) The genitive adjective changes for gender and case in Jāyasī and Tulsī regularly while only sometimes in Nūr Muhammad.

Jāyasī : *tōra* is the common form (there being only one instance of *tohāra* : *tahā̃ tohāra maī̃ kīnha bakhānū* 'there I gave thy description,' p. 396), *e.g.*, *kā tora purukha* 'what is thy man?' (p. 140), *tōrai gharahi mā̃jha dasa panthā* 'there are ten ways in thy own house' (p. 232), *jehi bidhi asatuti tōri* 'in which way thy praise (should be done)' (p. 370).

Tulsī : *tōra kahā jehi dina phura hōī* 'the day on which thy word will turn out to be true' (p. 163), *karagata vēda tatva saba tōrē* 'all the principles of the Vedas are under your control' (p. 25), *pūjihi nātha anugraha tōrē* 'it will be fulfilled, my lord, by thy favour' (p. 158), *taba dhari jībha kaṛhāvaū̃ tōrī* 'then I shall get hold of you and will get your tongue cast out' (p. 163).

Nūr Muhammad : *tohāra* (*tehāra, tihāra*) form is more common, *e.g.*, *āvana bhaeu tohāra* 'came your arrival' (p. 14), *piya toharā* 'thy husband' (p. 41), *līnhā sarana* (fm.) *tohāra* 'took thy refuge' (p. 32), *prīta* (fm.) *tohāra* 'thy love' (p. 136), *sundara sīla tehārō* 'thy conduct is good' (p. 92), *tehārō binatī* (fm.) *māneū̃* 'agreed to your supplication'

(p. 104), *nāma tihārō* 'thy name' (p. 48); *tōra bakhāna* 'thy description' (p. 49), *mukh tōra* 'thy face' (p. 62).

NOTE.—Stray cases of *tērā* forms are also found, *e.g.*, *caracā tērō* 'thy talk' (p. 49), *nihōrā tērō* 'thy kind act' (p. 84), *sēvā tērī* 'thy service' (p. 57), *cēri hōtiū tērī* 'I would become thy maid' (p. 79).

tumhāra is found in all the three texts.

Jāyasī: *kanta tumhāra marama maī līnhā* 'my beloved, I came to know your reality' (p. 147), *karai tumhārā khōja* 'searches you' (p. 147), *pai tumhāra nahī rōā pasījā* 'but your hair did not become wet' (p. 503), *tumharē darasana lāgi* 'for your sight' (p. 501), *tumharei maṇḍapha* 'in your own bower' (p. 460), *mati hīna tumhārī* 'your thought is low' (p. 490), *tumharī jōti* 'by thy light' (p. 551).

Tulsī: *jehi bidhi hōihi parama hita nārada sunahu tumhāra* 'O Narada, the way in which there would be your best good' (p. 60), *bhayeu tumhāra tanaya soi* 'the same has become your son' (p. 159), *sātha tumhārē* 'in your company' (p. 183), *tumharē hṛdaya* 'in your mind' (p. 179), *tumharehi bhāga* 'by your luck only' (p. 186), *tumhāri mātu baidēhī* 'Sita is your mother' (p. 186), *jari tumhāri caha savati ukhārī* 'your co-wife wants to dig up your root' (p. 164), *raī tumharī sēvā basa rāū* 'the king is under the control of your service' (p. 165).

Nūr Muhammad: *hai sadana tumhārā* 'is your house' (p. 22), *jiu tumhārā* 'your life' (p. 21), *naina tumhārē tasa karaī* 'your eyes may do thus' (p. 62), *jiu sō niara tumhārē* 'am near you by my life-breath' (p. 76), *prīta tumhārī (hai)* 'your love is', *pai tumharī ãkhiyā matavārī* 'but your eyes are bewitching' (p. 176), *dōṣa tumhārī ãkhina kērā* 'the fault is of your eyes' (p. 62), but *bhajana* (masc.) *tumhārī* 'your prayer (p. 72). In one instance the spelling is *tomhārā* (*gulāba tomhārā* 'your rose', p. 37).

B. Modern Awadhi

§ 238. Lakhīmpurī has the following forms:

	sg.	pl.
	tui (tuɦi)	**tum**
Genitive adj.	**toːr**	**tumaːr (tumɦaːr)**

(*a*) There are no separate forms for the dir. and obl., the same form serves for both, only, **tuɦi** is not used as a subject. For example: **tui gʌwaː** 'thou went', **tui kaː diɦeũ** or **tuɦi kaː diɦeũ** '(I) gave to you'; **tum gʌjeu** 'you went', **tum kaː diɦeũ** 'I gave to you.'

(*b*) The genitive adjective changes for gender and case like the ordinary adjective, *e.g.*, **toːr kuːkur mʌri̥ gaː** 'thy dog died', **toːreː kuːkur kə khaːi kə diɦen** '(we) gave (something) to eat to your dog', **toːri̥ kutijaː mʌri̥ gʌi** 'thy bitch died', **toːriː kutijʌ kə khaːi kə diɦen** '(we) gave (something) to eat to your bitch'. Similarly, we have **tumaːr**, obl. **tumʌreː, tumaːri̥ : tumʌriː.**

Sometimes a short aspiration is heard after **-m-** in the case of this adjective.

(*c*) In Lakhīmpurī the singular **(tui)** is used only for the younger, chiefly children and the servants. It expresses either deep affection or contempt. Parents would always address their grown up sons and daughters as **tum** 'you'.

(*d*) The forms of this pronoun in S., L., U., Br. and R. are the same as in Lakhīmpurī, only in U., R., part of S. and L. **toːr** is pronounced as **twaːr** and **tui** as **toi.** F. and Bgh. have **tʌ̃i** for Lmp. **tui** and **twaːr** for **toːr.** B. for the singular direct has **twʌi** or **tui** and **tuː** for the singular oblique while for the plural it has **tum** like Lmp. Bgh. has **tumɦ.** G. has **twʌĩ** for the singular but generally uses **tuː** for both the numbers and **toɦaːr** as the genitive adjective. Fy., Sl., P. and A. have only one form **tuː** (sometimes **tũː** in Fy.) and **toɦaːr** for both the numbers. For the accusative-dative they have an additional form **toɦʌĩ (toɦʌ̃j)** which alternates with **toː kaː** or **tõɦ kaː** In these dialects when a specification is necessary **sʌb** is added after this pronoun to indicate the plural, *e.g.*, **tuː sʌb, tõɦ sʌb kaː, toɦʌĩ sʌb kaː**

(*e*) The dialectal difference about the change of gender of adjectives (see § 219) exists in the case of this genitive adjective also. Only the 1st and 2nd person pronouns have separate adjectival forms in the genitive.

C. Origin

§ 239. (*a*) Modern **tuː, tũː,** Early *tũ* all go back to forms of *tvam* in Pkt. *tumaṃ* etc. (Pischel § 420).

(*b*) Modern **tui, tʌĩ,** Early *tuĩ*, *taĩ* have parallels in Prakrit and are connected with *tvayā*.

(*c*) Modern **toː,** Early *tō* represents OIA *tava* (Chatterji § 549), and Modern **twʌi twʌĩ,** Early *tōhi* are oblique forms with *-hĩ*. **toːr,** *tōra* was *tō* + *kara*, while *tērā* was *tō* + *kēraka*, **toɦaːr** was *tō* + *kāra* with an emphatic *-h-*.

(*d*) *tum*, *tumha* goes back to Pkt. *tumhē*; *tumhahĩ* is the oblique with *-hĩ* and **tumaːr,** *tumhāra* simply *tumha* + *kāra*.

Third Person, Remote Demonstrative and Correlative Pronoun.

A. Early Awadhi

§ 240.	sg.	pl.
direct		
J.	*vaha*, *sō*	*vei*, *unha*, *tei*, *tinha*
T.	*sō*	*tē*, *tinha*, *una*, *unha*, *ō*, (*sē*).
N.	*sō*, *vaha*	*sō*, *vai*, *una*
oblique		
J.	*ohi*, *ō*, *tehi*, *tāhi*, *tā*, *tāsu*	*unha*, *tinha*,
T.	*ohi*, *tā*, *tehi*, *tāhi*, *tāsu*.	*tinahĩ*, *tinha*, *tinhahĩ*, *unha*, *unhahĩ*
N.	*va*, *tā*, *vohi* (*vahi*), *tehi*, *tāhi*, *tāsu*	*una*, *tina*, (*tena*), *unhaĩ*, *tinhai*
adjective		
	tauna	

The forms of these three pronouns are so confused together that it is impossible to distinguish one from another.

(*a*) The direct is used as the Nominative or inanimate object.

In Jāyasī *vaha* is generally used as the personal pronoun and as demonstrative while *sō* as the correlative. For instance: *jabahī gharī pūjai vaka mārā* 'as soon as the hour was completed, he would strike' (p. 64), *calā vaha āvā* 'he came near' (p. 112), *nā vaha milā na bēharā* 'neither is he united nor separate' (p. 11), *vaha binauba āgai hoi* 'he will come forward and supplicate' (p. 15). In one instance (*siṅghala-dīpa jāi vaha pāvai* 'by going to the island of Singhala he will obtain her' (p. 118) *vaha* has been used as the direct object; *sō pāvai vaha sīpa* 'he will get that mother of pearl' (p. 50), *sō rahai* 'he will remain' (p. 10), *dūri so niara niara sō dūrī* 'what is far becomes near, what is near becomes far off' (p. 35), *jō vei cahā so kīnhesi* 'what He wanted, He did' (p. 10).

NOTE.—*vaha* is found as *uha* in one case (*dhanapati uhai* 'he alone is rich', p. 7).

In Tulsī *sō* is the form for the direct singular and *tei* as the subject of trans. past. part. verb, *e.g.*, *sō suni tiya risa gayeu sukhāī* 'on hearing of the woman's anger, he became extremely unhappy (lit. dry)' (p. 167), *sō* is also used as the direct inanimate object, *e.g.*, *sō janabu satasaṅga prabhāū* 'take that to be due to the company of the good' (p. 4), *āyasu hōi so karaū gosāī* 'I should do that which my lord advises' (p. 161), *pīra tei gōi* 'she concealed the pain' (p. 168), *tei kachu kāna na kīnha* 'she did not listen to anything' (p. 177), *gavana tei kīnha* 'he went' (p. 201).

In Nūr Muhammad *vaha* is generally used as the third person or demonstrative pronoun and *sō* as correlative, *e.g.*, *pitā rāja para bhā vaha rājā* 'he became king over the father's kingdom' (p. 7), *sapanē mō sō hōta hai jau sautukai na hōi* 'that happens in dream which may never happen in direct perception' (p. 11), *jā mana āi basai jō kōī, tā kahā prāna piyārā sōī* 'he who comes and stays in one's heart, is as dear to one as life-breath' (p. 13).

In Jāyasī, the plural form of this pronoun is used, with plural verb generally and with participial singular transitive verb, *e.g.*, *vei hērahī* 'they see' (p. 49), *vei tō phirē utaru asa pāvā* 'they obtained such an answer and returned' (p. 90), *vei tau uḍē auru bana tākā* 'they flew away and aimed at another forest' (p. 112), *niṭhura tēi jō para māsa khāvā* 'they are cruel who eat others' flesh' (p. 126), *hajarata khvāja khijira tei pāē* 'he (respectful plural) met Hazrat Khvājā Khizra' (p. 26), *tei mohī pantha dīnha ũjiārā* 'he (respectful plural) showed me the well-lighted path' (p. 24); *niramara pantha kīnha tinha jinha re diā kichu hātha* 'they have paved a clear way who have given something by (their own) hand' (p. 300); *janu unha jōga tanta aba khēlā* 'it appears that they have played a trick of Yōga now' (p. 431), *nāgaphāsa unha mēlī giā* 'they have put a serpent-noose on their necks' (p. 538).

In Tulsīdās *tē* and *ō* are the regular direct plural forms while *tinha* and *unha* are used as subjects of transitive participle verbs, *e.g.*, *tē ki sadā saba dina milahī* 'they are found always' (p. 181), *aba tē dina bītē* 'now those days are past' (p. 164), *tē priya tumhahī* 'those are dear to you' (p. 163), *sundara suta janamata bhaī ōū* 'they also brought forth beautiful sons' (p. 85), *rēkha tinha khācī* 'they drew a line' (p. 165), *sīsa tinha nāē* 'they bowed their heads' (p. 159), *tinha nija ōra na lāuba bhōrā* 'they will not have any consideration' (p. 5), *citrakētu kara ghara una ghālā* 'he (respectful) destroyed the family of Citrakētu' (p. 38), *chana mahā sakala kaṭaka unha mārā* 'in a moment they destroyed the whole army' (p. 305).

NOTE—In one case *sē* has been used (*sē karata mitāī* 'they befriend', p. 326).

In Nūr Muhammad *sō*, *vai* and *una* are used in the plural without any difference, *e.g.*, *sō rahē āṭha jasa cērē* 'they were like the eight disciples' (p. 11), *āgē vai pagu rākhahī* 'they put forward the footstep' (p. 97), *mirtaka rahē jīva una pāē* 'they were dead, they got life' (p. 168).

(*b*) Of the forms of the oblique singular in Jāyasī *ō* and *tā* are always used with postpositions, *e.g.*, *jō dukha sahai hōi sukha ō kā* 'he who bears misery, to him happiness would come' (p. 476), *dēo pūji puni ō paha̋ āī* 'having worshipped the deity (she) came to him' (p. 501), *rahā na ō sa̋u dōsari ka̋dhī* 'there was no one with him to give a shoulder' (p. 590), *sō rājā vaha tā kara dēsū* 'he was the king and that was his country' (p. 39), *tā kaha̋ āna hāṭa kita lāhā* 'how can he have a gain in another market' (p. 56), *rōa̋ rōa̋ tanu tā sa̋u ōdhā* 'every hair of his body was closely connected with her' (p. 577), *baḍahara sō anūpa ati tākē* 'its *baṛahal* fruits were unrivalled' (p. 41). *ohi* and *tehi* are mostly used with postpositions, *e.g.*, *ohi sa̋u maī pāī jaba karanī* 'when I obtained competence from him' (p. 26), *ohi huta dēkhai pāeũ* 'through him I was able to see' (p. 27), *nā koi hoihai ohi kē rūpā* 'there shall be no one like him' (p. 11), *kīnhesi tehi kaha̋ bahuta birāsū* 'for him he created many objects of enjoyment' (p. 5), *tehi taī adhika* 'more than that' (p. 195), *prathama jōti bidhi tehi kai sāji* 'the creator first created his light' (p. 14), *tehi kara gurū* 'his preceptor' (p. 26), *bīju tehi māhā* 'lightning in that' (p. 2), *tehi para* 'on that' (p. 64). They are used sometimes without postpositions, *e.g.*, *ohi na kāhu kai āsa nirāsā* 'to him there is no hope or despair from anybody' (p. 7), *nā ohi kuṭūba* 'there is no family of his' (p. 10), *tehi sājū* 'his trappings' (p. 5), *tehi prīti* 'owing to his love' (p. 14). *tāhi* is used without a postposition, *e.g.*, *dōsa tāhi jehi sūjha na āgū* 'the defect is his who cannot see before himself' (p. 138), *bāta na pūchī tāhi* 'did not ask him anything'

(p. 507). *tāsu* is used as genitive only, *e.g.*, *janama bhā tāsū* 'his birth came' (p. 81).

NOTE.—At one place ***tāū*** is used meaning 'her' (***nāgamatī nāgini mati tāū*** 'Nāgamatī—her intellect was that of a she-serpent', p. 138).

Tulsīdās uses *tā* always with postpositions and *tehi* mostly with postpositions while *ohi* and *tāhi* without postpositions, for instance :

tā sanu āi kīnha chalu '(he) came and practised deception on (with) him' (p. 286), *tā tẽ* 'owing to that' (p. 164), *tā kahū̃ bibudha nadī baitaranī* 'for him (there is) Baitaranī, the river of the gods' (p. 286), *cāri padāratha karatala tākẽ* 'the four achievements are under his palm' (p. 175), *tehi para* 'above that', *tehi tẽ* 'owing to that' (p. 170), *tehi avasara* 'at that time' (p. 161); ***āna bhā̃ti nahī̃ pāvõ ōhī*** 'I shall not get her otherwise' (p. 60), ***dēu daiu phiri*** *sō phalu ōhī* 'may fate give him that fruit again' (p. 164), *kāhū̃ baiṭhana kahā na ōhī* 'no one asked him to sit down' (p. 286); *ajasa peṭārī tāhi kari* 'having made her an object (box) of infamy' (p. 162), *bhẽṭata bharata tāhi ati prīti* 'Bharata embraces him with great affection' (p. 232), *dharama nīti upadēsia tāhī* 'to him should virtue and polity be advised' (p. 185), *bacana bāna sama lāgahī̃ tāhī* 'to her the words struck as arrows' (p. 176). *tāsu* is the genitive, *e.g.*, *bānī savinaya tāsu sohā̃ī* 'humble words of her liking' (p. 169), *tāsu nirādara* 'his disrespect' (p. 174).

In Nūr Muhammad *vā* and *tā* are always used with postpositions, *e.g.*, *sabada bacana amrita rasa vā kē* 'the words of his speech are like nectar' (p. 153), *ēkahu bāra na vā kai tākō* 'nobody aims at him even once' (p. 56); *buddhasēna rahu tā kō nā̃ū* 'his name was Buddhasēna' (p. 12), *tā mahā̃ lākha bastu kī ḍhērī* 'in that there were heaps of lakhs of things' (p. 9), *rījhā tā para nirpa sarēkhā* 'the handsome king became enamoured of her' (p. 13), *pūcheū̃ tā sō* 'I asked her' (p. 3). *vohi* (*vahi*) is used with or without postpositions, *e.g.*, *jāū vohī kē dēsa kahā* 'I am going to her country' (p. 21), *basai mana vōhī* 'the mind takes an abode in her' (p. 43), *vohi ḍōlaī saba ḍōlaī* 'on her motion every one moves' (p. 46), *vahi darasana kā hāū maī bhukhā* 'I am hungry for her sight' (p. 28). *tehi* is generally used with postpositions, *e.g.*, *adhara tehi ka jō likhai citērā* 'if the painter paints her lower lip' (p. 13), *tehi nita sādhai jōga* 'for her he will practise Yōga' (p. 7), *tehi māhī* 'in that' (p. 8), but *rājakūara tehi rākhā nāū* 'his name was fixed up as *Rājakūara*' (p. 7), *puni ānata tehi apanē niyarē* 'then brings him near herself' (p. 10), *rāja doū jaga kō tehi chājā* 'the kingship of both the worlds fits him' (p. 1). *tāhi* is generally used without postpositions and expresses an accusative-dative sense, *e.g.*, *dīnhā rasanā tāhi bakhānō* 'He gave me the tongue that I should praise Him' (p. 1), *raṃcika tāhi na bhāvai* 'not even little appealed to him' (p. 13), but *hōta dharama nita tāhi majhārā* 'virtuous deeds are always done in that' (p. 14). Only a few cases of *tāsu* (genitive) are found, *e.g.*, *tāsu badana* 'her face' (p. 10), *tāsu bakhāna* 'her description' (p. 69).

The plural oblique form *unha* (*una*) has been used with postpositions in all the three texts, *e.g.*, Jāyasī: *taisa cahia puni unha kahā* 'again, to them such (a treatment) should be meted out' (p. 528), *unha kē raṃgā* 'their colours' (p. 70), *nā unha kai vaha rūpa sohāī* 'neither was there her (respectful) beauty' (p. 445), *unha mahā ēka gurū jo kahāvā* 'amongst them there was one, called their teacher' (p. 431); Tulsī: *maī unha kara dāsā* 'I am his (respectful) slave' (p. 300), *samujhi parī mohi unha kai karanī* 'I was able to understand his deed' (p. 304); Nūr Muhammad: *una nita māgu saraga sukha bāsū* 'for them always beg for a happy residence in Heaven' (p. 136). The form *tinha*, *tina* (*tena*) is found in Jāyasī both with and without postpositions, *e.g.*, *disiṭa pāpa saba tinha kē bhāgē* 'all their sins were gone by the sight' (p. 425), *tinha mahā* 'in them' (p. 75), *ḍarapahī rāi ḍēkhi tinha ṭhāḍhē* 'on seeing them standing, kings got frightened' (p. 63), *paduma gandha tinha aṅga basāhī* 'their bodies gave out a fragrance of lotus' (p. 49). In Tulsī and Nūr Muhammad, however, they are seen always with postpositions, for instance, Tulsī: *tinha kē mana mandira basahu* 'reside in their mind-temples' (p. 208), *jē tinha mahū̃ baya biridha sayānē* 'those amongst them who were older in age and wise' (p. 200), Nūr Muhammad: *pūcheū̃ tina kara tā sõ nāū̃* 'I asked their name' (p. 3), *sō karihai tina kara bistārā* 'he will have their amplification' (p. 69), *lōha phā̃da tina kē gala hīrē* 'iron-snares will be diamonds on their necks' (p. 141), *cahū̃ disa tina para bhãvara bhavāhī* 'on all sides the bees hovered on them' (p. 8). The accusative-dative forms *unhahī*, *unhaī* and *tinhahī*, *tinhai* have been used without postpositions by Tulsī and Nūr Muhammad both, *e.g.*, Tulsī: *tasa phalu unhahī dēū̃* 'I shall give her (respectful) a similar recompense' (p. 170), *tinhahī suhāi na nagarabanāvā* 'to them the city-decorations did not appeal' (p. 162), *tinhahī bilōki bilōkati dharanī* 'having seen them looks towards the ground' (p. 203), *tinhahī ko mārai binu bhagavantā* 'excepting the Lord, who can kill them' (p. 305); Nūr Muhammad: *aura na kījai unhaī nirāsū* 'and do not make them helpless' (p. 136), *jīu tinhai hai prīta tumhārī* 'your affection is life to them' (p. 51), *tinhai lai āvā* 'brought them' (p. 68).

(*c*) These forms are also used as Remote demonstrative pronouns. For instance:

Direct singular—Jāyasī: *asa vaha suā amōla* 'that parrot is so priceless' (p. 127), *sō pāvai vaha sīpa* 'he will get that mother of pearl' (p. 50), *āi so nārī* 'that woman came' (p. 134), *sō rājā* 'that king' (p. 39); Tulsī: *sō baidēhī sōvati mahī* 'that Sita sleeps on the ground' (p. 193), *soi bharōsa mōrē mana āvā* 'that very assurance came to my mind' (p. 8), *voha sukha* 'that happiness' (p. 85); Nūr Muhammad: *sō dina gayeu* 'that day has passed' (p. 52), *darapana bīca rahī vaha rānī* 'that queen was in the mirror' (p. 12), *vō prēmī kahaī* 'that lover says' (p. 6).

Direct plural—Jāyasī : *tehi sira phūla caḍhahī vei* 'those flowers are put on that head' (p. 53), *dahū haū lōni ki vei padumanī* 'whether I am handsome or the rival is Padminī' (p. 134); Tulsī : *tē dina bītē* 'those days have passed' (p. 164); Nūr Muhammad : *gavanata haī vei lōi* 'those people go' (p. 54).

NOTE.—sg. *vei* and pl. *unha* (*una*), *tinha* are not used as demonstrative pronouns.

Oblique singular—Jāyasī : *ohi jaga bichurahī kitu* 'how will they be separated in that world' (p. 31), *ōhī chāha raini hoi āvai* 'by that very shade, night comes up' (p. 40), *tehi nāca* 'in that dance' (p. 60); *jaga kahā jiana dīnha tehi mūṭhī* 'with that hand he gave life to the world' (p. 17), *tā dina byādha bhaeu jiu-lēvā* 'on that day the fowler became the murderer' (p. 116); Tulsī : *tehi avasara āē laṣana* 'at that time Lakshmaṇa came' (p. 161); Nūr Muhammad : *tā mukha kērā* 'of that face' (p. 11), *tā pagu raja kē ūpara* 'on the dust of her feet' (p. 99), *cētā vōhi samai cali āī* 'Cētā came at that time' (p. 69), *jō vahi mukha kō paragaṭa dēkhā* 'he who saw that face clearly' (p. 18), *bhā tehi bacana hutē saṃsārā* 'the Universe was created by that word' (p. 5), *tehi ṭhāī* 'in that place' (p. 6).

Oblique plural—Jāyasī : *unha bānahī* 'by those arrows' (p. 177), *tinha tālahī* 'in those ponds' (p. 50), *tinha purukhanha kahā* 'to those men' (p. 308); Nūr Muhammad : *sapata ahai una ākhina kērī* 'oath of those eyes' (p. 71), *tena sarīra kō cīnhā* 'who recognises those bodies' (p. 59).

NOTE.—*unhahī, unhaī, tinhahī, tinhaī* are not used as demonstrative pronouns.

(*d*) Instances of the correlative adjective *tauna* 'that' are found in Nūr Muhammad, *e.g.*, *kehi hita āni dharāyeu tauna sunāvahū mōhī* 'why did you allow yourself to be caught tell me that' (p. 88), *siddha hōi apanē gana, sunai anāhada tauna* 'he who hears that Anāhada sound becomes an accomplished being' (p. 121).

B. MODERN AWADHI

§ 241. Lakhīmpurī has the following forms:

	sg.	pl.
dir. masc.	**uː, wʌɦu**	**ui**
,, fem.	**waː, wʌɦ**	
obl.	**ui, wʌɦi**	**un (unɦ)**

For instance: **uː** or **wʌɦu kʌɦisi̥** 'he said', **waː** or **wʌɦ kʌɦisi̥** 'she said', **ui kʌɦin** 'they (men or women) said', **ui kaː deːkhen** or **wʌɦi kaː deːkhen** '(we) saw him (her)', **un kaː** or **unɦ kaː deːkhen** '(we) saw them (men or women).'

(*a*) All these forms (excepting obl. pl.) are used as pronominal adjectives also, *e.g.*, **uː lʌrikaː** or **wʌɦu lʌrikaː** 'that boy', **waː gaːi** or **wʌɦ gaːi** 'that cow', **ui** or **wʌɦi lʌrikʌ ko** 'to that boy', **ui** or **wʌɦi gaːi ko** 'to that cow', **ui lʌrikaː** 'those boys', **ui gaːiː** 'those cows' The pronominal adjective for obl. pl. also is **ui** (and not **un, unɦ**), *e.g.*, **ui lʌrikʌn ko** 'to those boys', **ui gaːin ko** 'to those cows'.

(*b*) There is considerable dialectal difference with regard to the forms of this pronoun. S., L., Br., R. and U. agree with Lmp. except that in Br., dir. pl. is **woɦi** besides **ui**, in R., obl. sg. **wʌi** besides **wʌɦi** and **ui** and in U. (as well as in south L.) **wʌɦi** is pronounced as **woɦi** and there is one more obl. sg. form **uɦi**. The dir. sg. masc. is sometimes **woː**. In F. masc. and fm. forms coincide in the sg. **wʌɦ** or **waː** and the obl. sg. is **wʌɦi** or **wʌi**. In B. the sg. differs from Lmp. in having no difference of gender or case, **uː** being the common form with **uɦ** in the obl. sometimes. For instance: **uː kʌi** or **uɦ kʌi** 'his or her'. G., Fy., Sl., P. and A. do not observe any distinction of gender.

The masc. dir. sg. in all these is **uː** (P. has **oː** also) and the obl. sg. is **oɦ** (G.), **wʌɦi, oː** (Fy.), **wʌɦ wʌi** (Sl.), **oɦe** (P. and A.). The dir. pl. in G. is **wʌi,** in Fy. **wʌɦi,** in Sl. **wʌi.** In P. and A. **pãːc** or **sʌb** is added to the sing. to specify the plural. The obl pl. is **un** in all the Eastern dialects; only Fy. has **wʌn** and P. (also A.) **on, onɦ** besides **un.** Besides there is an accusative-dative form **unɦʌi**. Bgh. in the singular has **waː** dir. and **woː (wʌɦi)** obl.—and in the plural **ui** dir. and **un, unɦ** obl.

(*c*) As in Lakhīmpurī, the forms of this pronoun are used as adjectives also in all the dialects. In U. and parts of F. and R. the obl. is used as the subject also of past participle tenses.

(*d*) Remote Demonstrative Pronoun

The third person pronoun is also used as the remote demonstrative pronoun, there being no separate forms for the latter. The forms of this pronoun are used also as the correlative pronoun besides the forms of the correlative pronoun (see § 247).

C. Origin

§ 242. Like other Mod. IA languages we have three varieties of forms, *viz.* (1) *s-* , (2) *t-* and (3) *u-*, *w-* or *o-*. Possibly nowhere else do we find a variety so abundant as here. In Sanskrit there were forms of the Third person pronoun *saḥ*, *tat* etc. (which appear to have combined two pronouns: note *sasmin* in Vedic, Pischel p. 300) and of the Demonstrative pronoun *asau*, *amū* etc. (where also a combination of two pronouns is shown). A distinction of gender was maintained. We find that the distinction of gender is losing ground in the Prakrits. Early Awadhi has already entirely lost it. Of the three varieties of forms

(1) those with initial *s-* are connected with *saḥ* and *sā*, and E. Aw. *sō* (modern **soː**) *exactly* represents *saḥ* of

Sanskrit[1]. On account of frequency of use and being a monosyllable it has maintained itself. Its use for the plural is modern (post-Middle-Indian) on the analogy of nouns. *sẽ*, used as plural only, is on the model of *tẽ*, *kẽ*, *yẽ*.

(2) *t*- pronouns are attested by the variety of forms in the Prakrits. Nominative **taun** goes back to *taṃ* + *uṇa* (< *tat punaḥ*) of the Prakrits, Nom. sg. **teɪ** in Eastern Awadhī dialects is Māg. Nom. -*ē*, *tehi* is its oblique *tā* with post-positions was another oblique derived from *tasya*, a later and fresh form of the same is *tāsu*[2] and *tāhi* is the superimposed oblique. Nominative plural *tẽ* (**teɪ**) is in line with other pronouns while **tiɪ** is a new formation. *tei* appears to be the emphatic of *tẽ*. *tinha*, *tenha*, *tinh*, *tin* are the oblique forms based on the ancient genitive plural -*nām* like nouns.

(3) It is difficult to find the derivation of the pronouns in *u*-, *w*- or *o*-. We have no forms in old Indo-Aryan (except *avōḥ* in R. V., *vide* Chatterji § 572) or in Middle Indo-Aryan which might be called the ancestors of our modern forms. Chatterji observes that the *ava* base, though not attested by literary dialects, must have been current dialectically. It was current in Iranian and Dardic. But it seems a little strange that none of its forms should have been shown by the Prakrits which have such a variety of pronominal forms. Their first use is found in the Apabhraṃśa (Chatterji, p. 837). I should offer another explanation as an alternative. The proximate demonstrative has initially *i*- *e*-; on its analogy the remote demonstrative came to be indicated by forms with *u*- *o*- as the initial sound. Once *this way* of expression is taken into a language, the

---

[1] Prof Chatterji, however, thinks that Hin **soɪ** < *sau* < *saō* < **sa-ka-ḥ*, while Skt. *saḥ* > *sō* > *su*.

[2] Prof. Chatterji thinks that *tāsu* and other -*s*- forms are loan-words from literary Apabhraṃśa.

variety of forms would result from an analogy with the forms of the Proximate demonstrative pronoun :

Proximate	Remote
ī	*ū*
ē	*ō, vē*
yehu	*wahu, ohu*
yā	*wā̃ (vā)*
ehi	*ohi, wahi*
inha	*unha*

In Modern Awadhi the western dialects observe the distinction of gender just as in adjectives. In Early Awadhi no distinction of gender in pronouns is attested by the texts which all belong to the Eastern Hindi area. The same applies to the Proximate Demonstrative.

Proximate Demonstrative Pronoun

A. Early Awadhi

§ 243. The forms of this pronoun are generally found in all the three texts as adjectives and seldom as pronouns except in Tulsīdās. The orthography transcribes *ya* and *e* and *ye* separately, but like modern Awadhi, there does not appear to have been any difference in pronunciation in Early Awadhi as well.

		sg.	pl.
direct			
	J.	*yaha, yahu*	
	T.	*yaha, yahu, eha, ehu*	*ē, yē*
	N.	*yaha*	*yei, yaha*
oblique			
	J.	*ehi*	
	T.	*ehi*	*inhahī, inahī inha*
	N.	*ehi, yā*	*ina*

(*a*) Direct—Jāyasī : *yaha pachitāu calaū̃ binu sēvā* 'this is the regret that I am going without having served you' (p. 90), *kō yaha bāta pitā saū̃ cālai* 'who can start this talk with father' (p. 399), *ratanasēna yahu tahā̃ narēsū* 'this

Ratnasena is a king there' (p. 616). In one instance the form *iha* is found (*tā kara ihai jo khānā pianā* 'this only is his meat and drink', p. 7). *Tulsī* : singular—*yaha suni* 'having heard this' (p. 168), *yaha bicāri* 'having considered this' (p. 179), *yaha bicāru ura āni nṛpa* 'the king having put this thought in his mind' (p. 158), *ēka kahahī yaha bāta alīhā* 'some say that this (thing) is untrue' (p. 176), *mohi sama yahu anubhayeu na dūjē* 'no one else has experienced this as much as I have' (p. 158), *bimala baṃsa yahu anucita ēkū* 'in the untarnished family, this one is improper' (p. 161), *bhayeu punīta āju yahu gēhū* 'this house has become sanctified to-day' (p. 161), *yahu kucāli kachu jāna na kōī* 'this evil machination nobody know' (p. 166), *eha sudhi pāi prayāga nivāsī* 'inhabitants of Prayāg, on getting this news' (p. 199), *satya kahehu giribhava tanu ēhā* 'you have truly said that this body was born from a mountain' (p. 38), *jadyapi eha samujhata haũ nīkē* 'although I understand this well' (p. 226), *bharata bhuāla hōhī ehu sācī* 'Bharata will become a king, this is true' (p. 165), *sakhā parama paramāratha ēhū* 'my friend, this is the best objective' (p. 193); plural—*ēka kahahī ē sahaja suhāē* 'some said : these are naturally beautiful' (p. 204), *ē dōū dasaratha kē ḍhōṭā* 'both of these are the fondled children of Daśaratha' (p. 96), *yē priya sabahī jahā̃ lagi prānī* 'these are dear to all living beings' (p. 94). Nūr Muhammad : *ēka kahā yaha bhā matavārā* 'one said : he has become mad' (p. 62), *gurujana sõ yaha binatiya mōrī* 'this is my prayer before the elders' (p. 4), *yei dasa kāmini saṃgī, haī jōgī tohi jōga* 'O yogin, these ten loving women are thy fit companion' (p. 83), *haī hatyāre nayana yaha tērē* 'these, thy eyes, are murderous' (p. 62). In one case the form is *iha* (*ihai agama kō pantha* 'this is the path to the unreached', p. 26).

(*b*) Oblique—Jāyasī : *jei na hāṭa ehi līnha besāhā* 'whoever did not purchase anything in this market' (p. 56), *ehi misa laharai dēi* 'for this reason, sets up waves'

(p. 98), *ehi bana rahata gaī hama āū* 'our life-span has finished up in this forest' (p. 112).

NOTE.—The oblique has been used as inanimate object in several cases, *e.g.*, *ghara paiṭhata pūchaba ehi hārū* 'when I enter the house, they will ask about this necklace' (p. 103), *āvahu ehi bana chāḍi parāhī* 'come let us leave this forest and run away' (p. 112). In an emphatic (inclusive) form we find direct: *ēhū kahā asa mayā karēhū* 'do show favour on this also' (p. 470) and in one case the form is *ei*: *ei bikha-cārai saba budhi ṭhagī* 'this food-poison robbed me of all wisdom' (p. 113).

Tulsīdās: singular—*ehi tē adhika dharamu nahī dūjā* 'there is no better virtue than this' (p. 181), *pālava baithi pēḍu ehi kāṭā* 'the tree has been cut by this (her) sitting at the top' (p. 175), *ehi tau rāma lāi ura līnhā* 'Rāma himself has embraced this one' (p. 233), *ehi avasara* 'at this time' (p. 160), *ehi pāpinihi sūjhi kā pareū* 'what did this sinner think?' (p. 175). In one case the form is *yehi* (*rāma-pēma-bhājana bharata baṛē na yehi karatūti* 'Bharata was loved by Rāma and was great not on account of this accomplishment' p. 283). In another case the direct *yahu* has been used as oblique (*yahu kula ucita rāma kahā ṭīkā* 'in this family, it is proper to give coronation to Rāma', p. 164); plural—*inha kai dasā na kaheū bakhānī* 'I have not given details of their state' (p. 40), *jani sapanehu inha kē basa hōhū* 'do not be under their control even in dream' (p. 186), *ehu saba bhā inha ākhina āgē* 'all this has occurred before these very eyes' (p. 222), *taru-bara bāsa inhahī bidhi dinhā* 'the Creator gave these, residence under a (good) tree' (p. 204), *inahī harasaprada barasā ēkā* 'to these the rainy season gives great joy' (p. 320).

Nūr Muhammad: *ehi kārana maī līnheū* 'for this reason, I have taken' (p. 43), *ēhi samujha ḍara mānata jīū* 'understanding this he is afraid at heart' (p. 58). In one case the form is *yēhi* (*rahiyē yēhi nagara bairāgi* 'O yogin, live in this town', p. 3) and in another *ihi* (*ihi kājā* 'for this reason', p. 30), *yā tē bhalō na aura* 'nothing is better than this' (p. 43), *yā tẽ tehi kachu hātha na āvā* 'owing to this he obtained nothing' (p. 60), *yāhī sõ* 'by this very (thing)' (p. 56), *yāhū para* 'even on this' (p. 45), *ina kē bīca* 'between these' (p. 3)

NOTE—In a few cases direct *yaha* is found used with an oblique substantive, *e.g.*, *yaha sapanā kī bāta para* 'on this mention of the dream' (p. 11), *yaha jaga mõ* 'in this world' (p. 171).

B. MODERN AWADHI

§ 244. Lakhīmpurī has the following forms:

	sg.	pl.
dir. masc.	**iu, jʌɦu**	**iː**
,, fem.	**jaː, jʌɦ**	
obl.	**iː, eɦi**	**in, inɦ.**

For instance: **iu** or **jʌɦu gʌwaː** 'this (man) went', **jaː** or **jʌɦ gʌi** 'this (woman) went', **iː hʌĩ** 'these (men or women) are'; **iː kaː** or **eɦi kaː khʌwaːoː** 'feed this (man or woman)', **in** or **inɦ kaː khʌwaːoː** 'feed these (men or women)'.

(*a*) Of the dialects S., L., U. and F. agree with Lmp. Br. and R. have **eɦu** masc. dir. sg. and **jaː** fem. dir. sg. and the other cases are the same as in Lmp. Br. has dir. sg. masc. **iu** and dir. pl. as **iː** or **jʌi,** everywhere else it has **iː.** G., Fy., Sl., P. and A. do not observe distinction of gender, the dir. sg. being **iː** everywhere and the obl. sg. **iː** or **jaː** (*e.g.*, Fy. **jʌ kʌre**) **eɦi** and **eː.** The dir. pl. is **jʌi** (G., Fy., Sl.) and **eː** (P. and A). The obl. pl. is **iː** in G., Fy. and Sl. and **en** in P. and A. Bgh. has **jaː** dir., **jʌɦi** or **jaː** obl. sg., **eː, enɦ** dir. pl., **jʌn, jʌnɦ** obl. pl.

(*b*) In all the dialects the forms of this pronoun are used as adjectives also except that in Lakhīmpurī the dir. pl. is used as the obl. pl. also in adjectival uses. For instance: **iː lʌrikaː aːjeː** 'these boys came', **iː lʌrikʌn ko maːrʌu** 'beat these boys'. In U. the obl. pl. is used as the subject of past participial verbs, *e.g.*, **inß maːraː** 'these beat (me)', **inß lʌrikʌn hʌm kaː maːraː** 'these boys beat us'.

C. Origin

§ 245. Sanskrit had two bases *idam* and *etad*. In Awadhi we do not find any descendants of the former. *yahu*, *ehu* both go back to *ēṣaḥ* and *iu* is further decay of the same form. The existence of *iu* and *ehu* side by side in modern Awadhi can be explained by the difference in time at which their ancestors came into the language—*eso* and *ehu* must have been used side by side. In *yaha*, *eha* and *yā* there is the history of *ēṣā*. *ē* goes back to *ēlē*; *yē*, *yei* and **jʌi** also are closely connected with it.

iː appears to be a fresh formation. The oblique *inha* (*ina*, *in*) is a regular form from **ī** and *inhahī* is a superimposed oblique.

Relative and Correlative Pronouns

A. Early Awadhi[1]

§ 246.

		sg.	pl.
direct			
	J.	*jō*, *jei*	*jei*, *jō*, *jinha*
	T.	*jō*, *jehi*	*jē*, *jinha*
	N.	*jō*, *jeī*	*jina* (*jena*)
oblique			
	J.	*jā*, *jehi*, *jāsu*	*jinha*
	T.	*jā*, *jehi*, *jāhi*, *jāsu*	*jina*, *jinha*, *jinhahī*, *jinahī*;
	N.	*jā*, *jehi*	*jina*
adjective		*jauna* (*javana*)	

(*a*) Direct singular—In all the three texts *jō* is found as the subject or as inanimate direct object while *jei* (*jehi*) as

[1] The forms of the correlative have been shown above under § 240.

the subject of transitive participle verbs only. For instance:

Jāyasī: *dōsara nāhĩ jo sarabari pāvā* 'there is no one else who has obtained equality' (p. 8), *marai jo calai gaṅga gati lēĩ, tehi dina kahā̃ ghaḍī kō dēĩ* 'he who is going to die and to take the shelter of the Ganges, to him who is it that appoints the auspicious day and the hour?' (p. 242), *jō ḍolāu sō ḍōlā* 'what he moves, moves' (p. 11), *sasi caudasi jō daī savā̃rā, tēhū cāhi rūpa ũjiārā* 'the moon of the 14th date which the Creator has made beautiful—his beauty was brighter than its' (p. 21); *jei mukha dēkhā tei hā̃sā* 'whoever saw the face, laughed' (p. 33), *duhū̃ jaga tarā nā̃ũ jei līnhā* 'whoever took (remembered) the name, crossed both the worlds' (p. 15), *jei jiu dīnha* 'who gave life' (p. 2).

Tulsīdās: *baranaũ raghubara-bimala-jasu, jō dāyaku phala cāri* 'I describe the untarnished glory of the best of Raghus, which gives the four fruits' (p. 157), *munirāja kara joi joi āyasu hōi . . . bēgi karahu soi sōi* 'whatever be the order of the great sage, quickly obey that' (p. 159), *anna so joi joi bhōjana karaī, soi soi tava āyasu anusaraī* 'whoever eats that food, he will obey your orders' (p. 74), *jō jehi bhāva nīka tehi sōi* 'whatever appears good to one, for him that is good' (p. 5), *baia so lunia lahia jō dīnhā* 'whatever is sown is reaped, whatever is given is obtained' (p. 163), *jehi rāura ati anabhala tākā, soi pāihi ehu phalu paripākā* 'he will obtain the fruit of this who has aimed at your evil' (p. 165). *dīnha hamahī jei lōcana-lāhū* 'who gave to us a gain for our eyes' (p. 205).

Nūr Muhammad: *jō asa bhāria bhāra uṭhāī* 'who lifts such a heavy load' (p. 22), *jō nabha au mahi kō bala harā* 'who robbed the earth and the sky of their strength' (p. 22), *jō baca bhākhai adhara tumhārā* 'which words your lip speaks' (p. 14), *kāḍhai sōī bara jō hōī* 'he who will draw up will be the bridegroom' (p. 17), *jeĩ nidrā rasanā para līnhā, bandhu mā̃sa teĩ bhōjana kīnhā* 'he eats the flesh of his relatives who remains quiet (lit. who takes sleep on his tongue)' (p. 143), *paṭa bāhara jeī pāva pasārā* 'who stretches the feet beyond the cloth' (p. 43).

Direct plural—

Jāyasī : *bhā jaga adala dīna jō āyē* 'on whose accepting the religion, justice was established in the world' (p. 16), *bhae dharamī jei pāḍhata sikhē* 'those who were well-read, became virtuous' (p. 15).

Tulsīdās : *jē* is used with all verbs while *jinha* only with past participle verbs, *e.g.*, *jē nija bhagata nātha tava ahahī* 'O Lord, those who are your own devotees' (p. 67), *jē pura gā̃va basahī maga māhī, tinhahī nāga-sura-nagara sihāhī* 'the cities of the *Nāgas* and the gods praise those cities and villages which lay on their way' (p. 201), *jē priya parama kaikaī kērī* 'who were very dear to Kaikēi' (p. 176), *jinha paṭhaē bana bālaka aisē* 'who sent such boys to the forest' (p. 192), *prathama jāi jinha bacana sunāē, bhūṣana basana bhūri tinha pāē* 'Those who first gave the news, they got many ornaments and clothes' (p. 160).

Nūr Muhammad : *jina bina khambha akāsa sā̃vārā* 'who (respectful) has arranged the sky without pillars' (p. 1), *jena pahirā añjana pahirāvā* 'those (eyes) which have put on the collyrium-clothes' (p. 71).

(*b*) Oblique singular—In all the three texts *jā* has been used always with postpositions. For intance:

Jāyasī : *kīnha sabai asa jā kara* 'whose creation all this is' (p. 2), *jā kahā̃ hōi aisa kanahārā* 'for whom there is such a leader' (p. 24), *jā saũ vei hērahī cakhu nārī* 'towards whom those women look with their eyes' (p. 49).

Tulsī : *jā tē̃ avadha anātha na hōī* 'by which Avadha may not be without a Lord' (p. 194), *sādhu samāja na jā kara lēkhā* 'who is not counted in the assembly of the good' (p. 231).

Nūr Muhammad : *jā kahā̃ karatā darasa dekhāeu* 'to whom, O Lord, you showed yourself' (p. 2), *kīnhā dina kāraja hai jā sō̃* 'He has created day, by which action is possible' (p. 1), *jā kē hiẽ larika budhi hōī* 'who has childish thoughts in his mind' (p. 4).

jehi in Jāyasī is found both with and without postpositions while in Tulsī and Nūr Muhammad it is generally found with postpositions, *e.g.*, Jāyasī: *kīnhesi amī jiai jehi pāī* 'He created nectar by obtaining which one is enlivened' (p. 6), *kīnhesi daraba garaba jehi hōī* 'he created wealth by which one has pride' (p. 5), *ādihu anta rāja jehi chājā* 'whose rule is grand from beginning to end' (p. 8), *sō pai marama jānu jehi nāhī* 'he only knows the value (secret) who has not (got them)' (p. 12), *calai utāila jehi kara khēvā* 'whose paddling (of the oars) is very rapid' (p. 26), *jehi kai asa panihārī sō rānī kehi rūpa* 'what beauty must that queen have, whose water-carriers are such' (p. 49), *dīnhesi kaṇṭha bōli jehi māhā* 'He has given a throat in which there is speech' (p. 12); Tulsīdas: *soi saba bhā̃ti mōra hitakārī jehi tē̃ rahai bhuāla sukhārī* 'he is in every way my benefactor with whom the king remains happy' (p. 188), *jehī na hōhī dukha dīna* 'by which (my mothers) are not distressed by misery' (p. 189); Nūr Muhammad: *jehi ka prēma mahā̃ hiyā* 'whose heart is in love' (p. 6), *jehi dēkheũ nisa māha* 'whom I saw at night' (p. 12).

NOTE.—Both in Tulsīdās and in Nūr Muhammad *jā* and *jehi* are found used as adjectives, *e.g.*, *jā mana jāmā prēma rasa* 'in which mind love sentiment has taken a root' (N. p. 6), *jā dina prēma hākārai āvā* 'on which day, love comes to call' (N. p. 24), *jehi jehi jōni karama basa bhramahī* 'in whichever birth we have to roam according to our *karma*, (T. p. 166), *tōra kahā phura jā dina hōī* 'your word will turn out to be true on which day' (T. p. 163), *jehi ṭhāũ* 'at which place' (N. p. 2). *jehi rānī kara* 'of which queen' (N. p. 20).

jāhi and *jāsu* are used without postpositions, the former in the sense of accusative-dative and the latter of genitive, *e.g.*, *aribasa daiva jiāvai jāhī*, 'whom fate keeps alive under the enemy' (T. p. 165), *jāhi dīna para nēha* 'who has affection for the poor' (T. p. 3), *jāhi dharahī muni dhyāna* 'whom the sages keep in mind' (T. p. 55); *barabhā ḍarai catura-mukha jāsū* 'Brahmā who has four faces is afraid' (J. p. 587), *jāsu bhajana binu jarani na jāī* 'without the prayer of whom, the fire (anguish) is not removed' (T. p. 159).

NOTE.—In one case the form is *jisu*: (*saba sidhi sulabha japata jisu nāmū*, 'by meditating upon his (whose) name all the accomplishments become easy' (T. p. 52).

Oblique plural—*jinha* (*jina*) is used with postpositions while accusative-dative *jinhahī* (*jinahī*) without postpositions, *e.g.*, *dara nisāna saba jinha kē bājā* 'at whose doors the military music always played' (J. p. 72), *para hita-hāni lābha jinha kērē* 'for whom gain consists in others' loss' (T. p. 4), *para hita ghṛta jinha kē mana mākhī* 'whose minds are like flies in the butter in the shape of others' good' (T. p. 4), *kahā bahuta jena kī mati phērī* 'turned their thoughts by saying a great deal' (N. p. 100); *rāma carana-paṅkaja priya jinhahī* 'to whom the lotus-feet of Rāma are dear' (T. p. 190), *sumirata jinahī rāma mana māhī* 'whom Rāma remembers in his mind' (T. p. 242).

(*c*) The relative adjective *jauna* (*javana*) 'which' is found in the texts and changes for gender, *e.g.*, *jaunahi bhā̃ti* 'in whichever way' (J. p. 297), *bañcehu mōhi javani dhari dēhā, soi tanu dharahu* 'take that body having put on which you have deceived me' (T. p. 62).

B. MODERN AWADHI

§ 247. Lakhīmpurī has the following forms:

	sg.	pl.
Relative.		
dir.	**ɟoː, ɟʌun**	**ɟoː, ɟʌun, ɟiː**
obl.	**ɟiː, ɟeɦi**	**ɟin, ɟinɦ**
Correlative		
dir.	**soː, tʌun**	**soː, tʌun, tiː**
obl.	**tiː, teɦi**	**tin, tinɦ**

For instance : **joː** or **jʌun jʌis kʌriː soː** or **tʌun tʌis paːiː** 'as one will do so one will get', **joː** or **jʌun** or **jiː jʌiɦʌĩ soː** or **tʌun** or **tiː maːrn̥ khʌiɦʌĩ** 'those who will go will be beaten'; **jiː kaː** or **jeɦi kaː bolaːoː tiː kaː** or **teɦi kaː khaːi ko deːu** 'give (something) to eat to him (or her) whom you call', **jin kaː** or **jinɦ kaː bolaːoː tin kaː** or **tinɦ kaː khaːi ko deːu** 'give them (something) to eat whom you invite'.

(*a*) Of the dialects S., L., U. and F. agree with Lmp.; in B., R. and Br. **jeɦi** only is used as obl. sg. and **jeː** instead of **jiː** in the dir. pl.; similarly in the correlative **teɦi** and **teː**. Of the Eastern dialects G. has commonly **jʌun : tʌun** and **jeː : teː** for both the numbers in the direct and **jeː, jeɦi, teː, teɦi** sg. and **jenɦ, tenɦ** in the obl. Similarly, Fy. and Sl. have **jeː, seː** very commonly and **jʌun, tʌun** rarely. P. has

	sg.	pl.
dir.	**joː, jʌwʌn**	**joː, jʌwʌn, jeː**
obl.	**jeː, jeɦi**	**jen**
dir.	**tʌwʌn**	**tʌwʌn**
obl.	**teː, tʌwʌneː**	**tʌwʌnen**

Similarly, A. Br., R. and Fy. have an accusative-dative case in the plural **jinɦʌi, tinɦʌi**. Bgh. has **jʌun tʌun** dir. and **jjʌɦi'tjʌɦi** obl. sg. and **jjʌnɦ** for dir. and obl. plural.

(*b*) The forms of the Third Person pronoun are freely used in place of those of the Correlative, *e.g.*, **jʌun, uː**.

(*c*) In all the dialects the forms of this pronoun are used as pronominal adjective also. Such dialects as have a change in adjectives for gender (see § 219) change this adjective also, *e.g.*, Lakhīmpurī **jʌuni̥ lʌũr̥ijaː : jʌuniː lʌũr̥ijaː** etc. In Lmp. **jiː : tiː** are commoner than **jin jinɦ : tin tinɦ** while in R. the latter are commoner than the former.

Of the Eastern dialects G. and P. report change of gender in the case of this adjective, G. **jʌuniː : tʌuniː**, P. **jʌwniː : tʌwniː**.

C. ORIGIN

§ 248. The initial sound of this pronoun is *j*-Skt. *y*- of ancient relative. **joː** (*jō*) represents Skt. *yaḥ*, Pkt. *jō* while **jeː** (sing.) is the Māg. Nominative sg. **jʌun** (*jauna*) represents *yaḥ punaḥ* (Chatterji, p. 842) which was regarded in Middle Indian as one group. *yaḥ* maintains itself as *jō* being a monosyllable while *yaḥ punaḥ* has disintegration first into *ja uṇa* and then into *jauna*, **jʌun**. The interchange of the vocable -*u*- with *va* through *vu* is a regular feature.

Early Awadhi *jei*, *jehi*, *jeĩ* shown under the direct case are really oblique forms (being used as subject in participial construction) derived as Māg. *jē* + *hi* the regular oblique termination. The other oblique *jā* is *yasya* through *jassu*, *jāsu*, *jāhu*, *jāh*, *jā*. We find *jāsu* used side by side with *jā* —the latter has lost its oblique sense and requires a postposition. *jāhi* should be taken as a superimposed oblique. Modern oblique **jiː** and pl. dir. **jiː** are modern formations; the use of *jō* for plural in the texts is modern, on the analogy of nouns; *jē* (dir. pl.) represents Skt. *yē* and *jei* is its emphatic form. *jina*, *jinha*, *jena*, *jenha* are oblique forms of the plural, on the analogy of nouns, based on -*nāṃ* and *jinhahĩ* is a superimposed oblique.

Interrogative Pronoun

A. EARLY AWADHI

§ 249.

		sg.	pl.
direct			
	J., T., N.	*kō*, *kei*	*kē*
oblique			
	J., T., N.	*kā*, *kehi*, *kāhi*, (*kāsu*)	
inanimate			
	J., T., N.	*kā*, *kāha*	
adjective			
	J., T., N.	*kavana* (*kauna*)	

(*a*) Direct—*kō* is used with all verbs while *kei* (*kehi*) with past participle verbs only, *e.g.*, *kō pũchai* 'who asks?' (J. p. 123), *kō sari mō saũ pāvaĩ* 'who can obtain equality with me?' (J. p. 83), *bharata sarisa priya kō jaga māhī* 'who is so dear as Bharata in this world?' (T. p. 160), *kō na kusaṅgati pāi nasāī* 'who is it that does not perish when fallen in bad company?' (T. p. 167), *tā kō mūrata kō likhi pārai* 'who can paint her picture?' (N. p. 13), *kō piya tērā* 'who is thy beloved?' (N. p. 58), *kei yaha basata basanta ujārā* 'who has made this flourishing spring desolate?' (J. p. 445), *kei tava nāsā kāna nipātā* 'who has cut your nose and ears?' (T. p. 304), *kei ḍārā* 'who has put?' (N. p. 123).

(*b*) Oblique—*kā* is always used with postpositions, *e.g.*, *kā saũ karaũ barōka* 'with whom shall I perform the engagement ceremony?' (J. p. 83), *asa nāraṅga dahũ kā kahã rākhē* 'no one knows for whom such oranges have been kept?' (J. p. 201), *kahe na dhyāna dhana kā para dīnhē* 'the lady does not say on whom she has fixed her attention?' (N. p. 36), *mana sõ kā kahã sumirai kōū* 'who may remember whom in his mind?' (N. p. 107); *kehi* and *kāhi* are used with or without postpositions, *e.g.*, *dahũ kei jōga daī asi gaḍhī* 'for whom, has the Creator created her fit?' (J. p. 83), *kehi kahã kavãla bigāsā* 'for whom has the lotus bloomed?' (J. p. 183), *gāla karabu kehi kara balu pāī* 'whose support shall I get, to be able to be proud?' (T. p. 163), *nahī jānahũ bāura kehi nētī* 'I do not know for whom he is mad?' (N. p. 55); *kahau so pīra kāhi binu khãgā* 'tell us your trouble, without whom are you miserable?' (J. p. 223), *vyaratha kāhi para kījia rōṣū* 'on whom should anger be shown uselessly?' (T. p. 224).

kāsu is genitive, *e.g.*, *kahia hōi bhala kāsu bhalāī* 'please say, whose good can come about?' (T. p. 261).

(*c*) The inanimate interrogative pronoun is used to denote 'what?'. It is used in the direct, the oblique of the animate serves for the oblique of the inanimate also. For instance: *kā baranaũ* 'what shall I describe?' (J. p. 61), *karaũ kā bhāī* 'hullo! what shall I do?' (T. p. 28), *kā jānai sukha bhōga bhulānā* 'what shall a man who forgets himself in the enjoyment of happiness, know?' (N. p. 11), *na janaũ kāha hoihi kabilāsā* 'I do not know what shall happen in Kailāsa?' (J. p. 468), *aba dhaũ bidhihi kāha karanīyā* 'what will the Creator do now?' (T. p. 214)

(*d*) The pronouns given above are also used as adjectives, *e.g.*, *kahu kehi raṅkahi karaũ narēsū* 'tell me which poor person I shall make a king?' (T. p. 167), *kehi dēsa* 'in which country?' (N. p. 40).

The adjective *kavana* (*kauna*) is very generally used in all the texts. It changes forms for gender in Jāyasī generally and in Tulsīdās always while never in Nūr Muhammad. It changes for case in all the texts. For instance:

Jāyasī: *kaunu utara pāubi* 'what answer shall we have?' (p. 97), *na janaũ kaũnu pavanu lei āvā* 'God knows which wind has brought (it)?' (p. 104), *kauni mati malī* 'what opinion has been held?' (p. 223), but *kavana bhā̃ti* 'in which way?' (p. 11).

Tulsī: *kāranu kavanu* 'what is the reason?' (p. 172), *kavani bipati bari bhārī* 'what great calamity?' (p. 312), *kavani āsā* 'what hope?' (p. 177), *kavanē avasara* 'on what occasion?' (p. 169).

Nūr Muhammad: *kavana pantha taĩ līnhā* 'what path hast thou taken?' (p. 58), *kavana jāta hai* 'what is thy caste?' (p. 45), *kauna bhalāī* 'what goodness?' (p 29), *rākhai kaunē māna* 'in which way will (he) keep?' (p. 92).

B. Modern Awadhi

§ 250. Lakhīmpurī has the following forms:—

animate

	sg.	pl.
dir.	**koː, kʌun**	**koː, kʌun**
obl.	**kiː, keɦi**	**kin, kinɦ**

inanimate

dir.	**kaː**
obl.	**kaːɦeː, keɦi**

For instance: **koː** or **kʌun aːwaː hʌi** 'who has come?', **huāː koː** or **kʌun rʌɦʌĩ** 'who were there?', **kiː kaː** or **keɦi kaː bolaːeu** 'whom (sg.) did you call?', **kin kaː** or **kinɦ kaː bolaːeu** whom (pl.) did you call?'.

(*a*) Of the dialects, S., L. and U. agree with Lmp., F. has obl. sg. as **kʌɦi.** B. has obl. sg. as **keɦ** and obl. pl. as **kʌun.** Br. dir. is like Lmp., only **kʌun** is pronounced as **kʌuːn**; obl. sg. is **keɦi, koɦi** and obl. pl. does not differ from Lmp. In R. obl. sg. is **kʌɦi.** All the Eastern dialects have only one form for the dir. sg. and pl. *viz.*, **keː**; this is also sometimes used as obl. otherwise **keɦi** or **keɦ** is used in the sg. and **ken** in the pl. **kʌun** is rarely used in the Eastern dialects, the form in P. being **kʌwʌn.** Bgh. has **kʌun** dir., **kjʌɦi** obl. sg. and **kiʌn, kjʌnɦ** as both dir. and obl. plural. Inanimate dir. is **kaːɦ,** obl. **kʌiː.** In G. the obl. forms **kʌuneː, kʌuniː** are used.

(*b*) In all the dialects the inanimate dir. 'what?' is **kaː.** The obl. differs. Lmp., S., L., U., F., B., Br. have **kaːɦeː,** R. **kaːɦeː, kʌɦi,** G., Fy., Sl., P. and A. have **keɦi, kaːɦeː, kethuaː** and **kethaː, kaːɦeː** or **keɦaː,** *e.g.*, **kethaː se bãdʌrowʌn ko hãːkiː** 'with what shall I drive the monkeys?'.

(*c*) All the dialects use **kʌun** as the pronominal adjective and modify it according to case and gender (§ 219) as they do in the case of ordinary adjectives. For instance:

Lmp. **kʌuni̯ lʌũɽijaː** 'which girl?', **kʌuniː lʌũɽijʌ kə** 'to which girl?', **kʌuneː lʌrikʌwʌ kə** 'to which boy?', S.E. Sultānpurī: **kʌuneː tʌraː** 'in which manner?', **kʌuneː saːmaːn se** 'with what preparation?'.

C. Origin

§ 251. The history of the Interrogative pronoun is closely allied with that of the Relative pronoun, *e.g.*, **koː** represents *kaḥ*, **keː** < Skt. *kē*; *kei*, *kehi*, are oblique forms, *kā* is based on *kasya* ; *kauna* < Pkt. *ka+uṇa* ; Mod. **kʌɦi** <Early Aw. *kāhi* ; **koɦi** is absolutely modern.

Here, however, we find that the distinction between animate and inanimate is observed in Modern Awadhi and is attested by Early Awadhi. This is very clear for the direct—animate *kō*, inanimate *kā*. What is the derivation of this *kā*? Skt. had *kiṃ* for the neuter, but that has survived only as *ki* indeclinable. Besides *kā*, Early Aw. has *kāha*. Is this *ha* merely emphatic? The forms **kethaː**, **kethuaː** and **kaːɦeː** also are untraced historically.

Reflexive Pronoun

A. Early Awadhi

§ 252.

direct

J., T. *āpu* (*āpuna*), N. *āpa*

oblique

J., T. *āpu*, *āpuhi*, N. *āpa*, *āpuhī*

adjective

masc. dir. J., T. *āpana*, *āpuna*, *apāna*,
N. *āpana*, *apanō*, *āpanō*, *āpunu* (*āpa*),
fm. J., T. *āpani*, fm. obl. T., N. *apanī*, *āpanī*
masc. obl. J., T. *apanē*, N. *apanē*, *āpanē*, *apānē*,

(*a*) Direct—*e.g.*, *guru hoi āpu kīnha jaga cēlā* 'himself becoming the preceptor, he made the world his pupil' (J. p. 132), *sabahi khiāvai āpu na khāī* 'he feeds all but himself does not eat' (J. p. 7), *rāma jāsu jasa āpu bakhānā* 'whose glory Rāma himself has sung' (T. p. 12), *āpu lasana para baiṭheu jāī* 'himself he went and sat near Lakshmana' (T. p. 192), *tīnha vidhavapana apajasu āpū* '(she) herself obtained widowhood and infamy' (T. p. 227), *āpa dharama dēhī hai rājā* 'the king himself is incarnation of Dharma' (N. p. 15), *rājā rahai āpa tehi māhī* 'the king himself lives in that' (N. p. 8).

NOTE 1. Besides being used as a subject, *āpu* is found used as (animate) object also in the following instances: *gunī na kōī āpu sarāhā* 'no skilful person praises himself' (J p. 130), *nindahi āpu sarāhi nisādahī* 'having admired Niṣāda, they censure themselves' (T. p. 236).

NOTE 2. In Tulsī there is one instance of *āpuna* (*āpuna caleu* 'himself went' p. 79).

(*b*) Oblique—*āpu* or *āpa* is used with postpositions while *āpuhi* (-*ī*) without them, *e.g.*, *āpu āpu kahā hōihi* 'every one will be (busy) for one's own self' (J. p. 97), *āpu āpu mahā rōdana karahī* 'weep amongst themselves' (J. p. 113); *jāni āpu para nēhu* 'having known (their) affection for himself (Lakshmaṇa)' (T. p. 211), *bōlē bacana āpa mahā mīṭhē* '(they) spoke sweet words amongst themselves' (N. p. 101), *ēka pāva dē āpa para* 'putting one foot on thyself' (N. p. 51); *risa āpuhi budhi aurahi khāī* 'anger harms self while wisdom another' (J. p. 145), *jō jānai sata āpuhi jārā* 'he who knows the truth, burns himself (his self)' (J. p. 323), *baṛabhāgini āpuhi anumānī* 'having considered themselves very lucky' (T. p. 240), *jaga au āpuhi kasa pahicānō* 'how do I take myself and the world?' (N. p. 3), *cēlā āpuhī jāni* 'having considered myself to be a disciple' (N. p. 21), *āpuhī paragaṭa karai nidānā* 'ultimately (beauty) reveals itself' (N. p. 6)

(*c*) The adjective is frequently used. For instance: Jāyasī: *jō piu āpana kahai so jhūṭhā* 'he who says 'the beloved is mine' is a liar' (p. 144), *āpuna nāhī kayā* 'the body is not one's own' (p. 307), *dōsa apānā* 'the fault is ours' (p. 116), *pahara pahara sō āpani bārī* 'after every watch, every one on one's turn' (p. 64), *kita āuna puni apanē hāthā* 'whence would the coming back be in our hand (control)' (p. 96), *au apanē apanē ghara rājā* 'and (they are) kings in their own houses' (p. 67).

Tulsī: *āpana mōra nīka jō cahahū* 'if you want your own good and mine' (p. 181), *taka puni sambhu samujhi pana āpana* 'there Śiva considering his vow' (p. 30), *sabahi apana sudhi bhōrī bhaī* 'everyone lost an idea about oneself' (p. 136),. . *saba āpani karanī . . . baranī* 'she described her own action' (p. 220), *jō pāvãru apanī jaṛatāī, tumhahī sugāi* 'the wretched man who suspects you owing to his own ignorance' (p. 229), *kṛpā bhalāī āpanī, nātha kīnha bhala mōra* 'my lord has acted well towards me by his own kindness and goodness' (p. 273), *phirata sanēha magana sukha apanē* '(they) move about imbued with affection and in their own happiness' (p. 15), *apanē calata* 'as far as lay in my power' (p. 165).

Nūr Muhammad : *jaba maī āpana nāma bhulāvaũ* 'when I lose memory of my own name' (p. 25), *kaṭa cāhai apa mahimā, laṭa āpana marajāda* 'the loin wished its greatness while the lock of hair its own respect' (p. 138), *apanē citra citērā dēkhi* ... 'the painter seeing his picture' (p. 71), *dhana jō mitra āpanō cīnhā* 'blessed is he who recognises his friend' (p. 54), *bāta samēṭahu āpunū* 'finish your talk' (p. 24), *apanī apanī āṭa tē* 'with one's own money (in the folds of his cloth)' (p. 9), *āneu apanē gēha* 'brought (her) to his house' (p. 17), *gaī āpanē grēha* 'went to her house' (p. 52), *tohi lai calahū apānē gāū* 'shall take you to my village' (p. 102).

NOTE 1. The Sanskrit forms ***sva*** and ***nija*** have also been occasionally used.

NOTE 2. ***āpusa*** (***sakhina matā āpusa mō̃ kīnhā*** 'the friends settled amongst themselves', p. 100).

(*d*) Honorific pronouns are not found in Jāyasī or Nūr Muhammad. But we find in Tulsīdās both *āpu*[1] as the honorific pronoun and *rāura* (*rāvara*) as honorific genitive

[1] Greaves (Grammar of the Rāmāyan, p. 15) denies the existence of *āpa* as honorific and rightly criticises Growse's translation of the 2nd Caupāī after Dohā No. 177 on p. 67 of the Rāmāyan, but the instances quoted here do prove the use of *āpu* as honorific.

adjective. For instance: *saba samēta pura dhāria pāū, āpu ihā amarāvati rāū* 'Please step into (enter) the city with all; you are here and the king is in Amarāvatī' (p. 254), *prabhu priya pūjya pitā sama āpū* 'you are just like my father—my master, adorable and dear' (p. 271), *gyāna ambu nidhi āpuna ājū* 'you yourself are the ocean of knowledge' (p. 271); *rājana rāura nāma jasa* 'O King, your name and glory' (p. 159), *rāuri māyā* 'your *māyā*' (p. 170), *sarāhana rāvarī* 'your praise' (p. 236), *hita sabahī kara raurē hāthā* 'every one's good is in your hands' (p. 270).

B. Modern Awadhi

§ 253.

ʌponaː

This pronoun expresses a reflexive sense for emphasis and is used with all personal pronouns and with nouns without any change in form, *e.g.*, **raːm ʌponaː tʌu bʌn kaː cʌleː gʌjeː dʌsʌrʌth kə roːwʌi kə ɡɦʌr chãːɽi̥ geː** 'Rām himself went away to the forest but left Daśaratha at home to lament', **ʌponaː tʌu khaːini̥ piini̥** '(he) himself ate and drank', **ʌpənaː tum coraːeu ʌu hʌm kaː coːriː lʌgaːeu** 'you yourself stole (the money) and attributed the theft to me' **mʌi ʌpɔnaː mʌrʌũ cʌɦʌi jiʌũ tum seː kaː mʌtlʌbu̥** 'whether I myself die or live what have you to do with me', **ui ʌpənʌ kə bʌɦut bɦʌlaː buraː kʌɦini̥** 'he rebuked himself very much'.

(*a*) This pronoun also expresses the combined sense of 'you and I' sometimes, *e.g.*, **bɦaːiː ʌpʌnʌ se kaː mʌtlʌbu̥** 'my friend, what have we to do with it?'

(*b*) The form of this pronoun in all the dialects is the same. When the sense of 'all alone by one's self' is to be expressed we have **aːpui aːpu̥** in Lmp. and other Western and Central dialects while **ʌpunʌi** in the Eastern dialects.

(*c*) This pronoun is also used as an adjective, *e.g.*, Lmp. **ʌpʌn, ʌpʌni̥, ʌpʌneː, ʌpʌniː.** In the Eastern dialects the form is **aːpʌn,** *e.g.*, Fy. **aːpʌn kitaːb, aːpʌn lʌrikaː** 'one's book, one's son'.

(*d*) There are no honorific pronouns in Modern Awadhi like Hindustani **aːp** or Bihari **rʌuwãː.** When honour or respect is shown, special care is taken to use the plural pronoun and verb. Sometimes the Hindustani form **aːp** is borrowed as **aːpu̥.** With this the verb used is that for the second person plural instead of the third person verb or the passive verb of Hindustani. For instance: Lmp. **aːpu̥ aːeu**, Hindustani **aːp aːijeːgaː** 'please do come', Lmp. **aːpu̥ ɟaːu,** Hin. **aːp ɟaːijeː** 'please go'.

In Bgh. owing to the influence of Bhōjpurī **ʌpənaː** dir. and **ʌponeː** obl. are used as honorific pronoun, *e.g.*, **ʌpənaː mwʌɦĩ bwʌkorʌu bɦʌr nʌɦĩː diːn** 'your honour never gave even a goat to me', **ʌpənaː keːr** 'your honour's'.

C. Origin

§ 254. The forms with *a*- (**ʌ**-) and *ā*- are all based on Skt. *ātman* which in Mid. Indian came to have two developments *appa* and *atta* (Chatterji § 591). The -*p*- form is found in Awadhi, Early Aw. *āpu* <*appo*. The modern form **ʌpənaː** is based on the genitive pl. *appāṇaṃ* which is used as an adjective in a variety of forms, but the presence of old Nominative is attested by modern emphatic forms such as **aːpui aːpu.** The use of *ātman* is also verified by a noun in Awadhi **ʌpaː** 'selfness'; *āpusa* <*appassa*.

The honorific use of this word is not Awadhi properly. That it was used honorifically in Mid. Indian is shown by the word *attā* 'mother-in-law, a respected lady'. In Early Awadhi we find the honorific adjective *rāura*, *rāvari* etc. This is a borrowing from Bhōjpurī where the pronoun **rʌuãː** is freely in use. *rāura* is based on *rājan* and has the -*ra* of the postposition *kara*. These forms are distinct from Hin. *rāwal* <*rājakula*.

Indefinite Pronouns

A. Early Awadhi

§ 255. *aura* and its equivalents

direct

aura, *auru* (*aurana* pl. only); *āna*

obl.

aurahi (*aurana* pl. only); *ānahi*

adjective *parā-*

Forms of *aura* 'other' are found in all the three texts. For instance

Jāyasī: *aura jo hōi so bāura andhā* 'anybody else who be, is mad and blind' (p. 10), *aura jo dīnha jagata mahā̃* 'whatever else has been given in this world' (p. 8), *aura jo bhūlē āutahi* 'others who have lost (the way) while coming' (p. 16), *budhi aurahi khāī* 'wisdom eats (destroys) another' (p. 145), *kō auru narēsā* 'which other king?' (p. 162), *vei tau uḍē auru bana tākā* 'they flew and aimed at another forest' (p. 112).

Tulsī: *auru karai aparādha kou aura pāu phala bhōgu* somebody else commits a fault and another obtains the enjoyment of the fruit (punishment)' (p. 187), *aura karahi kō bharata baṛāī* 'who can give more praise to Bharata', (p. 257), *aurau jē hari bhagata sujānā* 'others also who are wise and are devoted to Hari' (p. 18).

Nūr Muhammad: *darasa dēkhi jō jiya tajaũ yātē bhalō na aura* 'if having seen (her) I give up life, nothing else will be better than this' (p. 43), *tohi taji aurahi dhyāna na lāvai* 'he will not fix his attention on any one else except you' (p. 62), *aurana kahā calahu vahi vōrā* 'the others said: let us go to that side' (p. 56), *aurana sō mānuṣa niyarānā* 'the man approached the others' (p. 34).

(*a*) Besides *aura*, forms of *āna* and *parā-* are found in Tulsīdās and Nūr Muhammad, *e.g.*, *āna upāya banihi nahī̃ bātā* 'in any other way, nothing fruitful will result'

(T. p. 190), *sapatha tumhāra bharata kai ānā* '(I take) your oath and another of Bharata' (T. p. 174), *mohi taji ānahi barihi na bhōrē* 'she will surely not choose anybody other than me' (T. p. 61), *suni dui bāta āna sō̃ rānī* 'O queen, after having heard two words from another' (N. p. 62), *daraba jo āna kō* 'another's money' (N. p. 109); *pisuna parāya pāpa kahi dēhī* 'backbiters who give out other's sin' (T. p. 222), *munihi mōha mana hātha parāē* 'owing to his infatuation, the sage's heart was in other's hands' (T. p. 61), *dēkhi na sakahī parāi bibhūtī* 'cannot look at another's prosperity' (T. p. 162), *jaba bhayeu parāvā* 'when it became another's' (N. p. 104).

§ 256. *kōī*

direct animate

kōī, kāhu, kou

oblique

kāhu, kāhi, kehu, kāhuhi

direct inanimate

J. *kichu*, T. *kachu, kichu*, N. *kachu, kichu, kucha*

(*a*) direct animate—In Jāyasī the most common forms are *kōī* and *kāhū*; I have found only two instances of *kōū*. For instance: *na kōī rahā* 'nobody survived' (p. 5), *nā koi hoihai ohi kē rūpā* 'nobody will be like him' (p. 11), *asa jaga dāna na kāhū dīnhā* 'no one in the world has given such a gift' (p. 23), *sērasāhi sari pūja na kōū* 'no one has reached the equality of Sher Shah' (p. 23), *nayana bā̃ka sari pūja na kōū* 'the eyes are charming, nothing equals (them)' (p. 174).

In Tulsīdās *kou* is frequently used while *kōī* and *kāhū* are less in use, *e.g.*, *kou nṛpa hōu* 'anybody may become king' (p. 163), *dāru bicāru ki karai kou* 'does any one pay an attention to the wood?' (p. 8), *jasa karai na kōī* 'as nobody does' (p. 177), *kāhu na mohī kahi prathama janārā* 'no one gave me an indication of it before' (p. 175).

In Nūr Muhammad *kou* and *kōi* both are frequently used while *kāhu* is less in use, *e.g.*, *tehi sama kōu na āhi* 'there is no one like him' (p. 1), *kou ṭhāṛhā hai dhyāna lagāẽ* 'some one is standing with fixed attention' (p. 16), *na kōpehu kōī* 'please do not, any one of you, be angry' (p. 4), *mōti kāṛha na pārai kōī* 'no one can draw the pearl out' (p 17), *rasa sugandha kahā chāṛā kāhū* 'some one gave up taste (tasteful meal) and good smell' (p. 12).

(*b*) oblique—In Jāyasī the most general form is *kāhū* which is used with postpositions, *e.g.*, *ohi na kāhu kai āsa nirāsā* 'he has neither hope nor despair from (of) any person' (p 7), *kōī karai besāhanā kāhū kēra bikāi* 'some one was making a purchase while another's article was selling' (p. 56), *rini kāhū kara līnhesi kāḍhī* 'he borrowed money of some one' (p. 120). *kāhuhi* is used without postpositions, *e.g.*, *kāhuhi bhōga bhuguti sukha sārā* 'to some one enjoyment of objects of pleasure and the best of happiness' (p. 7); there is only one instance of *kāhi* (*bāura karihai kāhi* '(he) will make some one mad' p. 132), and two instances of *kehu*, viz., *koi kehu pāsa āsa kai gavanā* 'some one has gone to some one with hope' (p. 130), *jaū na hōta asa bairī, kehu kāhū kai āsa* 'if there were not such an enemy, would any one have dependence on another?' (p. 129).

In Tulsīdās, only two forms *kāhu* and *kāhuhi* are found, the latter is always found without postpositions while the former is with postpositions except when it comes as accusative, *e.g.*, *kāhuhi dōsa dēhu jani tātā* 'dear (son) do not blame any one' (p. 221), *sanamukha bimukha na kāhuhi kāū* '(it) is not against any one who comes before it' (p. 261), *apanē calata na āju lagi anabhala kāhu ka kīnha* 'as far as I could, I have never done harm to (of) any one till now' (p. 165), *tehi nisi nīda parī nahī kāhū* 'that night, no one had sleep' (p. 172).

In Nūr Muhammad, only *kāhū* is found and it is used with postpositions, *e.g.*, *hai kāhū kō prēma biyōgī* '(he) is lovelorn of somebody' (p. 55), *jaga mō̃ kāhū sātha* 'with anyone in this world' (p. 81).

(*c*) direct inanimate—For instance, Jāyasī: *katahũ kathā kahai kichu kōī* 'somewhere, some one was reciting a story' (p. 59), *tasa jaga kichū na pāeũ upama dēũ ohi jōga* 'I have obtained nothing such in this world as could be compared with her' (p. 217);

Tulsī: *kou kichu kahai na kou kichu pūchā* 'no one said anything, nor did anyone ask anything' (p. 252), *kachu jāna na kōī* 'nobody knew anything' (p. 166), *kachu kahaũ* 'I say something' (p. 167);

Nūr Muhammad: *jō kōū kachu lēvai cāhai* 'if any one wanted to take anything' (p. 9), *kachu na sunāeu bāta* 'did not say a word' (p. 26), *kichu upāya nahi āvai* 'no means have I' (p. 51), *kichu hamāra cintā hai tōhī* 'have you any anxiety for me?' (p. 84), *tapiya kahā rājā kachu sūjhā* 'the hermit said: O king, have you seen anything?' (p. 21).

§ 257. *saba*

direct *saba*

oblique *saba, sabahi*

(*a*) direct—*maṅgala kalasa sajana saba lāgī* 'all began to arrange the auspicious *kalaśas* (jars)' (T. p. 160), *nṛpa saba rahahī kṛpā abhilāṣē* 'all the kings remain desirous of his favour' (T. p. 158), *saba sumirata hai tāhi* 'all that remembers him' (N. p. 1), *rasanā hōi rōma saba mōhī* 'if all my hair becomes tongue' (N. p. 2), *sabu pāyeũ* 'obtained all' (T. p. 158), *karateũ jiu tana mana saba vārana* 'I would have sacrificed all—life, body and mind' (N. p. 3).

(*b*) oblique—in Jāyasī the oblique is found used with postpositions except *sabahi* used as accusative-dative, *e.g.*, *saba kahã bhuguti rāti dina bāṭā* 'he gives enjoyment to every one, day and night' (p. 7), *vaha saba saũ saba ohi saũ baratā* 'all are knitted with him and he with all' (p. 10), *madira madira saba kē caupārī* 'there are sitting-halls in the houses of all' (p. 57), *jāvãta jiu saba kara bhakha-dātā* 'you are the giver of meals of all beings that are' (p. 107), *tā kara disiṭi sabahi uparāhī* 'his glance is on every one' (p. 7), *sabahi khiāvai āpu na khāī* 'he feeds all, but himself he does not eat' (p. 7).

In Tulsīdās and Nūr Muhammad *saba* is used with postpositions and *sabahi* (accusative-dative) without them, *e.g.*, *saba kē ura abhilāṣu asa* 'such was the desire in everyone's heart' (T. p. 158), *sabahi rāmu priya* 'Rāma is dear to every one' (T. p. 158), *sabahi suhāi* 'if it is pleasant to all' (T. p. 164), *saba kahā sūdhī bāṭa calāvai* 'he puts everyone on the right path' (N. p. 9), *tehi sumirana mō sabahi anandā* 'by remembering Him, delight (comes) to everyone' (N. p. 56).

B. Modern Awadhi

§ 258. **ʌur**

This pronoun expresses the sense of 'more', 'other', 'another (else)' and is constant in form in all the dialects, *e.g.*, Lmp. **ʌur kaː cʌɦiː** 'what more is wanted?', **thoːreː mʌnʌiː hiãː hʌĩ ʌur huãː** 'a few men are here, others are there', **ʌur aːiː hʌĩ** 'other (women) have come'.

(*a*) When used as an adjective it changes for gender and case as indicated in § 219. For instance: Lmp. **ʌur, ʌuri̥, ʌureː, ʌuriː**.

(*b*) There are two other adjectives **pʌraːr** and **aːn** used in the same sense of 'other'. For instance, Lmp. **pʌraːriː meɦʌruʌ kə nə deːkhʌi kə cʌɦiː** 'one should not look at another's wife', **pʌraːreː dɦʌn seː kʌunu̥ pʌroːjʌnu̥** 'what business (have we) with another's property?', **hʌm aːneː gãːu kə gʌjeː rʌɦʌn** 'I had been to another village'

§ 259. Lmp. **koːiː**

It means 'some one', 'any one' and is constant in form, *e.g.*, **koːiː aːwaː hʌi, koːiː aːiː hʌi** 'some one (male or female) has come', **koːi ko no maːrʌu** 'do not beat any one', **koːiː naːiː rʌɦʌĩ** 'there were no people'.

(*a*) This does not change even as an adjective, *e.g.*, **koːiː ʌdmiː** 'some man', **koːiː meɦʌruaː** 'some woman'.

(*b*) B.S. and L. have **koːiː,** U.,F., Br., R. **koːuː (koːɦuː)**, G., Fy., Sl., P. and A. have **keːuː (keːɦuː)**

(*c*) Like interrogative inanimate **kaː** 'which thing?' indefinite inanimate **kuchu̥** direct and **kaːɦeu** oblique mean 'something, anything'; the form for this in Eastern dialects is **kuchuː** dir. For instance: Lmp. **hʌm kuchu̥ naːiː kiɦen** 'I did not do anything', **hʌm kaːɦeu se peːʈu̥ bɦʌri̥ liɦen** 'I filled my stomach with something.'

§ 260. **sʌb**

It means 'all' and has one constant form for both the genders and cases, *e.g.*, **sʌb kiɦini̥** 'all did it', **sʌb kaː khʌwaːoː** 'feed all' It does not change as an adjective also, *e.g.*, **sʌb meɦʌruʌn se gʌunʌiː gʌwaːoː** 'cause all the women to sing', **sʌb ʌdmin se hʌm seː koːiː mʌtlʌb naːiː** 'I have nothing to do with all men'.

(*a*) All the dialects have the same form **sʌb.** The Eastern dialects have an accusative-dative form **sʌbʌi** (emphatic **sʌbːʌi** or **sʌbːʌj).**

C. Origin.

§ 261. (*a*) The forms of **ʌur, aːn, pʌraːr,** mostly adjectives, are attested by Early Awadhi and go back to Skt. *apara*, *anya* and *para* (*-kāra*) respectively.

(*b*) The forms **koːiː** (*kōī*), **koːuː** (*kou*) and **keːuː** all go back to OIA *kō'pi*. We find that instead of being elided the last vowel has been strengthened; this might be due to emphasis. This pronoun is always used emphatically corresponding to English 'anyone', 'not one' etc. **-uː** from *-pi*. *-vi* is not regular. It is decidedly on the analogy of Nom. sg. of the nouns. **keːuː** is based on Mag. Nom. sg. *kē*.

(*c*) A distinction between animate and inanimate is maintained in this pronoun. **kichu** keeps the *-i* of *kiṃ* while *kachu* and *kuchu* do not have it. The forms should be traced to some form of the pronoun *kiṃ cid*, Probably it is *kaścid*; cf. Aśoka *kici* and *kicchi*. Final *-u* is perhaps a particle (Chatterji, p. 845). See also Turner: Nep. Dic. under **kuchu.**

(*d*) **sʌb** (E. Aw. *saba*) goes back to *sarva* and **sʌbʌi** (E. Aw. *sabahi*) is the oblique form. The *-b* becomes long in emphasis and in other languages (*e.g.*, Nepali) it becomes aspirated. The expected form is ***saːb**, however.

Compound Pronouns

A. Early Awadhi

§ 262. The relative pronoun is combined with forms of *kōī*, *saba* with *kōī* and *aura* with *kōī*, *e.g.*,

Jāyasī : *saba kōū* 'everyone' (p. 123), *saba kichu* 'everything' (p. 11).

Tulsī : *jehi kēhī* 'to whomsoever' (p. 270), *jō kachu* 'whatsoever' (p. 158), *saba kou* 'everyone' (p. 170), *saba kāhū* 'to every one' (p. 176), *saba kēhī* 'to all' (p. 241), *auru kou* 'anyone else' (p. 187).

Nūr Muhammad : *jō kōi* 'whoever' (p. 15), *jō kou* 'whoever' (p. 74), *jō kacha* 'whatever' (p. 1), *jō kichu* 'whatever' (p. 56), *saba kāhū para* 'on everybody' (p. 8), *saba kōū* 'everyone' (p. 44).

B. Modern Awadhi

§ 263. The relative pronoun is combined with **koːiː** and **sʌb** and **sʌb** with **koːiː**, *e.g.*, Lmp. **sʌb koːiː** 'everyone', **ȷoː koiː** 'whoever', **ȷiː sʌb aːjeː** 'all who came'. **sʌb** is also added to personal pronouns, *e.g.*, **hʌm sʌb** 'we all', **tum sʌb** 'you all', **ui sʌb** 'they all'. **ʌur** also is combined with **koːiː** or **sʌb,** *e.g.*, **ʌur koːiː** 'anybody else', **ʌur sʌb** 'all else'.

(*a*) The dialects have corresponding forms. For instance: Fy. **jeː keuː khiːsaː jaːnʌt hoːi teː kʌħʌi** 'whoever may be knowing a tale should relate (it)', P. **jʌwʌn kuchụ,** Br. **joː kouː,** R. **sʌb kuchʌu.**

Pronominal Adjectives

A. Early Awadhi

§ 264. The texts have pronominal adjectives of manner, quantity and number based on the demonstrative, relative-correlative and interrogative pronouns. For instance:

(*a*) of manner

Jāyasī: *asa diyā* 'such a lamp' (p. 78), *asi kathā* 'such a tale' (p. 78), *asi jā kari dasā* 'whose condition is such' (p. 55), *jasa aṁcala jhīnai mahā̃ diyā, tasa ũjiāra dekhāvai hiyā* 'as the lamp under a thin linen, similarly shines the light in the heart' (p. 78), *jasa cā̃da* 'as the moon' (p. 24), (*vaha*) *aisa rahā* 'he was such' (p. 11), *aisī bithā raini saba jāgai* 'she wakes for the whole night owing to such a disease' (p. 378).

Tulsī: *abhilāṣu asa* 'such a desire' (p. 158), *asi nīti* 'such a polity' (p. 161), *tasi mati jasi bhābī* 'as the fate, so the thoughts' (p. 164), *kasi kubēsatā phābī* 'what manner of bad appearance came up' (p. 167), *aisehu kājā* 'even in such a cause' (p. 173), *aiseu bacana kaṭhōra suni* 'even on hearing such harsh words' (p. 183), *tulasī, jasi bhavitavyatā taisī milai sahāya* 'O Tulsī, one gets such help as the ordination is' (p. 71), *chabi jaisī . . . sōha na taisī* 'as the beauty is . . . so it does not shine' (p. 8).

Nūr Muhammad: *asa sapanā maĩ dēkheũ* 'I saw such a dream' (p. 5), *jasa pũjia hōī* 'as the capital be' (p. 30), *acaraja aisa* 'such a marvellous thing' (p. 5), *hērahu aisiya rānī* 'find out such a queen' (p. 117), *jaisō rahai tayasa puni hōi* 'as (it) was so it will become' (p. 33), *nahī jānahī sira parihai kaisō, khēlahu hōi khēlanā jaisō* 'it is not known what manner (of fate) will befall us, let us have (such) a play as (we want)' (p. 53).

(*b*) of quantity

Jāyasī : *etanā bōla* so much speech' (p. 555), *etanī bōli* 'in this much speech' (p. 289), *duijahī jōti kahā̃ jaga ōtī* 'where in the world, is there that much light on the second date?' (p. 168), *dukha tētā* 'that much of misery' (p. 158), *itē rūpa bhai kaniā* 'that girl was of so much beauty' (p. 80).

Tulsī : *etanā kahata* 'while he said so much (p. 232), *janu etania birañci karatūtī* 'as if this much was the whole capacity of the creator' (p. 158), *etanai kaheu bharata sana jāī* 'say only this much to Bharata' (p. 218), *ētehu dukha* 'even on so much misery' (p. 221), *kahi jāta na jētā* 'as much (love) as cannot be described' (p. 253), *kētika bātā* 'what amount of regard' (p. 256), *kētika bārā* 'what delay' (p. 161).

Nūr Muhammad : *hai ētō upakāra* 'there is so much of good deed' (p. 61), *ētō sugharāī para* 'on this much of good finish' (p. 92), *dukha jētō pāvā* 'as much misery as (it) got' (p. 67), *jētō . . . tētō* 'so much . . . as' (p. 52), *ketikō prīta* 'how so much affection' (p. 51), *jata . . . jōgū, tata . . . bhōgū* 'as much *yōga*, so much of enjoyment' (p. 169).

(*c*) of number

Jāyasī : *rakata ka bū̃da kayā jata ahahī* 'as many drops of blood as are in the body' (p. 577), *jāvata kēsa rōva pakhi pakhā* 'as many hair (on the head and on the body) birds and feathers as (there are in this world)' (p. 13), *ehi dharatī asa kētana līlē* 'this Earth has swallowed how many such (parrots)' (p. 110).

Tulsī : *raghupati-carana-upāsaka jētē* 'as many devotees of the feet of the Lord of Raghus (as there are)'

(p. 12), *saila himācala ādika jētē, citrakūṭa jasu gāvahĩ tētē* 'as many mountains, Himalayas, etc., as there are, all of them sing the glory of Citrakūṭa' (p. 211), *dēkhē jitē, hatē hama kētē* 'how many did we see, conquer and kill?' (p. 301).

Nūr Muhammad: *sundaratā kō lacchana jētē, pyārī cērē tērē tētē* 'as many characteristics of beauty as there are, all those are thy servants, my dear' (p. 91), *jētika ahaĩ kāya ruda aṅgū, vētika karahũ tāla miradaṅgū* 'as many noises as there are in the limbs of the body, I shall make them offer tempo to the drum' (p. 34), *jaita phūla phala patriya cāhī, tãvata āgama pura mõ āhī* 'as many flowers, fruits and leaves as are required, all those are in Āgamapura' (p. 14), *jāvata jōgī rahā samājā, tāvata kīnhā prēmiya rājā* 'as many Yogis as were in the assembly, the king made all of them lovers' (p. 22).

B. Modern Awadhi

§ 265. Awadhi has pronominal adjectives based on the demonstrative, relative, correlative, and interrogative pronouns. These are of manner (quality), of quantity and of number.

(*a*) Adjective of manner

Lmp. **ʌis** 'of this sort', **wʌis** 'of that sort', **ʝʌis . . . tʌis** 'such as', **kʌis** 'of which sort?'.

S., L., U., F., Br. and R. agree with Lmp. B. has **ʌs** 'of this sort', **wʌs, tʌs** 'of that sort', **ʝʌs** 'as', **kʌs** 'of which sort?'. Similarly G., Sl. and Fy. agree with Lmp.

(*b*) Adjective of quantity

Lmp. **etɪaɪ** or **ʌtɪaɪ** 'so much', **otɪaɪ** 'that much', **ʝetɪaɪ tetɪaɪ** 'as much as', **ketɪaɪ** 'how much?'.

S., L., U., F., Br., Fy. and Sl. agree with Lmp. The latter two with B. and G. have **etʌnaɪ** 'so much', **otʌnaɪ** or **tetʌnaɪ** 'that much', **ʝetʌnaɪ** 'as much', and **ketʌnaɪ** 'how much' (besides **kʌtik**).

R. has, besides the Lmp. set, **etʌraː** 'so much', **wotʌraː** 'that much', **ɟetʌraː tetʌraː** 'as much as', **ketʌraː** 'how much?'.

(*c*) Adjective of number

Lmp. **etːeː** 'so many', **otːeː** 'so many', **ɟetːeː tetːeː** 'as many as', **ketːeː** 'how many?'.

S., L., U., F., Br. agree with Lmp.; B., G., Fy. and Sl. have **etʌnaː, otʌnaː, ɟetʌnaː tetʌnaː** and **ketʌnaː.** R. has, besides the Lmp set, **etʌreː wotʌreː, ɟetʌreː tetʌreː, ketʌreː.** (All the dialects have **ɟʌi** 'as many', **tʌi** 'so many', **kʌi** 'how many' which do not change for gender or case).

The above adjectives change for case and gender as shown in § 219. For instance:

Lmp. **ʌiseː din maː gɦʌr bʌiʈhʌu** 'sit at home on such a day', **wʌisi̥ kitaːb phiri̥ naːiː deːkhi̥ pʌriː** 'never was a book of that sort seen again', **etːeː ãːʈʌ se̥ hʌmaːri̥ bɦuːkh naːiː ɟaːiː** 'my hunger will not be satisfied with so much flour', **hʌm otːiː roːʈiː khaːjcn** 'I ate that much bread', **tum ketːaː kaːmu̥ kiɦeu** 'how much work did you do?', **tumɦʌreː ketːeː lʌrikaː ʌu ketːiː lʌũɽijaː hʌĩ** 'how many sons and daughters have you got?', **ɟetːeː lʌrikaː tumɦʌreː hʌĩ tetːeː hʌmʌreː** 'I have as many sons as you have', **ɟetːiː lʌũɽija hʌmʌreː hʌĩ tetːiː koːi ke̥ naːiː** 'no one has so many daughters as I have'.

C. Origin

§ 266. (*a*) of manner—we have two varieties of forms (1) in **-ʌs** (*asa*) and (2) in **ʌis** (*aisa*). The latter go back to *-dṛśa* forms of OIA, *e.g.*, *yādṛśa* > *jāisa* > *jaisa* > **ɟʌis.** The former are later and simpler formations.

(*b*) of quantity—there are three varieties of forms (1) in **-tːaː** (E. Aw. *-eta*), (2) **-tʌnaː** and (3) **-tʌraː.**

In Sanskrit there were *-yat* adjectives which in the Prakrits became *-anta*. All these adjectives go back to those, the (1) forms directly while (2) and (3) by later additions of **-naɪ** and **-raɪ.**

(c) of number—the plural form of *-yat* adjectives was used in Sanskrit also for denoting number. We find the *Ardha-tatsama* forms of the same in *jāvata*, *tāvata* of Early Awadhi. **jʌi, kʌi**, etc., represent Sanskrit *yati kati*, etc.

CHAPTER V

POSTPOSITIONS[1]

Introductory

§ 267. The decay of old case-forms and the growth of postpositions goes side by side in a language. The history of postpositions in IA is complicated because of the fact that as these are used very often and in a variety of senses, as Bloch pointed out (Bloch: *Langue Marathe* § 197), they become semantically weak and undergo greater phonetic modification than ordinary words. There is another factor to be taken into consideration; as soon as the old auxiliary words seem to fail to indicate the required meaning, fresh words are borrowed from the literary dialects. This is

[1] What is a postposition? Any morphemic word which is generally put after other words and gives a meaning with those words only, it has no independent meaning of its own without reference to those words. It is different from terminations in as much as it does not undergo changes of form by incorporation with the previous words. If we adopt this as a characteristic of a postposition, we should not regard such words as have an independent meaning still, as postpositions.

I prefer to retain the word postposition in spite of a suggestion from Dr. Grahame-Bailey (B.S.O.S., V page 515) to use 'preposition' because the words in question are most generally post- and not pre-, as also because of the fact that I believe that the word 'postposition' has come to have a settled meaning and too frequent a change in scientific terminology and symbols is apt to injure the science. For the same reason, I retain the terms 'direct' aud 'oblique' in preference to 'prepositional' or postpositional'

clear from the fact that we have in modern Bengali a number of modern loan-words for this purpose (*vide* Chatterji § 509). It is also clear from such words as **khaːtir** and **bidɦi** in Modern Awadhi. This brings about two results :

(1) It is possible that a fresh loan-word and its ordinary form may both be employed at one time in the sense exactly the same and thence-forward may undergo common phonetic changes. We find in Tulsīdās *maha* (possibly from *semi-tatsama* **madha*—cf. Av. *maɽa*) and *mājha* (< *madhya-*) and to-day we have their successors **maː** and **mʌɦiaː.**

(2) A loan-word has a certain hesitation about it in phonetic adaptation in the language and may have different developments in different dialects. For instance Lmp. **khaːtir** (Per. *khāṭir*) is found in North Gonda as **khʌrtir.** The change from *-t-* to *-rt-* is explained only by the theory of hesitation.

This accounts for the variety of the forms of the same postpositions.

§ 268. Jāyasī and Tulsī do not generally employ postpositions. The noun or pronoun in its base form or in the case form expresses the required sense of case-relationship. There has been a gradual development of the use of postpositions as is shown by the following statistics.

In Jāyasī in the first twc hundred lines there are 91 such nouns as would require postpositions according to the practice in Modern Awadhi, but we find postpositions employed only after 24 nouns, *i.e.*, after about 26 p. c. of the nouns. In Tulsī who follows closely in time, there are 184 nouns (in the first three hundred lines) which would require postpositions according to modern usage, but only 45 are followed by postpositions, or about the same percentage as in Jāyasī. But when we come to Nūr Muhammad who composed his work after about two hundred years (1157 A.H.) from Jāyasī (947 A.H., 1540 A.D.), we find that in the first two hundred lines of his work, there are 175 such words as would require postpositions after them according to the practice of Modern Awadhi and we find postpositions employed after 137 nouns, *i.e.*, a little over 78 p. c.; with this compare the percentage of Jāyasī and Tulsī (26 p. c.). Nūr Muhammad thus comes very near Modern Awadhi (compare also § 270).

A postposition in Modern Awadhi is used generally to denote all case-relationships except the Nominative. It is found after the oblique case, if one exists, otherwise after the direct, *e.g.*, **raːɟʌ sə̥, raːɟʌn sə̥, sʌb maː, ʌcche sə̥, khaːi mə.**

§ 269. In the old texts we find postpositions employed oftener with pronouns than with nouns. For instance in Jāyasī in the first three hundred lines there are 96 pronouns which would require postpositions and these are employed after 33 pronouns. The percentage of the use of postpositions with pronouns is thus 34 as against 26 of nouns. Similarly the percentage of the first three hundred lines of Tulsī (61 : 27) is 44 after pronouns as against 24 of nouns. Not only this. Further we find that there is no case of *-hi* form of the noun (in any of the three texts) with a postposition but there are 16 (in Jāyasī), 7 (in Tulsī) and 9 (in Nūr Muhammad) cases of *-hi* form of the pronoun with a postposition. Thus even such cases as appear distinctly significant (without postposition) as regards noun have lost their case-significance as regards pronouns.

This practice is intelligible. The pronouns on account of their more frequent use become weak semantically sooner than the nouns and thus require auxiliary words. Even in the Prakrit stage we find many alternative forms of pronouns and a greater confusion in case-endings than in the case of nouns. A frequent use of pronouns can be examplified by usages of Modern Hindi. The pronoun comes first at the speaker's tongue. For instance: one generally asks **ʌreː woɦ leː aːjeː** 'Hullo, have you brought that?', and only when the person spoken to asks 'what?' that the article is named.

The earlier and more frequent use of postpositions after pronouns explains the incorporation of the postposition in pronouns earlier than in nouns.

Modern Awadhi has **moːr** 'mine', **toːr** 'thine', **hʌmaːr** 'ours', **tumaːr** 'yours', **pʌraːr** 'another's', where the genitive postposition (*kara*) has been inextricably incorporated in the pronoun, but there is no case of a noun incorporating it.

§ 270. As we see above, some of the postpositions have undergone so much phonetic change that they are hardly recognisable as derivatives of particular words, *e.g.*, **me** < *madhya*, **po** < *pakṣē*. But if we remember the fact that they are put in a very frequent use, we can see the possibility of such a violent sound-change. With some of the postpositions, it is not possible to find the evidence of literary documents for their predecessor-forms. But it may be noted that the auxiliary words being a popular device would be recognized only later in literary works.

Accusative-Dative[1]

A. Early Awadhi

§ 271. J. and T. generally use the oblique case in *-hi*, *-hĩ* (or *-i*) to express this sense, but sometimes they employ postpositions. These are never found after the oblique in *-hi*, *-hĩ*, *-i*.

(*a*) J. *kaha*, *e g.*, *saba kaha* 'to all' (p. 6), *jaga kahã* 'to the world' (p. 17), *sunai kaha* 'for hearing' (p. 12).

(*b*) T. generally has *kaha* (*e g.*, *tinha kaha* 'to them', p. 19), *kahũ* (*tinha kahũ* 'to them', p. 7), *kāhu* (*e.g.*, *saba kāhu* 'to all', p. 19), but sometimes *kaũ* (*tuma kaũ* 'to you',

[1] The postpositions for these two cases have the same forms in Awadhi.

F. 28

p. 90), *kō* (*sabahī kō nikō* 'good to all people', p. 17) and even *ka* (*tulsī ka* 'to Tulsī', p. 17).

NOTE:—*kahā̃* and *kahū̃* sometimes appear without nasalisation. An example of direct object—*prabhu kahā̃ cīnhā̃* 'recognised the master.'

(*c*) N. generally has *kahā̃* (*e.g. sūraja kahā̃* 'to the sun', p. 3) and rarely *kō* or *kō̃* (*dvāra kō* 'to the door,' p. 5, *nibala kō̃* 'to the weak', p. 8).

NOTE:—This *kō* or *kō̃* is, I believe, *kau* or *kaū̃* and has been wrongly transcribed in the Dēvanāgarī version of the manuscript which is in Persian characters where کو can be read as either *ko* or *kau*.

B. MODERN AWADHI

§ 272. Lakhīmpurī has **kə** and **kaː**. For instance: **raːmuː gopaːl kə maːrisi̥** 'Rāmū beat Gopāl'—Accusative, **gopaːl kə kuchu̥ khaːi kə deːu** 'give something to Gopal to eat'—Dative. The postposition is not employed after inanimate object.

§ 273. Of the two the long form (**kaː**) is used after

(1) monosyllables containing

(*a*) a final long vowel, *e.g.*, **ɟiː kaː**

(*b*) a short vowel, followed or not by a consonant, *e.g.*, **gɦʌr kaː**

(2) dis-syllables containing two short syllables each ending in a vowel, *e.g.* **keɦi kaː**.

The short form (**kə**) is used after all other words, **coːr kə**. **mʌrd kə**, **ʌɦir kə**[1], **aːgi kə**, **nʌuwʌ kə**.

NOTE 1. If the last vowel of a word preceding the short form of the postposition is long, it is pronounced short (*e.g.*, **gɦoːɽaː se̥ > gɦoːɽʌ se̥, aːgiː se̥ > aːgi se̥**).

---

[1] Professor Bloch suggests that the differentiation probably happened at a time when final short vowel, *-a*, *-i*, etc., was actually spoken in **mʌrd** (*-a*), **ʌɦir** (*-a*), **gɦʌr** (*-a*)

NOTE 2. If the word after which a long postposition is used, is lengthened by adding a suffix or otherwise, the long postposition can no longer be used (*e.g.*, **gɦʌr kaː** 'to the house', but **gɦʌrʌɦẽ ko,** 'to the house only', **iː kaː** 'to this', but **iːmʌ ko**, 'of this')

These rules apply to all sets of long and short postpositions in such dialects as possess them.

§ 274. S. and Western L. have **ko** and **kaː**, U. and F. only **kaː**, B. and Bgh. have **ko**, **kaː** and **kʌiɦãː** and partly use **kʌi** in the East; G. has **ko**, **kaː** but **kʌiɦãː** is found in specimens of the North and **keː** in the specimens of the East—**kaː** or **kãː** is, however, the most common. Fy. and Sl. have **kaː** but Fy. specimens show **kʌi** also (**sʌb wʌɦi kʌi gʌrijaːwʌi lʌgeː** 'all began to abuse him) and S. E. Sl. **keː** (**raːt keː** 'at night'); Br. and R. have **kaː** and **kʌiɦãː** while P. and A. have **kaː** generally but **keː** in the Eastern parts.

NOTE:—The dative-sense 'for' is expressed by such words as **khaːtir** etc. (See below § 286).

Genitive[1]

A. EARLY AWADHI

§ 275. The oblique in *-hi*, etc., is seldom used to denote this case; the noun-stem generally with postpositions and sometimes without it is used.

(*a*) J. has *kara* (fem. *kari*), *kēra* (fem. *kērī*) elongated sometimes to *kērā* (*kērī*) and *ka* (*kā*), *kē* and *kai*.

Of these *kara* (*kari*) is the usual one and generally does change for the gender of the following noun, *e.g.*, *haũ saba kabitanha kara pachalagā* 'I am the follower of all poets' (p. 33), *sōnai kara saba puhumi akāsū* 'the floor and the roof both (were) of gold' (p. 73), *dharama pantha kara*

[1] The postpositions for this case agree with the following noun, pronoun, etc., in gender and case and not with the preceding noun, etc.

karahī bakhānū 'are making the elucidation of the path of virtue' (p. 59), *tā kari disiṭi* 'his glance' (p. 7). *kēra* is used sometimes, *e.g.*, *dirisa gosāī kēra* 'the sight of the Lord' (p. 27), *sulēmā kēri āgūṭhī* 'the ring of Suleman' (p. 17).

ka (*kā*) singular direct and *kē* singular oblique or plural is also frequently used. For instance:

nisi ka bichōhā 'separation of (at) night' (p. 50), *sabhā ka rūpa* 'the appearance of the assembly' (p. 72), *ūca gaḍha tākā* 'his fort was high' (p. 61), *mādira mādira saba kē caupārī* 'everyone had sitting-halls in every house' (p. 67), *duhū kē bhāra* 'by the burden of both' (p. 25), *pāna phūla kē rahahī adhārī* 'subsist only on leaves and fruits' (p. 75).

kai is generally used with feminine nouns as in Tulsīdās. For instance:

kēlā kai ghaurī 'clusters of bananas' (p. 52), *gharī rahāṭa kai* 'wheel of the water-mill' (p. 52), *siṃghala kai hāṭā* 'market of Singhala' (p. 56), *bāsuki kai piṭhī* 'the back of Vāsuki' (p. 61), *gāḍhē kai sāthī* 'friend in need', *paurī navau bajara kai sājī* 'all the nine thresholds are made of cement' (p. 63), *laṅka dīpa kai silā* 'the stone of Laṅkadīpa' (p. 47).

(*b*) T. has *kara* (fem. *kari*) *kēra* (elongated to *kērā* particularly at the end of lines), fem. *kēri* (*kērī*), obl. singular and plural dir. and obl. *kērē*; *ka* (elongated to *kā* at times) as masculine dir. and *kē* (*kē̃*) masculine sing. obl. and plural dir. and obl., *kī* (*ki*) fem., rarely *kō* (masculine singular) and *kai* generally feminine. The distinction of gender is generally maintained but sometimes in the *kara* set masculine postposition is used before feminine nouns. For instance:

santanha kara sātha 'the company of the good' (p. 22), *jā kari taī dāsī* 'whose slave thou art' (p. 81), but also *jama kara dhārī* 'the stream of Yama' (p. 45), *saba kara bidā* 'the departure of all' (p. 49), *tehi kara punya* 'the merit of his' (p. 45).

In the *kēra* set the distinction of gender is maintained throughout. For instance:

mitra tāpasa nṛpa kērā 'friend of the hermit-king' (p. 75,) *bhṛgupati kēri garaba-garuāi* 'the height of the pride of the lord of Bhṛgūs' (p. 111), *carana kamala bandaū̃ tinha kērē* 'their lotus-feet I bow down to' (p. 10).

In the set *ka*, *kī*, *kē*, the gender is distinguished. For instance:

jō jehi khāni ka 'whosoever was of whichever source' (p. 3), *ati hita saba hī kā* 'very beneficial to all' (p. 97), *kathā raghubara kī* 'the story of Raghubara' (p. 7), *ugharahī bimala bilōcana hī kē* 'the clear eyes of the heart open up' (p. 3) *mana jā kē* 'in whose mind' (p. 59), *rāma kō nāma* 'the name of Rāma' (p. 15).

kai is generally followed by a feminine noun but sometimes by masculine also, *e.g.*, *dasā sambhu kai* 'Śambhu's condition' (p. 27), *bhagavanta kai bhagati* 'the devotion to (of) the Lord' (p. 25), *nārada kai upadēsa* 'the advice of Nārada' (p. 43), *dui kai cāri māgi maku lēhū* 'you may beg for four (boons) instead of two' (p. 168), *rāma janama kai hētu anēkā* 'various causes of the birth of Rāma' (p. 56). With the last may be compared *rāma janama kara hētu* 'the cause of Rāma's birth' (p. 68), where the same word is preceded by a masculine postposition. In *praśna umā kai* 'Uma's question' (p. 52), the feminine *kai* is all right as *praśna* (masculine in Sanskrit) is treated of as feminine by Tulsīdās throughout his work[1]

(c) N. has *kō* masculine sg. (sometimes *ka* and *kā* also), *kē* masculine singular and plural dir. and obl., *kī* (*ki*), *kai* feminine, *kara* masculine sg. dir., *kērā* masculine singular dir., *kērī* feminine, and *kērē* masculine sg. obl. and plural

---

[1] T. has once *kṛta* used as a postposition, *viz.*, *jinha kṛta mahā mōha mada pānā* 'those who are under the influence of infatuation' (p 54)

dir. and obl. The distinction of genders is maintained generally. For instance:

jaga kō rājā 'the king of the world' (p. 1), *phulavārī kā dvārā* 'the door of the flower-garden' (p. 6), *jehi ka bakhāna* 'whose description' (p. 2), *sapanē kī bāta* 'the talk of the dream' (p. 11), *pahilī rāta kī mūrata* 'the image of the first night' (p. 10), *indrāvati kai gīu* 'the neck of Indrāvatī' (p. 5), *tina kara nāū̃* 'his name' (p. 3), *sāgara bhau kērā* 'the ocean of Bhava' (p. 2), *hāṭa mahīpati kērī* 'the market of the king' (p. 9), *jaga kērē cērē* 'the disciple of the world' (p. 2).

Sometimes, however, the distinction of gender is missed:

adharama kō jara mūla 'the root of absence of duty' (p 9), *tapī kara bāhu* 'the arm of the hermit' (p. 4), *tākō mūrata* 'her image' (p. 13), *tā kī mātha* 'on her forehead' (p. 18).

NOTE.—*kō* should be read as *kau* [see note to § 271 (*c*)].

B. MODERN AWADHI

§ 276. Lakhīmpurī has **ko, kaː; kʌr, keːr**—masc. dir. sg., **ke̥, keː, kereː** masc. obl. sg. and pl. dir. and obl., **ki̥, kiː, keːriː** fm. dir. and obl. For instance:

gopaːl ko (or **keːr**) **lʌrikaː mʌri gaː** 'Gopāl's son has died', **gopaːl ke̥** (or **kereː**) **lʌrikʌ ko maːrini̥** 'they beat Gopāl's son', **gopaːl ke̥ caːriu lʌrikaː jiʌti̥ hʌĩ** 'Gopāl's all the four sons are living', **gopaːl ki̥ lʌũṛijaː** 'Gopāl's daughter'

S. and L. agree with Lmp.; U. and F. have no short forms **ko** and **ki̥** and **ke̥**. B. is like Lmp., but has **kʌj** in Eastern specimens; G. does not use **keːr** but **kʌr** is found in specimens; it uses **kʌj** very generally. Fy. possesses **kaː, kiː** but generally uses **kʌr** forms (**o kʌriː phiraːk, ke kʌreː saːtheː, baːsːaːɦ keːri biṭijaː**). It also uses **kʌj** mostly before feminine nouns. Sl. uses **kʌr** and **kʌj** generally irrespective of the gender (**un kʌr meɦʌruaː, okʌreː hiãː, un kʌj khopʌriː, un kʌj likhaː, un kʌj din**). Br. like Lmp. distinguishes gender and has the same postpositions. Similarly R. (**kjaːr** for **keːr,** however) P. and A. generally use **kʌr, keː** and **kʌj.** Bgh. has **keːr,** masc. dir. **ke,** masc. obl. **keː**, fem. dir. **kiː,** obl. **kʌi.**

Accusative-Dative-Genitive

C. ORIGIN

§ 277. The postpositions for these three cases are put together for derivation. We have:

Modern Awadhi **ko, kaː (kãː), kʌiɦãː, kʌi** and **kʌr, keːr.**

Early Awadhi *kahā̃, kahū̃, kāhū̃, kaū̃, kō* (*kō̃*) and *kara, kēra, kā, kē, kai, kṛta.*

These go back (1) to some forms of *kṛ* and (2) to *kakṣa.*

(*a*) For **ko, kaː** and obl. **keː**, the best suggestion is to derive them from *kṛta*, (*kṛtaka*) which is once found in Tulsīdās in this sense [see footnote § 275 (*b*)]. **keː** dir. in the Eastern dialects of Modern Awadhi is the Māgadhī (Nom. sg.) form of the same word. **kiː** and **kʌi** are the feminine forms.

But *-ṛ-* normally becomes *-i-* and here we have it as *-a-*. Is it because of a peculiar treatment in a loan-word?

(*b*) **kʌr** (fm. **kʌri**) is derived from *kāraka* and **keːr (keːri, keːriː)** from *kārya, kāryaka.* The later derivation requires an epenthesis which occurs already in Apabhraṃśa: *kārya* > *kāyara* > *kaira.* We have such a development in a number of words, however, and we should remember, that this was a loan-word.

(*c*) Modern Awadhi **kʌiɦãː** and Early Awadhi *kahā̃, kahū̃, kāhū̃, kaū̃, kō* go back to *kakṣa.* In **kʌiɦãː**, we see the transference of aspiration to the last syllable. We should suppose **kʌɦiãː** < *kakṣyaka* (cf. **pʌɦiãː** and **mʌɦiaː**) or we may derive it as Aw. *kahā̃* + *iyā̃.*

A possible derivation of these *-h-* forms of the postposition was from *kṛ* (*kṛta* etc.) by attributing inter-vocalic *-h-* to the device of avoiding hiatus (Bloch, pp. 31 and 182). But the long *ā* in *kāhū* and *-kh-* in Old Bengali *kakhu* (Chatterji, p. 760) are insuperable difficulties.[1]

Instrumental-Ablative[2]

A. Early Awadhi

§ 278. The oblique in *-hi*, *-hī*, *-i* is not generally used to denote this sense; the noun-stem with or without postpositions is used.

(*a*) J. has *sõ*, *saũ*, *bhai*, *tẽ*, *taĩ*, *sẽti*, *huta* (*huti*) and *cāhi*. Of these *saũ* is most common, *e.g.*, *aratha sõ* 'with meaning' (p. 127), *cāri basērē saũ caṛhai sata saũ caṛhai jo pāra* 'he who is allowed to truthfully take four days to get up to it' (p. 63), *saba sau* 'from all' (p. 10), *bhai* (*āchahī sadā sugandha bhai* 'are always with good smell', p. 53). *taĩ* is generally used in comparison, *ēka ēka taĩ rūpa bakhānī* 'one famous for beauty more than another' (p. 75), *chārahī taĩ* 'from ashes' (p. 5), *pēma tẽ* 'with love' (p. 348), *rājā sẽti* '(talked) with the king' (p. 310), *naraka sitẽ* 'from hell' (p. 337). *cāhi* also shows comparison, *e.g. eka eka cāhi ēka eka balī* 'one even stronger than another' (p. 69), *laṅkā cāhi ũca gaḍha* 'the fort higher than Laṅkā even' (p. 61). *huta* denotes either 'from' (*uṭhē puhumi huti* 'rose from the Earth', p. 40), or 'through', *e.g.*, *ohi huta dēkhai pāeũ darasa gosāĩ kēra* 'through him I was able to have the sight of the Lord' (p. 27).

(*b*) T. has *sana* (sometimes *sanu* and *sõ*), *tẽ* (sometimes as *tē*, *taĩ*), *sē* and *sī*.

Of these *sana* is the most common and indicates both the instrumental and ablative meaning. For instance: *sō mō sana kahi jāta na* 'that cannot be said by me' (p. 4), *satī*

---

[1] Cf. also Sindhī *-khẽ*

[2] The postpositions for these two cases do not differ in form.

sana prīti 'love with Satī' (p. 29), *sivā sana bhākhā* 'spoke to Śivā' (p. 20), *gura sana kiē durāva* 'by keeping the secret from the teacher' (p. 25), *muni sana bidā mãgi* 'having obtained permission (to depart) from the sage' (p. 26).

tē̃ generally indicates the sense of 'from' and 'than', *e.g.*, *tehi tē̃ kachu guna dōṣa bakhānē* 'because of that I have described a few merits and demerits' (p. 5), *ēka tē̃ ēkā* 'some more than the others' (p. 28).

sē (masc.) and *sī* (fem.) indicate likeness only, *e.g.*, *rāhu sē* 'like Rāhu' (p. 4), *ramā sī* 'like Ramā' (p. 18). Sometimes *sō̃* is used in this sense, *e.g.*, *sītānātha sō̃* 'like the husband of Sītā' (p. 17).

(*c*) N. has *sō̃* (sometimes *saũ* or *sō*), *tē̃* (sometimes *tē*), *hutē̃* (sometimes *hutē*), *sētī̃* and *sē*.

Of these *sō̃* is the most common and expresses both the instrumental and ablative senses, *e.g.*, *dāyā sō̃* 'with compassion' (p. 2), *jiya sō̃* 'with heart' (p. 3), *nibarana sabarai saũ dukha pāvā* 'the weak obtained misery from (at the hands of) the strong' (p. 2).

tē̃ is less common. For instance: *jībha tē̃* 'with the tongue' (p. 3), *cahū̃ disa tē̃* 'from all the four directions' (p. 3).

hutē̃ means 'by reason of', 'through', *e.g.*, *bhā tehi bacana hutē̃ saṁsārā* 'the Universe came to be through that Word', *bacana hutē̃ yaha jagata mō̃ kīrati paragaṭa āhi* 'by reason of the Word, the fame is flashing in this world' (p. 5), *prēma hutē̃ dōū kahã dīnhā alakha milāya* 'the Invisible united the two because of their love' (p. 3).

sētī̃ is comparatively rare. For instance: *dāyā sētī̃* 'with compassion' (p. 4), *haũ hīnā vidyā budhi sētī̃* 'I am bereft of knowledge and wisdom' (p. 4).

sē is unusual, *e.g.*, *paragaṭa hōi tahã sē sōī* 'he comes out from there' (p. 10).

NOTE:—*sō* or *sō̃* should be read as *sau* or *saũ* [see note to § 271 (*c*)]

B. Modern Awadhi

§ 279. Lakhīmpurī has **sẹ** and **seː**, *e.g.*, **uː hʌm kaː ḍʌṇḍʌ sẹ maːrisi̥** 'he beat me with a stick', **baːdʌr sẹ bū̃ːdiː girī̃ː** 'drops (of rain) fell from the cloud'; sometimes **seneː**, *e.g.*, **kaːɦeː seneː** 'with what?'. S. and L. have **tẹ**, **teː** besides **sẹ**, **seː** and also **seneː**, **teneː.** U. and F. have **seː** and **teː** (sometimes **beː** and **bheː**). B. has **sẹ**, **seː** and **setiː**, also **teːneː.** G. has **seː** and **seːtiː** in specimens of the North. Fy. and Sl. have only **seː**, Br. has **seː** and **teː** and sometimes uses **kʌiɦā̃ː** also in an instrumental sense (**wʌɦi kʌiɦā̃ː ʌnaːɟ lʌi aːjeː** 'with that (money) brought the corn') R. has **teː**, **teːniː**, P. **seː**, **seːniː** and **seːneː,** A. generally **seː**, Bgh. **seː**, **teː**.

P. expresses the sense of 'than' by **lʌgeː** (see below § 286) also, *e.g.*, **tʌu hī̃jā̃ː lʌgeː mʌɟeː maː rʌɦʌb** 'then I shall be better off (there) than here'.

Note:—The idea of 'with' indicating company is expressed by some such word as **sʌŋgh, saːtheː** (see below § 286).

C. Origin

§ 280. Mod. Aw. **sẹ**, **seː**, **tẹ**, **teː**, **seneː teːneː**, **setiː**. **sʌntiː**, **seniː**, **beː**, **bheː**.

E. Aw. *sō̃*, *saũ*, *sana*, *sanu*, *sā* (*sī*), *sētī̃*, *tē* (*tē*, *taĩ*), *bhai*, *hũta*, *hutē̃* (*hutē*) and *cāhi*, *kari*.

Of these Mod. Aw. **sẹ**, **seː**, **seːniː** probably go back to *sahitēna* and **seːtiː**, E. Aw. *sētī̃* to *santakēna* (cf. Pāli *santakō*, *e.g.*, *parasantakō* 'belonging to another') *anta* > *ē*, possibly influenced by *sē*; while E. Aw. *sō̃*, *saũ*, *sana*, *sanu* to *samaḥ* and *samēna*; **beː bheː**, *bhai* are derivable from the absolutive of *bhū*. E. Aw. *sā*, *sī* in the sense of 'like' has a modern correspondent in Hindustani usage **muɟɦ saː** 'like me' (**muɟɦ siː** feminine) etc. and should go back to *sama* 'equal'. Mod. Aw. **tẹ**, **teː**, **teːneː** and E. Aw. *tē̃* (*tē*, *taĩ*) are probably connected with $\sqrt{tan}$ – *tatēna*.

hũta, *hutẽ* (*hutē*) have correspondents in *huntō*, *huntē* in the Apabhraṁśa and are connected with √*bhū*—**hontō* Mg. *hontē*, or **hontēna*.

cāhi is connected with √*cāh*- 'to desire', 'to wish'. and is the absolutive form of the root Similarly *kari* is the absolutive of √*kar* 'to do'

Locative

A. Early Awadhi

§ 281. In Jāyasī and Tulsī the oblique -*ē* and -*hi* etc. is quite frequently used to express the locative sense. Otherwise the noun-stem with or without the postpositions is used.

(*a*) J. has *mahã* and *māhã* generally (sometimes *mãjha*, *māhã* and *mãjhiārā*) for 'in' and *para*, *ūpara*, *pāhã* and *pai* generally and *uparāhī̃* sometimes for 'on, over'. For instance :

bīju tehi mãhā 'the lightning in that' (p. 2), *nakhatanha mãhā* 'in the stars', *saba mãha* 'in all' (p. 75), *tinha mahã* 'in them' (p. 75); *ghara mãjhiārā* in the house' (p. 232), *jaũnā mãjha* 'in the Jamunā' (p. 164); *khãḍa khãḍa ūpara* 'above every part' (p. 74), *gaṛha ūpara tāĩ* 'upto the above (of) the fort' (p. 63), *sīsa uparāhī̃* 'over the head' (p. 70).

(*b*) T. has *mahã* (*maha*), *mahũ* (*mahu*), *māhī̃* (*mahi*) generally and *mãjha* (*mãjhā*), *majhāri* and *madhya* sometimes for 'in' and *para* for 'on', and *tara* 'below.' For instance :

chana mahã 'in a moment' (p. 47), *raghubaṁsinha maha* 'amongst the descendants of Raghu' (p. 108), *bhōga mahũ* 'in enjoyment' (p. 12), *trētā juga māhī̃* 'in the Trētā age' (p. 26). *jaga mãjhā* 'in the world' (p. 221), *tinha tarubaranha madhya* 'in (amongst) those good trees' (p. 249). *muni-manḍalī madhya* 'in company of sages' (p. 250); *dīna para* 'on the poor' (p. 3), *aṭanha para* 'on the upper floors' (p. 149), *sindhu mãjhārī* 'in the whole ocean (p. 78), *milehī̃ mãjha* 'in the middle of the process of obtaining' (p. 175); *sura-taru tara* 'under the tree of the gods' (p. 5).

(*c*) N. has *mahā̃* (*mā̃ha*, *māhā̃*, *mahī̃*, *māhū̃*) usually and *mõ* quite frequently and *majhāra*, *mẽ*, and *ma* rarely for 'in', *para* usually, *ūpara* frequently and *uparāhā̃* (*uparāhī̃*) sometimes for 'on, above' and *tara*, *tarẽ* for 'under'. For instance :

gīu mahā̃ 'in the neck' (p. 5), *bārī mā̃ha* 'in the garden' (p. 5), *dou hāthana-māhā̃* 'in both the hands' (p. 5), *tehi māhī̃* 'in that' (p. 8), *hāṭa mõ* 'in the market' (p. 9), *bhāṣā mō* 'in vernacular' (p. 4), *phā̃da majhārā* 'in the snare', *sabhā majhāra* 'in the assembly' (p. 115), *ādarasa majhāra* (p. 10), *sindhu mẽ* 'in the ocean' (p. 4), *artha ma* 'in meaning' (p. 102); *rāja para* 'over the kingdom' (p. 7), *para trīyā para* 'on another's woman' (p. 9), *mohi ūpara* 'over me' (p. 2), *pāṭa uparāha* 'on the kingship' (p. 7), *mukha uparāhī̃* 'on the face' (p. 3)', *biricha tara* 'under the tree' (p. 3), *pā̃va tara* 'under the foot' (p. 8), *bircha tarē* 'under the tree' (p. 106).

NOTE.—*mō* should be read as *maū̃* [see note to § 271 (c)]. In one instance *viṣa mau* 'in poison' (p. 73), we find the correct form.

B. MODERN AWADHI

§ 282. Lakhīmpurī has **mo, maː** and **mʌiɦā̃ː** 'in' and **po, pʌr, pʌriɦā̃ː** 'on'. For instance : **kheːt mo gaːi cʌrti hʌi** 'the cow is grazing in the field'; **birowaː pʌr** 'on the tree', **kaːɦeː mʌiɦā̃ː** 'in what', **duaːre po** 'on the door'.

NOTE.—The long forms **mʌiɦā̃ː, pʌr** and **pʌriɦā̃ː** can be used after such words also as have the short postposition after them.

S. and L agree with Lmp.; U. and F. have **maː, mʌiɦā̃ː** and **pʌr, pʌriɦā̃ː,** B. has all Lmp. forms except **po.** G. town does not possess **mʌiɦā̃ː** but specimens of the North and South-Eastern portions of the district show it; it has **pʌj** also for 'on' (**dukaːn pʌj, dʌrwaːɟe po**). **Fy**. has **maː, mãː, mʌɦʌ̃** and **po**, Sl. **maː**, and **mãː** and **pʌj**, Br. **maː, mãː, mʌiɦjãː** and **pʌi**, R. **maː, mʌiɦjãː** and **po**. P. and A. generally have **mãː, po**; Bgh. has **maː**.

C. Origin

§ 283. Modern Awadhi **mo maː (mãː), mʌiɦãː (mʌɦijẽː), po, pʌi (pʌj)** and **pʌr, pʌriɦãː**.

Early Awadhi *maha* (*mahã*), *māhã*, *māhĩ*, *mahũ*, *mãjha*, *madhya*, *mõ* etc.; *para*, *ūpara* *pāhã*, *pai*, *uparāhĩ*, *uparāhã*, *uparāta*; *tara*, *tarẽ*.

Of these all *m*- forms go back to *mádhya*, (*-ka* or *-ra* in some cases); the forms with *-r*, *-r-* to *upari*, *uparitra* and *upariṣṭha*, **pʌi (pʌj)** to *prati*; *pāhã* and **po** as well as *pahi*, *pahũ* etc. of Early Awadhi in Tulsīdās to some forms of *pakṣa*, or *pārśva*. *tara* and *tarẽ* go back to *tala*, *talē* (*talakē*).

Other Postpositions

§ 284. These are used after the genitive forms of the personal pronouns, after the genitive postpositions in case of such nouns as can take the short postposition, and after the noun or pronoun directly in other cases.

A. Early Awadhi

§ 285. Besides the case-postpositions mentioned above, the texts have the following which are more or less used as postpositions.

(a) Jāyasī *saṅga* (*sãga*) in the sense of with (*e.g.*, *jehi sãga* 'with whom', p. 25.) *saũ* in the sense of 'before, in front of' (*e.g.*, *jā saũ* 'in front of whom', p. 49), *tāĩ* 'for' (*e.g.*, *jaga kai tāĩ* 'for the world', p. 25), *lāgi* (*lagi*) meaning 'upto' (*e.g.*, *lāgi akāsā* 'upto the sky', p. 40, *jab lagi tab lagi* until . . . then'), and *lei* or *lahi* in the same sense (*jau lahi* until', p. 58, *saraga lei lāvā* 'sown upto heavens', p. 73), and *sari* 'like' (*e.g.*, *sērasāhi sari* 'like Sher Shāh' p. 23), *nāī* 'like' (*e.g.*, *bīju kai nāī* 'like lightning' p. 49), *bhari* 'whole' (*e.g.*, *janama bhari* 'throughout life' p. 15).

(*b*) Tulsīdās has a large number. Frequently he uses *pahī* (*paha̐*) and *pāhī* and sometimes *pāsa* to indicate 'nearness', the sense of **tīr** of Lakhīmpurī. For instance:

kumbhaja ṛṣi pāhī 'to (near) the sage born of the jar (Agastya)' (p. 26), *jasa bara mai baraneũ tuma pāhī* 'the bride-groom such as I have described to you' (p. 34), *mahēsa pahī calī* 'went towards Śiva' (p. 28), *sambhu paha̐* 'near Śambhu' (p. 41), *bibhīṣana pāsa* 'near Bibhīṣaṇa' (p. 77).

He uses *lāgi* (*lagi*), *liya* and *badi* in the sense of 'for', exactly in the sense in which Lakhīmpurī has **khātir**. For instance: *barahī lāgi* 'for the bride-groom' (p. 46), *bhagatana hita lāgī* 'for the good of the devotees' (p. 10), *kachu kahana liya* 'for saying something' (p. 217), *rāura badi* 'for your sake' (p. 279). *lagi* (sometimes *lagē*) and *lai* are used to indicate the idea of 'upto' or 'even', *e.g.*, *baṛī bāra lagi* 'upto a great deal of time' (p. 60), *kaha̐ lagi* 'upto where' (p. 16), *pāya̐ lai parahī* 'even do they fall at the feet' (p. 163).

saṅga (*sa̐ga*) indicates 'with', 'in company of' (*e.g.*, *daccha kumārī saṅga* 'with the daughters of Dakṣa', *rāma kubhā̐ti saciva sa̐ga jāhī* 'Rāma was going in an untoward way with the minister', p. 172) and *bhari* 'throughout' (*e.g.*, *bhari māgha nahāhī* 'bathe throughout Māgha', p. 25), while *bīca* (*bica*) means 'in the middle of' (*e.g.*, *bīthinha bica* 'in the middle of the rows', p. 85).

(*c*) N. has *pāsa* 'near' (*e.g.*, *tina pāsa* 'near them' p. 9), *sanga* (*sa̐ga*) and *sātha* 'with' (*mohi saṅga* 'with me', p. 5, *rānī sātha* 'with the queen', p. 7), *lāga* 'for' (*e.g.*, *jōga lāga* 'for the *yōga*', p. 16), and *laga* and *tāī* for 'upto' (*e.g.*, *jau laga* 'until that', *jaba laga*, p. 21, *aba tāī* 'uptill now', p. 20), *bīca* 'in the middle' (*e.g.*, *sapana bīca* in the middle of the dream' p. 10), *nita* 'for' (*e.g.*, *tumhai nita* 'for you' p. 72).

All the texts use *nāī* (*nyāyī*) in the sense of 'like', 'as', *e.g.*, T. *raurihi nāī* 'like yourself' (p. 158)

B. Modern Awadhi

§ 286. (1) To express the sense of 'for' Lakhīmpurī uses **khaːtir,** *e.g.*, **hʌmoriː khaːtir duːdɦu̥ lʌjaːoː** 'bring milk for me', **wʌɦi kiː khaːtir** 'for him', **raːm khaːtir** 'for Rām'. When the idea of 'officiating' is to be denoted the word **bʌdi̥** is employed, *e.g.*, **hʌmoriː bʌdi̥** 'for me—officiating me'. S. and L. agree with Lmp., U. and F. use **bʌreː** and **mudːeː** for **khaːtir.** B. agrees with Lmp., G. uses **wʌɦʌtːeː** and **khaːtir** both, and reserves **bʌdi̥** for officiating. In the North, G. has **khʌrtir** for **khaːtir.** Fy. and Sl. have **khaːtir.** Br. has **tʌĩː, khaːtir** and **bʌdeː** with no nuances in meaning; R. , P. and A. have **tʌĩː, bʌreː, sʌntiː** and **khaːtir.**

(2) To express the sense of 'with' *i.e.*, 'in company of', the dialects generally use **sʌŋgɦ** and **saːth** (or **saːtheː** in Eastern dialects, *e.g.*, Sl. **toɦoreː saːtheː** 'with you'). For instance:

Lmp. **hʌmoreː sʌŋgɦ, ui keː sʌŋgɦ, raːm sʌŋgɦ.**

(3) To express the sense of 'near', the dialects use **tiːr** or **lʌgeː.** For instance, Lmp. **hʌmoreː tiːr** 'with me', 'near me'; **dukaːn lʌgeː** 'near the shop' The postposition **lʌgeː** (sometimes **lʌg**) expresses the sense of 'upto' also, *e.g.*, **birowaː lʌgeː pʌɦũcʌu tʌu** 'first reach upto the tree'.

(*a*) **lʌi** also expresses the sense of 'upto' but is particularly used after adverbs, *e.g.*, **kʌɦã̃ː lʌi** 'upto where?'

(4) To express the sense of 'owing to', 'on account of' **maːreː** is used in all the dialects, *e.g.*, Lmp. **kaːmeː maːreː** 'owing to work', **ui keː maːreː** 'because of him'. **tumɦoreː maːreː** 'on account of you'.

(5) To express the sense of 'through' **d̪ʌgʌr** 'way' is used, *e.g.*, **moɦoreː d̪ʌgʌr nikʌri̥ aːoː** 'come

along through the gate'. **kʌuniː ɖʌgʌr** 'through which way'.

(6) To express the sense of 'like' Lakhīmpurī uses **tʌnaː**, central dialects generally have **tʌnaː** or **tʌraː** and the Eastern ones use '**bidɦi**', *e.g.*, Lmp. **hʌmʌriː tʌnaː** 'like me', **lʌrikʌwaː tʌnaː** 'like a boy'

(7) To indicate the idea of 'entirety', the postposition **bɦʌreː** is placed after the noun and then the necessary case-postposition, for instance: **gãːu bɦʌre ko** 'to the whole village'. After a noun in direct case **bɦʌri̥** is placed irrespective of gender, *e.g.*, **gãːu bɦʌri̥ aːwaː** 'the whole village came'; **lʌũɽijaː bɦʌri̥ aːĩː, ʌdəmiː rʌɦi̥ geː** 'all the girls have come away, (only) the men have stayed back'.

(8) To express the sense of 'in front' or 'before' the dialects have **sʌmʌɦeː** and **aːgeː**, *e.g.*, **hʌmʌreː sʌmʌɦeː** 'in front of me', **hʌmʌreː aːgeː** 'before me'.

C. Origin

§ 287. Of the other postpositional words:

Mod. Aw. **khaːtir**, **khʌrtir** come from Ar. *khāṭir* and **wʌɦʌtːeː** from *vāsṭē*.

bʌdi < √*vand*- 'praise, honour'? (*rāura badi* 'in honour of your worship, for you').

sʌntiː < Pkt. *santē* 'being. *nita* < *nimitta* 'cause'. **bʌreː** < some derivative of √*vr̥*-, **tʌĩː** < *sthānē*?

sʌŋgɦ < *saṅgha* 'a collection'. E. Aw. *saṅga* (*sãga*) is Skt. *saṅga* and if the Mod. Aw. **sʌŋgh** were connected with that, the aspiration would be inexplicable.

tiːr < Skt. *tīra* 'bank'.

lʌgeː and E. Aw. *lāgi*, *lagi*, are derivatives of *lagna* (*lagnakē* and *lagia*).

lʌi, E. Aw. *lai* and *lahi* go back to the absolutive of √*labh*-; **maːreː** may be connected with *māritēna*. **ɖʌgʌr**

means 'way' in Mod. Aw. = Skt. *mārga* and is possibly a Deśī word. We may compare the use of Marāṭhī *māgẽ*.

sarisa < *sadṛśa* 'like'.

tʌraɪ is Arabic *ṭaraḥ* ; is **tʌnaɪ** a corrupt form of it? In this connection the substitution of *r* by *n* in child's language may be noted (*vide* Part I § 161).

bidɦi < Skt. *vidhi* 'way, means'.

bhʌreɪ and **bɦʌri̥**. E. Aw. *bhari* are derivatives of root √*bhṛ*-.

sahũ and *saũ* of E. Aw. are connected with Skt. *saṁmukha*. We have another derivative of the same word in Mod. Aw. **sʌmʌɦeɪ** 'in front'; **aɪgeɪ** < *agra-kē*. *pāsa* comes from Skt. *pārśva* and *nāī*. *nyāyī* from *nyāyena*.

CHAPTER VI

VERBS

Root[1]

§ 288. (*a*) The roots are either active or passive in sense, *e.g.*, **lʌkʌṛiː kʌṭʌti̥ hʌi** 'the wood gets cut' (passive), **uː lʌkʌṛiː kaːṭʌti̥ hʌi** 'he cuts the wood' (active). The passive roots are all intransitive, the active roots are either transitive or intransitive. Roots have a simple (*e.g.*, **kaːṭʌb** 'to cut') and a causal form (*e.g.*, **kʌṭaːwʌb** 'to cause to be cut'). All denominative roots are intransitive, *e.g.*, **lonaːb** 'to taste saltish', **lʌjaːb** 'to feel ashamed.'

(*b*) The root of a verb may be obtained by separating **-bu̥** (*e.g.*, **hoːbu̥** 'to be'); **-ʌbu̥** (*e.g.*, **kʌrʌbu̥** 'to do') or **-wʌbu** (*e.g.*, **bʌjaːwʌbu̥** 'to beat a musical instrument') as the case may be from the direct case of the verbal noun (see below § 335),

§ 289. Most of the roots used in Awadhi are already found in OIA and Mid. IA. There are a few roots borrowed from Persian-Arabic, *e.g.*, **newaːjʌb** 'to be merciful' Pers. *nawāz*, **daːgʌb** 'to scorch' Pers. *dāǧ*, **gudʌrʌb** 'to pass' Pers. **guđar, baldab** 'to change' A. *badal*. In some cases the ancient participle has been taken and used as a root', *e.g.*, *hataba* 'to kill' in the Rāmāyan, based on *hataḥ* 'killed'. *bhāgab* 'to run away' on *bhagnaḥ* 'broken'. What appear as passive roots to-day are based on the ancient passive forms, *e.g.*, *chījai* 'to waste away' < *chidyatē* : *chijjai*, *bājai* 'strikes' : *vādyatē* > *bajjai*. If a root is both

[1] Early Awadhi does not differ from Modern Awadhi in the treatment of roots.

passive and active, *e.g.*, *bharab* 'to be filled' or 'to fill', it is derivable from two different forms (Pkt. *bharīai* and *bharai* respectively). The derivation from two different sources explains the alternation of consonants also, *e.g.*, *ṭūṭab* 'to break' (passive) and *tōrab* 'to break' (active) are derivable from *truṭyate* and *trōṭayati*, *-ṭy-* > *-ṭṭ-* > *ṭ-*, while *-ṭ-* intervocalic becomes *r* in Awadhi.

Auxiliary Verb

A. Early Awadhi

§ 290. The auxiliary verb is seldom employed; the participle by itself expresses the complete sense of the verb generally. The following are the forms, sometimes used as the auxiliary but generally as the substantive verb.

Present tense

Jāyasī, Tulsī and Nūr Muhammad all have *ah-*, *h-* forms, *e.g.*, Jāyasī: *haũ* (p. 528), *ahaũ* (p. 517), *ahau* (p. 435), *hai* (p. 10), *ahai* (p. 33), *ahahi* (p. 147), *āhi* (p. 348), *hahī* (p. 151); Tulsī: *ahaũ* (p. 379), *hahu* (p. 296), *hahī* (p. 144), *ahahī* (p. 456); Nūr Muhammad: *haũ* (p. 25), *hasi* (p. 55), *ahasi* (p. 43), *hahu* (p. 32), *hai* (p. 1), *ahai* (p. 2.), *āhi* (p. 5), *ãhai* (p. 45).

Jāyasī does not generally use *tatsama* forms. but still at one place he uses *nāsti* (p. 8).

We find three instances of *āch-* verb in Jāyasī: *āchahī* (p. 181, p. 585) and *ācha* (p. 245), and *achata* 'remaining' in Tulsīdās (*e.g.*, p. 158).

Past tense

All the three texts have *bha-* forms, Jāyasī in addition has *ah-* and *h-* forms and Tulsī *h-*, *rah-* forms, *e.g.*, Jāyasī: *ahā* (p. 225), *hatē̃* (p. 150), *hatā* (p. 113), *hata* (p. 120), *huta* (p. 171), *ahē* (p. 342), *ahī* (p. 35), *bhā* (p. 16), *bhaeu* (p. 78), *bhai* (p. 78), *bhaē* (p. 79); Tulsī: *bhaī* (p. 85), *bhayeu* (p. 324), *hī* (p. 379), *rahī*, *rahē* (p. 146); N. Muhammad: *bhaeũ*

(p. 63), *bhā* (p. 6), *bhaī* (p. 9), *bhaeu* (p. 8), *bhaila* (p. 67), *bhaē* (p. 11), *bhaena* (p. 59), *bhaĩ* (p. 19), *bhaĩna* (p. 59).

NOTE.—Jāyasī uses *āthĩ* once.

Future tense

All the texts have *hō-* forms, *e.g.*, Jāyasī: *hōeū* (p. 21), *hoihai* (p. 249), *hōihi* (p. 312), *hōhai* (p. 416), *hōhihī* (p. 245); Tulsī: *hōihi* (p. 28); N. Muhammad: *hōihi* (p. 26), *hōba* (p. 55), *hōbai* (p. 58).

For the Imperative and Conjunctive *hō-* forms are used, *e.g.*, *hōai* (J. p. 573), *hōi* (J. p. 348), *hōhu*. (N. p. 32).

B. MODERN AWADHI

§ 291. The following are the forms of the auxiliary verb.

(a) Present Indicative

Lakhīmpurī

	sg.	pl.
1st person	**hʌū**	**hʌn**
2nd person	**hʌi**	**hʌu**
3rd person	**hʌi**	**hʌĩ**

The dialects of Sitapur, Lucknow, Unao, Fatehpur, Bahraich, Barabanki, Gonda and Western Sultanpur all have **h-** forms. S., L., U. and F. agree entirely with Lmp.; B. and G. substitute **hoɪiɪ** for the 1st per. pl. and **hʌs** for 2nd pers. sg.; Br. has 1st pers. **hʌ̃w, hʌn,** 2nd pers. **hʌwʌi, hʌwʌo** and 3rd pers. **hʌwʌi, hʌwʌĩ.** R. has the forms of Lmp. except 2nd pers. sg. **hʌsi̥,** 3rd pers. sg. **aɪj,** 3rd pl. **ʌɦĩɪ** or **aɪɦĩɪ.** Fy. and Sl. have **ʌɦ-** forms *viz.*, 1st pl. **ʌɦiɪ, ʌɦʌn,** 2nd sg. or pl. **ʌɦʌu, ʌɦaɪ,** 3rd sg. **ʌɦʌi** or **aɪj** and 3rd pl. generally **ʌɦʌ̃j, (ʌɦĩɪ, ʌɦin).** Bgh. has **h-** and **ʌh-** forms: 1st **ʌɦeū, hʌĩ**; 2nd **hʌi,** and **hʌu, ʌɦʌu,** 3rd **aɪj ʌi** and **hʌĩ, ʌɦẽɪ.** In P. we find **baɪṭ-** forms: 1st. pl. **baɪṭen,** 2nd sg. or pl. **baɪṭʌi, baɪ,** 3rd sg. **baɪṭʌi,** 3rd pl. **baɪṭʌ̃j** but **ʌɦ-** also (*e.g.*, **tʌĩ ʌɦʌsi** 'thou art', **ʌɦʌi**

3rd sg.). In A. both **ʌɦ-** and **baːt̪-** forms are found and in Mirzapur mostly the latter.

(b) Past Indicative

Lakhīmpurī

	sg.	pl.
1st pers.	**rʌɦʌũ**	**rʌɦʌn**
2nd pers.	**rʌɦʌi**	**rʌɦʌu**
3rd pers.	**rʌɦʌi**	**rʌɦʌĩ**

All the dialects have **rʌɦ-** forms for this tense. Only in the Western portion of Unao and Fatehpur which border on Kanaujī and in Bgh., we find **hʌt-** forms (masc. pl. all persons **hʌteː**, **hʌtiː** fm., sg., **hʌtaː** masc., **hʌtiː** fm.; the **hʌ-** of these forms is elided after participles). In Partabgarh the present tense **baːt̪en** (1st pl.) is used as an alternative with **rʌɦeː.** There are dialectal differences in **rʌɦ-** forms. S., L., U., F., Br. and R. agree with Lmp., only R. has **rʌɦisi̥** for 2nd sg. B. and G. have 1st pl. **rʌɦin,** 2nd sg. **rʌɦis**; G. Fy. and Sl. have 3rd sg. **rʌɦaː** (masc.) and **rʌɦiː** fm. while Sl. and A. as well as Mirzapur have 3rd pl. as **rʌɦen** or **rʌɦin.** Sl. 1st pl. is **rʌɦʌwãː** and 2nd sg. or pl. **rʌɦjaː.** In Bgh. the **rʌɦ-** forms are also used: **rʌɦeũ rʌɦen, rʌɦaː rʌɦeu, rʌɦaː rʌɦen.**

(c) Future Indicative

Lakhīmpurī

	sg.	pl.
1st pers.	**hoiɦʌũ**	**hoibaː, hoːib**
2nd pers.	**hoːiː, hoiɦʌi**	**hoiɦʌu**
3rd pers.	**hoːiː**	**hoiɦʌĩ**

All the dialects have **hoː-** forms, only in West U. we have **hoiɦʌĩ.** But there is a difference with regard to the forms containing **-ɦ-** or **-b-**. In Lmp. and in S., L., U., F. and Bgh. we have **-b-** only in 1st pl., In B., Br., R. and G. also **-b-** form is found only in the 1st pers. pl. B. **hoibʌi, hoːb,** Br. **hoːbʌi,** R. **hoːb,** G. **hoːb.** In Fy., Sl., P., A. and Mirzapur **-b-** forms replace **-ɦ-** forms in the 2nd person also: Fy.

1st **hoɪbʌi,** 2nd **hoɪbjaɪ,** P., A., M. 1st and 2nd **hoɪb, hoɪboɪ.** In 3rd pers. sg. R., Sl. and P. have **hoɪe.** Bgh. 1st. **hoɪeũ, hoɪbʌi**; 2nd **hoiɦes, hoɪwaɪ**; 3rd **hoɪiɪ, hõiɦʌĩ.**

(d) Imperative (Present)

Lakhīmpurī

	sg.	pl
2nd	**hoɪ**	**hoɪu**
2nd	**rʌɦu**	**rʌɦʌu**

All the dialects have the forms **ho-** and **rʌɦ-**, the former emphasises the momentary character of action while the latter the continuity of the same. Such dialects as do not use a singular, *viz.*, Eastern, substitute **rʌɦaɪ** for **rʌɦʌu**.

(e) Future Imperative

Lakhīmpurī

	sg.	pl.
2nd	**hoɪeɪ**	**hoɪeu**
2nd	**rʌɦeɪ**	**rʌɦeu**

This future Imperative is used to denote distant future as compared with the ordinary Imperative. Of the two forms **hoɪ-** lays emphasis on the momentary character of the action and **rʌɦ-** on the continuity of the same, *e.g.*, **tum khaɪti̥ rʌɦeu** 'you continue eating' while **tum khaɪti̥ hoɪeu** 'you be eating'. All the dialects possess this mood. Some dialects modify their terminations as shown below :

G. 2nd per sg. **hoɪis, rʌɦis,** Sl. and P. pl. **hoɪjaɪ rʌɦjaɪ**, Bgh: **hwaɪs** sg., **hwaɪu** pl.

(f) Past Conditional

Lakhīmpurī

	sg.	pl.
1st	**hoɪtiũ**	**hoɪten, hoɪiti̥**
2nd	**hoɪti̥**	**hoɪtiu**
3rd	**hoɪti̥**	**hoɪtĩɪ**

All the dialects have **hoɪ-** forms. S and L. agree with Lmp., U. and F. have 1st **hoɪteũ, hoɪteɪ,** 2nd **hoɪteɪ,**

hoːteu, 3rd **hoːt, hoːteː**; B. agrees with Lmp. while R. and Br. have 1st **hoːteũ, hoːit,** 2nd **hoːteː, hoːtuː,** 3rd **hoːt (hoːtʌi), hoːtẽː.** G. 1st **hoːit,** 2nd sg. **(twʌĩ) hoːtis,** pl. **(tũː) hoːtiu,** 3rd **hoːt, hoːtĩː.** Fy. 1st **hoːit,** 2nd **hoːteu,** 3rd sg. **hoːt,** pl. **hoːtẽː.** Sl., P. and A. agree with Fy. except in 2nd per. where **hoːtjaː** is found.

C. ORIGIN

§ 292. The auxiliary verb of Awadhi is based on the forms of Skt. $\sqrt{as}$- 'to be', $\sqrt{bh\bar{u}}$- 'to become', $\sqrt{v\d{r}t}$ 'to exist', $\sqrt{rah}$[1]- 'to depart, separate' and $\sqrt{\bar{a}\text{-}k\d{s}\bar{e}}$[2] 'to abide'.

The auxiliary, used generally as the copula in a sentence, has almost the same place in speech as a pronoun. It is in very common use but occupies an unimportant position semantically. So we find a great variety of forms. Most of the forms are based on $\sqrt{as}$-. There are two sorts of forms of this: (1) those which retain the initial *a-* as *a-* or *ā-* and (2) those which have lost it. The texts appear to have a preference for the retention of the initial vowel. Most of the forms of either variety are fresh forms, only a few cases go back to ancient forms, *e.g.* *āhi* < *asti*[3] through *atthi*, *āthi*, but *ahahi* is a fresh formation, taking *ah-* as the root, also *hate* with *hat-* as the root. Even in early Indo-Aryan $\sqrt{as}$- was substituted by $\sqrt{bh\bar{u}}$- for the Future and the Conditional. We find the same in Awadhi. Besides, the past tense in Awadhi has recourse either to $\sqrt{bh\bar{u}}$- or to $\sqrt{rah}$-. Both the *hō-* and *bh-* forms are attested by Early Awadhi: beside *huta* < *bhūta*, we find *bhā* which is decidedly a later formation. Modern Awadhi has discarded $\sqrt{bh\bar{u}}$- for the past tense and has almost universally substituted $\sqrt{rah}$-. $\sqrt{v\d{r}t}$- is not attested

[1] Turner: *Nepali Dictionary* (p. 531) under ***rahnu***.

[2] *Ibid* (p. 191) under ***chanu***, also see B.S.O.S. Vol. V, Part I (p. 137).

[3] Chatterji derives it from ****asati***.

by Early Awadhi; its use in Modern Awadhi is restricted to one district. But it is found in Bhōjpurī quite regularly, cf. Awadhi **baɽʌi,** Bhōj. **baɽʌj.** *ăch-* appears to have been infrequently used in Early Awadhi, but it is entirely absent in Modern Awadhi.

Tenses

§ 293. In Awadhi we find the Indicative mood, the Imperative mood and the Conditional. The Indicative merely expresses the action—past, present and future. The Imperative denotes order in the case of the second person and permission or approval in the case of others. This is with reference to the present (immediate future) or to the Future (distant future). The Conditional refers to the Past where the condition has not been satisfied. Thus there result six tenses in Awadhi; those are known as simple.

Besides the above, Awadhi makes periphrastic tenses by combining the Participles with the forms of the Auxiliary Verb—six with the Imperfect Participle and six with the Perfect Participle. In effect there are eighteen tenses, *viz.*:—

A. Simple Tenses

1. Present Indicative.
2. Past Indicative:
3. Future Indicative.
4. Imperative.
5. Future Imperative.
6. Conditional.

B. Periphrastic Tenses

(*a*) *With the Imperfect Participle*

7. Present Imperfect Indicative—Imp. Part. and Present Indicative of the Auxiliary Verb.

8. Past Imperfect Indicative—Imp. Part. and Past Ind. of the Auxiliary Verb.

9. Future Imperfect Indicative—Imp. Part. and Future Ind. of the Auxiliary Verb.

10. Imperfect Imperative—Imp. Part. and Imperative of the Auxiliary Verb.

11. Future Imperfect Imperative—Imp. Part. and Fut. Imperative of the Auxiliary Verb.

12. Imperfect Conditional—Imp. Part. and Conditional of the Auxiliary Verb.

(b) With the Perfect Participle

13. Present Perfect Indicative—Per. Part. and Pres. Ind. of the Auxiliary Verb.

14. Past Perfect Indicative—Per. Part. and Past Ind. of the Auxiliary Verb.

15. Future Perfect Indicative—Per. Part. and Future Ind. of the Auxiliary Verb.

16. Perfect Imperative—Per. Part. and Imperative of the Auxiliary Verb.

17. Future Perfect Imperative—Per. Part. and Fut. Imperative of the Auxiliary Verb.

18. Perfect Conditional—Per. Part. and Conditional of the Auxiliary Verb.

In Early Awadhi one does not find the same abundance of the use of periphrastic tenses as in Modern Awadhi. In Nūr Muhammad we find more instances of periphrastic tenses than in Jāyasī or Tulsīdās but even his practice is far from Modern Awadhi.

In Modern Awadhi the terminations of the various tenses are shown below and applied to **deːkhʌb** 'to see' (root **deːkh-**) for illustration. Where a distinction between the transitive and intransitive is made, forms of **mʌrʌb** 'to die (root **mʌr-**) have been put in.

Participles

A. Early Awadhi

§ 294. (*a*) In the texts we find *-ata* as the most general form of the Imperfect Participle used with both the numbers and all the persons, *e.g.*,

J. *nimikha na lāga karata ohi* 'creating, He did not take a second' (p. 4), *satta kahata rājā jiu jāū* '(my) life may end, O king, (by) telling the truth' (p. 150);

T. *rāu avadhapura cahata sidhāē* 'the king wants to go to Ayōdhyā' (p. 145), *karata manōratha bahu mana māhī̃* 'entertaining many longings in his heart' (p. 359):

N. *citavata dṛṣṭi pāra hoi jāī* '(on) seeing, the vision goes across' (p. 8), *uṭhata karējā sō nita dhūā̃* 'smoke always arises from (my) heart (lit. liver)' (p. 155).

(*b*) J. and T. change *-ata* to *-ati* for the feminine, *e.g.*, *haũ jānati haũ* 'I know' (J. p. 508), *lāgati avadhi bhayāvani bhāri* 'Ayōdhyā appears extremely terrifying' (T. p. 189), *sirāti na rāti* 'the night does not end' (T. p. 217). In periphrastic passive formations, however, the distinction of gender is sometimes absent, *e.g.*, (*sādhumahimā*) *sō mō sana kahi jāta na kaisē̃* 'that (greatness of the good people) is not described by me, in a manner' (T. p. 4), *prīti na sō kahi jāta* 'that affection is not described' (T. p. 195).

(*c*) A few instances of the passive participle in *ita*, *-iata* have been noticed in Jāyasī and Tulsīdās: J. *jōga jōri vaha pāita bhōgū* 'that enjoyment is obtained by concentrating on *yōga*' (p. 229); T. *girā aratha jala bīci sama, kahiyata bhinna na bhinna* 'word and meaning, like waves of water, are said to be different but are not so' (p. 33), similarly *pūjiata* 'is worshipped' (p. 13), *sarāhiata* 'are admired' (p. 233), *dēkhiata* 'are seen' (p. 331, p. 409).

(*d*) This participle is freely used to denote the Present Indicative in the Rāmāyan and less frequently in the Indrāvatī without the help of any auxiliary. In the Rāmāyan and Padmāvat, its use with the forms of the auxiliary verb is very rare (see §§ 314 and 316). In the Indrāvatī the auxiliary is in greater use but still the Imperfect Participle without the auxiliary is found considerably. There does not appear to be any distinction of sense between the real Present

Indicative (based on the Ancient Present) and that indicated by this participle.

NOTE.—Note 2 under § 296 is applicable to Early Awadhi also, *e.g.*, ***auru jo bhūlẽ āvatahi*** 'others who have forgotten (the path) while coming (lit. during the coming)' (J. p. 16)

§ 295. The following forms of the Perfect Participle are found in Early Awadhi texts :

(*a*) in *-ā*, (*b*) in *-ē*, (*c*) in *-ī*, (*d*) in ***-eū***, (*e*) in ***-iū***, (*f*) in *-inha*, (*g*) in *-esi*, *-isi*, (*h*) in ***-ehu***, *-eu*, (*i*) in ***-ihu***, (*j*) in *-enhi*, *-inhi*, ***-ena***, *-eni*, ***-ina***, (*k*) in ***-ī***, (*l*) in *-eu*, (*m*) in *-ehi*, (*n*) in *-ala*, *-ila*.

Of these the first three forms (*a*), (*b*) and (*c*) are used both as adjective and as verb; as adjective (*a*) qualifies a masc. sg. noun, (*b*) a masculine pl. noun and (*c*) qualifies a fm. sg. or pl. As verb, these forms are used irrespective of person. If the root is transitive, the participle used agrees with the number and gender of the object, and if the root is intransitive, it generally agrees with the number and gender of the subject. For instance :

Jāyasī : *taba lagi rānī suā chapāvā* 'the queen concealed the parrot till . . .' (p. 89), ***rānī sunā*** 'the queen heard' (p. 109), *ehi jhūṭhī māyā mana bhūlā* 'in this false *māyā* (my) mind has wandered' (p. 113), *hama na dēkha* 'I did not see' (p. 431) ; *tehi ghara dui dīpaka ũjiārē, pantha dēi kahā dai sãvārē* 'in that house the Creator prepared the two bright lamps to show (lit. give) the Path' (p. 25), *bhā bihāna paṇḍita saba āē* 'it became morning and all the learned men came' (p. 81), ***ohi saũ mai pāī jaba karanī, ugharī jībha kathā kabi baranī*** 'when I obtained the capacity from him, my tongue became unsealed and the poet (I) narrated the story' (p. 26), *jīva tumha bhaī* 'you became life' (p 568).

Tulsīdās: ***satī maruta hari sana baru mãgā*** 'Satī while dying asked for a boon from Hari' (p. 32), ***sō phalu bhalī*** *bhāti hama pāvā* 'well have I obtained the fruit of that' (p. 51), *tadapi malina mana bōdhu na āvā* 'even then understanding did not come to my defiled mind' (p. 51), *gaē mātu pahī rāmu gosāī* 'Lord Rāma went to (his) mother' (p. 177), *dīnhi asīsa lāi ura līnhē, bhūsana basana nichāvari kīnhē* '(she) gave blessings, embraced him closely and showered ornaments and clothes (on the servants) as gifts' (p. 177), *maī pani nija guru sana sunī kathā so sūkara khēta* 'I, however, heard that story from my teacher at Sūkara-khēta' (p. 18), *dukha dampatihī umā harasānī* 'Uma became pleased (but) the couple (her parents) got sorrow' (p. 33).

Nūr Muhammad : *ēka rāta sapanā maī dēkhā* 'one night I saw a dream' (p. 4), *jākō tuma sapanē mō dēkhā* 'whom you saw in dream' (p. 75), *uṭhā cahū disa tē vāvailā* 'lamentation rose up from all the four quarters' (p. 3), *hama nā rahē karabalā ṭhāī* 'I was not in Karbalā' (p. 3), *eka disa bādhē turai birājaī* 'on one side the tied horses looked beautiful' (p. 9), *gaṛha para caṛhī kamānaī durajana dēkhi ḍērāya* 'the wicked on seeing the strung bows on the fort, got frightened' (p. 8), *jaga sō patijhārī ritu gaī* 'the autumn season went away from the world' (p. 52).

NOTE 1.—The final *-ā, -ē, -ī* is sometimes found short, particularly for metre, *e.g.*, J. *dīnha, kīnha* (p. 2), *lāga* (p. 4), *bhai* (p. 78), *gai* (p. 19); T. *baiṭha, kīnha līnhu bhae* (p. 63), *bhai, gai, līnhi*; N. *kīnha* (p. 1) Verbs of very general occurrence have shorter forms: *bhā, bhē, gā, gē* are found in all the three texts; cf. 297 (z). In Jāyasī on p. 583, *baiṭhu haī, baiṭhu* (sg.) has been used with a pl. auxiliary, it ought to have been *baiṭha*.

NOTE 2 – Transitive roots used intransitively are treated of as intransitive In one case in Jāyasī (*padumāvati hāsā* 'Padmāvatī laughed', p. 429) the masc. form of the participle has been used with a feminine noun, possibly for rhyming or it might be an instance of *bhāva prayoga*. In Nūr Muhammad however there are many instances where the masculine form is found instead of the expected feminine.

NOTE 3.—In Jāyasī and Tulsīdās the use of the uninflected forms (*a*), (*b*), and (*c*) is found in abundance for indicating the past tense, but in Nūr Muhammad it is much less. He uses the inflected forms generally.

Forms (*d*) in *-eū* and (*e*) in *-iū* are used with a 1st person sg. subject, (*d*) with masculine nouns and (*e*) with feminine. Sometimes, however, even when the subject is masculine, the form of the participle is feminine in order to conform with an object in the feminine gender (*sū suni samujhi sahiū saba sūlā* 'I (Bharata) heard and understood all that, and put up with the torture' (T. p. 259). For instance:

J. *āeū ehi hāṭā* 'I (Brāhmaṇa) came to this market' (p. 121), *āiū ehi sāthā* 'I (a female friend of Padmāvatī) came with her' (p. 103). In one instance (*jāgi uṭheū*[1] 'I (Padmāvatī) got up from sleep', p. 439), form (*d*) is found with a feminine subject.

T. *anucita bacana kaheū agyātā* 'Not knowing you, I (Parushurāma) have uttered improper words' (p. 121), *dēkhiū khōja lōka tihū nāhī̃* 'I (Śūrpaṇakhā) have searched throughout, but (a man suitable to me) does not exist in the three worlds' (p. 300).

In one instance (*aba ura rākhehu jō hama kaheū* 'keep in your mind what we have said', p. 37), form (*d*)—the nasalisation being absent due to rhyme—is found with a subject in the plural number.

N. Here no instances of form (*e*) have been found; even with fem. subjects the masculine form (*d*) is used: *āhō yaha nita barajeū jōgī* 'O Yogin, I have prohibited you on this account'—the female gardener speaking to the Prince, (p. 43); *sumireū sirajanahārahī̃ jaba dēkheū asa rūpa* 'I

[1] We should, however, note that J. and N. were written originally in Persian characters which did not distinguish between *e* and *i* and hence these mistakes might be due to the scribes in Devanāgarī characters.

remembered the Creator when I saw such beauty'—the Yogin speaking (p. 19).

Form (*f*) in *-inha* is found only in Tulsīdās and has been used with fem. subject of the 1st person plural, *e.g.*, *hama saba......bhainha dhanya* all of us (women) became blessed' (p. 244). From this a corresponding masculine form in *-enha* can be deduced which would correspond with Modern Awadhi *-en* (§ 297).

Form (*g*) in *-esi* is found in all the three texts in transitive verbs, while that in *-isi* is found only in Tulsīdās where it always goes with a feminine noun in the 3rd pers. singular. The *-esi* form in Jāyasī and Tulsīdās is found with 3rd sing. or 2nd sing., while in Nūr Muhammad only with the 3rd pers. For instance:

J. (*tũ*) *abahũ na samputa khōlesi* '(thou Padmāvatī) has not yet opened the socket' (p. 551); (*suā*) *kahesi calaũ jau lahi tana pãkhā* '(the parrot) said: I should go away while I have wings in my body' (p. 107).

T. (*madana*) *marana ṭhāni mana racesi upāī* '(Cupid) made up his mind to die and contrived means' (p. 41), (*kaikēyī*) *māresi mōhī kuṭhāũ* '(Kaikēyī) hit me at a bad point' (p. 169).

(*mantharā*) *kahesi kathā sata savati kai* '(Mantharā) narrated hundreds of stories of co-wives' (p. 164); *būṛha bhayasi* '(thou) hast grown old' (p. 393).

NOTE.—In Tulsīdās this form of the participle always implies a contempt for its subject.

N. *gagana ki sōbhā kīnhesi tārā* '(the Creator) made the stars, an ornament of the sky' (p. I).

Forms (*h*) in *-ehu* (*-eu*) and (*i*) in *-ihu* are used with the 2nd pers. plur., (*h*) in the masculine and (*i*) in the feminine. *-eu* is found very seldom in Jāyasī and Tulsīdās while it is frequently found in Nūr Muhammad. The fem. form is not found in Nūr Muhammad. For instance:

J. *hatiā dui jo caḍhāehu kādhai* 'the two murders that you have borne on your shoulder' (p. 470), *āeu milai calehu mili sūā* 'O parrot, you came to meet and have moved away after the meeting' (p. 404), *jo gaihu kālhi dēo kara bārī* 'that you went to the deity's garden yesterday' (p. 442), *pūji manāihu bahuta bināti* 'after having adored him, you coaxed him by many prayers' (p. 442).

T. *muni asa kṛpā na kīnhehu kāū* 'O sage, never did you show such a favour before' (p. 90), *ḍahaki ḍahaki paricehu saba kāhū* 'you have become hardened by overcoming every one' (p. 62), (*tumha*) *kīnhihu prasna jagata hita lāgī* '(you) have put the question for the sake of the world's good' (p. 53), *rahihu baurānī* 'you were mad' (p. 64).

N. *hō dhana jā kō nāma sunāyehu* 'O lady, he whose name you have uttered (lit. made me hear)' (p. 49), *jō jōgī kahā samujheu āju* 'if you understood the Yogin today' (p. 75).

NOTE.—On p. 25, in the Rāmāyan an instance occurs (*kīnhahu praśna* 'you have put the question') where the termination *-ahu* appears for *-ehu* and is obviously a misprint.

Forms (*j*) and (*k*) are used with a subject in the 3rd pers. plur.; of these (*k*) in *-ī* is used only with a feminine subject and generally when the verb is intransitive, while (*j*) is found with the masculine generally and with the feminine when the verb is transitive. *-enhi* is found in Jāyasī, *-enhi* and *-inhi* in Tulsīdās without any distinction and *-ena*, *-eni* and *-ina* (fm.) in Nūr Muhammad. There is only one instance in Tulsīdās where *-eni* is found (*raheni tahā* 'there they lived', p. 90 of the 1915 edition), but this reading has been discarded in the later edition. For instance:

J. *chāḍenhi lōga kuṭūba saba kōū* 'all left their people and family' (p. 263), *dharī tīra saba kāṁcuki sārī* 'on the bank (the women) put their sārīs and bodices (p. 99), *jāi pāli para ṭhāḍhī bhaī* '(the women) went and stood on the bank' (p. 95).

T. *daccha-sutanha upadēsinhi jāī* '(he—respectful plural) went and advised the sons of Dakṣa' (p. 38), *jehi ripu chaya soi racenhi upāū* 'they contrived means by which the enemy might be destroyed' (p. 75), *bṛnda bṛnda mili calī logāī* 'the women started in groups' (p. 85).

N. *sumirena indrāvati kara nāū* 'they remembered the name of Indrāvatī' (p. 26), *bahuta amī adharana para diheni sindhu mō̃ prāna* 'many men abandoned their lives for the sake of the nectar-lips' (p. 49), *samujhāina saba sakhī sayānī* 'all the wise friends advised (her)' (p. 75), *bhai na bilamba sakhī saba āī* 'there was no delay, all the friends came' (p. 52).

NOTE.—*ī* is sometimes shortened to *-i* for the sake of metre, *e.g.*, J. *calī*, (p. 415), T. *cali* (p. 28).

Form (*l*) in *-eu* is found in all the three texts with the 3rd person singular subject, *e.g.*, Jāyasi: *jō gā tahā̃ bhulāneu sōī* 'whoever went there lost (the way)' (p. 153), *naeu* "became subdued' (p. 19); Tulsī: *nārada jāneu nāma pratāpū* 'Nārada came to realise the powerful effect of the Name' (p. 16), *ratha samēta rabi thākeu* 'the sun stayed with his chariot' (p. 86); Nūr. Muhammad: *jā kahā̃ karatā darasa dekhāeu* 'to whom the Creator showed the path' (p. 2), *jagata bhaeu ādhiyāra* 'the universe became dark' (p. 3).

Form (*m*) in *-ehi* is found with the 2nd pers. sing. and only in Tulsīdās, *e.g.*, *rē saṭha sunehi subhāu na mōrā* 'O knave, thou hast not heard about my nature' (p. 116).

In one case *-ē* is found (*jānē nahī̃ marama saṭha mōrā* 'O knave thou did not know my secret' p. 344)

Only a few instances of form (*n*) are found in Nūr Muhammad and obviously they are borrowed from Bihārī, *e.g.*, *tāpala rahai* 'remains heated' (p. 58), *gaila sakhī tahā̃ bahila bayārā* 'the friend went, there the breeze blew' (p. 161).

Similarly Braj forms and Bhōjapurī forms are found occasionally in Tulsīdās as loan-words.

B. Modern Awadhi

§ 296. The Imperfect Participle in Lakhīmpurī has three forms, (*a*) in **-ʌtḭ**, (*b*) in **-itḭ** and (*c*) in **-ʌtiː**. Form (*b*) is used with the 1st pers. pl. in both the genders, *e.g.*, **hʌm deːkhitḭ hʌi** 'we (masc. or fem.) are seeing' and (*c*) in **-ʌtiː** with the fem. pl. of the 2nd and 3rd pers., *e.g.*, **tum dekhʌtiː hʌu** 'you (females) are seeing', **ui dekhʌtiː hʌĩ** 'they (females) are seeing'. For all other cases, *i.e.*, singular in both genders and plural masculine in the 2nd and 3rd pers. the form (*a*) in **-ʌtḭ** is used.

(*a*) The final **-ḭ** of forms (*a*) and (*b*) is found in Sitapur, Lucknow (western and southern) and in parts of Unao only, in other districts it is absent.

The use of the form (*c*) in **-ʌtiː** is extended to 1st pers. pl. also in Unao and other places bordering on Kanaujī area, *e.g.*, **hʌm deːkhit hʌi** 'we (men) see', **hʌm dekhʌtiː hʌn** 'we (women) see'. In parts of Kheri district bordering on Hardoi, (*b*) is found ending in **-iʌtḭ** (**ɟʌiʌtḭ, cʌɦiʌtḭ, khʌiʌtḭ,** etc.). In Barabanki and parts of Sultanpur, form (*b*) in **-it** is not used, the (*a*) form has taken its place. The dialects of Bahraich and Sultanpur as well as parts of Fyzabad distinguish the gender in the Imperfect Participle in the 3rd person sg. and pl., *e.g.*, **deːkhʌt hʌi** (masc.), **deːkhʌtḭ hʌi** (fem.), **deːkhʌt hʌĩ** (masc.), **deːkhʌtḭ hʌĩ** (fem.).

Note 1.—Of the forms of the auxiliary, present tense **hʌi** and past tense **rʌɦʌi** (and their corresponding forms in the dialects) are used with **-itḭ** or **-iʌtḭ** forms of the 1st pers. plural.

Note 2.—The Imperfect Participle is sometimes used as a verbal noun also, *e.g.*, Lmp. **hʌmʌreː khaːtḭ me dundu ne mʌcʌːoː** 'do not make a noise while I am eating (lit. in my eating)'. It emphasises the imperfection of the act.

§ 297. The Perfect Participle in Lakhīmpurī has the following forms :—

(*a*) in **-aː**, *e.g.*, **deːkhaː** 'seen,' **pʌɽɦaː** 'read', **mʌraː** 'died', **gʌwaː** 'went.'

(*b*) in **-eː**, *e.g.*, **deːkheː**, **pʌɽɦeː**, **mʌreː**, **gʌeː**

(*c*) in **-iː**, *e.g.*, **deːkhiː**, **pʌɽɦhiː**, **mʌriː**, **gʌiː**

(*d*) in **-eũ**, *e.g.*, **deːkheũ**, **pʌɽɦeũ**, **mʌreũ**, **gʌeũ**

(*e*) in **-iũ**, *e.g.*, **mʌriũ**, **gʌiũ**

(*f*) in **-en**, *e.g.*, **deːkhen**, **pʌɽɦen**, **mʌren**, **gʌen**

(*g*) in **-isi̥**, *e.g.*, **deːkhisi̥**, **pʌɽɦisi̥**

(*h*) in **-eu**, *e.g.*, **deːkheu**, **pʌɽɦeu**, **mʌreu**, **gʌeu**

(*i*) in **-in**, *e.g.*, **mʌrin**, **gʌin**

(*j*) in **-ini̥**, *e.g.*, **deːkhini̥**, **pʌɽɦini̥**

(*k*) in **-ĩː**, *e.g.*, **mʌrĩː**, **gʌĩː**

As regards the use of these forms, the dialects show a difference between transitive and intransitive verbs. Forms (*a*) and (*c*) are used to qualify a subject in the singular number of masc. and fem. gender respectively, when the verb is either intransitive by itself or bears an intransitive or passive sense, *e.g.*, **mʌi gʌwaː hʌũ** 'I have gone' (masc.), **mʌi gʌiː hʌũ** 'I have gone' (fem.), but **mʌi deːkhaː hʌũ** 'I am one who has been seen' (masc.), **mʌi deːkhiː hʌũ** 'I am one who has been seen' (fem.), **mʌi pʌɽɦaː** (or **pʌɽɦiː**) **hʌũ** 'I am read—literate' (masc. or fem.). Similarly in the plural, forms (*b*) and (*c*) are used, *e.g.*, **hʌm gʌeː hʌn** 'we have gone' (masc.), **hʌm gʌiː hʌn** 'we have gone' (fem.), **hʌm deːkheː hʌn** 'we are those who have been seen' (masc.), **hʌm deːkhiː hʌn** 'we are those who have been seen' (fem.). In the same manner they are used with the subjects in the 2nd and 3rd person.

In the case of transitive verbs form (*b*) in **-eː** is used with the subject of any number and person (except 3rd plur.) and gender, *e.g.*, **mʌi deːkheː hʌũ**, **tui deːkheː hʌi**, **uː** or **waː deːkheː hʌi**, **hʌm deːkheː hʌn**, **tum deːkheː hʌu** Here it always bears an active sense. Forms (*d*) in

-eũ and (*e*) in **-iũ** are used with 1st pers. sg. **mʌi** only, (*d*) with both genders when the verb is transitive and with masculine when the verb is intransitive, *e.g.*, **mʌi deːkheũ** 'I (masc. or fem.) have seen', **mʌi gʌeũ** 'I went' (masc.) and (*e*) in fem. gender only when the verb is intransitive, *e.g.*, **mʌi gʌiũ** 'I went' (fem.). Form (*f*) in **-en** is used when the subject is in 1st pers. pl., irrespective of the gender, and the verb is either transitive or intransitive, *e.g.*, **hʌm deːkhen hʌi** 'we have seen', **hʌm gʌjen hʌi** 'we have gone'. Form (*g*) is used when the verb is transitive and the subject is either in 2nd pers. sg. or in 3rd pers. sg., *e.g.*, **tui deːkhisi̥ hʌi** 'thou hast seen', **uː** or **waː deːkhisi̥ hʌi** 'he or she has seen'.

Forms (*h*) in **-eu** and (*i*) in **-in** are used when the subject is in the 2nd person plural, (*h*) in both genders with a transitive verb and in masc. gender with an intransitive verb, *e.g.*, **tum deːkheu hʌi** 'you have seen' (masc. or fem.), **tum gʌeu hʌi** 'you have gone' (masc.) and (*i*) in fem. gender only when the verb is intransitive, *e.g.*, **tum gʌiu hʌi** 'you have gone' (fem.). Form (*j*) in **-ini̥** is used when the verb is transitive and the subject is in the 3rd pers. plur. irrespective of gender, *e.g.*, **ui deːkhini̥ hʌi** 'they have seen' (masc. or fem.). Form (*k*) is used with 3rd pers. plur. fem. only, when the verb is intransitive and is used independently without an auxiliary, *e.g.*, **ui gʌĩː** 'they went', but **ui gʌiː hʌĩ** 'they have gone'.

NOTE 1.—With forms (*d*) to (*j*), the auxiliary **hʌi** (present) and **rʌɦʌi** (past)—and their corresponding forms in the district dialects (*e.g.*, **baː, baːʈʌi**) are used and not other forms of the present or past, *e.g.*, **mʌi deːkheũ hʌi** and not **mʌi deːkheũ hʌũ**.

The dialects of the districts show considerable divergence with regard to the use of the forms of the perfect participle. Forms (*a*) and (*c*) are used, irrespective of the verb being transitive or intransitive, in all persons and numbers, in all the dialects except Lmp. and S. In the Eastern dialects, sometimes, the distinction of gender also is not observed, *e.g.*, Fy. **hʌm deːkhaː rʌɦen** 'we had seen'. Sl. **hʌm deːkhaː ʌɦiː** 'we have seen'. B. **hʌm deːkhaː hʌi** 'we have seen', L. **hʌm khaːwaː** 'we ate', U. **hʌm dekhaːwaː rʌɦʌi** 'we had shown', Sl. **tũː deːkhaː rʌɦjaː** 'you keep seeing', U. **tum kaiseː bʌtaːwaː** 'how did you tell?', P. **ʌɦir kʌɦaː** 'the Ahīr said', G. **aːdɦiː raːt bhaː** 'midnight came', **meɦraːruː cʌlaː gʌi** 'the woman went away', B. **raːjaː balaːwaː** 'the king called', U. **sãːp kaːʈi khaːwaː rʌɦʌi** 'the serpent had bitten', **waː dɦʌriː rʌɦʌsi̥** 'she had put', Sl. **wʌj deːkhaː rʌɦẽː** 'they had seen', U. **un khʌbʌri̥ paːiː** 'they got the news', **caːriu bɦaːiː jaːneː naːiː paːwaː** 'the four brothers could not know'. Form (*b*) is used with the plural when the verb is intransitive and with 1st sg. and 2nd sg. where they exist (western and central dialects), with 1st pl. and 2nd pl. in all the dialects and also with 3rd pl. even in the case of transitive verbs in the Eastern dialects, *e.g.*, Br. **mʌi deːkhaː hoːũ** 'if I may have seen', R. **tui deːkheː hʌi** 'thou hast seen', Sl. **hʌm deːkheː ʌɦiː** 'we have seen', Sl. **tũː deːkheː hoːteu** 'had you seen', Fy. **wʌj deːkheː rʌɦʌĩ** 'they had seen'.

This form appears as nasalised in the extreme East, *e.g.*, A. **hʌmaːr bɦaːj aːjẽː** 'our brothers have come'. Form (*d*) in **-eũ** (Br. **-ew̃**) and Form (*e*) in **-iũ** are used in Western and Central dialects like Lmp., in the Eastern dialects they are rare and do not maintain a distinction of transitive and intransitive, (*d*) being used as the masculine and (*e*) as feminine. Forms (*f*) in **-en** and (*j*) in **-ini̥** (**-in**) are used both with the 1st plural and the 3rd plural, the form in **-un** also is found on the Kanaujī borders of Sitapur and Unao, *e.g.*, B. **hʌm laːin** 'we brought', **hʌm gʌin** 'we went' S. **hʌm jhothʌri̥ ɖaːrini̥** 'we thrashed him', F. **hʌm lʌuʈi̥ aːun** 'we came back', Sl. **wʌj deːkhen** 'they saw', P.

wʌj deːkhen hʌi 'they have seen', U. **wʌi kʌṭaːuːi** 'they got (it) cut', M. **oː aːjen ʌu kʌhen** 'they came and said', **oː jaːi laːgen** 'they started to go', **dui beṭʌwaː rʌhen** 'there were two sons'. Form (*g*) in **-isi̥** is found as **-esi̥ (es)** in parts of Lucknow, Unao, Fatehpur and in R., B. and P. On the borders of Kanaujī it is also found as **-osi.** In P. and other Eastern dialects it is found with intransitive verbs also, *e.g.*, G. **twʌĩ mʌris** 'thou died', **twʌĩ khaːj laːgisu̥** 'thou began to eat', P. **deːkhes rʌhʌi** 'had seen', U. (Kanaujī border) **diːnhosi̥** 'gave' **kiːnhosi̥** 'did'. Forms (*h*) in **-eu** and (*i*) in **-iu** are found used in all the dialects, with this difference that the Eastern dialects use (*h*) with masculine subject and (*i*) with feminine subjects, irrespective of the verbs being transitive or intransitive, *e.g.*, P. **tũː hoːteu** (masc.) and **tũː hoːtiu** (fem.) 'had you been'. Form (*k*) is used with 1st. pl. (fm.) and 2nd pl. (fm.) also in the case of intransitive verbs in U. and F., *e.g.*, **hʌm mʌrĩː** 'we died', **hʌm gʌĩː** 'we went'.

(*x*) Such intransitive roots as contain a long syllable (*e.g.*, **laːg** 'to appear', **bʌiṭh-** 'to sit', **sʌrmaː-** 'to be ashamed'), generally elide the terminations **-aː** and **-eː** and substitute **-i̥** for **-iː** (fm. sg.). In the Eastern dialects this **-i̥** also does not appear sometimes, *e.g.*, **laːgaː laːg, bʌiṭheː bʌiṭh, laːgiː laːgi̥, bʌiṭhiː bʌiṭhi̥**. A specimen from Unao gives **pʌiṭhi, laːgi** as masc. pl. where **-i** should represent **-e.**

(*y*) Roots in **-aː,** however, before accepting the above change have the augment **-n-** between the root and the terminations, *e.g.*, **sʌrmaːnaː sʌrmaːn, sʌrmaːniː sʌrmaːni̥.**

Monosyllabic roots ending in **-aː** (*e.g.*, **aː-** 'to come', **laː** 'to bring') neither insert **-n-** nor have the shorter forms by eliding the terminations.

(*z*) **jaː** 'to go', **hoː** 'to become', **deː** 'to give'. **leː** 'to take' and **kʌr** 'to do' have their perfect participle forms with **gʌ-, bhʌ-, dih-, lih-** and **kih-** respectively. In the case of **kʌr-** both are optionally used (*e.g.*, **kʌreũ** or **kiɦeũ**). **gʌ** and **bɦʌ** have shorter forms also, **gʌwáː gaː**, **gʌeː geː**, **gʌiː gʌi**, **bɦʌwaː bɦaː**, **bɦʌeː bɦeː**, **bɦʌiː bɦʌi**.

NOTE 2.—For the insertion of **-w-** see below § 341 (*d*) In the Central dialects and in south L., U. and F., we find the **-n**, **-nɦ** forms of the Perfect Part. of **kʌr-**, **deː-**, **leː-** (**kiːn**, **kiːnɦ**, **diːn**, **diːnɦ**, **liːn**, **liːnɦ**).

C. ORIGIN

§ 298. The Imperfect participle is based on the ancient present participle (*śatṛ*) in *-anta*. There are three forms in Modern Awadhi, **-ʌt**, **-ʌti̥** and **-iti̥** (**iʌti̥**). The Eastern form in **-ʌti̥** and the Western in **-ʌtiː** are mere feminine forms. The fm. form **-ʌti̥** is attested by the Rāmāyan. What is the basis of the masc. **-ʌti̥** form? It is found in some dialects of Western Hindi also. This goes back, most probably, to the Māgadhī and Ardha Māgadhī Nom. sg. in *-ē*, as opposed to *-ō* of the Western Prakrits. The *-ē* developes into **eː**, **i**, **-i̥** and then loses ground. It appears that the *i* (**i̥**) had already disappeared in the dialects represented by Jāyasī, Tulsīdās and Nūr Muhammad. The final *-a* in the participle is merely orthographic and not of actual speech. Another possible derivation is from the loc. sg. (*e.g.*, *dēkhantē*) of the participle, but in view of the fact that the Nom. sg. form is at the basis of the Western Hindi participle, this derivation appears improbable.

(*a*) The **-iti̥** (**-iʌti̥**) participle is based on the passive form of the ancient present participle (*paḍhianta*).

§ 299. The Perfect participle is based on the ancient passive past participle (*kta*), sg. masc. in **-ā** on Nom. sg. *-ao*, sg. fm. in **-ī** on Nom. sg. fm. in *-ī-* and pl. or obl. on the ancient plural in *-aē* or on the obl. in *-aē*. The other forms are inflected according to person, gender and number. What are these affixes? Eastern Hindi shares this principle of affixation with the Eastern Mod. IA languages. Three suggestions have been made to derive these affixes, *viz.*,

(1) the pronominal forms, (2) the terminations of the present tense and (3) the forms of the auxiliary verb. As far as Awadhi is concerned the last suggestion suits it the best as shown below :—

The affix for the 1st pers. sg. is (*d*) *-eũ* and (*e*) *-iũ* (fm.) This can be either the pronoun *haũ* as the enclitic, or the termination *-aũ* of the present or the auxiliary *haũ*, *e.g.*, *dēkhē -aũ* or *haũ* may become *dēkheũ* and *dēkhī-aũ* or *haũ dēkhiũ*. The affix for the 1st pers. pl. is (*f*) *-en* ; the form in the eastern dialects is *-in*. This, however, cannot be derived either from the pronoun *ham* or from the termination of the present tense (which as shown below § 303 is a passive form), but only from the auxiliary *han* (*dēkhē -han dēkhen*, later *dēkhin*, by the interchange of *e* : *i*). The affix for the 2nd sg. is generally (*g*) **-isi̥, -esi** which can go back only to the auxiliary *hasi.*[1] This was later extended in use to the 3rd sg. as well. The affix for the 2nd pl. is (*h*) *-eu* -masc. or (*i*) *-iu* fm. which goes back to the auxiliary *hau*, *hahu*, but can as well be derived from the termination of the present *-ahu*, *au*. The 3rd pers. fm. form (*k*) in *-ĩ* has merely nasalisation, to distinguish it from the singular. It is not peculiar to the 3rd pers. but used with the 1st and 2nd pers. also. The 3rd pl. masc. affix (*i*) **-ini̥, en** (E. Aw. *-enhi*, *-inhi*, *-ena*, *-eni*, *-ina*) is derived by Hoernle (p. 346) from *nhi* (< *nti*) but the nasal in such a position does not survive; the *-nhi* is not attested at all. The Prakrit, Apabhraṁśa (see Pischel, p. 323 and *Bhavisayatta Kahā* G.O.S., p. 24) as well as E. Awadhi attest only *-hĩ*.

It is only in Sindhī, Ṣiṇā, Bengali and Gypsy that *-n-* is found in the 3rd pl. present. But is it a development of *-nt-*? Neither does the pronoun nor the auxiliary appear to be at the source. The obl. pl. of the nouns and

[1] Bloch (Survivance de Skr. **asti** en Indian Moderne—BSL. XXXIII Fas. I, pp. 55-65) derives this from the ancient auxiliary **asti** > **asi** which is also a good explanation.

pronouns ends in *-an* (E. Aw. *-anha*, *-anhi* etc.). Can that have something to do with this form of the participle?[1] E. Awadhi affix (1) *-eu* has the direct case of the noun, while (*m*) *-ehi* can be derived from the participle plus *ahi*, *usi*. The (*n*) *-la* forms are loan-words from the neighbouring Bihārī dialects and go back to *-illa* suffix of Middle Indo-Aryan.[2]

§ 300. That the auxiliary is again being incorporated into the participles is fully corroborated by modern Awadhi. For instance: Lmp. **kʌɦãː ɟaːti̥ hʌu** appears in regular speech as **kʌɦãː ɟaːtiu** 'where are you going?', F. and Bgh. **kheːltiː tĩː** 'were playing' for **kheːltiː hʌtĩː**, **tum kʌhãː geː tjoː** 'where had you been?' for **tum kʌhãː geː hʌtjoː, biaːɦ ke khwaːɟ kaː gaː ten** 'I had been in search of marriage' for . . **gaː hʌten, waː baːt ɟoː kuãː maː kʌɦʌtiu tiu** 'that thing which you were saying in the well' for . . . . . **kʌɦʌtiu hʌtiu.** Similar examples have been found in Western Hindi also in abundance

Present Indicative

A. Early Awadhi

§ 301. The following are the terminatians:

	sg.	pl.
1st person	*-aũ*, *-õ*	(*-ahĩ*)
2nd person	*-asi*	*-ahu*
3rd person	*-ahi*, *-ai*, *-u*	*-ahĩ*, *-aĩ*

1st sg. *-aũ* is the termination in all the three texts, *-õ* being found only in a few instances in Nūr Muhammad. For instance.

Jāyasī: *dui māraga dēkhaũ eni naṭā* 'I see two paths in this market' (p. 124). *sēva karaũ tehi ṭhāũ* 'I serve at her place' (p. 131).

Tulsī: *tātẽ mai tohĩ barajaũ rājā* 'O king, therefore, I forbid you' (p. 73), *āju saṭhahi haṭhi māraũ ōhĩ* 'to-day I shall forcibly kill the scoundrel' (p. 393).

---

1 See Chatterji, p. 936.

2 Ibid, § 426.

Nūr Muhammad : *kahaũ na pōthī khelaũ khēlā* 'I do not write (lit. say) a book, but I play a game' (p. 4), *sadā karēja sarōnita piyaũ* 'I always drink the blood of the heart' (p. 78), *baranõ rājā kī phulavārī* 'I describe the king's garden' (p. 8).

1st pl.—No instances of 1st pl. active forms are available either in Tulsīdās or Nūr Muhammad, only in Jāyasī we have three instances, *viz.*, *jaũ re jiahī mili keli karahī* 'if we live, let us sport together' (p. 570), *marahī to* 'if die then' (p. 570), *calahu mahēsa dekhahī eka gharī* 'let us go, Mahēśa, and see for a moment' (p. 579). In Tulsīdās in *kahahu kahihi kē kīnhi bhalāī* 'tell me, whom shall we mention as having done good (to us)' (p. 288), *kahihi* at the first instance appears as an active form, but it is really passive, standing for *kahia*.

2nd sg.—For instance :

Jāyasī : *kahasi paṃkhi khādhuka mānāvā* 'sayest (thou) that man is an eater of birds' (p. 126), *naina jo dēkhasi pūchasi kāhā* 'why dost thou ask what thou see-est' (p. 468);

Tulsī : *saṃkara bimukha jiāvasi mōhī* 'thou keepest me alive when Śankara is displeased (with me)' (p. 30).

NOTE.—In one instance, *viz.*, *chatrabandhu taī bipra bolāī, ghālai liē sahita samudāī* 'O wretched Kṣatriya, thou killest the Brāhmaṇas after having invited them all' (p. 76), *-ai* appears as the termination of 2nd sg.

Nūr Muhammad : *abahī ahasi sarēkhā, jahã cāhasi tahã jāsi* 'now thou art young, thou goest wherever thou wantest' (p. 43).

2nd pl.—Only in Tulsīdās there are a few instances of this form being used as Present, otherwise it is found as Imperative or Conjunctive. Tulsī, for instance, *cāhahu sunai rāma guna gūṛhā* 'You want to hear the great (secret) qualities of Rāma' (p. 25).

3rd sg.—*-ahi* forms are found in Tulsīdās and Jāyasī only as alternating with *-ai* and *-a* forms, in Nūr Muhammad one finds only *-ai*. For instance:

Jāyasī : *āvahi rōi jāhi kai rōnā* 'weeping he comes and weeping goes' (p. 126), *kīnhesi amī jiai jehi pāī* 'He has created nectar by obtaining which (one) revives' (p. 6), *kō sari mō saū pāvai* 'who can obtain equality with me' (p. 83), *kharaga dāna sari pūja na kōi* 'not one reaches his equality in sword and charity' (p. 67). In one instance, *taki para bāju rāja ghariārā* 'on that rings the king's bell' (p. 64), the termination appears as *-u*.

Tulsī : the aspirated form is much less in use than the unaspirated one, *nāhina ḍaru bigarahi paralōkū* 'I have no fear that my other world is spoilt' (p. 239), *uṛai abīra manahū arunārī* 'the *abīra* (the red powder) is in the air and everything appears red' (p. 85), *ḍagai na saṃbhu sarāsana kaisē* 'how is it that the bow of Śambhu does not stir' (p. 108), *baha samīpa surasarī suhāvani* 'near by, flows the beautiful Ganges' (p. 58).

Nūr Muhammad : *sukha pāvai mānusa sabai saba kō hōi nibāha* 'man gets happiness, and every one's business goes uninterrupted' (p. 2). *tākō sarana tāki jō āvai* 'he who comes aiming at his refuge' (p. 152).

3rd pl.—*ahī* only is found in Jāyasī, *-ahī* generally in Tulsī but *-aī* also sometimes while *-aī* generally in Nūr Muhammad, *e.g.*,

Jāyasī : *kīnhesi paṃkhi uḍahī jahā cahahī* 'He created the birds (which) fly where (they) want' (p. 4), *utarahī caḍnahī lōga cahū phērī* 'people get down and get up on all sides' (p. 48).

Tulsī : *basahī nagara sundara nara nārī* 'handsome men and women reside in the city' (p. 59), *parama krōdha mījahī saba hāthā* 'all wring their hands owing to great anger' (p. 365), *manu kupantha pagu dharaī na kāū* 'they do not put their heart or foot on a wrong path' (p. 100)

Nūr Muhammad : *eka disa bā̃dhē turai birājaī* 'on one side the horses, tied down, look beautiful' (p. 8), *dhana kē rōvata rōvaī cērī* 'when the lady weeps, the maid-servants weep' (p. 26), *lēhī dhanī nidhanī pachatāhī̃* 'the rich take them while the poor feel sorry' (p. 9).

The forms of this tense are regularly used as Present Indicative in Jāyasī and Tulsī but in Nūr Muhammad the Present Imperfect Indicative is taking its place. As shown above [§ 294 (*d*)] the Imperfect participle is alternatively used to denote the Present.

The Present Indicative, like Modern Awadhi, is employed to denote the Present Conjunctive by prefixing some word meaning 'if', *e.g.*, *sāta saraga jaũ kāgada karaī* 'if the seven heavens, He turns into paper' (J. p. 13), *jō bilōki rījhai kũari* 'if on seeing, the princess is enamoured' (T. p. 60), *ēka manuja bhējē jau jāũ* 'If I go when (he) has sent only one man' (N. p. 65).

B. Modern Awadhi

§ 302.

Lmp.

	sg.	pl.
1st	**-ʌũ (deːkhʌũ)**	**-iː (deːkhiː)**
2nd	**-ʌi (deːkhʌi)**	**-ʌu (deːkhʌu)** **-oː (kurʌwoː)**
3rd	**-ʌi (deːkhʌi)**	**-ʌĩ(deːkhʌĩ)**

I pl. U. and West S. **-iʌi (dekhiʌi),** Bgh. **ʌn (deːkhʌn)**; II sg. Br. **-eː (deːkheː),** Bgh. **deːkhʌs**; II pl. East Sl. and P. **-jaː** or **-aː (deːkhjaː** or **deːkhaː),** Br. and P. **-eː (deːkheː),** Bgh. **deːkhʌn** or **deːkhʌb**; III sg. Bgh. **deːkhi.**

This tense is no longer used in common speech (except in the case of the substantive verb 'to be') to indicate the Present Indicative. instead the Present Imperfect Indicative is used, *e.g.*, for 'I see' **mʌi deːkhʌti̥ hʌũ** is used and not **mʌi deːkhʌũ,** but for 'I am', **mʌi hʌũ.** It,' however, survives in songs (*e.g.*, **soːwʌu ki jaːgʌu moriː aːdɦi bɦʌwaːni jʌgʌto keriː raːniː . . . bʌli jaːũ** 'are you sleeping or waking, revered Bhavānī, queen of the world, I bow') as the Present Indicative and in stories as the historic present or habitual past, *e.g.*, **mʌɦtaːriː roːjṳ chʌpːʌn pʌrkaːl ke bɦoːjʌn bʌnaːwʌi** 'the mother used to prepare food of fifty-six varieties daily', **raːjaː kʌceɦəri sḛ aːjeː deːkhʌĩ kaː koːi kḛ juːtaː dɦʌreː** 'the Raja returned from the Court and what does he see—that some one's shoes were there.'

The forms of the Present Indicative are also employed as the Present Conjunctive. The condition is shown by prefixing the sentence by some word meaning 'if', *e.g.*, **joː mʌi tum kaː dhoːkhaː deːũ tʌu kʌɦeu** 'If I deceive you, blame me', **joː uː deːkhʌi tʌu eːkṳ tʌmaːcaː maːrḭ diɦeu** 'if he sees, give him a slap.'

Note.—After roots mentioned in 343 (*d*) (**kurʌ**-etc.) the termination of the 2nd pl. **-ʌu** is found as **oː** (*e.g.*, **kurʌwoː, naːoː, aːoː kheːoː, dɦoːwoː, soːwoː**).

C. Origin.

§ 303. The forms of the Present Indicative are based on the ancient Present tense (*laṭ*), only there has been some levelling in MIA.

1st sg.—Skt. *-āmi*, Pkt. *-āmi* gives Marāṭhī *-eṃ*, Bg. *-i*, *-ɪ*; Gypsy, Gujaratī and Hindi have *-ṽ*, *-ũ*. Can the labial nasal *-m-* become *-ṽ-* *-ũ* and efface *-i*, thus *-mi* becoming *-ũ*? This appears unlikely. It is certain that the plural termination Skt. *-āmaḥ* Pkt. *-āmō* is at the base of the singular. The shifting of the number has to be explained. But we should remember that the 1st person subject is very seldom expressed and that when it was expressed it used to be generally in the plural number. Generally the 1st plural was used in the passive construction, as is clear from the absence in Awadhi of any active termination (see below). These facts explain the shift.

1st pl.—In Modern Awadhi we find **-iː** and sometimes **-iʌi.** This goes back to the passive MI. *-īai* (*e.g.*, *paḍhīai*). In Early Awadhi we find one form in *-ihi* which can be traced to the above passive. In Jāyasī we find three forms in *-ahĩ*. These should be connected with West. Hindi, modern **-ẽː (deːkhẽː).** The same termination is found in the 3rd pl. derived from *-anti.* Is it a case of substitution, but why?

2nd sg.—The termination **ʌi, -eː** cannot go back to E. Aw. *-asi* directly; there is only one instance of **-ʌi** in E. Aw. One has to assume that side by side with *-asi*, a form in *-ahi* was in use in Early Awadhi; this is found in the Imperative as an alternative with *-asi* in Tulsī and is attested by Apabhraṃśa (Bhavisayattakahā G.O.S., p., 24).

2nd pl.—Skt. *-atha*, Pkt. *-ahu*, Ap. *-ahu*, E. **Aw.** ***-ahu***, Mod. Aw. **-ʌu, -aː.** The **-ʌu** form is regular from *-ahu* . The change from Pkt. *-aha* to *-ahu* appears to be on the analogy of 1st pl. *-āmō.* Modern **-aː** < *-aha*, cf. Marāṭhī *-ā* (Bloch, p. 233). Or the accent on the penultimate syllable might be responsible for the dropping out of the final *-u* of *-ahu*, the ***h*** in **-aː** is still sometimes heard.

3rd sg.—Skt. *-ati*, Pkt. *-ai*, E. **Aw.** *-ai* (*-ahi*), Modern **-ʌi.** As shown above (Part I, Chaper II) Awadhi generally retains vowel-combinations, only rarely have they contraction; the final *-i* here is retained after *-a-*. The *-ahi* forms in Early Awadhi further show that there was some emphatic aspiration which also might have been responsible for keeping the vowel-combination here intact. The E. Aw. *-a* form is, in all probability, the past participle used as historic present or habitual past.

3rd pl.—Skt. *-anti*, Pkt. *-anti*, Ap. and E. Aw. ***-ahĩ***, Modern **-ĩ.** What is this *-h-*? It is attested by Apabhraṃśa.

Past Indicative

§ 304. As shown above various forms of the Perfect Participle are used to denote the past tense both in Early and Modern Awadhi. For instance in Lakhīmpurī :

	sg.	pl.
1st	**-eũ (deːkheũ)**	**-en (deːkhen)**
2nd	**-eː (deːkheː), -isi̥ (deːkhisi̥)**	**-eu (deːkheu)**
3rd	**-isi̥ (deːkhisi̥)**	**-ini̥ (deːkhini̥)**

Bgh. has the following forms :

	masc. fem.	mas.	fem.
1st	**deːkheɦũ**	**deːkhiː**	**deːkhen**
2nd	**deːkheɦ**	**deːkhiɦ**	**deːkheɦ**
3rd	**deːkhɑː**	**deːkhiː**	**deːkhen**

Lakhīmpurī maintains a distinction between the transitive and intransitive, as shown by the following forms of **mʌr-**

1st	masc.	**-eũ (mʌreũ), -ɑː (mʌrɑː)** ;	**-en (mʌren)**
	fem.	**-iũ (mʌriũ), -iː (mʌriː)**	,,
2nd	masc.	**-ɑː (mʌrɑː)**	**-eu (mʌreu)**
	fem.	**-iː (mʌriː)**	**-iu (mʌriu)**
3rd	masc.	**-ɑː (mʌrɑː)**	**-eː (mʌreː)**
		-iː (mʌriː)	**-ĩː (mʌrĩː)**

The dialectal variation has been shown above (§297).

(*a*) This tense refers to a momentary action which happened in the past, *e.g.*, **ɟʌb mʌi huʌ̃ se̥ cʌleũ tʌb tum huɑ̃ː nɑːiː rʌɦʌu** 'when I started from there, you were not in the place'.

If a continuous action in the past is meant to be indicated, a root indicating continuity is employed, *e.g.* **mʌi bʌiʈɦeũ** 'I sat', **mʌi bʌiʈɦ rʌɦeũ** 'I remained seated'. The difference between this tense and the Present Perfect Indicative and the Past Perfect Indicative is chiefly this that the effect of the last two lasts after the action while it does not last in the case of this tense. The Past Indicative may, however, be used to denote an action just completed (for which English uses Present Perfect), *e.g.*, **uː mʌnʌiː jiː kaː tum puːchʌtị rʌɦʌu aːi gʌwaː** 'the man about whom you were inquiring has arrived'. Thus, here, the momentary action of 'arriving' is emphasised, not its effect. If the effect were to be emphasised, the Present Perfect would be used.

(*b*) Used conjunctively this tense refers to a future action, *e.g.* **jo mʌi bʌjaːr gʌeũ tʌu tumɦʌriː khaːtir ṭʌpkaː lʌjʌiɦʌũ** 'If I go (lit. if I went) to the market, I shall bring mangoes for you'.

NOTE.—In Lmp. in the case of √**laː-** 'to bring', the terminations of the intransitive (**-aː, -iː** etc.) are found in spite of the root being transitive. *e.g.* **mʌi rupʌjaː laːiũ** 'I (fem.) brought money.' Is it that a root involving motion, *i.e. gatyarthaka*, has the same treatment as the intransitive roots?

Future Indicative

A. EARLY AWADHI

§ 305. The following are the terminations:

	sg.	pl.
1st	*-ihaũ, -aba, -abaũ abai, abi*	*-aba, abi, -abā, abai, ibē*
2nd	*-ihasi, -aba*	*-ihahu, -aba, -ibī, -abī, -abō*
3rd	*-ihai, -ihi, -ī, -aba,*	*-ihahĩ, (-ihaĩ), -ihĩ, -aba*

1st sg.—In Jāyasī we find *-ihaũ, -aba* and *-abaũ,*; in Tulsī *-ihaũ, -aba* and *-abi* while in Nūr Muhammad *-aba* and *-abai*. For instance:

Jāyasī: *deihaũ bhuguti dehaũ jaya-mālā* 'I shall give enjoyment and the victory-garland' (p. 403), *ghara kaisai paiṭhaba maĩ chũchē, kaunu utara dēbaũ tinha pũchē* 'empty how shall I enter the house? when they ask, what answer shall I give?' (p. 121).

Tulsī: *tasa kahihaũ hiya hari kē prērē* 'so shall I say, impelled in the heart by Hari' (p. 18), *hari ānaba maĩ kari nija māyā* 'I shall seduce him away by my deceit' (p. 74), *bhāsā-baddha karabi maĩ sōī* 'I shall render it in (popular) language' (p. 18).

Nūr Muhammad : *karaba maĩ sēvā* 'I shall render service' (p. 32), *anta ēka dina hōbai khēhā* 'ultimately one day, I shall be (turned into) ashes' (p. 35).

1st pl.—Jāyasī *-aba*, *-abi*, Tulsī *-aba*, *-abā*, *-abai* and *-ibē*, N. Muhammad *-aba* ; for instance :

J. *puni sāsura hama gavanaba kālī* 'then tomorrow, we shall go to our fathers'-in-law' (p. 96), *kaunu utaru pāubi kita mōkhū* 'what answer shall we get, whence will the deliverance be?' (p. 97).

T. *hamahū kahaba aba ṭhakurasohātī* 'we also shall now say words flattering to the master' (p. 163), *jiyata na karabi savati sevakāī* 'while I am alive, I shall not serve my rival' (p. 165), *dēbā*, *dekhibai*, *dekhibē*.

N. *hama kehi kārana karaba sĩgārā* 'why shall we adorn ourselves?' (p. 25).

2nd sg.—the instances are found in Tulsidas only :

jaihasi taĩ samēta parivārā 'thou shall go (to hell) with thy family' (p. 76), *tinhahĩ milē taĩ hōba punītā* 'on meeting them, thou shall be purified' (p. 337).

2nd pl.—J. *-ihahu* and *-aba*, T. *-ihahu* (*iahu*), *-aba* and *-ibī*, N. *-aba*. For instance :

J. *kā kahihahu jaba dekhihahu rōhū* 'what will you say when you will see the herring?' (p. 312), *kaisai dhūpa sahaba binu chāhā* 'how will you bear the sun without shade?' (p. 247).

T. *jaba lagi tumha aihahu mohĩ pāhĩ* 'till you come to me' (p. 27), *bhujabala bisva jitaba tumha jahiā* 'when you will conquer the universe by the might of your arms' (p. 63), *ehi rāja sāja samēta sēvaka jānibī* 'know me to be your servant with all the king's equipment' (p. 140), *ē dārikā paricāri tu kari pālabi* 'please protect these daughters, taking them as your maids' (p. 140), *aparādha chamibō* 'forgive the fault.'

NOTE.— *-ibi*, *-abī* and *-ibō* are used more as imperatives and are honorific.

3rd sg.—J. *-ihi*, *-ī*, *-ihai* and *-aba*, T. *-ihi*, *-ī* and *-aba*, N. *-ihi*, *-ī* and *-ihai*. For instance:

J. *kaisai nīda parihi bhuī māhā̃* 'how will sleep come, on the ground' (p. 247), *milī so kaunahu phēru* 'then that will come together in some way' (p. 396), *bāura karihai kāhi* 'he will make someone mad' (p. 132), *guna auguna bidhi pū̃chaba* 'the Lord will ask merit and demerit' (p. 15).

T. *tinhahī kathā suni lāgihi phīkī* 'to them the story will appear insipid on hearing' (p. 7), *aba na tumhahī māyā niyarāī* 'Māyā will not come near you now' (p. 63), *jehi bana jāi rahaba raghurāī* 'in whichever forest Rāma will go and live' (p. 198).

N. *saba bilāya jāihi eka bārā* 'once all will disappear' (p. 1), *kaisē̃ rahana kaliṃjara hōī* 'how will abode be (possible) in Kalinjar' (p. 23), *puni tō lai apanē ghara jaihai* 'then will take you and go to his place' (p. 41).

3rd pl.—*ihī* only is found in J., it and others are found in T.; for instance:

J. *tīnaū̃ lōka jarihī tehi lāgī* 'with that all the three worlds will burn up' (p. 457).

T. *sunihahī sujana sarāhi subānī* 'the good people will hear it and admire it in good words' (p. 7), *dekhiahī rūpa nāma ādhīnā* '(they) will see the form under the name' (p. 14), *sīya biyāhaba rāma* 'Rāma (honorific pl.) will marry Sītā' (p. 106); *-ihī* (*rākhihī*) is very uncommon.

NOTE 1 —In Tulsī and Nūr Muhammad two or three instances of *-gē* futures, *e.g.*, *pāvahugē* (T. pp. 62, 384), *karahīgē* (T. pp. 330, 378), are found but they are borrowed forms.

NOTE 2.—The note under § 306 showing **eː + i > jaː** does not operate in Early Awadhī, *e.g., deihaũ* (T. p. 28 line 19). Sometimes the *-i* of the termination is elided, *e.g., deihaũ, dẽhaũ* (J. p. 403).

B. MODERN AWADHI

§ 306.

Lmp.	sg	pl.
1st	**-iɦʌũ (dekhiɦʌũ)**	**-ibaː (dekhibaː)**
		-ib (deːkhib)
2nd	**-iɦʌi (dekhiɦʌi)**	**-iɦʌu (dekhiɦʌu)**
3rd	**-iː (deːkhiː)**	**-iɦʌĩ (dekhiɦʌĩ)**

(*a*) There is a dialectal variation with regard to **-ɦ-** or **-b-** forms. Except in the tracts bordering on Kanaujī [where **-iɦʌĩ (dekhiɦʌĩ)** form is found with 1st plural also, *e.g.*, West Unao], the Western dialects, *viz.*, Lmp., S., L., U., F. and Bgh. have **-b-** forms only for the 1st plur. In the Central dialects, *viz.*, B., Br. and R., the **-b-** forms are creeping into the second person also. In the Eastern dialects (G., Fy., Sl., P., A., M.) **-b-** forms are found in the 1st and 2nd persons regularly, **-ɦ-** forms being found only in the 3rd person.

1st pl.—S., L., U. and F., **-ʌb, -ibeː (deːkhʌb, dekhibeː)**, Bgh. **deːkhib, deːkhʌb, dekhəbʌi,** Br. and R. **-ʌb**, B. **-əbʌi (dekhəbʌi)**, G. **-ʌb** commoner than **-əbʌi**, Fy. **-ʌb** or **-əbʌi** and after **-aː** roots **-ub (aːub, bʌtaːub),** Sl. **-ʌb** (and **-ub** after **-aː** roots only), L. **-ʌb**, so also A. and M.

2nd sg.—Br. and R. **-ibeː**, G. **-əbeː (dekhəbeː)**, Bgh. **dekhiɦeː**; 2nd pl.—B., Br. and R. have **-iɦʌu**, so also has Gonda largely and S.W. Sultanpur and Fyzabad, else Fy. **-boː,-bʌo**, Sl.**-bjaː** P.,A., M. **-baː**, **-ibaː, boː**, S.E.G. **-boː**.

3rd sg.—R. **-eː (deːkheː)**, so also Fy., Sl., A., M., P. and S. W. Sl. have **iː (deːkhiː)**, Bgh. **deːkhiː**.

3rd pl.—Br. **-iɦẽː (dəkhiɦẽː)**; Fy., Sl. and other Eastern dialects **-iɦʌĩ (dekhiɦʌĩ)**

NOTE.—In the case of roots **deː** 'to give' and **leː** 'to take', the initial **-i** of **-iɦʌũ, -iɦʌi, -iɦʌu, -iɦʌĩ,** is combined with **-eː, eː+i** thus resulting in **-jaː,** *e.g.*, **djaːɦʌũ, djaːɦʌi, djaːɦʌu, djaːɦʌĩ.**

(*b*) This tense simply refers to a future action, *e.g.*, **hʌm miṭhaːiː khʌibaː** 'we shall eat sweetmeats'. As compared with this, the Fut. Imperfect Ind. refers to an action which will be in the process of being done (**mʌi miṭhaːiː khaːtị hoiɦʌũ** 'I shall be eating sweetmeats' and the Fut. Perfect Indic. to an action which will have been completed (**mʌi miṭhaːiː khaːeː hoiɦʌũ** 'I shall have eaten sweetmeats'). In the case of verbs indicating continuous action, this tense indicates merely the beginning of the action, *e.g.*, **ɟʌb tum ʌiɦʌu tʌb ɦʌm pʌṛɦibaː** 'when you come, I shall read', *i.e.*, I shall begin reading after your arrival. The tense can be used conjunctively also (**ɟo ʌiɦʌu tʌu dekhiɦʌu** 'if you will come, then you will see'). As such it has a little more probability of the action than in the case of the conjunctive sense indicated by the Past tense [*vide* § 304 (*b*)].

C. ORIGIN

§ 307. The Future Indicative of Awadhi is based on the ancient future (*lṛṭ*) and on the *tavya* participle, the *h*-forms going back to the former while *-b-* to the latter. The development of *-sy-*, as *-ss-* and *-s-* > *-h-* appears to be rather rapid, considering that *-s-* is generally retained in Mod. IA. But the sounds in a suffix might have had a different treatment.

All the dialects of Awadhi have the *-b-* form at least in the 1st pl., the more we proceed to the East, the more we find the *-b-* forms in use. These have a great variety; *-ibā*, *-ib*, *ibē*, *-ibai* etc. all of which may not be strictly derivable from *tavya* (*itavya*): *-abba*, *-iabba*; it appears that the dialects after adopting this participle to indicate the future have developed it individually, so that now in Mirzapur **-box** forms are used with the 1st person and **-bex** with the second person. No dialects of Modern Awadhi use **-b-** forms in the 3rd person, but in Early Awadhi, these are found optionally with all the persons and numbers. The 3rd sg. form in *-ī* should be connected with *-ihi > ii*.

Imperative

A. Early Awadhi

§ 308. The following are the terminations:

	sg.			pl.
1st	*-aũ*, *-ō̃*			
2nd	*-u*, *-a*,	*-asi*	*-ahi*	*-ahu -ō*
3rd	*-au*, *-ao*,	*-ai*		*-ahī*

1st sg.—*aũ* is found in all the three texts while *-ō̃* only in Nūr Muhammad. For instance:

J. *haũ aba banōbāsa kahā̃ jāũ* 'may I now go to an exile into the forest?' (p. 90);

T. *āpu sarisa khōjaũ kahā̃ jāī* 'where should I go and seek one like myself' (p. 67);

N. *āpana auguna kāha sunāvaũ* 'how should I speak of my own demerits' (p. 84), *jñāna manda kimi kahō̃ bakhānō̃* 'my knowledge is little, how should I describe in detail' (p. 15).

2nd sg.—*u* forms are found in all the three texts; in Nūr Muhammad in a few cases we have *-a*; *-asi*, *-ahi* are found only in Tulsīdās. For instance:

J. *mohī yaha lōbha sunāu na māyā* 'do not speak to me of attractions and attachments' (p. 249);

T. *rāma-nāma mani-dīpa dharu* 'put the bejewelled lamp of the name of Rāma' (p. 14), *taba lagi janu kachu kahasi bahōrī* 'till then do not say anything again' (p. 171), *bēgi priyā pariharahi kubēṣū* 'my beloved, leave this ugly appearance soon' (p. 167).

N. *māru na chīra bhāta mō̃ lātā* 'do not strike thy foot in milk and rice' (p. 21), *taja mana cinta baṛhāva hulāsū* 'leave anxiety and increase gladness' (p. 12).

2nd pl.—all the texts have *-ahu* forms, only in Nūr Muhammad *-ō* forms are found sometimes ; for instance :

J. *dhāvana tahā̃ paṭhāvahu, dēhu lākha dasa rōka* 'send messengers there and give an amount of ten lakhs' (p. 223).

T. *mā̃gahu āju juṛāvahu chātī* 'beg (them) to-day and cool your breast (heart)' (p. 166) ;

N. *hoi dayāla gaurīpatī, puravahu kāja hamāra* 'O lord of Gaurī, be compassionate and accomplish my business' (p. 32), *kai kirapā mohi pāra utārō* 'take pity and put me across' (p. 2).

3rd sg.—*au* is found both in Jāyasī and Tulsīdās while *-ai* only is found in Nūr Muhammad ; *-ao* is a variant form of *-au* in Jāyasī and *-ai* is sometimes found in Tulsīdās. For instance :

J. *dahū̃ vaha rasa kō pāu ko nāhī̃* 'whether any one may get that tasty juice or not' (p. 179), *jāi parā jahā̃ pāo na thāhā* 'went and fell (there) where (he) may not obtain the bottom' (p. 525).

T. *kou nṛpa hōu hamahi kā hānī* 'any one may become a king, what have I to lose?' (p. 163), *jārai jōgu subhāu hamārā* 'may fate burn my habit' (p. 163).

N. *kā jānai sukha bhōga bhulānā* 'what may one who has forgotten (himself) in the enjoyment of happiness, know' (p. 11).

3rd pl.—We find only one or two examples in Nūr Muhammad: *guru jana sō̃ yaha binatiya mōrī, kōpa na mānahī̃ bhaū̃ha sikōrī* 'this is our request to the elders, may they not show anger and frown' (p. 4).

NOTE.—The passive imperative is found considerably used in all the texts, particularly with a first person plural subject [see § 347 (*c*)].

The use of this tense is exactly like that of the Imperative of Sanskrit where 'order' is denoted by a form of the second person and 'permission' is sought by a form of the other two persons.

B. Modern Awadhi

§ 309. The forms of the Imperative are the same as of the Present Indicative, but there is a distinction from the latter in the 2nd person singular, *e.g.*, in Lmp. Pres. Ind. **deːkhʌi,** Imperative **deːkhu,** Pres. Ind. **ɟaːi,** Imperative **ɟaː.** The termination of the 2nd sg. here being **-u** (and zero in the case of **-aː -eː -oː** roots) while in the Pres. Ind. it is **-ʌi** (and **-i** in the case of **-aː, -eː, -oː** roots). Besides G. 3rd sg. Imp. is **-ʌu** (**deːkhʌu**). This difference of the termination warrants a separate treatment of the Imperative.

The Western dialects and B. and G. have **-u** (and zero) like Lmp., R. and Br. have zero (**deːkh, ɟaː**) in all roots, while the Eastern dialects do not possess a 2nd person singular and hence do not show any difference from the Pres. Indic. Bgh. has **deːkhʌs** sg. and **deːkhʌb** pl. The exact Imperative sense is expressed only in the 2nd person, *e.g.*, **tui ɟaː** 'go', **bɦaːgʌu** 'run away'. In other persons it has a permissive sense, *e.g.*, **mʌi kʌrʌũ** 'let me do', **uː kʌrʌi** 'let him do'.

Note.—As shown above (Part I § 160) the Imperative is distinguished from the Present Indic. by a difference in tone also.

C. Origin

§ 310. The Imperative shows a difference from the Present Indicative only in the 2nd pers. sing. and 3rd pers. sg. The 2nd sg. form with zero termination goes back to *-a* (*gaccha* etc.) which lost its pronunciation sometime in late MIA. The *-u* termination which occurs in Sindhī as well (see Bloch p. 238) cannot go back to MIA. *-asu* (*kahasu*), nor can it be said that the ancient *-u* (*kuru*, *śṛṇu*) has survived; we find that Apabhraṃśa has it (*e.g.*, *usaru*, p. 25, Bhavisayatta *kahā* G. O. S). Hoernle (p. 338) sees it as 'perhaps a corruption of *-a*'! The 3rd sg. *-au* attested by a dialect in Modern Awadhi also as well as by Bhōjapurī, goes back regularly to *-atu* (*gacchatu*). Other forms go back to the Present Indicative which began to replace the forms of the Imperative as early as the earliest MIA.

Future Imperative

A. Early Awadhi

§ 311. The use of this tense as shown in § 312 is different from the ordinary Imperative. The following are the terminations

	sg.	pl.
2nd	*-esu*	*-ehu*

For instance :

J. *au mukha saũ baca kahesu parēvā* 'O bird, then thou wilt say words with (thy) mouth' (p. 495), *āehu caḍhi so gagana puni sātā* 'then you will come by climbing up the seven skies' (p. 435);

T. *tinhahĩ dekhāi dihesu taĩ sītā* 'to them thou wilt show Sītā' (p. 337), *karehu so jatana bibēka bicārī* 'you will have recourse to that means after a mature consideration' (p. 27);

N. *nisa mō̃ rākhahu bhōrē̃ āehu, dhirja dharehu jaisō phula pāehu* 'put it at night and then you will come early in the morning, and have consolation with whatever fruit you will get' (p. 17).

Note.—As shown under § 312 the terminations of this tense are not found with roots based on the past participle (*e.g.*, ***hōehu*** and not *bhaehu*)

B. Modern Awadhi

§ 312. This indicates an imperative of a distant future as compared with the ordinary Imperative, *e.g.*, **deːkhʌu** 'see!' **deːkheu** 'see—future'. The forms in Lakhīmpurī are :

	sg.	pl.
2nd person	**-eː (deːkheː)**	**-eu (deːkheu)**

As such they do not appear to differ from the Past Indicative (cf. § 304). But two points should be noted :—(1) that out of the two forms that we have in Lakhīmpurī for the Past. Indic. in 2nd pers. sing., *viz.*, **-eː** and **-isi̥**, only one, *i.e.*, in **-eː**, is employed for the Future Imperative, the other one in **-isi̥** is never so used ; and (2) with roots that have separate forms for the Present and the Past [§ 297 (*2*)] the Future Imperative has its terminations after the Present root, *e.g.*, **ɟaː-** Present, **gʌ-** Past ; now **ɟaːeu** 'go—Future Imperative', **gʌeu** 'went—Past Indicative'. Similarly **hoːeu** 'be—Future Imperative', **bhʌeu** 'were—Past Indicative'.

This difference warrants a separate treatment of this tense. All the dialects possess this tense. They agree in not employing the **-isi̥** or its corresponding form in **-es, -osi̥** etc. for indicating the Future Imperative and in adding the terminations after the root of the Present where a difference of roots exists. A specimen from Gonda (Balrampur) has two forms in **-isu̥** (**aːisu̥, kiñisu̥**). Standard Hindi expresses the sense of this tense by what appears to be the verbal noun, *e.g.*, **tum deːkhnaː** 'you will see'.

C. Origin

§ 313. The Future Imperative is found only with reference to the 2nd pers. sg. and pl. Its sense is connoted by the infinitive in W. Hindi (*e.g.*, **tum ɟaːnaː** 'you will go') and by the forms derivable from the Future Indicative, in Bengālī, Maithilī and Bhōjpurī (Chatterji § 651). Awadhi, however, has special terminations—sg. **eː, esu : isu̥**, pl. **-eu, eñu**. These appear to go back to the *-aya* > *ē*, conjugation of MIA in the Imperative, examples of which are quoted by Pischel (pp. 331—32).

Past Conditional

A. Early Awadhi

§ 314. The Imperfect Participle is used to denote this tense and the use is like that in Modern Awadhi (§ 315). The participle is, however, inflected sometimes. The following terminations, thus, after the root, result :

	sg.	pl.
1st	*-ateũ, -atiũ*	
2nd	—	*-atehu*
3rd	*-teu*	—

1st sg.—*ateũ* is found in all the texts, only in Nūr Muhammad *-atiũ* is sometimes found with a subject in the feminine gender, *e.g.*,

J. *anu rānī haũ rahateũ rā̃dhā* 'O queen! very gladly would I have remained (here)' (p. 405);

T. *jaũ janateũ binu bhaṭa bhubi bhāī* 'had I known, brothers, that the Earth is devoid of heroes' (p. 108);

N. *jō maĩ cahateũ āpana nā̃ũ* 'if I had wanted my fame' (p. 25), *nā tō cērī hōtiũ tērī* 'or else, I (fem.) would have become thy servant' (p. 79).

2nd pl.—the forms have been found only in Tulsīdās: *jaũ tumha avatehu muni kī nāī* 'had you come like an ascetic' (p. 120).

3rd sg.—the simple Imperfect participle (masculine or feminine) is used in all the texts but J. in addition has *-teu* forms and N. *-tai*. For instance:

J. *kusala hōtu jau janama na hōtā* 'It would have been well, if there had been no birth' (p. 314), *dhāi siṁgha baru khāteu mārī* 'it would have been better, if a lion had attacked and eaten me up' (p. 382);

T. *hōta janama na bharata kō* 'if there had been no birth of Bharata' (p. 284), *jaũ pai jia na hōti kuṭilāī* 'if there had been no wickedness in the heart' (p. 231);

N. *hōtai mukuta hamāra* 'there would have been my deliverance' (p. 16), *mō mahā tā mukha lēta basērā* 'her face would have resided (for some time) in me' (p. 11), *ātamajā jō hōta eka* 'if there had been a daughter' (p. 16), *mana au prāna doū hara lētī* 'she would have snatched away both life and heart' (p. 18).

NOTE.—The uninflected participle can be used with any person, *e.g.*, Jāyasī: *kai tasi rahati āhi jasa bārī* (Padmāvatī says) 'or I would have remained just I was in childhood' (p. 382).

B. MODERN AWADHI

§ 315. Lmp

	sg.	pl.
1st	**-ətiũ (dekhətiũ)**	**-əten (dekhəten), -iti̥ (deːkhiti̥)**
2nd	**-ʌti̥ (deːkhʌti̥)**	**-ətiu (dekhətiu)**
3rd	**-ʌti̥ (deːkhʌti̥)**	**-ətĩː (dekhətĩː)**

The following are the variations in the districts:

1st sg.—The Western dialects as well as B. agree with Lmp., R. and Br. have **-ətũ (dekhətũ)**, Bgh. masc. **dekhətjehũ,** fem. **dekhətihũ.**

1st pl.—the final **-i̥** of **-iti̥** is not found in the Eastern dialects except in G., B. has **-ətin** for **-əten,** particularly in Eastern tracts; Bgh. masc. **dekhətjen,** fem. **dekhətin.**

2nd sg.—P. Br. and R. **-əteː (dekhəteː),** G. **-ətis (dekhətis),** Bgh [illegible]sc. **dekhətjeɦ,** fem. **dekhətiɦ.**

2nd pl.—**əte** [illegible]**lekhəteu)** in Fy., G. (except West), P. and Br.; **ətjaː (dekhətjaː)** in Sl., **ətuː (dekhətuː)** in R.; Bgh. masc. **dekhətjẽɦ,** fem. **dekhətiɦĩ.**

3rd sg.—**ʌt (deːkhʌt)** in Br., R., Fy., S., P., G., A. and M. Fy. distinguishes between masc. **-ʌt** and fem. **-ʌti̥**; Bgh. masc. **dekhətjʌi,** fem. **dekhətjiː.**

3rd pl.—**ətẽː (dekhəteː)** in R., **-əteː (dekhəteː)** in G. (except West); Fy., Sl. P., A., M., **-əten (dekhəten)** or

-otin (dekhotin). Fy. distinguishes between masc. **-oteː** and fem. **-otīː (dekhotīː),** Bgh. masc. **dekhotjen,** fem. **dekhotin.**

(*a*) This tense denotes (in a conditional or purpose clause) an action which might have taken place in the past but which never did come off, *e.g.*, **ɟo mʌi ghʌr seː aːʈh bʌɟeː cʌldeːtiũ tʌu hiãː bʌkhʌt pʌr pʌɦuɲɟaːtiũ** 'had I started at eight from my house, I would have been here in time', **tum ʌis kʌrotiu ki̥ hʌm kaː hũʌ se̥ ʈʌrkʌi ko mʌukaː. milɟaːti̥** 'you should have acted in a manner that I should have got an opportunity to slip off from there'.

Compared with the Past Imperfect Conditional (§ 325) and Past Perfect Conditional (§ 331) this tense does not refer to the aspect of the incompletion or completion of the act. but simply denotes that it did not take place.

C. Origin

§ 316. The Past Conditional in Awadhi, like other Mod. IA. is based on the Imperfect participle. In some forms the enclitic personal terminations, which appear in the past tense also, are found incorporated while in others, they are not used. Awadhi does not present any special feature here.

Present Imperfect Indicative

A. Early Awadhi

§ 317. The following instances have been noted :—

Jāyasī : *haũ jānati haũ* 'I know' (p. 508), *prāna mukuta aba hōta hai* 'life-breath is becoming free now' (p. 561), *khana eka maha cāhata hahī̃ dhāī* 'in a moment, they want to make an attack' (p. 605).

Note.—In *aba kasa hāri karasi hai hẽ hari* 'how now, overcome thou sayest (dost), O Hari' (p. 551), the auxiliary has been combined with the Present Indicative form

Tulsī : *nīti dharma naī jānata ahaũ* 'I know my duty according to polity' (p 379), *nisi dinu dēva japata hahu jĕhī* 'O lord, on whom you meditate day and night' (p. 296), *jānati hahu basa nāhu hamārē* 'you know that the lord is in your control' (p. 163), *mānahū mōri karata hahī nindā* 'methinks (they) are speaking ill of me' (p. 316), *kou kaha calana cahata hahī ājū* 'somebody said, they are going today' (p. 144), *prasna karata mana sakucata ahahī* 'he is hesitating to ask' (p. 456).

Nūr Muhammad: *rōvata ahaū bircha para, mitra chāṛi gā pāsa* 'I am lamenting on the tree, the friend has left me' (p. 85), *jehi nisa dina sumirata hai kōū* 'if any one remembers any one, day and night' (p. 75), *mitra jo hai karatāra kē, marata nahī hai sōi* 'those who are friends of God, do not die' (p. 54).

B. Modern Awadhi

§ 318. For instance in Lakhīmpurī:

	sg.	pl.
1st	**deːkhʌtḭ hʌū**	**deːkhitḭ hʌi** or **deːkhitḭ hʌn**
2nd	**deːkhʌtḭ hʌi**	m. **deːkhʌtḭ hʌu** f. **dekhotiː hʌu**
3rd	**deːkhʌtḭ hʌi**	m. **deːkhʌtḭ hʌī** f. **dekhotiː hʌī**

(*a*) This tense refers to an action which is taking place in the Present and has displaced the Pres. Indic. entirely in common speech. The auxiliary is uttered with much less emphasis than the principal verb, and hence appears to have lost ground in several cases. For instance:

Lmp. **tum dekhotiu naːiː hiãː kaː hoi gaː** 'you do not see what has happened here' where **dekhotiu** stands for **dekhotiː hʌu**; Fatehpur: **ʌbʌi tum nʌɦīː ɟʌnteo** 'till now you do not know', Gonda: **hʌm dɦoːtiː naːɦīː chãːṭḭ sʌkitḭ** 'I cannot wash *dhōtī*', **hʌm soːɟɦ birʌɦaː ɟaːnitḭ** 'I know simple *Birahā* (songs)', U. **mʌi nʌɦīː lʌi sʌktiū** 'I cannot take', Allahabad: **hʌm kuchṳ naːiː kʌroten** 'I am doing nothing'. In all these instances the auxiliary has very much modified itself, so that the forms appear as if they were of the Past Conditional.

Past Imperfect Indicative

A. Early Awadhi

§ 319. Instances of this tense are much fewer than those of the Present Imperfect Indicative. For example:

Jāyasī: *sōvata ahā jahā̃ sukha sākhā* 'I was sleeping there where (one finds) branches of happiness' (p. 225).

Tulsī: *sundara suta janamata bhaĩ ōū* 'they also were delivered of handsome sons' (p. 85), *mātha nāi pūchata asa bhayaū* 'having bowed down, he began to ask' (p. 324), *rahē kahāvata parama birāgī* 'he was called a great hermit' (p. 146).

Note.—Greaves (Grammar of the Rāmāyana, p. 33) makes a distinction between the Imperfect Participle with $\sqrt{rah}$- which he calls Imperfect Past and the Imperfect Participle with $\sqrt{bha}$- which is termed by him as Inceptive Imperfect. But no such distinction appears to be justified. $\sqrt{bha}$- is combined in exactly the same sense as $\sqrt{rah}$- and is found so used in Bihārī languages even to-day. The usage in Rāmāyana only shows that both the roots were employed to make the Past Imperfect.

B. Modern Awadhi

§ 320. This tense refers to an action which was being done in the past, the imperfection being emphasised, *e.g.*, **mʌi bʌjaːrʌi jaːtḭ rʌɦʌũ** 'I was going to the Bazar' indicates that the action of going was continuing. The forms, for instance, in Lmp., are:

	sg.		pl.
1st	**deːkhʌtḭ rʌɦʌũ**		**deːkhitḭ rʌɦʌi** or **deːkhitḭ rʌɦʌn**
2nd	**deːkhʌtḭ rʌɦʌi**	m.	**deːkhʌtḭ rʌɦʌu**
		f.	**dekhotiː rʌɦʌu**
3rd	**deːkhʌtḭ rʌɦʌi**	m.	**deːkhʌtḭ rʌɦʌĩ**
		f.	**dekhotiː rʌɦʌĩ**

(*a*) In Unao and Fatehpur where we have **h**- forms of the auxiliary for the past, they are modified generally, *e.g.*,

F. **pandʌrʌɦ rupʌjaː kʌi ciːɟ milʌt tiː** 'the article was obtainable for fifteen rupees', **khelətiː tĩː** '(the girls) were playing', **tum kʌɦãː geː tjoː** 'where had you been?', **biaːɦ ke khwaːɟ kaː geː ten** 'I had gone in quest of the marriage (of my son)'.

Future Imperfect Indicative

B. Modern Awadhi

§ 321. This refers to an action which will be in the state of duration at some particular time. The forms, for instance, in Lakhīmpurī are :

	sg.	pl.
1st	**deːkhʌti̥ hoiɦʌũ**	**deːkhiti̥ hoibaː** or **deːkhʌti̥ hoibaː**
2nd	**deːkhʌti̥ hoːiː**	m. **deːkhʌti̥ hoiɦʌu** f. **dekhəti̥ː hoiɦʌu**
3rd	**deːkhʌti̥ hoːiː**	m. **deːkhʌti̥ hoiɦʌĩ** f. **dekhətiː hoiɦʌĩ**

Imperfect Imperative

A. Early Awadhi

§ 322. One instance of Present Imperfect Conjunctive is found in *calā jāta jasa hōi baṭōhī* 'as a traveller may be going' (N. p. 3).

B. Modern Awadhi

§ 323. This is found only with the **rʌɦ-** root and emphasises the incompleteness of the action wanted to be done. For instance, Lmp. **tui deːkhʌti̥ rʌɦu** '(thou) continue seeing', **tum deːkhʌti̥** (fm. **dekhətiː**) **rʌɦʌu** '(you) continue seeing'.

Imperfect Future Imperative

B. Modern Awadhi

§ 324. This also emphasises the incompleteness of the action to be done, but with reference to distant future. For instance Lmp., **tui deːkhʌti̥ rʌɦeː** 'thou will continue seeing', **tum deːkhʌti̥** (fm. **dekhətiː**) **rʌɦeu** 'you will continue seeing'.

Present Imperfect Conditional

B. Modern Awadhi

§ 325. This tense refers to the continuity of an action which did not happen. The forms, for instance, in Lmp., are:

	sg.		pl.
1st	**deːkhʌti̥ hoːtiũ**		**deːkhʌti̥ hoːten, deːkhʌti̥ hoːiti̥**
2nd	**deːkhʌti̥ hoːti̥**	m.	**deːkhʌti̥ hoːtiu,**
		f.	**dekhətiː hoːtiu**
3rd	**deːkhʌti̥ hoːti̥**	m.	**deːkhʌti̥ hoːtĩː,**
		f.	**dekhətiː hoːtĩː**

Present Perfect Indicative

A Early Awadhi

§ 326. The following instances have been noted:—

Jāyasī: *jō hai likhā so jāi na mēṭā* 'what is ordained cannot be falsified' (p. 596), *jahā̃ baiṭhu hahī rāu* 'where the king is sitting' (p. 583).

Tulsī: *taba lagi baiṭha-ahaũ baṭa chāhī* 'till then I am sitting in the shade of the banyan tree' (p. 27), *thakita hōhī saba lōga lugāī* 'all men and women become stupefied' (p. 89).

Nūr Muhammad: *hama tuma rākhā hai tehi nā̃ū* 'he has named us and you' (p. 55), *jāni parata rājā sravana, parī na hai yaha bōla* 'it appears that this word has not reached the king's ears' (p. 25), *āe suhā̃sa banē hai cērē* 'he came and smilingly became a disciple' (p. 2).

B. Modern Awadhi

§ 327. The forms in Lakhīmpurī, for instance, are:

	sg.	pl.
1st	**deːkheː hʌũ**	**deːkheː hʌn**
	deːkheũ hʌi	**deːkhen hʌi**
2nd	**deːkheː hʌi**	**deːkheː hʌu**
	deːkhisi̥ hʌi	
3rd	**deːkhisi̥ hʌi**	**deːkhini̥ hʌi**
1st	**mʌraː** (f. **mʌriː**) **hʌũ**	**mʌreː** (f. **mʌriː**) **hʌn**
	mʌreũ (f. **mʌriũ**) **hʌi**	**mʌren hʌi**
2nd	**mʌraː** (f. **mʌriː**) **hʌi**	**mʌreː** (f. **mʌriː**) **hʌu**
	mʌreː hʌi	**mʌreu** (f. **mʌriu**) **hʌi**
3rd	**mʌraː** (f. **mʌriː**) **hʌi**	**mʌreː** (f. **mʌriː**) **hʌĩ**

(*a*) The difference between this tense and the Past Indicative lies in the use. This refers to an action the effect of which lasts up to the present while the Past Indicative refers to an action which has no effect at present, *e.g.*, **mʌi kuʌ̃ mo giri̥ gaː hʌũ** 'I have fallen into the well' *i.e.*, I am still there, while **mʌi kuʌ̃ mo giri̥ gʌeũ** refers to the momentary action of falling but does not show that I am still there. Compared with the Past Perfect Indicative this tense refers to the recent past while the other to the remote past, *e.g.*, **mʌi gãːwʌi gʌwaː hʌũ** 'I have gone to the village' refers to nearer past than **mʌi gãːwʌi gʌwaː rʌɦʌũ** 'I had gone to the village'.

Past Perfect Indicative

A. Early Awadhi

§ 328. The instances are very rare:

Jāyasī: *jaba lagi guru maĩ ahā na cīnhā* as long as I had not recognised my teacher' (p. 540), *āeũ marana mīcu hati likhī* 'I have come to die, death was ordained' (p. 121), *ohī dhanukha bēdhā huta rāhū* 'Rāhu had been pierced by that very bow' (p. 171), *dharatī saraga milē huta dōū* 'the Earth and the sky both were united' (p. 474).

Tulsī: *gaī rahī* 'she had gone', *gaē rahē* 'they had gone', *gaī hī* 'she had gone' (p. 379).

B. Modern Awadhi

§ 329. As shown above (§ 297 note 1) the uninflected forms (**-aː, -iː, -eː**) of the Perfect Participle are accompanied by the regular auxiliaries of the various persons and the inflected forms (**-eũ, -iũ, iu** etc.) by the 3rd person sg. (**hʌi** and its equivalents **ʌɦʌi, baː** in the Present Perfect Indicative and **rʌɦʌi, rʌɦaː** in the Past Perfect Indicative).

As compared with the Past Indicative, the effect of the action denoted by the Past Perfect Indicative lasts beyond the time when the action took place. Moreover, the Past Indicative refers to nearer past than the Past Perfect Indicative, *e.g.*, of **mʌi gãːwʌi gʌjeũ** 'I went to the village', and **mʌi gãːwʌi gʌwaː rʌɦʌũ** 'I had gone to the village', the latter refers to remote past.

Note.—Unlike English Past Perfect (*e.g.*, I had gone) the Awadhi Past Perfect does not require comparison with another past verb.

Future Perfect Indicative

B. Modern Awadhi

§ 330. This tense refers to an action which will be necessarily completed by some particular time in the future, *e.g.*, **jʌleː tum hʌm kaː bolaːwʌi ʌiɦʌu tʌleː hʌm roːṭi khaːi cukeː hoibaː** 'I shall have taken my meal before you will come to call me'. It also sometimes is used to denote a possible but uncertain action of the past, *e.g.*, **kaːlɦi kaː tum iː kursiː pʌr bʌiṭheː rʌɦʌu ? hãː bʌiṭheː hoibaː** 'did you sit on this chair yesterday ?' 'Yes, I may have sat (on it)'.

Perfect Imperative

§ 331. This emphasises the completeness of the action wanted to be done, *e.g.*, **tui deːkheː rʌɦu,** 'you continue in the state of having seen.'

Perfect Future Imperative

§ 332. As compared to the Perfect Imperative this tense refers to distant future, *e.g.*, **tui deːkheː rʌɦeː** 'thou will continue in the state of having seen'.

Past Perfect Conditional

§ 333. This tense refers to a conditional completed action in the past which did not occur, *e.g.*, **ʝo mʌi sʌbʌi kitaːbʌi pʌɽɦeː hoːtiũ, tʌu aːʝ cʌin kʌrti hoːtiũ** 'had I completed reading all the books, I should have been enjoying this day'. The forms in Lakhīmpurī, for instance, are:

	sg.	pl.
1st	**deːkheː hoːtiũ**	**deːkheː hoːten, deːkhen hoːtiʊ̥**
2nd	**deːkheː hoːtiʊ̥**	**deːkheːhoːtiu**
3rd	**deːkheː hoːtiʊ̥, deːkhisiʊ̥ hoːtiʊ̥**	**deːkheː hoːtīː**

C. Origin

§ 334. The periphrastic tenses of Awadhi are formed by combining the Imperfect or the Perfect participle with the various tenses of the auxiliary verb and do not present any peculiarity historically. Their use in Early Awadhi is comparatively rare, but with the progress of the language greater and greater display of these tenses is found.

The Absolutive

A. Early Awadhi

§ 335. The Absolutive in Early Awadhi ends in *-i* only about half a dozen instances in Nūr Muhammad show *-a* for *-i*. This *-a* was merely orthographic. The form is generally used without any postposition; wherever a postposition is present, Jāyasī has *kai*, Tulsī *kai* generally and sometimes *kara* and *kari*, Nūr Muhammad *kai*, *kē*. For instance:

Jāyasī : *augāhi* 'having dived deep' (p. 2), *ṭūṭi* 'having broken' (p. 19), *mili kai* 'having united' (p. 60).

Tulsī : *chā̃ṛi* 'having left' (p. 88), *jāni*, 'having known' (p. 191), *sudhāri kai* 'having corrected' (p. 301), *jāi kara* 'having gone' (p. 338), *khāi kari* 'having eaten' (p. 399).

Nūr Muhammad : *samujhi* 'having understood' (p. 3), *cuni* 'having picked' (p. 5), *chāṛa* 'having left' (p. 4), *samhāri kai* 'having arranged' (p. 4), *thira kē* 'attentively' (p. 27).

The use of the absolutive is the same as in Modern Awadhi.

B. Modern Awadhi

§ 336. The Absolutive in Lakhīmpurī is formed by adding **-i̥** to a root ending in a consonant (*e.g.*, **deːkhi̥, hʌ̃si̥**) and **-i** to a root ending in a vowel (*e.g.*, **ɟaːi, khaːi**). The form thus arrived at is then used with **ko** or **kʌi** or **-kʌiɦãː**, *e.g.*, **deːkhi̥ ko** 'having seen', **hʌ̃si̥ kʌi** 'having laughed', **ɟaːi ko** 'having gone', **lʌi kʌi** 'having taken', **uː sʌb din hʌ̃si̥ kʌi baːt kʌrti hʌi** 'he always talks after smiling, *i.e.*, after having smiled'.

S., L., U., B., Br., R., G. and P. have the **-i** sound distinctively in this form, F., Fy., Sl., A., M. and Bgh. appear to drop it sometimes after roots ending in a consonant (*e.g.*, F. **niɦaːrkʌi** 'having seen', Fy. **hʌ̃s ke** 'having laughed', Sl. **deːkh ke** 'having seen', A. **utaːr kʌi** 'having brought down', M. **bãːʈ ke** 'having divided') but retain it always after roots ending in a vowel. The **-i** is sometimes pronounced as **-e** and generally **-jʌ** in the Eastern dialects. The elision of intervocalic *-r-* is witnessed in certain forms of the Absolutive in the Eastern dialects, Lmp. **dɦʌri**, B. **dɦʌiː** 'having put', Lmp. **bhʌri**, Sl. **bhʌi** 'having filled, *i.e.*, full', Lmp. **ɖaːri**, Fy. **ɖaːi** 'having thrown' [Compare Chatterji : *Origin and Development of Bengali*, p. 157 (1)]. The postposition employed by the Eastern dialects is **ke** or

kʌi. **kʌiñā̃ɪ** is restricted to Lmp., S. and B. **kʌi** is very common.

NOTE.—(1) The absolutive (without the postposition) is used to form compound verbs also (*vide* § 355).

(2) **kʌr-** 'to do', **deɪ-** to give' and **leɪ-** 'to take' have their absolutive as **kʌi, dʌi, lʌi** respectively.

C. ORIGIN

§ 337. The Absolutive of Awadhi is based on the OIA. *-ya*, MIA. *-ia*, resulting in Awadhi as *-i* > i̥ > Zero. In certain usages (*e.g.*, in compound verbs where it is compounded with *sakab*, *pāvab*, *milab*, to show ability or capacity to do an action) the absolutive stands for the old infinitive (Skt. *-tum*, MIA. *-iuṁ*) and the probability is that in such cases it has been derived from the ancient infinitive *-iuṃ*, *-iũ*, *-i.*[1]

The Verbal Noun

A. EARLY AWADHI

§ 338. The Verbal noun in Early Awadhi has two forms *viz.*, (*a*) *-ana*, (*b*) *-aba* both of which are found in the texts. The direct sometimes ends in *-u* ; and the oblique from these is found in *-anē* and *-abē*. An additional oblique form in *-ai* is also found.

The use of the verbal noun is the same as in Modern Awadhi. For instance :

Jāyasī : here we have very few instances of the direct form the oblique ends in *-ai—kita āuna puni apanē hāthā* 'how will return be within our power' (p. 96), *tā kara ihai jo khānā piyanā, saba kahā̆ dēi bhuguti au jianā* 'that he gives enjoyment and life to everyone in his meal and drink' (p. 7); *dīnhesi sravana sunai kahā̆ bayanā* 'He gave ears to

[1] Cf. my paper on 'The Verb in the Rāmāyṇa', Allahabad University Studies, Vol. II, p. 235.

hear word' (p. 12), *pūjai jāi sakala saṁsārū* 'the whole world goes to worship' (p. 360).

Tulsī: *karana cahaũ raghupati guna-gāhā* 'I want to make a narration of the merits of the lord of the Raghus' (p. 7), *calē saṅga himavantu taba pahũcāvana ati hētu* 'then Himālaya started to send them off with great regard' (p. 49), *milaba hamāra bhulāba nija kahahu ta hamahī na khōri* 'I shall not be at fault if you mention my meeting or your missing (the way)' (p. 73); *ṭūṭa cāpa nahī jurihi risānē* 'the broken bow will never be fit by being angry' (p. 118), *hãsibē jōga hãsē nahī khōrī* 'it is fit to be laughed at, there is no evil in laughing' (p. 7), *tōrai lāga* 'began to break' (p. 349), *jarai na pāvā* 'could not burn' (p. 471), *calai kara* 'of going' (p. 228).

Nūr Muhammad: *birtha khāba sōiba au jīvana, piunā jivanā lōhu ka pīvana* 'eating, sleeping and life are useless, drinking and eating is (merely) drinking blood' (p. 35), *jāgaba mohī bairī bhayeu* 'awakening has become an enemy to me' (p. 48); *bāta sunai kahã saravana dīnhā* 'He has given ears to hear' (p. 1); *kahai likhai ūpara cita dīnhā* 'I concentrated my mind on saying and writing' (p. 4).

NOTE. 1.—In Nūr Muhammad one form *roibō* 'weeping' ends in *-ibō* (p. 26).

NOTE. 2.—In Tulsīdās there are a few feminine forms of the verbal noun ending in *-ani*, *e.g.*, *avalōkani bōlani milani prīti parsapara hãsa* 'their manner of looking, speaking, and meeting as well as their mutual affection and laughs' (p. 24).

B. MODERN AWADHI

§ 339. There are two cases of this—the direct and the oblique. The direct in Lakhīmpurī ends in **-ʌbu̥** (**deːkhʌbu̥** 'seeing'), **-bu̥** (**ɟaːbu̥** 'going', **hoːbu̥** 'becoming'), or **-wʌbu̥** (**bʌɟaːwʌbu̥** 'striking the musical instrument'). All the dialects have this form in the direct, only R., Br., B., Fy. and other Eastern dialects generally have **-ubu̥** instead of

-wʌbu̥ (*e.g.*, **roːubu̥** 'weeping', **luṭaːubu** 'squandering'); U. has forms in **-ʌn** (**deːkhʌn**) also. The usage is found in such sentences as : F. **un kaː khaːbu̥ niːk nʌɦĩː laːgʌt** 'eating does not appear good to him', Lmp. **khaːbu̥ kaː peːṭu̥ bɦʌrʌbu̥ hʌi** 'it is not eating, it is merely filling the stomach'.

The oblique in Lmp. ends in **-ʌi** (**deːkhʌi**), **-i** (**ɟaːi, hoːi**), or **-wʌi** (**bʌɟaːwʌi**). All the dialects (except portions of Lucknow, Unao, Barabanki and Fatehpur) have this form, only in the Eastern dialects generally **-i** is pronounced as **jʌ** and sometimes **-e**. In the tracts mentioned above an oblique in **-ibeː** (**dekhibeː, ɟʌibeː, bʌɟʌibeː**) is found and on the border line of Kanaujī a form in **-ʌn** (**deːkhʌn, ɟaːn, hoːn, bʌɟaːwʌn**) is used.

(*a*) The oblique is used without a postposition to show a purpose, *e.g.*, **meɦʌruaː ḍɦũːṛʌi cʌliː** 'the woman started for the purpose of searching'. It is also used without a postposition to form compound verbs (*vide* § 349). It can take the various postpositions like any other noun, in order to express the various case-relations, *e.g.*, **unkaː pʌṛɦʌi se̥ kaː mʌtlʌbu̥** 'what business has he with reading', **hʌm kaː kuchu̥ khaːi ko deːu** 'give me something to eat', **paːniː bʌrsʌi ko bʌkhʌtu̥ aːwaː** 'the time of raining has arrived', **iu lʌrikaː deːkhʌi sunʌi mo niːk hʌi** 'this boy is good in seeing and hearing (*i.e.*, to all reports and appearances)', **khaːi khaːtir roːṭiː laːoː** 'bring loaves for eating'.

C. Origin

§ 340. The Verbal Noun has forms in (*a*) *-n*, (*b*) *-b* and in (*c*) *-ai*. The *-n* forms go back to the suffix *-ana* (*lyuṭ*). Hoernle derives the suffix from *-anīyar* and is supported in his view by Kellogg. I should, however, agree with Beames in deriving it from *lyuṭ*; it sometimes indicates a purpose, a sense which was expressed by the verbal noun in OIA also, and not by *-anīyar*. The *-b* forms should, like the future, be derived from *-itavya*. The transition of the meaning from 'to be done', for instance, to 'to do' is one more instance of a passive form losing its passive sense and so in effect becoming active.

Forms in *-ai* which are always used in the oblique case appear to be connected with the ancient infinitive of the causative roots, *e.g.*, *karāiuṁ* > *karāiũ* > *karai.*[1]

The Noun of Agency

A. Early Awadhi

§ 341. The commonest forms end in *-vāra* (fm. *-vārī*) and *-hāra* (fm. *-hārī*), *e.g.*,

Tulsī: *rakhavārē* 'protectors', *mēṭana-hāra* 'destroyer', *kōṭi manōja lajāvani-hārē* 'one who puts to shame crores of cupids' (p. 203);

Nūr Muhammad: *nirasanahāra aghāi* 'the man who looks is satisfied' (p. 8), *phūlanahũ tē sōhanavārī* 'more beautiful than the flowers' (p. 8).

Other forms end in *-ana* (fm. *-ani*), *e.g.*, *harana* 'one who captivates', *harani*. These are mostly found in Tulsīdās.

B. Modern Awadhi

§ 342. The most general form in all the dialects is in **-ʌijɑː**, **-wʌijɑː** (**dekhʌijɑː** 'one who sees', **khʌwʌijɑː** 'one who eats'). Besides in Lmp. and P. a form in **-ʌnʌɦʌr** (fm. **-ʌnʌɦʌriː** or **ʌnʌɦʌri̥**) is found sometimes, *e.g.*, **jʌnʌɦʌr** 'one who goes, *i.e.*, is about to go'; fem. **jʌnʌɦʌriː**. The **-eː** roots (**deː**, **leː**) have a form in **-wɑːl** found in Lmp., S. and B., *e.g.*, **dewɑːl** 'one who gives', **lewɑːl** 'one who takes'). A form made by adding **-wɑːlɑː** to the oblique of the verbal noun (**-ʌi**) is reported from R., G. and P., *e.g.*, **bɦʌrʌiwɑːlɑː** 'one who fills', **kʌrʌewɑːlɑː**

---

[1] Prof Chatterji, however, sees phonetic difficulty in this derivation. Grierson thinks this to be derived as the oblique of the absolutive.

'one who does'. This appears to be made on the analogy of standard Hindi **bhArnex waxlax**, **kArnex waxlax**.

The noun of agency has a shade of the future time of the action denoted by it, *e.g.*, **kozix sAfiAr JAwAijax hozi tAu bozlAi** 'if there be anyone going to the city, let him speak out'.

C. ORIGIN

§ 343. The Noun of Agency has several forms of which **-Aijax** is most common in Modern and *-vāra* in Early Awadhi. The **-Aijax** forms appear to be connected with the ancient noun of agency in *-tṛ* + the pleonastic affix *-ka*, *e.g.*, *paṭhatṛkaḥ* : *paṛhai-ō* : *paṛhai-ā* : **pAṛfiAijax** [see Hoernle (p. 149) who sees it as *āv* + *aiyā*]. The *-vāra*, **waxl** forms are all combinations of the verbal noun with *pālakaḥ* and the **-AnAfiAr**, *-anahāra*, *-anihāra* forms are the verbal noun in *-na* + *dhārakaḥ*. Forms in *-ana*, denoting the noun of agency, are *ardha-tatsama* forms, corresponding with *kartari lyuṭ*.

Phonetic Rules for Conjugation

A. EARLY AWADHI

§ 344. I have found no instances of the operation of rules (*a*), (*b*), (*c*) under § 345, in Early Awadhi. Other rules are illustrated by the following instances:

(*d*) Jāyasī : *paṭhavā* (p. 16), *niarā-v-ā* (p. 40).

Tulsī : *cita-v-ā* (p. 28, line 22), *pā-v-ā*, *janā-v-ā* (p. 28, line 20).

Nūr Muhammad : *calā-v-ā*, *pā-v-ā* (p. 2, line 16).

(*e*) *wa* > *u*, *e.g.*,

Jāyasī : *bina-uba* (p. 15), *pā-ub*, *āubi* (p. 97).

Tulsī : *pā-uba* (p. 46, line 17), *ā-uba* (p. 74, line 19).

Nūr Muhammad : *pā-uba* (p. 57, line 16).

(*f*) Jāyasī: *khā-ba* (p. 247), *dē-ba* (p. 76), *hō-ba* (p. 254).

Ṭulsī : *jā-ba* (p. 57, line 16), *dē-na* (p. 168, line 12), *hō-ba*, (p. 67), line 12;

Nūr Muhammad : *jā-ba* (p. 57, l. 13) *lē-ba* (p. 31, l. 18), *hō-bai* (p. 35, l. 16).

NOTE.—In several instances *-i* appears as *-ya*, ī as *-yā* (*jāi* : *jāya*, *jāī* : *jāyā*) and ē as *-ye* or *-ya* particularly after vowels (*jagāehi*, *pāyaū*).

B. MODERN AWADHI

§ 345. (*a*) All roots ending in **-n**, **-r** or **-l** optionally elide initial **-ʌ** or **-ɵ** of the terminations, *e.g.*, **maːn-** 'to acquiesce' **+ʌti̥** : **maːnʌti̥** or **maːnti**, **maːn- +ɵtiː** **-mʌnɵtiː** or **mʌntiː**, similarly **cʌrʌti̥** : **cʌrti**, **haːlʌti̥** : **haːlti**.

(*b*) All roots ending in **-i** (*e.g.*, **ɟi-** 'to live') combine **-i** with **-i-** or **ɵ-** of dissyllabic terminations into **iː**, *e.g.*, **ɟi- -iɦʌũ** > **ɟiːɦʌũ**, **ɟi -ɵtiː** > **ɟiːtiː**, but **ɟi -ib** > **ɟiib**, **ɟi -iti̥** > **ɟiiti̥**.

(*c*) All roots ending in **-u** (*e.g.*, **chu-** 'to touch') combine **-u** with initial **u-** or **ɵ-** of the terminations into **uː** (*e.g.*, **chu -u** > **chuː**, **chu -ɵtiː** > **chuːtiː**).

(*d*) All roots ending in **-ʌ** (*e.g.*, **kurʌ-** 'to pile', **bɦʌ-**' became'), **-aː** (*e.g.*, **naː-** 'to pour', **sʌrmaː-** 'to be ashamed'), **-eː** (*e.g.*, **kheː-** 'to steer'), and **-oː** (*e.g.*, **ɖɦoː-** 'to carry', **soː-** 'to sleep') add **-w-** between the root and a termination beginning with **aː-** (*e.g.*, **kurʌwaː**, **bɦʌwaː**, **naːwaː**, **sʌrmaːwaː**, **kheːwaː**, **ɖɦoːwa**, **soːwaː**)

(*e*) All roots ending in **-ʌ**, **-eː** (except **leː**, **deː**) and **-oː** (except **hoː**), and transitive roots in **-aː** (except **khaː**) and **aː** 'to come' add **-w-** before a termination beginning with **ʌ-** (*e.g.*, **kurʌwʌti̥**, **naːwʌti̥**, **aːwʌti̥**, **kheːwʌti̥**, **ɖɦoːwʌti̥**, **soːwʌti̥**) or **ɵ-**, **-wɵ** then becoming **u** (**kurʌutiː**, **nʌutiː**, **ʌutiː**, **kheutiː**, **ɖɦoutiː**, **soutiː**).

(*f*) All intransitive roots ending in **-aː** (except **aː** 'to come') and **khaː** 'to eat', **leː** 'to take', **deː** 'to give' and **hoː** 'to become' elide the initial **ʌ-** or **ɵ-** of the terminations (*e.g.*, **ɟaː -ʌti̥ : ɟaːti̥, ɟaː -ɵtiː : ɟaːtiː, khaːti̥, khaːtiː, leːti̥, leːtiː, deːti̥, deːtiː, hoːti̥, hoːtiː**).

The Causative

A. Early Awadhi

§ 346. The Causative in Early Awadhi is generally formed by augmenting *-ā* to the root and then conjugating it like a transitive verb, *e.g.*,

Jāyasī: *sunāvahī* (p. 16), *milāeū* (p. 397), *cuāvahī* (p. 548);

Tulsī: *sunāvā* (p. 17, last line), *janāvā* (p. 28, l. 20), *sicāvā* (p. 33, l. 12);

Nūr Muhammad: *samujhāvaī* (p. 26, l. 5), *rovāvahī* (p. 26, l. 6), *hãkarāyeu* (p. 65, l. 2), *sunāyeu* (p. 65, l. 2).

There are a few instances where the ablaut of the vowel in the first syllable (*a* : *ā*, *i* : *ē*, *u*, *ū*: *ō*) expresses the causative sense, *e.g.*,

Tulsīdas: *ṭārā* (simple *ṭarā*) (p. 124, l. 14), *mēṭē* (simple *miṭē*) (p. 130, l. 12), *bōrahi* (simple *būṛahi*).

In the case of *baiṭhaba*, *baisaba* and *dēkhaba*, *-ār* is augmented, *e.g.*, *baiṭhārē* (T. p. 25, l. 7), *baisārē* (J. p. 193), *dekharāvā* (J. p. 310), (T. p. 88, l. 16). *dēkhaba* makes the causal in the ordinary way also, *e.g.*, *dekhāyē* (T. p. 124, l. 20).

I have not come across any example of the double causative, except perhaps *kahavāvā* 'made to call' (N. p. 25, l. 4), where the simple causative would have done.

NOTE.—The causative of √*khā-* 'to eat' is *khiā* 'to feed' found in Jāyasī and Nūr Muhammad, *e.g.*, *sabahi khiāvai āpu na khāī* 'He feeds all, but himself does not eat' (J. p. 7).

B. Modern Awadhi

§ 347. The causative is formed generally by adding the suffix **-aː** to the simple root and then conjugating it like any other transitive root in -**aː**, *e.g.*, **hʌ̃sʌb** 'to laugh': **hʌ̃saːwʌb** 'to make one laugh', '**deːkhʌb** 'to see': **dekhaːwʌb** 'to make ono see.'

The following verbs, however, form their causative by modifying the vowel, or the vowel and consonant of the root:

(*a*) lengthening the vowel: **pʌsʌr-**: **pʌsaːr-**, **ukhʌr-**: **ukhaːr-**, **nikʌr-** : **nikaːr-**, **khĩc-** : **khĩːc**; similarly **kʌṭ-**, **bʌ̃dɦ-**, **mʌr-**, **lʌd-**, **cir-**, **buɟh-**, **ɟʌr-**.

(*b*) changing **i** into **eː** and **u** into **oː**, **phir-**: **pheːr-**, **khul-** : **khoːl-**, similarly **ruk-**, **gɦur-**, **ɟur-**.

(*c*) modifying both the vowel and the consonant:

(1) alternation of **ṭ**, **ṛ** and **r**: **phʌṭ-**: **phaːr-**, **chuːṭ-**: **choːr-**, **ɟuṭ-**: **ɟoːr-**, **phuːṭ-**: **phoːr-**, **ṭuːṭ-**: **toːr-**, **buːṛ-**: **boːr-**.

(2) alternation of **k** and **c-**: **bik-** : **bẽːc-**.

In the case of **bʌiṭh-** 'to sit' **aːr** is added (in the Western and Central dialects) after **aː** to form the causal **bʌiṭhʌb** : **bʌiṭhaːrʌb**.

NOTE.—It should be noted that all the roots mentioned above (except **nikʌr-**, **mʌr-**, **ruk-**, **rʌɦ-**) are sets of passive-active verbs rather than simple-causative

Sometimes, there are found uses of a double causative. This is restricted to consonantal roots, *e.g.*, **hʌ̃sʌb** :, **hʌ̃saːwʌb**, **hʌ̃sʌwaːwʌb**, and is formed by adding **waː** to the simple causative.

In the case of a set of simple causative and double causative, the former is generally used in a case where the remote agent actively helps the immediate agent to do the action, *e.g.*, **gopaːl raːmu ke paːniː pijaːinɟ** 'Gopāl caused Rāmū to drink water' (*i.e.*, Gopāl actively helped Rāmū—perhaps by giving water); and the double when the remote agent is merely the director of the action through another, *e.g.*, **gopaːl ʌmbikʌ sẹ raːmu ke paːniː**

pijʌwɑːiniː 'Gopāl caused Rāmū to drink water by the help of Ambikā'. In effect, thus, in a double causative there are more than two agents.

The double causative is, however, very seldom used as the nice distinction between the two causatives is not generally required.

NOTE.—The idea of the causative in some cases is expressed by quite a differernt root, *e.g.*, **jaːb** 'to go' but **pʌṭhʌwʌb** 'to cause to go, *i.e.*, to send', **ɪːwʌb** 'to come' but **aːnʌb** 'to cause to come, *i.e.*, to bring', **rʌɦʌb** 'to remain' but **raːkhʌb** 'to keep'.

NOTE.—**khaː** 'to eat' makes its ordinary causative in Western and Central dialects (**khʌwaː**) but in the Eastern dialects it is found as **khiaː**.

C. ORIGIN

§ 348. The suffix *ā* of the Causative goes back to *-ā-p*: *-āv*: *-v* being represented in some forms still in Modern Awadhi by *-w*. In the roots forming their causatives by ablaut, the correspondence with ancient causatives can be seen; Skt. *prasarati*: *prasārayati*, Aw. **pʌsʌrʌi** : **pʌsaːrʌi.** On the analogy of the ablaut of *a* : *ā*, the ablaut of *i* : *ē*, *ū* : *ō* is also found.

The *-r* is an augment to the suffix *-ā* and is found only in a few roots. It corresponds with *l* of Western Hindi, and with the *-r* normally found in Sindhi, with the causatives. Its origin is obscure.[1]

The Passive

A. EARLY AWADHI

§ 349. (*a*) Early Awadhi attests some roots which are passive in meaning, *e.g.*, *bujhāī* 'is extinguished' (J. p. 375),

---

[1] See J. A. S. B., 1896 Part I, pp 1—5 where Grierson connects *l*, *r*, *ḍ* etc. to Pkt. suffix *-illa* added to nouns and adjectives; and draws analogy of Skt *kr—ṇō—ti* etc., which are said to be denominatives by Brugmann.

miṭahī 'are effaced' (T. p. 3, l. 11), *ugharahī* 'are opened up' (T. p. 3, l. 11), *sūjhahī* 'become visible' (T. p. 3, l. 12). Such roots, though they take the active forms, always express the passive sense.

(*b*) Some active roots form the passive by augmenting *-ā*, *e.g.*, *samuda sukhāhī* 'oceans are dried up' (J. p. 19), *rahē kahāvata parama birāgī* 'he was called a great hermit' (T. p. 146). Denominative verbs come under this class of the passive, *e.g.*,

Jāyasī : *lajāneu* 'was ashamed' (p. 179), *juḍāna* 'became cool' (p. 346).

Tulsī : *ḍerānā* 'became afraid' (p. 58, l. 5), *juṛānē* 'become cool' (p. 60 l. 20).

Nūr Muhammad : *bhulānē* 'became forgetful' (p. 15, l. 23), *arujhānē* 'became entangled' (p. 15, l. 23).

NOTE.—The augment in the case of the Causative also is *-ā* but these denominatives are treated of as intransitive and so add *-n-* between the root and the terminations of the Past tenses. The context also indicates the difference.

(*c*) Besides the above, Early Awadhi attests some forms of the synthetic passive. The Passive Imperfect Participle has been shown above [§ 294 (c)]. Moreover, we find an impersonal passive present-imperative ending in *-ia*, *-iahi* (*-iai*), *-iē*, *-ījai*, *ījia*, *ījiai*, *-ījē*. Of these *-ia*, *-iai* (*iahi*), *-ījia* and *-ījiai* are found in Jāyasī, *-ia*, *-iahi*, *iē*, *-ījai* in Tulsī and *-ījē* in Nūr Muhammad. In Nūr Muhammad, however, I have found only two instances of this form (*viz. kījē* 'make', *lījē* 'take', p. 27, l. 2).

In Jāyasī and Tulsī there are many more examples. Jāyasī : *jaṃbuka kahā jaū caḍhiahi rājā, siṃgha sāji kai caḍ ia ta chājā* 'If one were to attack a jackal, O king, it will be best if he attacks after making preparation for (the attack of a) lion' (p. 530), *āju kālhi bhā cāhia* 'it should come about to-day or to-morrow (p. 442), *kharaga dēkhi pānī hoi ḍhariai* 'on seeing the sword, one (or you) should trickle down as water' (p. 536); *bhalehi āe aba māyā kījia, pahunāī kahā āesu dījia* 'it is well that you have come, be favourable and order (me to put forward) hospitality' (p. 286), *ghāli kasauṭī dījiai* 'give (her) after putting (him) on the touchstone' (p. 610).

Tulsī : *sunia kathā sādara rati mānī* 'let the story be heard with respect and affection' (p. 19), *cahia amiya jaga jurai na chāchī* 'nectar is wanted, but even whey is not available in this world' (p. 7), *jānia bhagati na pūjā* 'neither devotion nor worship is known' (p. 81); *bāyasa paliahi ati anurāgā* 'let the crow be nurtured with great affection' (p. 5), *bēṣa pratāpa pūjiahi tēū* 'they also are worshipped owing to their guise' (p. 6); *gai nisa bahuta sayana aba kījai* 'night has passed sufficiently, let thee sleep' (p. 74). Similarly *kariē, hariē* etc.

NOTE.—As shown above these forms of the Passive are sometimes Imperative in sense, and sometimes denote merely the Present tense or the Conjunctive.

(*d*) Besides the synthetic passive, instances of the analytic passive also are found in Early Awadhi, *e.g.*,

Jāyasī : *gagana nakhata jasa jāhī na ganē* 'so many stars in the sky as cannot be counted' (p. 177), *jau pīsata ghuna jāihi pīsā* 'while grinding barley, the insect also will be ground' (p. 487), *sahi na jāi jōbana kara bhārū* 'the weight of youth cannot be borne' (p. 382).

Tulsī : *bidhi karataba kachu jāi na jānā* 'Fate's action is not known at all' (p. 180), *ārati prīti na sō kahi jātī* 'that agony and affection is not described' (p. 195), *khaga mṛga haya gaya jāhī na jōī* 'birds, deer, horses, and elephants are not seen' (p. 210), *barani na jāhī mañju dui sālā* 'the two beautiful houses cannot be described' (p. 209); *mohi lakhi parata bharata mata ēhū* 'to me it appears that it is Bharata's opinion' (p. 270), *ehi pāpinihi būjhi kā pāreu* 'what was understood by this sinner?' (p. 175).

Nūr Muhammad : *ḍara sõ uttara jāi na dīnhā* ' owing to fear, the answer is not given ' (p. 58), *nā tõ mārī jāū* ' otherwise, I shall be killed ' (p. 58), *sapana na būjhā jāi* ' the dream is not explained ' (p. 5).

NOTE. – see § 354 (5) *paraba*.

B. MODERN AWADHI

§ 350. (*a*) Some roots are passive in sense by themselves, *e.g.*, **kAṭ-** ' to be cut ', **bÃdh-** ' to be bound ', **jaː lAkAṛiː ɟAldiː naːiː cirAtị** ' this wood does not split (*i.e.* is not split) soon ', **juː ghAṛaː bhArAi tAb cAliː** ' let this jar fill (*i.e.* be filled), then we shall go '. Most of such roots have merely a passive sense, their causative expressing the active, *e.g.*, **kAṭ- : kaːṭ-**. But a few (*e.g.*, **bhAr-**) have an active or passive sense according to the context. For instance, in the above instance it has been used as passive, but in **gopaːl iu ghAṛaː bhArAi tAb cAliː** ' let Gopāl fill this jar, then we shall go ' it is active.

NOTE.—**cAh-** ' to want ' is used passively in the case of 3rd person singular only, *e.g.*, **rupAjaː cAhiː** ' money is wanted '.

(*b*) A passive is formed sometimes by adding the suffix **-aː** to transitive roots and then conjugating them like intransitive roots [for distinction see above § 345 (*e*) and (*f*)], *e.g.*, **juː Admiː ãːdhAr dekhaːtị hAi** ' this man appears (lit. is seen) blind ', **tum rãːṛAi ɟAnaːtiː hAu** ' you appear to be (lit. are perceived) widows '. This passive, however, in Awadhi is found with a restricted number of roots only, mostly such as denote perception or knowledge (**sunaːb** ' to be heard ', **Aghaːb** ' to be satiated ') but sometimes with a few other roots (**buɟhaːb** ' to become extinguished '). Denominative verbs (formed by adding **aː-**, *e.g.*, **miːṭh** ' sweet ' : **miṭhaːb** ' to taste sweet ', **loːn** ' salt ' : **lonaːb** ' to taste saltish ', **khAṭṭaː** ' sour ' : **khAṭaːb** ' to appear sour ', **piAr** ' yellow ' : **piAraːb** ' to become yellow ', **hAraː**

'green' : **hʌriaːb** 'to become green', **lʌɦʌr** 'wave': **lʌɦʌraːb** 'to appear full of waves, thence metaphorically, prosperous') come under this passive.

NOTE—In **baːt** 'word' : **bʌtlaːb** 'to talk a word', there is an addition of **l** before the suffix **-aː-**. In the Central and Eastern dialects **-i-** (**bʌtiaːb**) or **-u-** (**bʌtuaːb**) instead of **l** is found.

(*c*) It should be noted that the suffix **aː** denotes the causative also; but the difference lies in the fact that causatives are transitive and the passive (including the denominative) is intransitive and hence there is difference in conjugation, *e.g.*, **dekhaːwʌti̥** 'shows' : **dekhaːti̥** 'appears'. Where the form does not show the difference, the context indicates it, *e.g.*, **dekhaːeũ** may mean either 'showed' or 'appeared' according to the context

(*d*) The analytic or periphrastic passive is formed in Awadhi with the help of three verbs : **jaːb** 'to go', **aːwʌb** 'to come' and **pʌrʌb** 'to fall'. For instance: **ʌb sʌb ɖaːkuː maːreː jʌiɦʌĩ** 'now all dacoits killed will go *i.e.*, now all the dacoits will be killed', **jʌb duːdɦu̥ piʌi mə aːwʌi tʌb sewaːdu̥ jaːni̥ pʌrʌi** 'when milk drinking in comes then taste knowing falls *i.e.*, when milk is drunk then only its taste may be known'. With **jaːb** the Perfect Participle (the forms changing according to gender or number as required) is employed, and the agent is put in the instrumental case, if it is meant to be indicated. With **aːwʌb** the oblique case of the verbal noun (followed by a locative postposition) is employed and the agent is put in the genitive. In the case of **pʌrʌb**, the absolutive (without the postposition) is employed and the agent appears in the dative case.

(*e*) A sort of impersonal passive is formed from intransitive verbs (and transitive verbs intransitively used) by employing **jaːb** with the Perfect participle (3rd sg.) and expresses the additional aspect of ability to do an act, *e.g.*, **ui**

seː aːwaː naːiː jaːtị 'he is unable to come', **kaː tum seː khaːwaː naːiː jaːtị** 'can't you eat?' This additional aspect of 'ability' is present sometimes in the case of the transitive verb also, *e.g.*, **tum ʌis duːbʌr hoi geu ki deːkheː naːiː jaːtiu** 'you have become so lean that you cannot be looked at, *i.e.*, the glance turns away from you.'

(*f*) The active construction is the normal feature of the language. The passive is used only to lay an emphasis either on the object of the active construction or on its attribute (**jaː ḍħoːl phuːṭị jʌnaːtị hʌi** 'this drum appears to be broken') or on the action itself (**mʌi seː cilːaːwaː naːiː jaːtị** 'I cannot shout'). The subject occupies a very secondary place and is mostly understood.

C. Origin

§ 351. The suffix of the Passive, *-ya-*, is represented in MIA. as *-īa* and *-ijja*, and in Early Awadhi (see § 349) as *-i-* or *-ij-* found in the passive imperfect participle and in the passive imperative; the *-iahi* (*-iai*), *-iē* go back to passive MIA. *-īai* (*karīai*), the present tense denoting the imperative. In *-ia*, the 3rd sg. termination *-a* is found after the passive root. Similarly *-ījai*, *-ījē* go back to MIA. *-ijjai* and in *-ījia* and *ījiai*, a sort of double passive is visible from the form, *e.g.*, Pkt. *dijjīai* 'is given.' In Modern Awadhi, the synthetic passive is found in certain root-forms only and in the Imperfect participle of the 1st pl. Besides *cahī* 'is wanted' is passive.

§ 352. The denominative in *-ā* is passive. The origin of this is the ancient denominative affix *-āya-* (*e.g.*, *vīrāyate* 'acts like a brave person'). This is clearly distinguished in Mod. IA. from the causative which is always transitive. Further, in the past tense, the denominative has the augment *-n* (see § 297), *e.g.*, **sʌrmaːneũ** 'I became ashamed'. This **-n-** does not appear in the causative, *e.g.*, **khʌwaːeũ** 'I fed'; similarly a causative requires *-w-* before a termination of the imperfect participle (*e.g.*, **sArmaIwAtị**) 'putting to shame') while a denominative does not (*e.g.*, **sArmaIti** 'getting ashamed').

353. The analytic passive is the regular passive of the modern language; occasional instances of it are found in Early Awadhi also. It began with the compounding of verbs like *yā* 'to go' with other verbs (*e.g.*, *vēḍhiuṃ jāi* 'is encompassed', *vilihiuṃ jāi* 'is painted', *Karpūramañjarī*, I. 30) and became stereotyped in this sense by and by and ousted the synthetic passive.

Compound Verbs

A. Early Awadhi

§ 354. The use of compound verbs is not very common in Early Awadhi, but it is still found quite frequently. We have found instances of the following verbs, used with the participles, the verbal noun or the absolutive of the principal verb, as compound verbs. The shades of meanings expressed are the same as in Modern Awadhi.

(1) *uṭhaba*, *e.g.*, *jāgi uṭheũ asa dēkhata, sakhi kahu sapana bicāri* 'seeing thus I woke up. My friend, think out and explain the dream' (J. p. 439), *dalaki uṭheu suni hr̥daya kaṭhōrū* 'the hard heart, on hearing, began to break' (T. p. 168).

(2) *cahaba*, *e.g.*, *sunu mati kāja cahasi jau sājā* 'take (my) counsel, if thou desirest to accomplish the business' (J. p. 276), *bhai cāhai asi kathā salōnī* 'the story is going to be so charming' (J. p. 78), *tasa sara sāji jarai caha rājā* 'having prepared such a pyre, the king wants to burn (himself)' (J. p. 457), *nija nayananhi dēkhā cahahĩ nātha tumhāra biyāhu* 'Lord, (they) wish to see your marriage with their own eyes' (T. p. 42), *jō nahāi caha ehi sara bhāī* 'brothers, whoever wants to bathe in this tank' (T. p. 22), *nātha lasana pura dēkhana cahahĩ* 'My lord, Lakṣmaṇa wishes to see the town' (T. p. 95), *karu sōi jō cāhasi kīnhā*

'do what you like to do' (N. p. 68), *āpuhī phēra cinhāvai cahā* '(He) desires to make people know him' (N. p. 6).

(3) *jāba, e.g., suni vei bayana lāji chapi jāhī* '(they) conceal (themselves) becoming ashamed on hearing her words' (J. p. 186), *janu chui gaeu pāka baratōrū* 'as if a ripe boil (at the point of the breaking of a hair) got touched' (T. p. 168); *chūṭi jāe sumirahu tuma mōhī* 'it will be loosened, should you remember me' (N. p. 4).

(4) *dēba, e.g., dāruna sasura na nisarana dīhī* 'the harsh father-in-law will not permit (us) to go out' (J. p. 96), *phiri nahī jhūlana dīhī sāī* 'later, the master will not allow (us) to swing' (J. p. 97), *tinhahī dekhāi dihesu tai Sītā* 'to them thou wilt show Sītā' (T. p. 337), *rājaī rāja kāja taji dīnhā* 'the king's work was given up by him' (N. p. 11).

(5) *paraba, e.g., sūjhi na parata pantha ãdhiārā* 'the dark path would not have come to be seen' (J. p. 14), *ehi pāpinihi būjhi kā pareū* 'what was it that came to be realised by this sinner' (T. p. 175), *jāni parata rājā sravana parī na hai yaha bōla* 'it appears that this word has not been heard by the King' (N. p. 25). This gives a passive sense.

(6) *pāraba, e.g., tumha khēvahu jau khēvai pārahu* 'if you are able to ply, ply' (J. p. 314), *tumhahī achata kō baranai pārā* 'while you live, who can describe (it)' (T. p. 117), *tabahū barana na pārau tōhī* 'even then I cannot describe you' (N. p. 2).

(7) *pāvaba, e.g., chūṭa na pāu mīcu kara bãdhā* 'one tied to death cannot be released' (J. p. 394), *kō dēkhai pāvai vaha nāgū* 'who can be allowed to see that serpent' (J. p. 208), *durlabha sāja sulabha kari pāvā* 'was able to gather easily the requisites difficult to obtain' (T. p. 459), *jarai na pāva dēha birahāgī* 'the body is not allowed to burn in the separation-fire' (T. p. 355).

(8) *rahaba, e.g., bēdhi rahā sagarau saṃsārā* 'the whole world remains pierced' (J. p. 177), *rahā lukāi* 'remained in hiding' (T. p. 380).

(9) *rākhaba*, *e.g.*, *kuhū kuhū kai kōila rākhā* 'the cuckoo went on cooing' (J. p. 43), *hōihi soi jo rāma raci rākhā* 'that which Rāma has created, will come about' (T. p. 28).

(10) *lāgaba*, *e.g.*, *lāgī saba mili hērai, būḍi būḍi eka sātha* 'all of them diving together again and again, began to make a search' (J. p. 103), *rāma nāma siva sumirana lāgē* 'Śiva began to remember Rāma's name' (T. p. 31), *kahē lageu pōthī tabai, pāya tapī kara bā̃ha* 'having obtained the arm of the ascetic, (he) began to compose the book' (N. p. 4).

(11) *lēba*, *e.g.*, *khēli lēhu jō khēlahu āju* 'if you play, do play to-day' (J. p. 96), *daccha liyē muni bōli saba* 'Daksa invited all the hermits' (T. p. 31), *ahai ṭhāṛha mohi līnha bolāi* '(he) is standing there and has called me' (N. p. 4).

(12) *sakaba*, *e.g.*, *chui kō sakai rājā kai bārī* 'who can touch the king's garden' (J. p. 201), *dēkhi na sakahī parāi bibhūtī* '(they) cannot look (with equanimity) at another's prosperity' (T. p. 162,) *kita kai sakaū̃ vakhāna tumhārā* 'how can I make a description of yours' (N. p. 2).

B. MODERN AWADHI

§ 355. Compound verbs are in very common use and express various aspects. The helping verb loses its own meaning and merely helps to express a certain shade of the principal verb. The accent being on the principal verb, the helping word is pronounced with less force and has a tendency to lose its sounds. Four forms of the principal are thus compounded :

(*a*) the absolutive (§ 336)

(*b*) the oblique case of the verbal noun (§ 339 *a*).

(*c*) the Perfect participle in -**ax** (§ 297).

(*d*) the Imperfect participle in -**Ati̥**, -**At** (§ 296).

The absolutive is combined with

(1) **jaːb, cukʌb, leːb** and **d̨aːrʌb** to express definite completeness of an action, *e.g.*, **hʌmaːr ghʌrụ jʌrị gaː** 'my house burnt down', **jʌb mʌi khaːi cukʌũ** 'when I finish eating', **mʌi huãː aːi leːũ tʌu bʌtaːwʌũ** 'let me come over there then I shall say' **uː caːrị gilaːs paːniː piː d̨aːrisị** 'he drank up four (whole) tumblers of water'.

Of these **cukʌb** expresses thoroughness and **d̨aːrʌb** an unexpected nature of the action.

(2) **pʌrʌb, uṭhʌb, bʌiṭhʌb** to express suddenness or surprise, *e.g.*, **uː pʌgolaː aːgi mo kuːdị pʌraː** 'that mad man jumped down into the fire', **tum eteːː joːr sẹ boːleu kị lʌrikaː jaːgị uṭhaː** 'you spoke so loudly that the child woke up', **etːe mo mʌi kʌhi bʌiṭheũ** 'in the meanwhile I spoke up'.

(3) **sʌkʌb, paːwʌb, milʌb** ' to express ability to do an act, *e.g.*, **mʌi rupʌjaː laːi sʌkʌtị hʌũ** 'I can bring money', **mʌi kʌi pʌihʌũ tʌu kʌrihʌũ** 'if I am able to do (it), I shall do it', **mʌi kaː naːiː kʌi milaː** 'I could not do it'.

NOTE.– **jaːb** expresses 'ability' also [see above § 350 (*e*)]

(4) **khaːb** and **maːrʌb** to express an offence or infliction of an undesirable thing, *e.g.*, **ui kaː kutːaː kaːṭị khaːisị** 'a dog has bitten him', **mʌi dʌs pʌnʌ ki ciṭːhiː likhị maːreũ** 'I wrote out a letter of ten pages'.

(5) **cʌlʌb** to express the beginning of an action, *e.g.*, **uː hʌm kaː dekhotʌi maːri cʌlaː** 'no sooner did he see me, than he began to beat'.

(6) **deːb** to express the intensity of an action, *e.g.*, **moːrị bãːh chãːṛị deːu** 'do leave my arm'.

The oblique case of the verbal noun is combined with

(1) **deːb** to express permission, *e.g.*, **mʌi kaː roːṭiː khaːi deːu** 'allow me to take my meal'.

(2) **laːgʌb** to express inception of an action, *e.g.*, **ʌb ui hʌmoreː hiãː aːwʌi laːg bʌĩ** 'they have started coming to my place now'

(3) **cʌɦʌb** to express near completion of an act, *e.g.*, **bɑːrɑː bʌɟʌi cʌɦʌti̥ hʌĩ** 'it is about twelve o'clock.'

(4) **pɑːwʌb** to express the indulgence or permission to do an act, *e.g.*, **uː kʌɦʌi nɑːiː pɑːwɑː** 'he was not allowed to say'.

The Perfect Participle in **-ɑː** is combined with

(1) **kʌrʌb** to denote frequency of an action, *e.g.*, **hʌm ɑːwɑː kʌribɑː** 'I shall come frequently'.

(2) **cʌɦʌb** to denote wish, *e.g.*, **ui ɟɑːwɑː cʌɦʌti hʌĩ** 'they are desirous of going'.

The Imperfect Participle in **-ʌti, -ʌt** is combined with **rʌɦ-** to express continuity, *e.g.*, **uː pʌɽɦʌti̥ rʌɦɑː, boːlɑː nɑːiː** 'he continued reading (and) did not speak'.

NOTE.—Though the root **-rʌɦ-** is employed as an auxiliary to denote the past tense, it denotes continuity as a compound verb. If it were merely an auxiliary the form in the above instance ought to have been **rʌɦʌi** and not **rʌhɑː.**

C. ORIGIN

§ 356. In OIA. the various aspects and shades of meaning were expressed either by suffixing or prefixing the roots. With the disintegration of the system of conjugation and the levelling of terminations these could no longer serve the purpose. Modern Indo-Aryan has, therefore, adopted a method of compounding two verbs where one expresses the main semanteme while the other expresses the shade or aspect. It is interesting to note that Dravidian has a similar use of compound verbs, on which Chatterji remarks: 'It is very likely that here we have another contribution of Dravidian in the formation of Modern Indo-Aryan speeches' (p. 1050).

CHAPTER VII

ADVERBS

§ 357. Adverbs of Awadhi are based on nouns (*e.g.*, **jʌldiː** 'soon'), pronouns (*e.g.*, **jʌiseː** 'as'), adjectives (*e.g.*, **pʌɦileː** 'at first') or on ancient adverbs (*e.g.*, **aːju̥** < *adya* 'to-day') or adverbial expressions (*e.g.*, **tʌɦi kʌi** : *tasmin kṛtē* 'after that').

PIA. adverbs were mostly formed by suffixes added to pronouns or were merely case-forms of nouns or adjectives (*vide* Whitney : *Sanskrit Gram*, Chap. XVI). Modern adverbs have either descended from old adverbs or are fresh formations from nouns and adjectives, *e.g.*, *adya* > *ajjō* > **aːju̥** and **jʌldiː** < Pers. *jaldī*.

Adverbs of Time

A. Early Awadhi

§ 358. 'now' : *aba* (J. 10, T. 6), *-hī* (N. 4); 'then' : *taba* (J. 78, T. 6), +*hū̃* (N. 2), *tabai* (N. p. 4), *tabaī* (N. p. 37); 'when?' : *kaba*, +*hū̃* (J. 346, N. 27); 'when' : *jaba* (J. 40, T. 4, N. 6); 'to-day' : *āju* (J. 196, T. 165), *āja* (N. 3); 'yesterday or tomorrow' : *kāli*, *kālhi* (J. 96, 271, T. 161), *kālha* (N. 52); 'always' : *niti* (J. 111), *nita* (T. 157), *nitta* (N. 7), *nitu* (N. 59); 'formerly' : *agumana* (J. 537), *agamō̃* (N. 109), *āgē* (T. 289), *āgehā̃* (N. 85), *pahilē* (N. 13); 'then' : *tahiā* (J. 110, T.); 'when' : (*jahiā* (T.); 'in the morning' : *bhōra* (J. 271, N. 4), *bhōrē̃* (N. 17), 'in the evening' : *sā̃jha* (J. 375, N. 14); 'again' : *puni* (T. 5), *bahuri* (T. 4), *bahōrī* (T. 162), *phiri* (T. 171), *phira* (N. 38), *phēra* (N. 40), 'immediately' : *turata* (T. 324), 'soon' : *bēgi* (T. 161).

B. Modern Awadhi

§ 359. (*a*) based on nouns : Lmp. uses **saːiti̥** 'moment', *e.g.*, **iː saːiti̥** 'just now', **ui saːiti̥** or **tiː saːiti̥** 'then, at that time', **jiː saːiti̥** 'when (relative)', **kiː saːiti̥** 'when?'. Some dialects use **khʌn** 'moment' or **berijaː**, **sʌmʌu**, **ɟʌmʌj**, or even **ṭeːm** 'time'; the Eastern dialects generally use **juːn** 'time', *e.g.*, **iː juːn** 'now', **uː juːn** 'then'. Other nouns used adverbially are: **jʌldiː** 'lit. haste, but hastily, soon'. **phurti : and cʌṭkʌiː** also mean 'haste' but are similarly adverbially used; **etːiː deːr mo** 'meanwhile', **deːr sẹ** 'late', **sʌb din** 'always'.

(*b*) based on pronouns: Lmp. has **ʌb** 'now', **tʌb** 'then', **jʌb** 'when (relative)', **kʌb** 'when?' The corresponding forms in B., Fy. and other Eastern dialects are **ʌbːʌj**, **tʌbːʌj**, **jʌbːʌj** and **kʌbːʌj**. G. has **ʌbɦʌj**, **tʌbɦʌj**, **jʌbɦʌj**, **kʌbɦʌj**. Other adverbs of the type are: **ʌb kiː** or **ʌb tiː** 'once again', **jʌleː : tʌleː** 'till then'.

(*c*) based on adjectives: **pʌɦileː** 'previously', **aːgeː** 'formerly', **paːcheː** 'later', Lmp. **etːe mo**, Fy. **jʌtʌre mo** 'meanwhile'.

(*d*) based on ancient adverbs: **aːjụ** (**aːj**) 'to-day', **kaːlɦi̥** 'yesterday or to-morrow', **pʌrʌũ** 'day before yesterday or day after to-morrow', **nʌrʌũ** 'two days before yesterday or two days after to-morrow', **baːdi̥** or **baːdi̥ ko** 'afterwards', Lmp. **phir**, Fy. **phin**, **phun**, M. **puni** 'again'; **ʌgəmʌn** 'formerly—in ancient times', **turto** 'at once', **nit** 'always', **bɦorʌɦẽː** 'in the morning', **ãːsʌũ** 'this year', **paːr saːl** 'last year'

NOTE.—Sometimes a play upon tone expresses the idea of 'soon', *e.g.*, **aːoː** 'come!', but **aːoː** 'come soon!' would have a higher pitch on the last syllable and a lengthening also which would appear as **aːoːo**.

C. ORIGIN

§ 360. (*a*) **saːiti** : Ar. *sā'at*, **khʌn** : *kṣaṇa*, **berijaː** < *vēlā* + pleonastic *-ikā*, **sʌmʌu** : *samayo*, **ṭeːm** : Eng. *time*,

juɪn : *yōni*? (see *Nēpālī Dic. juni*, p. 220). **phurtiɪ, cʌṭkʌiɪ** and **deɪr** are nouns used in the language quite generally. Early Awadhi *bahuri, bahōri, phiri, phēra* are absolutive forms of the roots; *sãjha* : *sandhyā bhōra* 'morning, dawn'; *bēgi* is derivable from Skt. *vega*.

(*b*) The forms in **-b** (**ʌb** etc.), Early Awadhi *-ba*, appear to be the combinations of the initial pronominal syllables *a-, ta-, ja-, ka-* with *-evva* : *evaṃ* (*vide* Chatterji, p. 856). **ʌbɪʌj,** etc., are fresh formations or possibly the oblique cases in *-hi* resulted as such; **ʌbɦʌj,** etc., have an emphatic **-ɦ-**. **jʌleɪ, tʌleɪ** show the addition of *lahi* > **leɪ**. Early Awadhi has two forms *jahiā, tahiā* (attested by Modern Bhōjpurī) which denote time.

(*c*) **pʌɦileɪ,** etc., are the locative cases of *pahila* < *paḍhilla*, etc.; **etɪeɪ, etʌreɪ** also are locative cases of pronominal adjectives.

(*d*) **aɪjụ** : *adya*; **kaɪlɦi, kaɪli**, *kālha* : *kalyē*, the aspiration being emphatic. The ancient words *hyaḥ* and *śvaḥ* have left no trace. *śvaḥ*, however, appears under **pʌrʌũ** < *paraśvaḥ*. It is interesting to note that *-śv-* > *-ss-* has lost trace in Awadhi, possibly after becoming *-h-*; **nʌrʌũ** is on the analogy of **pʌrʌũ**. The distinction between past (*hyaḥ*) and future (*śvah*) also has gone out. **baɪdi̥** comes from Arabic *ba'd* 'after'. In *phin, phun* we find a curious blending of *phiri* and *puni* both of which exist in some dialects. *agumana, agamõ* and **ʌgomʌn** are connected with *agra-*; **turtə** and **nit** have correspondents in Early Awadhi *turata* and *nitta* (*niti, nita, nitu*) and should be *ardha-tatsama* forms of *tvaritam* and *nityam*.

Adverbs of Place

A. Early Awadhi

§ 361. 'here' : *ihā̃* (J. 104, T. 170, N. 2), 'there' : *uhā̃* (J. 273, T., N. 69), *tahā* (J. 57, T. 324), *tahā̃* (J. 97,

T. 343, N. 3), *tahawā̃* (J. 113, T. 345); 'where' : *jahā̃* (J. 24, T. 3), *jahā̃* (J. 80, T. 4, N. 4), *jahawā̃* (J. 225, T. 345), 'where?' : *kahā̃* (J. 33, 17), *kahā̃* (J. 90, T. 342, N. 8), *kahawā̃* (J. 225, N. 11), 'before, in front' : *āgai* (J. 107), *āgē* (J. 123, T. 324), *āgẽ* (T. 328, N. 10), *agahuṛa* (T. 167), *āgū* (J. 245), *āgẽha* (N. 105), *agā̃* (N. 146), *saũhu* (J. 296, N. 11), *sauhaĩ* (N. 79), 'behind' : *pāchē* (J. 138, T. 286), *pāchẽ* (N. 17); 'near' : *niara* (J. 332, N. 14), *niarē* (J.), *niyarẽ* (N. 13), 'far off' : *dūri* (J. 265, T. 289), *dūrei* (N. 159), *dūrū* (N. 14); 'on this side' : *ita* (T. 173), 'on that side' : *uta* (T. 173), 'on which side?' : *kita* (N. 2), 'inside' : *bhītara* (T. 14, N. 7), 'outside' : *bāhara* (T. 14, N. 7).

B. Modern Awadhi

§ 362. (*a*) based on nouns : Lmp. combines **waːr** 'side' with the pronominal adjectives **jiː, tiː, iː, ui, kiː** in order to indicate direction, *e.g.*, **iː waːr** 'on this side, here'. R. combines **kʌĩtiː** 'side', *e.g.*, **keː kʌ̃itĩː** 'whither?' B. and G. have the combinations of **ʌlʌ̃g** or **oːr** with the adjectives, *e.g.*, G. **jʌuniː ʌlʌ̃g** 'on which side', **wʌɦi oːr** 'thither'. In Fy. and Sl. as well as in parts of Gonda we find some forms where the pronominal adjective and the noun have become incorporated, *e.g.*, **eɦʌr, oɦʌr, jeɦʌr, keɦʌr,** B. **ʌkelʌ̃g** 'on one side', G. **kʌɦewʌr** 'whither', **eɦʌwʌr** 'hither'. In A. and M. similarly we find **eṭhãː** 'here', **oṭhãː** 'there', **keṭhãː** 'where?'.

(*b*) based on pronouns or pronominal adjectives : Lmp. has **hiãː** 'here', **huãː** 'there', **jʌɦãː tʌɦãː** 'where...there', **kʌɦãː** 'where?'. In Eastern dialects we have these as well as elongated forms, *e.g.*, Fy. **kʌɦʌ̃waː** 'where?'; other dialects agree with Lmp. Besides we have **ʌisiː** 'on this side, hither', **wʌisiː, jʌisiː tʌisiː, kʌisiː**; A. has **eɦkiː** 'hither', **oɦkiː** 'thither'.

(*c*) other adverbs : **bɦiːtʌr** 'within', G., P., Fy. **bɦitːʌr** or **bɦitʌreː**; **baːɦer** or **bʌɦiriː** 'outside', **upːʌr** 'above', **tʌreː** or **khaːleː** or **tʌrkhʌleː** 'below',

aːgeː 'before', P. **aːgẽː**; **paːcheː** (P. **pʌchwãː**) 'behind', **neːreː** or **nʌgiːceː** (B. **lʌgiːceː**) 'near', **duːrḁ** (Eastern **duːr**) 'far', **pʌlːeː** (R. **pʌlːaː**) 'beyond', **ʌnto** 'elsewhere'.

NOTE.—The multiplicative adverbs 'twice', 'thrice', etc., have been shown above under Numerals (§ 231). The idea of a 'second time' is indicated either by **dosʌraːi ko** or by combining the ordinal number with a word expressive of 'time, turn', *e.g.*, **dosʌriː daːĩ**. Similarly **tisʌraːi ko** or **tisʌriː daːĩ**.

C. ORIGIN

§ 363. (*a*) **waːr, oːr, kʌĩtiː** and **ʌlʌ̃g** are normal words for 'side' in the language, some of these have already coalesced with the qualifying adjectives. In **eṭhãː**, etc., we can see *sthāna* > *ṭhāna* incorporated in the same manner.

(*b*) **jʌɦãː**, etc., of which we find short (*jaha*) and long (*jahawā*) forms also in Early Awadhi, should be connected with MIA forms in *-ttha* (*ettha* etc.), *-tha* > *-ha* [see Chatterji (p. 858)., also *Nep. Dic.* (p. 81 under *kahā̃*)].

(*c*) **bhiːtʌr** < *abhyantare*, **baːɦer** cf. Skt. *bahiḥ*, **upʌr** : *upari* with emphatic elongation of **p-**, **tʌreː** : *talē*, *khālē* cf. Skt. *khallaḥ* 'creek' (*Nep. Dic.* p. 121 under *khālci*); **neːreː**, *niara*, *niarē* are connected with *nikaṭe* while **nʌgiːceː** and **lʌgiːceː** may be connected with **laṅghitya* 'that can be crossed, near'. Professor Turner, however, accepts Hoernle's derivation from Persian *nazdīk* (*Nep. Dic.* p. 334, under *nagic*) to which **nʌjik** found in Bgh. and Chattis. is surely related. **duːrḁ** : *dūra* ; **pʌlːeː** may be compared with *pallava* 'extension'. **ʌnto**, *anata* go back to *anyatra*. Early Awadhi *saũha*, *saũhai* are connected with *saṁmukha* and *ita*, *uta* may be learned words corresponding to Skt. *itaḥ* etc., or connected with *atra*, **itra* etc.

Adverbs of Manner

A. Early Awadhi

§ 364. Three varieties of forms, in *-imi*, in *-is* and in *-asa* are found in all the texts, as far as pronominal adverbs are concerned:

imi 'in this manner' (J. 323), *jimi* 'in which manner' (J. 326, T. 4), *timi* 'in that manner' (T. 286), *kimi* 'how?' (J: 91, T. 18, N. 8); correspondingly *asa* (J. 11, T. 9), *tasa* (J. 8, T. 18), *jasa* (J. 17, T. 18, N. 2), *kasa* (J. 96, T. 161, N. 3), and *aisẽ* (T. 289), *aisai* (J. 103), *aisõ* (N. 69), *taisẽ* (N. 100), *jaisẽ* (J. 66, T 166), *jaisõ* (N. 69), *kaisẽ* (T. 166, N. 56), *kaisai* (J. 110). Besides in Tulsidas we find *bhā̃ti* or *bidhi* added to pronominal adjectives in order to indicate manner, *e.g.*, *kehi bhā̃ti* 'in which manner?' (p. 162), *ehi bidhi* 'in this manner' (p. 17). Sometimes *nā̃ī* is found similarly added, *e.g.*, *parabata kai nā̃ī* 'like a mountain' (J. 332), *raurihi nā̃ī* 'like yourself' (T. 158). Other adverbs of this class are: *sajaga* 'alert' (T. 166), *nidharaka* 'fearlessly' (T. 173), *bali* 'forcibly' (T. 174), *bariā̃ī* 'forcefully' (T. 326), *bihālā* 'out of sorts' (T. 326); 'how?' *kita* (J. 56), *kittu* (J. 31), *kata* (T. 163).

Note.—Adverb of quantity 'a little': *naku* (J. 98), *rañcaka* (N. 19).

B. Modern Awadhi

§ 365. (*a*) based on nouns: the Western dialects, R. and P. as well as a part of B. combine a noun indicating manner (Lmp. and S. **tʌnaː**, L., U., F., R., Br. and P. **tʌnaː** or **tʌraː**, P. **bidɦ** also) with some adjective, *e.g.*, Lmp. **iː tʌnaː** 'in this way', **ʌcːhiː tʌnaː** 'well'. Other dialects do not possess adverbs of manner based on nouns.

(*b*) based on pronominal adjectives: Lmp. **ʌiseː** 'in this way', **wʌiseː**, **jʌiseː...tʌiseː**, **kʌiseː**, some dialects (B., G., Br., Sl. and part of P.) have **ʌs**, **wʌs**, **jʌs**...

tʌs, kʌs ; others (P., Fy., Sl., A., M.) have **ʌisen, wʌisen, jʌisen...tʌisen, kʌisen**, or **kʌsʌs** or **kʌsʌk**.

(*c*) Other adverbs : **haːliː** 'rapidly', **dɦiːreː** or **dɦiːmeː** (P. **rugus rugus**) 'slowly', **jɦʌʈːo** 'hurryingly', **niɦureː** 'bowingly', Fy. **kʌlːeː kʌlːeː** 'slowly', Lmp. **ewʌĩ** 'in this way'.

Note.—Adverbs of quantity are based on the adjectives of quantity, pronominal or otherwise, *e.g.*, 'more' : **ʌur**, G. **sʌigʌr**, P. **adɦikaːr, ʌwʌr** ; 'little' : **tʌni** or **tʌnik**, Br. **kiɲc, rʌɲc** ; 'not at all' : **birkulːi**, Fy. **berkul**.

C. Origin

§ 366. (*a*) **tʌnaː** and **tʌraː** both go back to Pers *ṭaraḥ*, *-n-* being a variant of *-r-*, *bidhi* < *vidhi, bhā̃ti* < *bhakti* (*Nep. Dic.*, p. 473) and *nāĩ* < *nyāyēna*.

(*b*) **ʌs** etc., are based on pronominal adjectives [see § 266 (*a*)] only in modern language there are fresh suffixes *-n* and *-k* in some dialects. For Early Awadhi *-mi* forms Hoernle (p. 314) and Chatterji (p. 860) suggest a derivation from Apabhraṁśa forms *jemva* etc. (see Pischel § 261).

(*c*) Other adverbs are either onomatopoetic or *deśī* words (*e.g.*, **jɦʌʈːo**), or are based on nouns, with or without prepositions, *e.g.*, **haːliː** 'haste' (Ar.), *bali* : *bala*, *bihālā* : Pers. *bēḥāl*. **ewʌĩ** may be compared with *ēvamēva* and may be an *ardha-tatsama* form of it.

Miscellaneous Adverbs

A. Early Awadhi

§ 367. 'Why?' : *kāhē*, *kāhẽ* (N. 65), 'no (prohibitive)' : *jani* (J. 142, T. 4), *jini* (N. 55), 'no, not (denial)' : *na* (J. 110, T. 4, N. 2), *nahī* (J. 90, T. 7, N. 4), *nāhī̃* (J. 112), *nāhīna* (T. 163), 'why not?' : *kina* (T. 158, N. 77), 'surely' : *abasi* (T. 177), 'without' : *binu* (J. 222, T. 4), *binā* (N. 14), *bāju* (J. 222), *bihūna* (J. 323).

NOTE.—Adverbs are compounded and used as in Modern Awadhi (§ 368-69). The postpositions for 'upto' are: *lahi* (J. 107), *lagi* (J. 61, T. 115), *laga*, (N. 31), **tai** (J. 97, N. 66).

B. MODERN AWADHI

§ 368. **kaːɦeː** 'why?', **hãː** 'yes', **naːiː, naːɦiː,** Sl. **naːj,** Fy. and F. **nʌɦiː,** P. **nʌɦin,** R. **naːɦĩː** 'no, not'; **naː** 'not—prohibitive', Eastern **jin; saːiti̥** 'perhaps', **tʌni** 'a little—invitative'.

NOTE.—Adverbs are sometimes compounded, *e.g.*, **jʌɦã̄**...... **tʌɦã̄** 'at some places', **jʌb . . . tʌb** 'sometimes, frequently', **cʌɦʌi jʌb** 'whenever', **cʌɦʌi jʌɦãː** 'wherever', **cʌɦʌi . . . jʌiseː** 'howsoever'.

§ 369. (*a*) Comparison of adverbs is expressed in the same manner as of adjectives (§ 225), *e.g.*, Lmp. **mʌi iu kaːm tum seː jʌldiː kʌi sʌkʌtiũ** 'I can do this thing earlier than you'.

(*b*) Adverbs of time and place can be employed with postpositions **seː (se̥)** to denote the idea of 'from', with **kaː (ko)** to denote the idea of 'of' and with **lʌi, lʌgi̥ (lʌg), tʌku̥, tʌluk** to denote 'upto', *e.g.*, **ʌb seː ʌis kaːmu̥ naː kiɦeu** 'do not do such a thing from now', **kã̄ɦʌ ko aːmu̥ laːeu** 'the mango of which place have you brought?', **kʌb tʌluk ʌiɦʌu** 'upto what time will you come back?', **kʌɦãː tʌk jʌiɦʌu** 'up to what place will you go?'.

NOTE.—Where English uses an adverb (*e.g.*, very, much) to modify an adjective, Awadhi employs the ordinary adjective, *e.g.*, Lmp. **iu gʌgoraː bʌɽaː gʌruː hʌi** 'this jar is very heavy', **jaː baːlʈiː bʌɽiː gʌruː hʌi** 'this bucket is very heavy', **jʌisi̥ ʌcːhiː waː meɦʌruaː hʌi tʌisi̥ iː sʌɦʌr me eːkʌu naːiː** 'no lady is so pretty in this town as that one', **ui aːdɦeː mãːdeː hʌĩ aːdɦeː niːk** 'he is half ill and half well'

C. ORIGIN

§ 370. **kaːɦeː** should be connected with some form of *kiṃ* (possibly *kathaṃ*), though the suffix is not clear.

na < *na*; *nahī*, *nāhī̃* go back to *na* plus an emphatic enclitic which may be a form of $\sqrt{as\text{-}}$ 'to be'. *natthi* is regularly found in MIA and means 'is not'. Professor Turner suggests contamination of Skt. *nahi* (*Nep. Dic.*, p. 337 under *nahī*). The derivation of *jani*, *jin* from *yat na* is suggested by Professor Chatterji. **sazitị** is connected with Pers. *šāyad*; **tʌni** may be compared with *tanuka* 'a little'.

NOTE.—The compounding of adverbs or the use does not show any divergence from that of the earlier stages

CHAPTER VIII

CONJUNCTIONS

A. Early Awadhi

§ 371. (*a*) Cumulative—'and' : *au* (J. 101, N. 1), *aru* (T. 326), *auru* (J. 149), *aura* (N. 3).

(*b*) Alternative—'may be' : *baru* (T. 165), *baruka* (T. 176), 'or' : *ki* (T. 166) ; 'otherwise, or' : *nāhī ta* (J. 132, T. 163), *nā tō* (N. 20), *nā tau* (N. 36), *na ta* (T. 346).

(*c*) Adversative—'but' : *pai* (T. 5), 'even then': *tadapi* (T. 18), 'though' : *jadapi*.

(*d*) Subordinative—'if' : *jau* (*jaũ*) (J. 29, 20, T. 9, 7, N. 21), *jõ* (N. 6), *joha* (N. 117), *jo* (N. 16), 'if...then' : *jau...tau* (J. 29, T. 11, 165, N. 77); (if)...then: *ta* (T. 165); 'as if' : *janu* (J. 107, T. 18), *jānaũ*, *janaũ* (J. 204), *manahũ* (T. 158), *dahũ* (J. 107), *dhaũ* (T. 177).

B. Modern Awadhi

§ 372. (*a*) Cumulative—'and' **ʌu**, Fy. **ʌu** or **ʌo**, *e.g.*, **ui ʌu hʌm duːnʌu jʌneː bʌjaːrʌi jʌibaː** 'He and I, both persons, will go to the market', **ui aːeː ʌu chin bɦʌri̥ bʌiṭhi̥ kə cʌl diɦeː** 'he came and went away after sitting for a while'. Sometimes a mere **ʌ** (**u** or **o** dropped out) stands in rapid speech.

(*b*) Alternative—'either or' **cʌɦʌi...cʌɦʌi**, **ki**, *e.g.*, **cʌɦʌi hiãː bʌiṭhʌu cʌɦʌi huãː** 'either sit here or there', **iu ljaːɦʌu ki uː** 'will you take this or that?' The form of **cʌɦʌi** is **caːɦʌj** in the Eastern dialects and **caːɦʌu** in U. and South L; 'neither. . . nor' is expressed by **nʌ ... nʌ**, *e.g.*, **nʌ hʌm iu leːib nʌ uː** 'neither shall I take this nor that'; 'otherwise' is expressed by **naːi tʌu** (**naːɦĩː tʌu**), *e.g.*, **hʌm kaː rupʌja deːu naːi tʌu maːrib** 'give me money or else I shall beat (you)', **ki** 'or', *e.g.*, **ʌis hʌi ki naːiː** 'is it so or not?'

(*c*) Adversative—'but' Lmp. **ʌkel** or **leːkin**, Fy. and Sl. **mulaː**, P. **munaː**, G. **mudaː**, B. **bʌkiː**, *e.g.*, Lmp. **ui hʌĩ tʌu ʌmiːr ʌkel deːti koːi ko naːɦĩ** 'he is rich but he never gives (anything) to anybody'.

(*d*) Subordinate—'that' **ki** (Eastern dialects generally **ke**), north B. and G. **mʌneː**, *e.g.*, Lmp. **hʌm kaː uː bʌtaːisi̥ ki̥ gãːu mo coːriː hoi gʌi** 'he told me that a theft had occurred in the village', B. **tʌun ʈaːr diɦin mʌneː kaːtik mo aːeː tʌb raːm raːm sun leːiː** 'he turned him away (saying) that come in Kārtik (month), then I shall hear Rām Rām'; 'so that' **ɟiː maː, ɟeɦi maː**, *e.g.*, **uː pʌuɽɦi̥ rʌɦaː ɟiː maː pʌɽɦʌi nʌ ɟaːi ko pʌrʌi** 'he lay down in bed so that he may not have to go to school', 'if' **ɟo**, Sl. **ɟʌu**, 'if then' **ɟo. . . tʌu**, 'then' **tʌu, to**, *e.g.*, **ɟo mʌi ɟaːũ** 'if I go', **ɟo soːi ɟaːũ tʌu ɟʌgaːi diɦeu**, 'if I go to sleep, do wake me up', **tʌu kaː bɦaː** 'what happened, then?'; 'as if' **ɟʌnʌu** or **mʌnʌu** or **dɦʌũ** *e.g.*, **ʌis cupːiː saːdɦin ɟʌnʌu mʌri̥ geː hoːĩ** 'he kept so quiet, as if he were already dead.'

C. ORIGIN

§ 373. (*a*) The cumulative conjunctions in use in Awadhi are connected with Skt. *apara*, in some cases (**ʌu**) the *-ra* has dropped out while in others (*aru*) the *p* > *v* > *u* has changed place.

(*b*) Early Awadhi *baru* goes back to *varaṃ* and *baruka* may be *baru* plus an enclitic *ka*. I should prefer this derivation to that from Pers. *balke*; **ki** < *kiṃ*. **cʌɦʌi** and **caːɦʌj** are the Imperative forms of the verb **cʌɦʌb, caːɦʌb** 'to desire'. **tʌu, tʌ** etc., should be connected with *tataḥ*.

(*c*) Early Awadhi *tadapi* and *jadapi* are *ardha-tatsama* forms of *tadyapi* and *yadyapi* which also are found in the Rāmāyana. *pai* may be connected with *paraṃ* (see Hoernle: *Gram. of the Gaudian Languages*, § 561) or may be the absolutive form (*pāi*) of *pāwab* 'to obtain'. *pāi* > *pai* will mean 'having obtained', 'obtaining' and can easily be used in the sense of a conjunction. **ʌkel** (cf. Hindi **ʌkeːlaː** 'all alone') is derived from Pkt. *ekkalla* by a metathesis of the vowels (see *Nep. Dic.*, p. 57 under *eklo*). **lekin** and **bʌkiː** are from Persian *lēkin* and *bāqī*. The words **mulaː, mudaː** and **munaː** are connected together and may have some affinity with *mūla* 'root'. We may compare Beng. *moddā* 'main' which Chatterji derives from Arabic.

(*d*) The subordinative conjunction **ki (ke)** is in all probability a borrowing from Persian idiom in modern language. OIA had *yat* in the beginning of a clause or *iti* at the end, with neither of which can *ki* be connected. This *ki* cannot go back to Skt. *kim* which is interrogative and survives as a conjunction in the sense of alternation. **mʌneː** (on the borders of Nepal) is connected with Nepali **bhʌne** (*Nep. Dic.*, p. 468) through *mhane*.[1] The word *bhanē* 'I say' is found almost similarly used in Pāli also. *jau* . . . *tau* are connected with *yadā* . . . *tadā* through *jaõ* . . . *tao*. *janau*, *manau* etc., are forms of *jānab* 'to know' and *mānab* 'to think' in the sense of 'I know, know' and their use may be compared with *jāne* and *manye* in Sanskrit. *dahū̃* and *dhaū̃* may be similarly connected with *dhyāwab* 'to think'. That words in such uses have a rapid modification of syllables is amply illustrated, *e.g.*, **kʌjʌni** < **kaː jaːniː** 'I do not know' in such expressions as **kʌ jʌni kʌɦʌ̃ se aːi gʌwaː** 'I do not know wherefrom he has come up'.

---

[1] Prof. Chatterji compares Beng. *mene*—a particle of emphasis or mere indication and derives it from OIA *manāk*.

CHAPTER IX

EMPHATIC FORMS

§ 374. Two varieties of emphatic forms, Inclusive and Restrictive, are obtained by adding terminations to the nouns, postpositions, adjectives, numerals, pronouns, verbs and adverbs. For instance: **haːthiː aːwaː** 'the elephant came' but **haːthiu aːwaː** 'the elephant *also* came' and **haːthin aːwaː** 'the elephant *only* came'.

Inclusive Forms

A. Early Awadhi

§ 375. In Early Awadhi the Inclusive and Restrictive forms are found abundantly. The affix for the Inclusive form is *-hu* (*-u*). The *-hu* forms are very common in Jāyasī while *-u* in Nūr Muhammad; *-u* combined with the previous *-a-* appears as *-o*. Tulsīdās comes between these two. For instance:

(*a*) Nouns—*janamahu* 'throughout life' (J. p. 23) *sapanehu* 'even in dream' (T. p. 163), *gaurihu* 'Gaurī also' (N. p. 17), *phūlanahũ tẽ* 'more than even flowers' (N. p. 8).

(*b*) Adjectives—*bhaleu* 'the good also' (T. p. 5), *aurau* 'others also' (T. p. 18).

(*c*) Numerals—*sātau* 'all the seven' (J. p. 3), *cāriu* 'all the four' (J. p. 16), *dou* 'both' (T. p. 169), *tihũ* (*pura*) 'in all the three (towns)' (T. p. 171), *chatīsau* 'all the thirty six' (N. p. 16), *cāriu* 'all the four' (N. p. 2), *sātō* 'all the seven' (N. p. 12); *chavō* 'all the six' (J. p. 68), *barahō* 'all the twelve' (J. p. 68).

The idea of indefiniteness of a number is signified in Early Awadhi by adding *-ka*, *e.g.*, *cārika* 'about four' (T. p. 234), *pacāsaka* 'about fifty' (T. p. 200), ***kōṭika*** 'crores' (T. p. 165), cf. *kachu eka* 'a few' (T. p. 343).

(*d*) Pronouns—*mōhũ* 'to me also' (J. p. 363), ***hamahũ*** 'we also' (J. p. 254), *tēhu* 'they also' (J. p. 19), cf. ***tehu*** (J. p. 39), *uhau* 'that also', *kaunau* 'somebody' (J. p. 69), cf. ***kaunahũ*** (J. p. 396); *mahũ* 'I also' (T. p. 259), ***hamahũ*** 'I also' (T. p. 163), *teu* 'she also' (T. p. 288), ***tuhũ*** 'thou also' (T. p. 170), *tinhahũ* 'them also' (T. p. 14), ***mahũ*** (N. p. 76), *hamahũ* (N. p. 59), ***sōũ*** 'he also' (N. p. 107), *kuchau* 'somewhat' (N. p. 122), *tōhũ* 'thou also' (N. p. 59).

(*e*) No instances of the emphatic forms of the post-positions have been found.

(*f*) Verbs—Examples of the Inclusive forms of the verb are rare: *muehũ* 'dead also' (J. p. 597).

(*g*) Adverbs—*abahũ* 'even now' (J. p. 13), ***kabahũ*** 'ever' (J. p. 346), *katahũ*, *katahũ* 'anywhere' (J. p. 59); ***sãcehu*** 'truly' (T. p. 11), *kabahũ* 'ever' (T. p. 5), *ajahũ* 'even now' (T. p. 122), cf. *ajahũ* (T. p. 170), *aisehu* 'even so' (T. p. 289); *kabahũa* 'ever' (N. p. 115), *tabahũ* 'even then' (N. p. 2), *kahũ*, *katahũ* 'anywhere' (N. p. 15), ***kaisehũ*** 'some how' (N. p. 14).

B. Modern Awadhi

§ 376. The general affix for the Inclusive emphatic form is **-ʌu** after a stem ending in a consonant or **u, uː** (the **-u** of the stem changes to **-w** and **-uː** becomes short) and **-u** after one ending in any other vowel (the vowel if long or whispered becomes short).

Note— **-ʌɦuː** (instead of **-ʌu**) is optionally added to stems of one syllable or of two short syllables. If a dissyllabic or a long monosyllabic stem ends in a consonant, **-ʌu** and not **-ʌɦuː** will be added (**gɦʌr** : **gɦʌrʌu** or **gɦʌrʌɦuː**, **paːr** : **paːrʌ'** *never* **paːrʌɦuː**). For instance :

(*a*) Nouns—**kitaːb** 'book' : **kitaːbʌu** 'the book *also*' **gãːu** 'village' : **gãːwʌu, baːruː** 'sand' : **bʌruʌu, raːjaː** 'king' : **raːjʌu, seːṭhi̥ː seːṭhiu, dɦoːbiː** 'washerman' : **dhoːbiu, pãːɽeː** : 'a particular caste of Brāhmaṇa' : **pãːɽeu, kutːʌn** 'to the dogs' : **kutːʌnʌu.**

(*b*) Adjectives—**laːl** 'red' : **laːlʌu** 'red *also*', **gʌruː** 'heavy' : **gʌruʌu, kʌrijaː** 'black' : **kʌrijʌu, niːki̥** 'good' (fem.) : **niːkiu, bɦaːriː** 'heavy' : **bɦaːriu, piʌreː** 'yellow' (pl.) : **piʌreu.**

(*c*) Numerals—**eːk** 'one' : **eːkʌu** 'one *also*', **nʌu** 'nine' : **nʌwʌu** 'all the nine', **baːraː** 'twelve' : **baːrʌu** 'all the twelve', **saːṭhi̥** 'sixty' : **saːṭhiu** 'all the sixty', **ʌsːiː** 'eighty', **ʌsːiu** 'all the eighty', **nʌbːeː** 'ninety' : **nʌbːeu** 'all the ninety'.

NOTE 1.—To add the significance of *indefiniteness* to a number **-ʌn** (**-n** after a vowel) and **-ʌk** (**-k** after a vowel) are added, *e.g.*, **biːs** 'twenty', **biːsʌn** 'scores', **pʌcaːs** 'fifty', **pʌcaːsʌn** 'fifties'; **biːsʌk** 'about twenty', **saːṭhik** 'about sixty'.

NOTE 2.—**dui** 'two' has **duiu** and also **duːnʌu.**

(*d*) Pronouns—If there are two forms of a pronoun, one shorter than the other (*e.g.*, **koː, kʌun**), the affix is added to the longer form (**kʌun-ʌu**). The personal pronouns and the demonstrative pronouns add **-ʌɦuː** (**-ɦuː**) instead of **ʌu** (**-u**) as illustrated below:

mʌi	**mʌɦuː**	
hʌm	**ɦʌmʌɦuː**	
tui	**toɦuː**	B. G. Fy. etc. **tuɦãː**
tum	**tumʌɦuː**	
uː, waː, wʌɦ	**wʌɦʌu**	B. G. Fy. etc. **uɦʌu**
ui	**wʌɦuː**	
un	**unʌɦuː**	
iu, jaː, jʌɦ	**jʌɦʌu**	B. G. Fy. etc. **iɦʌu**
iː	**jʌɦuː**	
in	**inʌɦuː**	

(*e*) Postpositions—In Lakhīmpurī the Inclusive (or Restrictive) affix can be added either to the noun, adjective or pronoun or to the postposition which follows, *e.g.*, **uː gɦʌr seː gaː** 'he went from (his) house', **uː gɦʌrʌu (gɦʌrʌɦu) se̥ gaː** or **uː gɦʌr səu gaː** 'he went from the house also'.

The Western dialects and R. and Br. agree with Lmp. in this practice while B. and the Eastern dialects do not; they add the termination only to the noun, adjective, pronoun or adverb, not to the postpositions.

(*f*) Verbs—the regular affix (Inclusive or Restrictive) is added to the participles, verbal noun and absolutive, *e.g.*,

deːkhʌt (deːkhʌti̥) :	**dekhotʌu**	(imperf. part.)
deːkhaː	**deːkhʌu**	(perf. part.)
deːkhiː	**deːkhiu**	,,
deːkheː	**deːkheu**	,,
deːkhʌb	**dekhʌbʌu**	(Verbal noun)
deːkhi̥	**deːkhiu**	(absolutive)

In the case of the simple conjugated tense-forms the sense of the Inclusive (or Restrictive), however, is expressed in a different way, *e.g.*,

uː deːkhʌi 'he may see' : **uː dekhibʌu kʌrʌi** 'he may see also'

mʌi deːkheũ 'I saw' **mʌi dekhibʌu kiɦeũ** 'I saw also'

uː deːkhiː 'he will see' **uː dekhibʌu kʌriː** 'he will see also'

hʌm dekhibaː 'we shall see' **hʌm dekhibʌu kʌribaː** 'we shall see also'.

In other words, the corresponding forms of **kʌrʌb** 'to do' are combined with a form obtained by adding the suffix **-ib** (in some dialects the suffix is **-ʌb, dekhʌbʌu**) plus the Inclusive (or Restrictive) termination to the root.

If the tense-form already contains the suffix (*viz.*, the **-b** future) the suffix is not added. The periphrastic tenses and the compound verbs add the regular termination to the participle or the absolutive as the case may be, *e.g.*, **mʌi deːkhʌt hʌũ** 'I am seeing', **mʌi dekhotʌu hʌũ** 'I am seeing also', **mʌi kiɦeː hʌũ** 'I have done', also **mʌi kiɦeu hʌũ** 'I have done also', **uː giri̥ pʌraː** 'he fell down' : **uː giriu pʌraː** 'he fell down also'.

(*g*) Adverbs—all adverbs take the regular affix except the following which add **-ʌɦũː**

ʌb 'now' :	**ʌb-ʌɦũː** 'even now'
tʌb 'when'	**tʌbʌɦũː** 'even then'
ɟʌb 'when'	**ɟʌbʌɦũː** 'whenever'
kʌb 'when?'	**kʌbʌɦũː** 'ever'
kʌɦãː 'where?'	**kʌɦũː** 'nowhere, anywhere'

The aspiration changes place sometimes, *e.g.*, **ʌbʌɦũː** or **ʌbɦʌũː**. The regular affix is found in such instances as : **ɟʌldiː** 'soon', **ɟʌldiu** 'soon also', **ʌbtiː** 'this time', **ʌbtiu** 'this time also', **tʌɦʌũ** 'there also', **upːʌrʌu** 'above also', **ʌsʌu** 'in this way also'. It is found in some dialects with **ʌb** etc., but then the **b** is lengthened, *e.g.*, **ʌbːʌu** 'even now', **tʌbːʌu**, **ɟʌbːʌu**, **kʌbːʌu**.

C. ORIGIN.

§ 377. The Inclusive emphatic affix **-u** (Early Awadhi *-hu*) goes back to *khalu* and has come down to Modern Awadhi through * *khlu* > *khu* > *hu* (see Pischel § 148). *khalu* was employed in Sanskrit to give an idea of certainty, assuredness. By and by it appears to have assumed the meaning of inclusion. The **ʌ-** before **-u** in Modern Awadhi should be taken as pleonastic, coming from *-ka*. The aspiration is still present in most of the emphatic pronominal forms and may be sometimes heard in a feeble degree in other forms also. The lengthening of *-u* to *-ū* can be explained only by the stress due to emphasis. That the stress was on the last syllable appears to be indicated by the disappearance of *-a* of *khalu*. In the case of the verb, the emphatic form in certain cases is arrived at by putting the verbal noun with emphasis and then combining it with the required conjugated form of **kʌrʌb**. This device is modern. In adverbial forms the lengthening of a consonant (*e.g.*, **ʌbːʌu**) also comes in to indicate emphasis.

NOTE.—The **-ʌn** affix added to Numerals appears to be merely a plural of the numeral, while **-ʌk, -k** comes from *-eka*. The latter is attested by Early Awadhi. The last vowel of the numeral is retained where it exists (*e.g.*, **saːṭhik**) before appending *eka*—*e* going out. In other cases *e* > *a*.

Restrictive Forms

A. EARLY AWADHI

§ 378. The affix for this emphatic form is *-hi* (*i*) generally and *-na* after a stem ending in *-i*, *-ī*.

For instance:

(*a*) Nouns—*gharahi mā̃jha* 'in the house itself' (J. p. 232), *chārahī taī* 'with mere earth' (J. p. 5), *gā̃ūhi gā̃vā̃* 'in every village' (J. p. 263), *bārahī bārā* 'many a time' (T. p. 18), *māṭina* 'in the very earth' (N. p. 59).

(*b*) Adjectives—*pahilai* 'at the first' (J. p. 3), *bahutai* 'many a' (J. p. 2), *thōrihi* 'only a little' (T. p. 174), *biralai kōī* 'only a rare person' (N. p. 18), *aurai* (*tana mana*) 'some other (body and mind)' (N. p. 12).

(*c*) Numerals—*ēkai* 'one only' (J. p. 29), *ēkahi bāra* 'only at one time' (T. p. 163), *ēkai ēkahi* (N. p. 8)

(*d*) Pronouns—*tumahī̃ saū̃* 'with you yourself' (J, p. 247), *uhai* 'he himself' (J. p. 321), *ihai* 'this only' (J. p. 286), *soi* 'he himself' (J. p. 41), *'sabai* 'everyone' (J. p. 41); *mahī̃* 'I myself' (T. p. 259), *soi* 'that very' (T. p. 173), *ihai* (T. p. 160), *tei* 'they only' (T. p. 205), *tumhahī̃* 'you only' (T. p. 226), *hamārehi* 'ours only' (T. p. 201), *tumharihi kṛpā* 'by your own favour' (T. p. 207); *tuhī̃* 'thyself' (N. p. 76), *tumahī̃* 'you yourself' (N. p. 76) *uhai* (N. p. 2), cf. *uhaī* (N. p. 14), *ihai* (N. p. 26).

(*f*) Verbs—Examples are rare, *jiatahī* 'while living' (J. p. 479).

(*g*) Adverbs—*jaũhi* 'whenever' (J. p. 484), ***jabahi*** 'whenever' (J. p. 19), *tahiai* 'at that very time' (J. p. 110), *ājuhi* 'to-day only' (J. p. 101), *turatahī* 'at once' (T. p. 343), *bēgihi* 'at once, soon' (T. p. 175), *taisehi* 'similarly' (T. p. 9), *dūrihi tē* 'from the very far off' (T. p. 287), ***abahī*** 'just now' (N. p. 4), *tabaī* 'then' (N. p. 37), *dūreha* 'far off' (N. p. 159), *āgehī kērī* 'of former times' (N. p. 100), ***ṭhīkahī*** 'just' (N. p. 15).

B. Modern Awadhi

§ 379. The affix for this form is **-ʌi** after a consonantal stem, **-n** after a stem ending in **-i**, **-iː** and **e, eː** and **-i** after a stem ending in **-e, -eː** or any vowel except **-i -iː**. The **e, eː** stems, thus, have alternative forms in **-i** and **-n**. The **-u** stems add either **-ʌi (u > w)** or **i**. The long vowel is shortened before the affix.

Note.—**-ʌɦeː** (**-ʌɦiː** in the Eastern dialects) is optionally added to stems of one syllable or of two short syllables. If a dissyllabic or a long mono-syllabic stem ends in a consonant, **-ʌi** only is added (**gɦʌr : gɦʌrʌi** or **gɦʌrʌɦeː, gɦʌrʌɦiː, paːr : paːrʌi**—never **paːrʌɦeː**).

(*a*) Nouns—**kitaːb** 'book' : **kitaːbʌi** 'the book itself or only the book', **gãːu : gãːwʌi** or **gãːui, raːɟa : raːɟʌi, seːʈhi̥ seːʈhin, dɦoːbiː dɦoːbin, baːruː baːrui, pãːɽeː pãːɽen** or **pãːɽei, kutːʌn kutːʌnʌi**.

(*b*) Adjectives—**laːl** 'red' : **laːlʌi** 'red only', **kʌrijaː kʌrijʌi, niːki̥ niːkin, bɦaːriː bɦaːrin, gʌruː gʌruʌi** or **gʌrui, piʌreː piʌrei** or **piʌren**.

(*c*) Numerals—**eːk** 'one' : **eːkʌi** 'one only', **baːraː baːrʌi, saːʈhi̥ saːʈhin, ʌsːiː ʌsːin, nʌu nʌwʌi** or **nʌui nʌbːeː nʌbːei**.

Note.—**dui** has regular **duin** and also **dueː** (Eastern dialects **duiː**).

(*d*) Pronouns—If a pronoun has two forms, one long and another short, the affix is added to the long one (*e.g.*, **jeː jʌunẹ**, restrictive **jʌunui**). The personal and demonstrative pronouns add **-ʌɦeː (-ʌɦiː)** as shown below:

mʌi	**mʌɦeː**	R. B. G. Fy., etc.	**mʌɦiː**
hʌm	**hʌmʌɦeː**	,,	**hʌmʌɦiː**
tui	**toɦeː**	,,	**tuɦiː, tuɦĩː**
tum	**tumʌɦeː**		
uː, waː, wʌɦ	**wʌɦʌi**	,,	**uɦiː**
ui	**wʌɦeː**	,,	**wʌɦiː**
un	**unʌɦeː**	,,	**unʌɦiː**
iu, jaː, jʌɦ	**jʌɦʌi**	,,	**jʌɦiː**
iː	**jʌɦeː**	,,	**jʌɦiː**
in	**inʌɦeː**	,,	**inʌɦiː**

(*e*) Postpositions—See § 376 (*e*). **gɦʌr seː gaː** 'went from the house', **uː gɦʌrʌi (ghʌrʌɦe) sẹ gaː** or **uː gɦʌr sei gaː** 'he went from the house itself or from the house only' The dialectal difference noted in § 376 (*e*) is observed here also.

(*f*) Verbs—see § 376 (*f*). The following are the instances of the Restrictive forms:

deːkhʌt (deːkhʌtị):	**dekhətʌi** (imperf. part.)
deːkhaː	**deːkhʌi** (perf. part.)
deːkhiː	**deːkhin**
deːkheː	**deːkhen** or **deːkhei**
deːkhʌb	**dekhʌbʌi** (verbal noun)
deːkhị	**deːkhin** (absolutive)

uː deːkhʌi 'he may see', **uː dekhibʌi kʌrʌi** 'he may see only'; **mʌi deːkheũ** 'I saw', **mʌi dekhibʌi kiɦeũ** 'I saw only'; **uː deːkhiː** 'he will see', **uː dekhibʌi kʌriː** 'he will see only'; **hʌm dekhibaː** 'we shall see', **hʌm dekhibʌi kʌribaː** 'we shall see only'; **mʌi deːkhʌt hʌũ** 'I am seeing', **mʌi dekhətʌi hʌũ** 'I am seeing only'; **mʌi kiɦeː hʌũ** 'I have done', **mʌi kiɦei hʌũ** 'I have done only'; **uː giri̥ pʌraː** 'he fell down', **uː girin pʌraː** 'he did fall down, he fell down only'.

(*g*) Adverbs—**ʌb, tʌb, ɟʌb** and **kʌb** add **-ʌɦẽː** (**-ʌɦĩː** Eastern): **ʌbʌɦẽː** 'just now', **tʌbʌɦẽː** 'just then', **ɟʌbʌɦẽː** 'just when', **kʌbʌɦẽː** 'just when?' The aspiration may change place, so that we may have **ʌbʌɦẽː** or **ʌbɦʌẽː**. The forms **ʌbɦʌjen, tʌbɦʌjen, ɟʌbɦʌen** are double restrictives—as we find **-n** termination superimposed—but they have no difference in sense from **ʌbɦʌjẽː** etc. The forms in Eastern dialects are: **ʌbʌɦĩː, tʌbʌɦĩː, ɟʌbʌɦĩː** etc. Here also we sometimes find super-imposed forms **ʌbʌɦin, tʌbʌɦin, ɟʌbʌɦin.** Occasionally one comes across forms such as **ʌbʌɦinʌi** or **ʌbɦʌinʌi** which are further super-imposed forms but have no difference in sense. The regular **-ʌi** is found in such forms as **ʌbːʌi, kʌbːʌi** etc. and in **ɟʌldin** 'soon', **ɟʌɦʌĩ** 'wherever', **ʌisei** 'in this very way', etc.

NOTE.—Sometimes a Restrictive form is followed by the ordinary form, both the forms together indicating the Restrictive sense, *e.g.*, **kitaːbʌi ɟʌrĩː** 'the books were burnt', **kitʌbʌin ɟʌrĩː** 'only the books were burnt', **kitʌbʌin kitaːbʌi ɟʌrĩː** 'only the books were burnt', **hʌm aːjen** 'I came', **hʌmʌɦeː aːjen** 'I only have come', **hʌmʌɦen aːen** (double Restrictive) **hʌmʌɦen hʌm aːjen** 'only I have come'.

C. ORIGIN

§ 380. The Restrictive emphatic affix **-i** (Early Awadhi *-hi*) is derived from *-eva* > *ẽ* > *i*, the *-h* in Early Awadhi as well as in some forms of Modern Awadhi may be due to contamination with the particle *hi*. *eva* has possibly a double treatment, one in *evva* which survives as *-b* in the adverbs of time, but another in *ẽ* (cf. Amg. *em*=*evam*, Pischel § 149) which appears to be at the basis of the affix here.

The -**n** (old *na*) affix should be connected with Pkt. *ṇam* found in Ardhamāgadhī for *nūnam* (see Pischel § 150). The adverb **ewʌĩ** = *evameva* also contains *eva* as *-i*. The **ʌ**- before the affix *-i* shows that the affix came after a pleonastic suffix in the stem, *viz.*, *ka*.

Repetition, Reduplication, etc.

B. MODERN AWADHI

§ 381. Some grammatical forms are repeated and as such denote the sense of entirety, repeatedness, continuity or intensity.

(*a*) Nouns, Pronouns and Adjectives—the idea of entirety or plurality is indicated by repeating a noun, pronoun or adjective, *e.g.*, **hʌm gãːu gãːu gɦuːmen** 'I roamed about in many a village', **kutːaː kutːaː mʌri̥ geː** 'all that were dogs—all the dogs died', **ɟoː ɟoː aːwʌi ui kaː khaːi ko deːu** 'give meals to all those who come', **hʌriʌr hʌriʌr paːtaː biːn leːu** 'pick up all the green leaves'.

(*b*) Numerals—the repetition here is merely for emphasis or to denote the groups, *e.g.*, **chaː chaː ɟʌneː aːjeː** 'as many as six—quite unexpectedly—have arrived' or 'people have come in sixes.'

(*c*) Verbs—the Imperfect participle and the absolutive are repeated to indicate the repeated nature, frequency or continuity of an action, *e.g.*, **[illegible]ːkhʌdːeːkhʌcːʌleː ɟaːu** 'go on, continuing the action of seeing', **pʌɽɦi̥ pʌɽɦi̥ ciʈːhiː dɦʌrti̥ rʌɦaː** 'he continued putting away the letters after reading them one after another', **rupʌjaː giri̥ giri̥ pʌrti hʌi** 'the rupee falls down again and again', **huãː ɟaːi ɟaːi kaːmṷ bigaːreu** 'you spoiled the business by going there frequently'.

(*d*) Adverbs—these are repeated for emphasis, *e.g.*, **ɟʌb ɟʌb** 'whenever', **ɟʌɦãː ɟʌɦãː** 'wherever', **ɟʌiseː ɟʌiseː** 'as'.

NOTE — If a form followed by its postposition is to be repeated, the postposition is not repeated, it comes only after the second form, *e.g.* **gãːu mo,** repeated **gãːu gãːu mo; deːkhʌi mo,** repeated **deːkhʌi deːkhʌi mo.**

§ 382. The Echo-words or Expletive words begin in Awadhi with **u : wʌ** and **uː : waː,** with the former if the first syllable of the real word is short (**ʌdmiː udmiː** or **ʌdmiː wʌdmiː** 'man etc.') and with the latter if it is long (**roːʈiː uːʈiː** 'bread etc.', **khaːb waːb** 'meal etc.'). **wʌ** instead of **u** is found in a few dialects, *e.g.*, S. and U., while **waː** for **uː** is found only when the first syllable of the real word ends in **-aː.** The Echo-word sometimes carries the sense of 'et cet ra' or 'things like that' but more often it is meaningless and appears to give to the speaker only a facility in his current of speech. Generally nouns, adjectives and verbs have the echo-forms.

§ 383. Facility in the current of speech again appears to be at the basis of Reduplication of certain roots. The reduplicated root does not mean anything by itself but its addition to the principal root sometimes does give a shade of intensity of action. In Reduplication, the initial consonant of a root is repeated intact, but the vowel changes. If it is **-ʌ, aː** in the principal root, the reduplicated root will have **u, uː,** otherwise the reduplication-vowel is **ʌ, aː.** For instance:

bãːdɦʌb : bãːdɦʌb bũːdɦʌb 'to tie completely', **caːʈʌb : caːʈʌb cuːʈʌb** 'to lick', **hʌ̃sʌb : hʌ̃sʌb hũsʌb** 'to laugh', **kʌi : kʌi kui** 'having done', **lʌi : lʌi lui** 'having taken', **ɟiːtʌb : ɟiːtʌb ɟaːtʌb** 'to win', **kuːdʌb : kuːdʌb kaːdʌb** 'to jump', : **heːrʌb : heːrʌb huːrʌb** 'to search', **soːi saːi** 'having slept'.

NOTE.—In actual use we have not been able to detect any marked distinction between the Echo-words and Reduplication. They appear to be two different devices for the same thing.

§ 384. Different from Reduplication are certain forms which go in pairs. Here both the words have independent meanings, but in combination give an additional idea connoted by both in a general sense, *e.g.*, **hãːthiː** and **ghoːɽaː** separately mean 'elephants' and 'horses', but when brought together they not only mean 'elephants and horses' but also other high class conveyances or paraphernalia of a king. Similar expressions are: **boːl caːl** 'companionship', **ɟoːr toːr** 'contrivances', **naːc kuːd** 'merriments', '**kheːl tʌmːsaː** 'shows and spectacles', **rupʌjaː pʌisaː** 'money', **maːr kaːʈ** 'slaughter', **deːb leːb** 'to give and to take, *i.e.*, mutual help', **hʌgʌb muːtʌb** 'to ease oneself and to urinate, *i.e.*, affairs not fit to be mentioned in decent society', **nʌɦaːb dɦoːwʌb** 'to bathe and to wash, *i.e.*, to clean oneself', **kaːnaː phũːsiː** 'secret talk', **khaːb piʌb** 'eating and drinking', etc.

C. ORIGIN

§ 385. Repetition of a word is a normal feature in Sanskrit and MIA, *e.g.*, *deśē*, *deśē* 'in every country', *pītvā pītvā* 'having drunk again and again', *yadā yadā* 'whenever'.

Echo-words are found in Mod. IA throughout as well as in Dravidian (see Chatterji, p. 176) and they serve only as a help in the current of speech. Such a thing is not likely to find a place in literary works, however; we have found only one instance in Early Awadhi: *chanda wanda* (*Awadha Bilāsa*, leaf 9*b*)..

Similarly Reduplication is another device taken up for facility in speech and is found in other Mod. IA languages as well (see Chatterji § 775). People do require some such supports (called *takia-e-kalām* in Persian, meaning, literally, 'pillow of speech') and sometimes a whole clause is introduced, *e.g.*, 'isn't it' or 'you know' in English and **mʌi baːt kʌɦeũ** 'I say', **ɟaːneu ki naːi** 'isn't it', **hũ waːɦ bɦaːiː** 'O Yes, brother!' in Awadhi. These devices are restricted strictly to spoken languages, mostly to slang, and do not find place in written language

CHAPTER X

WORD ORDER

A. EARLY AWADHI

§ 386. Unfortunately no prose works are available. The only prose piece that is found is the arbitration deed said to have been written by Tulsīdās as an arbitrator to settle the dispute about the division of the property of Rājā Tōḍarmal after his death. The language of deeds is generally archaic and formal and so is also of this deed (*Tulsī Granthāvalī*, Part III, pages 36—38). The following sentences show the order:

āgē jē āgya dunahu janē māgā jē āgya bhai sē pramāna mānā dunahu janē . . . . . . likhītaṁ ananda rāma jē ūpara likhā sē sahī 'previously whatever order both the persons wanted (and) which order was put that has been accepted by both the persons . . . written by Anandarāma whatever is written above is correct.'

Here *āgē* adverb is quite in order with modern usage. The precedence of the object (*jē āgya*) before the subject, as well as the putting of the subject (*dunahu janē*) at the end are emphatic in such cases and are similarly found in the modern language as well. The order of words thus does not differ from that found in Modern Awadhi (see below § 388).

§ 387. As in Modern Awadhi so in the old language, the normal order of words is often violated. For instance:

(*a*) subject coming after the verb, *jabahi caḍhahi puhumī pati, sērasāhi jaga-sūra* 'whenever Shēr Shāh, the hero of the world, the king of the (whole) Earth, attacks' (J. p. 19), *mukuṭa bā̃dhi saba baiṭhā rājā* 'all the kings sat with their crowns on' (J. p. 72), *bōli apara kahehu sakhi nīkā* 'the other said: friend, (you) have well said' (T. p. 97), *pura pūraba disi gē dou bhāī* 'both the brothers went to the Eastern part of the city' (T. p. 97), *kaha māruta-suta sunahu prabhu* 'the son of the Air-god said: my lord, hear' (T. p. 375); *dīnhā utara mahīpa biyōgī* 'the love-lorn king gave the answer' (N. p. 25), *kahā ratana sō ēka sahēlī* 'a friend said to Ratana' (N. p. 90), *karaba mai sēvā* 'I shall do the service' (N. p. 32).

(*b*) object after the verb, *kīnhesi dharatī saraga patārū* 'He created the Earth, the sky and the nether world' (J. p. 2), *dēkhī sāsu āna anuhārī* 'saw the mothers-in-law much different' (T. p. 245), *suni siya sapana bharē jala lōcana* 'on hearing Sītā's dream (his) eyes were filled with water (tears)' (T. p. 245), *likhi pāti cētā kaha dīnhā* '(she) wrote the letter and gave it to Cētā' (N. p. 73), *lakhai na aiguna dēkhai sōbhā* '(he) does not look at (your) evils (and) sees (your) beauty' (N. p. 167).

(*c*) adjectival epithet after the noun, *pitā hamāra* 'my father' (J. p. 87), *jōbana mōra* 'my youth' (J. p. 87), *dīpa dui* 'two lamps' (J. p. 193), *kou kaha saṅkara cāpa kaṭhōrā* 'some one said that Siva's bow was hard' (T. p. 97), *kānanu kaṭhina bhayaṅkara bhārī* 'the forest is difficult (to pass through), terrifying and huge' (T. p. 181). *muni gyānī* 'the well-versed sages' (T. p. 264), *bōlē bāni sanēha suhāī* '(he) spoke words beautiful owing to affection' (T. p. 277), *hari lei calā parāna hamārā* 'he has taken my life and is gone' (N. p. 25), *auguna bharī sarīra hamārī* 'my body is full of evils' (N. p. 105), *pai tumharī ā̃khiyā̃ matavārī hama kaha khī̃ca surā disa ānaī* 'but your bewitching eyes, draw me and bring me towards wine' (N. p. 176).

B. Modern Awadhi

§ 388. The Awadhi sentence normally is small; it contains four or five words. Complex ideas are expressed by combining together several sentences by means of conjunctions or adverbial expressions.

The normal order of words is:

Subject, object, verb; *e.g.*, **mʌi duːdɦʊ piːɦʌũ** 'I shall drink milk'. A sentence may contain only the subject and the verb, *e.g.*, **mʌi ɟʌiɦʌũ** 'I shall go' In connected speech any of the above may be understood, so that, in effect a sentence may contain either the subject only, or the verb or the object. The adjectival adjuncts normally precede the noun or pronoun that they qualify attributively. Predicatively, however, they come after the noun or pronoun qualified as shown above (§ 224). The adverbial adjuncts generally come immediately before the verb, but adverbs of time and place are found, quite frequently, placed after the subject. Normally the indirect object precedes the direct object.

§ 389. The normal order of words in the language is, however, not rigidly fixed. Except for the postpositions which must follow the noun or pronoun concerned, other parts of speech may have a different order for emphasis and for expression of emotion. The subject may come at the end of a sentence, *e.g.*, **tʌ hũʌ te cʌl diɦin ui** 'then he started from there', **ɟaːdaː nʌ ljaːb hʌm** 'I shall not take more'. The vocative generally precedes the subject (*e.g.*, **raːniː hʌm tʌu pijaːseː bʌɦut hʌn** 'O Queen, I am very thirsty', **tʌu lʌɽikiː boːliː naːɦiː raːɟaː hiãː nʌ piʌu** 'then the girl said: no king! do not drink water here'), but it may follow the subject sometimes (*e.g.*, **hʌm daːdaː tumʌriː bɦaːgi̥ sḙ khaːiti̥** 'Father! I live—lit. eat—owing to your good fortune'). The adjectival epithet normally precedes the noun, but for emphasis it may follow it (*e.g.*, **mʌɦotaːriː kiː tʌnaː aːgi̥ laːgi gʌi jaː**

'O Mother, how did this fire come about to catch (the house)', **ui ṭhʌgʌunaː saːtʌu dʌureː cʌleː aːwʌĩ** 'those *seven* highway robbers were coming on, running'.

§ 390. The object normally comes between the subject and the verb, but for emphasis or when it is the particular topic of talk, it may come at the beginning (*e.g.*, **soː haːr hʌm eːk ʌurʌt ko dʌi diːn** 'that *necklace*, I gave away to a woman') or at the end (*e.g.*, **tʌu mʌi dʌi ḍaːreũ rupʌjaː** 'then I gave away the money', **goːbʌr bɦʌr̥i kʌj diɦis̥i hʌm kaː** 'he gave to me filled with dung'). The direct object may, in similar circumstances, precede the indirect, *e.g.*, **kʌɦin nʌ hoːi laːo thoːraː khaːi leːiː thoːraː jʌhu ko dʌi deːiː** '(she) said: let it be, let me eat a little and give a little to this one also'. The adjectival epithet of the object may be separated thus by the intervention of the verb, *e.g.*, **jaː iː kiː khaːt̥i hʌi kʌmaːi** 'he earns his livelihood by it' where **iː kiː** was expected near **kʌmaːiː**.

§ 391. Of all the parts of a sentence, the adverbial adjunct has the least fixed place. In the same sentence one adjunct may be after the subject and another before the verb, *e.g.*, **ui maːreː gusːʌ kẹ roːṭiː ḍeɦʌrijʌ mo ḍaːr̥i deːĩ** 'she, on account of anger, used to throw the bread in the big jar' where **maːreː gusːʌ kẹ** comes after the subject and **ḍeɦʌrijʌ mo** before the verb; or **choːṭ bɦaːiː jɦʌṭːo bʌɽeː bɦaːi ko kursiː pʌr bʌiṭhaːris̥i** 'the younger brother, soon, seated the elder brother on a chair' where **jɦʌṭːo** comes after the subject and **kursiː pʌr** before the verb. Sometimes, particularly when the subject is inanimate, the adverb may come even before the subject (*e.g.*, **tʌu hũaː bʌɽaː hʌlːaː mʌcaː** 'then there rose up a great uproar') or after the verb (*e.g*, **gʌi rʌɦʌi ui waːr** '(she) had gone to that side').

§ 392. The verb normally comes at the end of the sentence, but it may precede the subject (*e.g.*, **rʌɦu tui** 'remain thou'), or the object (*e.g.*, **kaː kiɦisi̥ ki nikaːrisi̥ tʌrwaːri̥** 'what did (he) do? that he drew out the sword', **tʌu ʌĩcini̥ tʌrʌwaːri̥ ki iː kaː maːɖ̣ːʌribaː** 'then (he) drew the sword: that I shall kill her'). This is merely for emphasis. When there are two verbs in a sentence, that of the absolutive clause normally precedes the principal verb, *e.g.*, **gulgulaː ɟɦãːpi̥ ko dɦʌri̥ diɦini̥** '(she) covered up the cakes and put them aside' where the first clause is absolutive and the second principal. The absolutive of **aːwʌb** 'to come' or **ɟaːb** 'to go', however, when it is unaccompanied by its postposition always comes after the principal verb, *e.g.*, **hũaː khaːu ɟaːi** 'go and eat there', **iu kaːmʊ̥ kʌrʌu aːi** 'come and do this thing'. In compound verbs the principal normally precedes the accessory, but for emphasis the order may be reversed, *e.g.*, **tʌu liɦini̥ chiːni̥** 'then (he) snatched away', **ʌu ĩːʈ leːu lʌi** 'and take up a brick'.

§ 393. The Conjunction (**ki, mula,** etc.) or the conjunctive epithet (**tʌɦi kʌi** 'then', etc.) introduces a sentence connected with the previous sentence. The reported speech is normally direct and may or may not be introduced by the particle **ki**, *e.g.*, **tʌb waː lʌɽikiː kʌɦisi̥ jaː ʌ̃guːʈhiː tʌu hʌmʌreː baːp ki hʌi** 'then that girl said this ring is my father's', **tʌb kʌɦini̥ ki jaː ʌ̃guːʈhiː hʌm kaː deːu** 'then (she) said: give this ring to me'. In connected narrative speech the last portion of a sentence may be repeated to introduce the next sentence, *e.g.*, **tʌb duːnʌu pʌrdeːs ko eːk eːk gɦoːɽʌ po cʌɽɦi kʌi cʌl diɦini̥** 'then both mounted on one horse each and started for foreign land', **cʌl diɦini̥ tʌu eːk ʈhʌgʌn kẹ purʌwʌ mo ʌʈeː ɟaːi** then when started, they reached a village of robbers', **un kiː sʌrʌɦoɟin diːkh** 'his sisters-in-law saw (him)', **tʌu diːkh tʌu un kʌɦʌi laːgĩː** 'then when (they) saw (him) they began to say'.

Instances of the indirect report are, however, sometimes found, though very rarely, *e.g.*, **gopaːl hʌri sẹ bʌtaːisi̥ ki̥ sʌŋkʌṭaː tumaːr ṭʌpkaː coraːini̥ hʌi** 'Gopal told Hari that Saṅkaṭā had stolen his mangoes' but **gopaːl mʌɦi seː kʌɦisi̥ ki tum hʌmaːr ṭʌpkaː coraːjeu** Gopāl told me that you stole my mangoes'.

§ 394. The subject may be a noun, a pronoun, or an adjective (with the noun understood). As noted above (§ 175) a subject may take a plural number (indicated by the verb being in the plural) to show respect. In connected speech the same subject may be in the singular or the plural in clauses side by side, *e.g*, **waː ʌ̃guːṭhiː lʌi kʌi ʌpʌneː gɦʌr gʌi ʌpʌniː mʌɦətaːri kə dekhaːini̥ jaːi** 'she took the ring and went home (and) showed (it) to her mother', where **gʌi** shows a singular subject and **dekhaːini̥** a plural one; **tʌu eːk jʌɦʌr ki purijaː phiri̥ ghoːrisi̥, jɦʌṭːə wʌɦʌi loṭijaː gɦũːgɦuṭụ maːri̥ kə raːjʌ kə dihini̥** 'then she again dissolved a small packet of poison, (and) soon drawing the veil she gave the same cup to the king' where **gɦoːrisi̥ and dihini̥** show a difference of number. Such instances are quite frequent in every day speech. Not only this, when subjects are understood, different subjects may be understood in different clauses of the same sentence, *e.g.*, **pʌɦileː baːt bʌnaːi gʌi ʌbtimə ḍaːriː maːri̥** 'at first (she) explained it away, this time (he) will kill (us) outright', where the subject of **bʌnaːi gʌi** is 'the daughter of the demon' and of **ḍaːriː maːri̥** 'the demon himself' The difference of number may be visible in the same sentence, *e.g.*, **mʌi goɦaːri lʌgaːi kə pʌkʌren** 'I raised an alarm and caught him' where **mʌi** (singular) is connected with **pʌkʌren** (plural). The expected verb was **pʌkʌreũ.** Such wrong grammar, however, is not frequent.

§ 395. If a verb has a subject in different genders, the gender of the nearest subject is taken up by the verb, and the number is plural, *e.g.*, **mʌɦətaːriː puːt hoi**

rʌɦeː jaːi 'the mother and the son reached (the place)' where **rʌɦeː** agrees in gender with **puːt** and not with **mʌɦotaːriː.** Similarly **paːrbʌtiː mʌɦaːdeːu dunijʌ ki cintʌ ko nikʌreː** 'Pārvatī and Mahādēva started to look after the world', **kumɦaːr ʌu kumɦaːrini̥ maːʈiː nikaːrʌi aːĩː** 'the potter and his wife came to dig out earth'.

§ 396. When two pronouns of different persons stand as the subject, the order is 1st, 2nd, 3rd and the verb also agrees with the 1st in preference to the 2nd or 3rd and with the 2nd in preference to the 3rd, *e.g.*, **aːoː hʌm tum khaːiː** 'Come let u eat', **hʌm tum bʌjaːrʌi jʌibaː** 'You and I shall go to the market', **tum ui pʌkʌreu** 'he and you caught'.

§ 397. The subject of a passive or causal clause is put before the subject of the simple clause, *e.g.*, **uː lʌɽikaː kuchu̥ gʌltiː kiɦisi̥** 'that boy committed some mistake'—active, **ui lʌɽikʌ se̥ kuchu̥ gʌltiː hoi gʌi** 'some mistake was committed by that boy'—passive, where **uː lʌɽikaː** is the subject of the active construction while **ui lʌɽikʌ se̥** is the agentive phrase in the passive construction; similarly **raːm gopaːl ko paːniː piaːisi̥** '(he) caused Gopāl to drink water through Rām'.

§ 398. In poetry and songs, the normal order of words is found generally disturbed, *e.g.*, **jʌtʌniː bjaːr hʌri kino kaː gʌijʌi kino kaː lʌi kʌi naːũ** 'at this time whom shall I sing about, whose name shall I take'—here **naːũ** (object) would normally be put before **lʌi kʌi**; **kaːɦ naːũ ui guruː tumɦaːreː** 'what is the name of your preceptor?'—here **tumɦaːreː** (adjective) should have preceded **guruː**; **bɦitʌr te nikʌsĩː jʌsoː-mʌti maːtaː** 'mother Yaśōdā came out from the inner apartments'—here **jʌsoːmʌti maːtaː** (subject) would precede **nikʌsĩː.**

C. Origin

§ 399. 'Like all languages that possess a rich store of inflections, Sanskrit affords a comparatively great freedom as to the order of words in the sentence' (Speijer: *Sanskrit Syntax* § 15). In the Sanskrit word the morphemes were combined with the semanteme so that each word was a unit by itself and carried with it its full significance. Hence the order of words did not matter for the connotation of the meaning. In spite of this we find a certain order generally—subject—object—verb; the attribute precedes the noun, the vocative generally heads the sentence (*ibid,* § 16). We find that this general order has been kept up more or less throughout modern Indo-Aryan [see Bloch: *Langue Marathe*, (p. 268), Chatterji: *Origin and Development of Bengali*, (p. 176)]. Only there is this difference between Sanskrit and modern IA, that in the former the terminations expressed the morphemes of case, number, gender, person, tense etc., while in modern IA some of these are expressed by post-positions or other form-words. Just as the morphemes necessarily accompanied the semanteme then (being incorporated in the word), similarly in Mod. IA they accompany the semanteme (closely following it). Granted this, the word-order is the same. For instance:

Skt. *devadattaḥ* | *kaṭam* | *karoti* |

Hindi **deːvʌdʌtːe** | **cʌʈaːiː** | **bʌnaːtaːhʌi** |

'Devadatta | mat | makes'.

Here no harm would be done if the words of the Sanskrit sentence change their places as the morphemes are incorporated in the semantemes; but normally the Hindi sentence would keep the order because the morphemes are not manifest. However, as shown above, the order may change sometimes in poetry, or even in prose for emphasis and there the context will be the only indicator of the syntactical relation. Let us take another case:

Skt. *viṭapāt* | *patrāṇi* | *kṣaranti* |

Awadhi **birAWA sẹ** | **paːtaː** | **jɦArAtị hAĩ** |

'From the tree | leaves | fall off'.

The three elements of the sentence in either languages may be changed without causing any confusion in sense. Or take another sentence :

Skt. *tataḥ* | *rāmaḥ* | *sitayā sārdham* | *vanaṁ* | *jagāma*

Awadhi **tau** | **raːm** | **siːtaː sAŋgɦ** | **bAn kaː** | **cAleː gAeː**

'Then | Rām | with Sītā | to the forest | went'.

Here also the sense will not be confused if the order of the various parts of the sentence is changed.

The word-order, thus, in essentials has remained the same in modern IA as in OIA.

FINIS

APPENDICES

APPENDIX I

SPECIMENS OF EARLY AWADHI (UNPUBLISHED) TEXTS

(*a*) Awadha Bilāsa

(*b*) Prēma Pragāsa

(*c*) Gura Anyāsa

(*d*) Yūsuf Zulekhā

(a) Awadha Bilāsa[1]

Page 1.

Srī Gaṇēśāya Namaḥ

Śrī pustaka Avadha Bilāsa likhyatē

dōhā

Bēda ukti anubhava jugati
Jñāna ratana kī khāni
Lāla gupta eha pragaṭa kie
Audha Bilāsa bakhāni.

Audha Bilāsa samudra hai
Sāhu sādhu taṭa jāhi
Ratana kathā Raghubīra kī
Lāla bahuta tā māhi.

Lāla succha trailōka kō
darapana Audha Bilāsa
Jō jaisahi hoi dēkhihai
Tā kaha taisā bhāsa.

Saba hī ruci nahi ēka hai
Kāhū kachū sohāe
Tā tē mai bahu mata racē
Audha Bilāsa banāe.

Pragaṭeu Avadha Bilāsa ghanu
Bidyā jñāna apāra
Khulē khajānē lāla kē
Lāla hṛdaya bhaṇḍāra.

Rāga raṅga rata Rāmu sō
Nau rasa jñāna prakāsa
Jasa prabhutā jaga maha calai
Tau paṭu Avadha Bilāsa.

[1] Text from a copy (in the Hindustani Academy, Allahabad) of the manuscript described in the Introduction above §6.

Translation

Salutation to Śrī Gaṇēśa

Awadha Bilāsa begins

The Vēdas, apt sayings, experiences, devices, a mine of precious stones of knowledge, Lāla says, these are hidden, (but) he has made these manifest by having composed the Audha Bilāsa.

The Audha Bilāsa is an ocean, whose (two) ends are *sāhu* (the trading class), and *sādhu* (the religious mendicant class). Gems of the story of Rāma, Lāla says, are abundantly found in it.

The Audha Bilāsa is a bright mirror for (reflecting) the three worlds. Whoever will look in it in whatever mood, he will find it reflecting similarly.

All tastes are not alike ; some like certain things (while others like a different thing). This is why I have included in the Audha Bilāsa, many shades of thought.

The cloud of the Audha Bilāsa has made manifest boundless knowledge and wisdom, and has opened in the storehouse of Lāla's mind, treasures of precious stones (of beautiful thoughts).

Love, sport, devotion to Rāma, the nine sentiments, and the light of knowledge, all those qualities which rule the world, have been cleverly incorporated in the Audha Bilāsa.

Koū kāhu kī bāta suni
Lagē sarāhana tāhi
Avadha Bilāsahi enha paḍhai
Tau kā acaraja āhi.

Bhaktanha kaha haya bhakta eha
Rasikanha kō rasa rūpa
Jñānī kō hai jñāna yuha
Audha Bilāsa anūpa.

Bahuta kathā bahu grantha kī
Ukti anūṭha ananta
Paḍhihai jō sō hōihaya
Kahata Lāla gunavanta

Kāhē kō bahutai cahai
Pōthī bhāra anēka
Saba guna mē kina rākhiyē
Avadha Bilāsahi yēka.

Raghubaṁsī Raghubaṁsa jē
Lavakusa baṁsa prakāsa
Tinha kē Lāla bisēkha
Paḍhibō Audha Bilāsa.

Pōthī Audha Bilāsa kī
paḍhatahi sunata sohāta
Āe miluta hai bahuta tahā
Lāla bāta para bāta.

Kamalanha jō ruci māni ali
Taji taji āna nevāsa
Lāla rasika jē hōhigē
Paḍhihai Avadha Bilāsa.

P. 2.
Jō eha Avadha Bilāsa kō
Gāvai kari bisrāma
Tā kē hiya maha hōe kē
Sunihai Sītā Rāma.

Some one begins to admire things on hearing from some one else; what wonder if he reads them in the Avadha Bilāsa.

To the devotees, this unparalleled Audha Bilāsa is devotion itself, to the men of feeling, it is an embodiment of sentiments, and to the wise, it is knowledge.

He, who will read numerous stories from various books, and innumerable apt sayings, says Lāla, will become a man of qualities.

But, why should one so much like the burden of numerous volumes of books? Why should not one keep, for all these qualities, the Avadha Bilāsa alone?

Of all those born in the line of Raghu, Lava and Kuśa were luminaries of the line; in the Avadha Bilāsa, Lāla, you will read about them at length.

As you read the book of Audha Bilāsa, or hear it, you begin to like it, for therein you occasionally meet with numerous apt sayings.

As the black bee likes to dwell in the lotus, leaving aside other abodes, similarly those, who are men of feeling, will read the Avadha Bilāsa (leaving aside other compositions).

In the heart of him who sings this Avadha Bilāsa with ease, Sītā and Rāma will sit and hear (the Avadha Bilāsa).

Bacana racana muktā ratana
Kūda kalā itihāsa
Lāla hēma kutakā racē
Bhūkhana Avadha Bilāsa.

Ābhūkhana hai bhagata kō
Rāṃadāma guna hīra
Lāla alaṅkṛta dēkhi kai
Rijhata hai Raghubīra.

Grantha grantha para saba karata
Lēta grantha kī chāha
Lāla koī anabhava ......
Rāma kṛpā kī bāha.

Rāmāena satakōṭi hai
Rāmahi jānata tāhi
Jō kachu pragaṭa na gupatahi
Rākhata nāgari nāri.

Jāni būjhi nāhī dharata
Kaṭhina aratha kō daura
Rāma nāma jō jakta maha
Grantha calaya saba ṭhaura.

Gūḍha kāvya Jayadēva kabi
Tulasī Sūra bakhāna
Kēśava Bidyāpati bikaṭa
Lāla sarala mana māna.

Bātai saba Brahmāṇḍa kī
Racō Lāla mana āni
Bisva rūpa jē bisvamai
Audha Bilāsahi jāno

Adṛṣṭa bāta apaṭhita asṛta
Alapa jñāna jehi dēha
Tā kō Audha Bilāsa rasa
Aṭapaṭa lāgahi ēha.

With the pearls and precious stones of beautiful sayings, the *kūda* (*kunda* flower ?) of art and history, and the gold of *kūtaka* (probably *kūṭaka* 'tricky compositions' or *kautuka* 'pleasures'), Lāla has prepared this ornament of the Avadha Bilāsa.

This is an ornament for the devotee, being a string of diamonds of the qualities of Rāma. Lāla says, Rāma is pleased to see one decorated with this ornament.

All place one book upon the other (in the matter of authority), and take the shelter of books (in their reasonings), but here is Lāla's practical experience, for Rāma has placed his kind hand upon him.

The Rāmāyaṇa (story of Rāma) is a hundred-crore-fold, only Rāma knows it, as the clever woman gives out something, and always keeps it a secret.

Knowingly and wilfully, I do not compose in it anything hard to understand, so that my book may be popular at all places, like the name of Rāma.

For poetry difficult to appreciate, Jayadēva, Tulasī and Sūra are well-known; and, Keśava and Vidyāpati are simply prolix, while Lāla is as easy as one would like.

Lāla has commented upon all the subjects of the Universe. Whatever the Universe is, or whatever the Universe is contained of, all that you will find to be identical with the Audha Bilāsa.

To him, who has seen little, read little, and heard little, who has little knowledge in his self the pleasure of reading the Audha Bilāsa seems meaningless.

Paṇḍita hai sō jānihai
Kathā prasaṅga prabīna
Mūrakha mana maha mānihai
Lāla kahā eha kīna.

Tīratha avadha je avadha hai
Rāma avadha autāra
Taisō bhakthā kī avadha
Avadha Bilāsa apāra.

Dōe dēha hai Avadha kī
Sukṣima thūla prakāsa
Dhāma rūpa asthūla hai
Sukṣima Avadha Bilāsa.

Jō eha Avadha Bilāsa kō
Avadhahi jānai kōi
Tā kē sunatahi hōta hai
Avadha gaē phala sōi.

kai kou jānata santa jana
Rāma janāvahi jāhi.
....
....

Svāratha paramāratha bisavai
Bānī Lāla prakāsa
sō vai bātai kavana hai
Jō nahi Avadha Bilāsa.

I. 3.

Basīkarana mōhana kṛkhana
Sabadāvana guna nēka
......mantra saṁsāra maha
Avadha Bilāsa hai ēka.

Paranābhī basi mā hṛdaya
Madhyā kaṇṭhaki māhi
...hara pragaṭa su baikharī
Bānī cāri kahāhi.

He, who is wise, and is clever at stories and discourses, will know its worth; and, he, who is stupid, will think 'what has Lāla done here?'

As Avadha is the end of all the holy places, and as Rāma is the end of all the incarnations (of the supreme), so also the endless Audha Bilāsa is the end of the vernacular (compositions).

Avadha has two bodies obviously, *sūkṣma* or the inner, and *sthūla* or the outer, and the shrine is the outer one, while the Audha Bilāsa is the inner one.

Whoever accepts this Avadha Bilāsa with the belief that it is Avadha itself, he reaps the advantages of visiting the holy shrine by only hearing the Avadha Bilāsa.

Either certain saints know this fact, whom Rāma makes aware of it, ...

The message of Lāla covers both the fields: egoistic, and the altruistic. What are those subjects that are not contained in the Avadha Bilāsa?

The art of subduing, of alluring and of attracting, all these have many good qualities; but in the world of master-charms, the Avadha Bilāsa is unique.

Paranābhī dwells in the heart, *madhyā* in the throat, in . . . (?) appears the *baikharī*, these are said to be the four varieties of the speech.

Bhākhā ārakhī mānukhī
Baikhārī paramāna
Ārakhi kahiē Saṁsakṛta
Bhākhā mānukha jāna.

Suddha pragaṭa laukika bayana
Suni samujhai saba kōi
Kaṭhina sabda hai Saṁsakṛta
Bhākhā kahiē sōi.

Dēsī Prākṛta Saṁsakṛta
Pārasi yārabi jāna
Jaha jaha jākī Lāla kahi
Bhākhā sabahī jāna.

Ihai jāni bānī bimala
Kahata Lāla sudha buddha
Kaṭhina kābya eha Saṁsakṛta.
Bhākhā kahiyē suddha.

Gūḍhahi bhalī na prakāsa
Bānī Lāla biyāja.

....

....

Nava Bilāsa diṭha guna bhayō
Patita pāra kṛta kāja
Lāla sindhu saṁsāra maha
Avadha Bilāsa jahāja.

Sai paṇḍita sai sādhu kō
Jē tō saṅga bakhāna
Tā tē Avadha Bilāsa kō
Lāla paḍhē hoi jñāna.

Saṁbata sattraha sai barakha
Sudi Baisākha sukāla
Lāla Avadha madhi rahi racī
Audha Bilāsa risāla.

Baikharī of human beings has got the following varieties, *ārakhī* (S. *ārṣa*) or of the gods, and *bhākhā* or vernacular. *Ārakhī* is otherwise named as Saṁskṛta, and *mānukhī* as *bhākhā*.

Pure and open are the earthly discourses (conducted in *bhākhā*), which everyone understands when he hears them, while Saṁskṛta is full of difficult words. These are called the (two-fold varieties of) language.

Dēsī, Prākṛta, Saṁskṛta, Pārasī, and Yārabi, *i.e.*, the Arabic, know each one (of these) to be a language. Lāla says, wherever whichever (of these) may be in use, that is Bhākhā.

Being aware of this fact, Lāla uses, knowingly, the pure dialect (*i e.*, *bhākhā*). Difficult poetry is composed in the Saṁskṛta, while poetry of easy construction is done in the *bhākhā*.

It is not proper to make the secret manifest through language. ... ...

The new Bilāsa of substantial worth has proved to be a ship in the ocean of the world, for carrying the fallen across it.

As much as one is said to gain in the company of a hundred wise men, and a hundred saints, the same amount of knowledge he can also gain by reading the Avadha Bilāsa.

In the Sambata year 1700, in the auspicious bright half of Baisākha, staying in Avadha, Lāla composed the tasteful Audha Bilāsa.

caupāī

Prathamahi gura Ganapati sira nāvō
Puni Hari Hara Surasatī manāvō.

Jau ei kṛpā kaṭākṣanha hērē
Tau kachu jñāna hōi jiya mērē.

Brahmā Bēda ādi Mahāmāyā
Pranavō tāhi jakta jinha jāyā.

Sanaka Sanātana Sanayakumārā
Aura Sananda cāri parakārā.

Bāluka rūpa rahai Brahmagyānī
Jīvanmukta nirāabhimānī.

Ādi bhakti jē Śrī Hari pyārī
Bandava tāhi bhagati bistārī.

Pranavō Pāratha Prabhu kē saṅgī
Hari samāna bapu rūpa saraṅgī.

Bandau cāri mukti haya sōī
Pāvata bhagata avara nahi kōī.

P. 4.

Eka salōka sāmīpa sohāī
Eka sājujasārūpa kahāī.

Indrādika dēvatā jētē
Mō para kripā karahu saba tētē.

Hōhu dayāla dasau dṛgapālā
Grahu titha paya tata krama kālā.

Cāri khāni kē jē jata prānī
Siddha sādhu mūrakha aru gyānī.

Aṇḍaja svēdaja jarāeja jānā
Udbhija khāni e cāri bakhānā.

Avadha Bilāsa kathā mana mānī
Baranō tāhi dēhu mohi bānī.

In the very beginning, I bow to my preceptor, and to Gaṇapati; then, I pray to Hari, Hara, and Sarasvatī; for if these looked at me with kindly glances. some knowledge will grow in my heart.

I bow to Brahmā, and the Vēdas, and the basic Mahāmāyā, who begot the world I bow to Sanaka, Sanātana, Sanatkumāra, and Sanandana, the four sages.

Who knowing the Brahma, live in the guise of boys; who are bondless in this life, and who are free from vanity. Then, I bow to the basic Devotion, Śrī, the spouse of Hari, with considerable devotion.

I bow to Pārtha, the comrade of the Lord, whose body and appearance were similar to those of the Lord. I bow to the four-fold scheme of salvation, which devotees alone get, and none others.

One is Sālōkya, or attaining the same region with the Lord, the other is Sāmīpya, or attaining proximity to the Lord, the third is Sāyujya, or being one with the Lord and the fourth is Sārūpya, or being of the same appearance with the Lord. All the gods including Indra, be ye all kind to me.

Ye, all the ten regents of the directions, planets, *tithas* (*tithis*?), *paya* (?), *krama* (?) and Time, be ye all kind to me. All the creatures of the four-fold creation, *siddhas*, and the mendicant class, the foolish and the wise, I bow to you all.

Aṇḍaja or born initially in the form of egg, *svēdaja* or born of perspiration of the body, *jarāyuja* or born from the womb, and *udbhija* or plants, these are the four main types of creatures. I describe the story of the Avadha Bilāsa in my own way, give me voice (for it).

Nārada Byāsa Basiṣṭa bakhānā
Pārāsara Sukadēva sayānā.

Bhāradvāja rikhi Bālamīka muni
Kasi...pa Bisvāmitra Atri puni.

Gautama Saunaka aura Pulastī
Śaubhari Suragura Sukra Agastī.

Durbāsā Bhṛgu Pivana Sudāmā
Inha sabahinha kaha karau pranāmā.

Dhruba Prahlāda bhakti siratājā
Aṁbarīka Rupamaṅgata rājā.

Bali Jaḍa Bharata au Janaka Bidēhī
Bhagati Bibhīkhana Rāma sanēhī.

Baranau Hanūmāna dukha bādhaka
Rāma bhagata sabahī sukha sādhaka.

Arajuna Udhau Bidura samētā.
Rāmānanda ādi bhae jētā.

Bandau gōpa gōpikā nārī
Banakuñjana Hari saṅga bihārī.

Bidhu Maṅgala Jayadēva sayānā
Candrahāsa Hari kē mana mānā.

Jinha kē hiē Rāma bisrāmā
Tinha kē Lāla karata paranāma.

Paṇḍita jē bakatā kabirāī
Aru jō kathā sunaya mana lāī.

Tinha sō binaya karau kara jōrī
Suni mama grantha dēhu jani bōrī.

Jō kachu cūka mōhi hoi pārī
Tau tumha lījahu tāhi sudhārī.

Jo bigarō parakāja savāraya
Te apanō paralōka sudhāraya.

Nārada, Vyāsa, Vasiṣṭha, Parāśara, wise Śukadēva, sages Bharadvāja and Vālmīki, Kaśyapa, Viśvāmitra, and Atri,

Gautama, Śaunaka and Pulastya, Śaubhari, Suragura (Bṛhaspati), Śukra, and Agastya, Durvāsas, Bhṛgu, Pivana (?), and Sudāmā, I bow to these all.

Dhruva and Prahlāda, the crown of the devotees, Ambarīṣa and king Rukmāṅgada. Bali, Jaḍa Bharata, bodyless Janaka, and the devotee Bibhīṣaṇa, the lover of Rāma (I bow to these all).

I appraise the pain-ending Hanumāna, who is a devotee of Rāma, and a means for the attainments of all the comforts. I bow to Arjuna, Uddhava, Vidura, Rāmānanda, and all others who have been devotees.

I bow to the Gopas, and the Gopikā maidens, who roamed in the groves in the company of the Lord. Lāla bows to the Moon, the Mars, the wise Jayadēva, and the Candrahāsa, the pet of Hari, the persons in whose hearts Rāma abides.

To the wise men, the speakers, the great poets, and to those who hear this story attentively, I bow to them all with folded hands, that they may not drown my book when they have heard it.

If I might have committed any mistake, you will correct it. and accept my composition. One who corrects the mistake of another, makes his place secure in the other world.

dōhā

Gyānī guna suni kō karai
Paṇḍita karaya bicāra.
. . . Lāla bhulē nahī
Jhagarā karahi ki māra.

P. 147.

caupāī

Yā bidhi rājā rikhihi livāī
Nagara Ajodhyā pahucē āī.

Utima māsa devasa jaba jānā
Putra iṣṭa taba jagyahi ṭhānā.

Sāgara chīra jahā̃ ārambhā
Gāḍē jāe jagya kē khambhā.

Baḍē baḍē muni rikhi au rājā
Āe jurē jahā̃ baḍo samājā.

Bēda bihitu saba bidhi bistārā
Dāna diē kō ganaya apārā.

Kausilyā Kēkaī Sumānī
Bayaṭhē gāṭhi jōri nripa rānī.

Sundara jagya bēdi mana mohai
Tāpara agini dēvatā sōhai.

Aura jagya samagrīhī sājā
Tē bahutai lē bayaṭheu rājā.

Pañca ratana habi gabi hai jētā
Pañcāmṛta sāmīdha samētā.

Patra puhupa phala basana anēkā
Patra dhāta gandha bibidhi bibēkā.

Mōti mūgā kanaka anūpā
Pañca ratana ēi cuni rūpā.

Tila jau dhāna ghīva guḍa lēi
Khīra supāri hēma draba ēi.

Who would bother himself with the qualities of a wise man? Pandita alone ponders over these . . . it is not good . . either to quarrel or to make a fuss over it.

P. 147.

Thus, the king, accompanied by the sage, reached the city of Ajodhyā; when he knew the month and the day to be auspicious, he commenced the performance of the sacrifice, *Putreṣṭi* (for obtaining a male issue)

Where the sea of milk began trom, he fixed the pillars of the sacrifice. In that great congregation, all the great saints, sages, and kings assembled.

The king performed all the rituals as commanded by the Vēdas, and he gave alms to such a great extent that none can make a correct estimate of it. The king sat with his queens, Kauśalyā, Kēkayī and Sumānī (Sumitrā), having tied the ends of his garment to the garments of the queens.

The beautiful platform of the sacrifice attracted the mind; Fire-god was beautifully placed over it. The king had collected also the other constituents of the sacrifice in large quantities, and with these, he sat (to perform the sacrifice).

His collection consisted of *pañca-ratana* or the five gems, oblations, *gavya*, *i.e.*, the products of the cow, the *pañcāmṛta* (mixture of milk, sugar, butter, curds and honey) fuel for the sacred fire, leaves, flowers, fruits, various kinds of garments plates of metals, and many varieties of perfumes.

He collected pearls, coral stones, unique gold, (rubies) and silver, which constitute *pañca-ratna* (five jewels). Black sesamum, barley, paddy, clarified butter, with molasses, milk and areca-nuts, all these constitute the golden ingredients.

Dūdha ghīva dadhi madhu guḍa lahiē
Ambṛta pāca nāma eha kahiē.

Gōbara mūtra gaū kē hōī
Dūdha ghīva dadhi gabi kahi sōī.

Āvāhana kari kari jo bolāē
Pūjā lēna dēvatā āē.

Bājā bajata bibidhi cahu vōrā
Manu pāvasa gājata ghana ghōrā.

Sāthē sāta saekarē rānī
Gāvata gīta kōkilā bānī.

Nācata naṭī bhaī maga ṭhāḍhī
Dāmini sī damakata duti bāḍhī.

Ṭhaura ṭhaura guni jana lie bājā
Gāvata rāga nīrta kari sājā.

Bipranha Bēda paḍhē aru gāē
Mānahu Bēda dēha dhari āē.

Rājā tahā bhaē Daśāvantā
Muni Baśiṣṭa rikhi Śriṅgī santā.

Aura sabai muni sākala lēhī
Vai dou hōma tapasa saba dēhī.

Jagya raccha caudaha niḥpāpā
Tinha kō jagya bhītara lai thāpā.

Brahmā Bisna Rudara tahā sōhai
Indra Kubēra Candramā mōhai.

Sūraja Pāvaka au Dṛgapālā
Bidyādhara Gandharba bisālā.

Lōkapāla aru Baruna Ganēsa
Apa āpana disa bayaṭha sudēsa.

Puruba Indra Agini aṅganēē
Dacchina Jama nairitu Racha sēē.

Pachima Baruna bāebyan Bāyū
Uttara bayaṭha Kubēra sohāyū.

Take milk, clarified butter, curds, honey, and molasses these are called *pancāmṛta*; and if the mixture consists of the refuse of the cow, its urine, its milk, its clarified butter, and its curds, it is called *gavya*.

The deities who had been invoked, came to accept the offerings. In all the four directions, various kinds of instruments were being played upon, as though in the rainy season. heavy clouds were thundering.

Seven hundred queens together were singing songs in the note of the cuckoo. The nautch-girls, in the course of dancing, paused in the passage and the increased glow of their persons shone like lightning.

At places, skilled masters with the accompaniment of instruments, sing various melodies, that are being supplemented again by dance. The Brāhmaṇas chanted Vedic hymns in such a manner as if the Vēdas themselves had appeared in person.

There happened to be king Dasavanta (Daśaratha) and sages Vasiṣṭha and Śṛṅgī. While these latter performed the sacrifice, other sages took the charge of offering oblations, warming their body.

The fourteen spotless protectors of the sacrifice were brought in and put in position. Brahmā, Viṣṇu and Rudra were present there, and Indra, Kubēra and Moon-god attracted the attention.

The Sun-god, the Fire-god, and the rest of the regents of the several directions, and the great Gandharvas, Vidyādharas, and the Lords of the (fourteen) worlds, and Varuṇa and Gaṇeśa, everyone sat in his proper place.

In the east was seated Indra, in the south-east, Fire-god, in the south, Yama, in the south-west, Rakṣas (the demon who is the regent of that direction), in the west, Varuṇa, in the north-west the Wind-god and in the north, Kubēra.

P. 148.

Īsānē Śaṅkara sukhadāī
Brahmā sarga Sēkha bhna pāī.

E drigapāla nāma dasa āē
Puni navagraha bayaṭhē juhā̃ pāē.

Jehi jehi ṭhaura dēratā bhākhē
Tāha tāha bipra Bēdavā rākhē.

Joi joi nāma dēvatā hōī
Biprahi nāma dharata gae sōī.

Dēvanha kē ruci kō jo ahārā
Dēta gaē tinha kō byauhārū.

Kēsari candana phūlanha pūjē
Hōhi prasanya kṛtāratha dūjē.

Sila chamā khaṭa karmanha māhī
Tē sabu brāhmana ṭahala karāhī.

Padhai paḍhāvai dei aru lēī
Jagya karai karavāvai jēī.

E khata karma bipra kē hōi
Jāmaha ē khaṭakaramī sōī.

Putra sōi jō Bēda bakhānai
Gāetrī japa tapa brata ṭhānai.

Atharā Bisna bhagata jō hōī
Tā brāhmaṇa sama aura na kōī.

dōhā

Candaṇa phūlai ūkha phalu
Khā̃ḍa barai pai māhī.

Lāla bipra puni Bisnabā
Tā samu tula kou nāhī.

caupāī

Hōma karata santuṣṭa hutāsana
Bhaē prasanya jo putra prakāsana.

Dibya rūpa pāvaka adhikāī
Jagya purukha pragaṭē jahā̃ āī.

In the north-east was seated the auspicious Śiva Brahmā was given the heavens, and S'ēṣa, the earth. These ten regents named (above) came. Then the nine planets sat where they were offered seats.

Wherever I have named deities, at each of those places Brāhmaṇas were seated, who had knowledge of the Vēdas. Whatever were the names of the deities, the same were given to those Brāhmaṇas; whatever food was especially liked by those deities, the same was offered to these.

They were worshipped with saffron, sandalwood-paste, and flowers; they were pleased, and also grateful. Such Brāhmaṇas as performed their six-fold duties with a good disposition and with forbearance, were appointed to serve them.

Studying, teaching, giving (charity) and taking (it), offering of oblations, and helping others in performing sacrifices, these are the six-fold duties of a Brāhmaṇa. One who possesses these qualities is called a *ṣaṭkarmī.*

The same is the son who propounds the Vēdas, who repeats Gāyatrī, and who engages in invocations and penances, or else who is a devotee of Viṣṇu. None is equal to such a Brāhmaṇa.

Although the sandal-tree may bear blossom, and the sugarcane may bring forth fruits, or sugar may burn in water, there is none equal to a Brāhmaṇa who is devoted to Viṣṇu.

When offerings were thrown in the sacred fire, the deity who had the capacity to bestow upon one an issue, was pleased. Sacrifice appeared there with a divine appearance which was accentuated by the fire around him.

Adbhuta rūpa agni maha rājai
Kanaka thāra dou hātha birājai.

Tā maha sundara khīra ahārā
Lēhu lēhu kahi hātha pasārā.

Muni rikhi uṭhi ādara kai lieū
Ubhai bhāga kari rājahi dieū.

Śīsa caḍhāe liē nripa rānī
Dhanya dhanya rikhi kahi muni bānī.

Pūrana jagya bhayō jaba jānā
Dīnha dacchinā kari sanamānā.

Bhūmi bhōga bahutai diyo grāmā
Pāe parai saba kē nripa bāmā.

Āju bhaē saba kāja hamārē
Āvata hī rikhi pāe tumhārē.

Bipra kṛpā kari āvahi jākē
Pūrana hōe manōratha tākē

Jā ghara bipra dharai pagu āī
Tā ghara kīrati hōi baḍāī.

Bipra prasāda Indra bhae lōgā
Bipra prasāda putra dhana bhōgā.

dōhā

Banitā basana sugandha au
bhōjana gīta jo pāna
Mandira bājī Lāla kahi
Āṭha bhōga ehi jāna.

P. 230.

dōhā

Dhōtī bastī navalakā
Gajakaru nētī jāna
Bhāthī sōdhana dēha kē.
E khaṭakarma bakhāna.

His unique appearance shone in the fire; gold-dishes looked pretty in both of his hands, and in those dishes, there was good-looking *khīra* (a preparation of milk). He stretched his hands with the cry, "Take this, take this!"

The sages stood up and accepted it with veneration, and having divided it into two, they offered it to the king. The king and the queens placed it on their forehead and accepted it, and the sages declared, "Blessed are the king and the queens!"

When (the king) knew that the sacrifice was over, he honoured (the Brāhmaṇas) and gave them presents. He gave them many villages to enjoy the blessings of the earth. The queens placed their heads at the feet of all the guests, and said,

"Today, all our desires have been fulfilled, when, sages, your feet came to this place. In whosesoever house the Brāhmaṇas kindly come, his desires are fulfilled.

"In whichsoever house the Brāhmaṇas come and place their feet, that house is highly praised (by all). By having pleased the Brāhmaṇas, they have (in the past) become Indra, and by having pleased the Brāhmaṇas they have been blessed with issues and riches."

Maidens, clothes, perfumes, food-stuff, music, drinks, palaces, horses, know these to be the eight-fold blessings, says Lāla.

Dhōtī, bastī, navalakā, gajakara, nētī, and *bhāthī* these are said to be the six processes of bodily purification.

caupāī

Nētī ḍōri nāsikā pōvai
Dhōtī basana nīla mala dhōvai.

Navalī nala phērai ju uṭhāī
Udara madhya gura tē lakhi pāī.

Bhāthī karai nāka sura aisē
Dharai sunāra dhātu kaha jaisē.

Aicai ēka ēka svara chāḍai
Ati hī bēgi bēgi hãsi māḍai.

Bastī mūla dvāra jala karakhai
Gajakuranī gaju jyau jala barakhai.

P. 231.

Aba sunu prāṇāyāma bakhānau
Jōga grantha kē mana mata ānau.

Sādhai sādhu jōga jau kōī
Rahai dēsa jahā̃ dunda na hōī.

Sadā subhaccha rahai tā ṭhaurā
Dharamarāja kaha dhāvana daurā.

Rākhai saṅga ēkāī ēvā
Sārati samujhi karai saba sēvā.

Rahai jāe ēkānta bicārī
Jahā̃ nahī̃ bahutai nara nārī.

Chāḍai saba jañjāla samētā
Rahai sumaṭha suṭhi dvāra sakētā.

Nahi ati nīca nahī ati ũcā
Āsana saina bhūmi kara sũcā.

Prathumahi kusa tāpara mṛga-chālā
Puni kambala ūpara rudramālā.

Ati kōmala sama ruci sukhadāī
Padumāsana baiṭhē mana lāī.

Nēti denotes that process in which a rope is passed through the nose; *Dhōtī* denotes that in which (the outlet for) the filth is washed with a blue cloth; *Navalī* denotes that in which the intestines are moved in the belly—one sees this latter with the aid of a preceptor.

Bhāthī denotes that in which such a sound is produced by the nostrils as is produced by the goldsmith in the course of blowing the metal. The inhalation should be done by one nostril, and the exhalation by the other. This should be repeated in quick succession, and with a laugh.

Bastī denotes that in which water is passed through the anus. *Gajakaranī* denotes that in which water is blown like an elephant. Now I describe the *prāṇāyāma*, hear the same. I now recollect the opinions of the treatises on *yoga*.

When a mendicant performs *yoga*, the land becomes free from strife. In that land, good eatables are always available, and messengers of Dharmarāja are always on tour in that land.

He (the *yōgī*) should keep only one person with him, who may render all sorts of services befitting the requirements of the ascetic. The ascetic should make his abode in a secluded place, which may not be frequented by men or women.

He (*i.e.*, the ascetic) should renounce everything with its train of cares. He should live in a *maṭha* which should have a narrow opening. He should sit and sleep on the ground (which should be) neither at a very high level nor at a very low level.

He should first prepare a bed of Kuśa-grass, thereon he should spread the skin of a deer, and again thereon, he should spread a woollen carpet. He should wear a rosary of Rudrākṣa (probably in the neck). Thus, having prepared a very soft, even and comfortable seat, he should sit in the posture of the lotus (Padmāsana), with a centred attention.

Uṭhi baiṭhē ila uta nahi ḍōlai
Bala nahi karahi bahuta nahi bōlai.

Kaṭi aru grīva sīsa sama rākhai
Nāsā agra driśṭi abhilākhai.

Sūchama kachuka rākhi mukha āgē
Dēkhai tāhi palaka nahi lāgē.

Jaba lagi naina sajala bhari hōi
Trāṭika dhyāna kahata hai sōi.

Agya nāsa racchā kari tana kē
Ṭikā karai kapaṭa taji mana kē.

Jagya dāna japa tapa brata pūjā
Hōma pāṭha saradādika dūjā.

Jōga dhyāna au dānahu diē
Niḥphala hōhi tilaka binu kiē.

Prāṇāyāma karai tehī ṭhaurā
Aicai pavana dāhinē vōrā.

Iṅgalā piṅgalā karai bicārā
Bāē dāhina nākē dvārā.

Iṅgalā piṅgalā sukhamā nārī
Nāsā madhya rahata sukhakārī.

Dakṣina puṭa nāsā svara jānā
Tāhi piṅgalā kahata sayānā.

Bāē ilā jānīē sōī
Madhya sukhamanā nārī hōī.

Tinha kē tīni dēvatā gāē
Sūraja Candra Brahma tāhā chāē.

Enha kō bhēda gurū sō jānai
Jōtakha saguna sabai pahicānai.

Bhinna bhinna jau kahau banāī
Bātahi bāta grantha baḍhi jāī.

Khoḍasa bēra pranau mana māhī
Pūrata japai adhika kachu nāhī.

He should sit with his chest forward. He should not roam here and there. He should not apply excessive physical force (in doing the *prāṇāyāma*). He should not talk much. He should keep his loin, neck, and head in a straight line; and he should concentrate his vision on the tip of his nose.

Placing some subtle thing in his front, he should constantly gaze, without letting his eyelids fall, till the eyes are moisted. This is called *Trāṭika* meditation.

The tip of the nose protects the body. Having done away with mental deceits, he should place the mark on his forehead. Sacrifices, charity, invocations, penances, fasts, worships, oblations, reading of sacred texts, observing the second day of *Śarada* and other seasons,

Practising of *yōga*, meditations, and giving of alms, all these are fruitless without having made a *tilaka* (the mark). There he should practise *prāṇāyāma*. He should inhale by the right nostril.

Through the left and the right nostrils, he should respectively meditate on Iṅgalā, and Piṅgalā. Iṅgalā, Piṅgalā, and Sukhamā (Suṣumṇā) are the relief-giving veins which are found in the nose.

The sound that is produced in the right nostril is called Piṅgalā by the wise; similarly that produced in the left nostril is called Ilā. In the middle is located the Sukhamanā (Suṣumṇā) vein.

They are said to be ruled by three deities respectively; the sun-god, the moon-god, and Brahmā are ruling there. When distinctions between these are known with the help of a preceptor, the sciences of astrology and of omens become known.

If I describe the various aspects (of the *yōga* system), the dimensions of the book will easily increase. (Therefore I am brief here.) He should utter the *praṇava* sixteen times in his heart. Having done this he need not utter it any more.

Rākhai mūdi pavana nahi jāī
Causaṭhi mantra japai taba tāī.

P. 232.

Bāē svara chāḍai taba sōī
Bēra batīsa mantra japa hōī
Aicai pavana so pūraka kahiē
Rākhai rōki so kumbhaka lahi
Chāḍai tāhi so rēcaka jānī
Tāsō prāṇāyāma bakhānı.
Mantra sahita tehi kahata sagarbhā
Binā mantra soi jāni agarbhā.
Rākhai āni prāna bhū māhī
Tṛkuṭī dhyāna kāla bhau nāhī.
Prāṇāpāna karai gatirōdhana
Prāṇāyāma sōi aghaśōdhana
Sanē sanē sādhai ehi bhātī
Karu abhyāsa devasa aru rātī.
Pūrata tajata rōki jaba dharaī
Pañca sāta rasa rasa saba karaī.
Jaisē nayā ghōra gaja hōī
Dauraba cāla sıkhāvai kōī.
Ekahi bēra karai haṭha ṭhānī
Sō jōgī rōgī hoe jānī.
Prāna apāna bāyu sama dhārai
Nāsā madhya madhya sañcārai.
Mana aru pavana tṛkuṭa kari mēlā
Rahai unamanahi dhyāna akēlā.
Jōgī jahā karai nija bāsā
Dēkhai parama jōti parakāsā
Anahada sunai jōti mana lāvai
Ajapā japai bahuri nahi āvai.
Kāla karma kī kāṭaı phāsī
Sō jōgī kahiē abināsī.

He should keep his mouth closed, so that the breath may not escape, and by that time he should utter the spell (of *praṇava*) sixty-four times. Then he should leave the breath by the left nostril, covering a time occupied by thirty-two repetitions of the spell.

The process of inhaling is called *pūraka*, that of holding the breath, *kumbhaka*, and that of exhaling, *rēcaka*. These constitute what is known as *prāṇāyāma*.

When the *prāṇāyāma* is accompanied by spells, it is known as *sagarbha*. When it is devoid of spells, it is known as *agarbha*. The ascetic should store up his vitality in the eye-brows. By the meditations of the *tṛkuṭi*, there is no fear of death.

If one controls the movements of *prāṇa* and *apāna* (two of the life-winds) the same is *prāṇāyāma*, which is a purifier of sins. It ought to be gradually practised thus. It should be repeated day and night.

When inhalation, exhalation, and holding of breath are being practised, they ought to be done each five or seven times. They ought to be done slowly, as one (slowly) teaches a rough horse or elephant the art of galloping or trotting.

If one does it in one stretch by force, know the same ascetic to have become sickly. One should hold the life-winds *prāṇa* and *apāna* in equal quantities, and he should cause them to flow in the nose.

Having brought together the mind and the life-winds in the *tṛkuṭi* he should remain in a detached mood. with a centred meditation. Where the ascetic has made his abode, there he sees the dazzling ray of light.

One who hears the *anahada* (S. *anāhata*) sound, and concentrates his mind at the ray of light. and utters the unutterable and does not come back, and who breaks the tie of Kāla and Karma, he should be called an immortal ascetic.

Dina dina mana tana mē bilamāvai
Rākhai rōki rōki jaha dhāvai.

Tana cañcala tau cañcala pavanā
Pavana capala tē mana kō gavanā.

Mana kē calē bindama cali jāī
Binda calē bahu buddhi nasāī.

Buddhi gaē hoe sabai bigārā
Nityānitya bibēka bicārā.

Bayaṭhē bāraha aṅgula bāī
Nikasai dasa bhītara kō jāī.

Dvai dvai aṅgula ṭūṭata svāsā
Tā tē hōta dēha kō nāsā.

Sōvata calata aṭhāraha jāhī
Causaṭhi dhāvata mithu(na)nha māhī.

Sādhana pavana jōga karu ēī
Rākhai rōki jāna nahi dēī.

Sō jōgī jīvai bahu kālā
Dēkhai Lāla jagata kē khyālā.

Halukā alapa ahāra karāī
Bhūkhahi marai na pēṭa bharāī.

P. 233.

Ābila lavana khaṭāī chāḍai
Kēvala dūdha bhāta maha māḍai.

Jāgata rahai na bahutai sōvai
Baiṭhā rahata na phiratahi khōvai.

Rākhai bīda jatana kari lēī
Apanē jāna jāna nahi dēī.

dōhā

Kaḍuka kalaha maithuna saena
Tṛsanā bhōjana sañca
Ghaṭai ghaṭāē Lāla ē
Baḍhai baḍhāē pañca.

He should, day by day, pay his attention to the body, and hold it back when it goes elsewhere. When the body is tremulous, the life-winds will be unsteady, and by the life-winds being unsteady, the mind will be roaming (from one object to another).

By the mind being unsteady, the *bindu* or the seminal fluid begins to move, and by the moving of the seminal fluid, the intellect considerably diminishes. By the vanishing of the intellect, everything goes astray, and especially the power to distinguish between the eternal and ephemeral is lost.

The life-wind diminishes by twelve *aṅgula* (the thickness of a finger) by remaining seated, when you inhale, it diminishes by ten, and when you break your respiration, each time you lose by two. Therefore, the body perishes.

During sleep and during walk, it diminishes by eighteen, and by sixty-four in the course of running and in the course of sexual union. Therefore, you should perform this kind of *yōga*, *i.e.*, of controlling the life-winds. You should hold them and not let them go.

Such an ascetic lives a long life and sees the movements of the world. He should eat very light food, and that also in a small quantity; neither should he starve, nor should he fill his belly.

He should keep away the acid, the saline and the sour food; he should eat only milk mixed with boiled rice. He should (generally) keep awake, and should not sleep much. He should (generally) remain seated, nor should he lose by loitering. He should preserve the seminal fluid with care, and should not lose it in his knowledge.

Ring-worm, quarrel, sexual union, sleep, desire for eating, and storing these five become less by lessening and increase by increasing.

dōhā

P. 281

Nripa kaha asa āgē bhaē
Dātā yā jaga māhi
Lāla putra ehi bidhi diē
Tinha mē hamakō āhi.

caupāī

Aurau sunahu (?) jasa jākō
Śiva ausīna nāma rahō tākō

Jagya bahuta kīnhē tehi rājā
Padabī lēhu Indra kē kājā.

Karau na dāna kari dēva kahāvai
Sau jaga bhaē Indrapada pāvai.

Anta jagya rahe karata bhuālā
Bhau tehi dēkhi Indra kaha jvālā.

Liē Bṛhaspati gurahi bolāī
Hamarī anta avasthā āī.

Jōrē hātha dīna hoe bhākhā
Jau bala hōi kachū tau rākhā.

Suragura kahata calē taha jāī
Jagya karata tehi dēhi ḍigāī.

Rājā dayāvanta suni ata hī
Jīva dayā kachu karata hai tatahī.

Mai kapōta hoi calata hau āgū
Tuma saiyāna pāchu hoi lāgū.

Parihau jāe sarana so daihai
Mārata mōhi bacāe so laihai.

Taba tai kahu cha bhaccha hamārā
Rājā dēhu na karaba bicārā

P. 282

Pacchī hōi dōu uṭhi dhāyē
Rājā jagya karata taha āē

P. 281.

The king says, "In the past, such generous men have been in this world, that they have given their sons in this manner. What am I amongst them?"

Hear more about him. His fame was . . . His name was Śiva Ausīna. That king performed many sacrifices with the object of attaining the office of Indra.

(He said to himself), "I do not give alms. One who gives alms is called a deity, and by performing a hundred sacrifices, he attains the office of Indra. (The king with this idea commenced the series of sacrifices.) While he was performing the last of the series, Indra saw it, and was inflamed (with rage).

He summoned his preceptor, Bṛhaspati, and said, "The end of my life has arrived." And with joined hands and in a suppliant mood he requested, "If you have any power, do protect me."

The preceptor of the deities said, "Let us go there, and while the king is performing the sacrifice, let us move him (from the path of virtue). I have heard that he is of an extremely kind disposition, and that whenever any being asks him his protection, he is generous to him (in offering the same).

" I am leading you in the guise of a dove, and you follow me in the guise of a hawk. I shall fall before him (when chased by you), and he will offer me his protection, and will save me from death.

"Then you would say, 'This is my food. King, you should hand it over to me, without any hitch.' In the guise of birds, then, they both leapt up, and flew to the place where the king was performing the sacrifice.

Jhapaṭi saiyāna kapōta girāvā
Rājā kē kōchē maha āvā.

Tākō dēkhi dayā jiva āī
Racchā kiyō liyō hiya lāī.

Kahai saiyāna nṛpati taji dēhū
Bhaccha āju pāyō mai ēhū.

Eha ahāra pāvai tau karihai
Nā tau pañca jīva hama marihai.

Mārai pañca ēka kī racchā
Ehu kaho kauna dharma hai acchā.

Rājā kahai aura saba sajihai
Saranāgata āē nahi tajihai.

Ēka vōra saba dharamahi kījai
Ēka vōra jiva dānahi dījai.

Jīva dayā bahu bhāti bakhānā
Māsa ahāri ēka na jānā.

Diḍha mata jāni saina asa bhākhē
Apanō māsu dēu ehi rākhē.

Arē saiyāna bhalō kahi ētō
Dēhau māsu māgu cahai jētō.

Kāheko adhika lēba hama rājā
Dēhu kapōta samāna so kāja.

Rājā mana utasāha baḍhāvā
Apanā māsu utāri caḍhāvā.

Līni churā......jyau chōlē
Rāma Rāma kahi saba takā tōlē.

Taba taha guru kapōta hoi baisā
Palarā adhika adhika hoi taisā.

Brahmā Bisna Rudra tahā āē
Dēva danuja muni dēkhana dhāē.

Chīli chāli nṛpa māsu caḍhāvā
Dēkhi dēkhi saba acaraju pāvā.

The hawk pounced upon the dove, and brought it down. The dove fell into the lap of the king. Seeing the plight of the dove, the king felt compassionate. He offered it his protection, and clasped it to his heart.

The hawk says, "King, leave this dove, for only today I have got my food. After I have got it, I will satisfy my hunger; otherwise five lives including mine, will perish.

"You hereby kill five, and save one. Tell me, what good you are doing by saving the dove." The king said, "I will do everything, but I will not leave one who has sought my protection."

"Place at one end (of the scale) all the virtuous deeds you do, and at the other end the saving of one life (and both will weigh equal). Kindness to the creatures has been praised in various terms, none of which are known to the flesh-eaters."

Knowing the king to be firm in his determination, the hawk said, "If you protect this dove, give me your own flesh." The king said, "You have well said, I will give my flesh however much you may ask for."

The hawk said, "Why should I ask for more? Only give me flesh equal to the weight of the dove, and that will do." The king gathered courage and began to weigh his own flesh.

As soon as he took up the knife to take out flesh from his body, every one present there exclaimed, 'Rāma, Rāma!' On the scale, the dove sat, having become abnormally heavy, and the pan of the scale sank and sank, every time becoming heavier and heavier.

Brahmā, Viṣṇu and Rudra came over there: the deities, the demons, and the sages ran to see (what was going to happen). The king placed his flesh on the pan, having removed it from his bones, and everyone was struck with surprise when he saw it.

Asa kō aura karai kina kīnhā
Yā bidhi tana kāhū nahi dīnhā.

Jā tana sō tana lagē anēkā
Asva gaja nara kō karai bibēkā.

Jō tana bahuta tapani tapi pāyō
Sō tana para tana lāgi gavāyō.

Jō tana bahuta jatana kari rākhō
Rāja dēha durlabha bhai bhākhō.

Bhūkhana basana aragajā lāgā
Sō tana nṛpa tṛna sama kari tyāgā.

Sundara tana jāsō sukha mānī
Banitā bahuta rahata lapaṭānī.

Gārī dēhi risāe risāī
Kaikai tōhi kavana mati āī.

P. 283

Marō Maithirā duṣṭa kaṭhōrī
Srāpahi tāhi āguri kari phōrī.

Jinha kē Rāma lagē anabhāē
Tinha apanō paralōka nasāē.

Rāmahi bana enha dīnhā hōī
Aganahi kahana lagē saba kōī.

Srāpahi pasu pañchī sira tarahū
Rōvana marana karai gharabarahū.

Chaṭapaṭāhi jimi jala binu mīnā
Ucharahi mīna kōhi jala hīnā.

Sajjana sukhuda mitra rahe kōī
Girē pachāra khāe suni sōī.

Hinahināhi ghōrē dukha karahī
Naina nīra bhari bhari giri parahī.

Rāmahi jāta dēkhi pachatāē
Hāthinha tōri jajīra bahāē.

Who else would do it? Who else has done it? Nowhere has anyone given his body in this fashion, the body with which are attached so many other bodies, like those of horses, elephants, and men—who can count them?

" The body which was obtained after having done many penances, the same body the king spared for another body. The body which you keep with such a great care, and say that it is very difficult to attain the body of a king.

"And the body which was covered with ornaments, and clothes, and which was smeared with perfumed pastes, the same body the king gave away like a blade of grass.

The beautiful body from which numerous maidens derived pleasure, and therefore they clung to it. (Hereafter something seems to have been missed).

They in angor call Kaikēyī by evil names and say, "Kaikēyī, what didst thou think?"

" May extremely wicked Mantharā die!" They curse her by twisting their fingers. They said, " They, whom Rāma was not dear, have lost their heavens."

Pointing to Agana(?), everyone began to say, " This must be the man who sent Rāma to wilderness." Animals, birds, stones ('Sirā'?) and trees, all curse (Kaikēyī), and even the houses wept and lamented.

They were restless like the fish without water, as the fish toss up and down when water (of the tank) diminishes. There were gentlemen who were friends; when they heard the news, they fell aback.

The horses (of the king's stable) neighed and wept; they filled their eyes with water and fell down. When the elephants saw Rāma going (to the wilderness), they felt their helplessness; they broke the chains away.

Dārahi dhūri sīsa gaja dhūnī
Jiyaba Rāma binu bāta bihūnī.

Kalasā dhajā na dhīraje dharahī
Mahalanha para tē giri giri parahī.

Ṭhaura ṭhaura murachala bhaharānā
Girē kōṭa Rāmahi gae jānā.

Jinha jaha sunē tahā tē daurē
Kau ratha kau paga kau caḍhi ghōrē.

Panthahi rōki rōki rahe ṭhāḍhē
Calana na dēhi mōha ati bāḍhē.

Keu dē kṛyā paraga jau daihau
Māri hamahi āgē taba jaihau.

Keu mahārājahi kahi samujhāī
Rāmahi ajahu phēri lehu jāī.

Parajā pañca Rāma saga jaihai
Kāpara amala Bharata nṛpa kaihai.

dōhā

Lāla subhaṭa sēvaka kahai
hōē kōu mahārāja.
Hama na johāraba Rāma binu
rājai kīnha akāja.

caupāī

Dāsī dāsa kahai binu Rāmahi
Aba kō aura sabhārai kāmahi.

Gaḍhata paḍhata rahe dēta jo lētē
Taji taji kāja calē saba tētē.

Bhicchuka gunī kahai kahā jaiē
Rāma samāna dāni kaha paiē.

Lāgata āju Ajōdhyā kaisī
Sūna masāna bhayāvana jaisī.

They, excessively, threw dust on their heads, and said that it was untrue to think of living without Rāma. The jars and banners could not remain unmoved. From the (tops of the) palaces, they fell down.

At various places the *chaurī* came down, and the boundary-walls of the city fell down when they knew that Rāma had gone to wilderness. Whoever heard the news, he ran from the place where he was, either on a chariot or on foot, or again on the horse-back.

They barred the passage, and would not allow Rāma to proceed, so greatly they were feeling (his departure). Some sweared, "If you move a pace on, you will first kill us and then go forward."

Some requested the king, "Do bring Rāma back, even today, for the subjects and the gentry will go with Rāma, then, over whom will Bharata reign?"

The bolder of the servants said, "Whoever may be the king, we shall not bow down to any one except Rāma. It is the king who has done the mischief."

The maidservants and the servants said, "Without Rāma, who can take the management (of the state) in his hands?"

All those who were (doing any business) either making vessels, or reading, or were giving, or were taking, left their business and went to the spot.

The beggars and artisans said, "Where are we to go now? Where would we find a man as generous as Rāma. Today, Ajodhyā is looking as lonely and as dreadful as the cremation ground."

Keu kaha rāti dēkhi hama sapanā
Ghara taji taji sabahī calē apanā.

Khāna pāna sāhana sudhi bisarī
Paradē rahata nāri sou nisarī.

P. 284.

Rājā parē sōca kē sāgara
Rānī sabai bhaī dukha āgara.

Jñānī ēka Basiṣṭa sayānā
Rāmahi kahū gaē nahi jānā.

Sarajū birahini bhai dukha mānā
Rahi gai bahatē nīra jhurānā.

Thakē gañja kaṭarā bājārā
Uṭhi gai banika bhaī haṭatārā.

Sabakē sōca sōga bhae ēhī
Rahihai kavana bhāti Bayadēhī.

Sahasanhu laccha sakhī mē khēlī.
Kaisē bana Siya rahaba akēlī.

Keu kahai Rāma rahana kē nāhī
Sītahi bhalā chāḍi jaū jāhī.

Barajai sāsu kahai samujhāī
Sītā rahu gharahī jani jāī.

Kā jō Rāma pūta bana jaihai
Kusala chēma bēgē phiri aihai.

Jāta hai chāḍi bāpa aru maiyā
Tē kā kahahi rahaigē bhaiyā.

Dēsa bidēsa jāta hai kēū
Tiyau saṅga phirata kā tēū.

Sītā kahati māe sunu bātā
Tiya ko jīva pati kīnha bidhātā

Jenha patibrata nēma kari līē
Tē pati binu kaunē bidhi jīē.

Sēvā karai sadā rahai saṅgā
Agyā kabahu karai nahi bhaṅgā.

Some said that they had dreamt in night that every one had left his home (and accompanied Rāma), that he had forgotten eating, drinking and bathing. Even the ladies who were in *purdah*, left *purdah* and came out.

The king was amidst the sea of cares, and all the queens had become abodes of misery. There was one very wise man Vasiṣṭha who did not think that Rāma had gone elsewhere.

The Sarayū became deserted and felt the departure. Her water evaporated while she was flowing. The quarters, the streets, and the markets of the city looked worn and weary. The businessmen had departed and there was a complete strike (*hartāl*) in the city.

Everyone was lamenting, "How would Vaidēhī stay there? She has played amidst thousands of tens of thousands of playmates, how will the same Sītā live there alone?"

Some said, "Rāma is not going to stay there. It would have been better if he had left behind him his wife Sītā." The mother-in-law of Sītā forbade her (from going to the wilderness) and said, "Sītā, stay at home, and do not go (with Rāma)."

"How does it matter if my son, Rāma, goes to the wilderness? He will soon come back safely. He is going (to the wilderness), leaving his father and mother; vainly do they say that he will stay there.

"When somebody goes to a foreign country, does the wife also accompany him to that land?" Sītā says:

"Mother, hear me. For the wife, the Maker has made her husband her very life-spirit.

"A lady who has taken the vow of *pātibrata*, how can she live without the husband? She should always serve him and keep his company, and she should never disobey him.

Pārabatī Lachamī Brahmānī
Piya kē aṅgahi māha samānī.

Pati kē aradha aṅga rahai sōī
Aradhaṅgī kahiyata kinha kōī.

Jajña dāna tīrathahu Purānā
Banitā sãga lai karaba bidhānā.'

Bānaprasta gṛhasta āsramā
Banitā hī sō rahata hai dharamā.

Rāma calata Siya calī sabhāgī
Jaisē chāha saṅga hī lāgī.

dōhā

Pṛtama saṅga banabāsa bhala
Sahaba sīta bhala ghāma
Lāla piyārē piya binā
Indralōka kehi kāma.

....

Sukula paccha kī pañcamī
Phāguna māsahi jāna
Kiyē payāna Avadha tē
Lāla gamana mana māna.

Pārvatī, Lakṣmī and Brahmāṇī, all are one with the body of their respective lords. They live in the half of the body of their respective lords. Does not everybody call them '*ardhāṅgī*' or occupying half the body (of their lord)?

"It is enjoined (by the scriptures) that sacrifices, charity and visits to holy shrines should be done in the company of the wife. *Vānaprastha* and *Gṛhastha* stages of life are maintained with wife."

With the departure of Rāma, Sītā also made her departure as the shadow goes side by side (with the object).

Exile is a blessing (to a lady) when her lord is with her whether it is cold or it is sunny. Lāla says, 'Of what worth (to a lady) is the *Indra-lōka* without her dear lord ?'

... ...

Know the fifth day of the bright half of the month of Phāguna to be the day on which (Rāma), Lāla, made his departure from Avadha, of his own sweet will.

(b) Prēma Pragāsa

BY

DHARAṆĪ DĀSA

[Text from a manuscript completed on 21st date of Bhādō̃, year 1281 (Faslī), A.D. 1873, by Mahanta Rāmadāsa of Mājhī for Jānakīdāsī alias Baratā kuāra of the same place.]

Srī Gaṇēśāya namaḥ

Śrī pōthī Prēma pragāsa

Prathamahi paramēsvara kō nāmu
Jō saba santa karahi bisrāmu.

Alakha akhaṇḍita agama apārā
Jinha kīnhō eha sakala pasārā.

Sakala sriṣṭi kara bhōjan dātā
Juga juga abicala ēka bidhātā.

Sarba karma sō kartā karaī
Bāura nara aurana sira dharaī.

Jō jana tana mana prabhu rāga rātā
Tinha sō bilaga na rahata bidhātā.

bisrāma 1

Bīśambhara bisarāvai,
sō nara kūra kujāna
Jo kita sō cita lāvai,
pāvai pada nirbāna.

caupāi

Gura mahimā ati agama apārā
Gura binu būṛi marai savasārā.

Gura binu puni puni āvai jāī
Gura binu bhava jala parai bhulāī.

Gura binu pāpa pūni kara ās
Gura binu parai kāla kē phāsā.

Gura binu dēi (na) dēvā sēvā
Gura binu milai na mukti kai bhēvā.

Gura binu lōkācārahi lāgā
Gura binu saṁsaya bharama na bhāgā.

Translation

Salutation to Śrī Gaṇēśa

The book Prēma pragāsa (Light of Love) (begins).

First (let us utter) the name of the Almighty who gives relief to all saints ; He is Invisible, Perfect, Unfathomable (and) Boundless, He is one who has spread over all this (universe). He gives food to the whole creation, in every cycle of time He is Immovable, the Creator. He, the Doer, does all acts (while) the foolish people attribute them to others. The man who dyes himself in the Lord's colour (affection), from him the Creator never remains separate.

bisrāma 1

The man who forgets the Protector of the universe is an idiot and ignorant, (while) he who puts Him in his heart with regard obtains the place of Emancipation.

caupāi

The greatness of the teacher is unfathomable, unbounded; without the teacher one may get drowned in the world (-ocean). Without the teacher one comes and goes again and again; without the teacher one gets lost in the waters of existence. Without the teacher one expects sin and merit; without him one falls in the snare of Death. Without the teacher, one does not offer service to the deities ; without him one does not reach the secrets of Liberation. Without the teacher, one sticks to worldly affairs ; without him doubts and illusions do not go away.

bisrāma 2

Gura mahimā kō kahi sakē,
Gura dēvana kō dēva
Jō gura tattu lakhāiā
Dharanī sō gura sēva.

caupāi

Taba puni sakala sādhu sira nāvō
Jākō kriyā abhaya pada pāvō.
Jō budhivanta santa jaga māhī
Binatī kareū sakala jana pāhī.
Āpu ukti nahī ākhara kareū
... ...
Sō ākhara jani hāsa laḍāvahu
Jō laghu hōē samujhi sudhārahu.
Mūrakha kē mohi sōca na āvē
Hasē ki bilakhē jō mana bhāvē.

bisrāma 3

Paḍhata gunata sura sādhu jana,
khaṇḍita lēba merāi.
Sugharc hātha para pāthara,
mōla bahuta ṭhaharāi.

aslōka

Pañcavaṭī ca udayē purasya
śrīpurē madhyē ma tathā
Jaḥ jānāti caturasthānaṃ
dharanī tasya namaskrita.

caupāi

Harijana sēvaka jahā ke bāsā
Nāma ṭhāma guna karahi pragāsā.
Madhya dīpa mājhī asthānā
Surapura sama kē sarisa nidhīnā.

bisrāma 2

Who can describe the teacher's greatness ; he is the god of gods, O Dharaṇī, serve the teacher who has shown the quintessence.

caupāi

Then again I bow my head before all the saints, by their action (favour) I may obtain the place free from fears. Whoever are wise and saintly in the world, to all people I make a prayer I am not putting down my own ideas in these words . . . . . Please do not laugh at these words, whatever be deficient, please correct it after understanding (the same). I do not mind the fool ; he may laugh or be displeased, whatever he likes.

bisrāma 3

The gods, saints on reading and pondering over this will put in whatever is deficient; a stone placed on beautiful hands fetches considerable price.

śloka

Dharaṇī, bow to him who knows the abode of the wise in the middle of Śrīpura town at the entrance of which there is Pañcavaṭī (?).

caupāi

The servant of the people of Hari reveals the name, surroundings and qualities of the place where he resides. In the middle of the Dvīpa, there is a place Mā̃jhī, like the city of gods.

Cārihu vōra saghana amarāū
Tāla taḍāga kahō (-ō̃ ?) kita nāū.

Jahā̃ tahā̃ puhupa bāṭikā lāū
Byāpī kūpa tahā̃ bahuta badhāū.

Dēva (a-) sthala bahu dēkhie tahā
Harikō caracā nisu dina tahā.

bisrāma 4

Bastu kahā̃ lagì baranō,
jahā̃lagi hāṭa bikāhi.

Ēka devasa jaha dēkha,
janmo na bisarē tāhi.

caupāi

Śrīvāstava śrīpati kō dāsā
Karahī sahita parivāra nevāsā.

Ṭikaitadāsa tahā tapa-āgara
Kāetha kula mahimā ati sāgara.

Parasrāma suta tinha kahā̃ bhaiū
Sujasa bēli jinha basudhā kaiū.

Biṣṇu upāsika ati sura gyānī
Nirmala jasa cahu disā bakhānī.

Patanī tāsu birāmā māī
Purabila karanī bahuta kamāī.

Daā dharma diḍha dūnō prānī
Nirmala jasa cahu disā bakhānī.

Pāca putra bidhi tinha kahā̃ daiū
Pañcana māha ujāgira kieū.

Tina kē nāma kahata hau jānī
Bipra bēda mata kaheu bakhānī.

Tihakē nāma kahō (-ō̃) bilagāi
Jātē samujhi parē nara lōī.

Which place can equal it? On all the four sides, there is a thick mango-grove; the tanks and lakes, how shall I give their names. Here and there are flower-gardens planted, many wells and water-reservoirs have been constructed. One sees many temples there wherein people discourse upon Hari, day and night.

bisrāma 4

How far can I describe the articles that sell there in the market; whosoever has seen it even once, will not forget it throughout life.

caupāi

The Śrīvāstavas, slaves of Hari, reside there with their families. There (lived) Ṭikaita Dāsa, an abode of austerities and an ocean of the greatness of Kayastha family. A son, Paraśu Rāma was born to him, who spread the creeper of good fame on this Earth. He was a devotee of Viṣṇu and had knowledge of the gods; his spotless fame was praised in all the four quarters. His wife was mother Birāmā; she had earned considerable merit in previous births. Both the living beings were steadfast in compassion and virtue, their blameless glory went about in all the four directions. The Creator gave them five sons and made them prominent amongst the people. I give their names, (as) the Brāhmaṇa elucidates the doctrine of the Vedas. I mention their names individually, so that the people in general may understand (the same).

bisrāma 5

Lachirāma vō Chatrapati,
Dharanī Bēnīrāma.
Kulmani sahita pañca jana,
sādhu saghati bisrāma.

caupāi

Dharanī kē mana anubhava bhaiū
Prēma-pragāsa kathā eka ṭhaneū.
Sahijahi jīva upajō anurāgā
Sō antahu tē cihuki janu jāgā.
Utapati kahō kathā kichu āgē
Bhagti bhāva amī antara lāgē.
Saraguniā sarguna lai lāvē
Nirguniā nirgunahi sunāvē.
Saṁmata satrā sō cali gaiū
Tēraha adhika tāhi para bhaiū.
Śāhajahā chōḍī duniāī
Pasarī auragajeba dohāī.
Sōca bisāri ātamā jāgī
Dharanī dhareu bhēkha bairāgī.

bisrāma 6

Pukhya pañcamī sukula pacha,
pakha nichatra gura bāra.
Tehi dina kathā arambha bhau
mēhasi nagra majhāra.

bisrāma 257

Sāhasa tē sidhi pāiē,
jō mana niścē hōi.
Binu sāhasa Dharanī kahē,
sīdhi na pāvē kōi.

caupāi

Barisa devasa ehi bidhi cali gaiū
Mili mantrī rājē mata kieū.

bisrāma 5

Lachirāma and Chatrapati, Dharaṇī, Bēnīrāma; with Kulamani they were five men (who obtained) relief in the company of saints.

caupāi

Dharaṇī had an Experience in his mind, the story Prēmapragāsa occurred (in the mind). Naturally love came to the soul, it appeared as if it flared up inside. Now further I describe the genesis of the story, with devotion-nectar within (me). The devotee of the attribute-full (God) brings up the attribute-full while the worshipper of the attributeless talks about the attributeless. The Saṃvat year 1700 passed off, thirteen years over and above it have elapsed. Shāhjahān gave up worldliness and the call of the protection of Aurangzeb went round. The soul gave up all anguish and became awake, Dharaṇī put on the guise of a person disaffected from worldly affairs.

bisrāma 6

The fifth day of Pausha, in the bright fortnight, the Puṣya (?) asterism, Thursday; on that day this story was begun in the city of Mēhasi.

bisrāma 257

If there is a determination in the mind, one's wishes are accomplished by means of courage; Dharaṇī says, no one obtains accomplishment without courage.

caupāi

In this way, days and years passed off; the king and the minister together had counsel.

Kahe rājā aba cētahu rāju
Kuvarahi dēhu tilaka dida rāju.

Rāja kāja aba karī kumārā
Mai nija nāma japō karatārā.

Tehi dina kī bidhivata jata cīnhā
Sō bidhi sakala sampuraṇa kīnhā.

Brāhmana bōli gharī ṭhaharāī
Apanē hātha tilaka dihu rāī.

Pahilē nripati nripati āpu ca nāvā
Tau puni saka(la) śriṣṭi sira nāvā.

bisrāma 258

Citrasēna mahathā bhavō,
saṅginha māna baḍhāi.
Kuarī bhai paṭarānī,
Dharanī jana guna gāi.

caupāi

Jō jana kathā paḍhē mana lāī
Sumati baḍhē durmati bahi jāī.

Jō jana sunē sravana cita lāī
Tākō kartā Rāma sahāī.

Jō paḍhi ānahi kathā sunāvē
Tākī manasā dēva pujāvē.

Likhi likhāi jō ānahi dēi
Tiratha barata phala baiṭhē lēi.

Apanē hātha jē kathā utārē
Tākē bāḍhē gyāna apārē.

bisrāma 259

Rasika paḍhē rasa ūpajē,
mūrakha upajē gyāna.
Kādara nara hō sūruā,
jōgī pada nirbāna.

Pōthī Prēma pragāsa sampūrana.

The king says: 'Now look to the kingdom, give coronation to the Prince, give him kingship. The Prince will now perform the king's duties, I shall mutter the name of my Creator.' Whatever ceremonies were recognised for the day, they were all fulfilled. Having called the Brāhmaṇa and settled the auspicious moment, the king coronated (the Prince) with his own hand. The king made the (new) king bow first to himself and then to the whole creatien.

bīsrāma 258

Citrasēna became the Lord, honouring his companions, the princess became the coronated queen; Dharaṇī says the people sang praises.

caupāi

Whosoever mindfully reads the story, his good understanding increases and evil understanding flows away. The man who with his heart hears it, is helped by the Creator, Rāma. He who, after reading it, recites it to another, the God fulfills his aspiration. He who writes it out and hands it over to another obtains the fruit of (visiting) sacred places and of (keeping) vows. He who copies the story in his own writing, his knowledge increases limitlessly.

bisrāma 259

If the man of tastes reads it, he derives pleasure. The fools derive knowledge, the timid become brave and the *yōgī* obtains Emancipation.

The book Light of Love (is) completed.

(c) **Gura Anyasa**

BY

ŚIVA NĀRĀYAṆA

[Text collated from two manuscripts :—

MS. A mentions no date of writing but as colophon it has the date of transfer to Rāmsēvak Rām Mahant in the year 1307.

MS. B completed in 1290, Jēṭha, dark fortnight, 14th date, Friday ; given to Bābā Saburī Dāsa ; written by Ājōra Rāma.]

Santasarana

ṣantapatī jī sahāe

Sabada grantha Gura Anyāsa arambha hōta santabacana pramāna.

dōhā

Karatā sabha guna kāra kā
Gunakārana bhaubhāra,
Sriṣṭi-savārana cāriphala
Cālacalana bevahāra.
Caracā tākī jō sunai
Caurāsī sō bāca,
Gura bina sō nahi pāvai
Bina gura milata na sāca.

caupāi

Gura Anyāsa kahata jaba ānī
Taba gati mukuti hōta hai prānī.
Gura kē sabada pāi hoe santā
Bina gura sabada na pāvata antā.
Gura kē kripā te pari kichu būjhī
Bhau anusāra pantha paru sūjhī.
Kripā kīnha taba ādi kumārī
Kaṇṭhē baisi gyāna deti bhārī.
Gyāna hōta taba agama apārā
Taba Anyāsa kathā anusārā.
Sammata satraha sai ekānabē hōī
(E)gāraha sai sana paitālisa sōī.
Agahana māsa paccha ujiārā
Tithi tirōdasī sukra se bārā.

Translation

Refuge of the saints

May the Lord of saints help

The Book of Word, Gura Anyāsa, begins ; the Saint's word is authority.

Dōhā

The Creator of all qualitative things, the cause of qualities, the genesis (?) of existence, the decorator of the creation, the (bestower of) four fruits and the dispenser of worldly affairs ; one who hears discourse about him escapes the eighty-four (lacs of existences ?) ; without the teacher He cannot be obtained, without him none can obtain the Truth.

Caupāi

When Gura Anyāsa is recited, the living being gets deliverance. By obtaining the teacher's words, one becomes a saint ; without the teacher's word one does not reach the goal. By the teacher's favour something is comprehended, the path according to existence becomes visible. Then the primeval maid took compassion and sitting in the throat bestows weighty knowledge. Then unfathomable, unbounded knowledge comes and the *Anyāsa* story is begun. There was the samvat year 1791 and the Fasli year 1145. The month (was) Agahana, the bright half, the 13th date and Friday.

Tehi dina niramaya kathā punītā
Gura Anyāsa kathā sabha hītā.
Sāha Mahammada Ḍillī sulatānā
Kāsī,chatra Āgarē hai thānā.

dōhā

Tehi samai mō Sīvanarāena
Baṅgadēsa cali āu
Kaṇṭhē baisi Sarōsatī
Kathā Anyāsa banāu.

caupāi

Janmabhumī hai kanauji dēsā
Karma basī sē Baṅga parabēsā.
Tīratha paraāga subā jē hōī
Tehi kē amala Gājīpura sōī.
Gājīpura sarakāra kahāvē
Sube pariāga amala sei pāvē.
Jaharābāda paraganā āhī
Asakarana tappā tehi māhī.
Sē asathāna Cadavāra kahāvē
Sīvanarāena janma taha pāvai.
Janma pāi bhau gura kē māā
Taba Anyāsa asa kathā banāā.

dōhā

Āsapāsa Cadavāra maha
Gājīpura sarakāra
Bunda Naravanī kahata sabha
Bāgharāe kē bāra.

caupāi

Dukhaharana nāma sē gurū kahāvē
Baṛē bhāga sē darasana pāvē.

On that day the *Gura Anyāsa* story, sacred and beneficial to all, was composed. Shāh Muhammad was the Sultān of Delhi. Āgare (Agra?) is the place in the region of Kāśī.

dōhā

At that time Śiva Nārāyaṇa came away to Baṅga country (Bengal), Goddess Sarasvatī sat in (my) throat and I composed the Anyāsa story.

caupāi

The birthplace is Kanauj country, by the force of deeds I entered the Baṅga country. The sacred place Prayāg is the Sūbā (province), under it is Gāzīpur. Gāzīpur is known as Sarkār, it obtains orders from the Prayāg province. There is a *parganā*, Jaharābad, in it there is a *Tappā* (named) Asakarana. Its place is called Cā davār, there Śiva Nārāyaṇa was born. Having been born, he obtained the loving pity of the teacher and then he composed the Anyāsa story.

dōhā

All around Cādavār there is the Sarkār of Gāzīpur; the people of this place, the descendants of Bāgharāi, are called Naravanī (Rajputs).

caupāi

The teacher (of Śiva Nārāyaṇa) is known Dukhaharaṇa by name, by great luck one obtains his sight.

dōhā

Tinha kē carana ke cita dharē
Bhau Śivanarāena dāsa
Dukhaharana nāma kē sumiratē
pāvata niscala bāsa.

caupāi

Gura kē nāma hiā maha rākhī
Ehi bica santa sabhai kehu bhākhī.
Gura kē sabada hiā maha gaeū
Śivanarāena cali taha bhaeū.
Cali phiri kē dēkhata savasārā
Jānata ghaṭa ghaṭa gurū piārā.
Eka dina santa sabhā maha gaeū
Carcā sabada hōta taha rahaeū.
Caracā sunata bahuta sukha pāī
Śivanarāena suni mana lāī.
Sunata sunata mora mana patiāī
Dibbi gyāna taba cita maha pāī.
Gura kē caracā sunata punītā
Santa kahata gura nāma le nītā.
Sē suni sravana bahuta sukha pāī
Sunē dhyāna kari ante na jāī.
Kahata ki gurū bisna sama jānā
Jānahu aṁsa ēka nahi ānā.
Gura kē sumirata bisna sahāī
Binu gura dāā bisna na pāī.
Jaba gura dāā karata mana māhī
Taba sikha siddha hōta chana māhī.

dōhā

Jē pāā gura sabada tē
Sē kichu likhā banāe
Paṇḍita jana sē mīnatī
Bhulā māpha kari pāe.

dōhā

By meditating upon his feet, Śiva Nārāyaṇa became his slave; as soon as he remembers the name of Dukhaharaṇa, he obtains permanent abode.

caupāi

Keeping the teacher's name in the heart, in the meantime speaking to all the saints, with the teacher's words in the heart, Śiva Nārāyaṇa moved away from the place. He wanders about and sees the world, he knows that the teacher is dear to every body. One day he went to the assembly of the saints, there discourses on the Word were going on. On hearing the discourses Śiva Nārāyaṇa felt very happy and took it to heart. Hearing again and again my mind came to have faith and then in the heart I obtained supreme (godly) knowledge. The teacher's sacred discourse is heard and the saints always utter the teacher's name and talk of it. On hearing it the ears feel very happy ; on hearing meditation does not cease. It is said that the teacher should be taken as Viṣṇu, take him to be His part, nothing else. On remembering the teacher, one is helped by Viṣṇu, without the teacher's compassion one cannot have Viṣṇu. When the teacher becomes compassionate, the pupil in a moment becomes a *siddha* (perfect).

dōhā

Whatever I obtained from the teacher's words, that I have composed and written down ; I pray to the learned : 'may I obtain pardon for my mistakes'?

Sunata se sīvanarāena
Kahata se gurū hamāra
Paṇḍita jana sē mīnatī
Būjhaba ehī bicāra.

Jē paṛhē se to agama gati
Sunē mukuti kai rāha
Ura antara suni kē dharē
Bhau jala pāu nibāha.

Phēri na āvata jagata sē
Pāvata nihacalu bāsa
Kahata santa mana jāni kē
Sīvanarāena dāsa.

Subhaī khōje na mili sakē
Nahi pāē keu bāsa
Pāeu sīvanarāena
Chūṭi avari kī āsa.

Niraṅkāra kā bhāva asa
Calata dharē sabha aṅga
Sē nau barakha sunna maha
Kē hoe nāri anaṅga.

Jata andhī sama kandha hai
Bhāga bibhāgi bicāri
Sē taha hīna adhīna hoe
Jaba kahī baisata hāri.

Jōga jāpa jaha taha karai
Jaha taha mārata khāe
Kahi dēkhata parvāna nahī
Kahī rahai bhaṭakā khāe

Nāma marana savasāra maha
Kahi kahi bācata āe
Gura pratāpa tē Sīvanarāena
sādhu saṅghati maha pāe.

Siva Nārāyaṇa hears, my teacher speaks, my prayer to the learned is : 'keep this point into consideration.' Whosoever reads obtains the path to the Unfathomable, one who hears comes on the path of deliverance, one who keeps it in heart, after hearing it, is relieved of the waters of existence. He never returns to the world, he obtains the permanent abode. The slave Śiva Nārāyaṇa says so, having read the thoughts of the saints. Everyone is searching but none obtains, none gets the abode. Śiva Nārāyaṇa has got it and has given up the hope of other things.

The feeling of the Formless is such that one moves about endowed with all the limbs. (He remains) (?) in an empty space for nine years or has women and Love. The world (?) is as if blind, considering all matters. When at becomes defeated it sits quite humble and subdued. (People) practise *yōga* and mutter prayers at some places, at some other places they kill and eat. For this (latter) there is no authority; at places they suffer delusion. (People) come and loudly declare that in this world there is Name and Death. (This teaching) Śiva Nārāyaṇa obtained in the company of saints, by the grace of the teacher.

Ghara chāē adhiāra bhau
Ujiārē saba pāe
Nēkī badī ke kāranē
Sabha ghaṭa rahā chapāe.

Raṅga rūpa rēkhā nahī
Karata jagata ūjiāra
Sata gura milai to pāiē
Bina guru pāu na pāra.

Sē guna aparampāra hai
Sīvanarāena dāsa
Disṭi nihārē tāhi kaha
Pāvata niscala bāsa.

Nau nāma bhau ēka tē
Dasō nāma kē hātha
Sīvanarāena tōharē
Sadā rahō mai māth.

Sabada grantha Gura Anyāsa (gyāna dīpaka) sampurana bhaila.
Santa bacana paravāna, sabada kahē so māna.
Santa pāra pāra pāra pāra pāra pāra,
Caupāi aṭṭhāisa sau bāvana (2852)
Dōhā ēka sau sarasaṭhi (167)
Isloka 12.

The house being covered became dark, everyone obtains (Him) in light, (the soul) is enveloped in a body due to deeds, good and bad. He has no colour, no form, no lines (but) gives light to the universe ; one can obtain Him if one has a good teacher, without a teacher, one cannot find any clue. That teacher's qualities are unfathomable, slave Śiva Nārāyaṇa obtains permanent abode, having been seen by Him by a glance. From One, came about nine names, Śiva Nārāyaṇa says : " O tenth name, may my forehead be always in thy hand."

The Book of Word, *Gura Anyāsa* (the Lamp of Knowledge) became complete.

The words of the saints are authoritative ;
one should obey what is stated in the Saint's words.

The saints (are) across, across, across, across, across, across.

(In this book there are) 2852 caupāis,
167 dōhās
and
12 ślōkas.

(d) Yūsuf Zulēkhā[1]

P. 10 *Hijarī sana bāraha sai bā̃cā*
Baraneu pēma kathā yaha sā̃cā.
Aṭṭhāraha sai sattāīsā
Sam̐bata Bikrama Sēna narēsā.
Sattraha sai bāraha puna Sākā
Sattraha sai navvē īsā kā.
Sattāvana barakh bītē āāvū
Taba upajeu yaha kathā ka cāvū.
Sāta divasa mā̃ha kathā samāpata
Durmata nāmu raheu so sam̐bata.
Kieu tarana kō tēja umaṅkā
Sāthī kiyē chāḍa sabha saṅkā.
Bāē̃ ansa uṭha kē jaga māhī̃
Bharenha devasa aba kucha rasa nāhī̃.
Banā janama ko gōrakha dhandhā
Abahū̃ na samujhai yaha manu andhā.
Bāra bayasa ava tarana sohārā
Gayau bīta tīsara pana āvā.
P. 11 *Tēja nagārā kū̃ca kā*
karahu so citta sābhāra.
Agama pantha sāthī nahī̃
Kehi bidhi utaraba pāra.
Biradha bayasa mā̃ha kīnha bicār
Kehi bidhi hōī mōra udhārā.
Kahaū̃ tau tanta kathā ati sā̃cā
Jo Qurāna mā̃ sunā o bā̃cā.

[1]Text taken from the manuscript described in the Introduction § 6.

Translation

Page 10

When Hijarī year 1200 was read, I described this true love-story. Then it was the 1827th year of King Bikrama Sēna, and 1712th of the Sakas, and 1790th of the Christ. When fifty-seven years of my life had passed, I entertained the idea of telling this story. The story was completed in seven days. The name of the Sambata was 'durmata.' I indulged in the excesses of youth and leaving aside all cares, I made companions. Having arisen in this world from the left-side (of the supreme ?) I have completed my days, and now nothing substantial remains. The snare of Gōrakha is completed, and still my blind mind does not understand. The childhood and the youth have passed and third part of my life has arrived.

Page 11

Loud is the sound of the drum of departure,
my mind, note it carefully.
The way is unknown, and I have no company,
how will I complete it?

This thought came to me in old age ; in what manner shall I be redeemed ?

That is why I tell this most beautiful story, which I have already heard and read in the Qurān.

Sabha bhākhā m̐aha kathā sohāī
Baranaū̐ bhā̐ti bhā̐ti guruvāī.

Abarī au Arabī sura bānī
Pārasi au Turakī Nasarānī

Bhākhā m̐aha kāhū̃ nahi bhākhā
Mōrē ansa daiu likhi rākhā.

Sō aba kathā kahaū̃ cita lāī
Jehi tē̃ mōkha mukti hoi jāī.

Yūsufa nabī mudita jaga āvā
Tārana gana m̐aha canda sohāvā.

Jahā̐ lahi (ra) hā siddha avatārā
Sabha m̐aha rūpa dīnha ujiārā.

Kathā anūpa jagata m̐aha sōī
Prēma bhagati sata dharama samōī.

Yūsufa nabī anūpa jaga
Parghaṭa bhē sansāra,
Jākī kathā so tanta aba
Baraneū̃ tēja kartāra.

Jō yaha kathā sunai cita lāī
Nāsai pāpa punya adhikāī.

P. 12.

Bā̐jhini sunai so santati pāvai
Aggita niripa mā̐cha kara āvai.

Nirdhana hōe hōe dhana āgara
Nirguna sunai hōe guna sāgara.

Dukhī sunai tau sukha adhikāī
Bandī sunē mōkha hoi jāī.

Bichuṛai daī so dēya milāī
Rōgī sunai rōga hari jāī.

Nirdāī kaha dāyā āvai
Jōgī sunai jōga adhikāī.

This beautiful story has been said in all the languages.
and in various laudable ways :
in Ibarī (Hebrew), Arabī (Arabic), Suryānī (Syriac),
Pārasī (Persian), Turkī (Turkish), and Nasarānī (Christian).
But this has not been anywhere said in the vernacular,
and the same was left by the Maker to me as my share of the work,
therefore, I tell the story with all sincerety,
so that I may attain salvation and deliverance.
The prophet Yūsuf came to this earth joyfully,
as though he was the beautiful moon amidst the stars.
As far as there have been incarnations of seers,
the Maker gave him the most shining appearance.
The same story is unique in this world
which is rich in love, devotion and true religion.
Of all the prophets who graced this world
Yūsuf has not been equalled.
Now I describe his mystic (?) story
with the help of the Maker's powers alone.
Whoever hears this story attentively,
he destroys his sins, and adds to his virtuous deeds.

Page 12

A barren lady who hears it, gets an issue
who is respected by the kings (?).
If the hearer is a pennyless beggar, he becomes rich,
and if he is a man of no good, he becomes a man of qualities.
If a miserable man hears it, his share of happiness increases,
and if a man in bondage hears it, he is set free.
It brings them together. whom fate has separated,
and if a sick man hears it, the sickness disappears
If the hearer is merciless, he takes pity.
And if an ascetic hears it, his powers of *yōga* increase.

Kaisaũ bipata gāḍha jō hōi
Sunē kathā bidhi ḍārai khōi.
Sunai satī dina dina sata bāḍhai
Birahī biraha dīnha dukh ḍāḍhai
Pēmī sunai pēma adhikāvai
Paṇḍita sunai mahā rasa pāvai.

Jo koi sunai paḍhai likhai
Hōi siddha sansāra
Bansa sutana sukh pāvai
Dēya asīs Nisāra.

Kathā anūpa ihai jaga māhī
Dūsara kathā so yahi sãgha nāhī.
Nabī lāgi yaha kathā sohāī
Saraga lōka tē Daiu paṭhāī.
Ēka dausa Jibaraila jo āē
Hasana Husēna ko dukkha sunāē.
Mārinha tinha bairī nirdāī
Pānī bũda na dīnha kasāī.

P. 13.

Suni kai marana nabī dukha mānā
Rōē lāga dukhita hoe prānā.
Taba Jibaraila kathā yaha lāē
Āni aratha sabha bāci sunāē.
Jō imāma kaha ummata mārinha
Yūsufa bandha kũpa maha ḍārinha.
Kathā satta aba kahaũ sohāī
Jehi bidhi saraga lōka tē āī.
Cūk hōi tau lēhu sabhārī
Suddha asuddha so likheu bicārī.

However great may be the distress,
if one hears this story, the Maker reduces his distress to nothing.
If a lady devoted to her lord, hears it, her devotion increases day by day.
and if the hearer is away from his beloved, he sets fire to his pangs of separation.
If a lover hears it, his love increases,
And, if a wise man hears it, he finds great pleasure in it.

Whoever hears, reads, or writes it,
he becomes a seer in this world,
his family and his sons get repose,
so blesses Nisāra.

This story is singular in this world,
no other story can vie with it.
For the sake of the Prophet,
the Maker sent this beautiful story from the heavens.
One day, Jibrāil came,
and told the miseries of Hasan and Husain.
Their merciless enemies had killed them,
those butchers did not give them a drop of water.

Page 13

The Prophet was aggrieved to by the news of their death,
he began to weep, and his heart sank.
Then Jibrāil brought this story,
and having brought it, he explained its significance.
How they killed the followers of Imām
and how they inprisoned Yūsuf in a blind well.
The same true and beautiful story, I now say,
and also, how it came to this earth from the heavens.
If I commit any mistake, correct it.
I have written it after having considered the right and the wrong.

Baranau kathā anūpa aba
  Prēma bharī au sā̃ca
Mōkha mukata gati pāvahī
  Jōrē sunā au bā̃ca.

Kanaā̃ nagara jo Nūha basāvā
  Tahā̃ nabī Ya'qūba sohāvā.
Jaga mā̃ha lahā siddha avatārā
  Pūjai tāhi sakala sansārā.
Lauta nabī kai sutā sohāī
  So biyāha Isahāqa ke āī.
Bhē Isahāqa ke dui suta saṅgā
  Eka udara dui rabi sasi raṅgā.
Ēka Ạisa Ya'qūba so dūjā
  Tapa japa bidyā kōu na pūjā.
Mahā siddha tā kaha bidhi kīnhā̃
  Isrāīla nāma tinha dīnhā̃.
Upajē Śāma dēsa dou bhāī
  Rahē Kanaāna Ya'qūba sohāī.
P. 14. Bhējē tāhi so alakha sā̃dēsā
  Lāvai nigama pantha sabha dēsā.
Nīca ū̃ca kaha māraga lāvai
  Ōkara mū̃ha saba bhēda batāvai.

Karai tapasyā raina dina
  Tapa japa nēta au nēma
Jibarāīla āvahī tahā̃
  Āna baḍhāvaĩ pēma.

Sāta istirī sughara sohāī
  Bāraha putra daī adhikāī.
P. 331. So puni kathā ahai bistārā
  Kahaũ kathā Yūsufa kara sārā.

I now describe the unique story,
which is full of love, and is most true.
He attains salvation and deliverance,
who hears and reads it.

In the city of Kanaā̃ (Canaan), which was founded by Nūha,
there lived the good prophet Ya'qūba.
He was in this world, the incarnation of a seer,
he was worshipped as a god by the whole world.
The prophet had a daughter, Lūt by name,
she came to Ishāq in marriage.
Ishāq was blessed with twin-sons,
(as though) the sun and the moon were born together.
One was Aisa and the other was Ya'qūb,
and none could vie with them in the matter of meditation, invocation, or knowledge.
The Maker made them great seers,
and Isrāil was the man who gave them names.
Both the brothers were born in the country of Śāma (Syria)
and Ya'qūb remained well in Kanaā̃ (Canaan).

Page 14

The Lord used to send through him (Ya'qūb) the divine message. He brought the whole country to the divine path. He brought the high and low to the right path. His mouth emitted all the mystries. All day and night he indulged in meditation, and invocation, and followed a regular course of life. Jibrāil used to visit his place, and whenever he reached there, he would accentuate the divine love. (Ya'qūb had married) seven beautiful wives, who gave birth to twelve sons.

Page 331

That story is, again, a long one,
I tell the essence of the story of Yūsuf.

Dasaẽ barasa āe jamarājū
Yusūfa nabī prāna kē kājū.

Kahā alakha jō agyā kīnhā̃
Cahaũ parāna tōra maĩ līnhā̃.

Yūsufa kahā jo agyā hōī
Sō sabha lēū̃ sīsa para sōī.

Dēkhi lēũ maĩ darasa Zulēkhā
Taba hama (?) karahu jo āvai lēkhā.

Taba jamarāja kahā yaha bātā
Agyā nātha lakhau mukha rātā.

Aba tuma tajahu pēma vahi kērā
Karahu pema jō karahi nibērā.

Bahuta bhā̃ti binatī kai hārā
Pāvā na Zulēkhā rūpa tihārā.

Yūsufa cahā bahuta
Lakhai Zulēkhā rūpa
Pai Jamrāja na mānā
Agyā alakha anūpa.

Jaba lahi āī Zulēkhā pāsā
Taba lahi phūla gayau nija bāsā.

Āī nāra jo piu kē tīrā
Dēkhai parā jo sūna sarīrā.

Puni nihāri Yūsufa kaha dēkhā
Raheu na rūpa raṅga nahi rēkhā.

Mū̃dē nayena khulaī aba nāhī
Bayena harē mukha bōlata nāhī.

P. 332

Hātha pā̃ũ mukha saravana nāsā
Saba tana harata kiē jasa māsā.

Sūna sarīra parā bina jīū
Gā ṭhaga māri dēkhi mukha pīū.

In the tenth year, Death (Jamarāja) came for the life of prophet Yūsuf.
He announced the will of God, and said, " I want to take your life."
Yūsuf said, " Whatever may be your command I will obey it.
Only I want first a glimpse of Zulēkhā,
Then you may do whatever is proper."
Then, Jamarāja said,
" Accept the Lord's will with a brave face.
Now, leave the affection of that lady, and engage in the love that offers salvation."
Yūsuf requested for a glimpse of Zulēkhā in various terms,
but could not see your face, Zūlēkhā.' Yūsuf earnestly tried to see the face of Zūlēkhā,
but Jamarāja did not allow him,
for such was the firm command of the Lord.
Before Zūlēkhā came to his side the smell of the flower had departed from the flower (*i.e.*, the life-spirit had departed from the body).
When the lady came to the side of her lord, she looked at the dead body ; she again closely saw Yūsuf and found there neither the beauty, nor the charming complexion, nor again the beautiful lines on the face.
The eyes were closed ; they would not open.
The voice had departed the mouth would not speak.

Page 332

The hands, the feet, the ears and the nose, the whole body was as if mere flesh.
The empty body lay there life-less.
She was thunderstruck to see the face of her lord.

Dhasaka āki hie māhi samānā
Gaeu chāṛa jasa dēha te prānā.
Murachi rahī nārā jasa phirī
Raheu na cēta hareu jaba sirī.
Nāri dēkhi piu kara tana sūnā
Binā parāna sabha piṇḍa bihūnā.

Kaun haṁsa saravara hateu
Kehi disa gayeu parāi
Jehi bina sūna sarīra bhai
Kāhū na kahā so hāi.

Parī Zulēkhā hoi bina jīū
Bahuri na dēkhā āpana pīū.
Taba nahalāi sāja sabha kīnhā
Laikai saũpi chāra kaha dīnhā.
Chāra milāi so chāra uṛāvā
Thātī saũpi lōka paha āvā.
Jō jākara tehi saũpā sōī
Sāthī saṅgha rahā nahi kōī.
Tīna dausa dukha raheu apārā
Rahī Zulēkhā nathī bekarārā.
Piū kōpa kucha jānata nāhī
Rahī so nāri sūkhi paṭa māhī.
Tisarē dausa bhōra hoi gaeū
Taba puni cēta Zulēkhā bhaeū.

P. 333. *Dēkhā khōli naena cahū ōrā*
Kahā ke āja bhaeu kasa bhōrā.
Piu jāgata taba mōhī jagāvai
Āja saṅghī kahū disṭa na āvai.
Aba maī āja bhōra kai jāgī
Gaeu pīu kasa agasara bhāgī.
Piu kara mukha nahi dēkhaū ājū
Mohī taja kabahū karata na kājū

Shock violently struck her heart and it seemed as
though the life had also departed from her body.
As she turned, she swooned ;
she lay unconscious, and the radiance of her face
departed.
The lady saw the body of her lord lying lifeless.
Without life, the whole body lay empty.
" Which goose was in this lake, and to what direction
has it flown away, without whom the body is empty ?
Alas, no one tells me that."
Zulēkhā fell unconscious, and did not see her lord again.
They washed the dead body of Yūsuf,
and they adorned it well.
Then they delivered it to the earth.
They mixed that structure of dust with the dust.
And having thus returned the pledge
they came back.
They handed it back to one whose it was
and no companion accompanied him.
For three days, Zulēkhā was extremely pained,
and she could not be made to understand (the real
state of things).
She did not know the reason of her lord's displeasure,
and she withered away within doors.
The third day in the morning
Zulēkhā was restored to consciousness.

Page 333

She opened her eyes and saw about her,
and said, " Of what type is today's morning?
When my lord got up, he would wake me up,
but today, my mate does not come before my eyes.
Today I got up very early,
still, how is it that my lord has left all alone ?
Today, I do not see the face of my lord,
he would never do anything without me.

Jaba laga rahaũ sēja para
Kantha na chāṛahi mōhī.
Aba rāja āja kahā̃ gaeu
Lāla so mōhi bichōhi.

Kahā saṅghī vai saraga sidhārē
Tumakā̃ biraha āgi maha jārē.
Suni yaha bāta so khāi pachārā
Phira phira sīsa bhūmi para mārā.
Jahā̃ so pīu hōi nihicintā
Tahā̃ lai calahu jahā̃ mora mintā.
Calī sãghai sãgha biākula nārī
Jahā̃ kantha sūnē sō nārā.
Tehi kē ḍehara jāi sira nāvā
Pirathama kēsa tōri chitarāvā.
Chitarāesi mōtina kē hārā
Jūrā ṭūka ṭūka kai ḍārā.
Bāra khasōṭi tōri natha ḍārā
Abharana tōri bhūsahē sĩgārā.
Cūrī phōri sīsa taba phōrā
Chāra milāi dīnha vahi cūrā.

P. 334

Parī ḍhēra para chāra uṛāvahi
Bipata bipata mukha bayena sunāvai.

Nayena kāḍhi dō līnhesi
dīnhesi ḍhēra para ḍāri.
Jehi naenani piu tōhi lakheũ
dēkhaũ kāhi nihāri.

Kahā kantha tuma kaharā̃ gaeā̃
Naena baēna mukh sūna sabha bhaeū
Gāta gulāba dēkhi murajhāī
Sō tana chāra līnha aba khāī.

So long as I would remain in bed,
my lord would not leave me.
But, where has my King, my love, now gone,
having left me here?"
Her companions said that he had gone to the next world,
having scorched you in the fire of separation.
When she heard this news, she fell aback.
She would strike her head against the earth, again and again, and say,
" Wherever may that care-free lord of mine be,
Take me to that place, where my friend is."
Along with her, the sorrowful maidens went
where the dead body of her lord lay.
On the threshold of the tomb she placed her forehead,
and first of all she let her hair loose,
and she scattered the necklaces of pearls,
and then broke her braid of hair into pieces.
She tore the hair and broke the nose-ring,
and having broken her ornaments, she undid her toilet.
Having broken her bracelets, she broke her head
And threw those pieces of bracelets in the dust.

Page 334

She lay on the tomb and scattered dust
and cried, " I am in distress, I am in distress!"
She took out both her eyes,
And threw them over the tomb and said,
" These eyes with which, my lord, I looked at you,
whom should I now look with them?
What, my lord, where have you gone?
All your eyes and your mouth are lifeless.
Seeing the beauty of your body, roses drooped,
but now the same body is being eaten away by the earth.

Jehi mukha bōlahu amrita bānī
Amrita bōla vai kahā̃ herānī.
Nita mō para tuma karata jo dāyā
Kasa aba lā'la bhaeu niramāyā.
Maī pāpina tumha saṅgha na lāgī
Ahaū̃ karam kī sadā̃ abhāgī.
Mōhi chāṛi kita kīnha sidhārī
Naena ōṭa nā karata piyārī.
Jaba jamarāja parāna tora līnhā
Niṭhura lā'la mōhi khabari na dīnhā.
Maī jama tē asa karati nihōra
Lēhu lā'la sā̃gha prāna so mōrā.
Ēkahu chana nā mōhi bisārehu
Calata bāra kasa mōhi na pukārehu.

Naena ōṭa kahū̃ hōta raheu
Mōhi tē agyā lēhu
Aisē gaenha bidēsa kāha
Mōra na khōja karēhu.

P. 335

Cālisa barasa jo jōga kamāvā
Taba prītama maī tuma kā̃ pāvā.
Daraba aratha sabha dīheū luṭāī
Jōbana rūpa anūpa gā̃vāī.
Kīnha dayā taba alakha gosā̃ī
Dīnhā̃ rūpa soī sukha māhī.
Taba mahimā̃ maī tōra na jānī
Nisa dina rahiū̃ hiē abhimānī.
Sō aba kantha kahā̃ tohi pāyaū̃
Carana lāi sira tō̃hi manavō̃.
Tumha nita karahu mōra manuhārī
Maī nā karaū̃ kucha kāna tumhārī.

Your mouth would emit words like nectar,
but where have now those nectar-like words gone ?
You would always love me,
then, how is it, my lord, that you have become pitiless ?
I, sinner, did not accompany you (to the next world)
I have always been unfortunate.
Leaving me alone, where have you gone?
You would never let me be away from your sight.
When Death (Jamrāja) took away your life,
cruel lord, you did not inform me, for otherwise
I should have strongly urged him
that he should have taken my life also along with your life, my lord.
You never forgot me for a moment,
why did you not call me when you were departing (for the next world)?
Whenever you would go anywhere beyond the range of my sight, you would always take my permission.
But this time you went to a foreign land in a singular fashion, for you did not even care for me.

Page 335

When I had practised *yōga* for full forty years,
my dear. then it was that I got you.
When I had squandered all my fortunes,
and wasted my youth and beauty unequalled,
then it was that the Unseen took pity
and bestowed on me that beauty (of yours), amongst rejoicing.
Then I did not know your virtues,
and all day and night, I was haughty.
Now, my dear, where should I get you
that I may make you agreeable, by placing my head at your feet.
You would always beseech me,
but I would never lend my ear's to your request.

Kā aba karahū manāvõ kaisē
Binatī karahū kīnha tumha jaisē.
Tumha sāī maī cērī tōrī
Kā aba karahū āeū mati thōrī.
Nita sarīra rākheū tore caranā
Kā aba karahū daī kara karanā.
Sāta barasa bāda rākheū
Lāeu dōkha na mōhi
Auguna mōra chapāeu
Kaheu na kachu tuma mōhi.
Sāta barasa rākheū bāda māhī
Mana māha rōsa kiheu kucha nāhī.

P. 336
Calata bara torā rūpa na dekheū
Bacana na suneu na naena bisēkheū.
Sō lā'lana taji rahē abhāgī
Gaē lā'la maī sōi na jāgī.
Jaba tōhikā bāhara baharāī
Bairini nīda kahā tē āī.
Dekheū jāgi mādira torā sūnā
Nagara kōṭa ghara bhaeu bihūnā.
Āehu phūla chāṛi phulavārī
Kāṭa raheū bāga mā chāṛī.
Gāeu kantha sō bēgi so bhāgā
Pāchē raheu kalaṅka so lāgā.
Dēhu utara mōhi kantha sohāī
Phāṭai bhumi aba jāyū samāī.
Yaha kalaṅka aba dēhu miṭāī
Uṭhi kai lā'la lēhu sāgha lāī.
Aisā ratana milā jaga,
Chāra samāneu āi
Dhrika jīvana jō lā'la bina
Jaga mā jiyata rahāi.

What should I do now? How should I now make you agreeable?
I now request you as you had previously done.
You are my lord, and I am your bond-maid,
what should I do now? I have little understanding.
Ever did I lay my body at your feet,
what should I do now against the will of the Lord?
I kept you in captivity for full seven years,
but you did not blame me.
You would screen my evil doings,
and never chide me for them.
I kept you in captivity for seven years,
still you did not at all take it ill.

Page 336

At the time of your departure, I did not see your face,
nor did I hear your voice, nor did I see your eyes.
However, you forsook this unfortunate woman,
my lord, you went, and I did not wake up.
That sleep of mine which sent you out,
whence did that enemy sleep come?
When I woke up, I found thy temple lonely,
and the walls of the city, the dwelling, and all else deserted.
Flower, you came here, leaving the flower-bed;
I was a thorn scattered in the garden.
The Lord (the flower) disappeared immediately
while I, a dark spot, lagged behind.
Answer me, my beautiful lord,
may the earth split and I go inside it!
Wipe off this blemish upon me,
and get up and take me with you, my Love.
I got such a gem in this world,
but ultimately that was mixed with the dust;
Cursed be the life that even without the lord
continues to exist in this world.

Yaha ghara bāra so dēsa tumhārā
Bhaeu sūnu sabha jaga ādhiyārā.
Kauna batāihi bhēda karama thā
Bhūlē kauna dekhāehi panthā.
Kō tuma bina yaha pahāra uṭhāihi
Nēma dharama dina dina adhikāī.

P. 337

Aba tumha asa jaga upajē nāhī
Kauna so karī dukhī parachāhī.
Tumha samāna jaga phērī na āī
Kō asa rūpa gyāna budhi pāī.
Nibharama nīda raheu piu sōī
Nāri sovati cētā nā kōī.
Tumha nihacinta bhaeu piu jāī
Sōca hamāra tajeu sukhadāī.
Sahī lōka hai yaha sansārā
Tumha bina kōu na ahai hamārā.
Kehikā dēkhi mana hulasē piū
Tirakha bujhāi piyāsē jiū.

Vahai basanta vahi pāvasa
vahai phūla phala sōi
Sabha apanē ritu dēkhaba,
tumhaī na dēkhī kōi

Vahai mādira ō saravara tīrā
Karahi dhamāra sadā jehi tīrā.
Vahai phūla phūlai cahū ōrā
Vahi cāṭaka rāga khañjana mōrā.
Vahai pavana jō phira phira āvae
Vahai dausa vahi raini dekhāvae.
Eka na tumha jehi bina sansārā
Hoigā tīna bhuvana ādhiyārā.

This household and this country of yours,
all, are deserted, and the world looks gloomy.
Who will now tell (the world) the secrets of Providence,
and who will now guide (it) when it has forgotten the right path.
Who will now, without you, raise this mountain (of duties),
And who will without you lead a regular course of life day by day ?

Page 337

Now none will be born in this world like you.
And, who will now give shelter to the suffering ?
None will again come to this world, who like you,
will get such a good knowledge and understanding.
You were sleeping soundly ;
nobody awakened the wife who was asleep.
You have grown careless since you went
and you have forgotten my reposeful memory.
This world is the real world,
but in your absence, nobody is mine.
Whose sight, my dear, will gladden my heart now
that may quench a thirsty man's thirst ?

Spring is the same, and the same the Rainy season,
the same are the blossoms, and the same the fruits,
all will appear in their respective seasons,
but none will see you.

The same is temple, the same the bank of the lake
on whose banks we played naughtily.
The same flowers even now blossom on all sides ;
the same is the colour of the cātaka and the peacock.
The same wind blows again and again,
the same days and the same nights even now appear.
You alone are not here, for which reason this world,
and in fact all the three worlds look dark and dreary.

Vahi taravara vahi lāta sohāvana
Bhāvai na eka binā mana bhāvana.

P. 338

Eka dina hateu sobhāga sohāvā
Jehi dina tōhi kaha Nāyaka lai āvā.

Bhaī dhūma śabha Misira ke dēsā̃
Uṭhi dhāvā sabha raṅka narēsā̃.

Paṭhaeu Nīla karai aśanānā̃
Nara narēsa sabha dēkhi lobhānā̃.

Eka dina āja so dekheū̃,
sō mukha chāra chipāna,
Kā bhā rūpa anūpa vaha
jehi sansāra lobhāna.

Sapanē dēkhi bimōheū̃ tō̃hī
Upajā biraha tēja lakhi tō̃hī.

Āihū̃ Misira kantha tōhi lāgī
Kaheū̃ ki kā gūna kīnha abhāgī.

Pēma hamāra sā̃ca bidhi kīnhā̃
Pāhana sarūpa so hamakā̃ kīnhā̃.

Jaba prītama hamasē̃ mukha mōrā
Jīvana bhaeu darasa lakhi tōrā.

Cālisa barasa jōga mā̃ kīnhā̃
Suni kai nāū̃ sabhai kucha dīnhā̃.

Jaba torā nāu sunāvai kōī
Pāvai lākha dēū̃ jō hōī.

Bīsa barasa raheū̃ darasa adhārā
Bīsa barasa suni nāma sā̃bhārā.

P. 339.

Aba torā darasa harā bhuī mā̃hī
Nāū̃ tumhāra sunaba aba nā̃hī.

Dēkheū̃ (na?) darasa sunahū̃ nahī nāū̃
Kehi ke adhāra rahaū̃ yahi ṭhāū̃.

The same are the trees, the same the beautiful creepers
but none attracts me without the charming one.

Page 338

One day I was blessed with good fortune, the day on which Nāyak (God?) brought you (to me). There was rejoicing all over the country of Misira (Egypt). Everyone, whether a beggar in the street, or a king ran (to see you). They sent you to bathe in the Nile, and everyone, whether a layman or a king was pleased to see you.
And another day I find today, when the same face of yours is covered with dust. What has become of that singular beauty of yours which had enchanted the whole world?
When I saw you in a dream, I was at once in love with you,
and when I actually saw you, I was under the pangs of your separation.
For your sake, my lord, I came to Misira (i.e., Egypt)
and said, "For what reason have I been unfortunate?"
The Maker proved my love to be sincere,
He made me hard like stone.
When, dear, you turned your face from me,
my life would come back when I saw you.
I spent forty years of my life in *yōga*,
and when I heard your name I gave my all.
Whenever anyone would utter your name before me
he got from me a lakh, or whatever there was with me.
For twenty years I lived on your looks, and for another twenty years I lived on the sound of your name.

Page 339

Now, your looks have been covered by dust, and also I shall not hear your name now. Now, neither I have your glimpses nor do I hear your name. On whom should I depend for the purpose of staying here (in this world)?

Nā piu bōla sunāvahu
nā aba darasana dēhu.
Karahu dayā pata rākhau
Yaha jiu āpana lēhu.

Aba pati rahai jo jāī prānā
Dhirika jīva tuma bina jahā mānā.
Jīvana bhalā jaba lahi piu hōī
Binā pīu dhrika jīvana sōhī.
Piu bina sūna sabhai sansārā
Sukha sampati saba piu bina jārā.
Binā piu kōi saṅghātī nāhī
Kehi bidhi rahai prāna ghaṭa māhī.
Jarai jāi sukha sampati sājā
Binā pīu āvai nahī kājā.
Piu kē saṅgha jo hōi bhikhārī
Binā pīu sukha sampati balihārī.
Piu ke saṅgha bhalā bhikasai māhī
Binā pīu sukha bilasai nāhī.
Tuma bina kantha jagata ādhiyārā
Bhaeu ujāra sabhai sansārā.
Niṭhura prāna jō aba lahi raheū
Pāhana hiyā nithura dukha saheū.

P. 340

Khāi pachāra jo chāra para
Karai āha eka bār.
Pañchī prāna so uṛi gaeu
Rahī chāra māha chāra.

Neither do you, my dear, make me hear your voice,
nor you give me your glimpses.
Be kind and save me from blemish,
and accept this life which is yours.
Now, my honour will be saved only if my spirit departs.
Cursed be my spirit if it likes to stay without you.
Life is desirable only as long as the dear one lives,
and the same life is cursed without the dear one.
Without the dear one the whole world is dreary,
and without the dear one, all comforts and riches are worthless.
Without the dear one, none is a companion,
how should then the life spirit stay in the body ?
May the comforts and riches burn away !
For without the dear one, they are of no use.
It is better to be a beggar with the dear one,
but without the dear one the comforts and the riches should be thrown away ;
with the dear one it is better to dwell in miseries
but without him one should not indulge into luxuries.
Without you, my lord, the world is dark,
and the whole world is deserted.
My life spirit is piti-less, that it stays in my body even now,
and stone-like is my heart which has endured this disaster."

Page 340

When falling aback on the tomb
she released a sigh,
the bird-like life spirit of hers flew away,
and the dust was left with the dust.

APPENDIX II

MODERN AWADHI TEXTS

(a) **gulgulaːwaːliː kʌthaː** (Lakhimpur)

(b) **chʌndo** (Lakhimpur)

[These two specimens were given to the author by his mother in 1921 and appeared first in the author's monograph on Lakhīmpurī (published in 1923). The old lady spoke pure Awadhi. Alas! she is no more in this world, having breathed her last on June 1, 1931.]

(c) **cwaːrʌn ki kʌthaː** (Sitapur)

[From Jagannath, V. Jihurī, 2 miles to the south of Ramkōṭ, Dt. Sitapur.]

(d) **ṭhʌkurʌn ki bʌɦaːduriː** (Lucknow)

[From Ram Sahai of Amausī, Dt. Lucknow.]

(e) **ãdɦʌre ki beimaːniː** (Unao)

[From an inhabitant of a village, 2 miles to the north of Maurāwān, Dt. Unao.]

(f) **lʌrikini ki pʌti-seːwaː** (Fatehpur)

[From Sanwal Ahir of V. Catanpur, Pargana Kōṛā, Dt. Fatehpur, a place 4 miles from the boundary of Cawnpore district—by the courtesy of Fatehchand Varma.]

(g) **guruː kiɦeː ko phʌl** (Bahraich)

[From Tulsi Gaṛariyā, of Mankāpur, 6 miles to the west of Bahraich.]

(h) **baːmɦʌn ʌu bokʌraː keːr kʌthaː** (Barabanki)

[Collected by Pt. Lalta Prasad Sukul.]

(i) sijaːr au sijaːrin (Gonda)

[From Harmohan Singh of V. Mahaūbirāhim, Tahsil Utraulā, 28 miles from Gonda.]

(j) baːbaː ki kʌraːmʌt (Fyzabad)

[From Lachiman of V. Bichiā, 5 miles to the south-west of Fyzabad town.]

(k) kʌcehəriː maː bʌjaːn (Sultanpur)

[Statement of Jagwanti, wife of Ramanand, of V. Gãṛērī, Dt. Sultanpur, in the Court of Mr. Chintamani, Dy. Collector.]

(l) mukʌdimaː kʌi haːl (Partabgarh)

[Collected by Pt. Lalta Prasad Sukul.]

(m) bʌmhʌniː kʌi bʌjaːn (Allahabad)

[Statement of a Brahmin woman of a village on the Eastern boundary of Allahabad district, by the courtesy of B. Saligram, Reader, Collector's Court, Allahabad.]

(n) bhikhaːriː baːmhʌn kʌj kʌthaː (Allahabad)

[Collected by Pt. Lalta Prasad Sukul, from a resident of a village, 32 miles to the east of Allahabad towards Mirzapur.]

(a) gulgulaːwaːliː kʌthaː

eːk raːɟaː rʌɦʌĩ ʌu mʌɦɵtaːriː rʌɦʌi ʌu dulʌɦin rʌɦʌi. mʌɦɵtaːriː roːɟu chʌpːʌn pʌrkaːl ke̥ bɦoːɟʌn bʌnaːwʌi ʌu ʌpnaː khaːi ʌu ʌpneː lʌrikʌ kɵ khʌwaː-wʌi. dulʌɦin khaːtir eːk beɟɦʌri ki̥ roːʈiː sẽːkʌi, aːdɦiː roːʈiː ʌu loːnu sʌbeːreː deːi ʌu aːdɦiː sʌɲɟɦʌ kɵ. ui maːreː gusːʌke̥ roːʈiː ɖeɦʌrijʌ mɵ ɖaːri deːĩ ʌu loːnu gʌgʌri mɵ naːi aːwʌĩ. ʌisʌi kʌrti kʌrti baːraː bʌrsʌi gudʌri gʌĩː. tʌb eːk din buːɽɦaː gul-gulaː kiɦini̥. gulgulaː ɟhãːpi kɵ dɦʌri diɦini̥ ʌu ʌpnaː disʌi cʌliː gʌĩː. ɟaːti berijaː bʌɦu se̥ kʌɦi gʌĩː ki̥ 'dulɵɦini̥ ʌisiː deːkheː rʌɦeu.' bʌɦuː, ɟʌleː ui lʌuʈʌĩ tʌleː, tiːni̥ gulgulaː nikaːri liɦisi̥. khaːisi̥ naːiː, dɦʌri aːiː. tʌleː buːɽɦaː aːi gʌĩː. kulːaː ulːaː kʌi kʌi ʌpʌn ʌɽɦijaː deːkhini̥ ɟaːi. tʌu kʌɦini̥ 'dulʌɦin kaː iː mɵ ke̥ gulgulaː tum liɦeː hʌu?' dulʌɦin boːlĩː 'hʌm buaː hʌm naːiː liɦen hʌi kaː maːlum bilʌijaː lʌi gʌi hoːi, gʌi rʌɦʌi ui waːr.' tʌu bilʌijaː kʌɦisi̥ 'rʌɦu tui, tui kaː mʌi tiːni paːni se nɵ dɦoːi deːũ tʌu mʌi kaːɦe ki̥. tui liɦeː ʌu mʌi kaː coːriː lʌgaːjeː.'

tʌɦi kʌi ɟʌb sãːɟɦ bɦʌi tʌb raːniː ʌpʌni̥ khʌʈijaː bichaːini̥, dijaː baːri kɵ dɦʌrini̥. ɟʌb raːɟʌ ke̥ kʌceɦeri se̥ lʌuʈʌi mɵ deːr deːkhini̥ tʌu kʌhini̥

Translation

(a) A story about gulgulās[1]

There lived a certain king with his mother and wife. The mother used to prepare food of fifty-six varieties daily and she and her son used to partake of it. For the daughter-in-law, however, she baked a loaf of millet and gave half a loaf and salt to her in the morning and half in the evening. She, on account of anger, threw the bread into a big earthen pot and poured the salt into a jar. In this way twelve years passed. One day the old lady prepared *gulgulās*. She covered them and having done so she went out to ease[2] herself. While going she said to the daughter-in-law: "Daughter-in-law, keep an eye in this direction." Before the old lady returned, the daughter-in-law took out three *gulgulās*. She did not eat them but put them away. The old lady returned and after rinsing her mouth[3] went and looked at her wooden vessel.[4] Then she said: "Daughter-in-law, is it you who have taken the *gulgulās* from this?" The daughter-in-law replied: "I, mother, I have not taken any. Who knows but that the cat may have taken them, she has been that way." The cat, then, said: "All right, you wretch, I am not a cat if I do not wash you out altogether.[5] You took them and attributed the theft to me."

Thereafter when it became dark,[6] the queen arranged her bedding and lighted the lamp. When she saw that there was some delay in the king's return home from the court

[1] *gulgulā* is the name of a special Indian preparation made of flour and sugar, it is also called *puā* at some places.

[2] 'To go out or to go to the quarters' (literal trans.) is a euphemism for attending to nature's call.

[3] To rinse the mouth, *i.e.*, to wash the mouth, hands and feet.

[4] *aṛhiyā* is a big wooden vessel to put eatables in.

[5] *tīni pāni se dhōi dẽū*—lit. wash you away with three waters, *i.e.*, destroy you completely.

[6] Lit. when it became evening.

‘laːoː tʌleː soːi leːiː.’ iu kʌɦi kʌi soːwʌi laːgĩː. bilʌijaː kaː kiɦisi̥. koːi ki̥ pʌgijaː uʈhaːi laːiː ʌu unkiː khʌʈijʌ pə dɦʌri diɦisi̥, koːi ki̥ tʌrwaːri lʌi kʌi huʌĩ dɦʌri diɦisi̥, ʌu koːi ke̥ ɟuːtaː uʈhaːi laːiː so pʌlkʌ ke̥ tʌreː dɦʌrisi̥ aːi. ʌtːaː saːmaːn dɦʌri kʌi bilʌijaː ʌpnaː cʌliː gʌi.

raːɟaː ɟʌb kʌceɦeri se aːjeː deːkhʌĩ kaː koːi ke̥ ɟuːtaː dɦʌreː, koːi ki̥ tʌrwaːri, koːi ki̥ pʌgijaː. raːɟaː mʌn maː ʌnɟaːdeː ki koːiː mʌrdu raːniː tiːr aːwaː hʌi. tʌu ʌĩcini̥ tʌrwaːri ki iːkaː maːɖːʌribaː. tʌu dijaː boːlaː ‘raːɟaː sʌmuɟɦi kə maːreu.’ raːɟaː tiːni daːĩ tʌrwaːri uʈhaːini̥ ʌu dijaː tiːniu daːĩ tirbaːcʌku̥ diɦisi̥. tau raːɟaː tʌrwaːri dɦʌri̥ diɦini̥ ʌu loːʈaː lʌi kʌi pʌkhaːneː cʌleː gʌjeː.

etːiː deːr mə raːniː ɟaːgi pʌrĩː tʌu dijaː bʌɽɦaːi diɦini̥. dijʌ ke̥ dʌrwʌɟːe pə kũãː rʌɦʌi, raːɟaː huʌĩ kulːaː kʌrti rʌɦʌĩ. ɟʌb dijaː ʌpneː gɦʌr pʌɦũcaː tʌu mʌɦətaːriː kʌɦisi̥ ki ‘bɦʌijaː aːɟu bʌɽiː deːr lʌgaːjeu, mʌi khaːi kə liɦeː bʌiʈhi rʌɦiũ.’ dijaː kʌɦisi̥ ‘mʌɦətʌrijaː kuchu pũːchʌu naː, raːniː pʌr bʌɽiː bipʌti pʌriː hʌi.’ raːɟaː ʈhaːɽɦ hoi kʌi sunʌi laːg. mʌɦətaːriː kʌɦisi̥ ‘kaːɦeː bɦʌijaː?’ dijaː ɟʌis ɟʌis haːlu̥ bɦʌwaː rʌɦʌi tʌis sʌb bʌtaːi diɦisi̥. raːɟaː sʌb suni kʌi gɦʌr kaː aːjeː ʌu oːɽɦi kə pʌuɽhi rʌɦeː.

ɟʌb bɦoːru bɦʌwaː tʌu mʌɦətaːriː phiri chʌpːʌn pʌrkaːl ke̥ bɦoːɟʌn bʌnaːini̥ ʌu kʌɦini̥ ‘bɦʌijaː khaːu aːi.’ raːɟaː kʌɦini̥ ‘buaː pʌrsʌu.’ ui eːk thʌrijaː pʌrsini̥. raːɟaː kʌɦini̥ ‘dosʌriu pʌrsʌu.’ ui doːsʌri pʌrsini̥. raːɟaː kʌɦini̥ ‘tisʌriu pʌrsʌu.’ buːɽɦaː

she said to herself: "Let me sleep for a while." Having said so she went to sleep. And what did the cat do? She brought somebody's turban and placed it on her bedstead and took somebody's sword and placed it there She also brought somebody's shoes and put them under the bedstead. She put these things there and went away.

When the king returned from the court he saw that there were somebody's shoes and somebody's sword and turban. From it he concluded that some man had come to the queen. On this he drew his sword in order to kill her. The lamp spoke out: "O king, learn the truth before you kill her." The king thrice drew the sword out and the lamp forbade[1] him all the three times. He then put down the sword, took the *lōṭā*[2] and went away to attend to nature's call.

Meanwhile the queen woke up and put out[3] the lamp. There was a well before the door (of the house) of the lamp. The king was rinsing his mouth there. When the lamp reached home, his mother said: "My son, you are very late to-day, I have all along been sitting with the food ready." The lamp replied: "Dear mother, do not ask anything, great calamity has befallen the queen." The king stood there and listened. The mother asked: "What is the matter, dear son?" The lamp related everything that had happened. The king heard everything, came home and having covered himself up, lay down.

When it became morning, the mother again prepared food of fifty-six varieties and asked her son to eat it. The king asked her to serve. She served one dish. He asked her to serve another. She served another. He asked her to serve a third. The old lady said to him: "Come, let us

[1] *tirbācak dihisi*—lit. spoke three times, *i.e.*, in a decisive manner.

[2] *lōṭā* is a small brass or bronze vessel to contain water.

[3] *baṛhāi dihini*—(lit. lengthened or developed) is a euphemism for extinguished.

kʌɦini̥ ‘ɑːoː hʌm tum khɑːiː, dulʌɦin khɑːwɑː kʌri-ɦʌĩ.’ tʌu rɑːʤɑː kʌɦini̥ ‘nʌːiː tisʌriu pʌrsʌu.’ ʤʌb tisʌriu thʌrijɑː pʌrsi gʌi, tʌu rɑːʤɑː kʌɦini̥ ‘rɑːniː khɑːu ɑːi.’ rɑːniː kʌɦini̥ ‘sunʌu rɑːʤɑː bɑːrɑː bʌrsʌi biːti gʌĩː tʌb nʌ kʌbɦʌũː pũːcheu. ɑːʤu kɑː hʌi?’ iu kʌɦi kʌi ɖeɦerijʌ ki̥ roːʈiː ɑːgeː kurʌi diɦini̥ ʌu gʌgʌri kɵ loːnu ɑ̃ːgʌn mɵ nɑːi diɦini̥. buːʈɦɑː mɑːri kɵ khisijɑːi gʌĩː ʌu wʌɦeː tiːr mʌri kʌi rʌɦi gʌĩː. ‘ɑːʤɑː rɑːniː bʌɦut din rɑːʤi kiɦini̥.

ʤʌiseː un keː din bʌɦureː tʌiseː sʌb keː bʌɦurʌĩ.

take our meal, the daughter-in-law may eat food afterwards." But the king said, "No, serve a third dish also." When the third dish was also served, he asked the queen to come and eat. The queen replied, "Hear, O king, twelve years have passed and never did you ask me (to eat). What is the matter to-day?" Having spoken so, she brought out the bread from the earthen pot and put it all before him and poured out the salt from the jar in the courtyard. The old lady got very much ashamed and died on the very spot. The king and the queen reigned for many a day. May[1] everybody's good days return as did theirs.

[1] This is the prayer with which every story ends. It shows that a story may relate unhappy events but always has a happy end.

(b) chʌndo

soːwʌu ki ɟaːgʌu moːriː aːdɦi bɦʌwaːniː ɟʌgʌt keːriː raːniː, ʌkʌbʌr ʈhaːɽɦeː duaːr, hoː bʌli ɟaːũ. (1)

kiː tum ʌkʌbʌr pʌrchʌn aːjeu, ʌreː pʌrchʌn aːjeu, kiː tum dʌrsʌn aːjeu, bʌli ɟaːũ. (2)

naː hʌm maːtaː moːriː pʌrchʌn aːjen, ʌreː pʌrchʌn aːjen, naː hʌm dʌrsʌn aːjen, bʌli ɟaːũ. (3)

Translation

(*b*) A song[1] in praise of Bhawānī

Note 1.—Bhawānī is one of the seven powerful goddesses. She is sometimes also identified with Bhawānī, Siva's wife. Her abode is on the hills. The story goes that once Akbar thought of throwing her image (usually of stone) out and so he went to the temple of the goddess. The present song is the dialogue between the two.

Note 2.—For the sake of rhythm the words in a song undergo some changes which are not generally visible in ordinary speech. For instance, a short *a* is added to every word which ends in a consonant, final vowels are often lengthened and the long vowels in the middle of a word are often shortened.

Note 3.—The language of songs is often somewhat borrowed and archaic. For instance, in verse we have the obl. inf. in *-an* (*kaṭan*) side by side with *-ai* form (*jarai*).

1. "Are you sleeping or waking, my Ādhi Bhawānī[2], queen of the world, Akbar stands before your door, I bow to you[3]."

2. "Akbar, have you come here for the sake of *parchan*[4] or for *darsan*[5]?" I bow to you.

3. "My mother, I have come here neither to do *parchan*, yes, to do *parchan* nor to have your *darsan*, I bow to you."

[1] *chanda* is the term used for the songs in praise of gods and goddesses, chiefly goddesses.

[2] *Ādhi Bhawānī*—name of one of the seven sisters—the healer of all pains.

[3] *bali jāu*—I adore, I bow; this is the burden of the song.

[4] ***parchan*** < Sanskrit ***prakṣālana***; this signifies the special rite of pouring water—chiefly Ganges water—over the image of a god or goddess.

[5] ***darsan*** < Sanskrit ***darśana***, visiting, seeing, used only of gods and saints and elders to whom respect is due.

hʌm tʌu maːtaː moːriː lʌɽneː ko aːjen, ʌreː lʌɽneː ko aːjen, nikʌri nʌ lʌɽʌu mʌidaːn, bʌli ɟaːũ.
(4)

tumɦʌreː tʌu ʌkʌbʌr phʌuɟʌi bʌɦut hʌĩ, ʌreː phʌuɟʌi bʌɦut hʌĩ, hʌmʌreː tʌu negulaː ʌkeːl, bʌli ɟaːũ. (5)

tumɦʌreː tʌu ʌkʌbʌr ɖɦaːl tʌrwʌrijaː ʌreː toːbʌi bʌndukhijaː, hʌmʌreː phuːlʌn keːriː maːl, bʌli ɟaːũ. (6)

ɟaːi kʌɦeu ui durgaː bʌɦinin aːgeː, ʌŋgaːr maːtaː aːgeː, ui saːtʌu bʌɦinin aːgeː, tʌ̃buʌn aːgi uʈhaːwʌĩ, bʌli ɟaːũ. (7)

ɟʌrʌi laːgʌĩ tʌ̃buaː kʌʈʌn laːgʌĩ ɖoːriː, kʌʈʌn laːgʌĩ ɖoːriː, tʌb hʌm aːdɦi bɦʌwaːniː, bʌli ɟaːũ.
(8)

ɟʌrʌi laːgeː tʌ̃buaː, kʌʈʌn laːgĩː ɖoːriː, kʌʈʌn laːgĩː ɖoːriː, ʌb hʌm aːdɦi bɦʌwaːniː, bʌli ɟaːũ, ʌb hʌm ɟʌgʌt bɦʌwaːniː, bʌli ɟaːũ. (9)

ʌkʌbʌr bãːdɦi pʌʈijaː lʌrkaːwʌĩ, pʌʈijaː lʌrkaːwʌĩ, biːbiː sẹ daːnaː dʌraːwʌĩ, bʌli ɟaːũ.
(10)

hʌm tʌu ɟaːniː maːtaː kãːkʌr paːthʌr, ʌreː kãːkʌr paːthʌr, nikʌriː hʌĩ aːdɦi bɦʌwaːniː, bali ɟaːũ, nikʌriː hʌĩ ɟʌgʌt bʌkhaːniː, bʌli ɟaːũ. (11)

ʌbtiː beːr tum pʌlɟɦʌu bɦʌwaːniː, ʌreː pʌlɟɦʌu nʌɦʌraːniː, ʌb naːɦĩː pʌrbʌt aːib, bʌli ɟaːũ, ʌb naːiː pʌrbʌt aːib, bʌli ɟaːũ. (12)

soːwʌu ki ɟaːgʌu moːriː aːdɦi bɦʌwaːniː, ɟʌgʌt keːriː raːniː, ʌkʌbʌr ʈhaːɽɦeː duaːr, hoː bʌli ɟaːũ.

4. "My mother, I have come here to have a fight with you, yes, to have a fight, why not come out and fight, I bow to you."

5. "You Akbar, you have many armies, yes many armies, while I have the solitary *negulā*,[6]" I bow to you.

6. "You Akbar, you have shields and swords, yes rifles and guns, I have only the garland of flowers," I bow to you.

[Bhawānī now sends her messengers to her sisters and it is not long before they arrive to help her.]

7. "Go before sister Durgā, before Aṅgārmātā, yes before all the seven[7] sisters and ask them to set fire to the tents," I bow to you.

8. "When the tents begin to be burnt, when the strings begin to be cut down, yes to be cut down, then shall I be Ādhi Bhawānī," I bow to you.

9. The tents began to be burnt, the strings began to be cut. "Now I am Ādhi Bhawānī, now I am Bhawānī of the world," I bow to you.

10. They bind Akbar to a beam,[8] yes let him hang there and make his wife[9] grind corn, I bow to you.

11. "Mother, I thought you were only gravel and stone, yes only gravel and stone, but you have come out to be Ādhi Bhawānī, yes come out to be the celebrated goddess of the world, I bow to you."

12. "Be pleased, O Bhawānī, this time, yes pardon, O Empress of the world, never shall I come again to the hills, never shall I come again to the hills, I bow to you."

"Are you sleeping or waking, my Ādhi Bhawānī, queen of the world, Akbar stands before your door, I bow to you."

[6] *negulā*—the name given to the single boy-defender of the goddesses, who remains always with them.

[7] The goddesses are seven in number and all of them are sisters born of the same parents; *Durgā*, *Aṅgārmātā*, *Bhawānī* are three of them. Durgā is the goddess of small-pox, Aṅgārmātā burns everything and Bhawānī is the healing goddess.

[8] *paṭiyā* is the name given to the beams used to make a cot, there are four such in every cot.

[9] *bībī*—wife, here the Queen.

(c) cwɑːrʌn ki kʌthɑː

jɑːk sɑːɦ rʌɦʌĩ. tʌunkeː pichəwɑːreː roːcːwɑːrə ɑːwʌti̥ rʌɦʌĩ. tʌu phiri̥ jɑːk din phiri̥ ɑːjeː. tʌu sɑːɦ kʌɦin ki "dǰɑːkhʌu ɟiː rupʌjɑː diɦeː rʌɦʌn tʌun kʌɦẽː dɦʌrẽː." tʌu sɑːɦuni kʌɦini̥ "ɑ̃ːgʌn kȩ ɑːrem dɦʌrẽː." wʌɦi mɑː lɑːgiː rʌɦʌĩ bʌrːʌijɑː. tʌu sɑːcːwɑːr rʌɦʌĩ sunti. tʌu phiri̥ rɑːti ko cwɑːr ɑːjeː. tʌu phiri̥ eːkụ cwɑːr gʌwɑː wʌɦi mɑː hɑːthụ ɖɑːri̥ diɦisi̥. ui keː bʌrːʌijɑː kɑːʈi̥ khɑːini̥. tʌ uː bɦɑːgɑː. dwɑːsʌr kʌɦʌi lɑːg "uː tʌu uʈhɑːjeː sʌb liɦeː ɟɑːti. hʌmʌɦu lʌjɑːjiː ɟɑːi." tʌu wʌɦʌu lʌi kʌi bɦɑːɟɑː. jʌɦeː tʌnɑː sʌtʌɦũː kiɦin. wʌɦi din cwɑːr ʌponeː gɦʌrʌi cʌleː gʌjeː.

dwʌsʌreː din phiri̥ ɑːjeː. tʌb sɑːɦ ʌponeː ɑ̃ːgʌn mə ʌdmi kȩ buʈɑːũ eːku gʌʈʌɦɑː khodɑːin, ui mɑː siːrɑː bɦʌrəwɑːin. tʌu sɑːɦ sɑːɦuni tereː boːleː ki "ui phuːl kereː bʌrtʌn kʌɦɑ̃ː dɦʌreː?" tʌu phiri̥ sɑːɦuni kʌɦin "rɑːti kə nʌ buːɟɦɑː kʌrʌu. ɑ̃ːgʌn kereː ɖeɦukʌ m dɦʌrẽː." tʌ ui sɑːtʌu cwɑːr sunti rʌɦʌĩ. tʌb gɦʌr keː ɟʌb sʌb ɟʌneː soːi sɑːi gʌjeː tʌ wʌi cwɑːr sɑːtʌu ɑːjeː, tʌu ɑ̃ːgʌn kereː ɖeɦukʌm eːkụ pʌɦileː pʌiʈhɑː. tʌb dwɑːsʌr kʌɦʌti "iu tʌu sʌb bʌʈoːreː leːti hʌmʌɦuː bʌʈolːeːiː." tʌ wʌɦʌu phɑ̃ːdi pʌrɑː. jʌɦeː tʌnɑː sʌtʌɦũː phɑ̃ːdi pʌreː ui mɑː.

Translation

(c) The story of the thieves

There lived a banker.[1] Thieves used to resort to the back side of his (house) daily. Then again one day they came. The banker said : " See, the money that I had given to you, where have you placed it?" The banker's wife replied : " It is in the nook[2] of the courtyard." There were wasps in it. The seven thieves were hearing. At night the thieves came. One thief went and put his hand in it (the nook). The wasps stung him and he fled. The second thief said (to himself) : " He is taking all of it away, let me also take it." And he also fled after taking it. All the seven did in this manner. The thieves on that day went to their home.

On the second day, (they) came again. The banker had got a pit dug in which a man could get drowned and got it filled up with molasses.[3] The banker said to his wife : " Where are those vessels made of *phūl*[4]? The banker's wife replied : " Don't ask (such questions) at night. They are in the courtyard's cellar." All the seven thieves were hearing. When all the people of the (banker's) house had gone to sleep, the seven thieves came and one (of them) entered the cellar of the courtyard. Then the second said (to himself) : " He is collecting all of them. Let me also pick up." And he also got in. In this manner all the seven went in it (and got drowned).

[1] *sāh*—a banker, moneylender, usually of the *Vaiśya* caste.

[2] *ār*—a small recess in the walls, particularly on both the sides of the doors.

[3] *sirā*—The juice of sugar-cane is boiled first and then the solid part is separated to make sugar and the liquid part remains, this is known *sirā*.

[4] *phūl*—a metal made by a combination of several base-metals. it is one of the costly metals and makes beautiful vessels.

bɦorʌɦẽː beːreː eːkụ phʌkiːrụ aːwaː tʌ wʌɦi teː saːɦuni buːɟɦini "din bɦʌrem tum kʌi pʌseːriː naːɟu paːwʌti hʌu?" tʌ uː kʌɦisi̥ "hʌm tiːni pʌseːriː naːɟu paːiti hʌi." tʌu saːɦuni kʌɦini "djaːkhʌu iː cwaːr ko uʈhaːi kə taːl mo ɖaːri aːwoː, hʌm caːri pʌseːriː deːib." tauː ɖaːri aːwaː. tʌb saːɦuni kʌɦini̥ ki "tum nʌ maːlum kʌiseː ɖaːri aːwʌti u iu tʌu phiri̥ bɦaːgi aːwaː." jʌɦeː tʌnaː dwaːsʌr ɖ́aːrʌi gʌjeː tʌpːhiri̥ kʌɦini̥ saːɦuni "tum nʌ maːlum kʌiseː ɖaːrʌti hʌu iu deːkhʌu phiri̥ gɦuːmi aːwaː." jʌɦeː tʌnaː sʌtʌɦuː kʌiɦãː ɖaːri aːjeː tʌpːhiri̥ ɟʌb sʌtʌwãː ɖaːrʌi gʌjeː, tʌu ɦuãː eːkụ dɦoːbiː chãːʈʌti rʌɦʌi kʌpʌʈaː. tʌu cwaːr ko ui taːl mo ɖaːrin tʌb uː dɦoːbiː ɖeraːi ko bɦaːgaː. tʌb uː phʌkiːrụ kʌɦisi̥ "beːr beːr saːr bɦaːgi̥ ɟaːti rʌɦʌi ʌbʌkiː saːre k pʌkʌri liɦen." tʌ wʌɦi kaː maːri kʌiɦãː wʌɦeː taːl mʌiɦãː ɖaːri diɦin. tʌb uː saːɦuni tiːr gʌwaː, kʌɦʌi laːg "ɟʌun beːr beːr deːtiː rʌɦʌu tʌun ʌbʌkiː saːre ko maːri kə ɖaːri aːjen." tʌ wʌɦi kaː saːɦuni naːɟu diɦin caːri pʌseːriː.

At the time of dawn there came a Fakir. Then the banker's wife asked him: "How many *panserīs*[1] of corn do you get in a whole day?" Then he said: "I get three *panserīs* of corn in a day." The banker's wife said: "See, lift this thief and throw him in the tank, I shall give you four *panserīs*." He went and threw him. Then the banker's wife said: "I do not know how you throw, he has fled back again." In this manner, he (the Fakir) went to throw the second. Then the banker's wife said again: "I wonder how you throw, see, he has returned again." In this manner he threw all the seven. When he went to throw the seventh, there was a washerman washing clothes. When the Fakir threw the thief in the tank, the washerman fled out of fright. Then the Fakir thought: "the rascal[2] used to run away again and again; this time I have caught him." And killed him and threw him in the tank. Then he went to the banker's wife and began to say: "Him whom you gave (to me) again and again, I have killed and thrown away." Then the banker's wife gave him four *panserīs* of corn.

[1] *pasērī*, Hindustānī *pansērī*—a weight of five seers: a seer is of a little over two pounds.

[2] *sār*—lit. 'wife's brother,' thence a term of rebuke.

(d) ʈhʌkurʌn ki bʌɦaːduriː

gʌdʌr mo hʌm dʌs gjaːrʌɦ bʌrso ke rʌɦʌn. hʌm kaː sudɦi sʌb hʌi. baːsːaːɦ pʌkʌri gʌjeː rʌɦʌĩ. ʌ̃gʌreːʤ kʌɦini̥ "hʌm kaː cʌɦʌrːʌmu̥ deːu,"; baːsːaːɦ deːi laːg. ʌ̃gʌreːʤʌn deːkhini̥ baːsːaːɦ naːcʌi gaːwʌi mo pʌreː ɦʌĩ tʌb un kaː pʌkʌri lʌi geː. goːraː sʌbbeːli mo aːi gʌjeː.

munːaːsiŋgɦ hʌmaːr caːcaː rʌɦʌĩ. tiː baːsːaːɦ ke̥ kʌrindʌ ki naːk kaːʈini̥ rʌɦʌi. siːsmʌɦʌl waːleː mʌliɦaːbaːd ke̥ pʌʈhaːn bolaːini̥. dʌs sipaːɦiː, eːku̥ eːku̥ chuːraː ʌu eːku̥ eːku̥ ɖʌŋɖaː. munːaː ʌu pʌɲcʌm ʌu pʌɦʌlwaːn biaːɦu̥ kʌribʌi naːiː kiɦini̥ rʌɦʌi. tʌu pʌʈhaːnu̥ ui maː eːku̥ bʌɽaː beːɖɦʌbu̥ rʌɦʌi. uː kʌɦisi̥ "munːaːsiŋgɦ sunen rʌɦʌi tum bʌɽeː bʌɦaːdur hʌu, ʌ̃gʌreːʤʌn se̥ lʌɽeː rʌɦʌu. hʌmʌreː pʌʈhaːnʌn saːth nʌ lʌɽeu. dʌs din tumʌreː mʌkaːn mo aːjeː hoi geː." un kiː cʌupaːri bʌniː rʌɦʌi teɦi mʌ teː nikaːri diɦini̥ rʌɦʌi. ʌu eːku̥ bʌ̃gʌlaː rʌɦʌi tiː maː tiːniu bɦaːi rʌɦʌti̥ rʌɦʌĩ. tau kʌɦini̥ "kaːlɦi hʌm tum teː lʌɽʌb, phiri̥ nʌ kʌɦeu ki hʌm kaː maːrini̥."

tʌu bɦoːru̥ ʤʌb bɦaː tʌb dʌs ʈhʌĩː kʌnːjaː bʌmɦʌnʌn ki̥ bolaːini̥. un kaː miʈhaːiː khʌwaːini̥. unkaː caːri caːri pʌisaː ɖʌchinaː diɦini̥ ʌu ʤoː kuchu̥ bʌcaː tʌunu̥ ʌponaː tiːniu bɦaːi khaːi liɦini̥. kʌɦini̥ "ʌb sudɦʌrʌu hʌmaːr sipaːɦijaːnaː deːkhʌu." tʌb maːri laːʈhĩni̥ tiːniu bɦaːi giraːi diɦini̥. wʌɦeː sʌb coʈaːi gʌjeː. tʌu ʤʌmaːdaːr ʤʌunu̥ bʌɽaː tʌbʌrːaː boːlti rʌɦʌi, kʌɦini̥ "iː kiː naːk hʌm ʤʌruːr kaːʈʌb. juː hʌm kaː roːʈiː naːiː khaːi diɦisi̥." wʌɦiː naːk kaːʈi liɦini̥, kʌɦini̥ "hʌmaːr djaːkhʌu sipaːɦijaːnaː ʌb."

Translation

(d) The Bravery of Ṭhākurs

At (the time of) the mutiny I was ten (or) eleven years old. I have every recollection. The Bādshāh was captured. The English said : " Give us one-fourth (of your revenue)." The Bādshāh began to give it. The English saw that the Bādshāh was given to dance and music. Then they caught him (and) the white people occupied the quarters.

Munna Singh was my uncle. He had cut off the nose of the agent of the Bādshāh. (The Nawāb) of Shīshmahal called ten Paṭhān soldiers of Malihabad. (They had) each one knife and one *lāṭhī*. Munna and Pancam and Pahalwan (were bachelors) had not married. Then there was one Paṭhān amongst them who was very naughty. He said : "Munna Singh ! I had heard that you are very brave and that you had fought with the British. (But) you did not fight with us, the Paṭhāns. It is ten days that we came to your house." Their shed it was from which they had been turned out. There was a bungalow in which all the three brothers resided. Then (Munna Singh and his brothers) said : " We shall fight with you to-morrow. Do not say, later, that they killed us."

When it was morning, they called ten daughters of the Brahmins, fed them on sweetmeats and gave them four pice each as gift. And whatever (of the sweetmeats) remained, they ate up. (Then they) said : " Get ready now and see our soldiership." Then the three brothers by their *lāṭhī* strokes brought all of them down. They all got injured. Then the Jamādār who spoke very sharply, (with reference to him) (they said) : " We shall cut off this man's nose. He made it hard for us to eat our meals (lit. bread)." They cut his nose (and) said : " Now see our soldiership."

sʌɪl bɦʌre kị sʌɟaɪ bɦʌi. ɟʌb mʌɦinaɪ bɦʌri chuɪʈʌi ko rʌɦaɪ tʌb ʌdɦaɪr siŋgɦ ɖʌɪkodʌr te mili kʌi munɪaɪ siŋgɦ ko ɟjeɪl mo ɟʌɦʌr dewʌɪi ko mʌrwaɪi ɖaɪrinị.

They were sentenced for one year. When there remained one month for (their) release, Adhar Singh, in conspiracy with the Doctor, got Munna Singh poisoned in the jail and caused his death.

(e) ʌ̃dɦʌre kı̥ beimaːniː

jaːk sʌmʌi eːkṳ ãːdɦʌr aːdmiː rʌtːaː rʌtːaː cʌlaː ɟaːti rʌɦʌi. deːkhʌti rʌɦʌĩ ki meɦʌrijaː ʌu mʌnsʌwaː laːʈɦi m bʌiʈh cʌleː ɟaːti rʌɦʌĩ. tʌu meɦereːwʌĩ kʌɦaː mʌnsʌwaː tẹ ki "jʌɦi kaː laːʈɦi m bʌiʈhaː leːu". kʌɦin "ãːdɦʌr aːdmiː beimaːn hoːt hʌi jʌɦi kaː nʌ bʌiʈhaːwʌu laːʈɦi m." kʌɦin "naːiː bʌiʈhaːlːeːu, ɟʌb beimaːniː kʌrʌi tʌb hʌm teː bʌtaːjeu." un bʌiʈhaːlːiːn. tʌ un teː ʌ̃dɦʌrʌuː tẹ pũːchin "kʌɦãː pʌr tum utʌriɦʌu laːʈɦiː pʌr teː." kʌɦin "utʌri pʌrʌu ɟo ʌisiɦiː ɟʌiɦʌu." tʌ un kʌɦaː "laːʈɦiː bʌilṳ hʌmaːr aːi, hʌm kaːɦe ko utʌriː, tum utʌri pʌrʌu." pulis kẹ sipaːɦiː rʌɦʌĩ tʌ huãː raːɟʌ kẹ lʌgeː un kaː pʌkʌri lʌi geː. tʌu raːɟaː kʌɦeni "tumɦaːri peːsiː aːɟu nʌ hoːiː kaːlɦi hoːiː." tiːn koʈhʌrin mo tiɦũ ko jaːk jaːk ko bʌndo kʌi deɦin. tiːniu ɟʌgaː pʌr eːkṳ eːkṳ sipaːɦiː bʌiʈhaː deɦin. ui ɟʌːnin naː ki sipaːɦiː bʌiʈhʌĩ. raːɟaː kʌɦin "ɟʌunṳ iː raːti ko kʌɦʌĩ tʌun sʌbeːreː hʌm kaː bʌtaːjeu." ʌurʌt raːti ko kʌɦʌti rʌɦʌi ki "hʌmaːr mʌnsʌwaː kʌɦʌti rʌɦʌi 'iː kaː nʌ bʌiʈhaːoː' mulaː hʌm bʌiʈhaːi liɦin." tʌ mʌnsʌuː kʌɦin ki "meɦerijʌ k kʌɦaː nʌ kʌrʌi ko cʌɦiː, deːkhʌu hʌm kʌɦit rʌɦi geː ki 'iː kaː nʌ bʌiʈhaːoː,' beimaːniː kʌi gaː." ʌ̃dɦʌrʌuː kʌɦʌĩ "raːɟaː aːi ɟo nijaːu buːɟɦi ɟaːiː tʌu tiːni mo eːkṳ dewʌibʌi kʌriː." raːɟaː sʌbeːreː pʌɦʌr sipaːɦin te pũːchaː ki "ʌurʌt kaː baːt kʌɦis."

... ...

phirı̥ raːɟaː kaɦin "iː kaː kuchṳ nʌ deːu, iː kaː maːri ko kheːdːeːu."

Translation

(e) A Blind Man's Trickery

At one time, a certain blind man was going on a path. It was seen that a husband and wife, seated in a cart, were going. Then the wife said to the husband : "Take him in the cart." (He) said : "A blind man is dishonest usually, do not give him a seat." (She) said : "No, give him a seat, tell me when he practises dishonesty." He gave (him) a seat. Then (he) asked the blind man: "Where will you get down from the cart? You may get down if you go in this direction." He said: "The cart and bullock belong to me, why should I get down, you may get down." There were policemen, they caught them and took them to the king. The king said : "Your case will be put up to-morrow, not to-day." (He) shut up all the three, one by one, in three rooms. In all the three places (he) appointed a soldier each. They did not know that the soldier was sitting. The king instructed: "Whatever they say at night, tell it to me in the morning." The woman was saying at night : "My man was saying 'do not seat him,' but I gave him a seat." The husband said : "One should not do according to the woman's request, see I kept on saying 'do not seat him;' he did practise dishonesty." The blind man says : "He is a king, if he understands the case, he will cause one of the three (woman, cart and bullock) to be given (to me)." The king, in the morning, asked the soldiers: "What did the woman say?"

[Here follow the three statements of the three persons. one by one; these have been dropped to avoid repetition.]

Then the king said: "Do not give him (the blind man) anything, beat him and turn him out."

(f) lʌrikini ki pʌti-seːwaː

eːk bʌraːmɦʌn rʌɦʌi so woɦ mʌɦaːdeːo kʌi seːwaː kʌi cʌloː. tʌb mʌɦaːdeːo pʌrsʌndo bɦeː. hãː tʌb kʌɦen ki " mãːg leːo ɟo mãːgʌi kaː hoːi." hãː tʌb bʌraːmɦʌn kʌɦesi ki " hʌm kaː eːk lʌrikaː deːo." tʌb uiː kʌɦen ki " djaːb tʌu pʌi ɟʌb biaːɦ hui ɟaːiː tʌb lʌi ljaːb." tʌb bʌraːmɦʌn ʌponeː mʌn mẽː khjaːl kiɦesi ki " hʌm biaːɦ naː kʌrʌb, tʌb kʌiseː lʌi ljaːɦʌĩ." phir un keː baːlʌk diːnɦeni.

hãː tʌb ui baːlʌk sʌjaːn bɦeː tʌb biaːɦeː kaː loːg baːg dʌurʌĩ laːg, tab bʌraːmɦʌn inokaːr kiːn ki " biaːɦ nʌ kʌribeː." tʌb mʌɦotaːriː lʌrikaː kʌi kʌɦʌĩ laːg ki " mʌĩ ɟʌbʌrɟʌstiː biaːɦ kʌriɦʌũ." tʌb bʌraːmɦʌn maːreː kureːdɦ ke nikʌri kʌi cʌli bɦaː ki "ɟʌɦ biaːɦ ke t̪hʌĩː naː rʌiɦʌũ." ɟaːj ke eːk kuãː ke paːs pʌɦũci gaː. kuãː ke paːs caːri lʌrikiniː kheːlʌti tĩː. tʌb eːk sʌkhiː boːliː ki " kuch baːt kʌɦaː." tʌb eːk boːliː ki " tum ʌponeː sʌsureː ɟʌiɦaː to kaː kʌriɦaː." tab waː sʌkhiː boːliː ki " ɟʌb ɟʌiɦʌũ tʌb eːk cuːl lʌi ɟʌiɦʌũ, to ɟaːtʌi ɟaːt ɟudiː hui ɟʌiɦʌũ." tʌb duːsʌri sʌkhiː boːliː ki " ɟʌb mʌĩ ɟʌiɦʌũ tʌb bʌt̪hʌniː lʌi ɟʌiɦʌũ, tʌb hwʌn seː sʌb bʌt̪oːri lʌiɦʌũ." tʌb tiːsʌri boːliː ki " mʌĩ ɟʌiɦʌũ tʌb dijaːsʌraːiː lʌi ɟʌihʌũ. tʌb duʌrɦeː te aːgiː lʌgʌiɦʌũ." tʌb cʌuthi boːliː ki " mwaːr kʌŋt̪h[1] ɟo eːk pʌɦʌr ɟijʌt hoːiː to dui pʌɦʌr ɟiʌiɦʌũ."

tʌb waː bʌraːmɦʌn oiː lʌrikiː ke paːs cʌli bɦaː. tʌb lʌrikiː ʌponeː mʌkaːn me pʌɦũciː. tʌb bʌraːmɦʌn bʌit̪hi gaː ɟaːj. tʌb lʌrikiː ke gɦʌr keː maː baːp aːjeː tʌb pũːcheni ki "tum kʌɦãː rʌɦʌt ɦjaː.

[1] Obviously an error for kʌnt̪o.

Translation

(f) A Girl's devotion to her Husband

There was a Brahmin. He went to serve Mahādeva. And Mahādeva was pleased and (he) said: "Ask whatever you want to ask." Then the Brahmin said: "Give me a son." He said: "I shall surely give one but when he marries, I shall take him back." At that the Brahmin thought to himself: "I shall not marry him, how then will (the god) take him?" Then a son was given to him.

The boy grew up. People began to run for his marriage but the Brahmin refused (saying): "I shall not marry (him)." Then the boy's mother said: "I shall marry (my son) by force." The Brahmin went out (of the house) out of wrath: "I shall not remain here in place of marriage." Having gone he reached near a well. There were four maids playing near the well. One of the friends said: "Say something." Then one said: "When you will go to your father-in-law's, what will you do?" That friend said: "When I shall go, I shall carry an oven, and as soon as I arrive I shall get a separation (from other people of the family)." Then another friend said: "When I go, I shall carry a broomstick and shall sweep away everything and bring it with me." The third said: "If I go, I shall carry a match-box and shall set everything on fire from the very entrance." The fourth said: "If my beloved would be living for one watch, I shall endeavour to make him live for two watches."

The Brahmin went near that girl. And the girl reached her home. The Brahmin went and sat there. The girl's parents came and asked: "Where do you reside? What

kʌun ɟaːtiː aːɦiu." kʌɦaː ki "bʌraːmɦʌn aːɦiniː." tʌb lʌrikiː ke baːp pũːchesi ki "tum kʌɦeː kaː aːjʌu." tʌb waː bʌraːmɦʌn kʌɦesi ki "toːriː lʌrikiː ʌu moːreː lʌrikaː ki saːdiː hoːi cʌɦiː." tʌb ui lʌrikiː ke gɦʌr keː ui bʌraːmɦʌn kaː maːrʌĩ laːg ʌu kʌɦʌĩ laːg ki "saːreː hʌm ʌponiː lʌrikiː kaː biaːɦ toːreː lʌrikaː ke saːth nʌ kʌribeː." tʌb bʌraːmɦʌn ʌnːo paːniː chãːɽ diːnɦẽsi ʌu ɖeɦeriː mãː laːt lʌgaːe kʌi pʌr rʌɦoː ki 'lʌrikiː kaː biaːɦ nʌ kʌriɦaː to mʌi mʌri ɟʌiɦʌũ." waː phirijaːd raːɟaː khijãːː gʌi.

tʌb raːɟaː un kaː bolaːiniː ki "kʌɦeː kaː maːrjʌu jeɦ kaː." tʌb woɦ lʌrikiː keː gɦʌr keː kʌɦʌĩ laːg ki "saːɦeb jaː ɟʌbʌrɟʌstiː biaːɦ kʌrʌt hʌi moːriː lʌrikiː kaː." tʌb raːɟaː kul pũːchi kʌi kʌɦesi ki "biaːɦ kʌi djaː, ʌcːhaː hʌi." tʌb biaːɦ huĩː sʌɦiː huigaː. tʌb bʌraːmɦʌneː ʌponeː gɦʌr kaː cʌli bɦaː. ʌponeː gɦʌr mãː pʌɦũcoː tʌb bʌraːmɦʌni puːchʌi laːg ki "tum kʌɦãː geː tjoː ʌur kaː kʌri aːjoː." "lʌrikaː keː biaːɦ ke khwaːɟ kaː geː ten. biaːɦ sʌɦiː kʌr aːjen."

caste do you belong to?" (He) said: "I am a Brahmin." Then the girl's father asked: "Why have you come?" The Brahmin said: "It is necessary that your daughter and my son should marry together." At that the people of that girl began to beat the Brahmin and to say: "Rascal![1] we shall not marry our daughter to your son." The Brahmin, then, gave up eating and drinking and fixing a foot on the threshold lay down (saying): "If you will not marry (your) daughter (to my son), I shall die." The complaint was lodged at the king's.

The king called them (and asked): "Why did you beat him?" The girl's people said: "Sir, he is forcibly marrying our daughter." The king then asked everything and said: "Do marry (your daughter). It is nice." The marriage, thus was settled there. The Brahmin started for his residence. When he reached home his wife asked: "Where had you gone and what did you accomplish?" (He replied): "I went in search of the son's marriage and have settled it."

NOTE.—The story, later on, relates how when the daughter-in-law arrived she was able to prolong the life of her husband by propitiating the deities.

[1] See footnote No. 2 under (c), p. 445.

(g) guruː kiɦeː ko phʌl

dui ɟʌneː rʌɦʌĩ loːdɦ. tʌu unkeː guruː aːjeː tʌu kʌɦin "raːm raːm sunleːu, maːlaː pʌɦilːeːu." tʌun ʈaːr diɦin mʌneː "kaːtik mo aːwoː tʌb raːm raːm sunleːiː." unkʌi meɦoraːruː bɦʌgotin bɦʌi, ui ʈaːraː dʌi diɦini̥, kʌɦini̥, "maːgɦ mʌɦijãː." tʌb biːc mo meɦʌrʌruijaː keːr mʌrdʌwaː mʌri geː. phaːgun mo unkeː guruː aːjeː tʌb keː guruː kʌrʌi; guruː keɦi kʌi ceːlaː bʌnaːwʌĩ, ui rʌɦibʌi naːiː kʌrʌĩ. tʌb ui wʌisen rʌɦi geː.

tʌu kudːin baːdi unkʌi meɦoraːruː mʌriː tʌu sʌŋguti pʌriː raːm gɦʌreː. tʌb ui tʌu raːɟaː khiiãː beːʈiː ɟʌlʌmʊ liɦini̥ ʌu ui tʌu haːthiː bʌneː. tʌu kudːin baːdi ɟʌb saːdiː kʌrʌi ko bɦʌĩː tʌu haːthiː sunini̥ tʌu khuʈokaː kʌrʌi laːgẽː. tʌb bʌɦut kaːjʌl. bʌid wʌid bʌɦut bʌʈorini̥, naːɦĩː niːk hoːĩ. ɟʌb thoːren din bijaːɦ ko rʌɦi geː tʌu haːthiː bʌɦut duborijaːn. tʌb puːchini̥ ki "baːp ɟaːn haːthiː tʌu mʌraː ɟaːt hʌi." kʌɦini̥ "hãː beːʈiː mʌraː ɟaːt hʌi." tʌu kʌɦini̥ "phiri̥ koːiː ɟʌtʌn niːk kʌrʌu." tʌu haːthiː teːneː kʌɦojaːĩː ki "hʌm bijaːɦʊ uwaːɦʊ nʌ kʌrʌbʌi kuchʊ, nʌ kʌɦũː ɟaːbʌi kʌrʌb." tʌb kudːin baːdi baːbaː aːjeː. bɦʌbɦuːti uʈhaːi haːthiː pʌr bʌɦaːi diɦini̥ tʌb uː phiri̥ mʌnʌiː hoi geː.

Translation

(g) The fruit of accepting a preceptor

There were two persons, Lodh (by caste). Their preceptor came and said: "Hear (the *mantra*) *Rām Rām*, put on the rosary." But (he) put it off, namely: "Come in (the month of) Kātik, then I shall hear *Rām Rām.*" His wife became a devotee, he, however, put it off (and) said: "In (the month of) Māgh." Then in the meantime, the woman's husband died. In (the month of) Phāgun, his preceptor came, at that time who would accept the preceptor. Whom would the preceptor make the disciple, he no longer remained. So he remained (uninitiated) as he was.

Then after a few days, his wife died. Both of them came together in the Heavens (lit. Ram's house). She took birth at the king's as his daughter and he became an elephant. After a few days, when she was to marry, and the elephant heard (it), he began to worry (about it) (He was) very ill. Many physicians, etc., were brought together (but) he did not get better. When very few days for the marriage remained, the elephant became very much emaciated. Then (she) asked (her father): "Dear father, the elephant is dying." He (said): "Yes daughter, (he) is dying." Then (she) said: "Do cure him by any means." (She) went and told the elephant: "I shall not marry or do anything like it, nor shall I go anywhere." Then the saint came after some days (and) taking (sacred) ashes threw them on the elephant. At that he again became a human being.

(h) baːmɦʌn ʌu bokʌraː keːr kʌ́thaː

jaːkʌi bʌmɦʌnʌuː jaːk bokʌraː kʌiɦjãː kãːdɦeː pə̧ dɦʌreː bʌɟaːr mʌiɦjãː bjãːcʌi ko liːnɦeː ɟaːtị rʌɦʌĩ. rʌtːaː mãː tiːni bʌdmʌswaː mileː. ui bokʌrwʌ ko deːkhin ki saːrị lʌlcaːj uʈheː. mudaː bʌmɦʌnʌuː rʌɦʌĩ bʌɽeː ʈhiɦaːr tʌun un ʈeːneː bokʌraː chʌɽãːj ljaːbu kuchu ʌisụ wʌisụ kaːmụ naː rʌɦʌi. tʌɦũː un bʌdmʌswʌn mãː teːneː jaːkụ kʌɦʌi laːg ki "ɟʌs mʌi kʌrʌũ tʌisʌi sʌb ɟʌneː kiːnɦeo. tʌ bʌmɦʌnʌuː tə̧ bokʌrʌuː kaː hʌtijaːj ljaːb."

etnaː kʌɦʌtʌi khʌn bʌmɦʌnʌuː ui kʌĩtiː teː nikʌreː. tʌu wʌɦʌi bʌdmʌswaː un teːneː bwaːlaː ki "buɽhʌuː baːbaː jʌɦu kuːkurụ kʌpaːre pə̧ dhʌreː kaːɦeː cʌleː ɟaːt hʌo." suntʌi bʌmɦʌnʌuː risaːj uʈheː ʌu kʌɦʌi laːg "saːreː nʌɦi kʌeː, kaː twaːr diːdaː phuːʈi geː hʌĩ? jʌɦu kuːkur aːj? ʌs kuːkur kʌbʌũ deːkheː rʌɦʌi? cʌlu iː ʈhãːj teːneː, nʌɦĩː tʌu mʌriɦʌũ swãːʈaː tʌun kʌpaːr phuːʈi ɟaːiː." buɽɦʌuː bʌɦutʌi khʌphaː bheː ʌu ãːgeː cʌleː. etneː heː maː dusʌrkʌu aːwaː ʌur bwaːlaː "kaːkaː jʌɦu kuːkurụ kʌɦãː teːneː lʌi aːjeo?" etnaː suntʌi bʌmɦʌnʌuː keː aːgi laːgi gʌi ʌu bʌɦutʌi nʌraːɟ bɦeː mudaː ʌb bʌmɦʌnʌuː bɦitʌrʌi bɦiːtʌr swaːcʌi laːgi kị̊ "ɟetʌnʌɦeː saːrị̊ aːwʌt hʌĩ sʌbʌi jʌɦi kaː kukurʌi bʌtaːwʌt hʌĩ tʌunụ jʌɦi kjaːr kuchu bɦjaːdʌi nʌɦiː sʌmɟɦit." etʌneɦeː mʌiɦjãː tisʌrkʌu aːwaː ʌu kʌɦʌi laːg "dʌdːuː jʌɦu kuːkur kʌɦãː teːneː lʌi aːjeo?" jʌɦu suntʌi buɽhʌunuː khʌwkhjaːj uʈheː.

ui saːreː bʌdmʌswʌn kʌiɦjãː buɽhʌuː kheːdi bɦʌleː diːnɦin mudaː mʌn maː sʌk pʌri gaː ki

Translation

(*h*) The tale of the Brahmin and the Goat.

A Brahmin, with a goat on his shoulders, was carrying it to the market to sell (it). On the way, (he) met three crooks. As soon as they saw the goat, they got covetous (of it). But the Brahmin was very steady and so it was no easy job to snatch the goat away from him. Of the crooks one began to say : " Do as I do. Then we shall lay hands upon the goat."

While they were talking so, the Brahmin came that way. At that, that crook spoke to him : " Grandpa! why are you taking this dog over your head ?" The Brahmin, on hearing (this), got angry and said : " Rascal thou ! are you blind[1] ? Is this a dog ? Did you ever see a dog like this ? Get thee away from this place. Or else I shall so strike (you with) the staff, that your head will break." The old man became very angry and proceeded further. In the meantime the second (crook) came and said: "Uncle! where did you bring this dog from ?" Hearing this much, the Brahmin was (as if) seized with fire and he became very wrathful. But the Brahmin began to ponder to himself : " Whosoever, rascals are they, come, they tell this (goat) to be a dog : I do not understand the mystery of this." At this very time the third one came and said : " Brother ! where did you bring this dog from ? " On hearing this the old Brahmin foamed with rage.

Although the Brahmin put those rascals, the crooks, off, but he came to entertain (some) doubt in mind :

[1] lit. are your eye-balls broken.

"ɟʌunʌi djaːkhʌt hʌi eɦi kɑː kukurʌi kʌɦʌt hʌi. tʌunu ɟɑːni pʌrʌt hʌi ki mwɑːr buɽɦɑːpeː keː diːdɑː mʌɦi kɑː dɦwɑːkhɑː ɟʌruːr diːnɦin hʌi. jʌɦu ɟʌruːrʌi sɑːr kukurʌi ɑːj." etnɑː soctʌi buɽɦʌunuː ui bokʌrɑː kʌiɦjɑ̃ː bʌlːɑː hʌs ɟɦiʈiki diːnɦin ʌu ʈhɑːɽɦi hwʌi kʌi lɑːgi gʌrijɑːwʌi. ɟʌbʌi lʌgeː iː ʈhɑːɽɦi hwʌi kʌi lɑːgi gʌrijɑːwʌi, tʌbʌi lʌgeː ui bʌdmʌswɑː bokʌrwɑː kʌiɦjɑ̃ː uʈhɑːj kę lʌikeː bhɑːgi geː.

" Whosoever sees this calls it a dog. So it appears that my eyes of old age are surely deceiving me. Surely this wicked (goat) is a dog."

While the Brahmin thought so, he threw the goat away with a jerk like a small stick and, standing there, began to shower abuses. While standing he was showering abuses, the crooks lifted the goat and ran away with it.

(i) sijɑːr ʌu sijɑːrin

eːk ɟʌniː rʌɦĩː sijɑːrin. tʌb un kʌi mʌrdu mʌri gɑː. tʌb wʌi kʌɦin "hʌm okʌreː upːʌr sʌgɑːiː bʌiʈhʌb ɟekʌreː sʌu ʌkːili hoːiː." tʌu eːkṷ mʌɦɑː bɦʌdʌrgʌʈɦijɑː sijɑːr ɑːwɑː. uː kʌɦisi̥ ki̥ "hʌmʌreː eːk sʌi eːk ʌkːili hʌi." tʌb okʌreː upːʌr sʌgɑːiː bʌiʈhĩː.

tʌb wʌi gɑːbɦin bɦɑĩː. ɟʌb bijɑːi ko bɦɑː tʌu sĭjɑːr se̥ kʌɦin "cʌlʌu bʌtʌːoː ɟʌɦɑ̃ː tʌɦɑ̃ː bijɑːiː." tʌb uː ɟɑːi ko bʌtɑːisi̥ ɟʌɦɑ̃ː eːk ʈhʌĩː bɑːgɦ rʌɦʌt rʌɦɑː. tʌɦɑ̃ː bʌtɑːisi̥ ki̥ "jʌɦiː ʈhiɑ̃ː bijɑːu." kuch deːr bɑːdi bʌgɦowɑː ɑːwʌi lɑːg ɟʌɦɑ̃ː rʌɦʌt rʌɦɑː. tʌb sijʌriniʌuː deːkhin ʌu sijɑːr se̥ kʌɦin "kʌunʌu ʌkːil lʌgɑːoː ɟeɦi mɑ̃ː bʌgɦowɑː cʌlɑː ɟɑːi." tʌb uː kʌɦisi̥ "hʌm kʌun ʌkil lʌgɑːiː. hʌmʌreː ʌkil nɑːɦĩː hʌi." tʌb sijʌriniʌuː kʌɦin: "tuː tʌu kʌɦʌt rʌɦeu 'hʌmʌreː eːk sʌi eːk ʌkili hʌi'." tʌu sijɑːr kɑɦisi̥ ki̥ "ɟʌb seː hʌm toho kɑː sʌgɑːiː bʌiʈhɑːren tʌb seː sʌb ʌkil toɦʌreː gɦusʌri gʌi."

Translation

(i) The Jackal and his wife.

There lived a she-jackal. Her husband died. Then she said: "I shall enter into matrimonial alliance with one who has one hundred wisdoms." At that, there came a very wicked jackal. He said: "I possess one hundred and one wisdoms." She entered into matrimonial alliance with him.

Then she became pregnant. When it was time to be delivered she said to the jackal: "Come and tell me the place where I should be delivered." Then he went and indicated a place where a tiger used to reside. There he said: "Be delivered over here." After some time the tiger began to come to his place of residence. Then the she-jackal saw it and said to the jackal: "Do practise some wisdom, so that the tiger may go away." He said: "What wisdom shall I use; I have no wisdom." Then the she-jackal said: "You had said that you had one hundred and one wisdoms." The jackal replied: "Since I entered into matrimony with you, all my wisdom has entered you."

(j) baːbaː ki kʌraːmʌt

eːk buɽɦijaː rʌɦiː waɦi keː paːs eːk lʌɽikaː rʌɦaː. berkul gʌriːb rʌɦaː, bʌɦut gʌriːb, khaːne begir moɦotaːɟ. uː ghaːs khoːdi khoːdi ʌpəneː lʌɽikʌ ko ɟijaːwʌt rʌɦiː. tʌu kuch din keː baːdi lʌɽikaː sʌjaːnaː bɦaː. ʌpəneː baːp ki kʌ̃ʈijaː (bʌnsiː) lʌgaːwʌi laːg. phiri̥ kʌ̃ʈijaː lʌi kʌi cʌlaː tʌu kẽcuaː (caːraː) khoːdʌj laːg. ʌu dui roːʈiː beɟɦʌrʌ kʌi̥ powaːisi̥ ʌu lʌɦosun ʌu mircaː ʌu loːnu̥. tʌu eːk tʌlaːu mʌ̃ɦ kʌ̃ʈijaː lʌgaːwʌi laːg hʌi. girʌiː mʌchoriː eːk miliː dupʌɦʌr ko. tʌu mʌchori ko bɦũːɟi ko bhʌrtaː bʌnaːwaː tʌu bɦũːɟi ko khaːi laːg tʌu kʌɦisi̥ dui ʌdmiː hoːiti tʌu bʌtolaːi bʌtolaːi khaːiti. etʌremə eːk baːbaː aːi gʌjeː.

baːbaː kʌɦ·ni̥ "eːku̥ ʈukoɽaː hʌmoɦu ko deːu bʌcːaː tʌu hʌmʌɦuː khaːi leːit." tʌu lʌɽikaː kʌɦisi̥ ki "hʌm tʌu caːhʌti rʌɦen ki dui ʌdmiː hoːiti tʌu bʌtolaːi bʌtolaːi khaːiti." tʌb baːbaː pʌtaː ʈhekaːnaː puːchʌi laːgeː. tʌu kʌɦisi̥ "baːbaː hʌmʌreː lʌgeː rʌɦʌu." tʌu baːbaː oːkʌi̥ hʌɟaːmʌt bʌnwaːini̥ ʌu kʌpoɽaː pʌɦinaːini̥ tʌu wʌɦiː tʌlaːu po eːk mʌkaːn bʌni gʌwaː aːpʌi aːp. tʌb phini wʌheː duːnʌu hũʌ̃i rʌɦʌi laːgeː.

tʌu baːbaː kʌɦʌi laːgeː "bʌcːaː hʌm toɦaːr saːdiː kʌi deːiː tʌu kʌriɦʌu?" tʌb kʌɦini̥ "hʌmʌreː nʌ mʌɦətaːriː nʌ baːpu̥, hʌm tʌu bʌɦut gʌriːb hʌn. hʌmaːr bijaːɦu̥ keːu nʌ kʌriː." tʌu wʌɦiː tʌlaːu po eːku̥ ghoːɽaː aːpu̥ ruːpʌi bʌni gaː. tʌu wʌɦiː gɦoːɽʌ po wʌɦiː lʌɽikʌ ko bʌiʈhaːri ko ʌu dui khurəɟiː bʌnaːi ko duːnʌu khurəɟiː bhʌri kʌi pʌisaː bʌɦut laːdi diɦini̥. tʌu baːsːaːɦ kę eːk

Translation

(j) The Fakir's miracle.

There was an old woman. She had a son. He was very poor, very very poor, wanting in eatables. She used to nourish her son by digging up grass. After some time the boy grew up. He began to use his father's hook (to catch fish). When he started with the hook he would dig up the earthworms (to offer bait to the fish). He got two loaves of millet prepared and (took) garlic, chillies and salt. He just put the hook in a pool. He got one red fish at noon. He fried the fish and mashed it. Having so fried when he began to eat he said (to himself): "If we were two persons, I would eat and talk." At this very time a Fakir arrived.

The Fakir said: "(my) child, if you give a slice to me, I would also have a meal." Then the boy said: "I myself was saying 'if we were two, we would eat and talk at the same time'." At that, the Fakir asked the whereabouts and other details of the boy. He said: "O saint! reside with me." The Fakir got the boy shaved and clothed him. At that very pool a house appeared by itself. The two began to reside there.

The Fakir said: "(my) child, if I marry you, will you marry?" He said: "I have neither father nor mother, I am very poor. Nobody will consent to marry (his daughter with) me." At that a horse showed itself (by some miraculous power) at that pool. The Fakir seated the boy on it and loaded the horse with two bags stuffed fully with pice. (They) went to the city of a king. The king had

nʌgʌr mo geː tʌu bɑːsɑːɦ ke eːk lʌɽikiː rʌɦiː. tʌu jʌi ɟʌb gɦʌreː pʌɦũceː tʌu unkiː kʌceɦori ke̥ sɑːmneː pʌisɑː luʈʌub suruː kʌj diɦini̥. tʌb goɦorɑːini̥ ki "bɑːsːɑːɦ ṣɑːɦeb ʌponiː lʌɽiki ki sɑːdiː hʌmoreː sʌŋg kʌrbʌu." tʌu bɑːsːɑːɦ sɑːɦeb boːleː "nɑːiː." tʌu lʌɭikɑː ʌponeː mʌkɑːn ko cʌleː geː.

a daughter. When these people reached the residence (of the king), they began to shower away the pice. And shouted out: "Sire! king! Will you marry your daughter with us?" The king said: "No." The boy returned to his residence.

Note.—The story further tells that ultimately when rupees and *mohurs* were showered, the king, considering these people to be very rich, married his daughter to the boy. Immediately after the marriage, the boy somehow incurred the displeasure of the Fakir and everything vanished as it had come about. The boy again took to his profession of a fisherman. When the husband of the princess did not return, she started with a retinue on a search and to while away her time she used to hear stories from people of the places she went to. At last she arrives at the village of this boy, hears the life-story of her husband and recognises him and joyfully returns to the capital.

(k) kʌceɦoriː mɑː bʌjɑːn

gɦʌr mɑː hʌmɑːr sʌsur ʌɦʌi, biʈijɑː ʌɦʌi mʌn-seːruː ʌɦʌi.

sɑːɦeb teːrɑː roːɟ ki bɑːt hʌi, hʌmʌreː pʌroːseː eːk buɽɦijʌ ko gɦʌr ʌɦʌi. u buɽɦijʌ ke lʌgeː kʌbʌu kʌbʌu bʌiʈhi ɟɑːiti hʌi. biʈijɑː hʌmɑːri roːʈiː bʌnɑːisi̥ tʌu kʌɦisi̥ " cʌlʌu mɑːiː khɑːi ljɑː." tʌu hʌm kʌɦɑː "toɦɑːr dɑːdɑː kʌɦɑ̃ː?" kʌɦisi̥ "ɟɦɑ̃ːɽeː geː." hʌm kʌɦɑː " ɑːwʌi djɑː tʌu cʌliː." tʌu biʈijʌu hʌmɑːr moɦɑːrʌ ke ũːcɑː ũːcɑː nʌgʌrɑː hʌi tʌu bʌiʈhi gʌj. phiri̥ ɟɦɑ̃ːɽeː oːɽeː se ɑːjẽː tʌu goɦɑːr lʌgɑːini̥ tʌu hʌm ʌu biʈijɑː ciciɑːi ko dʌuren tʌu mʌɦɑːbiːr teːliu pʌhũci gɑː. tʌu hʌm nʌ ciːnɦiː nʌ ɟɑːniː. tʌu hʌmɑːr ɑːdmiː ʌu teːliː eːk ɑːdmi ko pʌkʌreː rʌɦen. hʌm nɑːiː ciːnɦi sʌkiti. rɑːt rʌɦiː ʌ̃dɦijɑːr. bʌɦut ʌdmiː chẽːkeː rʌɦeː. dʌrwʌɟeː pʌr rʌɟɑːiː miliː rʌɦiː.

Translation

(*k*) A Statement in the Court.

In my family, there is my father-in-law, (my) daughter and (my) husband.

Sir, the thing relates to the day, thirteen days off. In my neighbourhood, there is the residence of an old woman. Often I sit by that old woman. My daughter prepared food (lit. bread) and said: "mother come and eat." At that I said: "Where is thy daddy?" (She) said: "(He) has gone out to ease himself." I said: "Let him come and then I shall come." My daughter also sat down on the high platform on my threshold. When (he) returned after easing himself he gave out a shout (of danger) and at that my daughter and I cried and ran (towards the house). Mahabir, a Tēlī[1], also came round. I neither recognise nor know (the thief). My man and the Tēlī were holding a man. I cannot recognise (him). It was a dark night. Many men were obstructing (the view) The quilt was found at the door.

[1] Tēlī—caste of people who press out oil-seeds

(1) mukʌdimaː kʌi haːl

ʌchaː tʌu sunaː eːk mukʌdimaː kʌi haːl toɦ kaː bʌtaːiː. eːk meɦraːruː ʀʌɦiː tʌɴiː deːkhʌi maː niːki naːɦiː raɦiː. oːkʌʀ ᴍʌɴseːdɦuː oːkaː liaːe tʌu gaː munaː duin tiːn din maː bʌɦiaːj diɦisi̥. u becaːriː aːe ɴʌiɦʌreː mə ʀʌɦʌi laːgi̥. naiɦʌʀᴡʌo ᴍʌ ukəreː keuː naːɦiː ʌɦʌi. dui caːr din tʌu oːkʌʀ kaːkaː pitiː khaːe oːe kaː diɦin phin kʌɦen ki "ʌb hʌᴍʌʀeː maːn ko naɦĩː no cʌɦʌi ʌpəneː ᴍʌɴseːdɦuː keː hijãː ᴊaː cʌɦʌi ᴊʌɦãː ᴍʌɴ hoːe tʌɦãː ʌntʌi cʌliː ᴊaː. hʌᴍ sʌb ʌpəɴʌi eɦi kaːl maː bɦuːkhʌɴ ᴍʌʀʌtʌɦiː. tõɦ kaː khiaːᴡʌi kaː kʌɦãː dɦʌraː baːʈʌi" iː sʌni keː uː meɦraːruː uː gãːu choːɽi keː oɦi keː pʌʀoːseː dusʌʀeː gãːo maː ʀʌɦʌi laːgi ʌu in seː un seː udɦaːr baːʈɦiː laikeː aːpʌn din kaːʈʌi laːg. ʌisen oː kaː eːk bʌris biːti gaː. ᴊʌu deːkhisi̥ kiː ʌb udɦʌʀʌu baːʈɦiː kʌtʌɦũ seː nʌɦĩː milʌt tʌu ʌpəneː ɴʌiɦʌreː keː eːk baːmɦʌɴ keː lʌgeː gʌi. ʌu kʌɦisi̥ ki "bɦʌijaː ʌb tʌu kʌuniu tʌnaː nʌɦĩː cʌlʌt. kiː tʌu tuː sʌb keuː kʌɦaː ʌu hʌᴍ kaː kuchu̥ khaːj pijʌj kaː hʌᴍʌʀeː ᴍʌɴʌiwaː seː dijaːj djaː ki tʌu phiri cʌlaː hʌᴍ seː sʌʀkaːr maː eːk ɖʌʀkhaːs dewaːj dejaː nʌɦĩː tʌu ʌb hʌmaːr biːtʌb muskil baː". baːmɦʌɴ deotaː kaː eːkʌi haːl deːkhi kʌi bʌɽaː tʌʀʌs aːje ʌu kʌɦen kiː "ʌchaː cʌlaː ᴊʌu tʌu hʌᴍʌʀeː kʌɦaː maːneː tʌu tʌu hʌᴍ tõɦ kaː oː seː khaːe pijʌj kaː dijaːj deːbʌi ʌu ᴊo raːkhʌi pʌʀ tʌjaːr hoi ᴊaːe tʌb tõɦ kaː okʌʀeː hĩjãː ʀʌɦʌi ko pʌʀeː. ʌu hãː ᴊʌu uː naː tʌjaːr hoːiː tʌu cʌlaː hʌᴍ toː seː eːk ʈhi ɖʌʀkhaːs ɖipʈiː saːɦeb keː hijãː diaːj deːb wʌi ʌs ʌs maːmileː maː bʌɦut khijaːl kʌʀʌthĩː".

Translation

(*l*) The Account of a Case

All right, listen, I shall tell you the account of a case. There was a woman, but she was not good to look at. Her husband took her (with himself) (after marriage) but turned her out after two or three days. She, poor woman, came back to her father's and resided there. There is no one at her father's place either. Her uncles gave her food for a few days (lit. two or four days) and later said: "It is no longer within our means. Either go to your husband's or go elsewhere wherever you like. Nowadays, we ourselves are suffering from hunger, where have we got to feed thee?" Hearing this that woman quitted that village and took up her residence in a village near by. And (she) began to spend her days by borrowing from this or that person. When she found that she could no longer get anything by borrowing, she went to a Brahmin of her father's place and said: "Brother! it is impossible to go on now. Either all of you should speak to my husband and make him give me some thing to eat and drink or come and help me to put in a petition to the Government. Otherwise, it is difficult for me to carry on." The Brahmin-god on seeing her condition had compassion for her and said: "All right come, if he accepts my words, I shall make him give you something for you to eat and drink and if he will be ready to keep you, you will have to live with him. And yes, if he is not ready to keep you, come, I shall help you to give a petition to the Deputy Saheb He is very considerate in such cases"

(m) bʌmɦʌniː kʌi bʌjaːn

aːpus mãː kʌɟiaː bɦaː. gɦʌreː ke mʌnʌiː hʌmkeː nisaːr diɦin. hʌm ʌponeː pʌraːniː ke saːth bʌmbʌe ɟaːe ke ɟʌ̃gɦʌiː ke ʈiːsʌn kaː cʌleː. kuch durijaː hʌm pʌceː gʌjeː to lʌmbeː se eːk taːraː deːkh pʌraː. oɦ mãː hʌm nʌɦaːneː ʌu kinaːreː bʌiʈh ke daːnaː bijaː kʌrʌi laːgeː. itʌneː mãː . . . aːẽː ʌur hʌmʌreː mʌnseːdɦu se pũːchin ki "tuː kʌɦijaː gɦʌreː seː cʌljaː ?" phun dʌ kaː dʌ kaː kʌɦi keː un seː pʌdoːriː kʌrʌi laːgen. on hʌrken ki "kʌs bɦʌijaː kʌcːiː pʌkːiː boːlʌt ʌɦaː". tʌb ʌur phuːhʌr paːtʌr bʌkʌi laːgen. hʌm muɽijaː ke ugʌraː dɦʌrʌi ke kiɦaː. on dʌwʌɽ ke hʌmʌreː mʌnʌiː ke pʌnʌɦiː se maːrʌi laːgen hʌmaːr goɽɦʌraː ɖɦʌr-kʌuaː, nʌthijaː chiːn choːr liɦen. hʌm pʌceː pupuiː lʌgaːwaː ʌu gãːw deːs kʌi doɦaːiː deːj laːgen tʌb on goɽʌiteː bolaːj ke hʌmʌreː mʌnʌiː kaː dɦʌraːj diɦen.

Translation

(*m*) The Statement of the Brahmín Woman.

There was a quarrel amongst our people. The people of our family turned us out. I started with my man for Janghai Railway station in order to go to Bombay. When we had gone some distance, from far off a tank came to our sight. We bathed in it and started to eat food sitting at the bank. At this time (the aggressor) came and asked my husband : "When did you start from your home?" Later saying many things which I know not, he began to jest with him (my husband). He forbade : "Brother, why do you talk unbecomingly?" At that he began to speak further obscene words. We bent down and started to get off. He (the aggressor) came running and started beating my husband with shoes. And snatched away my anklets, bracelets and nose-ring. We shouted (for help) and sought protection of the village and the country. At that he (the aggressor) called the watchman and got my husband taken into custody.

(n) bɦikhaːriː baːmɦʌn kʌj kʌthaː

eːk ʈhe rʌɦẽː baːmɦʌn, to din raːt mãːgʌĩ. ʌis mãːg ɟãːc ke kuch dinaː khãːen pĩen. to eːk dinaː ʌur mãːgẽ gʌjẽː to wʌ̃ɦi dinaː kʌɦi gʌjẽː rʌɦẽː ʌpʌneː meɦraːruː se ki "aːgiː oːgiː ɟiaːeː rʌɦeː to ãːʈaː oːʈaː mãːgi ke liaːeː rʌɦʌb". to ɟʌb mãːg ũːg ke aːjen to ɟʌun kʌɦeː rʌɦen ki aːgiː oːgiː ɟiaːeː rʌɦeː tʌun aːgiː oːgiː ɟiaːeː nʌɦĩː rʌɦĩː. to aːgiː aːneː uɦãː pʌʈhʌi diɦin. to ãːĩː lʌi ke aːgiː to oː kʌɦen ki "eːk aːdmiː ko hʌm deːkhaː hʌi ki maːlpuʌi maːlpuaː khaːt baː". to oː kʌɦen ki "tumɦuː bʌnaːoː". tʌb uː ɟʌb bʌnaːwʌi kʌɦen to pãːc pʌseːriːke maːlpuaː bʌnʌen paːnʈhʌi. ɟʌb tʌjaːr hoi gʌwaː tʌb khaːe kaː bolaːen. tʌ ɖeːʈɦ maːlpuaː unkiː thaːriː me rʌkh diɦin ʌu pʌlthiː tiːr coraːi liɦen. to oː kʌɦen ki "kʌi reː pãːc pʌseːriː ki pãːcʌi ʈhe bʌnaː etʌnaː pisaːn liaːe rʌɦeː". duːnoː ɟʌneː seː ɟɦʌgʌʈaː hoi gaː. to kʌɦin ki "ʌisen naːɦĩː, eːk ʈheː sutʌreː ke mʌcʌwaː bichaːwaː to dunoː ɟʌneː oːɦiː pe leːʈiː. to ɟʌun ɟaːgʌi tʌwʌn khaːeː ʌu ɟiː soːi ɟaːeː tiː naː khaːeː".

Translation

(*n*) The Story of the beggar Brahmin.

There was a Brahmin. He used to beg day and night. Begging in this way he ate and drank for some time. Then again, one day he went a-begging. (Before he went) he had asked his wife to keep fire lighted (saying) "I shall bring flour etc. by begging." When he returned after begging, (he found that) she had not lighted the fire. He sent her to bring fire (from neighbourhood). When she came back with fire, she said: "I have seen a man, he eats only *mālpuā*[1] and nothing else." Then he said: "You may also make *mālpuā*[1]." When he asked her to make *mālpuā*, she made five out of five seers (of flour). When they became ready, she called (him) to eat and put one *mālpuā*[1] and a half in his vessel and stole away the rest by her side[2]. At that he said: "O! did you make only five; I had brought so much flour?" (And) both of them quarrelled. Then they said: "Not in this way; put a cot woven with cotton-threads[3] and let both of us lie on it. Whosoever keeps awake may eat (all the five *mālpuās*) and one who goes to sleep, should not eat."

***Note.*—The story is half-told.**

[1] ***mālpuā***—a cake of flour leavened with yeast, mixed up with dried fruits and sugar and fried in butter—greater delicacy than ***gulgulā*** [see note 1 under (*a*)].

[2] ***paithī***—a position of sitting, one foot on one thigh and the other under the other thigh.

[3] ***sutarē***—probably "of cotton-thread". This gives a very soft luxurious bed.

INDEX

PART 1. Sanskrit, Prakrit, Early Awadhi words and loan-words from other Indian and from foreign languages.

PART 2. Modern Awadhi and Hindustānī words.

NOTE.—(*a*) Generally derivatives have been put under respective roots, *e.g.*, *hōihi* under *hō*.

(*b*) *ṁ* before mutes has been transcribed as the nasal of the class of the mute, *e.g.*, *saṁga* as *saṅga*.

(*c*) the derivatives begin after the root (*ān* – , – *ahi* = *ānahi*) or after the root less the final vowel of he root (āju, – *ū* = ājū).

PART 1

Early Awadhi, Sanskrit, Prakrit etc.

F. 61

dh

P

bh

PART 2

Modern Awadhi and Hindustani Words

k

ch

bɦ

l

w